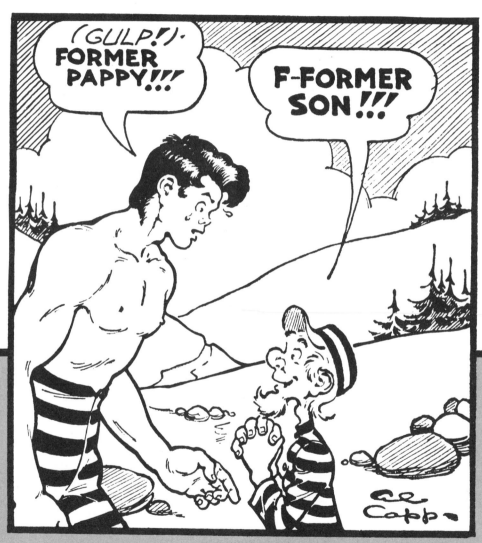

LI'L ABNER

(GULP!)- FORMER PAPPY!!!
F-FORMER SON!!!
Al Capp

Dailies

Volume Five: 1939

Al Capp

KITCHEN SINK PRESS

Princeton Wisconsin

Li'l Abner Dailies, Volume Five: 1939 by Al Capp is copyright © 1989 by Capp Enterprises, Inc., except "The Call From Dogpatch," copyright © 1989 by Stephen Lamar Harris, and "1939: Some Turning Points," copyright © 1989 by David Schreiner. All rights reserved. Entire contents copyright © 1989 by Kitchen Sink Press, Inc., No. 2 Swamp Rd., Princeton WI 54968. Nothing may be reproduced without written permission of the copyright holders, except for review purposes.

ISBN 0-87816-056-6 (hardcover)
ISBN 0-87816-057-4 (softcover)

This is the fifth volume of the complete **Al Capp's Li'l Abner**, reprinting the 1939 daily strip. The series is published by Kitchen Sink Press, **Denis Kitchen**, publisher. The series editor is **Dave Schreiner**. The cover was designed by **Ray Fehrenbach** and **Peter Poplaski** and colored by **Fehrenbach**, who also shot the strips, retouched and assembled them for publication. We wish to thank the Capp estate for their cooperation in publishing this series. We wish also to thank **Julie Capp Cairol** for her Introduction, **Stephen Lamar Harris** for his article about "Abbie an' Slats," and **Bill Blackbeard** of the San Francisco Academy of Comic Art for supplying us with the strips we needed for this volume.

Library of Congress Cataloging-in-Publication Data

Capp, Al, 1909-
    Li'l Abner : dailies.

    Includes index.
    Contents: v. 5. 1939
    I. Title.
PN6728.L5C29   1988   741.5'973   88-12831
ISBN 0-87816-056-6 (v. 5)
ISBN 0-87816-057-4 (pbk. : v. 5)

Introduction

by Julie Capp Cairol

One evening not long ago, I was introduced to some French visitors as "the daughter of Al Capp, creator of *Li'l Abner*." My new acquaintances politely inquired, "Who is Li'l Abner?" To which I spontaneously replied, "Li'l Abner—c'est moi!"

It's the simple truth. I *was* to be called "Abner" by my parents—but I turned out to be "Julie" instead; so Abner became the hero of my father's comic strip about hillbillies.

Since that evening with the French, I have often thought how sad it is that many people may never know *Li'l Abner*—a character who once played a role in the everyday lives of millions of people the world over, and who, for over four decades, gave them a break from routine.

It is difficult for me to be objective about *Li'l Abner* because I have always been immersed in it, even more so than the most faithful of its readers. My father's favorite way to begin a family dinner conversation was to say: "Wait until I tell you what happened to Abner today!" He would then proceed, with each *Gulp!* and *Haw Haw!* and *Bop!* and *Chomp!* in the script, to tell us the latest

In 1941, the Caplin family got together for a portrait. Standing, from left to right, are the three brothers: Elliott, Jerome, and Alfred, better known as Al Capp. In the front row are Julie Capp, one of Al's two daughters; Tillie Caplin, the matriarch of the family; Madeline Caplin, Al's sister; and Cathie Capp, Al's other daughter.

adventures of the Yokums and the other denizens of Dogpatch. We always knew, even as the tiniest of children, the right moment to laugh—because he always laughed first. If anyone who read the strip could have listened to his narration, they would have heard his characters speaking. He was a gifted draftsman, but above all he was a narrator, a creator of myths, fables, legends and traditions. Sadie Hawkins Day is still observed on many university campuses throughout the country. Al Capp has been compared to Rabelais, Dickens, Daumier and Twain. (John Steinbeck, in a preface to one of my father's books, made a plea for him to win the Nobel Prize for Literature. It was Steinbeck, however, who won the prize a few years later.)

Back at the dinner table, we heard all about the new characters that were to appear—each one clearly identifiable by his or her name: Rotten Joe Rattigan. Cousin Weakeyes Yokum. Big Barn-smell. Bet-a-Million Bashby. There are hundreds—maybe thousands—of others. Many of them were characterizations of well-known figures, fictional or otherwise: Joanie Phoanie, Eddie Ricketyback, Fearless Fosdick. Politicians, movie stars, billionaires, racketeers—they all paraded through and tried to corrupt or benefit Dogpatch, just as their real life counterparts did actual society. The strip became Al Capp's vehicle for social criticism.

Li'l Abner evolved from depicting the day-by-day adventures of a family in an isolated hill town, to a strip showing a society parallel to the one that existed in real life. Dogpatch became a town that wouldn't change for all the gadgets and commodities its society could bestow. Dogpatch's citizens loved their town because they somehow recognized all the trouble it took to become rich and famous. They might starve, but they wouldn't develop ulcers. Above all, they would rather rest than work, and it took a lot of work to become one of those personalities. When he got married, Abner himself got a job as a matress-tester; from 6 a.m. to 6 p.m. each day he was sleeping proof of the comfort of "Little Wonder Mattresses." He had just enough time at noon to eat lunch.

It was not long before the strip itself exploded. The frames needed more space, and started breaking into each other to the point that one would stand for six. The story of *Li'l Abner* brimmed over, it went beyond the newspaper's space and reality to reach the real world. All that was contemporary passed through Dogpatch. We can see that the cultural trends which brought freedom to the arts—surrealism, new forms of music and theatre, the musical comedy—had an echo in the strip and Al Capp took this freedom of form and used it critically and artistically, as did artists in other fields.

Doesn't the Sadie Hawkins Day race ring a beckoning bell, calling for Women's Liberation? And General Bullmoose's motto, "What's good for General Bullmoose is good for the U.S.A.!" exposes the treachery and venality of large corporations. All that was contemporary—except for World War II—passed through Dogpatch. (Dogpatch never did go to war; not in the daily comic strip, that is. My father contributed to the war effort with other work, and in person at innumerable hospitals. He wanted Dogpatch to be a kind of refuge both from and for the world—a reminder of peace. Only once do I recall a reference in *Li'l Abner* to the horrors people outside Dogpatch were suffering. In a 1940 Sunday page, Joe Btfsplk, "the world's most loving friend and worst jinx," announces to Abner that he is off to see "...a fella which needs me. Fella named Adolf.")

When Al Capp retired in 1977, he took *Li'l Abner* with him. He knew, we all knew, that Abner, his family, and the citizens of Dogpatch, could only continue to exist under Al Capp's touch. I am very grateful that Abner is back in this collection series. He lives again. To some he is an old friend; he is being introduced to others. To all he brings fun, happiness, and even a little wisdom. I like to think that my father, who died in 1979, may be also, in the hearts and minds of his readers, alive and well in the world he created, Dogpatch, U.S.A.

The Call From Dogpatch

Raeburn Van Buren at about the time he got the call from Dogpatch.

by Stephen Lamar Harris

When reminiscing about the telephone call that changed his life—and gave birth to the comic strip *Abbie an' Slats*—my late uncle Raeburn Van Buren was fond of saying that it came from Dogpatch.

The year was 1936, and Van was a famous magazine illustrator. His credentials included 350 stories for the *Saturday Evening Post* and a similar number for *Collier's*. He was forty-six, set in his ways, and stubborn as a Missouri mule. On the other end of the line was Al Capp, equally famous as the creator and artist of *Li'l Abner,* and equally as stubborn.

Capp had a business proposition. The 1930s were turning out to be a golden age of American comic strips. New ones were popping up daily, it seemed. Cartoonists and writers with clever ideas could make relative fortunes in a decade best remembered for economic ills. The beleagured citizenry looked for escape wherever it could, especially in the funny pages. And Capp, still flushed with the growing success of *Li'l Abner,* figured he had another escape route for them: a humorous strip about an orphaned boy from the tenements of "Noo York" who is forced to move to the country and live under the protective wing of his elderly cousin. A modern-day Tom Sawyer and Aunt Polly, if you will. Capp's proposition? If Van would draw the strip, Capp would write it, and the earnings, which Capp said might prove enormous, would be split down the middle.

My uncle balked. What could a comic strip offer him that he didn't already have as a major illustrator for magazines?

Security, Capp argued, who was eighteen years Van's junior. Magazine illustrators were on their way out. Photography was taking over, and so was radio. The only place for a man with Van's talent was in comics. Capp was impressed with Van's style—it was well-crafted with just the right touch of slapstick. It was a natural for the funny pages.

My uncle still scoffed at the offer. While Capp was famous in the world of comics, Van had never heard of him. In fact, he had never read or even seen *Li'l Abner.* Van's world was magazines and magazine illustrators. Although he had watched his income slide in recent years, 1935 had been a good year and 1936 held the promise to be as profitable. He was making twice the money of most doctors or lawyers. Besides, he was pushing fifty. Why change careers now? Why take a chance?

But Capp's call forced Van to look back on a creative life that had already spanned nearly thirty years. I don't know what went through my uncle's mind back then, but I'm sure he thought long and hard about his career; where it had been and where it was going. And I'm sure, too, that he was surprised at how successful it had turned out.

Raeburn Van Buren was born in Pueblo, Colorado, in 1891. His father, my great grandfather, was a frustrated inventor with the grand presidential moniker of George Lincoln Van Buren. The family called him Boppy. When he wasn't fiddling around with gadgets, he was farming or running a store. He didn't settle down until he brought his family to Kansas City, Missouri, around the turn of the century.

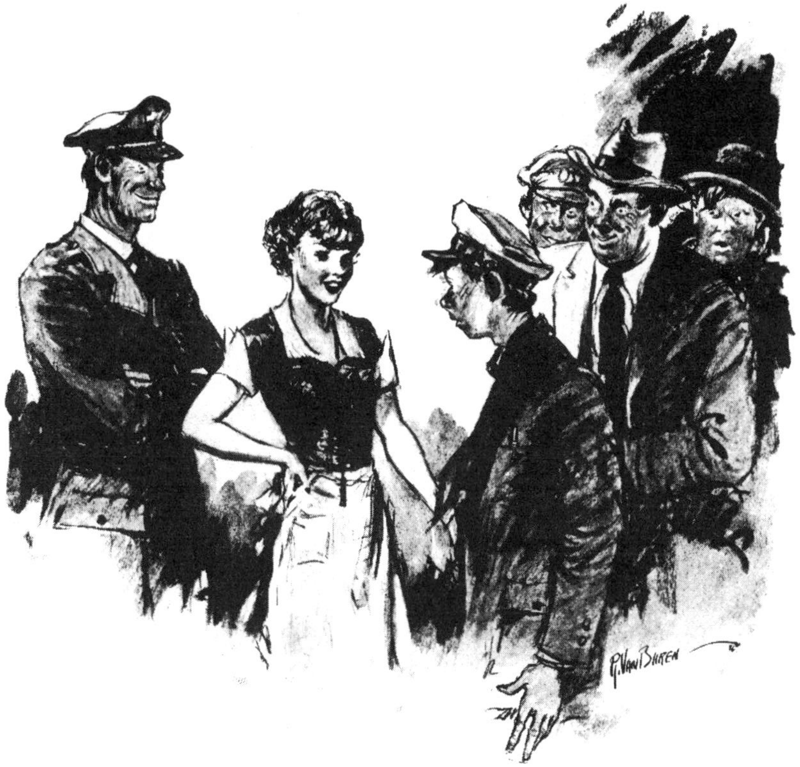

Van Buren illustration for, "Cheer for Your Own Side," by Harold Titus, SATURDAY EVENING POST, January 2, 1937.

In those days, Kansas City was a rowdy cowtown. Cowboys, riding their herds to the railyards and slaughterhouses in the north end, were a common sight; but certainly not as common as the bartenders and prostitutes who worked the scores of bars and brothels which filled that part of town. The famous outlaws and gunfighters were almost gone, and those that weren't were getting old and feeble and were nearly forgotten. Although Jesse James, who hailed from neighboring Clay County, had been dead for many years, his brother, Frank, could still be seen wandering the north side in the pay of the ruthless Pendergast brothers, who ran K.C. the way Tammany Hall ran New York City.

Back then the Pendergast machine was battled tooth and claw by one of the country's great newspapers, the legendary *Kansas City Star*—legendary because it was also the training ground for a number of famous writers and artists. Through its doors marched a legion of men destined for fame in city rooms of newspapers all over the country, in editorial offices of the great magazines and publishing houses, and in the writing cubicles of major Hollywood studios. The most famous of these alumni was Ernest Hemingway.

My uncle came under the tutelage of Harry Wood, the *Star's* art editor, who had created one of the early comic strips, *The Intellectual Pup*. Wood was an uneducated man with short legs and an almost larger-than-life torso. He was talented and had a heart as big as the city he covered. When my uncle, still in high school, showed up in the art department during the 1908 Christmas holidays, carrying samples of his work and looking for a job, Wood gave him a temporary assignment drawing ads. Van figured he had landed a permanent job and quit high school. After the holidays, Wood kindly thanked him and sent him home. You can imagine how Van felt. Taking pity on the youngster, Wood "rehired" him as a sketch artist, and paid him $15 a week from his own paycheck—not a small amount in those days.

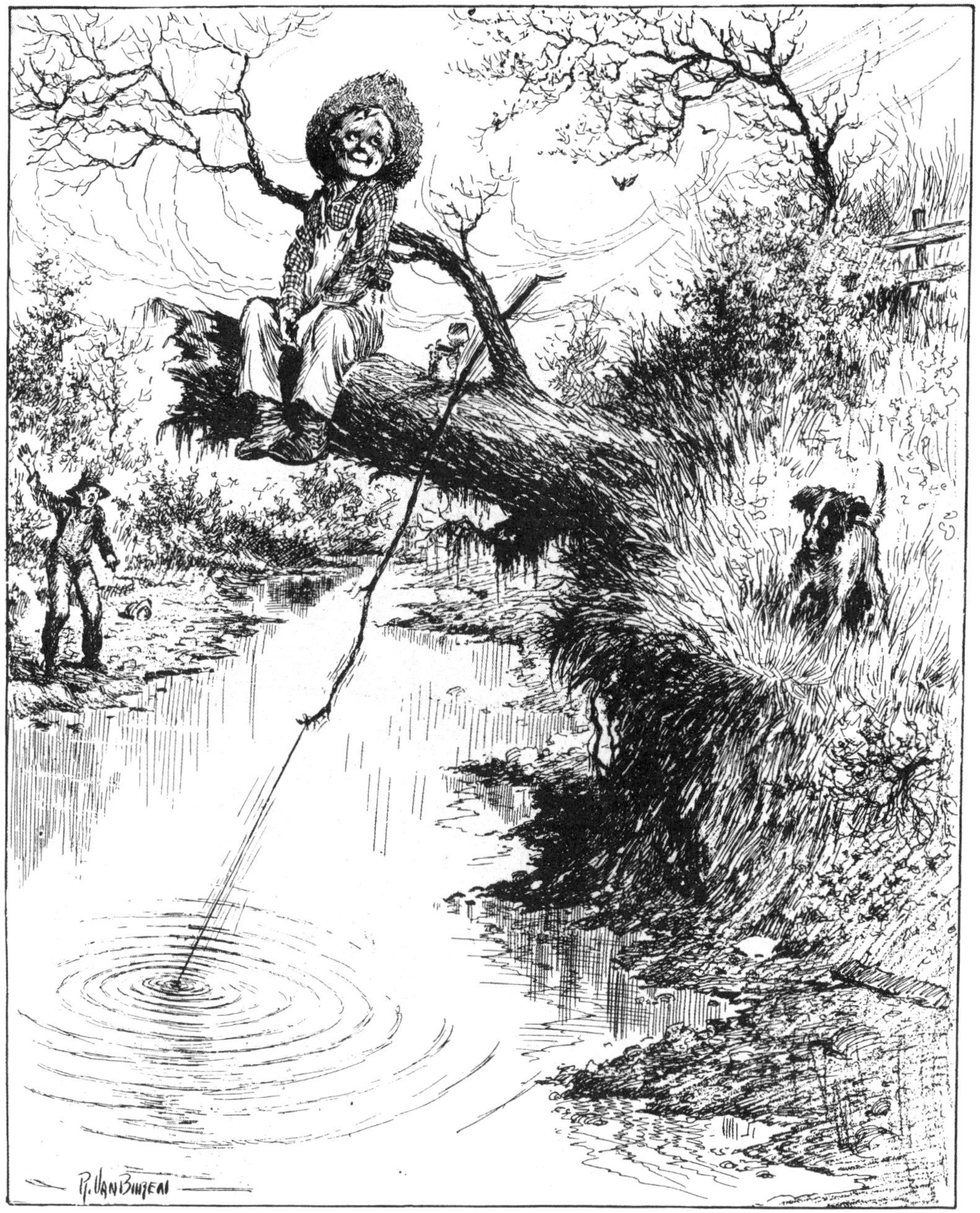

DRAWN BY R. VAN BUREN

In the Spring a Young Man's Fancy—

Full page illustration for PUCK, 1914.

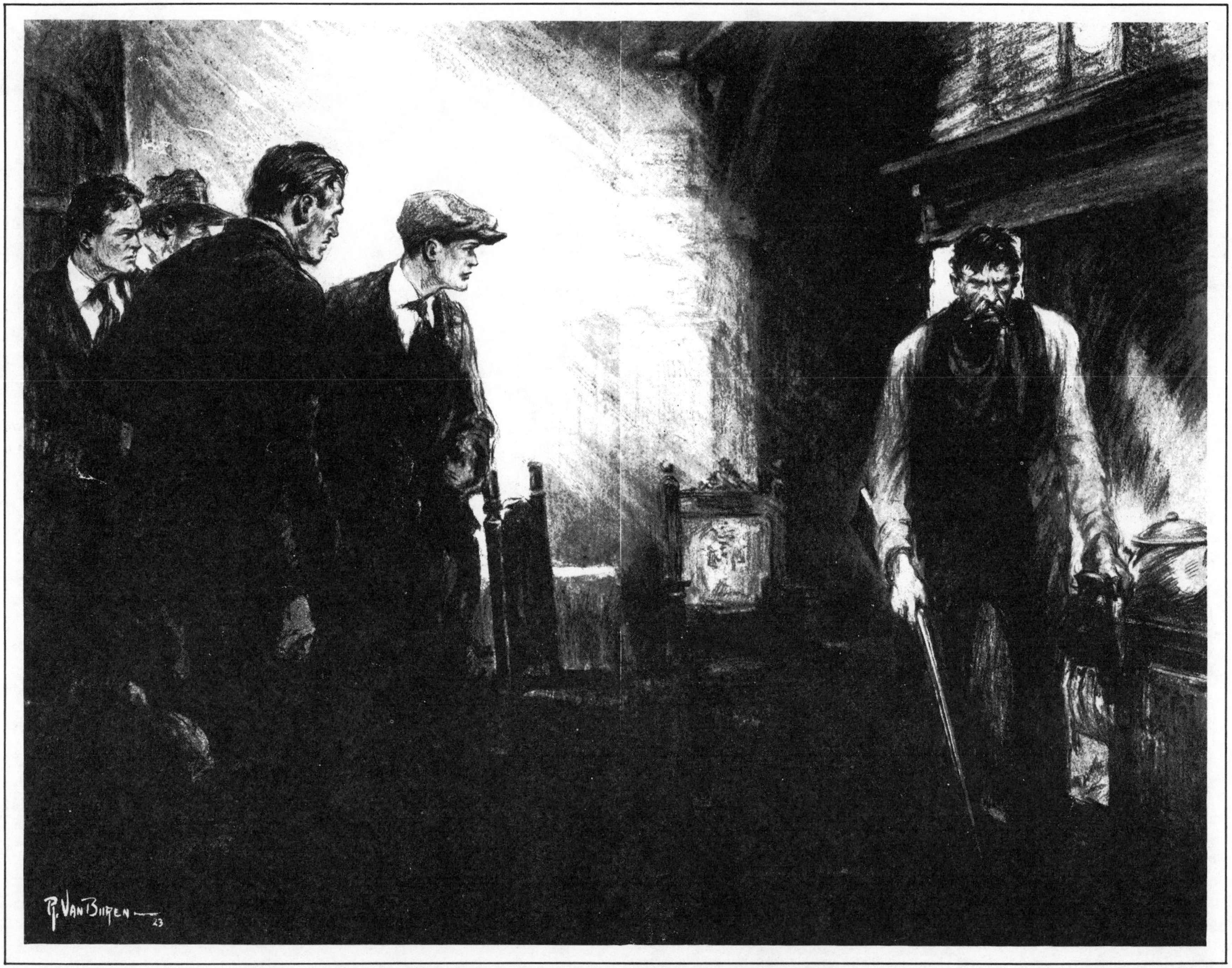
R. VAN BUREN 23

An example of Van Buren's "serious" illustration work.

When Van went out on his first murder assignment, it was with Courtney Ryley Cooper, then the *Star's* top reporter. Cooper had gained the admiration of his peers when, after getting his throat slit by a Pendergast henchman, he had the gash stitched in time to write about it for that night's late edition. Anyway, it was winter and an entire family had been slaughtered on their farm in Kansas. It was midnight and bitter cold when Cooper and my uncle arrived at the farm. Reporters from other newspapers were already prowling around the farmhouse.

"Let's go down to the barn," Cooper suggested. "I bet there's a stiff in there."

As they approached the barn, Cooper grabbed Van's arm and said, "Hold it!" He stuck a big chew of tobacco in his mouth and offered some to his nervous partner. "You'd better have some," he said. "You'll need it once we get inside." Van was sick to his stomach as it was, but he took the tobacco. Cooper spat out a dark stream of juice and picked up the lantern. Inside, a man was stretched out on the earthen floor. He was stiff, partially from the freezing temperatures and partially from rigor mortis. One arm was cocked in the air. Cooper spat again as they huddled over the body. Then he took his booted foot and pressed down on the arm. The body swung up into a sitting position. Van sprang back, crashing against the barn wall. Cooper looked at my uncle, so frightened, so inexperienced a sketch artist; his eyes wide, his heart pounding like a runaway freight train, his cheeks swollen with tobacco. The sorry sight made Cooper laugh so hard he had to sit down. It was the start of a friendship that would include collaboration on a score of short stories for *The Saturday Evening Post* and *Collier's*—Coop the writer, Van the artist.

The work my uncle did during his four years at the *Star* (1909-1913) provided the best education he ever got. A sketch artist was akin to a photojournalist. Instead of lugging a camera around, he carried a sketch pad and a fast pencil. The training he received—illustrating at least one story a day under extreme deadline pressures—was better, he claimed, than going to art school. In fact, when he arrived in New York he enrolled at the famous Art Students League, but quit after a few weeks because he felt the classes were tailored for bored rich girls with nothing better to do with their idle time than think themselves budding artists.

In New York, he roomed in a cheap apartment in the Lincoln Arcade. He shared a studio with fellow Missourians Thomas Hart Benton, Ralph Barton and William Powell. Benton became a great artist, Barton turned to caricature, and Powell attained fame in Hollywood as an actor. Van illustrated for the pulps—mostly Street and Smith publications—and several humor magazines, including *Life*, *Judge* and *Puck*.

"We ate a lot of beans in the Lincoln Arcade," Van once told me. He liked to describe the Arcade as a home for old ladies with parrots.

In 1918, he enlisted in the National Guard and served with New York City's "Silk Stocking Regiment" in World War I. He saw considerable frontline action. He was also art editor of the regiment's magazine, *Gas Attack*. His illustrations of American doughboys earned him the nickname "The American Bairnsfather" from the *New York Times*, after the British illustrator Bruce Bairnsfather.

When he returned home, his illustrations now more polished, more mature than ever, he set his sights on the major publications. Almost immediately he began selling to *Collier's*, *Cosmopolitan*, *Blue Book*, *Green Book* and *Redbook*. He bought a leather-bound ledger book and carefully entered every illustration he sold—from the story title and the magazine to the amount and whether he had gotten paid. In 1919, his first full year back from Europe, he earned $6,365. On April 21, 1921, he sold his first illustration to *The Saturday Evening Post*; "String Blood" for $150. In the 1920s, Van became one of the *Post's* most frequent contributors, sometimes landing the illustrations for two stories in one issue. His income from 1924 to 1930, his heyday as an illustrator, averaged a hefty $13,650. His best year was 1927, when he cleared $19,785. But when the Depression arrived his income—like most incomes during those trying times—declined. At $8,047, 1935 had been his best year in five. And when Capp phoned from Dogpatch, 1936 was looking as strong.

What Capp said about photography and radio made sense—*if* you were just starting out or your talent was borderline. Van was established, well-known and still financially well off. What turned the tables was the sudden departure from *The Post* of its editor-in-chief, George Horace Lorimer. One of the giants in the long history of American magazines, Lorimer had been at *The Post's* helm since 1898, when it had only 2,000 readers. He built the circulation into the millions. His handpicked successor was Wesley Stout, an alumnus of the *Kansas*

Another POST illustration, this time for "Women and Elephants," January 30, 1926.

City Star, but one who was not sympathetic toward magazine illustrators. His idea of illustrating short fiction was to use photographs—a trend that he had picked up from yet another *Star* grad, Sumner Blossom, editor of the popular *American* magazine.

So Capp was right. The golden age of American illustration was drawing to a close, so to speak. Van reluctantly joined forces with the creator of *Li'l Abner*, and launched a new career at a time when most men his age took to peering over the horizon toward retirement.

Once Van was convinced, the two men wasted little time in shaping the strip that was to become *Abbie an' Slats*. Capp told my uncle what he wanted, handed him seven weeks of continuity to illustrate, and then nervously waited to see how his characters would turn out. Van used real people as models for the leading characters. Abbie was an old school teacher he once knew. Slats, on the other hand, was the spitting image of himself—right down to the red hair and freckles. It got so that Van's own family began calling *him* "Slats." When he was satisfied with the results, my uncle shipped his drawings to Boston, where Capp lived. Capp shot back a happy reply: "There is no artist in the world who could do Abbie, no one else who could get the best of her as you have done. She is a grand old lady and thar's gold in her. Let's start gettin' it."

The two partners hammered out a contract, which basically split all the earnings in half. But when they met to apply the finishing touches, Capp's attorney, disgruntled at the split, cocked an eye at my uncle and said, "Artists are a dime a dozen." The comment rocked my uncle, and although he didn't walk out of the meeting, he later told Capp that "I gave my life to Abbie and Slats. When I left I was about as discouraged as I could be." The partnership was on the verge of falling apart, but Capp, who could ruffle feathers, could also smooth them back again. He cajoled my uncle, saying, "We are equal partners. We must work as one or we are licked both artistically and in a business way."

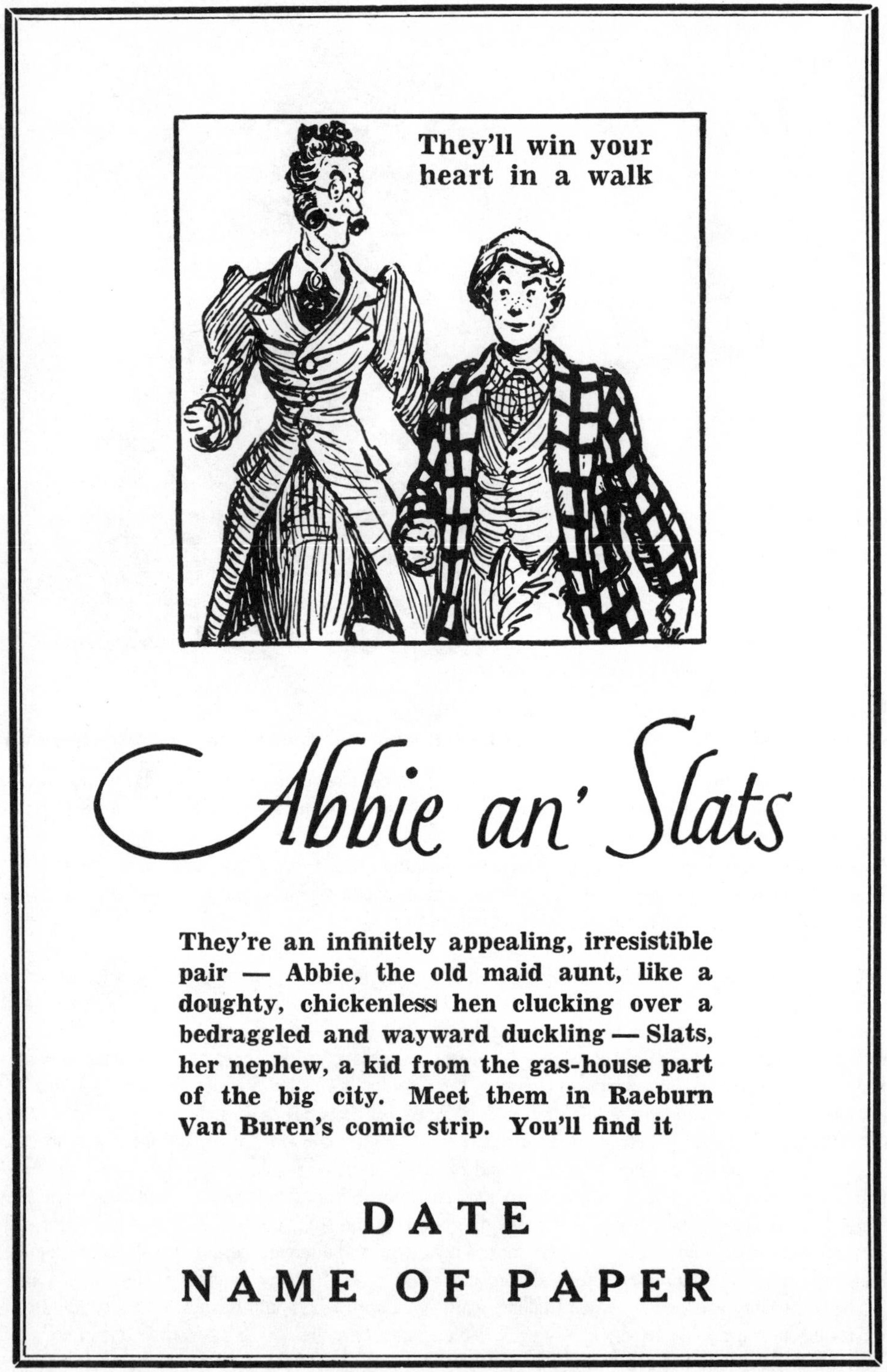
They'll win your heart in a walk
Abbie an' Slats
They're an infinitely appealing, irresistible pair — Abbie, the old maid aunt, like a doughty, chickenless hen clucking over a bedraggled and wayward duckling — Slats, her nephew, a kid from the gas-house part of the big city. Meet them in Raeburn Van Buren's comic strip. You'll find it
DATE
NAME OF PAPER

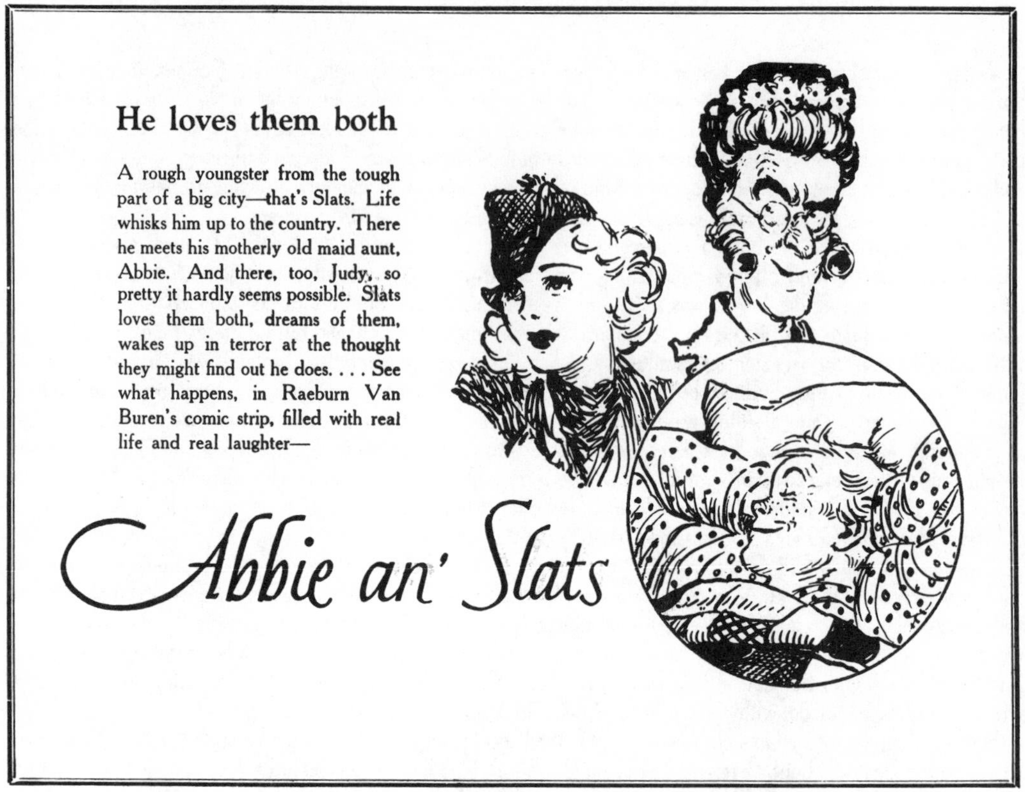
He loves them both
A rough youngster from the tough part of a big city—that's Slats. Life whisks him up to the country. There he meets his motherly old maid aunt, Abbie. And there, too, Judy, so pretty it hardly seems possible. Slats loves them both, dreams of them, wakes up in terror at the thought they might find out he does. . . . See what happens, in Raeburn Van Buren's comic strip, filled with real life and real laughter—
Abbie an' Slats

Promotional art for the new strip, ABBIE AN' SLATS, written by Al Capp and illustrated by Raeburn Van Buren. On the following pages, a sequence from the first daily strips.

Their next step was to sell the new strip to a syndicate. King Features made a good offer, and it was countered by United Features Syndicate. "I know the United offer is better all the way around," advised Capp, who was certainly better acquainted with cartoon syndicates than my uncle. "They will advance more money. They are unquestionably a far superior outfit. They NEED a hit strip now and we've got the hit strip of 1937. I know the syndicate and with George Carlin at the helm, I trust them implicitly. The only outfit which could do better with an initial guarantee is King and those guarantees of theirs have their drawbacks. King has killed off many a good strip, many a good artist."

The partners signed with United. The first daily appeared on July 7, 1937. *Abbie an' Slats* was an instant success and within a few years nearly threatened *Li'l Abner* in popularity. For the next eight years, the partnership bloomed, and then Capp, realizing he had to devote more time to his own strip, turned over the writing chores to his brother, Elliot Caplin. Caplin wrote the strip until its demise in 1971.

During Capp's courtship of my uncle, he had penned a brief letter that said, in part, "You and I have in Abbie a fortune and a long run of prosperity and pleasure."

If Van were alive today—he died in 1987 at the age of 96—he would certainly have agreed with that prophetic statement. *Abbie an' Slats* did bring him prosperity and pleasure and, as he said to me years later, "I was so glad to have answered that call from Dogpatch."

Stephen Lamar Harris, who was as close to his uncle, Raeburn Van Buren, as a son is to a father, is editor of General Electric's corporate magazine, Monogram.

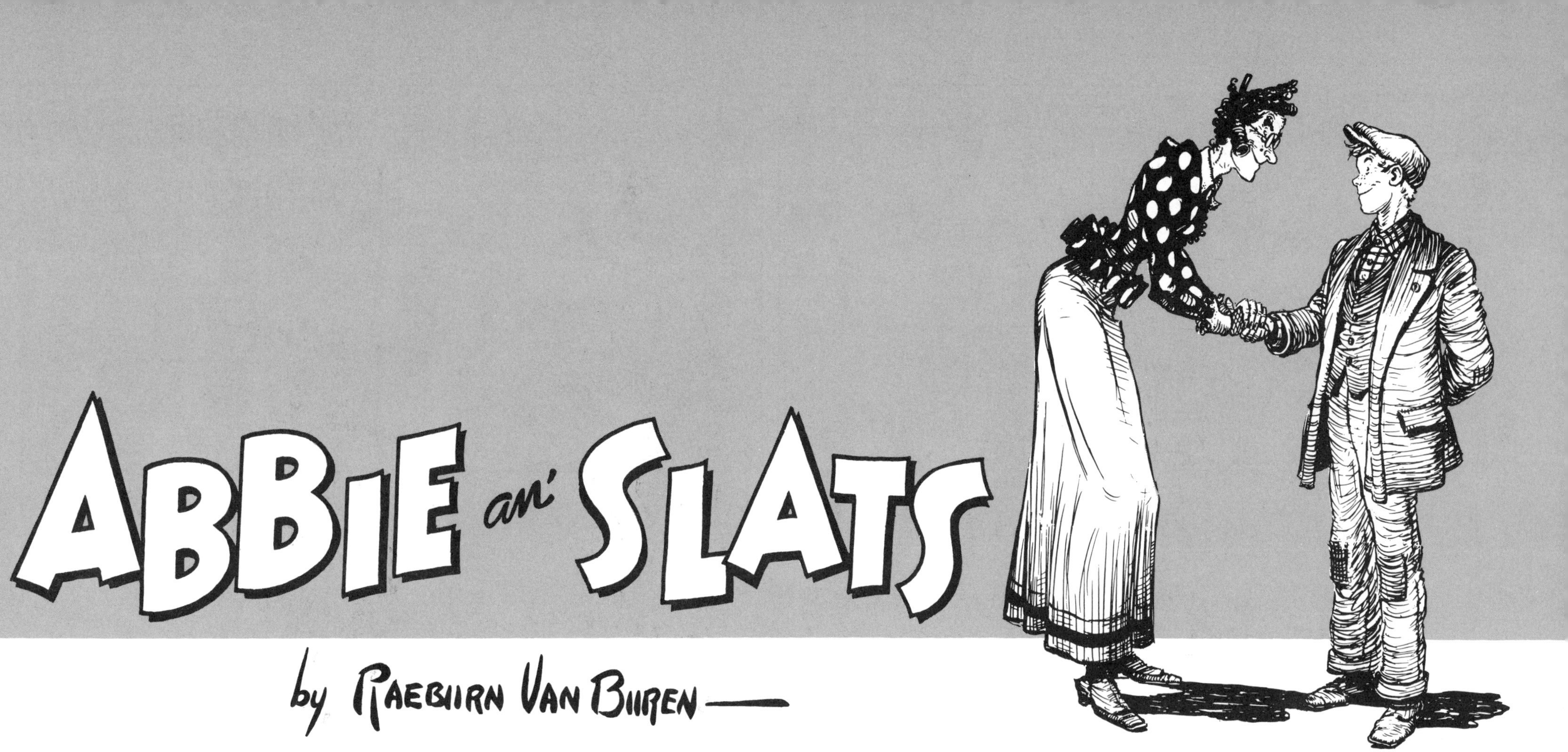
ABBIE an' SLATS
by RAEBURN VAN BUREN

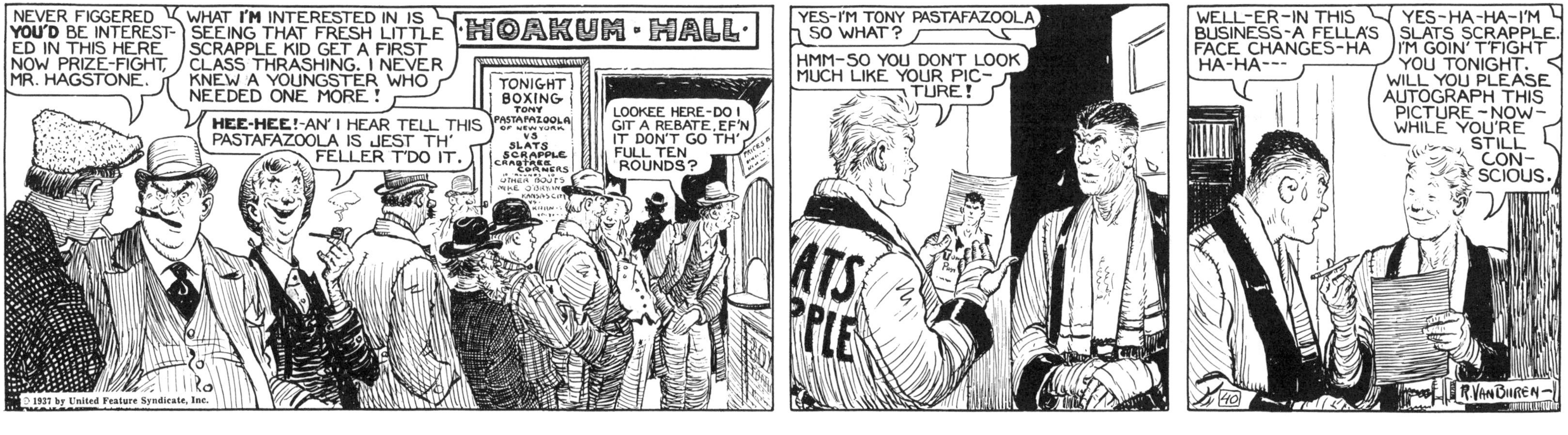
NEVER FIGGERED YOU'D BE INTERESTED IN THIS HERE NOW PRIZE-FIGHT, MR. HAGSTONE.
WHAT I'M INTERESTED IN IS SEEING THAT FRESH LITTLE SCRAPPLE KID GET A FIRST CLASS THRASHING. I NEVER KNEW A YOUNGSTER WHO NEEDED ONE MORE!
HOAKUM · HALL
TONIGHT BOXING TONY PASTAFAZOOLA OF NEW YORK VS SLATS SCRAPPLE CRABTREE CORNERS
HEE-HEE!-AN' I HEAR TELL THIS PASTAFAZOOLA IS JEST TH' FELLER T'DO IT.
LOOKEE HERE-DO I GIT A REBATE, EF'N IT DON'T GO TH' FULL TEN ROUNDS?
© 1937 by United Feature Syndicate, Inc.
YES-I'M TONY PASTAFAZOOLA SO WHAT?
HMM-SO YOU DON'T LOOK MUCH LIKE YOUR PICTURE!
WELL-ER-IN THIS BUSINESS-A FELLA'S FACE CHANGES-HA HA-HA---
YES-HA-HA-I'M SLATS SCRAPPLE. I'M GOIN' T'FIGHT YOU TONIGHT. WILL YOU PLEASE AUTOGRAPH THIS PICTURE-NOW-WHILE YOU'RE STILL CONSCIOUS.
R. VAN BUREN

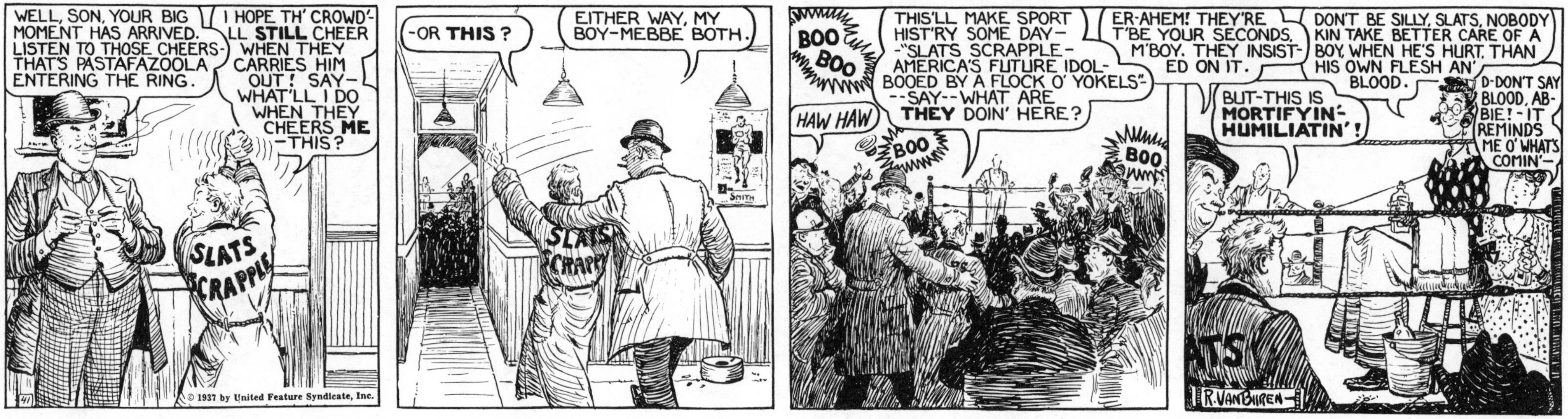
WELL, SON, YOUR BIG MOMENT HAS ARRIVED. LISTEN TO THOSE CHEERS-THAT'S PASTAFAZOOLA ENTERING THE RING.
I HOPE TH' CROWD'LL **STILL** CHEER WHEN THEY CARRIES HIM OUT! SAY-WHAT'LL I DO WHEN THEY CHEERS **ME** -THIS?
SLATS SCRAPPLE
41
© 1937 by United Feature Syndicate, Inc.
-OR **THIS**?
EITHER WAY, MY BOY-MEBBE BOTH.
SLATS SCRAPPLE
SMITH
BOO
BOO
HAW HAW
THIS'LL MAKE SPORT HIST'RY SOME DAY- -"SLATS SCRAPPLE-AMERICA'S FUTURE IDOL-BOOED BY A FLOCK O' YOKELS"- -SAY- -WHAT ARE **THEY** DOIN' HERE?
BOO
BOO
ER-AHEM! THEY'RE T'BE YOUR SECONDS, M'BOY. THEY INSISTED ON IT.
BUT-THIS IS **MORTIFYIN'-HUMILIATIN'**!
DON'T BE SILLY, SLATS, NOBODY KIN TAKE BETTER CARE OF A BOY, WHEN HE'S HURT, THAN HIS OWN FLESH AN' BLOOD.
D-DON'T SAY BLOOD, ABBIE! -IT REMINDS ME O' WHAT'S COMIN'-
ATS
R. VAN BUREN

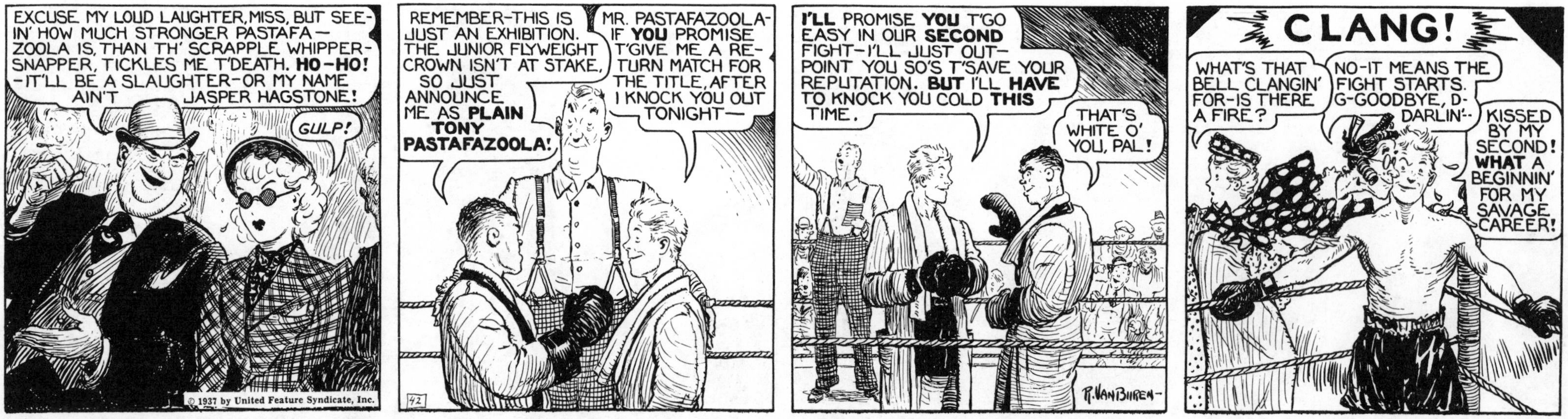
EXCUSE MY LOUD LAUGHTER, MISS, BUT SEEIN' HOW MUCH STRONGER PASTAFAZOOLA IS, THAN TH' SCRAPPLE WHIPPERSNAPPER, TICKLES ME T'DEATH. **HO-HO!** -IT'LL BE A SLAUGHTER-OR MY NAME AIN'T JASPER HAGSTONE!
GULP!
© 1937 by United Feature Syndicate, Inc.
REMEMBER-THIS IS JUST AN EXHIBITION. THE JUNIOR FLYWEIGHT CROWN ISN'T AT STAKE, SO JUST ANNOUNCE ME AS **PLAIN TONY PASTAFAZOOLA!**
MR. PASTAFAZOOLA-IF **YOU** PROMISE T'GIVE ME A RETURN MATCH FOR THE TITLE, AFTER I KNOCK YOU OUT TONIGHT-
42
I'LL PROMISE **YOU** T'GO EASY IN OUR **SECOND** FIGHT-I'LL JUST OUTPOINT YOU SO'S T'SAVE YOUR REPUTATION. **BUT** I'LL **HAVE** TO KNOCK YOU COLD **THIS** TIME.
THAT'S WHITE O' YOU, PAL!
R. VAN BUREN
CLANG!
WHAT'S THAT BELL CLANGIN' FOR-IS THERE A FIRE?
NO-IT MEANS THE FIGHT STARTS. G-GOODBYE, D-DARLIN'-
KISSED BY MY SECOND! **WHAT** A BEGINNIN' FOR MY SAVAGE CAREER!

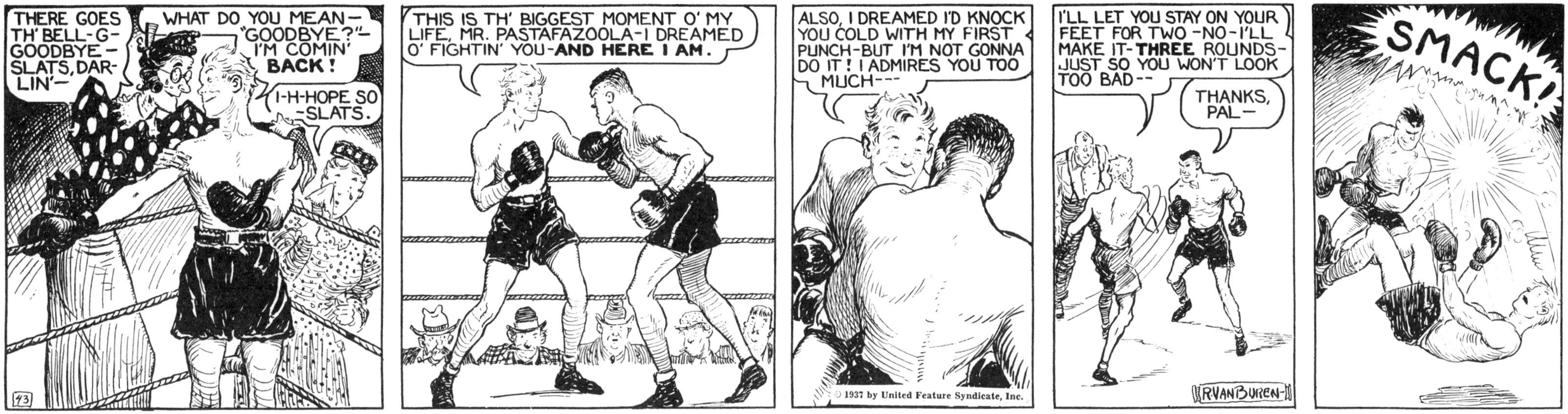
43
THERE GOES TH' BELL-G-GOODBYE-SLATS, DARLIN'-
WHAT DO YOU MEAN-"GOODBYE?"-I'M COMIN' BACK!
I-H-HOPE SO -SLATS.
THIS IS TH' BIGGEST MOMENT O' MY LIFE, MR. PASTAFAZOOLA-I DREAMED O' FIGHTIN' YOU-AND HERE I AM.
ALSO, I DREAMED I'D KNOCK YOU COLD WITH MY FIRST PUNCH-BUT I'M NOT GONNA DO IT! I ADMIRES YOU TOO MUCH---
© 1937 by United Feature Syndicate, Inc.
I'LL LET YOU STAY ON YOUR FEET FOR TWO-NO-I'LL MAKE IT-THREE ROUNDS-JUST SO YOU WON'T LOOK TOO BAD--
THANKS, PAL-
R.VANBUREN
SMACK!

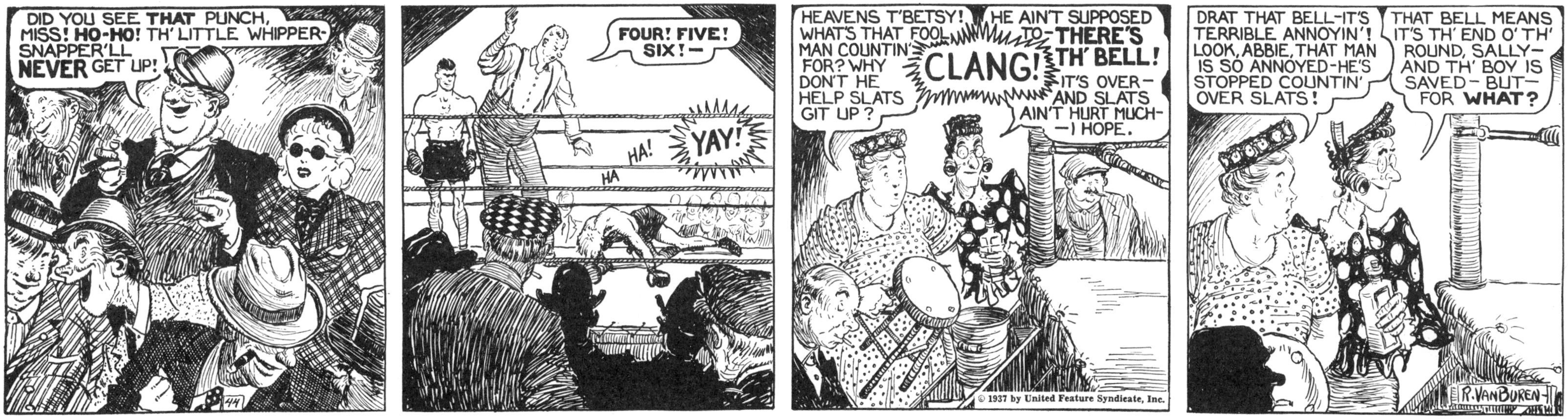
DID YOU SEE THAT PUNCH, MISS! HO-HO! TH' LITTLE WHIPPER-SNAPPER'LL NEVER GET UP!
44
FOUR! FIVE! SIX!-
HA! HA
YAY!
HEAVENS T'BETSY! WHAT'S THAT FOOL MAN COUNTIN' FOR? WHY DON'T HE HELP SLATS GIT UP?
HE AIN'T SUPPOSED TO-THERE'S TH' BELL! IT'S OVER-AND SLATS AIN'T HURT MUCH--I HOPE.
CLANG!
© 1937 by United Feature Syndicate, Inc.
DRAT THAT BELL-IT'S TERRIBLE ANNOYIN'! LOOK, ABBIE, THAT MAN IS SO ANNOYED-HE'S STOPPED COUNTIN' OVER SLATS!
THAT BELL MEANS IT'S TH' END O' TH' ROUND, SALLY-AND TH' BOY IS SAVED-BUT-FOR WHAT?
R.VANBUREN

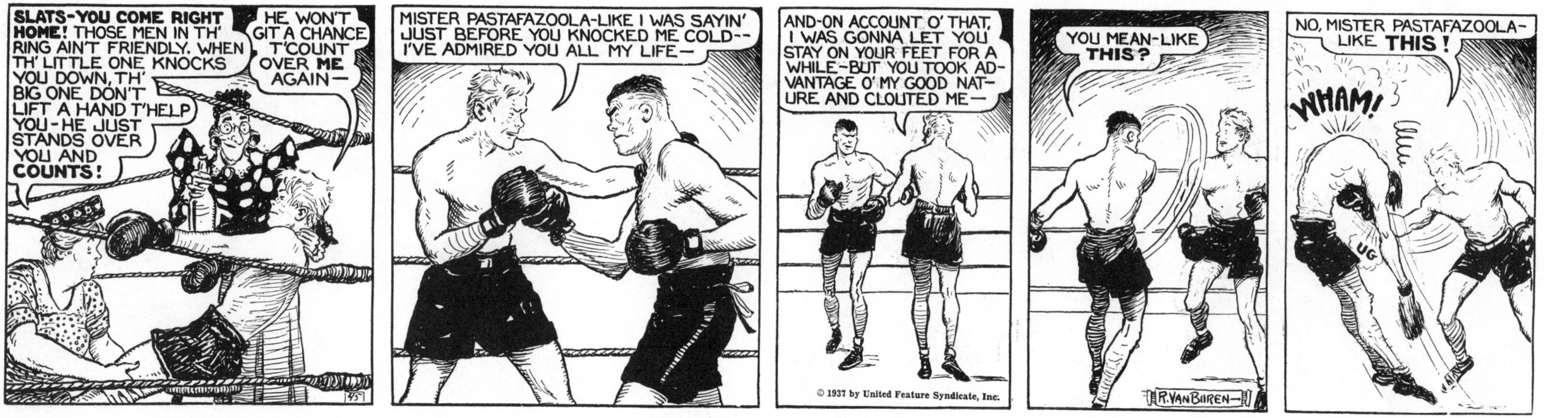
SLATS-YOU COME RIGHT HOME! THOSE MEN IN TH' RING AIN'T FRIENDLY. WHEN TH' LITTLE ONE KNOCKS YOU DOWN, TH' BIG ONE DON'T LIFT A HAND T'HELP YOU-HE JUST STANDS OVER YOU AND COUNTS!
HE WON'T GIT A CHANCE T'COUNT OVER ME AGAIN—
45
MISTER PASTAFAZOOLA-LIKE I WAS SAYIN' JUST BEFORE YOU KNOCKED ME COLD-- I'VE ADMIRED YOU ALL MY LIFE—
AND-ON ACCOUNT O' THAT, I WAS GONNA LET YOU STAY ON YOUR FEET FOR A WHILE-BUT YOU TOOK ADVANTAGE O' MY GOOD NATURE AND CLOUTED ME—
© 1937 by United Feature Syndicate, Inc.
YOU MEAN-LIKE THIS?
R.VANBUREN
NO, MISTER PASTAFAZOOLA-LIKE THIS!
WHAM!
UG

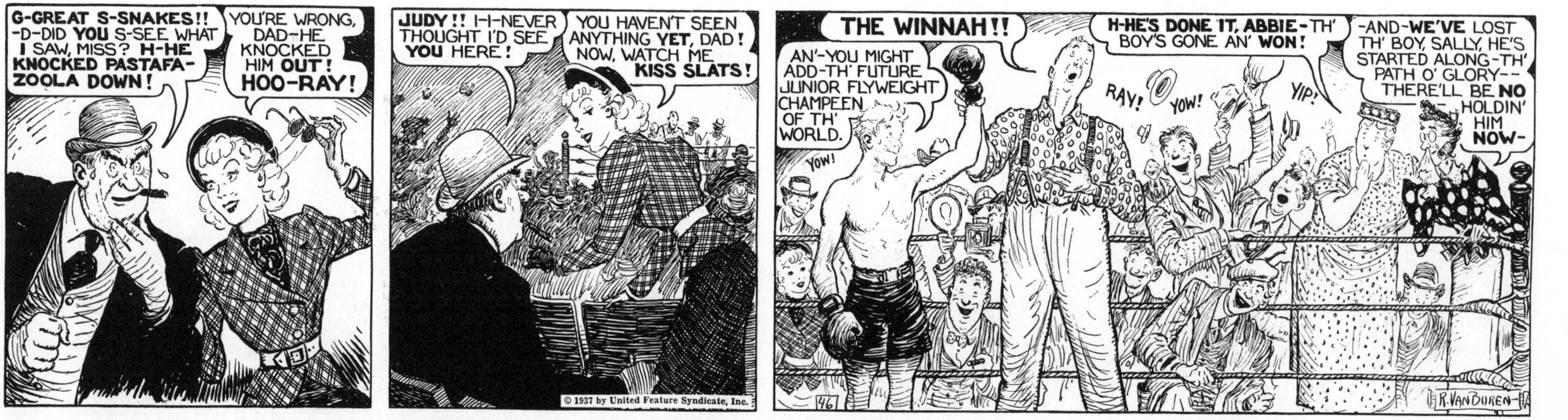
G-GREAT S-SNAKES!! -D-DID YOU S-SEE WHAT I SAW, MISS? H-HE KNOCKED PASTAFAZOOLA DOWN!
YOU'RE WRONG, DAD-HE KNOCKED HIM OUT! HOO-RAY!
JUDY!! I-I-NEVER THOUGHT I'D SEE YOU HERE!
YOU HAVEN'T SEEN ANYTHING YET, DAD! NOW, WATCH ME KISS SLATS!
© 1937 by United Feature Syndicate, Inc.
THE WINNAH!!
AN'-YOU MIGHT ADD-TH' FUTURE JUNIOR FLYWEIGHT CHAMPEEN OF TH' WORLD.
H-HE'S DONE IT, ABBIE-TH' BOY'S GONE AN' WON!
-AND-WE'VE LOST TH' BOY, SALLY. HE'S STARTED ALONG-TH' PATH O' GLORY-- THERE'LL BE NO HOLDIN' HIM NOW-
YOW!
RAY!
YOW!
YIP!
46
R.VANBUREN

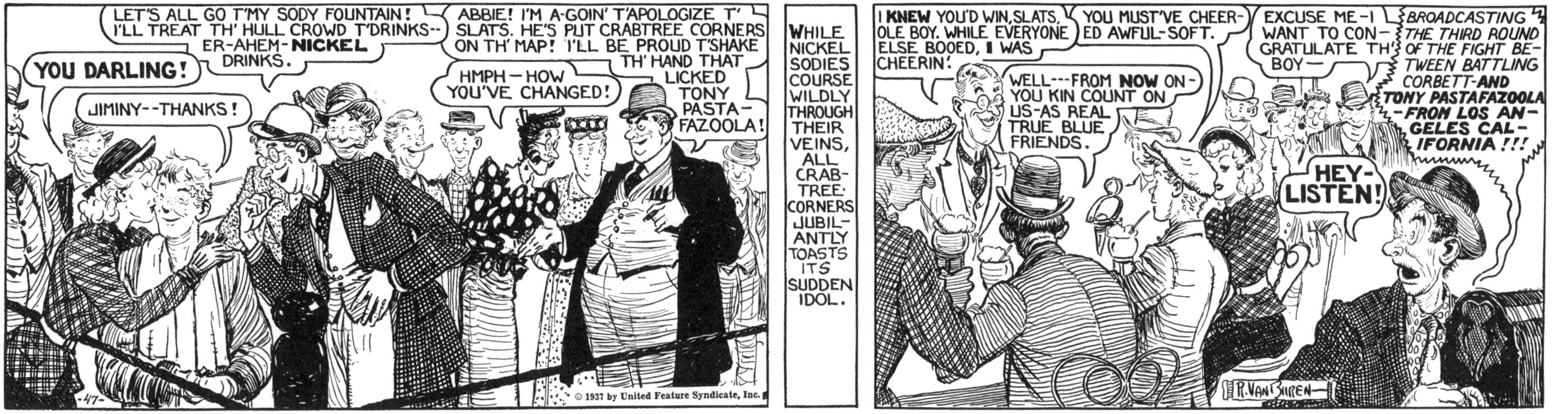
LET'S ALL GO T'MY SODY FOUNTAIN! I'LL TREAT TH' HULL CROWD T'DRINKS-- ER-AHEM-**NICKEL** DRINKS.
YOU DARLING!
JIMINY--THANKS!
ABBIE! I'M A-GOIN' T'APOLOGIZE T' SLATS. HE'S PUT CRABTREE CORNERS ON TH' MAP! I'LL BE PROUD T'SHAKE TH' HAND THAT LICKED TONY PASTA-FAZOOLA!
HMPH—HOW YOU'VE CHANGED!
-47-
© 1937 by United Feature Syndicate, Inc.
WHILE NICKEL SODIES COURSE WILDLY THROUGH THEIR VEINS, ALL CRABTREE CORNERS JUBILANTLY TOASTS ITS SUDDEN IDOL.
I **KNEW** YOU'D WIN, SLATS, OLE BOY. WHILE EVERYONE ELSE BOOED, **I** WAS CHEERIN'.
YOU MUST'VE CHEERED AWFUL-SOFT.
WELL---FROM **NOW** ON-YOU KIN COUNT ON US-AS REAL TRUE BLUE FRIENDS.
EXCUSE ME-I WANT TO CONGRATULATE TH' BOY—
*BROADCASTING THE THIRD ROUND OF THE FIGHT BETWEEN BATTLING CORBETT-**AND TONY PASTAFAZOOLA -FROM LOS ANGELES CALIFORNIA!!!***
HEY-LISTEN!
R. VAN BUREN

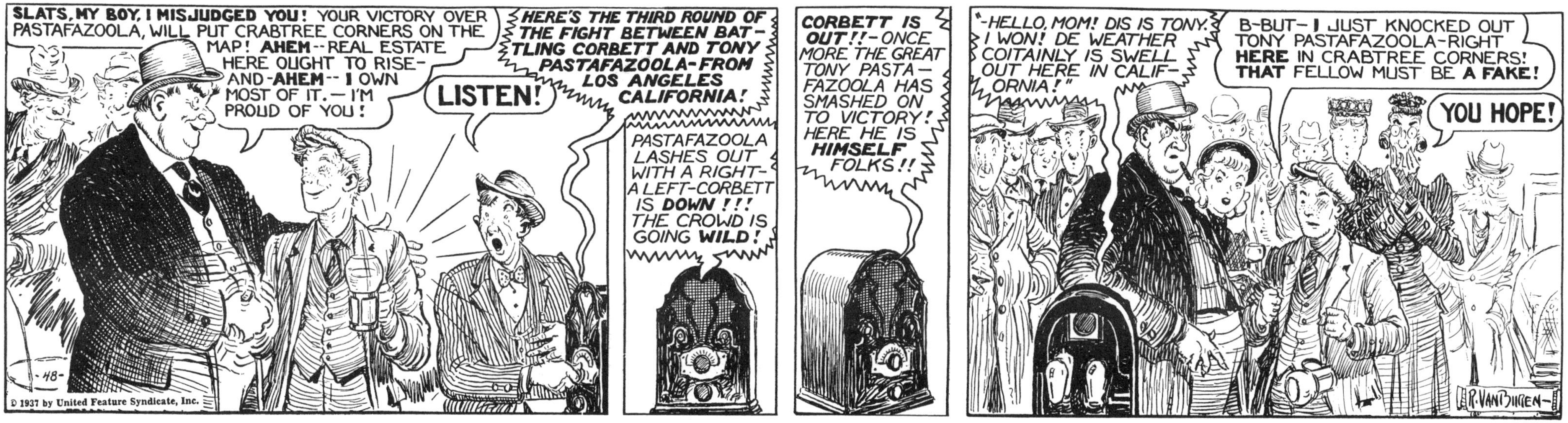
SLATS, MY BOY, I MISJUDGED YOU! YOUR VICTORY OVER PASTAFAZOOLA, WILL PUT CRABTREE CORNERS ON THE MAP! **AHEM**--REAL ESTATE HERE OUGHT TO RISE-AND-**AHEM**-- **I** OWN MOST OF IT.—I'M PROUD OF YOU!
LISTEN!
HERE'S THE THIRD ROUND OF THE FIGHT BETWEEN BATTLING CORBETT AND TONY PASTAFAZOOLA-FROM LOS ANGELES CALIFORNIA!
-48-
© 1937 by United Feature Syndicate, Inc.
*PASTAFAZOOLA LASHES OUT WITH A RIGHT-A LEFT-CORBETT IS **DOWN!!!** THE CROWD IS GOING **WILD!***
***CORBETT IS OUT!!**-ONCE MORE THE GREAT TONY PASTA-FAZOOLA HAS SMASHED ON TO VICTORY! HERE HE IS **HIMSELF** FOLKS!!*
"-HELLO, MOM! DIS IS TONY. I WON! DE WEATHER COITAINLY IS SWELL OUT HERE IN CALIFORNIA!"
B-BUT-**I** JUST KNOCKED OUT TONY PASTAFAZOOLA-RIGHT **HERE** IN CRABTREE CORNERS! **THAT** FELLOW MUST BE **A FAKE!**
YOU HOPE!
R. VAN BUREN

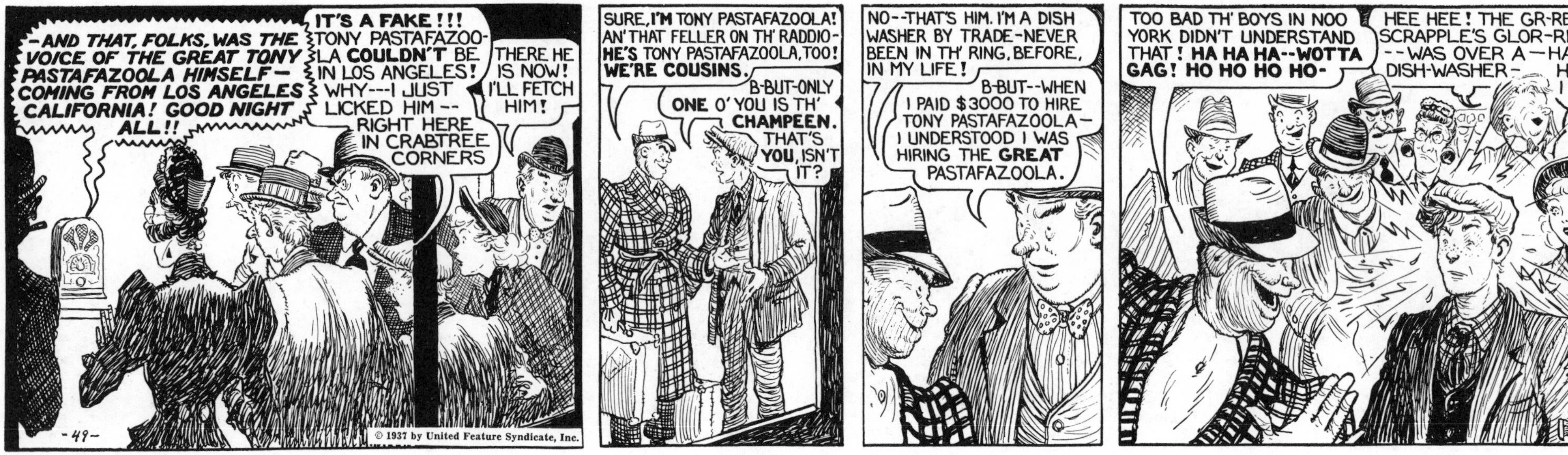
-AND THAT, FOLKS, WAS THE VOICE OF THE GREAT TONY PASTAFAZOOLA HIMSELF— COMING FROM LOS ANGELES CALIFORNIA! GOOD NIGHT ALL!!
IT'S A FAKE!!! TONY PASTAFAZOO-LA COULDN'T BE IN LOS ANGELES! WHY---I JUST LICKED HIM -- RIGHT HERE IN CRABTREE CORNERS
THERE HE IS NOW! I'LL FETCH HIM!
-49-
© 1937 by United Feature Syndicate, Inc.
SURE, I'M TONY PASTAFAZOOLA! AN' THAT FELLER ON TH' RADDIO- HE'S TONY PASTAFAZOOLA, TOO! WE'RE COUSINS.
B-BUT-ONLY ONE O' YOU IS TH' CHAMPEEN. THAT'S YOU, ISN'T IT?
NO--THAT'S HIM. I'M A DISH WASHER BY TRADE-NEVER BEEN IN TH' RING, BEFORE, IN MY LIFE!
B-BUT--WHEN I PAID $3000 TO HIRE TONY PASTAFAZOOLA- I UNDERSTOOD I WAS HIRING THE GREAT PASTAFAZOOLA.
TOO BAD TH' BOYS IN NOO YORK DIDN'T UNDERSTAND THAT! HA HA HA--WOTTA GAG! HO HO HO HO-
HEE HEE! THE GR-REAT SLATS SCRAPPLE'S GLOR-RIOUS VICT'RY --WAS OVER A—HAW HAW--- DISH-WASHER-
HAW HAW-- I KNEW ALL ALONG, IT WAS TOO GOOD T'BE TRUE! HEE-HEE!
R. VAN BUREN

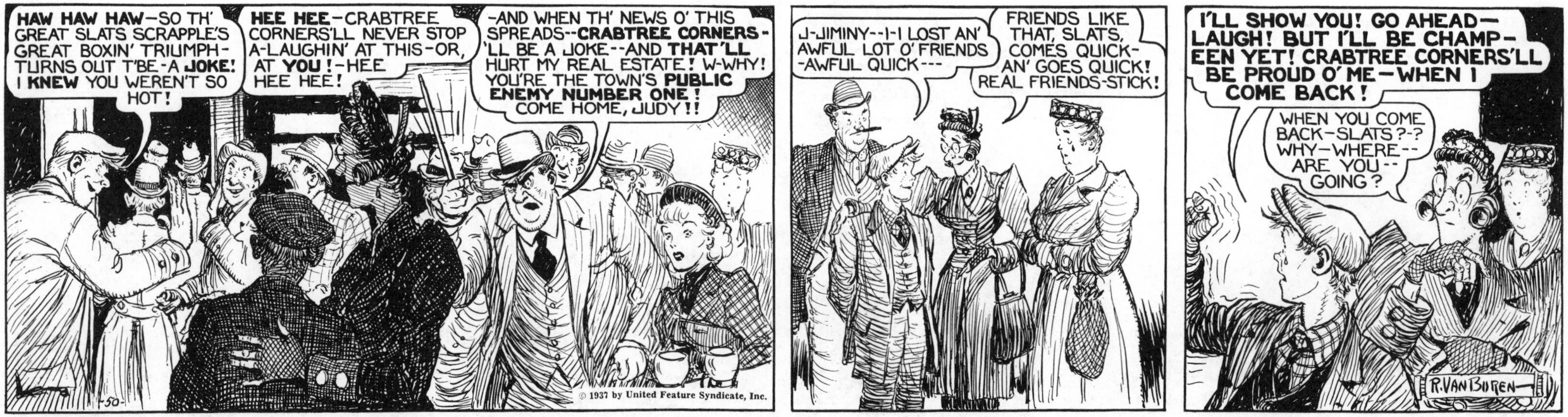
HAW HAW HAW—SO TH' GREAT SLATS SCRAPPLE'S GREAT BOXIN' TRIUMPH-TURNS OUT T'BE-A JOKE! I KNEW YOU WEREN'T SO HOT!
HEE HEE-CRABTREE CORNERS'LL NEVER STOP A-LAUGHIN' AT THIS-OR, AT YOU!-HEE HEE HEE!
-AND WHEN TH' NEWS O' THIS SPREADS--CRABTREE CORNERS-'LL BE A JOKE--AND THAT'LL HURT MY REAL ESTATE! W-WHY! YOU'RE THE TOWN'S PUBLIC ENEMY NUMBER ONE! COME HOME, JUDY!!
-50-
© 1937 by United Feature Syndicate, Inc.
J-JIMINY--I-I LOST AN' AWFUL LOT O' FRIENDS -AWFUL QUICK---
FRIENDS LIKE THAT, SLATS, COMES QUICK-AN' GOES QUICK! REAL FRIENDS-STICK!
I'LL SHOW YOU! GO AHEAD—LAUGH! BUT I'LL BE CHAMP-EEN YET! CRABTREE CORNERS'LL BE PROUD O' ME—WHEN I COME BACK!
WHEN YOU COME BACK-SLATS?-? WHY-WHERE--ARE YOU--GOING?
R. VAN BUREN

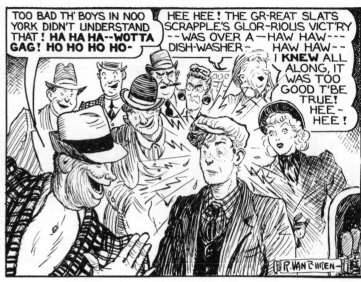

1939: Some Turning Points

by Dave Schreiner

"I found out through terrible, terrible agonies that you damn well better have that ending or you'll wind up wanting to kill yourself."

—Al Capp, in an interview with Rick Marschall, 1977.

The European War began the 1st of September, 1939, when Germany invaded Poland from the west. Two days later, England and France declared war on Germany and shortly thereafter, Russia invaded Poland from the east. Most of the rest of the world would be drawn into the conflict within two years.

The grimmest years of the 20th century were at hand.

With the start of the war, the isolationists and interventionists in the United States became even more polarized from each other than before. However, public opinion was moving glacially to a cautious position favoring England and France. It was felt that these allies should perhaps be materially helped, somehow, but only if America's neutrality was maintained. That is, the public was beginning to feel this way when or if it considered the question at all. After the initial actions and declarations of September, after Poland had fallen and been divided, the war just seemed to stop. Things would start to pop again in the spring of 1940, but in the latter part of 1939, America could still allow itself to be diverted by trivia and spectacle.

Radio was the cheapest source of daily entertainment around. The Depression had abated somewhat by 1939, so Americans had a tad more disposal income, but radio had become a fixture in the home by then, and listening to it was a congenial addiction. The decade was something of a golden age for the medium. Radio began to flex its muscles in a serious way with its as-it-happens news coverage of the coming war in Europe, but for years it had provided daily doses of music, soap opera, sports, shows for the kids, and comedy. By 1939, it had made stars of Bob Hope, Jack Benny, Fred Allen, and dozens of others.

If you had a bit more money, and were on the east coast, you could go to the world's fair in New York. It was called "The World of Tomorrow," and featured as its symbols two geometric objects called the Trylon and Perisphere. Fairgoers could buy souvenir doodads made from the miracle plastic, bakelite, and attend exhibits showing what life would be like in 1960. The fair was boycotted by Germany and visited by the king and queen of England, among many others.

1939 was a stellar year for Hollywood, both artistically and financially. The revenue giant was *Gone With the Wind*, which premiered in Atlanta, and then played to packed houses across the country. It achieved boffo box office because the book by Margaret Mitchell was *the* bestseller of the 1930s. The movie also rode the wave of an impressive publicity campaign which included a "nationwide" search for the actress to play the heroine, Scarlett O'Hara.

Al Capp put royalty and *Gone With the Wind* into *Li'l Abner* in 1939, along with ghosts, convicts, ancient hairy monsters, Lonesome Polecat, spies, headless men, mad professors, death rays that play swing music, and the third Sadie Hawkins Day.

The blond king's appearance in Dogpatch in April cunningly combined aspects of King George VI's coming visit to America in June and the abdication of King Edward VIII in 1936. The hoopla surrounding George and Elizabeth's tour of England's former colony made the creation of a visiting king a natural for Capp. (While in the United States, George and Elizabeth called on President Roosevelt, who made the isolationists nervous and Hitler angry by being the perfect host.) The blond king's love for Daisy Mae and his willingness to sacrifice "everything" for her, is an obvious reference to the blond Duke of Windsor's romance with the American Wallis Warfield Simpson. When the duke subsequently became King Edward VIII of England in 1936, he was forced to choose between keeping the crown or his divorced inamorata. He chose "the woman I love," and abdicated in favor of his younger brother, George. Then he married Mrs. Simpson. One of the most spectacularly trivial news events of that or any other decade, each step of the drama was avidly followed worldwide, and was certainly still quite fresh in the public's mind when Capp used it as a plot skeleton in *Li'l Abner.*

The actress Margo Mars stars in a cameo during the King in Dogpatch episode. The point is made that she is willing to give up the lead in "Pfft With the Breeze" in order to go after the incognito king. With this one panel, Capp made clear the depth of Margo's desire to his audience. It was public knowledge that "every" actress in Hollywood lusted after the female lead in *Gone With the Wind*. The producer, David O. Selznick, made all the top stars undergo screentests. His publicity department alleged that he searched the country for the "perfect" Scarlett, whether she be star or unknown. He finally settled on the English actress, Vivien Leigh.

Capp used *Gone With the Wind* again in a Sunday page sequence in 1942, and found himself in a peck of trouble. It began with Abner reading the book, then falling asleep and dreaming himself, Daisy, and Hannibal Hoops as the main characters. As Capp told it nearly 20 years later, Margaret Mitchell was not amused.

"I think the most luxurious trouble a strip ever got into," he told a National Cartoonists Society forum, "was some years ago when I read a book which along with all America I was enchanted with—*Gone With the Wind* by Margaret Mitchell...It was a thriller—a sort of *Dick Tracy*

without pictures. I loved *Gone With the Wind* and decided to send it flowers in my own way, which was to disembowel it in a series of four Sunday pages.

"Like all of you, I work five or six weeks ahead. The morning after the first of these burlesques appeared, my phone in Boston rang, and the operator told me I was being called from Atlanta, Georgia, by a John Marsh. I didn't know that Mr. John Marsh was Miss Mitchell's husband and a libel lawyer without much to do at the time. He asked me, 'Are you Al Capp, suh?' in a Southern drawl, and I told him yes that was my privilege. He said, 'Suh'—I must tell you that he called me 'suh' throughout the conversation, and at first I thought it a term of Southern respect. Later, I found out that it was an abbreviation for what he deeply felt about me—he said, 'Suh, my wife read your Sunday page, and suh, she didn't like it, suh.'

"...[H]e kept nagging me and said that the only way I could please his wife was to cancel the entire series. I patiently tried to explain the facts of syndicate life; that they were irrevocably in the papers and no power on earth...could possibly stop the pages. But he kept nagging, and as I had to go back to work, I ended the conversation with a short Anglo Saxon phrase of two words. It's very useful for getting rid of pests and for beginning lawsuits.

"About an hour later, United Features called me from New York to reveal for the first time that the gentleman was Miss Mitchell's husband and that my closing remark had somehow irritated him and that he intended to sue the syndicate and me jointly for one dollar for every newspaper in which this burlesque had appeared. We had actually infringed on their copyright. I had used an arrangement of English words—Gone With the Wind [In fact, Abner refers to the book as "Gone *Wif* the Wind"]—which then belonged to the Mitchells, as I've since always thought of them.

"He was going to sue me for one buck for every copy of every newspaper in which this infringement had appeared. Seventy-six million dollars! And in the opinion of the United Features lawyers, he had a damn good chance of collecting it. That didn't scare me, although it is true that my half would have amounted to somewhat more than a year's pay. But I tell you this in confidence—United Features is very cheap about sums like $38,000,000."

Capp and the syndicate settled out of court. Since it was too late to stop it, the parody ran for two more weeks, then abruptly ceased. In late December, Capp interrupted his current Sunday story and took two panels to apologize to "the Mitchells." The artist, in one of his own first appearances in the strip, is confronted at his drawing board

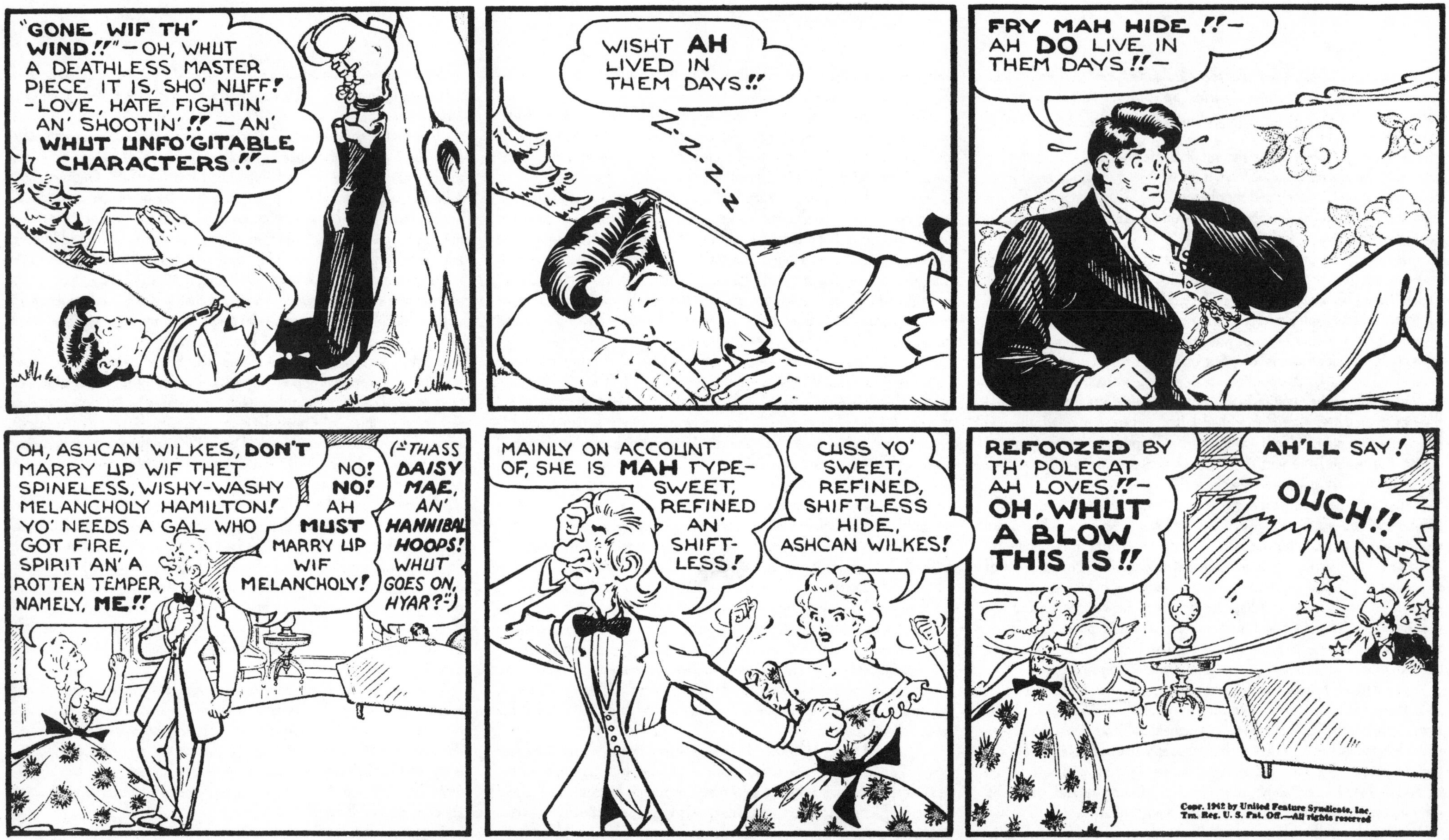
"GONE WIF TH' WIND!!" — OH, WHUT A DEATHLESS MASTER PIECE IT IS, SHO' NUFF! -LOVE, HATE, FIGHTIN' AN' SHOOTIN' !! — AN' WHUT UNFO'GITABLE CHARACTERS !!—
WISH'T AH LIVED IN THEM DAYS !!
Z-Z-Z-Z
FRY MAH HIDE !!— AH DO LIVE IN THEM DAYS !!—
OH, ASHCAN WILKES, DON'T MARRY UP WIF THET SPINELESS, WISHY-WASHY MELANCHOLY HAMILTON! YO' NEEDS A GAL WHO GOT FIRE, SPIRIT AN' A ROTTEN TEMPER, NAMELY, ME!!
NO! NO! AH MUST MARRY UP WIF MELANCHOLY!
(—THASS DAISY MAE, AN' HANNIBAL HOOPS! WHUT GOES ON, HYAR?—)
MAINLY ON ACCOUNT OF, SHE IS MAH TYPE-SWEET, REFINED AN' SHIFT-LESS!
CUSS YO' SWEET, REFINED, SHIFTLESS HIDE, ASHCAN WILKES!
REFOOZED BY TH' POLECAT AH LOVES!!— OH, WHUT A BLOW THIS IS !!
AH'LL SAY!
OUCH!!
Copr. 1942 by United Feature Syndicate, Inc.
Tm. Reg. U. S. Pat. Off.—All rights reserved

The first six panels from the 1942 Sunday page that got Al Capp in trouble with Margaret Mitchell and her lawyer husband. Abner has the starring role of Wreck Butler, opposite Daisy Mae's Scallop O'Hara. In November, Capp apologized to "the Mitchells," because, as Mammy said, "It's th' CODE OF TH' HILLS." The apology also forestalled a lawsuit.

by Abner and Mammy. Abner says, "Befo' goin' on wif *this* story, Mistah Capp—rec'lect thet story yo' did, *a while back*, good-naychurdly kiddin' a sartin book?" Capp says yes, and Mammy tells him, "Wal—sartin parties objected—sartin parties got thar feelin's hurt! Yo' gotta make it *right*, Mistah Capp!! *It's the Code of the Hills!!*" The last panel has Capp's and the syndicate's handwritten apology. It didn't have a punchline.

If George VI and his consort had read the comics page during their brief visit to America—and stranger things have happened, surely—they would have enjoyed a momentous event in the early history of *Li'l Abner*: the marriage of "Panther Eyes" herself, Sandra Petwell. Introduced in 1936, Sandra, with her eyes that shoot hypnotizing lightning bolts, was the first woman to capture Abner's undivided attention, if you ignore Mammy, Daisy, and Salomey, that is. She appeared briefly in the two following years, and finally, in 1939, she took center stage for her nuptials. It happens while Abner is trying to free the ghostly goodtime Charlie from his earthly ties. The episode, in which Charlie tries to tie up some mortal loose ends before heading into the sunrise, owes something to Thorne Smith's *Topper*, more to the 1937 movie made from that book, and its topicality derives from the 1939 sequel, *Topper Returns*. Another character Capp introduced in 1936 comes back to haunt Abner at the end of the decade: the nefarious Gat Garson. Abner's doppelganger yet again manipulates events so Abner goes to prison, but this time, the hero is nearly executed before being rescued. Abner's stay on death row was his second prison stretch of the year, and his fourth since 1936. That isn't counting time spent in local pokies, and must be a record for a guy as perpetually innocent as Abner. His first stretch of 1939 was spent with his parents—which is a first—and came after an agonizingly long adventure about Abner and a ne'er do well named Freddie Flophouse being mixed up by their parents at an early age. The complications and convolutions in this chapter seem to have defeated even Capp, a talented storyteller. After the story logically ends, he or the syndicate apparently felt the need to tie up all the bureaucratic loose ends in the strip for February 13, a Monday. It's certainly the least visual of any *Li'l Abner* strip, of any comic strip ever produced, with its four panels of text and no pictures. It could well have been this adventure and this strip that Capp had in mind when he talked to Rick Marschall about agonies and endings.

The whole affair points to Capp's growing dissatisfaction with the humorous soap opera format of *Li'l Abner*. The episodes with the king, the ghost, the Flophouse family, and with Garson all have moments of bright light. Watching Abner enter a car occupied by a headless man

(another dead end, as it turns out); seeing Abner react to the reappearance of Sandra; contemplating Abner masquerading as the toughest gangster of them all; appreciating the beautiful art in the ghost section—these are all beacons in *Li'l Abner*, 1939. But there is something lifeless about the stories wrapped around them. It's as if Capp is bored as a storyteller, as if he's going through the motions, filling the endless days with *product*, not comic strips he was truly happy with. A reader can perhaps sense that Capp is straining against the structure of the strip, trying to find his way out of the confines of *Li'l Abner's* format.

And why not? Capp is on record as saying his first love was the *comic* comic strip. Besides that, since 1937 he had been writing a soap opera with touches of humor for Raeburn Van Buren, *Abbie an' Slats*. The humor wasn't as broad as in *Li'l Abner*, and it was more realistic in plot, dialogue, and art, but it was essentially the same type of strip. With hindsight, we know Capp was groping toward satire, parody, burlesque, and the sublimely bizarre in *Li'l Abner*. Some early signs of what was to come surfaced in 1938. The internal battle went on in 1939, and Capp, suffering some setbacks along the way, nevertheless began to slowly change the strip into what he had wanted it to be in the first place.

For one thing, on September 5, 1939, Mammy ironed Pappy's pants—with Pappy in them. She'd never done that before. But she'd do it again.

For another, Capp brought Lonesome Polecat over from the Sunday page, where he had been hanging out with Hairless Joe since February of 1938. In tandem, they introduced Kickapoo Joy Juice to the daily strip audience. Combine Joe, Polecat, and Juice with Black Rufe, a "Thing" in armor from Scotland, and a society party, and you have a reprise of the Scragg family's invasion of a similar soiree in 1938. Only this one is wilder (not funnier, though).

Then there's the best Sadie Hawkins Day race yet, the third one. It introduces Mitzi Mudlark, *"the fastest critter on laigs in th' w-world."* There's the first SHD prediction by Ole Man Mose, and it's one of the only times Abner is able to figure it out and use it before the race (he has help, of course). The first Sadie Hawkins Eve dance appeared in 1939, and the race itself was the most frantic and narratively inventive affair yet. In 1940, Columbia Pictures would make a *Li'l Abner* movie, and Sadie Hawkins Day was its centerpiece. The filmmakers incorporated the prediction from Capp's 1939 race into their script, along with Abner's drag act and other incidents from this sequence.

Finally, Mammy engages in her first epic battle in the daily strips. This one's with Mother Ratfield, and it lasts for days. Mammy had

been doing mythic battle in the Sunday section almost from the moment it began in February of 1935, but the fantastic dimensions of her fistic prowess had never been fully explored in the dailies before. Many of her weekend battles were with various no-account residents of Skunk Hollow, Dogpatch's neighbor and worst civic enemy. Skunk Hollow is so tough, even Hairless Joe refuses to pass near it. The world's dirtiest wrestler, Earthquake McGoon, is typical of its citizenry, although he seems to be too uncivilized even for that town, being confined to the Badlands. Both McGoon and Skunk Hollow would soon debut in the dailies.

The Sunday page seems to have been Al Capp's spring training camp during this period. The daily and Sunday storylines did not overlap, and many characters who became staples of *Li'l Abner* had their first tryouts on Sunday. Capp also worked out ideas and formats here. The Sunday page was gag-oriented from the beginning. Typical stories ran from a week to four weeks. At first, the pages were given over to fisticuffs on Mammy's and Abner's part, and cowardice on Pappy's. Gradually, other elements were introduced: tall tales, dream sequences in which Li'l Abner became Li'l Nemo, the first jabs at Ham Fisher's *Joe Palooka*, and that nest of vipers over the hill in Skunk Hollow. On Sunday, Capp refined his central characters' personalities. He had the freedom from continuity on that day to let them evolve into the lovable types we're familiar with. Al Capp's vision of what *Li'l Abner* should be was coming into focus. By the time the war in Europe spread to the United States, he would have what he wanted—and his audience would want it, too.

Allen, Frederick Lewis, *Since Yesterday: The 1930s in America*, Harper & Row, New York, 1940

Capp, Al, "Work and Have Fun," *Famous Artists Cartoon Course*, Lesson 21.

Capp, Al, address to the National Cartoonists Society as recorded in *Nemo: the Classic Comics Library*, No. 18, April 1986.

Manchester, William, *The Glory and the Dream*, Volume 1. Boston: Little, Brown and Company, 1973.

Marschall, Richard, " 'Saying Something about the Status Quo,' An Annotated Interview with Al Capp," *Nemo: the Classic Comics Library*, No. 18, April 1986.

LI'L ABNER Mysterious Stranger By Al Capp

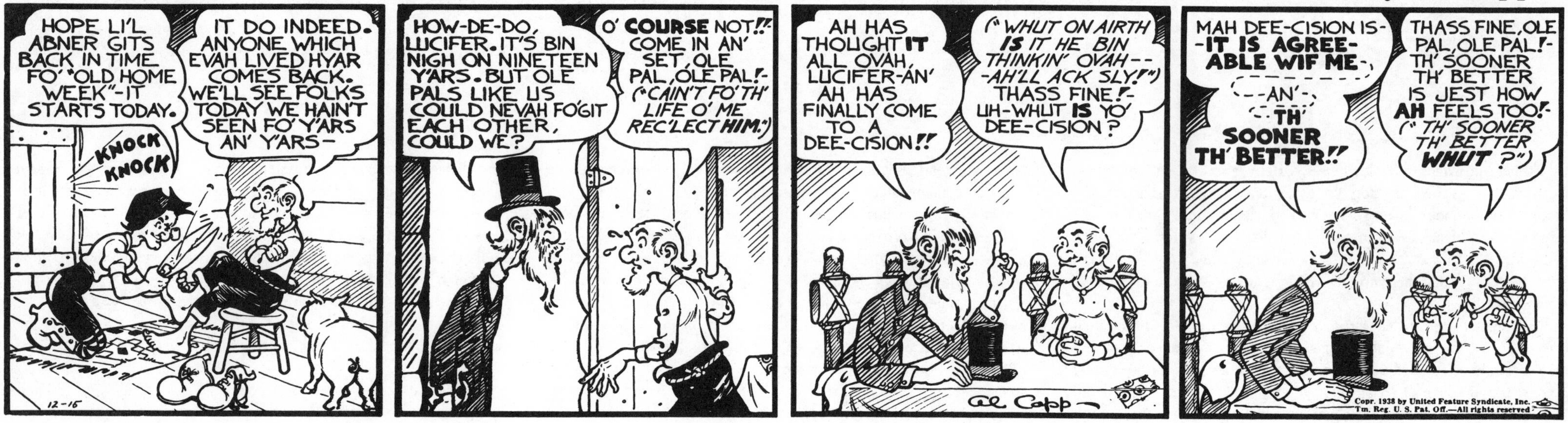

HOPE LI'L ABNER GITS BACK IN TIME FO' "OLD HOME WEEK"-IT STARTS TODAY.
IT DO INDEED. ANYONE WHICH EVAH LIVED HYAR COMES BACK. WE'LL SEE FOLKS TODAY WE HAIN'T SEEN FO' Y'ARS AN' Y'ARS—
KNOCK KNOCK
12-15
HOW-DE-DO, LUCIFER. IT'S BIN NIGH ON NINETEEN Y'ARS. BUT OLE PALS LIKE US COULD NEVAH FO'GIT EACH OTHER, COULD WE?
O' COURSE NOT!! COME IN AN' SET, OLE PAL, OLE PAL!- ("CAIN'T FO'TH' LIFE O' ME REC'LECT HIM.")
AH HAS THOUGHT IT ALL OVAH, LUCIFER-AN' AH HAS FINALLY COME TO A DEE-CISION!!
("WHUT ON AIRTH IS IT HE BIN THINKIN' OVAH---AH'LL ACK SLY!") THASS FINE!- UH-WHUT IS YO' DEE-CISION?
al Capp
MAH DEE-CISION IS- -IT IS AGREE-ABLE WIF ME- -AN'- -TH' SOONER TH' BETTER!!
THASS FINE, OLE PAL, OLE PAL!- TH' SOONER TH' BETTER IS JEST HOW AH FEELS TOO!- ("TH' SOONER TH' BETTER WHUT?")
Copr. 1938 by United Feature Syndicate, Inc. Tm. Reg. U. S. Pat. Off.—All rights reserved

LI'L ABNER Meet Jeeter Blugg By Al Capp

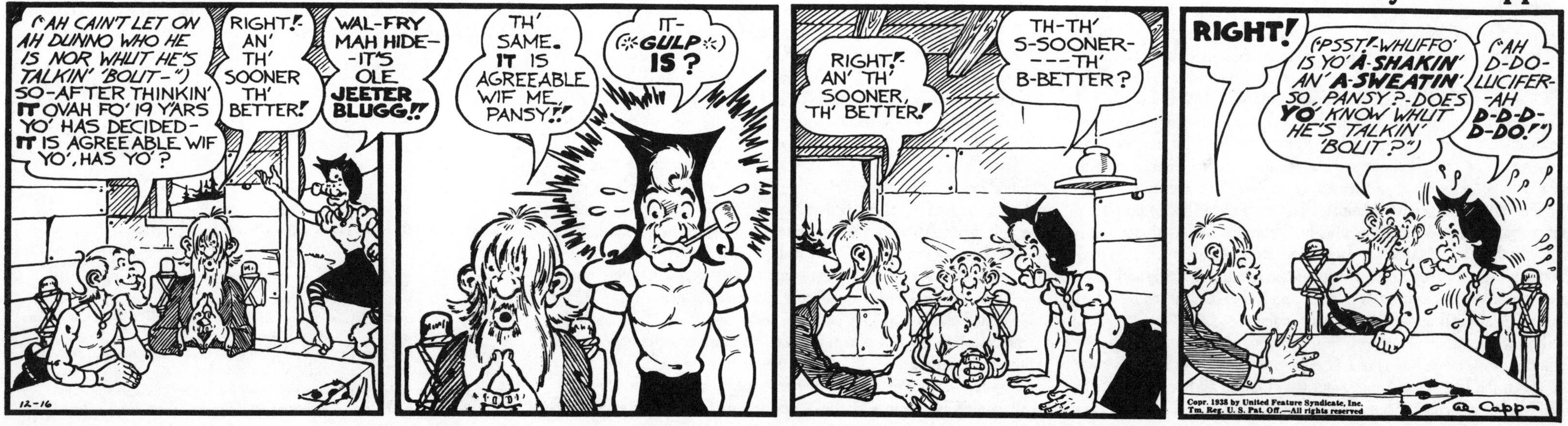

("AH CAIN'T LET ON AH DUNNO WHO HE IS NOR WHUT HE'S TALKIN' 'BOUT-") SO-AFTER THINKIN' IT OVAH FO' 19 Y'ARS YO' HAS DECIDED- IT IS AGREEABLE WIF YO', HAS YO'?
RIGHT!- AN' TH' SOONER TH' BETTER!
WAL-FRY MAH HIDE- -IT'S OLE JEETER BLUGG!!
12-16
TH' SAME. IT IS AGREEABLE WIF ME, PANSY!!
IT- (GULP) IS?
RIGHT!- AN' TH' SOONER, TH' BETTER!
TH-TH' S-SOONER- ---TH' B-BETTER?
RIGHT!
("PSST!-WHUFFO' IS YO' A-SHAKIN' AN' A-SWEATIN' SO, PANSY?-DOES YO' KNOW WHUT HE'S TALKIN' 'BOUT?")
("AH D-DO-LUCIFER- -AH D-D-D-D-DO!")
Copr. 1938 by United Feature Syndicate, Inc. Tm. Reg. U. S. Pat. Off.—All rights reserved
al Capp

LI'L ABNER

Like a Lamb to the Slaughter

By Al Capp

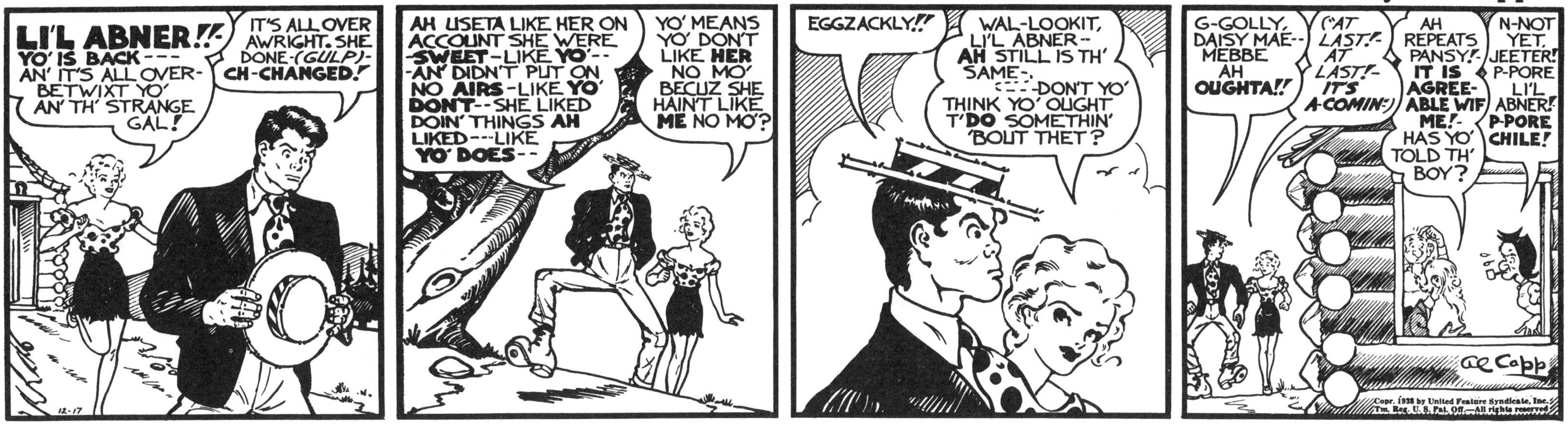

LI'L ABNER!!- YO' IS BACK--- AN' IT'S ALL OVER- BETWIXT YO' AN' TH' STRANGE GAL!
IT'S ALL OVER AWRIGHT. SHE DONE-(GULP)- CH-CHANGED!
12-17
AH USETA LIKE HER ON ACCOUNT SHE WERE -SWEET-LIKE YO'-- -AN' DIDN'T PUT ON NO AIRS-LIKE YO' DON'T--SHE LIKED DOIN' THINGS AH LIKED---LIKE YO' DOES--
YO' MEANS YO' DON'T LIKE HER NO MO' BECUZ SHE HAIN'T LIKE ME NO MO'?
EGGZACKLY!!
WAL-LOOKIT, LI'L ABNER- AH STILL IS TH' SAME-. ----DON'T YO' THINK YO' OUGHT T'DO SOMETHIN' 'BOUT THET?
G-GOLLY, DAISY MAE-- MEBBE AH OUGHTA!!
("AT LAST!- AT LAST!- IT'S A-COMIN'-)
AH REPEATS PANSY!- IT IS AGREE-ABLE WIF ME!- HAS YO' TOLD TH' BOY?
N-NOT YET, JEETER! P-PORE LI'L ABNER! P-PORE CHILE!
Al Capp
Copr. 1938 by United Feature Syndicate, Inc. Tm. Reg. U. S. Pat. Off.—All rights reserved

LI'L ABNER

Rain Inside and Out

By Al Capp

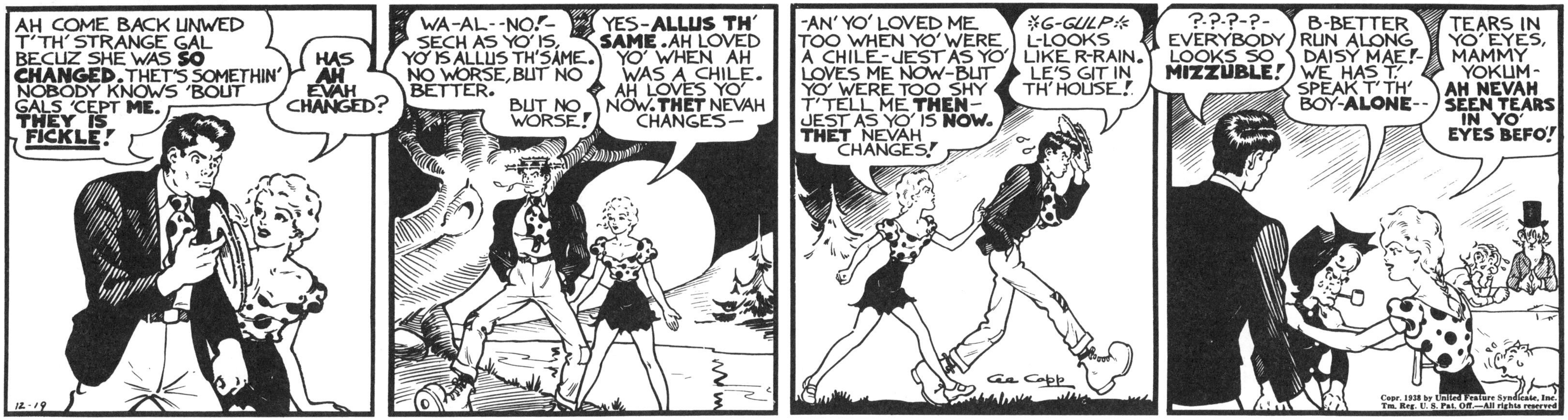

AH COME BACK UNWED T'TH' STRANGE GAL BECUZ SHE WAS SO CHANGED. THET'S SOMETHIN' NOBODY KNOWS 'BOUT GALS 'CEPT ME. THEY IS FICKLE!
HAS AH EVAH CHANGED?
12-19
WA-AL--NO!- SECH AS YO' IS, YO' IS ALLUS TH' SAME. NO WORSE, BUT NO BETTER.
BUT NO WORSE!
YES-ALLUS TH' SAME. AH LOVED YO' WHEN AH WAS A CHILE. AH LOVES YO' NOW. THET NEVAH CHANGES—
-AN' YO' LOVED ME TOO WHEN YO' WERE A CHILE-JEST AS YO' LOVES ME NOW-BUT YO' WERE TOO SHY T'TELL ME THEN- JEST AS YO' IS NOW. THET NEVAH CHANGES!
G-GULP L-LOOKS LIKE R-RAIN. LE'S GIT IN TH' HOUSE!
Al Capp
?-?-?-?- EVERYBODY LOOKS SO MIZZUBLE!
B-BETTER RUN ALONG DAISY MAE!- WE HAS T' SPEAK T' TH' BOY-ALONE--
TEARS IN YO' EYES, MAMMY YOKUM- AH NEVAH SEEN TEARS IN YO' EYES BEFO'!
Copr. 1938 by United Feature Syndicate, Inc. Tm. Reg. U. S. Pat. Off.—All rights reserved

LI'L ABNER A Pawn of Fate! By Al Capp

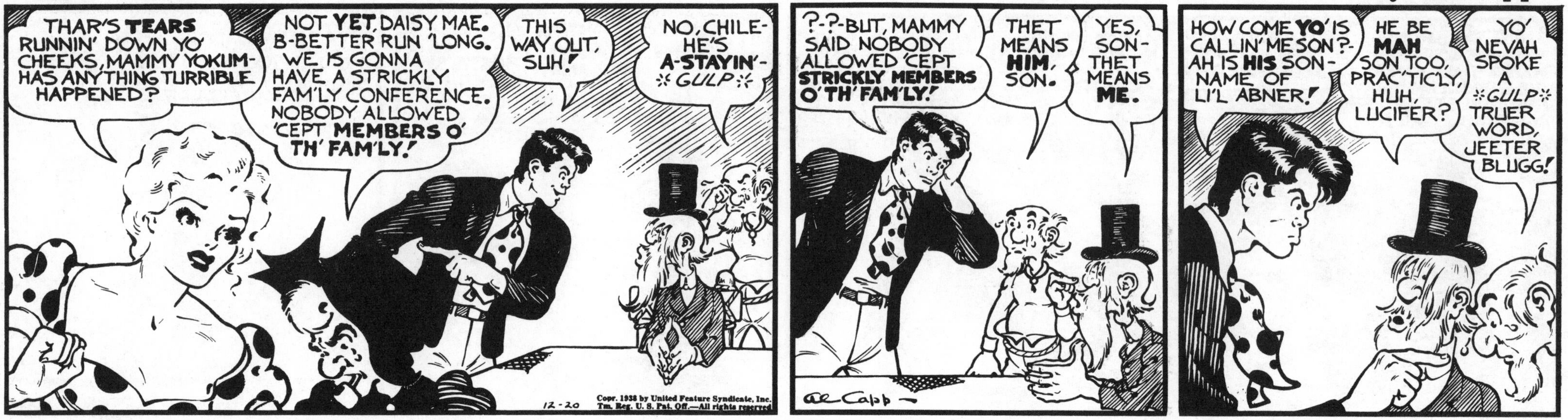

THAR'S TEARS RUNNIN' DOWN YO' CHEEKS, MAMMY YOKUM- HAS ANYTHING TURRIBLE HAPPENED?
NOT YET, DAISY MAE. B-BETTER RUN 'LONG. WE IS GONNA HAVE A STRICKLY FAM'LY CONFERENCE. NOBODY ALLOWED 'CEPT MEMBERS O' TH' FAM'LY!
THIS WAY OUT, SUH!
NO, CHILE- HE'S A-STAYIN'- GULP
12-20
Copr. 1938 by United Feature Syndicate, Inc. Tm. Reg. U. S. Pat. Off.—All rights reserved
?-?-BUT, MAMMY SAID NOBODY ALLOWED 'CEPT STRICKLY MEMBERS O' TH' FAM'LY!
THET MEANS HIM, SON.
YES, SON- THET MEANS ME.
AL CAPP
HOW COME YO' IS CALLIN' ME SON?- AH IS HIS SON- NAME OF LI'L ABNER!
HE BE MAH SON TOO, PRAC'TIC'LY, HUH, LUCIFER?
YO' NEVAH SPOKE A GULP TRUER WORD, JEETER BLUGG!

LI'L ABNER Child-Bridegroom! By Al Capp

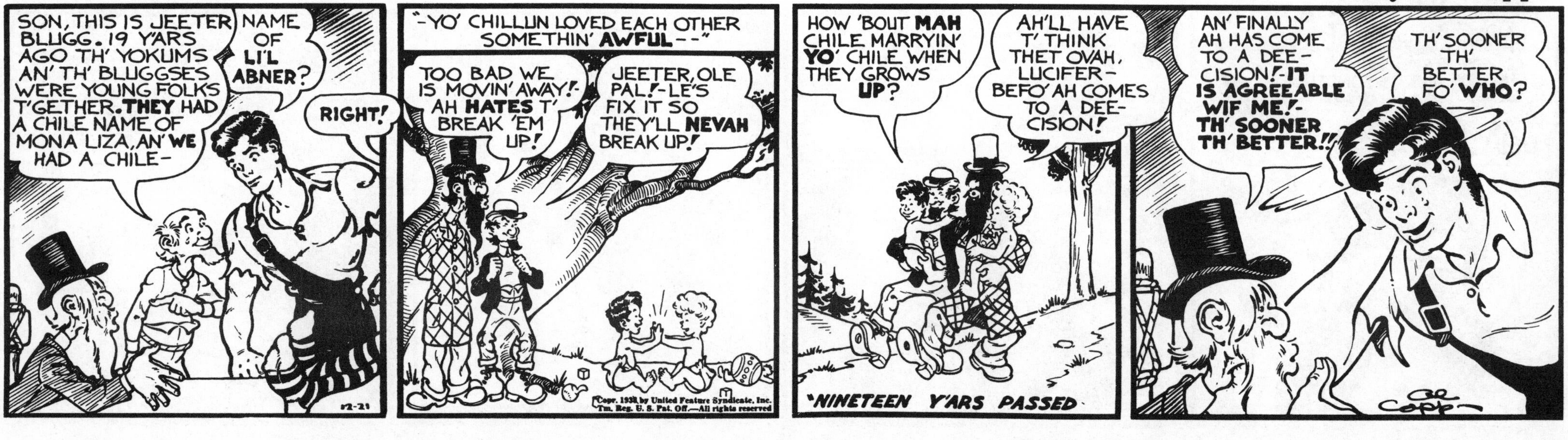

SON, THIS IS JEETER BLUGG. 19 Y'ARS AGO TH' YOKUMS AN' TH' BLUGGSES WERE YOUNG FOLKS T'GETHER. THEY HAD A CHILE NAME OF MONA LIZA, AN' WE HAD A CHILE-
NAME OF LI'L ABNER?
RIGHT!
12-21
"-YO' CHILLUN LOVED EACH OTHER SOMETHIN' AWFUL--"
TOO BAD WE IS MOVIN' AWAY!- AH HATES T' BREAK 'EM UP!
JEETER, OLE PAL!- LE'S FIX IT SO THEY'LL NEVAH BREAK UP!
Copr. 1938 by United Feature Syndicate, Inc. Tm. Reg. U. S. Pat. Off.—All rights reserved
HOW 'BOUT MAH CHILE MARRYIN' YO' CHILE WHEN THEY GROWS UP?
AH'LL HAVE T' THINK THET OVAH, LUCIFER- BEFO' AH COMES TO A DEE-CISION!
NINETEEN Y'ARS PASSED
AN' FINALLY AH HAS COME TO A DEE-CISION!- IT IS AGREEABLE WIF ME!- TH' SOONER TH' BETTER!!
TH' SOONER TH' BETTER FO' WHO?
AL CAPP

LI'L ABNER But Chile, Look at Her Now! By Al Capp

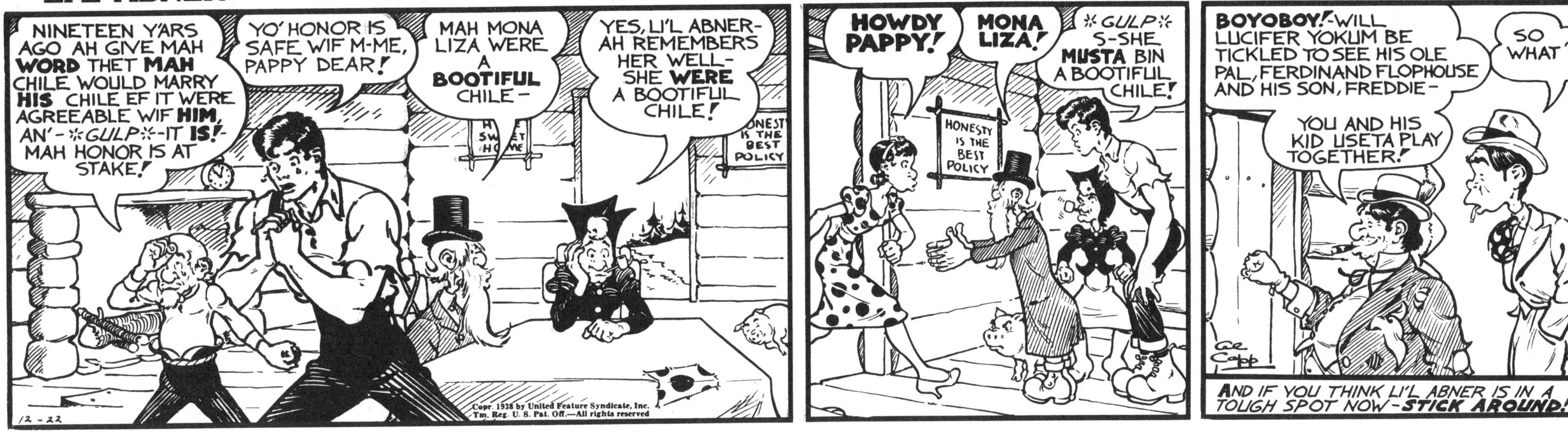
NINETEEN Y'ARS AGO AH GIVE MAH WORD THET MAH CHILE WOULD MARRY HIS CHILE EF IT WERE AGREEABLE WIF HIM, AN'-*GULP*-IT IS!-MAH HONOR IS AT STAKE!
YO' HONOR IS SAFE WIF M-ME, PAPPY DEAR!
MAH MONA LIZA WERE A BOOTIFUL CHILE-
YES, LI'L ABNER-AH REMEMBERS HER WELL-SHE WERE A BOOTIFUL CHILE!
12-22
Copr. 1938 by United Feature Syndicate, Inc. Tm. Reg. U. S. Pat. Off.—All rights reserved
HOWDY PAPPY!
MONA LIZA!
GULP S-SHE MUSTA BIN A BOOTIFUL CHILE!
HONESTY IS THE BEST POLICY
BOYOBOY!-WILL LUCIFER YOKUM BE TICKLED TO SEE HIS OLE PAL, FERDINAND FLOPHOUSE AND HIS SON, FREDDIE-
SO WHAT?
YOU AND HIS KID USETA PLAY TOGETHER!
Al Capp
AND IF YOU THINK LI'L ABNER IS IN A TOUGH SPOT NOW-STICK AROUND!-

LI'L ABNER September Morn By Al Capp

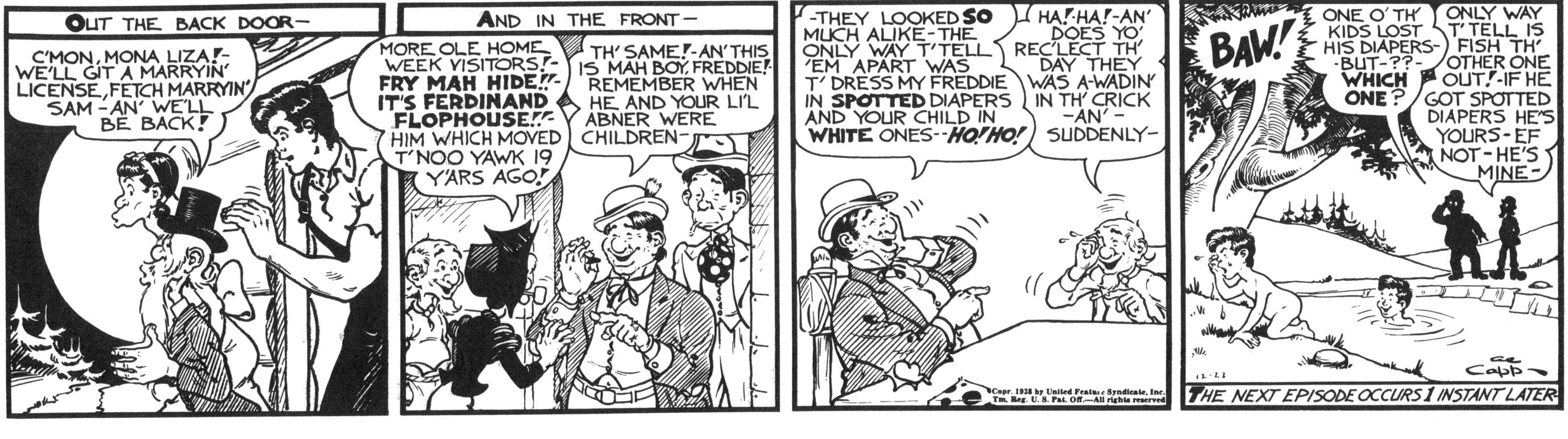
OUT THE BACK DOOR-
C'MON, MONA LIZA!-WE'LL GIT A MARRYIN' LICENSE, FETCH MARRYIN' SAM-AN' WE'LL BE BACK!
AND IN THE FRONT-
MORE OLE HOME WEEK VISITORS!-FRY MAH HIDE!!-IT'S FERDINAND FLOPHOUSE!!-HIM WHICH MOVED T'NOO YAWK 19 Y'ARS AGO!
TH' SAME!-AN' THIS IS MAH BOY, FREDDIE!-REMEMBER WHEN HE AND YOUR LI'L ABNER WERE CHILDREN-
-THEY LOOKED SO MUCH ALIKE-THE ONLY WAY T'TELL 'EM APART WAS T' DRESS MY FREDDIE IN SPOTTED DIAPERS AND YOUR CHILD IN WHITE ONES--HO! HO!
HA!-HA!-AN' DOES YO' REC'LECT TH' DAY THEY WAS A-WADIN' IN TH' CRICK -AN'- SUDDENLY-
Copr. 1938 by United Feature Syndicate, Inc. Tm. Reg. U. S. Pat. Off.—All rights reserved
BAW!
ONE O' TH' KIDS LOST HIS DIAPERS-BUT-??-WHICH ONE?
ONLY WAY T' TELL IS FISH TH' OTHER ONE OUT!-IF HE GOT SPOTTED DIAPERS HE'S YOURS-EF NOT-HE'S MINE-
12-23
Al Capp
THE NEXT EPISODE OCCURS 1 INSTANT LATER-

LI'L ABNER Spots Before Their Eyes! **By Al Capp**

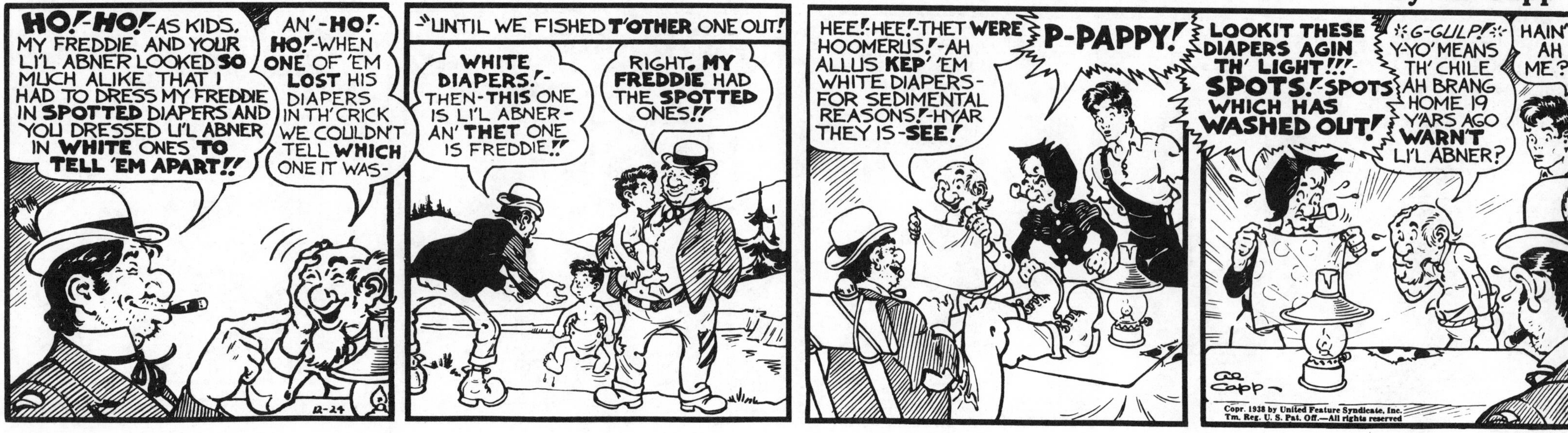
HO!-HO!-AS KIDS, MY FREDDIE AND YOUR LI'L ABNER LOOKED SO MUCH ALIKE THAT I HAD TO DRESS MY FREDDIE IN SPOTTED DIAPERS AND YOU DRESSED LI'L ABNER IN WHITE ONES TO TELL 'EM APART!!
AN'-HO!-HO!-WHEN ONE OF 'EM LOST HIS DIAPERS IN TH' CRICK WE COULDN'T TELL WHICH ONE IT WAS-
12-24
-UNTIL WE FISHED T'OTHER ONE OUT!
WHITE DIAPERS!-THEN-THIS ONE IS LI'L ABNER-AN' THET ONE IS FREDDIE!!
RIGHT. MY FREDDIE HAD THE SPOTTED ONES!!
HEE!-HEE!-THET WERE HOOMERUS!-AH ALLUS KEP' 'EM WHITE DIAPERS-FOR SEDIMENTAL REASONS!-HYAR THEY IS-SEE!
P-PAPPY!
LOOKIT THESE DIAPERS AGIN TH' LIGHT!!!-SPOTS!-SPOTS WHICH HAS WASHED OUT!
G-GULP! Y-YO' MEANS TH' CHILE AH BRANG HOME 19 Y'ARS AGO WARN'T LI'L ABNER?
HAIN'T AH ME?
Al Capp
Copr. 1938 by United Feature Syndicate, Inc.
Tm. Reg. U. S. Pat. Off.—All rights reserved

LI'L ABNER Comes the Dawn! **By Al Capp**

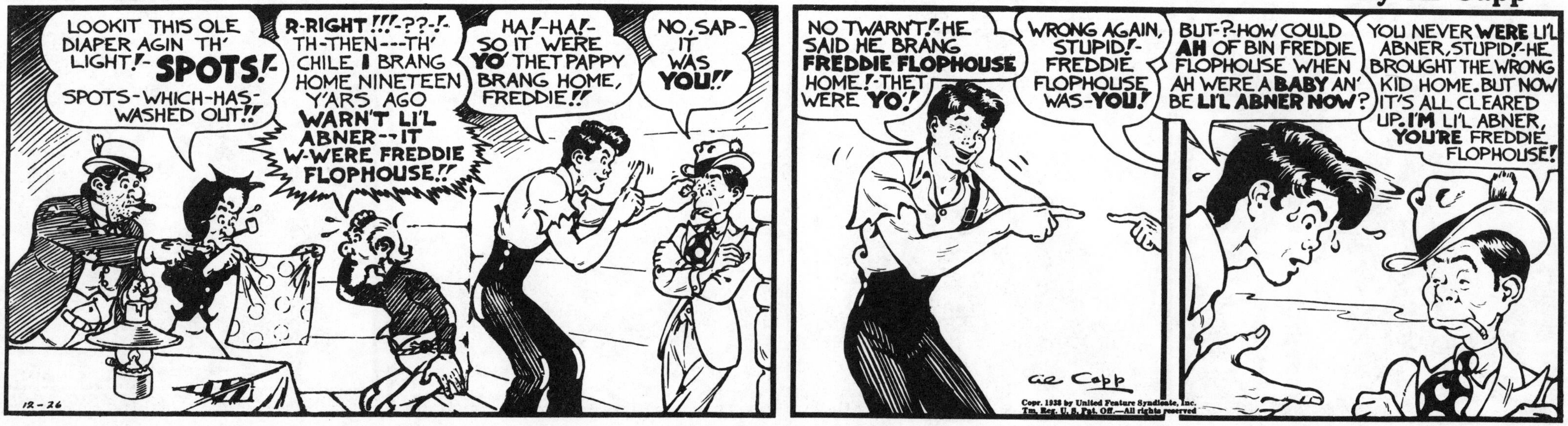
LOOKIT THIS OLE DIAPER AGIN TH' LIGHT!-SPOTS!-SPOTS-WHICH-HAS-WASHED OUT!!
R-RIGHT!!!-??-!-TH-THEN---TH' CHILE I BRANG HOME NINETEEN Y'ARS AGO WARN'T LI'L ABNER--IT W-WERE FREDDIE FLOPHOUSE!!
HA!-HA!-SO IT WERE YO' THET PAPPY BRANG HOME, FREDDIE!!
NO, SAP-IT WAS YOU!!
12-26
NO TWARN'T!-HE SAID HE BRANG FREDDIE FLOPHOUSE HOME!-THET WERE YO'!
WRONG AGAIN, STUPID!-FREDDIE FLOPHOUSE WAS-YOU!
Al Capp
Copr. 1938 by United Feature Syndicate, Inc.
Tm. Reg. U. S. Pat. Off.—All rights reserved
BUT-?-HOW COULD AH OF BIN FREDDIE FLOPHOUSE WHEN AH WERE A BABY AN' BE LI'L ABNER NOW?
YOU NEVER WERE LI'L ABNER, STUPID!-HE BROUGHT THE WRONG KID HOME. BUT NOW IT'S ALL CLEARED UP. I'M LI'L ABNER, YOU'RE FREDDIE FLOPHOUSE!

LI'L ABNER At Long Last— By Al Capp

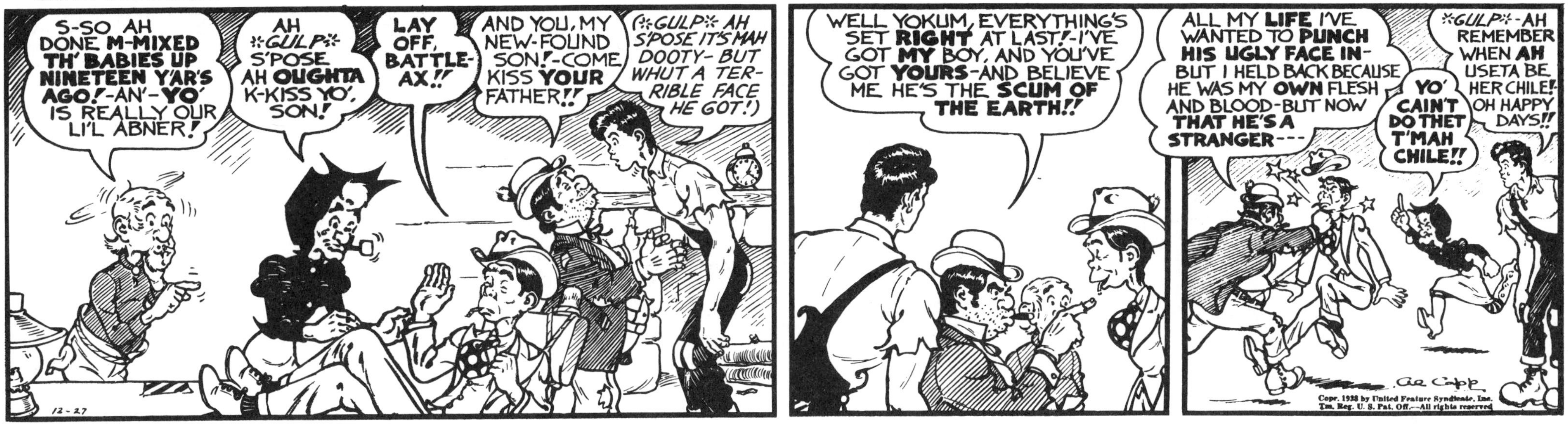
S-SO AH DONE M-MIXED TH' BABIES UP NINETEEN YAR'S AGO!-AN'-YO' IS REALLY OUR LI'L ABNER!
AH *GULP* S'POSE AH OUGHTA K-KISS YO', SON!
LAY OFF, BATTLE-AX!!
AND YOU, MY NEW-FOUND SON!-COME KISS YOUR FATHER!!
(*GULP* AH S'POSE IT'S MAH DOOTY- BUT WHUT A TER-RIBLE FACE HE GOT!)
12-27
WELL YOKUM, EVERYTHING'S SET RIGHT AT LAST!-I'VE GOT MY BOY, AND YOU'VE GOT YOURS-AND BELIEVE ME HE'S THE SCUM OF THE EARTH!!
ALL MY LIFE I'VE WANTED TO PUNCH HIS UGLY FACE IN- BUT I HELD BACK BECAUSE HE WAS MY OWN FLESH AND BLOOD-BUT NOW THAT HE'S A STRANGER---
YO' CAIN'T DO THET T'MAH CHILE!!
GULP-AH REMEMBER WHEN AH USETA BE HER CHILE!-OH HAPPY DAYS!!
Al Capp
Copr. 1938 by United Feature Syndicate, Inc. Tm. Reg. U. S. Pat. Off.—All rights reserved

LI'L ABNER Practically Nobody's Chile By Al Capp

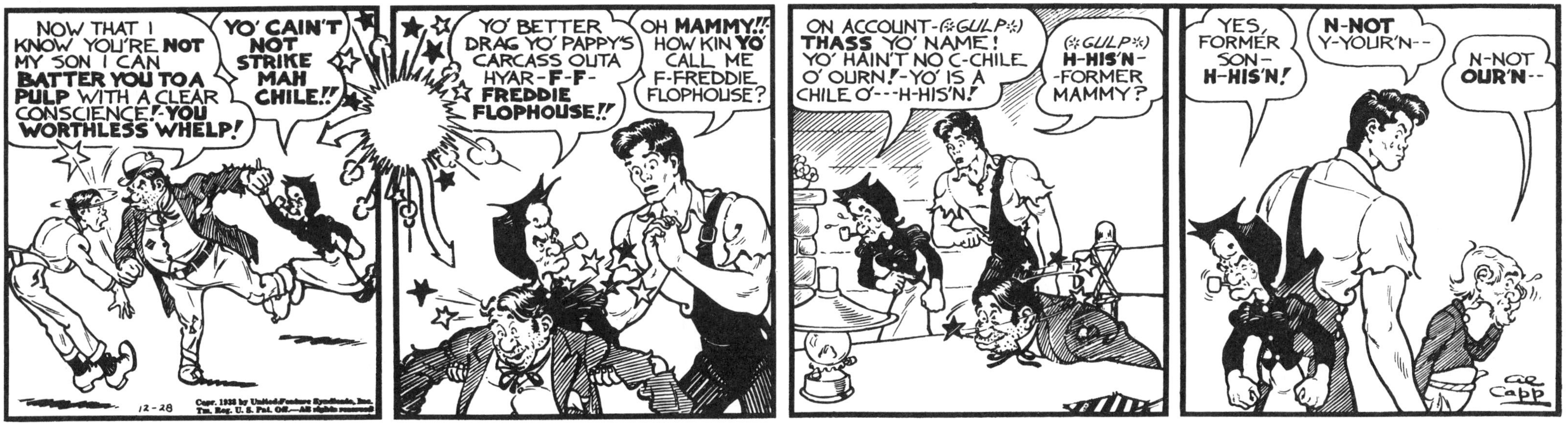
NOW THAT I KNOW YOU'RE NOT MY SON I CAN BATTER YOU TO A PULP WITH A CLEAR CONSCIENCE!-YOU WORTHLESS WHELP!
YO' CAIN'T NOT STRIKE MAH CHILE!!
12-28
Copr. 1938 by United Feature Syndicate, Inc. Tm. Reg. U. S. Pat. Off.—All rights reserved
YO' BETTER DRAG YO' PAPPY'S CARCASS OUTA HYAR-F-F-FREDDIE FLOPHOUSE!!
OH MAMMY!! HOW KIN YO' CALL ME F-FREDDIE FLOPHOUSE?
ON ACCOUNT-(*GULP*) THASS YO' NAME! YO' HAIN'T NO C-CHILE O' OURN!-YO' IS A CHILE O'---H-HIS'N!
(*GULP*) H-HIS'N- -FORMER MAMMY?
YES, FORMER SON- H-HIS'N!
N-NOT Y-YOUR'N--
N-NOT OUR'N--
Al Capp

LI'L ABNER Prepare for a Shock

By Al Capp

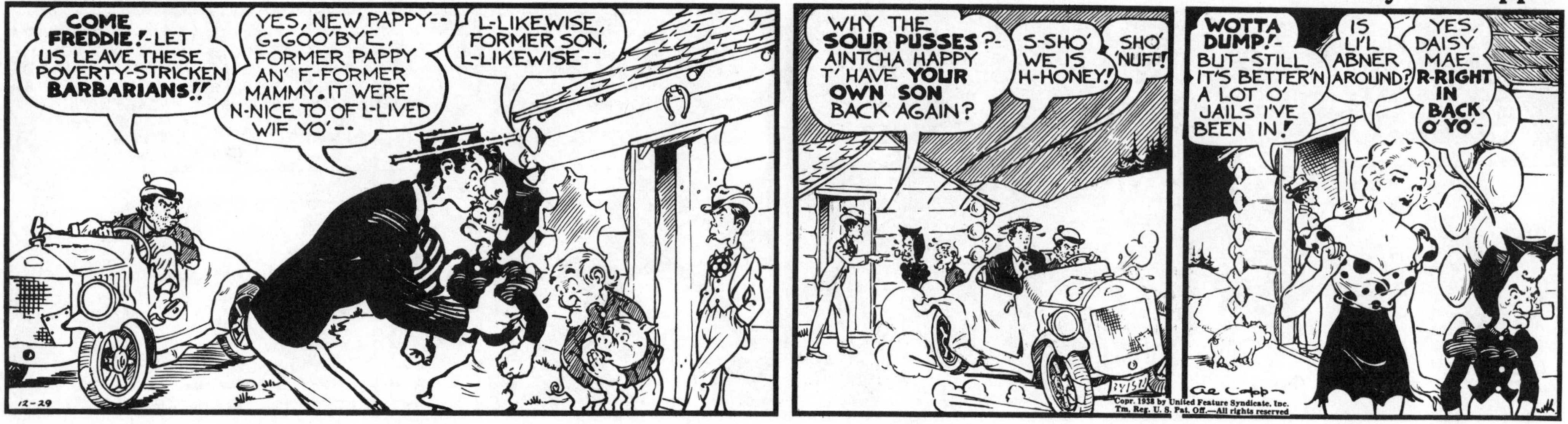

COME FREDDIE!-LET US LEAVE THESE POVERTY-STRICKEN BARBARIANS!!
YES, NEW PAPPY--G-GOO'BYE, FORMER PAPPY AN' F-FORMER MAMMY. IT WERE N-NICE TO OF L-LIVED WIF YO'--
L-LIKEWISE, FORMER SON, L-LIKEWISE--
12-29
WHY THE SOUR PUSSES?-AINTCHA HAPPY T' HAVE YOUR OWN SON BACK AGAIN?
S-SHO' WE IS H-HONEY!
SHO' 'NUFF!
WOTTA DUMP!-BUT-STILL IT'S BETTER'N A LOT O' JAILS I'VE BEEN IN!
IS LI'L ABNER AROUND?
YES, DAISY MAE-R-RIGHT IN BACK O' YO'-
Copr. 1938 by United Feature Syndicate, Inc. Tm. Reg. U. S. Pat. Off.—All rights reserved

LI'L ABNER Take a Powder, Old Folks

By Al Capp

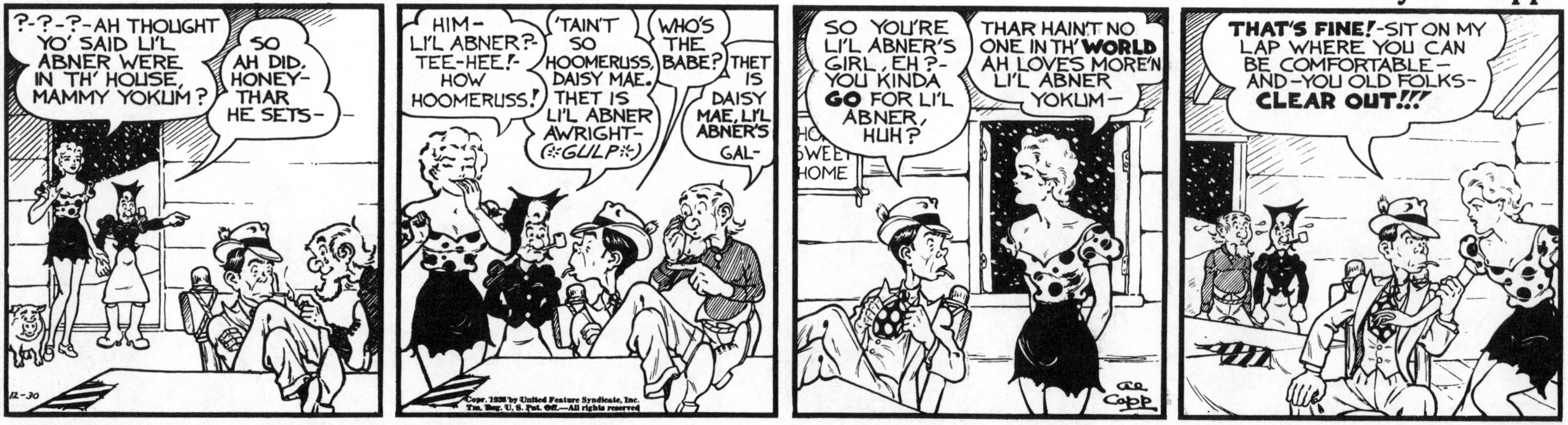

?-?-?-AH THOUGHT YO' SAID LI'L ABNER WERE IN TH' HOUSE, MAMMY YOKUM?
SO AH DID, HONEY-THAR HE SETS-
12-30
HIM-LI'L ABNER?-TEE-HEE!-HOW HOOMERUSS!
'TAIN'T SO HOOMERUSS, DAISY MAE. THET IS LI'L ABNER AWRIGHT-(GULP)
WHO'S THE BABE?
THET IS DAISY MAE, LI'L ABNER'S GAL-
Copr. 1938 by United Feature Syndicate, Inc. Tm. Reg. U. S. Pat. Off.—All rights reserved
SO YOU'RE LI'L ABNER'S GIRL, EH?-YOU KINDA GO FOR LI'L ABNER, HUH?
THAR HAIN'T NO ONE IN TH' WORLD AH LOVES MORE'N LI'L ABNER YOKUM-
THAT'S FINE!-SIT ON MY LAP WHERE YOU CAN BE COMFORTABLE-AND-YOU OLD FOLKS-CLEAR OUT!!!

LI'L ABNER The End of A Perfect Year! By Al Capp

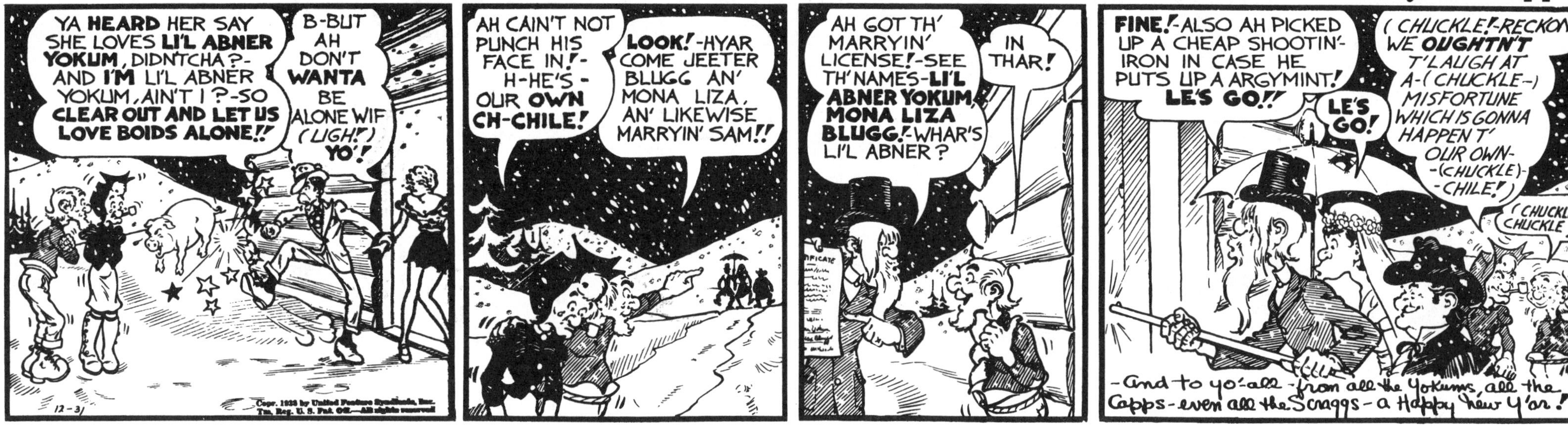
YA HEARD HER SAY SHE LOVES LI'L ABNER YOKUM, DIDN'TCHA?-AND I'M LI'L ABNER YOKUM, AIN'T I?-SO CLEAR OUT AND LET US LOVE BOIDS ALONE!!
B-BUT AH DON'T WANTA BE ALONE WIF (UGH!) YO'!
12-31
Copr. 1938 by United Feature Syndicate, Inc. Tm. Reg. U. S. Pat. Off.—All rights reserved
AH CAIN'T NOT PUNCH HIS FACE IN!-H-HE'S-OUR OWN CH-CHILE!
LOOK!-HYAR COME JEETER BLUGG AN' MONA LIZA, AN' LIKEWISE MARRYIN' SAM!!
AH GOT TH' MARRYIN' LICENSE!-SEE TH' NAMES-LI'L ABNER YOKUM, MONA LIZA BLUGG!-WHAR'S LI'L ABNER?
IN THAR!
FINE!-ALSO AH PICKED UP A CHEAP SHOOTIN'-IRON IN CASE HE PUTS UP A ARGYMINT! LE'S GO!!
LE'S GO!
(CHUCKLE!-RECKON WE OUGHTN'T T'LAUGH AT A-(CHUCKLE-) MISFORTUNE WHICH IS GONNA HAPPEN T' OUR OWN--(CHUCKLE)--CHILE!)
(CHUCKLE CHUCKLE)
-And to yo'-all-from all the Yokums, all the Capps-even all the Scraggs-a Happy New Y'ar!

LI'L ABNER. Give Me Your Answer True! By Al Capp

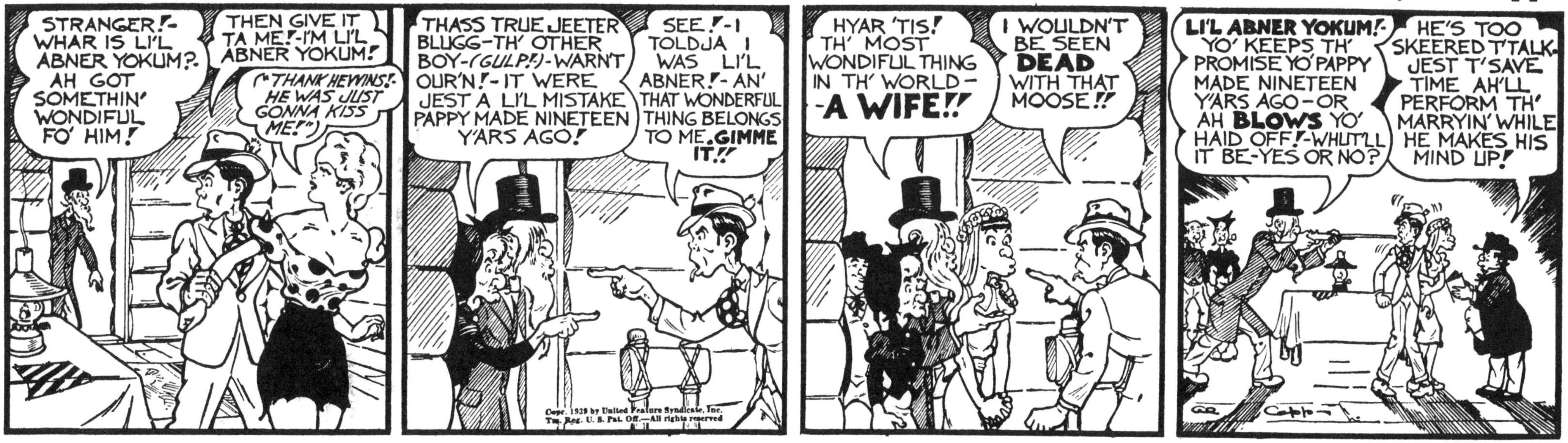
STRANGER!-WHAR IS LI'L ABNER YOKUM?-AH GOT SOMETHIN' WONDIFUL FO' HIM!
THEN GIVE IT TA ME!-I'M LI'L ABNER YOKUM!
("THANK HEVVINS!-HE WAS JUST GONNA KISS ME!")
THASS TRUE JEETER BLUGG-TH' OTHER BOY-(GULP!)-WARN'T OUR'N!-IT WERE JEST A LI'L MISTAKE PAPPY MADE NINETEEN Y'ARS AGO!
SEE!-I TOLDJA I WAS LI'L ABNER!-AN' THAT WONDERFUL THING BELONGS TO ME. GIMME IT!!
Copr. 1939 by United Feature Syndicate, Inc. Tm. Reg. U. S. Pat. Off.—All rights reserved
HYAR 'TIS! TH' MOST WONDIFUL THING IN TH' WORLD--A WIFE!!
I WOULDN'T BE SEEN DEAD WITH THAT MOOSE!!
LI'L ABNER YOKUM!-YO' KEEPS TH' PROMISE YO' PAPPY MADE NINETEEN Y'ARS AGO-OR AH BLOWS YO' HAID OFF!-WHUT'LL IT BE-YES OR NO?
HE'S TOO SKEERED T'TALK. JEST T'SAVE TIME AH'LL PERFORM TH' MARRYIN' WHILE HE MAKES HIS MIND UP!
Capp

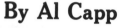

LI'L ABNER

Just Around the Corner

By Al Capp

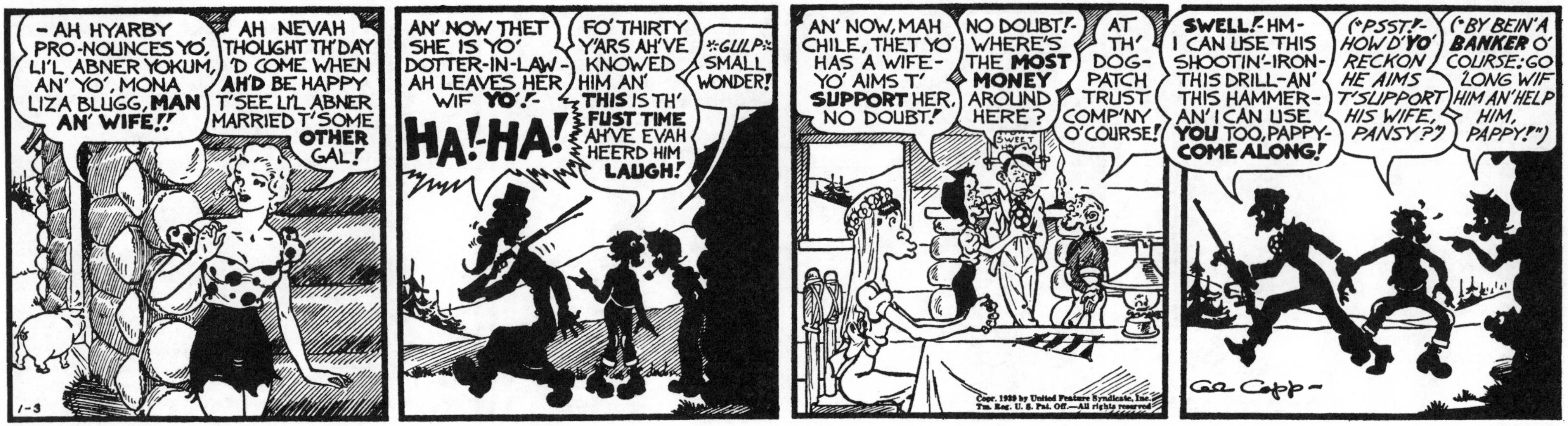

-AH HYARBY PRO-NOUNCES YO', LI'L ABNER YOKUM, AN' YO', MONA LIZA BLUGG, MAN AN' WIFE!!
AH NEVAH THOUGHT TH' DAY 'D COME WHEN AH'D BE HAPPY T'SEE LI'L ABNER MARRIED T' SOME OTHER GAL!
1-3
AN' NOW THET SHE IS YO' DOTTER-IN-LAW-AH LEAVES HER WIF YO'!-
HA!-HA!
FO' THIRTY Y'ARS AH'VE KNOWED HIM AN' THIS IS TH' FUST TIME AH'VE EVAH HEERD HIM LAUGH!
GULP SMALL WONDER!
AN' NOW, MAH CHILE, THET YO' HAS A WIFE-YO' AIMS T' SUPPORT HER, NO DOUBT!
NO DOUBT!-WHERE'S THE MOST MONEY AROUND HERE?
AT TH' DOG-PATCH TRUST COMP'NY O'COURSE!
Copr. 1939 by United Feature Syndicate, Inc. Tm. Reg. U. S. Pat. Off.—All rights reserved
SWELL!-HM-I CAN USE THIS SHOOTIN'-IRON-THIS DRILL-AN' THIS HAMMER-AN' I CAN USE YOU TOO, PAPPY-COME ALONG!
("PSST!-HOW D'YO' RECKON HE AIMS T'SUPPORT HIS WIFE, PANSY?")
("BY BEIN' A BANKER O' COURSE:GO 'LONG WIF HIM AN' HELP HIM, PAPPY!")
Al Capp

LI'L ABNER

Fatherly Pride

By Al Capp

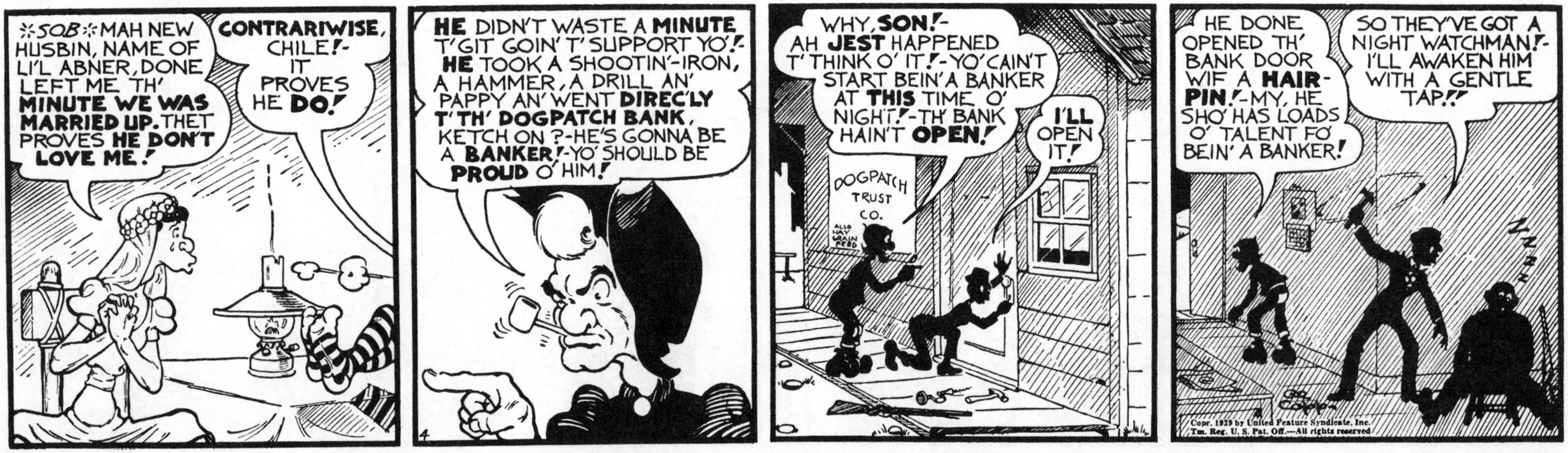

SOB MAH NEW HUSBIN, NAME OF LI'L ABNER, DONE LEFT ME TH' MINUTE WE WAS MARRIED UP. THET PROVES HE DON'T LOVE ME!
CONTRARIWISE, CHILE!-IT PROVES HE DO!
HE DIDN'T WASTE A MINUTE T'GIT GOIN' T' SUPPORT YO'!-HE TOOK A SHOOTIN'-IRON, A HAMMER, A DRILL AN' PAPPY AN' WENT DIREC'LY T' TH' DOGPATCH BANK, KETCH ON?-HE'S GONNA BE A BANKER!-YO' SHOULD BE PROUD O' HIM!
4
WHY, SON!-AH JEST HAPPENED T' THINK O' IT!-YO' CAIN'T START BEIN' A BANKER AT THIS TIME O' NIGHT!-TH' BANK HAIN'T OPEN!
I'LL OPEN IT!
DOGPATCH TRUST CO.
HE DONE OPENED TH' BANK DOOR WIF A HAIR-PIN!-MY, HE SHO' HAS LOADS O' TALENT FO' BEIN' A BANKER!
SO THEY'VE GOT A NIGHT WATCHMAN!-I'LL AWAKEN HIM WITH A GENTLE TAP!!
Copr. 1939 by United Feature Syndicate, Inc. Tm. Reg. U. S. Pat. Off.—All rights reserved

LI'L ABNER — His Master's Voice — By Al Capp

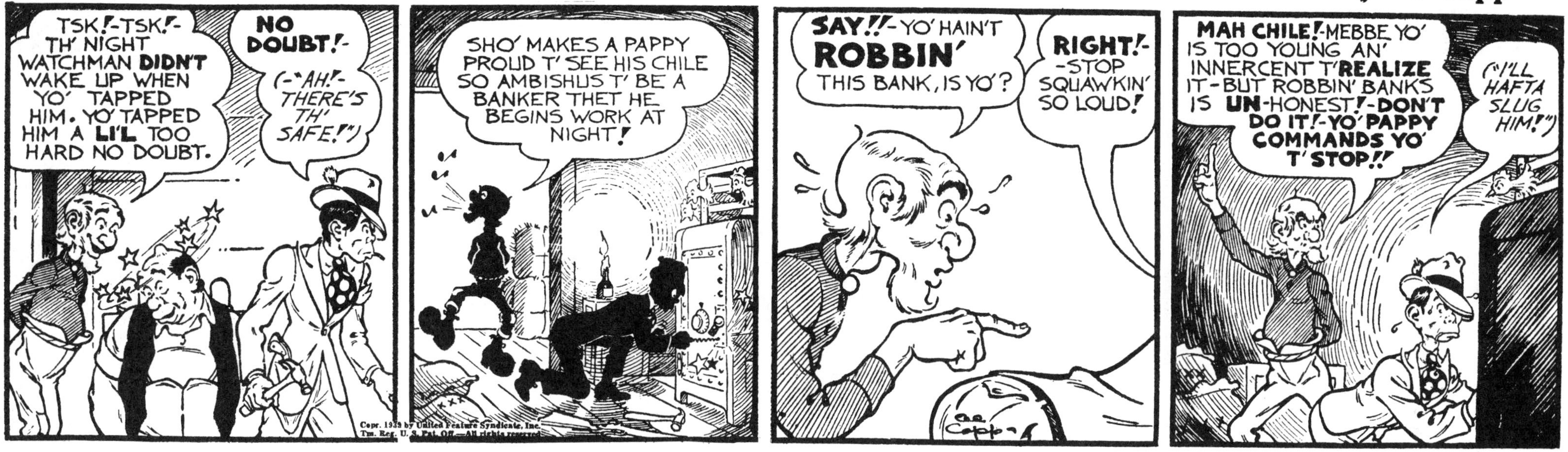

TSK!-TSK!-TH' NIGHT WATCHMAN DIDN'T WAKE UP WHEN YO' TAPPED HIM. YO' TAPPED HIM A LI'L TOO HARD NO DOUBT.
NO DOUBT!-
(-"AH!-THERE'S TH' SAFE!")
SHO' MAKES A PAPPY PROUD T' SEE HIS CHILE SO AMBISHUS T' BE A BANKER THET HE BEGINS WORK AT NIGHT!
Copr. 1939 by United Feature Syndicate, Inc. Tm. Reg. U. S. Pat. Off.—All rights reserved
SAY!!-YO' HAIN'T ROBBIN' THIS BANK, IS YO'?
RIGHT!-STOP SQUAWKIN' SO LOUD!
MAH CHILE!-MEBBE YO' IS TOO YOUNG AN' INNERCENT T' REALIZE IT-BUT ROBBIN' BANKS IS UN-HONEST!-DON'T DO IT!-YO' PAPPY COMMANDS YO' T' STOP!!
("I'LL HAFTA SLUG HIM!")

LI'L ABNER — Crime Wave in Dogpatch! — By Al Capp

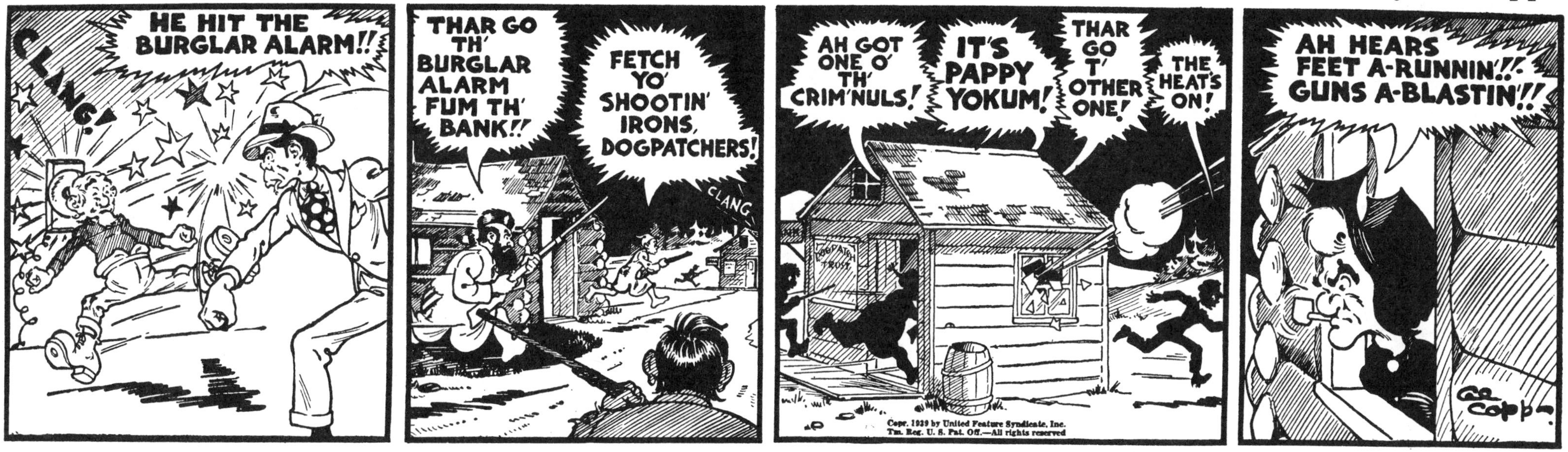

CLANG!
HE HIT THE BURGLAR ALARM!!
THAR GO TH' BURGLAR ALARM FUM TH' BANK!!
FETCH YO' SHOOTIN' IRONS, DOGPATCHERS!
CLANG
AH GOT ONE O' TH' CRIM'NULS!
IT'S PAPPY YOKUM!
THAR GO T' OTHER ONE!
THE HEAT'S ON!
DOGPATCH TRUST
Copr. 1939 by United Feature Syndicate, Inc. Tm. Reg. U. S. Pat. Off.—All rights reserved
AH HEARS FEET A-RUNNIN'!!-GUNS A-BLASTIN'!!

LI'L ABNER Crime Doesn't Pay By Al Capp

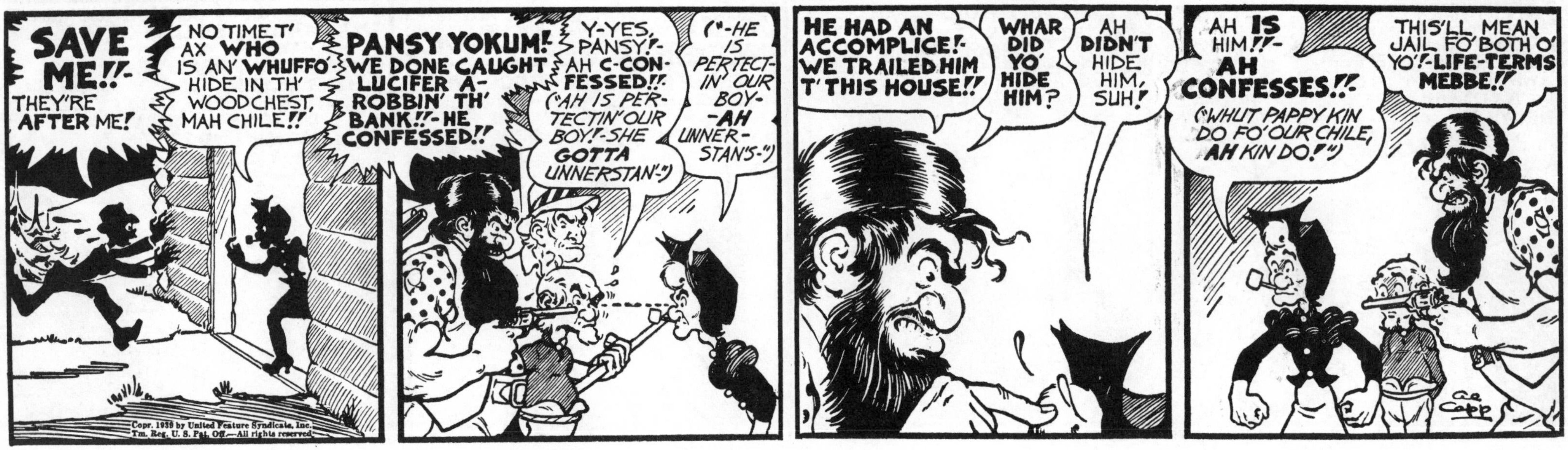
SAVE ME!!- THEY'RE AFTER ME!
NO TIME T' AX WHO IS AN' WHUFFO HIDE IN TH' WOODCHEST, MAH CHILE!!
PANSY YOKUM! WE DONE CAUGHT LUCIFER A-ROBBIN' TH' BANK!!-HE CONFESSED!!
Y-YES, PANSY!-AH C-CONFESSED!! ("AH IS PERTECTIN' OUR BOY!-SHE GOTTA UNNERSTAN'-")
("-HE IS PERTECTIN' OUR BOY- -AH UNNERSTAN'S-")
Copr. 1939 by United Feature Syndicate, Inc. Tm. Reg. U. S. Pat. Off.—All rights reserved
HE HAD AN ACCOMPLICE!-WE TRAILED HIM T' THIS HOUSE!!
WHAR DID YO' HIDE HIM?
AH DIDN'T HIDE HIM, SUH!
AH IS HIM!!- AH CONFESSES!! ("WHUT PAPPY KIN DO FO' OUR CHILE, AH KIN DO!")
THIS'LL MEAN JAIL FO' BOTH O' YO'!-LIFE-TERMS MEBBE!!
Al Capp

LI'L ABNER Rancid Romance! By Al Capp

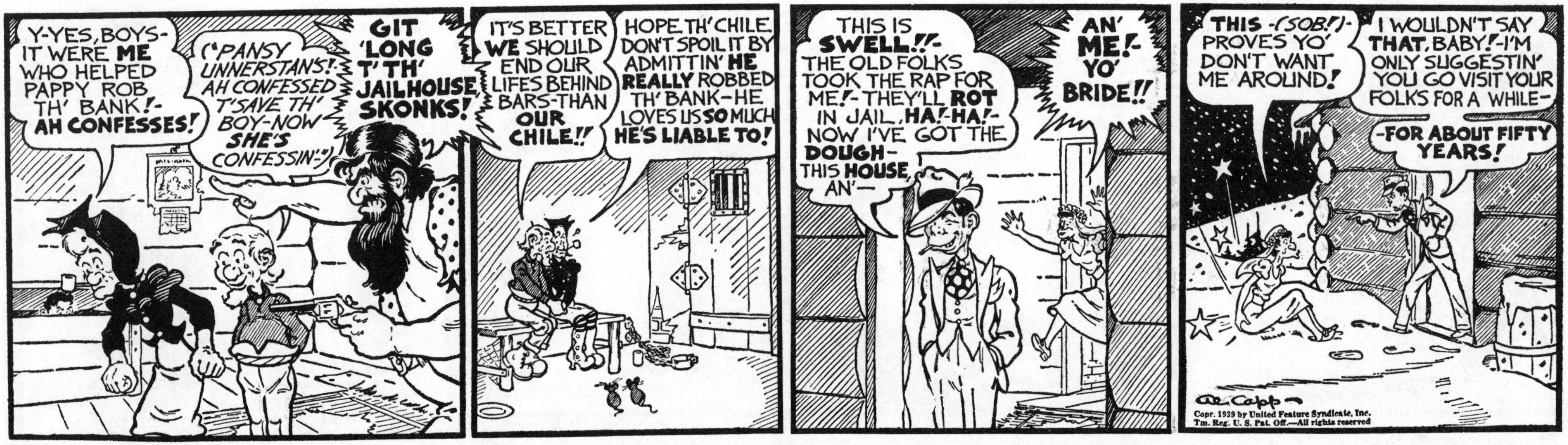
Y-YES, BOYS-IT WERE ME WHO HELPED PAPPY ROB TH' BANK!-AH CONFESSES!
("PANSY UNNERSTAN'S!-AH CONFESSED T'SAVE TH' BOY-NOW SHE'S CONFESSIN'-")
GIT 'LONG T' TH' JAILHOUSE SKONKS!
IT'S BETTER WE SHOULD END OUR LIFES BEHIND BARS-THAN OUR CHILE!!
HOPE TH' CHILE DON'T SPOIL IT BY ADMITTIN' HE REALLY ROBBED TH' BANK-HE LOVES US SO MUCH HE'S LIABLE TO!
THIS IS SWELL!!-THE OLD FOLKS TOOK THE RAP FOR ME!-THEY'LL ROT IN JAIL. HA!-HA!-NOW I'VE GOT THE DOUGH-THIS HOUSE, AN'—
AN' ME!-YO' BRIDE!!
THIS -(SOB!)- PROVES YO' DON'T WANT ME AROUND!
I WOULDN'T SAY THAT, BABY!-I'M ONLY SUGGESTIN' YOU GO VISIT YOUR FOLKS FOR A WHILE-
-FOR ABOUT FIFTY YEARS!
Al Capp
Copr. 1939 by United Feature Syndicate, Inc. Tm. Reg. U. S. Pat. Off.—All rights reserved

LI'L ABNER Flophouse Gets a Roundhouse! By Al Capp

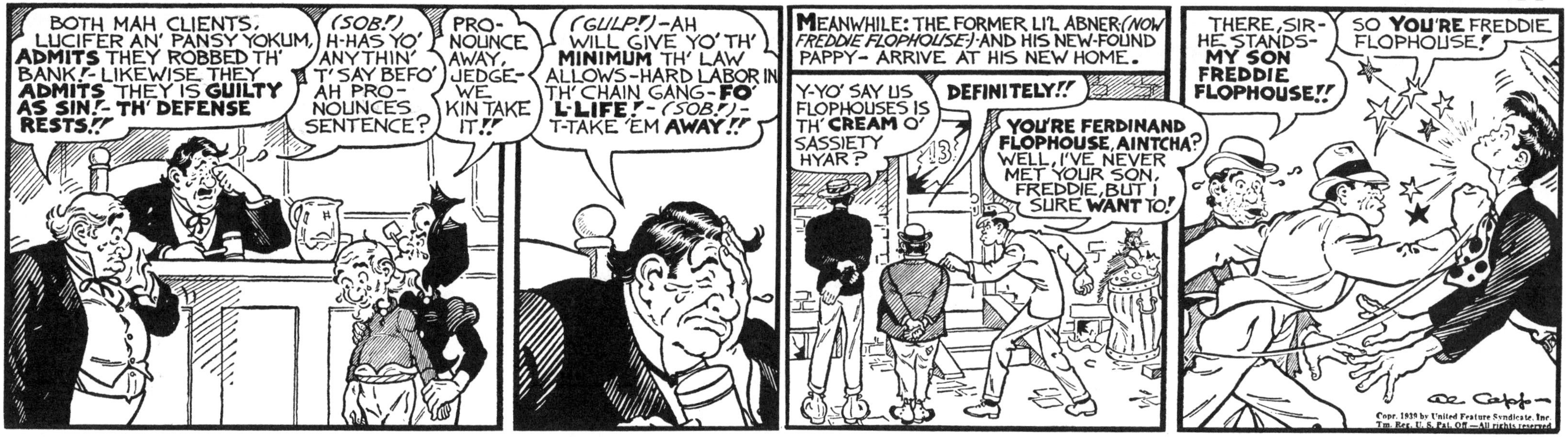

BOTH MAH CLIENTS, LUCIFER AN' PANSY YOKUM, **ADMITS** THEY ROBBED TH' BANK!- LIKEWISE THEY **ADMITS** THEY IS **GUILTY AS SIN!- TH' DEFENSE RESTS!!**
(SOB!) H-HAS YO' ANYTHIN' T' SAY BEFO' AH PRONOUNCES SENTENCE?
PRONOUNCE AWAY, JEDGE- WE KIN TAKE IT!!
(GULP!)-AH WILL GIVE YO' TH' **MINIMUM** TH' LAW ALLOWS-HARD LABOR IN TH' CHAIN GANG-**FO' L-LIFE!**-(SOB!)- T-TAKE 'EM **AWAY!!**
MEANWHILE: THE FORMER LI'L ABNER-(NOW FREDDIE FLOPHOUSE-)-AND HIS NEW-FOUND PAPPY- ARRIVE AT HIS NEW HOME.
Y-YO' SAY US FLOPHOUSES IS TH' **CREAM** O' SASSIETY HYAR?
DEFINITELY!!
13
YOU'RE FERDINAND FLOPHOUSE, AINTCHA? WELL, I'VE NEVER MET YOUR SON, FREDDIE, BUT I SURE **WANT** TO!
THERE, SIR- HE STANDS- **MY SON FREDDIE FLOPHOUSE!!**
SO **YOU'RE** FREDDIE FLOPHOUSE!
AL CAPP
Copr. 1939 by United Feature Syndicate, Inc. Tm. Reg. U. S. Pat. Off.—All rights reserved

LI'L ABNER His Lurid Past! By Al Capp

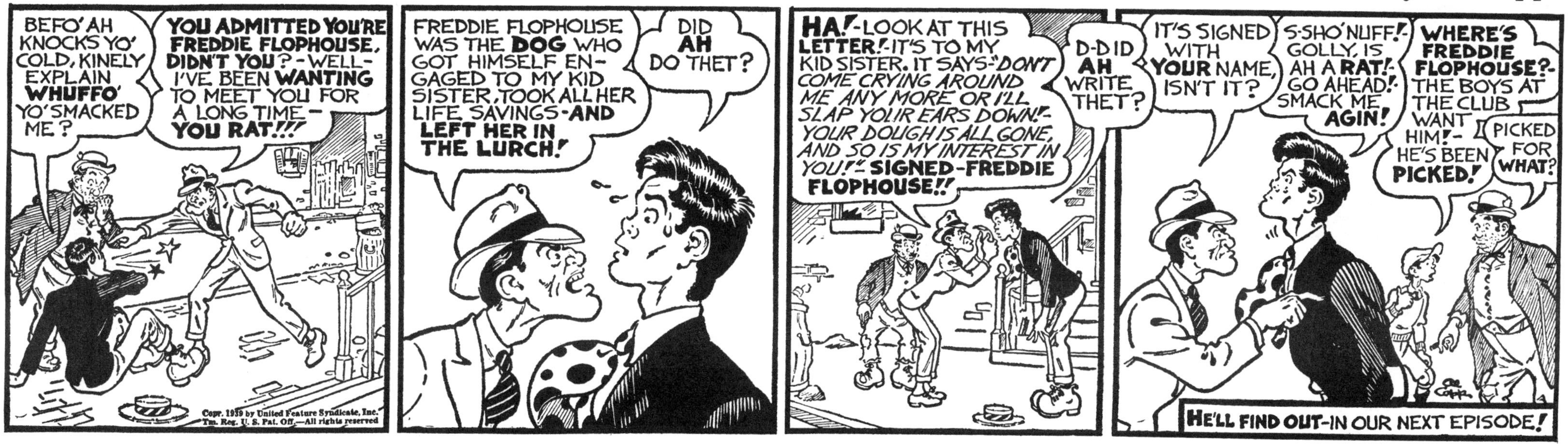

BEFO' AH KNOCKS YO' COLD, KINELY EXPLAIN **WHUFFO'** YO' SMACKED ME?
YOU ADMITTED YOU'RE FREDDIE FLOPHOUSE, DIDN'T YOU?-WELL- I'VE BEEN **WANTING** TO MEET YOU FOR A LONG TIME- **YOU RAT!!!**
Copr. 1939 by United Feature Syndicate, Inc. Tm. Reg. U. S. Pat. Off.—All rights reserved
FREDDIE FLOPHOUSE WAS THE **DOG** WHO GOT HIMSELF ENGAGED TO MY KID SISTER, TOOK ALL HER LIFE SAVINGS-**AND LEFT HER IN THE LURCH!**
DID **AH** DO THET?
HA!-LOOK AT THIS **LETTER!**-IT'S TO MY KID SISTER. IT SAYS-"*DON'T COME CRYING AROUND ME ANY MORE OR I'LL SLAP YOUR EARS DOWN!- YOUR DOUGH IS ALL GONE, AND SO IS MY INTEREST IN YOU!*"- **SIGNED-FREDDIE FLOPHOUSE!!**
D-DID **AH** WRITE THET?
IT'S SIGNED WITH **YOUR** NAME, ISN'T IT?
S-SHO'NUFF!- GOLLY, IS AH A **RAT!**- GO AHEAD!- SMACK ME **AGIN!**
WHERE'S FREDDIE FLOPHOUSE?- THE BOYS AT THE CLUB WANT HIM!- HE'S BEEN **PICKED!**
PICKED FOR **WHAT?**
AL CAPP
HE'LL FIND OUT-IN OUR NEXT EPISODE!

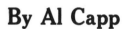

LI'L ABNER Friends in Need (of Money) By Al Capp

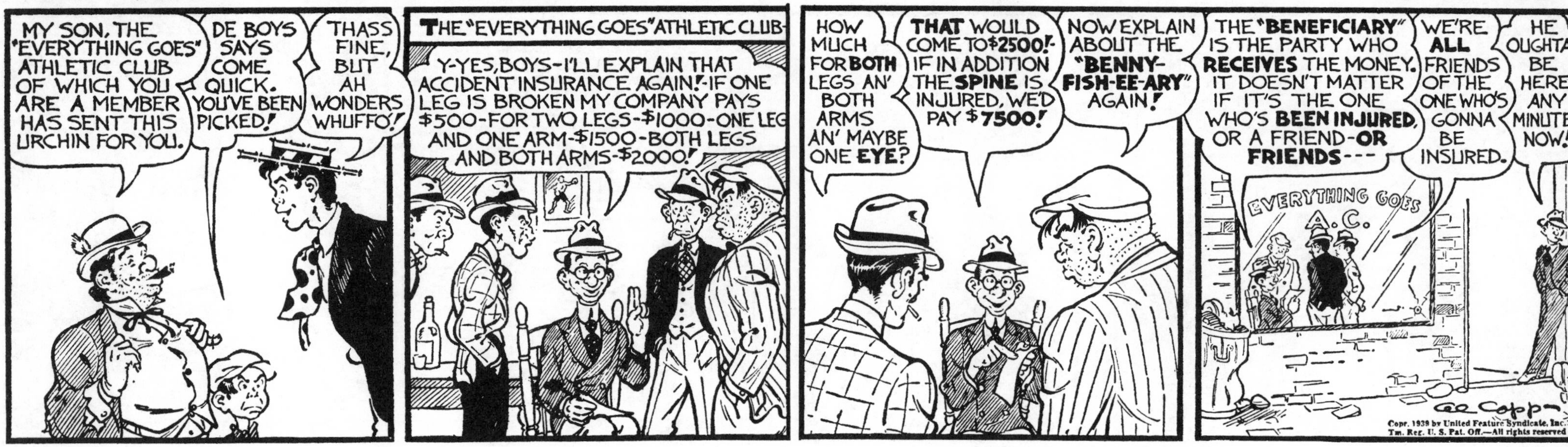
MY SON, THE "EVERYTHING GOES" ATHLETIC CLUB OF WHICH YOU ARE A MEMBER HAS SENT THIS URCHIN FOR YOU.
DE BOYS SAYS COME QUICK. YOU'VE BEEN PICKED!
THASS FINE, BUT AH WONDERS WHUFFO'!
THE "EVERYTHING GOES" ATHLETIC CLUB
Y-YES, BOYS-I'LL EXPLAIN THAT ACCIDENT INSURANCE AGAIN!-IF ONE LEG IS BROKEN MY COMPANY PAYS $500-FOR TWO LEGS-$1000-ONE LEG AND ONE ARM-$1500-BOTH LEGS AND BOTH ARMS-$2000!
HOW MUCH FOR BOTH LEGS AN' BOTH ARMS AN' MAYBE ONE EYE?
THAT WOULD COME TO $2500!-IF IN ADDITION THE SPINE IS INJURED, WE'D PAY $7500!
NOW EXPLAIN ABOUT THE "BENNY-FISH-EE-ARY" AGAIN!
THE "BENEFICIARY" IS THE PARTY WHO RECEIVES THE MONEY. IT DOESN'T MATTER IF IT'S THE ONE WHO'S BEEN INJURED, OR A FRIEND-OR FRIENDS---
WE'RE ALL FRIENDS OF THE ONE WHO'S GONNA BE INSURED.
HE OUGHTA BE HERE ANY MINUTE NOW!
EVERYTHING GOES A.C.
Copr. 1939 by United Feature Syndicate, Inc. Tm. Reg. U. S. Pat. Off.—All rights reserved

LI'L ABNER When Good Fellows Get Together By Al Capp

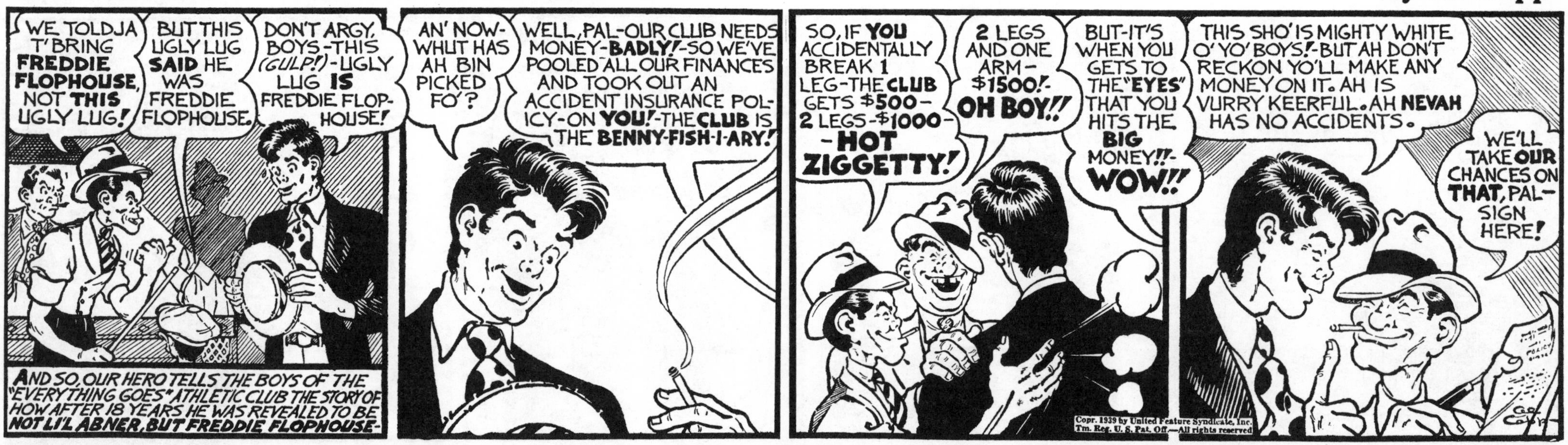
WE TOLDJA T'BRING FREDDIE FLOPHOUSE, NOT THIS UGLY LUG!
BUT THIS UGLY LUG SAID HE WAS FREDDIE FLOPHOUSE.
DON'T ARGY, BOYS-THIS (GULP!)-UGLY LUG IS FREDDIE FLOP-HOUSE!
AND SO, OUR HERO TELLS THE BOYS OF THE "EVERYTHING GOES" ATHLETIC CLUB THE STORY OF HOW AFTER 18 YEARS HE WAS REVEALED TO BE NOT LI'L ABNER, BUT FREDDIE FLOPHOUSE-
AN' NOW-WHUT HAS AH BIN PICKED FO'?
WELL, PAL-OUR CLUB NEEDS MONEY-BADLY!-SO WE'VE POOLED ALL OUR FINANCES AND TOOK OUT AN ACCIDENT INSURANCE POLICY-ON YOU!-THE CLUB IS THE BENNY-FISH-I-ARY!
SO, IF YOU ACCIDENTALLY BREAK 1 LEG-THE CLUB GETS $500-2 LEGS-$1000--HOT ZIGGETTY!
2 LEGS AND ONE ARM-$1500!-OH BOY!!
BUT-IT'S WHEN YOU GETS TO THE "EYES" THAT YOU HITS THE BIG MONEY!!-WOW!!
THIS SHO' IS MIGHTY WHITE O' YO' BOYS!-BUT AH DON'T RECKON YO'LL MAKE ANY MONEY ON IT. AH IS VURRY KEERFUL. AH NEVAH HAS NO ACCIDENTS.
WE'LL TAKE OUR CHANCES ON THAT, PAL-SIGN HERE!
Copr. 1939 by United Feature Syndicate, Inc. Tm. Reg. U. S. Pat. Off.—All rights reserved

LI'L ABNER Don't Worry—You're Protected! By Al Capp

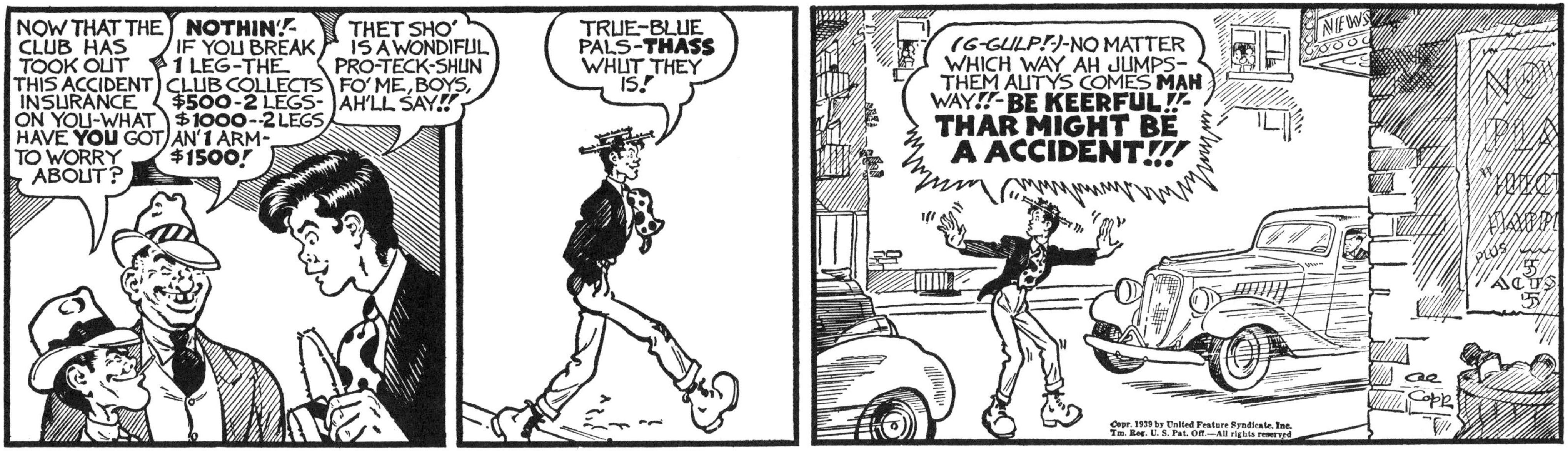

NOW THAT THE CLUB HAS TOOK OUT THIS ACCIDENT INSURANCE ON YOU-WHAT HAVE **YOU** GOT TO WORRY ABOUT?
NOTHIN'!- IF YOU BREAK **1** LEG-THE CLUB COLLECTS **$500-2** LEGS- **$1000**--**2** LEGS AN' **1** ARM- **$1500!**
THET SHO' IS A WONDIFUL PRO-TECK-SHUN FO' ME, BOYS, AH'LL SAY!!
TRUE-BLUE PALS-**THASS** WHUT THEY IS!
NEWS
(G-GULP!-)-NO MATTER WHICH WAY AH JUMPS- THEM AUTYS COMES **MAH** WAY!!-**BE KEERFUL!!**- **THAR MIGHT BE A ACCIDENT!!!**
Al Capp
Copr. 1939 by United Feature Syndicate, Inc. Tm. Reg. U. S. Pat. Off.—All rights reserved

LI'L ABNER Yokum-Trap! By Al Capp

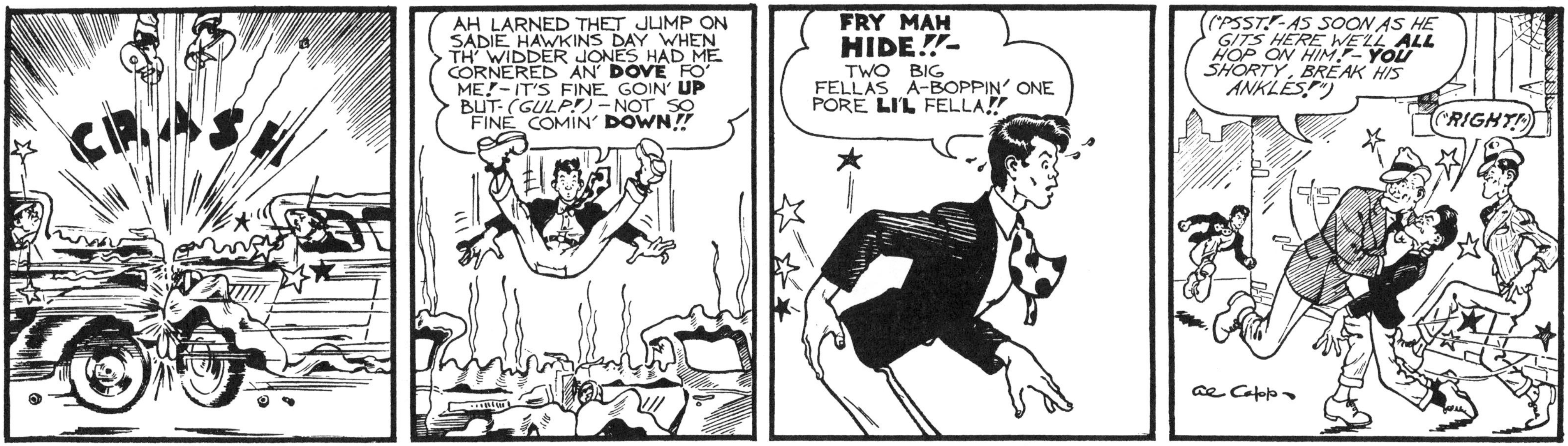

CRASH
AH LARNED THET JUMP ON SADIE HAWKINS DAY WHEN TH' WIDDER JONES HAD ME CORNERED AN' **DOVE** FO' ME!-IT'S FINE GOIN' **UP** BUT-(GULP!)-NOT SO FINE COMIN' **DOWN!!**
FRY MAH HIDE!!- TWO BIG FELLAS A-BOPPIN' ONE PORE **LI'L** FELLA!!
("PSST!-AS SOON AS HE GITS HERE WE'LL **ALL** HOP ON HIM!-**YOU** SHORTY, BREAK HIS ANKLES!")
("RIGHT!")
Al Capp

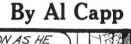

LI'L ABNER What Sight Greets Their Eyes? By Al Capp

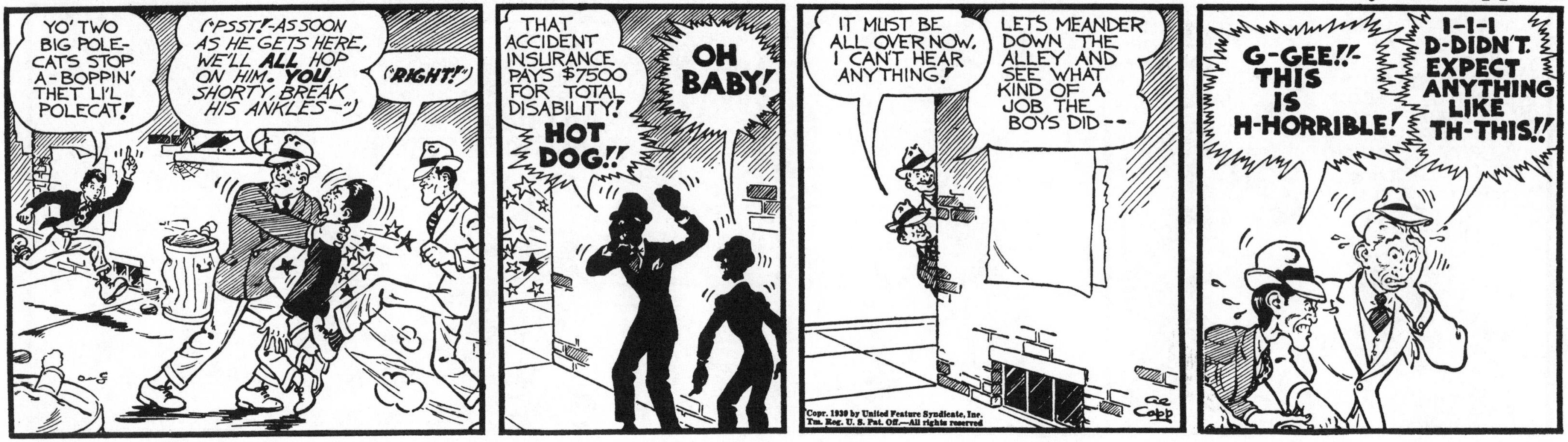
YO' TWO BIG POLE-CATS STOP A-BOPPIN' THET LI'L POLECAT!
("PSST!-AS SOON AS HE GETS HERE, WE'LL ALL HOP ON HIM. YOU, SHORTY, BREAK HIS ANKLES--")
("RIGHT!")
THAT ACCIDENT INSURANCE PAYS $7500 FOR TOTAL DISABILITY! HOT DOG!!
OH BABY!
IT MUST BE ALL OVER NOW. I CAN'T HEAR ANYTHING!
LET'S MEANDER DOWN THE ALLEY AND SEE WHAT KIND OF A JOB THE BOYS DID--
Copr. 1939 by United Feature Syndicate, Inc. Tm. Reg. U. S. Pat. Off.—All rights reserved
G-GEE!!-THIS IS H-HORRIBLE!
I-I-I D-DIDN'T EXPECT ANYTHING LIKE TH-THIS!!

LI'L ABNER Oh, Happy Day! By Al Capp

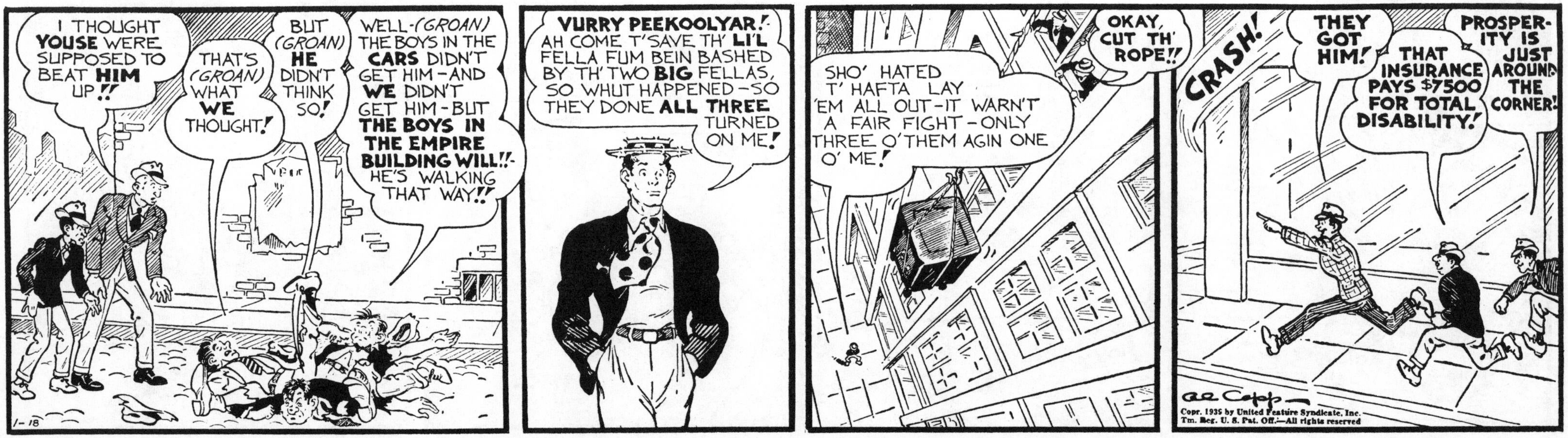
I THOUGHT YOUSE WERE SUPPOSED TO BEAT HIM UP!!
THAT'S (GROAN) WHAT WE THOUGHT!
BUT (GROAN) HE DIDN'T THINK SO!
WELL-(GROAN) THE BOYS IN THE CARS DIDN'T GET HIM-AND WE DIDN'T GET HIM-BUT THE BOYS IN THE EMPIRE BUILDING WILL!!-HE'S WALKING THAT WAY!!
1-18
VURRY PEEKOOLYAR!-AH COME T'SAVE TH' LI'L FELLA FUM BEIN BASHED BY TH' TWO BIG FELLAS, SO WHUT HAPPENED-SO THEY DONE ALL THREE TURNED ON ME!
SHO' HATED T' HAFTA LAY 'EM ALL OUT-IT WARN'T A FAIR FIGHT-ONLY THREE O'THEM AGIN ONE O' ME!
OKAY, CUT TH' ROPE!!
CRASH!
THEY GOT HIM!
THAT INSURANCE PAYS $7500 FOR TOTAL DISABILITY!
PROSPER-ITY IS JUST AROUND THE CORNER!
Copr. 1939 by United Feature Syndicate, Inc. Tm. Reg. U. S. Pat. Off.—All rights reserved

LI'L ABNER It's Done With Mirrors! By Al Capp

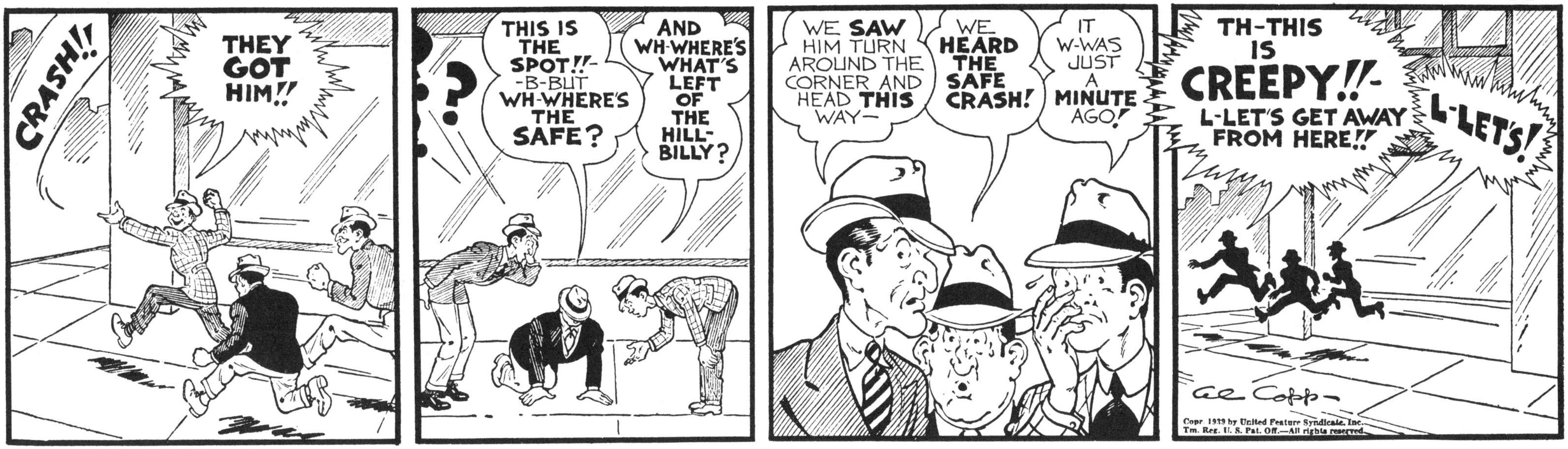
CRASH!!
THEY GOT HIM!!
THIS IS THE SPOT!!- -B-BUT WH-WHERE'S THE SAFE?
AND WH-WHERE'S WHAT'S LEFT OF THE HILL-BILLY?
WE SAW HIM TURN AROUND THE CORNER AND HEAD THIS WAY—
WE HEARD THE SAFE CRASH!
IT W-WAS JUST A MINUTE AGO!
TH-THIS IS CREEPY!!- L-LET'S GET AWAY FROM HERE!!
L-LET'S!
Al Capp
Copr. 1939 by United Feature Syndicate, Inc. Tm. Reg. U. S. Pat. Off.—All rights reserved

LI'L ABNER Honest Ab By Al Capp

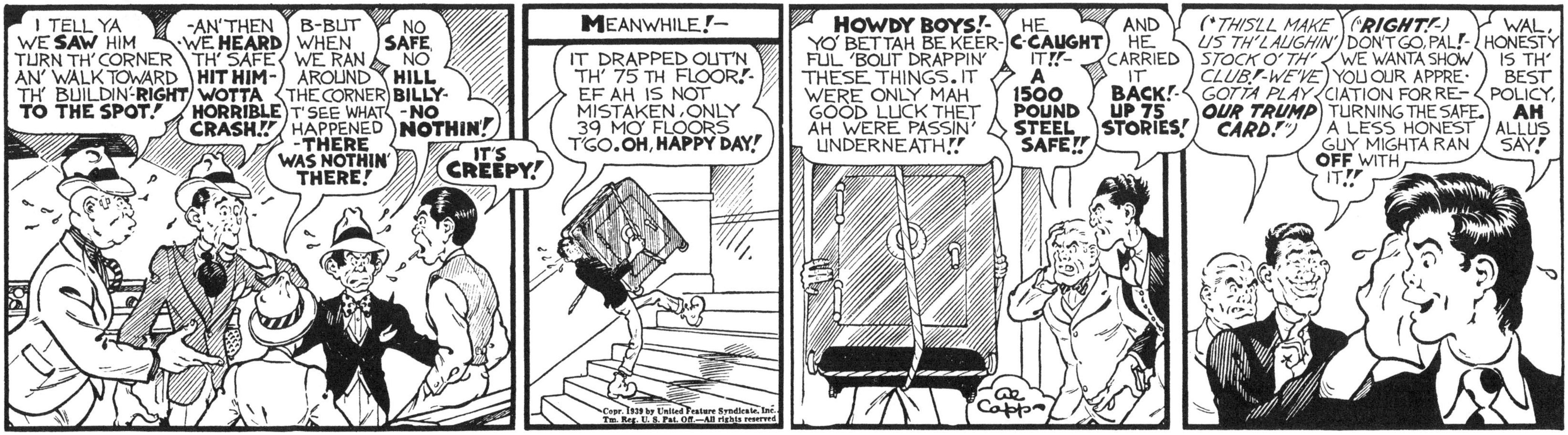
I TELL YA WE SAW HIM TURN TH' CORNER AN' WALK TOWARD TH' BUILDIN'-RIGHT TO THE SPOT!
-AN' THEN WE HEARD TH' SAFE HIT HIM-WOTTA HORRIBLE CRASH!!
B-BUT WHEN WE RAN AROUND THE CORNER T'SEE WHAT HAPPENED -THERE WAS NOTHIN' THERE!
NO SAFE, NO HILL BILLY- -NO NOTHIN'!
IT'S CREEPY!
MEANWHILE!—
IT DRAPPED OUT'N TH' 75 TH FLOOR!- EF AH IS NOT MISTAKEN, ONLY 39 MO' FLOORS T'GO. OH, HAPPY DAY!
Copr. 1939 by United Feature Syndicate, Inc. Tm. Reg. U. S. Pat. Off.—All rights reserved
HOWDY BOYS!- YO' BETTAH BE KEER-FUL 'BOUT DRAPPIN' THESE THINGS. IT WERE ONLY MAH GOOD LUCK THET AH WERE PASSIN' UNDERNEATH!!
HE C-CAUGHT IT!!- A 1500 POUND STEEL SAFE!!
AND HE CARRIED IT BACK!- UP 75 STORIES!
Al Capp
("THIS'LL MAKE US TH' LAUGHIN' STOCK O' TH' CLUB!-WE'VE GOTTA PLAY OUR TRUMP CARD!")
("RIGHT!-") DON'T GO, PAL!- WE WANTA SHOW YOU OUR APPRE-CIATION FOR RE-TURNING THE SAFE. A LESS HONEST GUY MIGHTA RAN OFF WITH IT!!
WAL, HONESTY IS TH' BEST POLICY, AH ALLUS SAY!

LI'L ABNER They Don't Make Buildings Like They Useta! By Al Capp

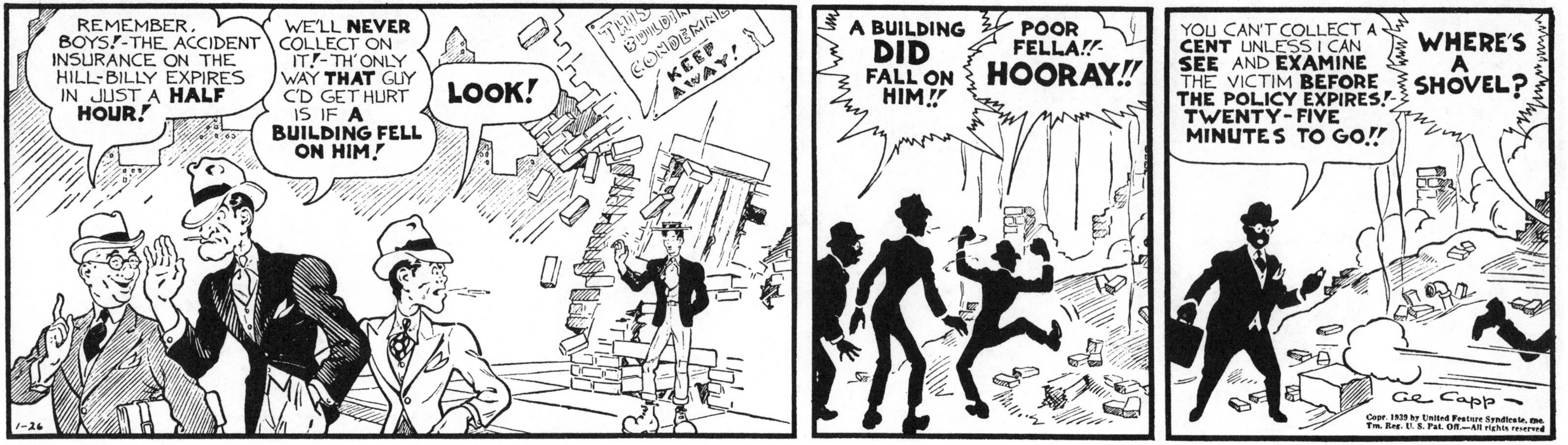
REMEMBER, BOYS!-THE ACCIDENT INSURANCE ON THE HILL-BILLY EXPIRES IN JUST A **HALF HOUR!**
WE'LL **NEVER** COLLECT ON IT!-TH' ONLY WAY **THAT** GUY C'D GET HURT IS IF **A BUILDING FELL ON HIM!**
LOOK!
THIS
KEEP AWAY!
1-26
A BUILDING DID FALL ON HIM!!
POOR FELLA!!-HOORAY!!
YOU CAN'T COLLECT A **CENT** UNLESS I CAN **SEE** AND **EXAMINE** THE VICTIM **BEFORE THE POLICY EXPIRES!-TWENTY-FIVE MINUTES TO GO!!**
WHERE'S A SHOVEL?
Al Capp
Copr. 1939 by United Feature Syndicate, Inc. Tm. Reg. U. S. Pat. Off.—All rights reserved

LI'L ABNER Asleep in the Deep By Al Capp

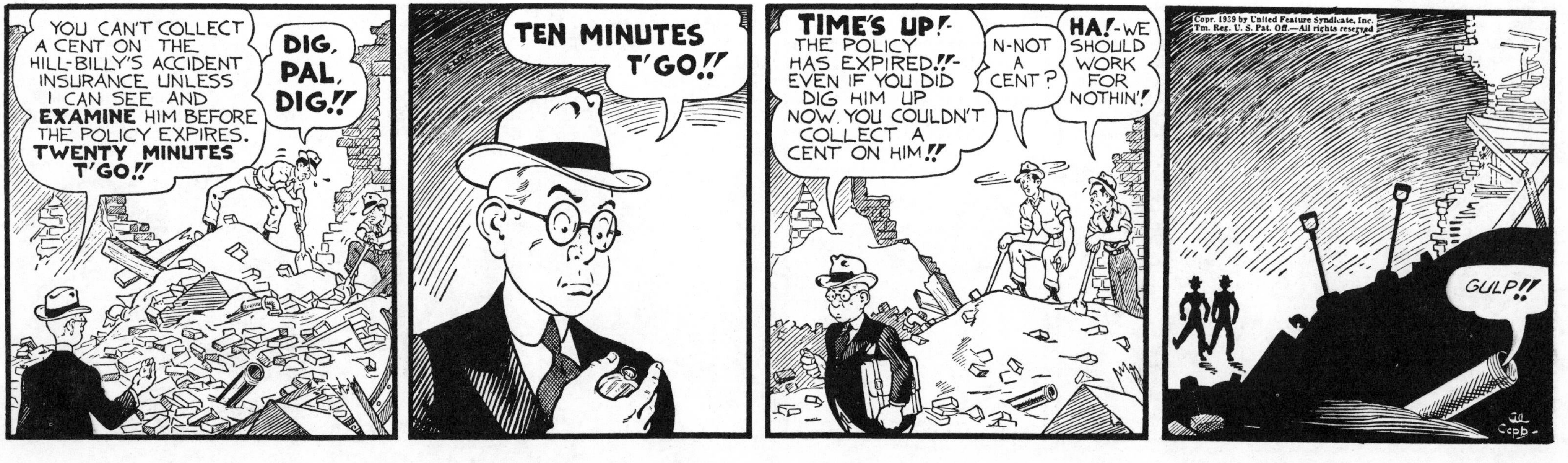
YOU CAN'T COLLECT A CENT ON THE HILL-BILLY'S ACCIDENT INSURANCE UNLESS I CAN SEE AND **EXAMINE** HIM BEFORE THE POLICY EXPIRES. **TWENTY MINUTES T'GO!!**
DIG, PAL, DIG!!
TEN MINUTES T'GO!!
TIME'S UP!- THE POLICY HAS EXPIRED!!-EVEN IF YOU DID DIG HIM UP NOW, YOU COULDN'T COLLECT A CENT ON HIM!!
N-NOT A CENT?
HA!-WE SHOULD WORK FOR NOTHIN'!
Copr. 1939 by United Feature Syndicate, Inc. Tm. Reg. U. S. Pat. Off.—All rights reserved
GULP!!
Al Capp

LI'L ABNER Rally in Our Alley!! By Al Capp

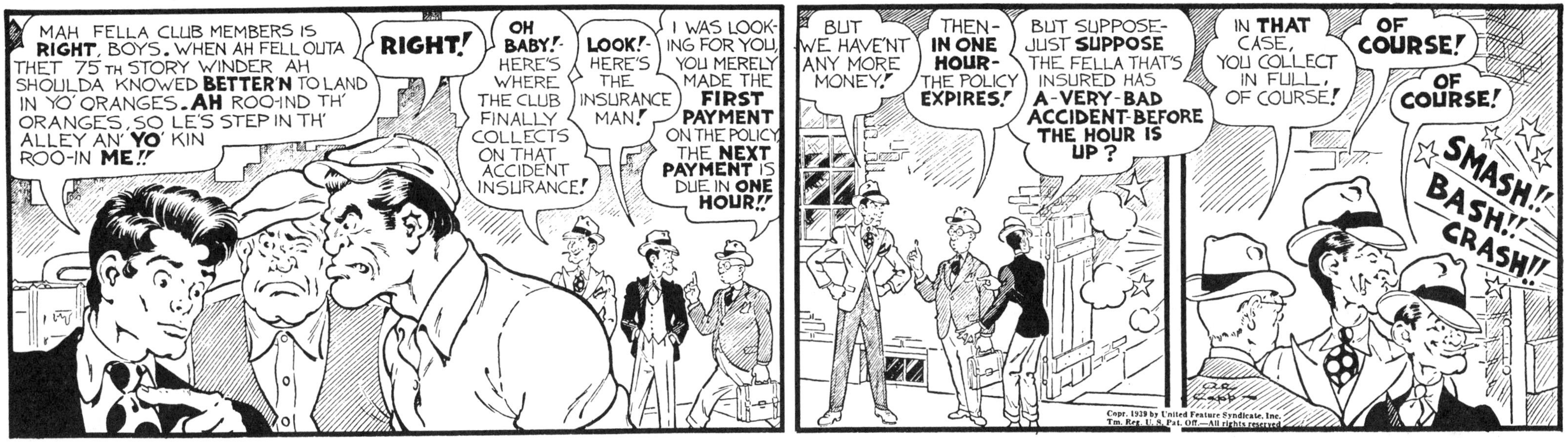

MAH FELLA CLUB MEMBERS IS RIGHT, BOYS. WHEN AH FELL OUTA THET 75TH STORY WINDER AH SHOULDA KNOWED BETTER'N TO LAND IN YO' ORANGES. AH ROO-IND TH' ORANGES, SO LE'S STEP IN TH' ALLEY AN' YO' KIN ROO-IN ME!!
RIGHT!
OH BABY!- HERE'S WHERE THE CLUB FINALLY COLLECTS ON THAT ACCIDENT INSURANCE!
LOOK!- HERE'S THE INSURANCE MAN!
I WAS LOOKING FOR YOU, YOU MERELY MADE THE FIRST PAYMENT ON THE POLICY. THE NEXT PAYMENT IS DUE IN ONE HOUR!!
BUT WE HAVE'NT ANY MORE MONEY!
THEN- IN ONE HOUR- THE POLICY EXPIRES!
BUT SUPPOSE- JUST SUPPOSE THE FELLA THAT'S INSURED HAS A-VERY-BAD ACCIDENT-BEFORE THE HOUR IS UP?
IN THAT CASE, YOU COLLECT IN FULL, OF COURSE!
OF COURSE!
OF COURSE!
SMASH!! BASH!! CRASH!!
Copr. 1939 by United Feature Syndicate, Inc. Tm. Reg. U. S. Pat. Off.—All rights reserved

LI'L ABNER It's a Small World By Al Capp

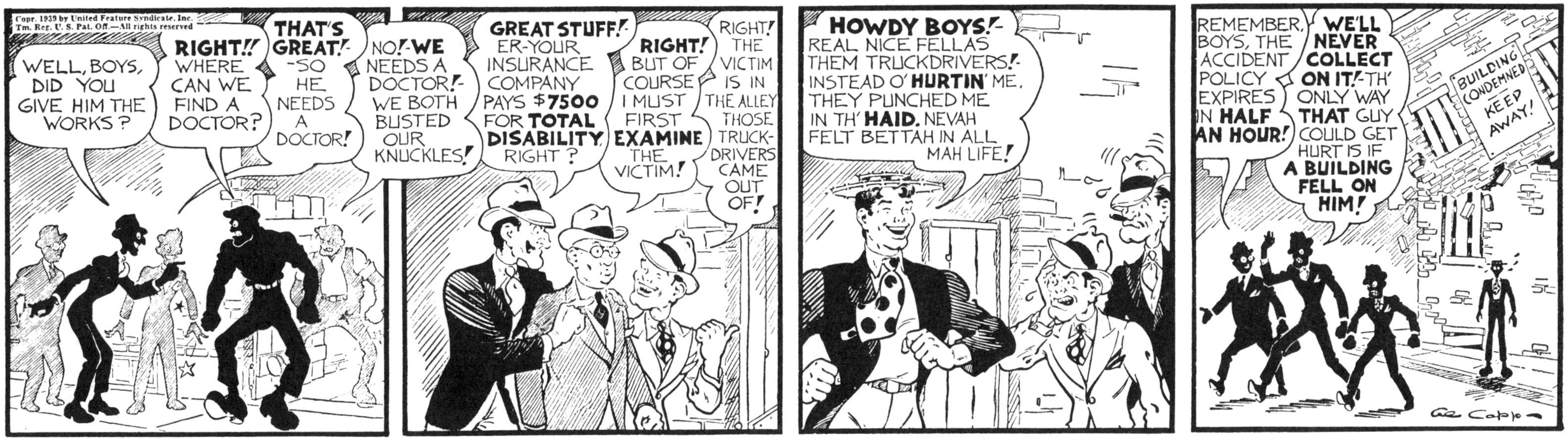

Copr. 1939 by United Feature Syndicate, Inc. Tm. Reg. U. S. Pat. Off.—All rights reserved
WELL, BOYS, DID YOU GIVE HIM THE WORKS?
RIGHT!! WHERE CAN WE FIND A DOCTOR?
THAT'S GREAT!- -SO HE NEEDS A DOCTOR!
NO!-WE NEEDS A DOCTOR!-WE BOTH BUSTED OUR KNUCKLES!
GREAT STUFF!- ER-YOUR INSURANCE COMPANY PAYS $7500 FOR TOTAL DISABILITY, RIGHT?
RIGHT! BUT OF COURSE I MUST FIRST EXAMINE THE VICTIM!
RIGHT! THE VICTIM IS IN THE ALLEY THOSE TRUCK-DRIVERS CAME OUT OF!
HOWDY BOYS!- REAL NICE FELLAS THEM TRUCKDRIVERS!- INSTEAD O' HURTIN' ME, THEY PUNCHED ME IN TH' HAID. NEVAH FELT BETTAH IN ALL MAH LIFE!
REMEMBER, BOYS, THE ACCIDENT POLICY EXPIRES IN HALF AN HOUR!
WE'LL NEVER COLLECT ON IT!-TH' ONLY WAY THAT GUY COULD GET HURT IS IF A BUILDING FELL ON HIM!
BUILDING CONDEMNED KEEP AWAY!

LI'L ABNER

Lucky Abner!

By Al Capp

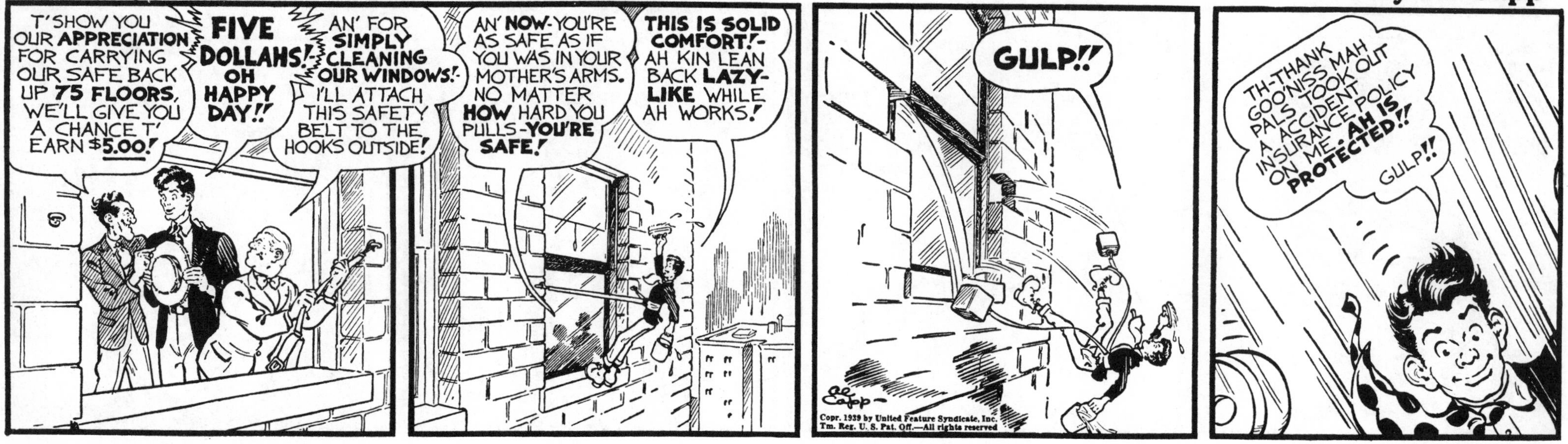

T'SHOW YOU OUR **APPRECIATION** FOR CARRYING OUR SAFE BACK UP **75 FLOORS**, WE'LL GIVE YOU A CHANCE T' EARN **$5.00**!
FIVE DOLLAHS!- OH HAPPY DAY!!
AN' FOR **SIMPLY CLEANING OUR WINDOWS!-** I'LL ATTACH THIS SAFETY BELT TO THE HOOKS OUTSIDE!
AN' **NOW**-YOU'RE AS SAFE AS IF YOU WAS IN YOUR MOTHER'S ARMS. NO MATTER **HOW** HARD YOU PULLS-**YOU'RE SAFE!**
THIS IS SOLID COMFORT!- AH KIN LEAN BACK **LAZY-LIKE** WHILE AH WORKS!
GULP!!
TH-THANK GOO'NISS MAH PALS TOOK OUT A ACCIDENT INSURANCE POLICY ON ME. **AH IS PROTECTED!!**
GULP!!

LI'L ABNER

He Did Them Wrong!

By Al Capp

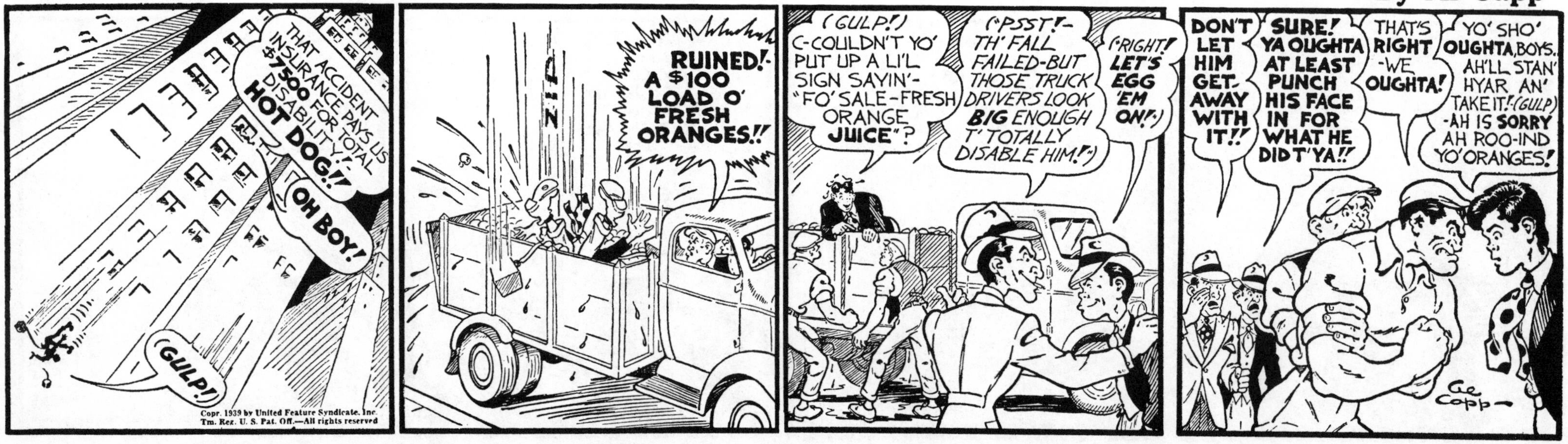

THAT ACCIDENT INSURANCE PAYS US **$7500** FOR TOTAL DISABILITY!- **HOT DOG!!**
OH BOY!
GULP!
RUINED!- A $100 LOAD O' FRESH ORANGES!!
(GULP!) C-COULDN'T YO' PUT UP A LI'L SIGN SAYIN'- "FO' SALE-FRESH ORANGE **JUICE**"?
("PSST!- TH' FALL FAILED-BUT THOSE TRUCK DRIVERS LOOK **BIG** ENOUGH T' TOTALLY DISABLE HIM!")
("RIGHT! **LET'S EGG 'EM ON!**")
DON'T LET HIM GET-AWAY WITH IT!!
SURE! YA OUGHTA AT LEAST PUNCH HIS FACE IN FOR WHAT HE DID T'YA!!
THAT'S **RIGHT** -WE **OUGHTA!**
YO' SHO' **OUGHTA**, BOYS. AH'LL STAN' HYAR AN' TAKE IT!-(GULP) -AH IS **SORRY** AH ROO-IND YO' ORANGES!

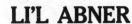

LI'L ABNER He Hain't What He Used to Be! By Al Capp

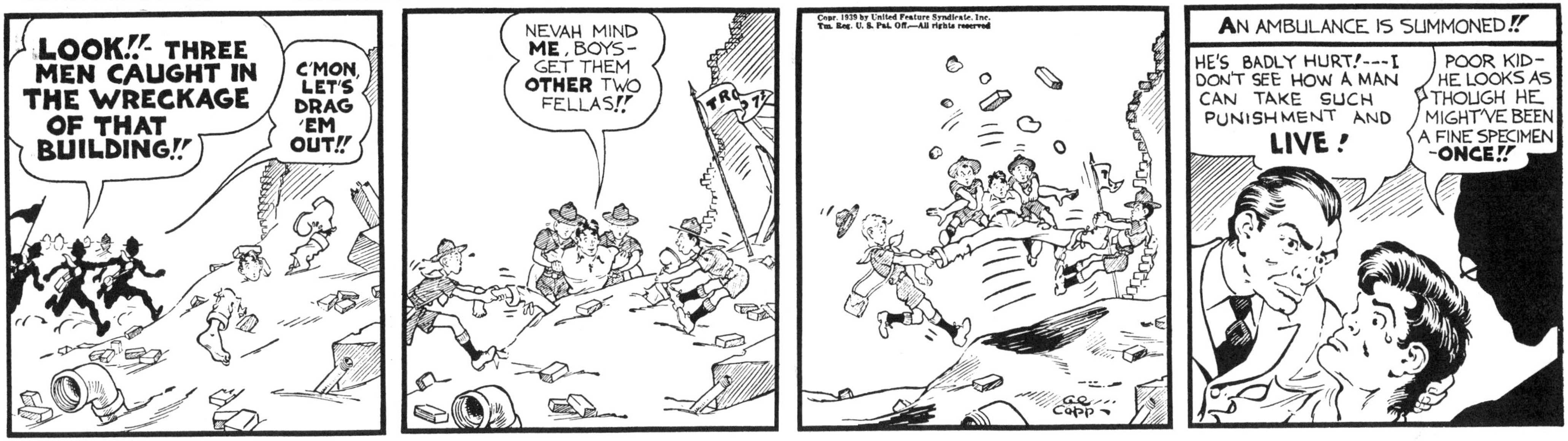

LOOK!!- THREE MEN CAUGHT IN THE WRECKAGE OF THAT BUILDING!!
C'MON, LET'S DRAG 'EM OUT!!
NEVAH MIND ME, BOYS- GET THEM OTHER TWO FELLAS!!
Copr. 1939 by United Feature Syndicate, Inc.
Tm. Reg. U. S. Pat. Off.—All rights reserved
Al Capp
AN AMBULANCE IS SUMMONED!!
HE'S BADLY HURT!---I DON'T SEE HOW A MAN CAN TAKE SUCH PUNISHMENT AND LIVE!
POOR KID- HE LOOKS AS THOUGH HE MIGHT'VE BEEN A FINE SPECIMEN -ONCE!!

LI'L ABNER Last One Out Is A Old Maid! By Al Capp

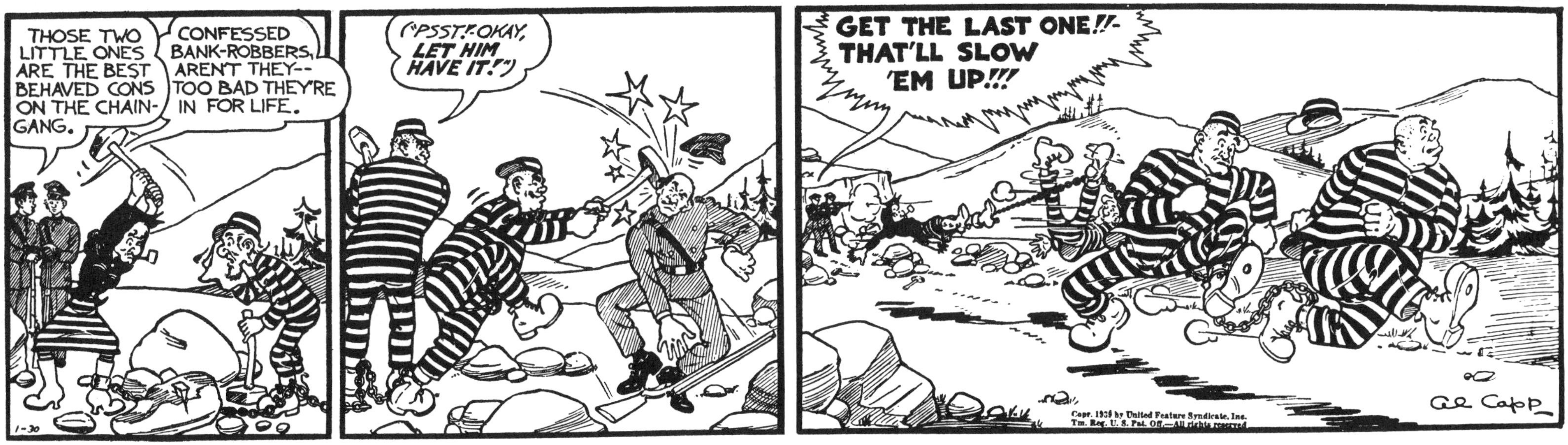

THOSE TWO LITTLE ONES ARE THE BEST BEHAVED CONS ON THE CHAIN-GANG.
CONFESSED BANK-ROBBERS, AREN'T THEY-- TOO BAD THEY'RE IN FOR LIFE.
1-30
("PSST!- OKAY, LET HIM HAVE IT!")
GET THE LAST ONE!!- THAT'LL SLOW 'EM UP!!!
Al Capp
Copr. 1939 by United Feature Syndicate, Inc.
Tm. Reg. U. S. Pat. Off.—All rights reserved

LI'L ABNER — Love Conquers All — By Al Capp

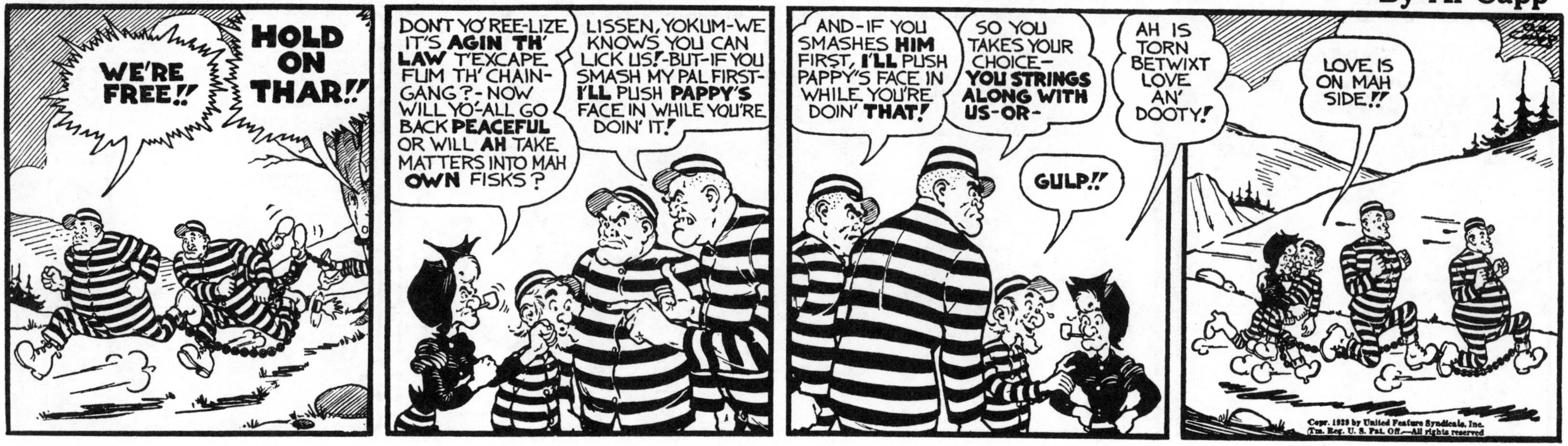
WE'RE FREE!!
HOLD ON THAR!!
DON'T YO' REE-LIZE IT'S AGIN TH' LAW T'EXCAPE FUM TH' CHAIN-GANG?-NOW WILL YO'-ALL GO BACK PEACEFUL OR WILL AH TAKE MATTERS INTO MAH OWN FISKS?
LISSEN, YOKUM-WE KNOWS YOU CAN LICK US!-BUT-IF YOU SMASH MY PAL FIRST-I'LL PUSH PAPPY'S FACE IN WHILE YOU'RE DOIN' IT!
AND-IF YOU SMASHES HIM FIRST, I'LL PUSH PAPPY'S FACE IN WHILE YOU'RE DOIN' THAT!
SO YOU TAKES YOUR CHOICE-YOU STRINGS ALONG WITH US-OR-
GULP!!
AH IS TORN BETWIXT LOVE AN' DOOTY!
LOVE IS ON MAH SIDE!!
Copr. 1939 by United Feature Syndicate, Inc. Tm. Reg. U. S. Pat. Off.—All rights reserved

LI'L ABNER — The Forgotten Mammy! — By Al Capp

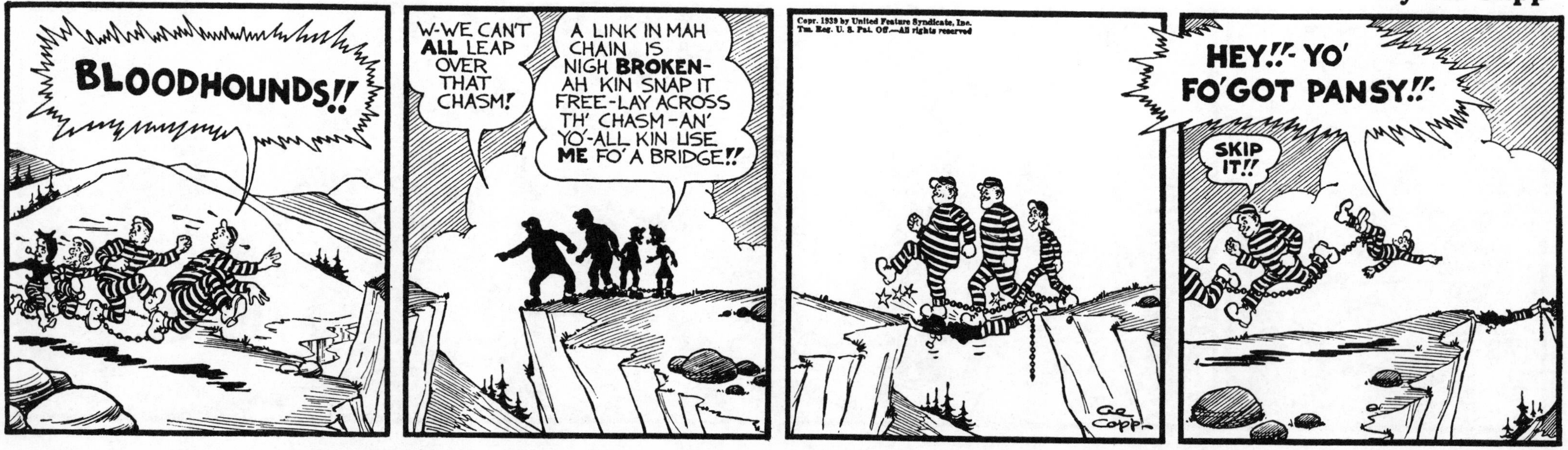
BLOODHOUNDS!!
W-WE CAN'T ALL LEAP OVER THAT CHASM!
A LINK IN MAH CHAIN IS NIGH BROKEN-AH KIN SNAP IT FREE-LAY ACROSS TH' CHASM-AN' YO'-ALL KIN USE ME FO' A BRIDGE!!
Copr. 1939 by United Feature Syndicate, Inc. Tm. Reg. U. S. Pat. Off.—All rights reserved
HEY!!-YO' FO'GOT PANSY!!
SKIP IT!!

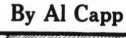

LI'L ABNER The Dead End Kids — By Al Capp

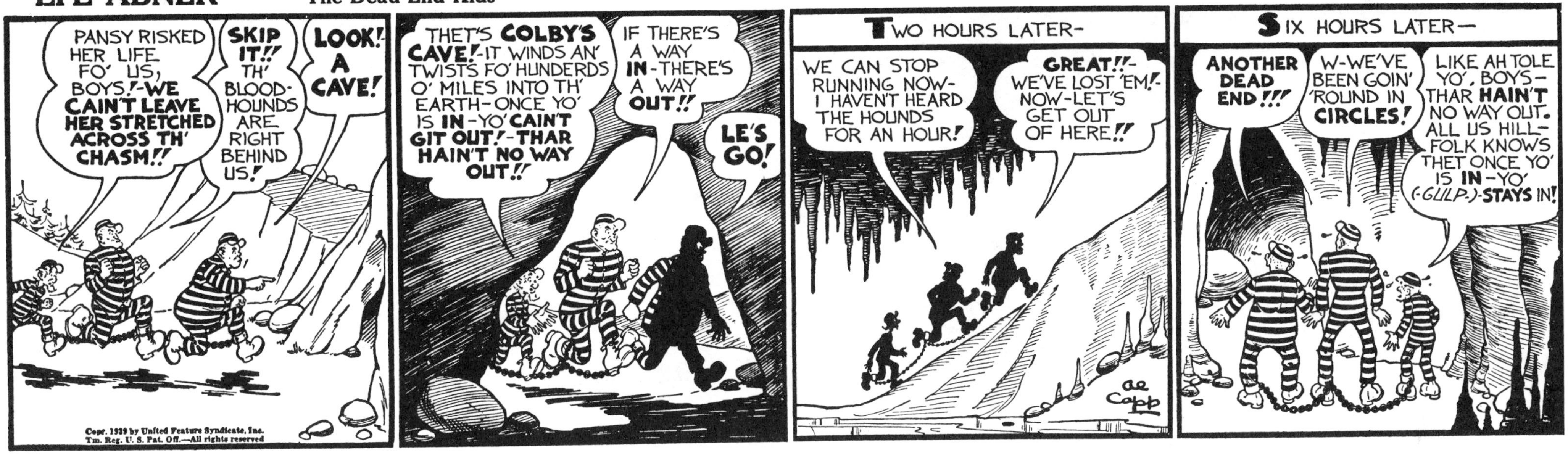

PANSY RISKED HER LIFE FO' US, BOYS!- WE CAIN'T LEAVE HER STRETCHED ACROSS TH' CHASM!!
SKIP IT!! TH' BLOOD-HOUNDS ARE RIGHT BEHIND US!
LOOK! A CAVE!
Copr. 1939 by United Feature Syndicate, Inc. Tm. Reg. U. S. Pat. Off.—All rights reserved
THET'S COLBY'S CAVE!-IT WINDS AN' TWISTS FO' HUNDERDS O' MILES INTO TH' EARTH-ONCE YO' IS IN-YO' CAIN'T GIT OUT!-THAR HAIN'T NO WAY OUT!!
IF THERE'S A WAY IN-THERE'S A WAY OUT!!
LE'S GO!
TWO HOURS LATER-
WE CAN STOP RUNNING NOW-I HAVEN'T HEARD THE HOUNDS FOR AN HOUR!
GREAT!!-WE'VE LOST 'EM!-NOW-LET'S GET OUT OF HERE!!
SIX HOURS LATER-
ANOTHER DEAD END!!!
W-WE'VE BEEN GOIN' 'ROUND IN CIRCLES!
LIKE AH TOLE YO', BOYS-THAR HAIN'T NO WAY OUT. ALL US HILL-FOLK KNOWS THET ONCE YO' IS IN-YO' (-GULP-)-STAYS IN!

LI'L ABNER Pappy a la Carte — By Al Capp

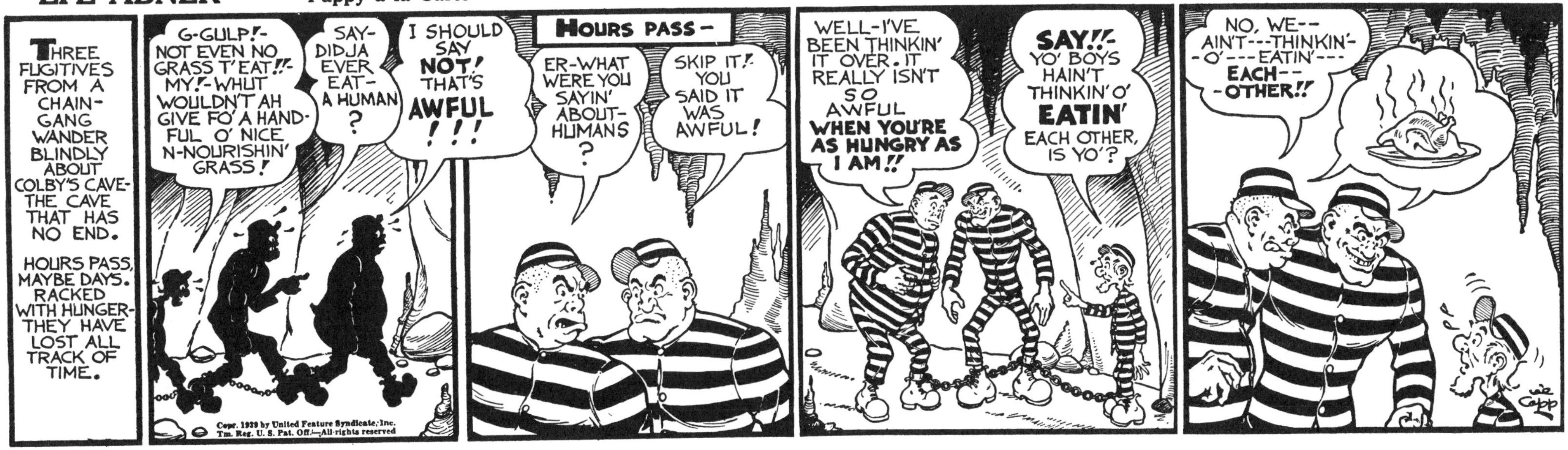

THREE FUGITIVES FROM A CHAIN-GANG WANDER BLINDLY ABOUT COLBY'S CAVE-THE CAVE THAT HAS NO END.
HOURS PASS, MAYBE DAYS. RACKED WITH HUNGER-THEY HAVE LOST ALL TRACK OF TIME.
G-GULP!-NOT EVEN NO GRASS T'EAT!!-MY!-WHUT WOULDN'T AH GIVE FO' A HANDFUL O' NICE N-NOURISHIN' GRASS!
SAY-DIDJA EVER EAT-A HUMAN?
I SHOULD SAY NOT! THAT'S AWFUL!!!
Copr. 1939 by United Feature Syndicate, Inc. Tm. Reg. U. S. Pat. Off.—All rights reserved
HOURS PASS-
ER-WHAT WERE YOU SAYIN' ABOUT-HUMANS?
SKIP IT!-YOU SAID IT WAS AWFUL!
WELL-I'VE BEEN THINKIN' IT OVER. IT REALLY ISN'T SO AWFUL WHEN YOU'RE AS HUNGRY AS I AM!!
SAY!!-YO' BOYS HAIN'T THINKIN' O' EATIN' EACH OTHER, IS YO'?
NO, WE--AIN'T---THINKIN'-O'---EATIN'---EACH---OTHER!!

LI'L ABNER Till Death Do Us'n Part! By Al Capp

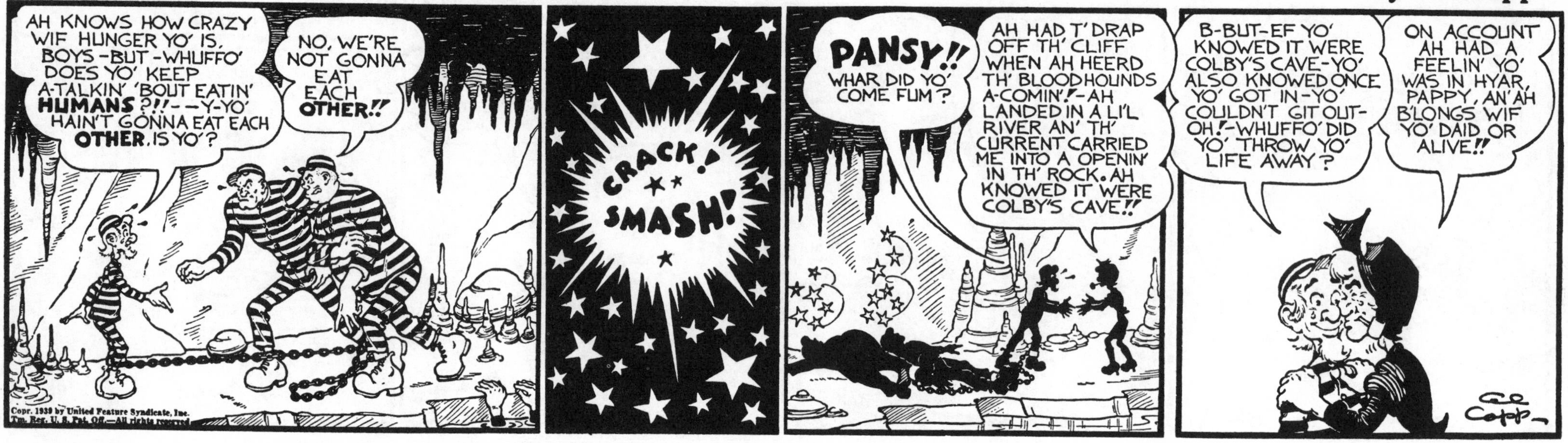
AH KNOWS HOW CRAZY WIF HUNGER YO' IS, BOYS-BUT-WHUFFO' DOES YO' KEEP A-TALKIN' 'BOUT EATIN' HUMANS?!!--Y-YO' HAIN'T GONNA EAT EACH OTHER, IS YO'?
NO, WE'RE NOT GONNA EAT EACH OTHER!!
Copr. 1939 by United Feature Syndicate, Inc. Tm. Reg. U. S. Pat. Off.—All rights reserved
CRACK! SMASH!
PANSY!! WHAR DID YO' COME FUM?
AH HAD T' DRAP OFF TH' CLIFF WHEN AH HEERD TH' BLOODHOUNDS A-COMIN'!-AH LANDED IN A LI'L RIVER AN' TH' CURRENT CARRIED ME INTO A OPENIN' IN TH' ROCK. AH KNOWED IT WERE COLBY'S CAVE!!
B-BUT-EF YO' KNOWED IT WERE COLBY'S CAVE-YO' ALSO KNOWED ONCE YO' GOT IN-YO' COULDN'T GIT OUT-OH!-WHUFFO' DID YO' THROW YO' LIFE AWAY?
ON ACCOUNT AH HAD A FEELIN' YO' WAS IN HYAR, PAPPY, AN' AH B'LONGS WIF YO' DAID OR ALIVE!!
Al Capp

LI'L ABNER Who Had the Right of Way? By Al Capp

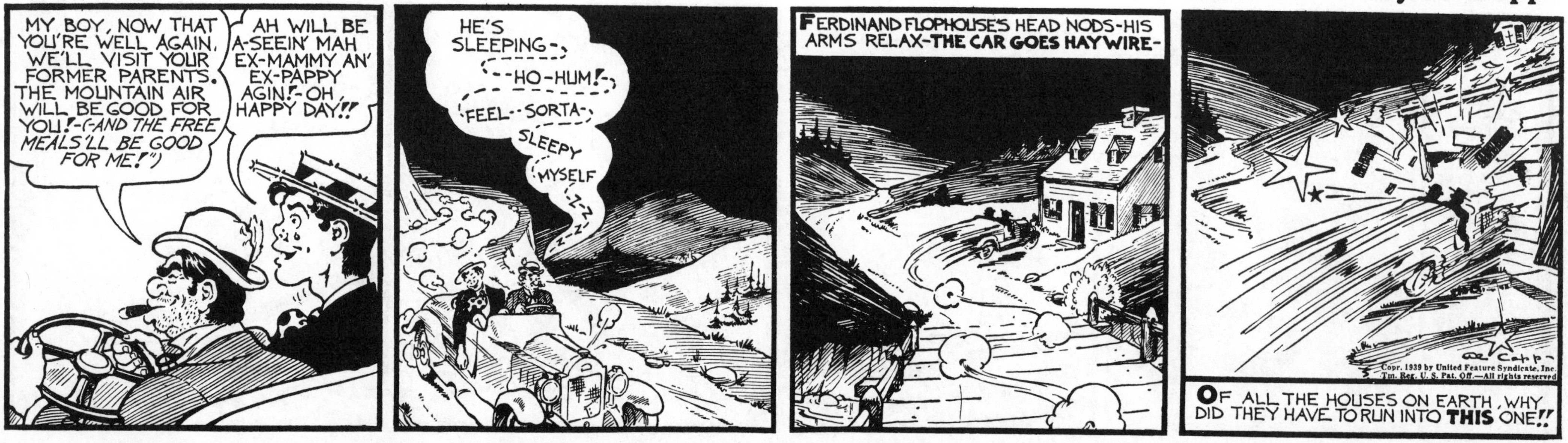
MY BOY, NOW THAT YOU'RE WELL AGAIN, WE'LL VISIT YOUR FORMER PARENTS. THE MOUNTAIN AIR WILL BE GOOD FOR YOU!-(-AND THE FREE MEALS'LL BE GOOD FOR ME!")
AH WILL BE A-SEEIN' MAH EX-MAMMY AN' EX-PAPPY AGIN!-OH, HAPPY DAY!!
HE'S SLEEPING--HO-HUM!-FEEL-SORTA-SLEEPY MYSELF
Z-Z-Z
FERDINAND FLOPHOUSE'S HEAD NODS-HIS ARMS RELAX-THE CAR GOES HAYWIRE-
Al Capp
Copr. 1939 by United Feature Syndicate, Inc. Tm. Reg. U. S. Pat. Off.—All rights reserved
OF ALL THE HOUSES ON EARTH, WHY DID THEY HAVE TO RUN INTO THIS ONE!!

LI'L ABNER — Condemned! — By Al Capp

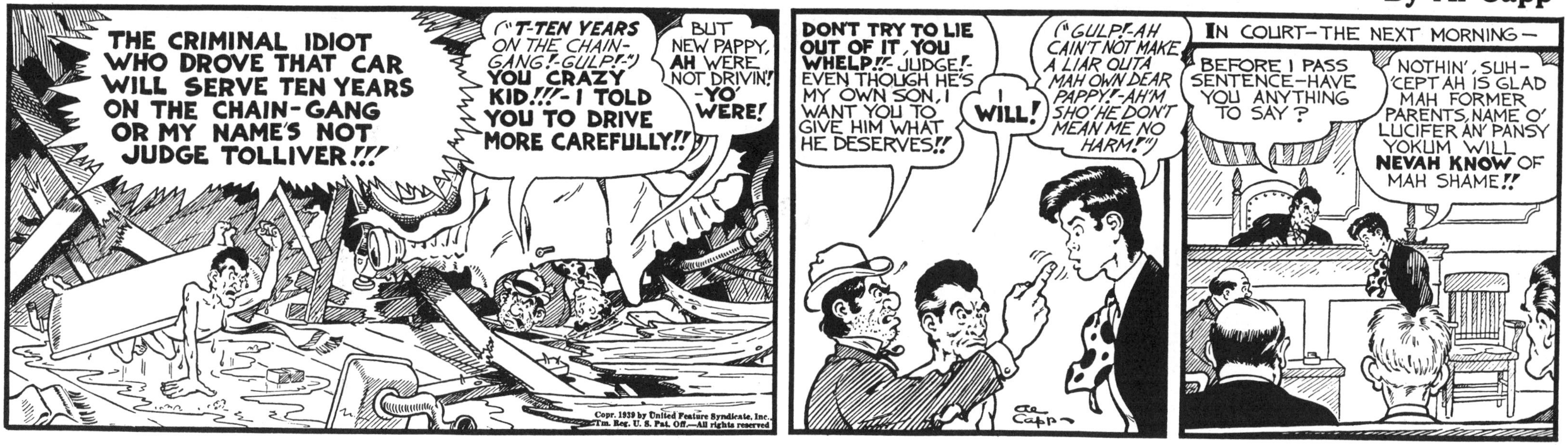
THE CRIMINAL IDIOT WHO DROVE THAT CAR WILL SERVE TEN YEARS ON THE CHAIN-GANG OR MY NAME'S NOT JUDGE TOLLIVER!!!
("T-TEN YEARS ON THE CHAIN-GANG!-GULP!-") YOU CRAZY KID!!!- I TOLD YOU TO DRIVE MORE CAREFULLY!!
BUT NEW PAPPY, AH WERE NOT DRIVIN'! -YO' WERE!
Copr. 1939 by United Feature Syndicate, Inc. Tm. Reg. U. S. Pat. Off.—All rights reserved
DON'T TRY TO LIE OUT OF IT, YOU WHELP!!- JUDGE!- EVEN THOUGH HE'S MY OWN SON, I WANT YOU TO GIVE HIM WHAT HE DESERVES!!
I WILL!
("GULP!-AH CAIN'T NOT MAKE A LIAR OUTA MAH OWN DEAR PAPPY!-AH'M SHO' HE DON'T MEAN ME NO HARM!")
IN COURT-THE NEXT MORNING-
BEFORE I PASS SENTENCE-HAVE YOU ANYTHING TO SAY?
NOTHIN', SUH-'CEPT AH IS GLAD MAH FORMER PARENTS, NAME O' LUCIFER AN' PANSY YOKUM WILL NEVAH KNOW OF MAH SHAME!!

LI'L ABNER — It's a Small World — By Al Capp

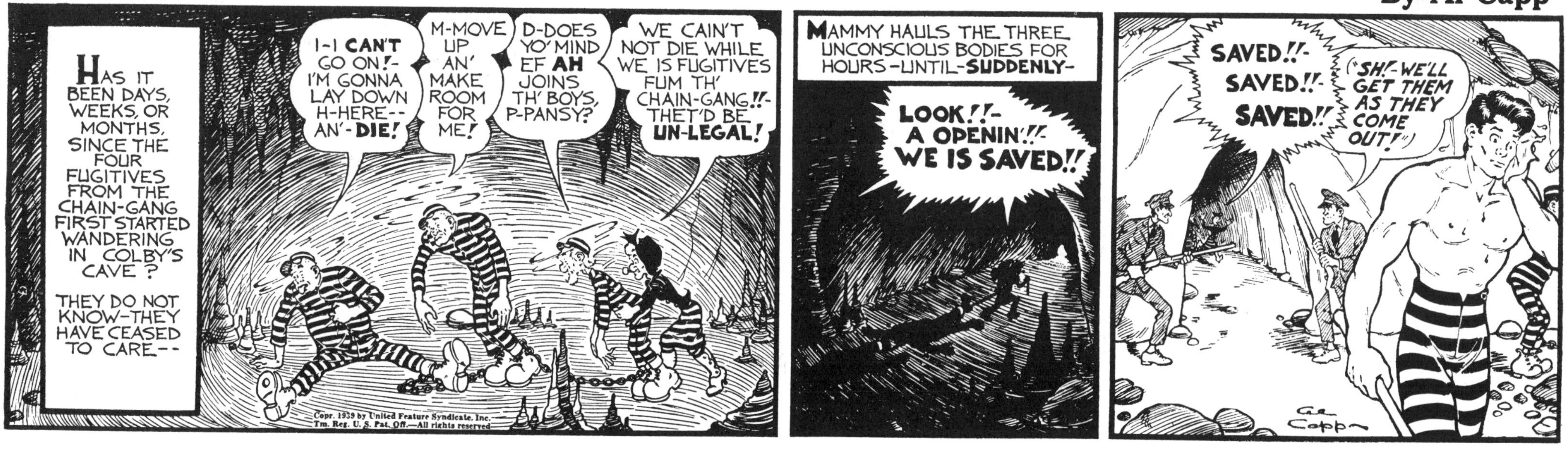
HAS IT BEEN DAYS, WEEKS, OR MONTHS, SINCE THE FOUR FUGITIVES FROM THE CHAIN-GANG FIRST STARTED WANDERING IN COLBY'S CAVE?
THEY DO NOT KNOW-THEY HAVE CEASED TO CARE--
I-I CAN'T GO ON!- I'M GONNA LAY DOWN H-HERE--AN'-DIE!
M-MOVE UP AN' MAKE ROOM FOR ME!
D-DOES YO' MIND EF AH JOINS TH' BOYS, P-PANSY?
WE CAIN'T NOT DIE WHILE WE IS FUGITIVES FUM TH' CHAIN-GANG!!- THET'D BE UN-LEGAL!
Copr. 1939 by United Feature Syndicate, Inc. Tm. Reg. U. S. Pat. Off.—All rights reserved
MAMMY HAULS THE THREE UNCONSCIOUS BODIES FOR HOURS-UNTIL-SUDDENLY-
LOOK!!- A OPENIN'!!- WE IS SAVED!!
SAVED!!- SAVED!!- SAVED!!
("SH!-WE'LL GET THEM AS THEY COME OUT!")

LI'L ABNER — Chain-Gang Blues — By Al Capp

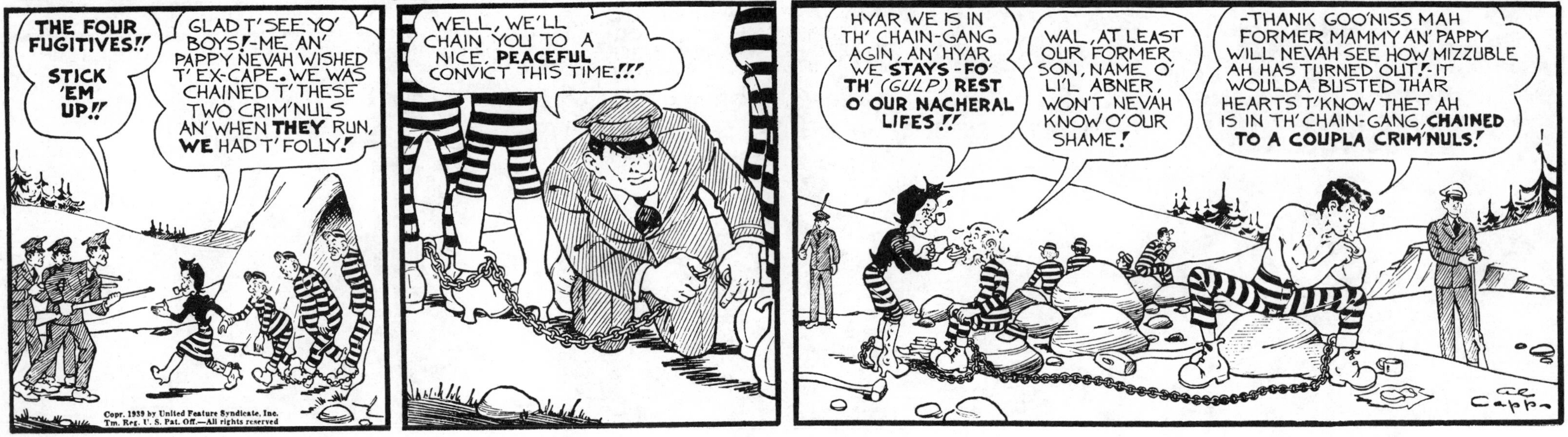

THE FOUR FUGITIVES!! STICK 'EM UP!!
GLAD T' SEE YO' BOYS! - ME AN' PAPPY NEVAH WISHED T' EX-CAPE. WE WAS CHAINED T' THESE TWO CRIM'NULS AN' WHEN THEY RUN, WE HAD T' FOLLY!
Copr. 1939 by United Feature Syndicate, Inc. Tm. Reg. U. S. Pat. Off.—All rights reserved
WELL, WE'LL CHAIN YOU TO A NICE, PEACEFUL CONVICT THIS TIME!!!
HYAR WE IS IN TH' CHAIN-GANG AGIN, AN' HYAR WE STAYS - FO' TH' (GULP) REST O' OUR NACHERAL LIFES!!
WAL, AT LEAST OUR FORMER SON, NAME O' LI'L ABNER, WON'T NEVAH KNOW O' OUR SHAME!
-THANK GOO'NISS MAH FORMER MAMMY AN' PAPPY WILL NEVAH SEE HOW MIZZUBLE AH HAS TURNED OUT! - IT WOULDA BUSTED THAR HEARTS T' KNOW THET AH IS IN TH' CHAIN-GANG, CHAINED TO A COUPLA CRIM'NULS!
Al Capp

LI'L ABNER — Oh, Happy Day (Gulp)!! — By Al Capp

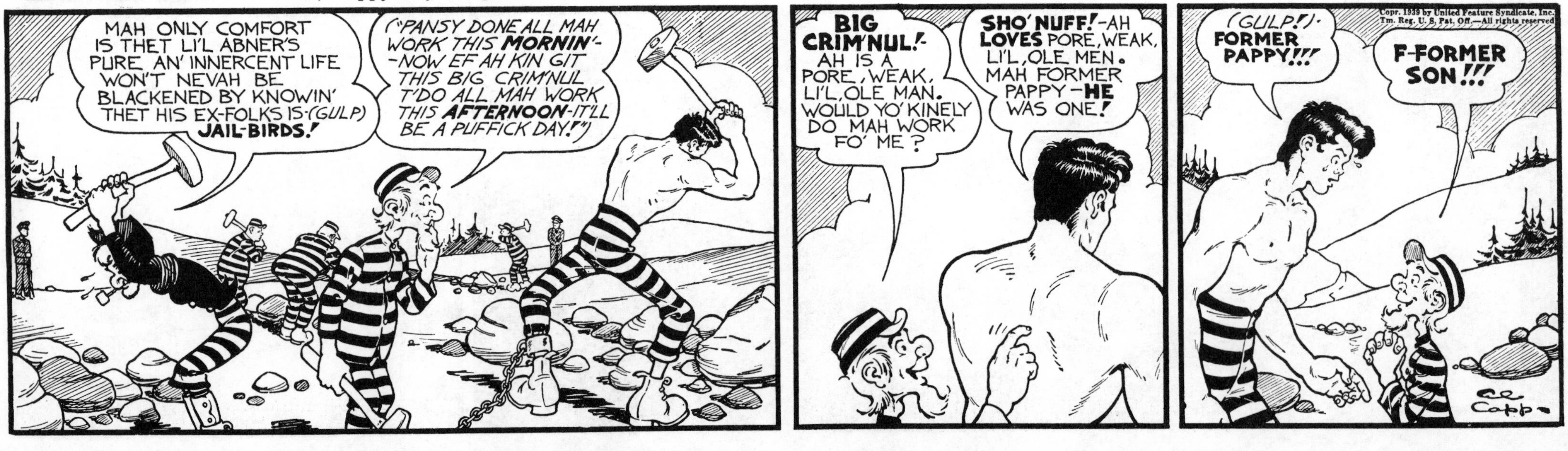

MAH ONLY COMFORT IS THET LI'L ABNER'S PURE AN' INNERCENT LIFE WON'T NEVAH BE BLACKENED BY KNOWIN' THET HIS EX-FOLKS IS - (GULP) JAIL-BIRDS!
("PANSY DONE ALL MAH WORK THIS MORNIN' - NOW EF AH KIN GIT THIS BIG CRIM'NUL T'DO ALL MAH WORK THIS AFTERNOON - IT'LL BE A PUFFICK DAY!")
BIG CRIM'NUL! - AH IS A PORE, WEAK, LI'L, OLE MAN. WOULD YO' KINELY DO MAH WORK FO' ME?
SHO' NUFF! - AH LOVES PORE, WEAK, LI'L, OLE MEN. MAH FORMER PAPPY - HE WAS ONE!
Copr. 1939 by United Feature Syndicate, Inc. Tm. Reg. U. S. Pat. Off.—All rights reserved
(GULP!) FORMER PAPPY!!!
F-FORMER SON!!!
Al Capp

LI'L ABNER That Man's Not Hyar Again! By Al Capp

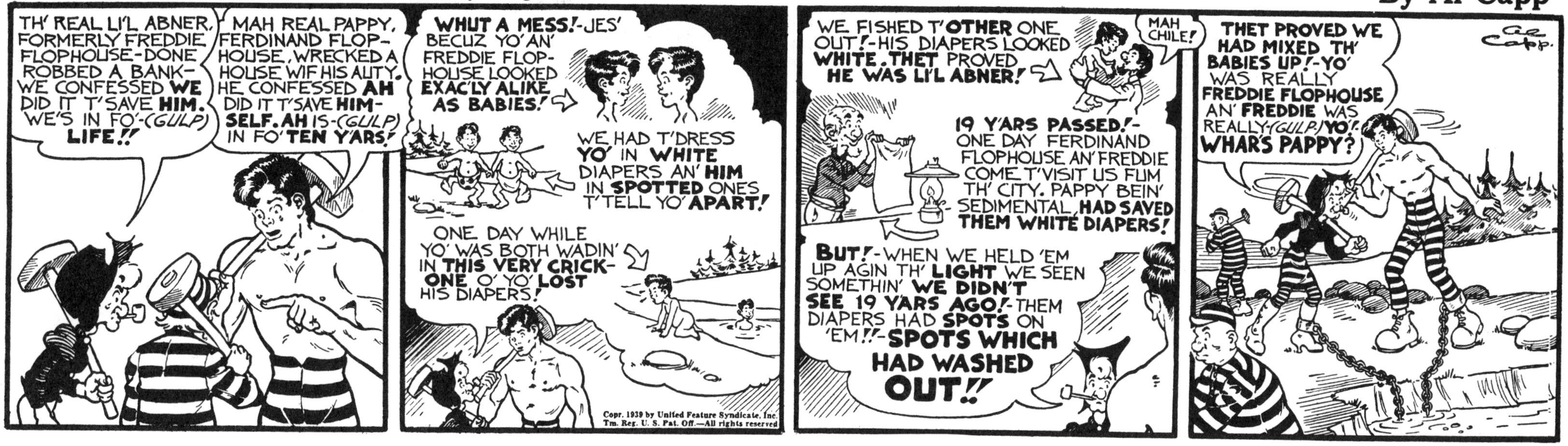
TH' REAL LI'L ABNER, FORMERLY FREDDIE FLOPHOUSE-DONE ROBBED A BANK-WE CONFESSED WE DID IT T'SAVE HIM. WE'S IN FO'-(GULP) LIFE!!
MAH REAL PAPPY, FERDINAND FLOPHOUSE, WRECKED A HOUSE WIF HIS AUTY. HE CONFESSED AH DID IT T'SAVE HIMSELF. AH IS-(GULP) IN FO' TEN YARS!
WHUT A MESS!-JES' BECUZ YO' AN' FREDDIE FLOPHOUSE LOOKED EXAC'LY ALIKE AS BABIES!
WE HAD T'DRESS YO' IN WHITE DIAPERS AN' HIM IN SPOTTED ONES T'TELL YO' APART!
ONE DAY WHILE YO' WAS BOTH WADIN' IN THIS VERY CRICK-ONE O' YO' LOST HIS DIAPERS!
Copr. 1939 by United Feature Syndicate, Inc. Tm. Reg. U. S. Pat. Off.—All rights reserved
WE FISHED T'OTHER ONE OUT!-HIS DIAPERS LOOKED WHITE. THET PROVED HE WAS LI'L ABNER!
MAH CHILE!
19 Y'ARS PASSED!-ONE DAY FERDINAND FLOPHOUSE AN' FREDDIE COME T'VISIT US FUM TH' CITY. PAPPY BEIN' SEDIMENTAL, HAD SAVED THEM WHITE DIAPERS!
BUT!-WHEN WE HELD 'EM UP AGIN TH' LIGHT WE SEEN SOMETHIN' WE DIDN'T SEE 19 YARS AGO!-THEM DIAPERS HAD SPOTS ON 'EM!!-SPOTS WHICH HAD WASHED OUT!!
THET PROVED WE HAD MIXED TH' BABIES UP!-YO' WAS REALLY FREDDIE FLOPHOUSE AN' FREDDIE WAS REALLY-(GULP) YO'!-WHAR'S PAPPY?
Al Capp

LI'L ABNER All's Well for the Moment By Al Capp

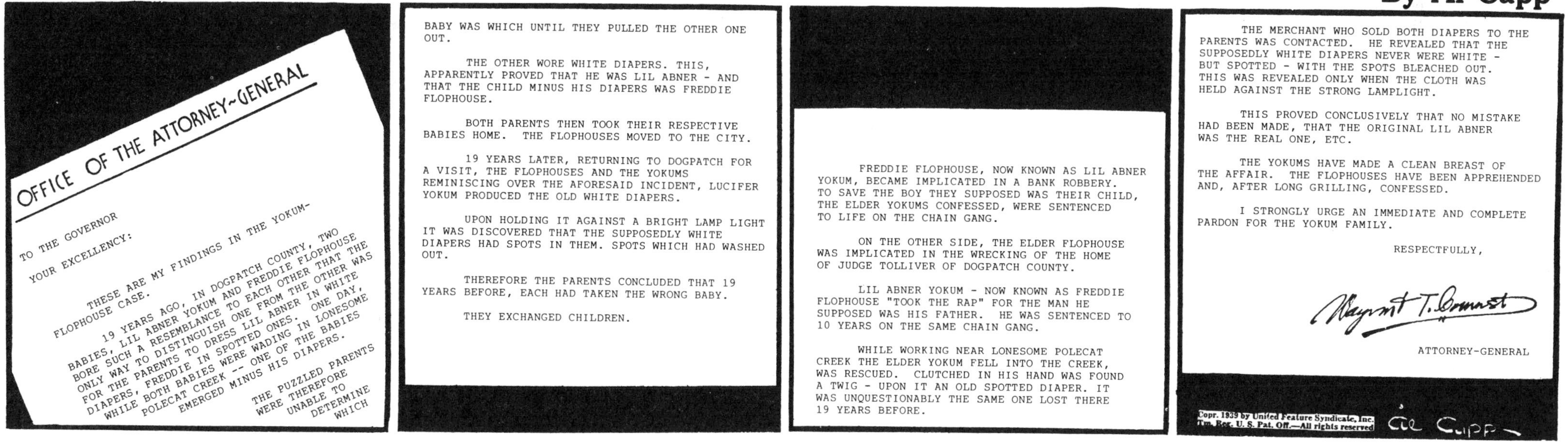
OFFICE OF THE ATTORNEY-GENERAL
TO THE GOVERNOR
YOUR EXCELLENCY:
THESE ARE MY FINDINGS IN THE YOKUM-FLOPHOUSE CASE.
19 YEARS AGO, IN DOGPATCH COUNTY, TWO BABIES, LIL ABNER YOKUM AND FREDDIE FLOPHOUSE BORE SUCH A RESEMBLANCE TO EACH OTHER THAT THE ONLY WAY TO DISTINGUISH ONE FROM THE OTHER WAS FOR THE PARENTS TO DRESS LIL ABNER IN WHITE DIAPERS, FREDDIE IN SPOTTED ONES. ONE DAY, WHILE BOTH BABIES WERE WADING IN LONESOME POLECAT CREEK -- ONE OF THE BABIES EMERGED MINUS HIS DIAPERS.
THE PUZZLED PARENTS WERE THEREFORE UNABLE TO DETERMINE WHICH BABY WAS WHICH UNTIL THEY PULLED THE OTHER ONE OUT.
THE OTHER WORE WHITE DIAPERS. THIS, APPARENTLY PROVED THAT HE WAS LIL ABNER - AND THAT THE CHILD MINUS HIS DIAPERS WAS FREDDIE FLOPHOUSE.
BOTH PARENTS THEN TOOK THEIR RESPECTIVE BABIES HOME. THE FLOPHOUSES MOVED TO THE CITY.
19 YEARS LATER, RETURNING TO DOGPATCH FOR A VISIT, THE FLOPHOUSES AND THE YOKUMS REMINISCING OVER THE AFORESAID INCIDENT, LUCIFER YOKUM PRODUCED THE OLD WHITE DIAPERS.
UPON HOLDING IT AGAINST A BRIGHT LAMP LIGHT IT WAS DISCOVERED THAT THE SUPPOSEDLY WHITE DIAPERS HAD SPOTS IN THEM. SPOTS WHICH HAD WASHED OUT.
THEREFORE THE PARENTS CONCLUDED THAT 19 YEARS BEFORE, EACH HAD TAKEN THE WRONG BABY.
THEY EXCHANGED CHILDREN.
FREDDIE FLOPHOUSE, NOW KNOWN AS LIL ABNER YOKUM, BECAME IMPLICATED IN A BANK ROBBERY. TO SAVE THE BOY THEY SUPPOSED WAS THEIR CHILD, THE ELDER YOKUMS CONFESSED, WERE SENTENCED TO LIFE ON THE CHAIN GANG.
ON THE OTHER SIDE, THE ELDER FLOPHOUSE WAS IMPLICATED IN THE WRECKING OF THE HOME OF JUDGE TOLLIVER OF DOGPATCH COUNTY.
LIL ABNER YOKUM - NOW KNOWN AS FREDDIE FLOPHOUSE "TOOK THE RAP" FOR THE MAN HE SUPPOSED WAS HIS FATHER. HE WAS SENTENCED TO 10 YEARS ON THE SAME CHAIN GANG.
WHILE WORKING NEAR LONESOME POLECAT CREEK THE ELDER YOKUM FELL INTO THE CREEK, WAS RESCUED. CLUTCHED IN HIS HAND WAS FOUND A TWIG - UPON IT AN OLD SPOTTED DIAPER. IT WAS UNQUESTIONABLY THE SAME ONE LOST THERE 19 YEARS BEFORE.
THE MERCHANT WHO SOLD BOTH DIAPERS TO THE PARENTS WAS CONTACTED. HE REVEALED THAT THE SUPPOSEDLY WHITE DIAPERS NEVER WERE WHITE - BUT SPOTTED - WITH THE SPOTS BLEACHED OUT. THIS WAS REVEALED ONLY WHEN THE CLOTH WAS HELD AGAINST THE STRONG LAMPLIGHT.
THIS PROVED CONCLUSIVELY THAT NO MISTAKE HAD BEEN MADE, THAT THE ORIGINAL LIL ABNER WAS THE REAL ONE, ETC.
THE YOKUMS HAVE MADE A CLEAN BREAST OF THE AFFAIR. THE FLOPHOUSES HAVE BEEN APPREHENDED AND, AFTER LONG GRILLING, CONFESSED.
I STRONGLY URGE AN IMMEDIATE AND COMPLETE PARDON FOR THE YOKUM FAMILY.
RESPECTFULLY,
ATTORNEY-GENERAL
Copr. 1939 by United Feature Syndicate, Inc. Tm. Reg. U. S. Pat. Off.—All rights reserved
Al Capp

LI'L ABNER Daisy Wilts! **By Al Capp**

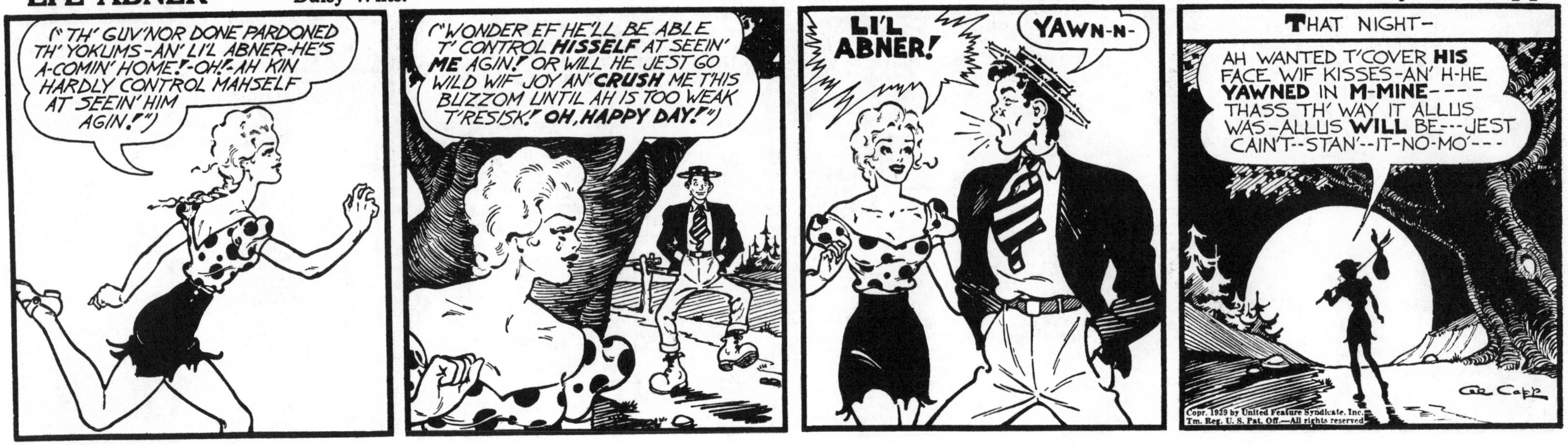
("TH' GUV'NOR DONE PARDONED TH' YOKUMS-AN' LI'L ABNER-HE'S A-COMIN' HOME!-OH!-AH KIN HARDLY CONTROL MAHSELF AT SEEIN' HIM AGIN!")
("WONDER EF HE'LL BE ABLE T' CONTROL HISSELF AT SEEIN' ME AGIN! OR WILL HE JEST GO WILD WIF JOY AN' CRUSH ME T'HIS BUZZOM UNTIL AH IS TOO WEAK T'RESISK! OH, HAPPY DAY!")
LI'L ABNER!
YAWN-N-
THAT NIGHT-
AH WANTED T'COVER HIS FACE WIF KISSES-AN' H-HE YAWNED IN M-MINE---- THASS TH' WAY IT ALLUS WAS-ALLUS WILL BE---JEST CAIN'T--STAN'--IT-NO-MO'---
Copr. 1939 by United Feature Syndicate, Inc. Tm. Reg. U. S. Pat. Off.—All rights reserved
AL CAPP

LI'L ABNER Mose is Never Wrong! **By Al Capp**

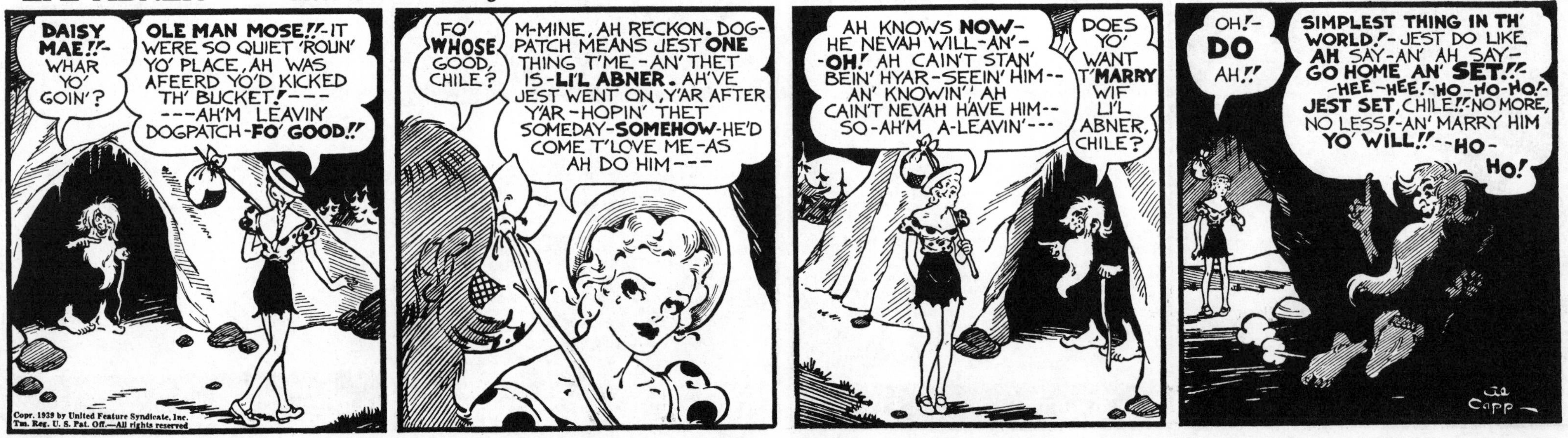
DAISY MAE!!- WHAR YO' GOIN'?
OLE MAN MOSE!!-IT WERE SO QUIET 'ROUN' YO' PLACE, AH WAS AFEERD YO'D KICKED TH' BUCKET!--- ---AH'M LEAVIN' DOGPATCH-FO' GOOD!!
FO' WHOSE GOOD, CHILE?
M-MINE, AH RECKON. DOG-PATCH MEANS JEST ONE THING T'ME-AN' THET IS-LI'L ABNER. AH'VE JEST WENT ON, Y'AR AFTER Y'AR-HOPIN' THET SOMEDAY-SOMEHOW-HE'D COME T'LOVE ME-AS AH DO HIM---
AH KNOWS NOW- HE NEVAH WILL-AN'- -OH! AH CAIN'T STAN' BEIN' HYAR-SEEIN' HIM-- AN' KNOWIN', AH CAIN'T NEVAH HAVE HIM-- SO-AH'M A-LEAVIN'---
DOES YO' WANT T'MARRY WIF LI'L ABNER, CHILE?
OH!- DO AH!!
SIMPLEST THING IN TH' WORLD!-JEST DO LIKE AH SAY-AN' AH SAY- GO HOME AN' SET!!- -HEE-HEE!-HO-HO-HO!- JEST SET, CHILE!!-NO MORE, NO LESS!-AN' MARRY HIM YO' WILL!!--HO- HO!
Copr. 1939 by United Feature Syndicate, Inc. Tm. Reg. U. S. Pat. Off.—All rights reserved
AL CAPP

LI'L ABNER — Mose Knows — By Al Capp

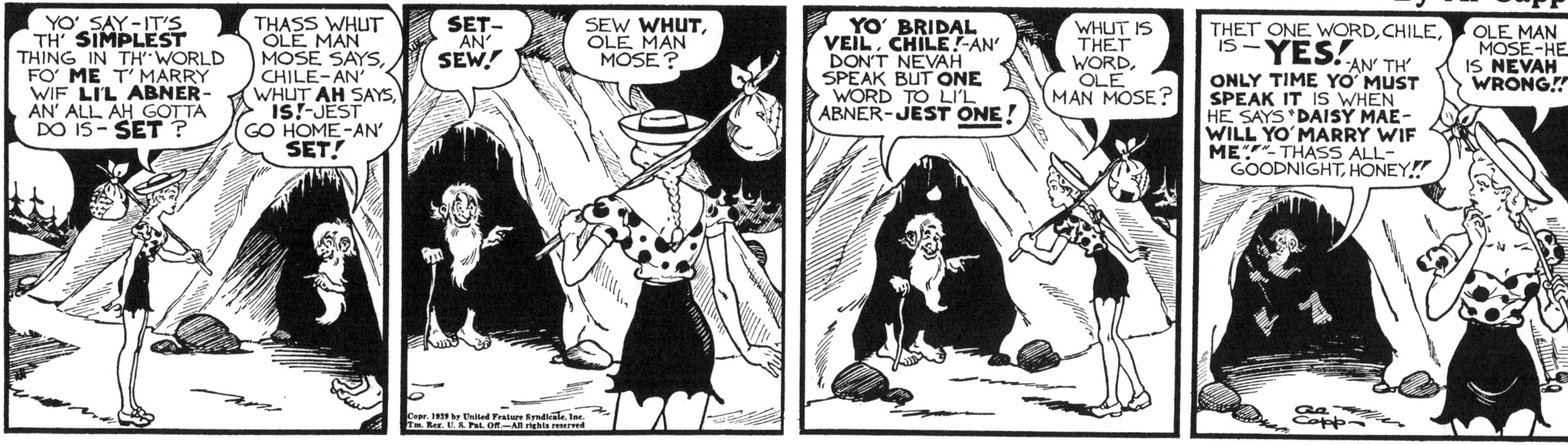

YO' SAY-IT'S TH' SIMPLEST THING IN TH' WORLD FO' ME T' MARRY WIF LI'L ABNER- AN' ALL AH GOTTA DO IS- SET ?
THASS WHUT OLE MAN MOSE SAYS, CHILE-AN' WHUT AH SAYS, IS!-JEST GO HOME-AN' SET!
SET- AN' SEW!
SEW WHUT, OLE MAN MOSE ?
Copr. 1939 by United Feature Syndicate, Inc. Tm. Reg. U. S. Pat. Off.—All rights reserved
YO' BRIDAL VEIL, CHILE!-AN' DON'T NEVAH SPEAK BUT ONE WORD TO LI'L ABNER-JEST ONE!
WHUT IS THET WORD, OLE MAN MOSE?
THET ONE WORD, CHILE, IS-YES!-AN' TH' ONLY TIME YO' MUST SPEAK IT IS WHEN HE SAYS "DAISY MAE-WILL YO' MARRY WIF ME"!"-THASS ALL- GOODNIGHT, HONEY!!
OLE MAN MOSE-HE IS NEVAH WRONG!!

LI'L ABNER — Love Hain't On His Side! — By Al Capp

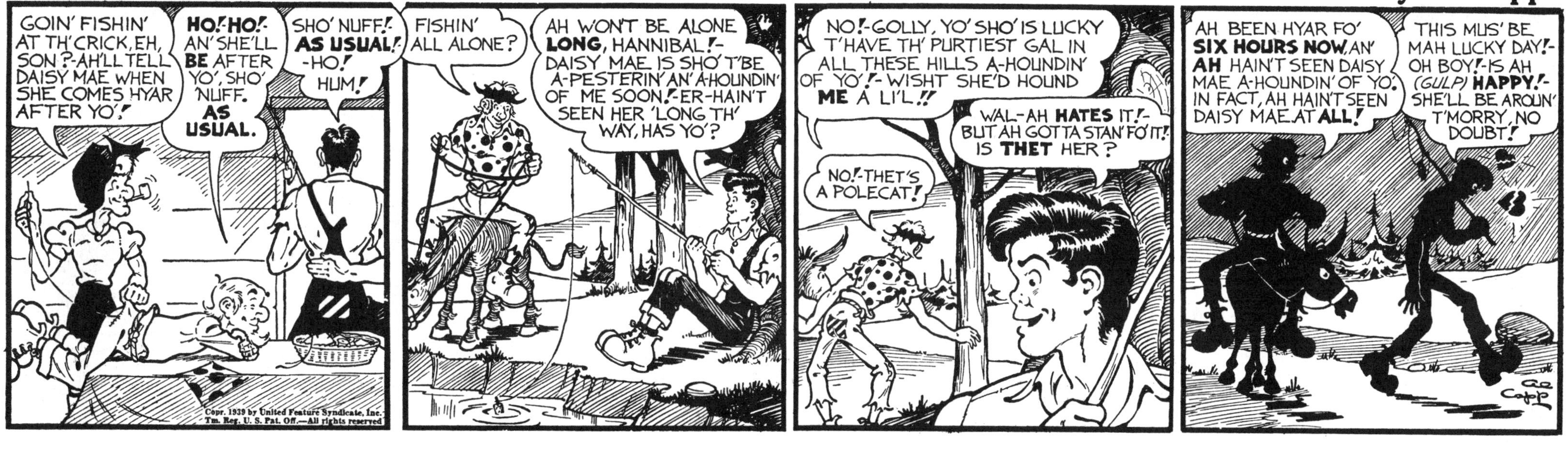

GOIN' FISHIN' AT TH' CRICK, EH, SON?-AH'LL TELL DAISY MAE WHEN SHE COMES HYAR AFTER YO'!
HO!-HO!- AN' SHE'LL BE AFTER YO', SHO' 'NUFF. AS USUAL.
SHO' NUFF!- AS USUAL!- -HO! HUM!
Copr. 1939 by United Feature Syndicate, Inc. Tm. Reg. U. S. Pat. Off.—All rights reserved
FISHIN' ALL ALONE?
AH WON'T BE ALONE LONG, HANNIBAL!- DAISY MAE IS SHO' T'BE A-PESTERIN' AN' A-HOUNDIN' OF ME SOON!-ER-HAIN'T SEEN HER 'LONG TH' WAY, HAS YO'?
NO!-GOLLY, YO' SHO' IS LUCKY T'HAVE TH' PURTIEST GAL IN ALL THESE HILLS A-HOUNDIN' OF YO'!-WISHT SHE'D HOUND ME A LI'L!!
WAL-AH HATES IT!- BUT AH GOTTA STAN' FO' IT!- IS THET HER?
NO!-THET'S A POLECAT!
AH BEEN HYAR FO' SIX HOURS NOW, AN' AH HAIN'T SEEN DAISY MAE A-HOUNDIN' OF YO'. IN FACT, AH HAIN'T SEEN DAISY MAE AT ALL!
THIS MUS' BE MAH LUCKY DAY!- OH BOY!-IS AH (GULP) HAPPY!- SHE'LL BE AROUN' T'MORRY, NO DOUBT!

LI'L ABNER Love Takes a Holiday! By Al Capp

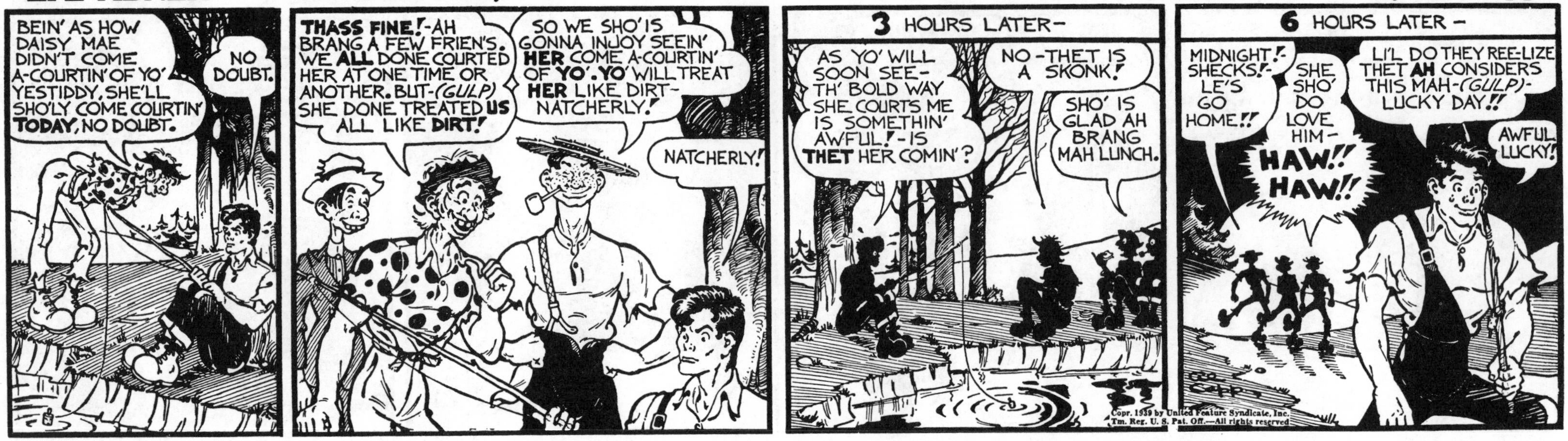
BEIN' AS HOW DAISY MAE DIDN'T COME A-COURTIN' OF YO' YESTIDDY, SHE'LL SHO'LY COME COURTIN' TODAY, NO DOUBT.
NO DOUBT.
THASS FINE!-AH BRANG A FEW FRIEN'S. WE ALL DONE COURTED HER AT ONE TIME OR ANOTHER. BUT-(GULP) SHE DONE TREATED US ALL LIKE DIRT!
SO WE SHO'IS GONNA INJOY SEEIN' HER COME A-COURTIN' OF YO'. YO' WILL TREAT HER LIKE DIRT-NATCHERLY!
NATCHERLY!
3 HOURS LATER-
AS YO' WILL SOON SEE-TH' BOLD WAY SHE COURTS ME IS SOMETHIN' AWFUL!-IS THET HER COMIN'?
NO-THET IS A SKONK!
SHO' IS GLAD AH BRANG MAH LUNCH.
Copr. 1939 by United Feature Syndicate, Inc. Tm. Reg. U. S. Pat. Off.—All rights reserved
6 HOURS LATER-
MIDNIGHT!-SHECKS!-LE'S GO HOME!!
SHE SHO' DO LOVE HIM-
HAW!! HAW!!
LI'L DO THEY REE-LIZE THET AH CONSIDERS THIS MAH-(GULP)-LUCKY DAY!!
AWFUL LUCKY!

LI'L ABNER Ole Man Mose Knows Whuffo! By Al Capp

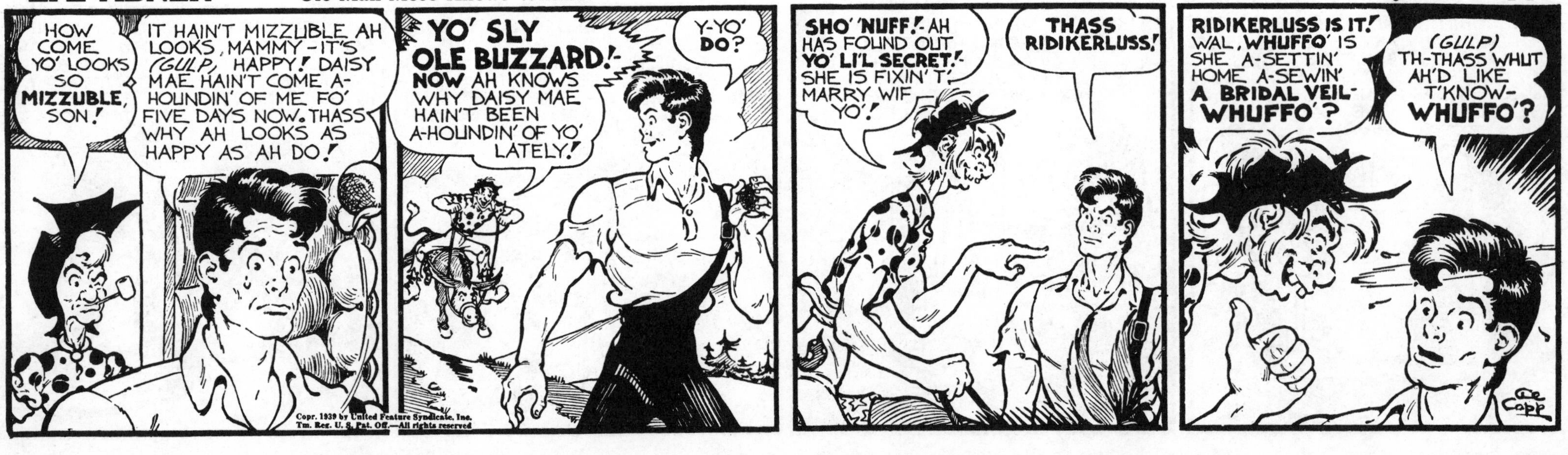
HOW COME YO' LOOKS SO MIZZUBLE, SON!
IT HAIN'T MIZZUBLE AH LOOKS, MAMMY-IT'S (GULP) HAPPY! DAISY MAE HAIN'T COME A-HOUNDIN' OF ME FO' FIVE DAYS NOW. THASS WHY AH LOOKS AS HAPPY AS AH DO!
Copr. 1939 by United Feature Syndicate, Inc. Tm. Reg. U. S. Pat. Off.—All rights reserved
YO' SLY OLE BUZZARD!-NOW AH KNOWS WHY DAISY MAE HAIN'T BEEN A-HOUNDIN' OF YO' LATELY!
Y-YO' DO?
SHO' 'NUFF!-AH HAS FOUND OUT YO' LI'L SECRET!-SHE IS FIXIN' T' MARRY WIF YO'!
THASS RIDIKERLUSS!
RIDIKERLUSS IS IT! WAL, WHUFFO' IS SHE A-SETTIN' HOME A-SEWIN' A BRIDAL VEIL-WHUFFO'?
(GULP) TH-THASS WHUT AH'D LIKE T'KNOW-WHUFFO'?

LI'L ABNER It's a Small World! By Al Capp

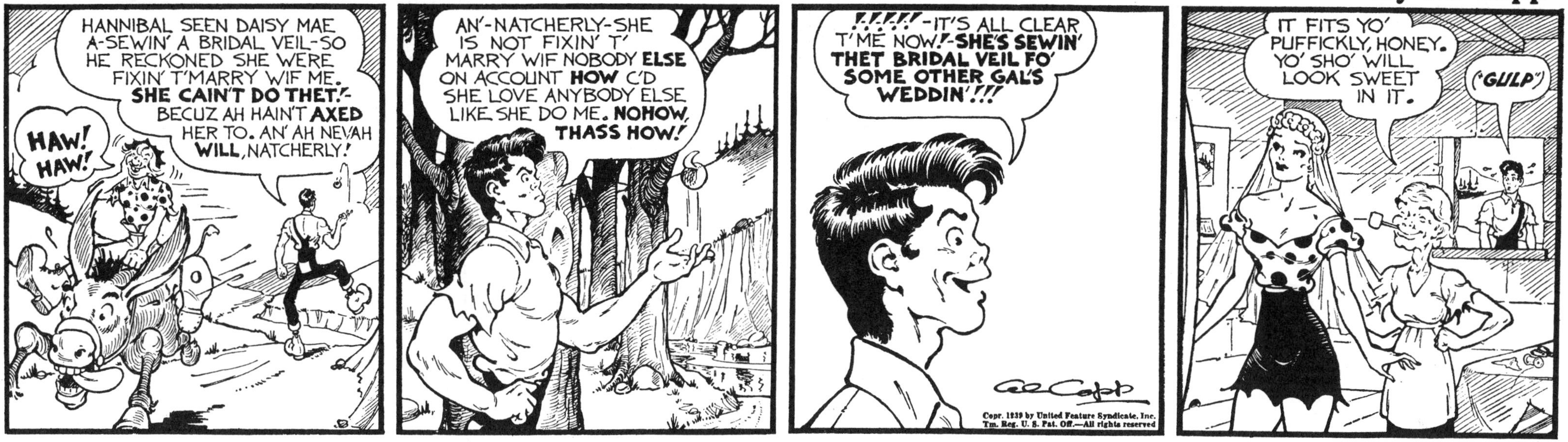
HANNIBAL SEEN DAISY MAE A-SEWIN' A BRIDAL VEIL-SO HE RECKONED SHE WERE FIXIN' T'MARRY WIF ME. **SHE CAIN'T DO THET!**- BECUZ AH HAIN'T **AXED** HER TO. AN' AH NEVAH **WILL**, NATCHERLY!
HAW! HAW!
AN'-NATCHERLY-SHE IS NOT FIXIN' T' MARRY WIF NOBODY **ELSE** ON ACCOUNT **HOW** C'D SHE LOVE ANYBODY ELSE LIKE SHE DO ME. **NOHOW, THASS HOW!**
-IT'S ALL CLEAR T'ME NOW!-**SHE'S SEWIN' THET BRIDAL VEIL FO' SOME OTHER GAL'S WEDDIN'!!!**
Al Capp
Copr. 1939 by United Feature Syndicate, Inc. Tm. Reg. U. S. Pat. Off.—All rights reserved
IT FITS YO' PUFFICKLY, HONEY. YO' SHO' WILL LOOK SWEET IN IT.
("GULP")

LI'L ABNER The Fish Is Biting By Al Capp

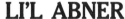

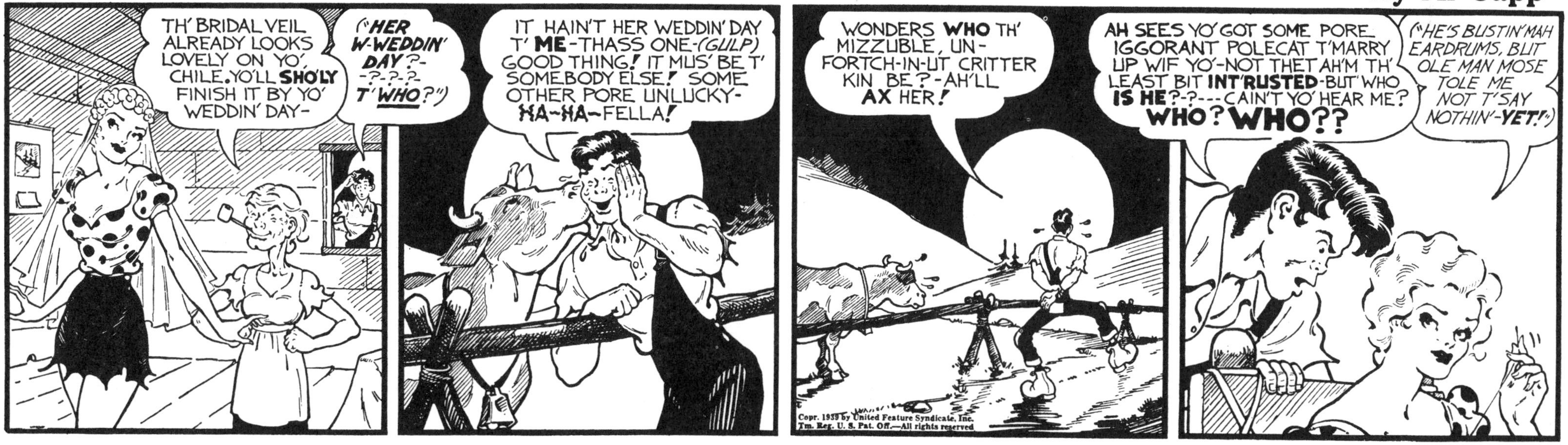
TH' BRIDAL VEIL ALREADY LOOKS LOVELY ON YO' CHILE. YO'LL **SHO'LY** FINISH IT BY YO' WEDDIN' DAY-
("HER W-WEDDIN' DAY?- -?-?-?- T' WHO?")
IT HAIN'T HER WEDDIN' DAY T' **ME**-THASS ONE-(GULP) GOOD THING! IT MUS' BE T' SOMEBODY ELSE! SOME OTHER PORE UNLUCKY- HA-HA-FELLA!
WONDERS **WHO** TH' MIZZUBLE, UN-FORTCH-IN-UT CRITTER KIN BE?-AH'LL **AX** HER!
Copr. 1939 by United Feature Syndicate, Inc. Tm. Reg. U. S. Pat. Off.—All rights reserved
AH SEES YO' GOT SOME PORE IGGORANT POLECAT T'MARRY UP WIF YO'-NOT THET AH'M TH' LEAST BIT **INT'RUSTED**-BUT WHO **IS HE**?-?---CAIN'T YO' HEAR ME? **WHO? WHO??**
("HE'S BUSTIN' MAH EARDRUMS, BUT OLE MAN MOSE TOLE ME NOT T'SAY NOTHIN'-YET!")

LI'L ABNER Like a Lamb to the Slaughter! By Al Capp

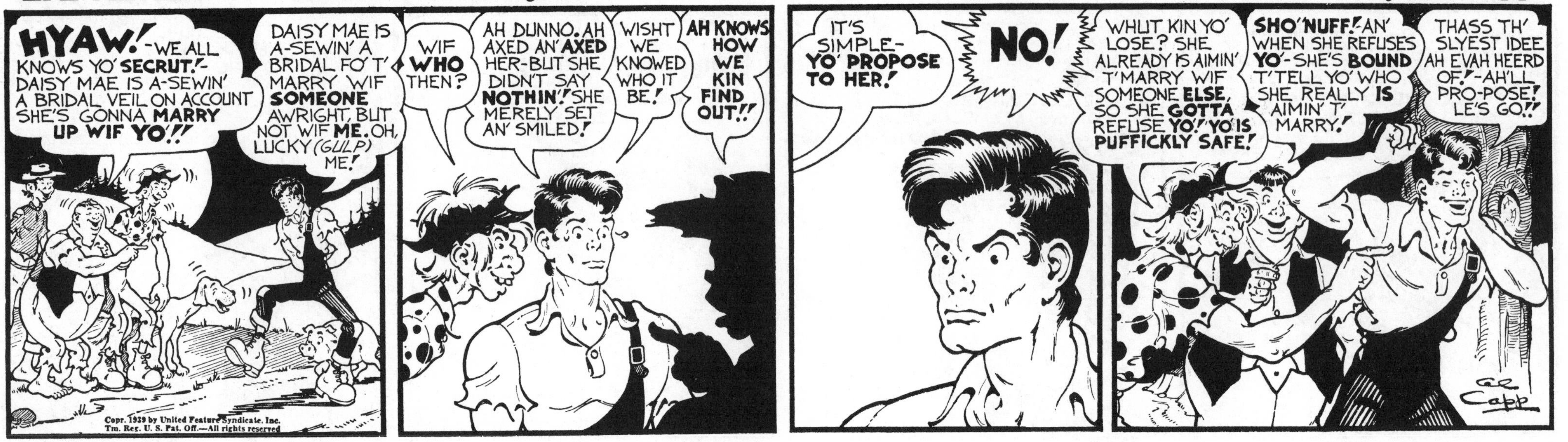

HYAW!-WE ALL KNOWS YO' SECRUT!-DAISY MAE IS A-SEWIN' A BRIDAL VEIL ON ACCOUNT SHE'S GONNA MARRY UP WIF YO'!!
DAISY MAE IS A-SEWIN' A BRIDAL FO' T' MARRY WIF SOMEONE AWRIGHT, BUT NOT WIF ME. OH, LUCKY (GULP) ME!
Copr. 1939 by United Feature Syndicate, Inc. Tm. Reg. U. S. Pat. Off.—All rights reserved
WIF WHO THEN?
AH DUNNO. AH AXED AN' AXED HER-BUT SHE DIDN'T SAY NOTHIN'! SHE MERELY SET AN' SMILED!
WISHT WE KNOWED WHO IT BE!
AH KNOWS HOW WE KIN FIND OUT!!
IT'S SIMPLE-YO' PROPOSE TO HER!
NO!
WHUT KIN YO' LOSE? SHE ALREADY IS AIMIN' T' MARRY WIF SOMEONE ELSE, SO SHE GOTTA REFUSE YO'! YO' IS PUFFICKLY SAFE!
SHO'NUFF!-AN' WHEN SHE REFUSES YO'-SHE'S BOUND T' TELL YO' WHO SHE REALLY IS AIMIN' T' MARRY!
THASS TH' SLYEST IDEE AH EVAH HEERD OF!-AH'LL PRO-POSE! LE'S GO!!
Al Capp

LI'L ABNER Now Comes the Surprise! By Al Capp

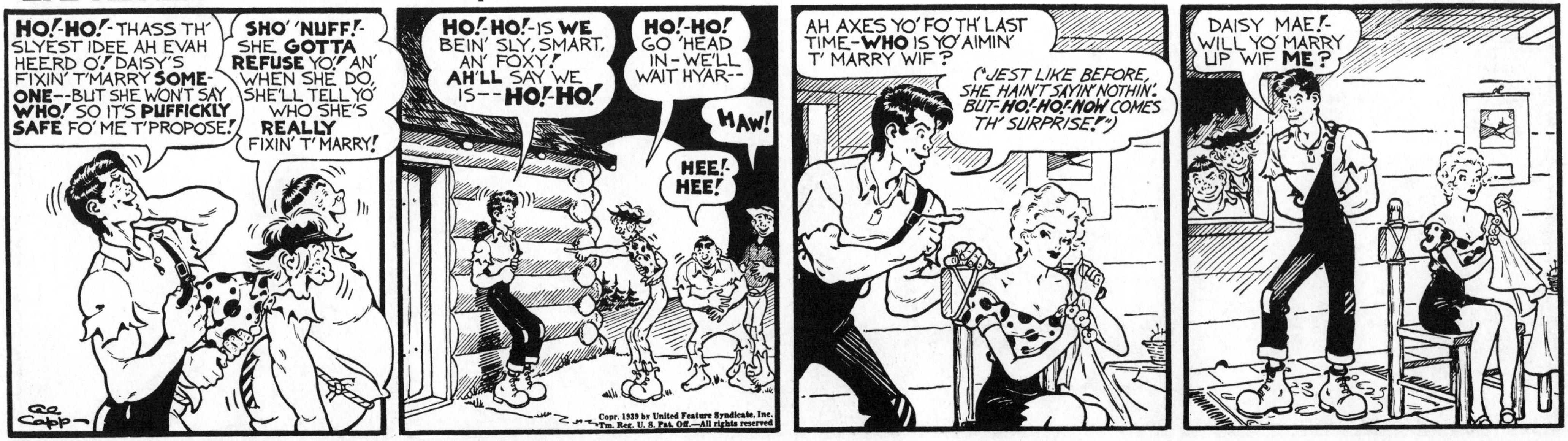

HO!-HO!-THASS TH' SLYEST IDEE AH EVAH HEERD O'! DAISY'S FIXIN' T'MARRY SOME-ONE--BUT SHE WON'T SAY WHO! SO IT'S PUFFICKLY SAFE FO' ME T'PROPOSE!
SHO' 'NUFF!-SHE GOTTA REFUSE YO'! AN' WHEN SHE DO, SHE'LL TELL YO' WHO SHE'S REALLY FIXIN' T'MARRY!
Al Capp
HO!-HO!-IS WE BEIN' SLY, SMART, AN' FOXY! AH'LL SAY WE IS--HO!-HO!
HO!-HO! GO 'HEAD IN-WE'LL WAIT HYAR--
HAW!
HEE!-HEE!
Copr. 1939 by United Feature Syndicate, Inc. Tm. Reg. U. S. Pat. Off.—All rights reserved
AH AXES YO' FO' TH' LAST TIME-WHO IS YO' AIMIN' T' MARRY WIF?
("JEST LIKE BEFORE, SHE HAIN'T SAYIN' NOTHIN'. BUT-HO!-HO!-NOW COMES TH' SURPRISE!")
DAISY MAE!-WILL YO' MARRY UP WIF ME?

LI'L ABNER GULP!! By Al Capp

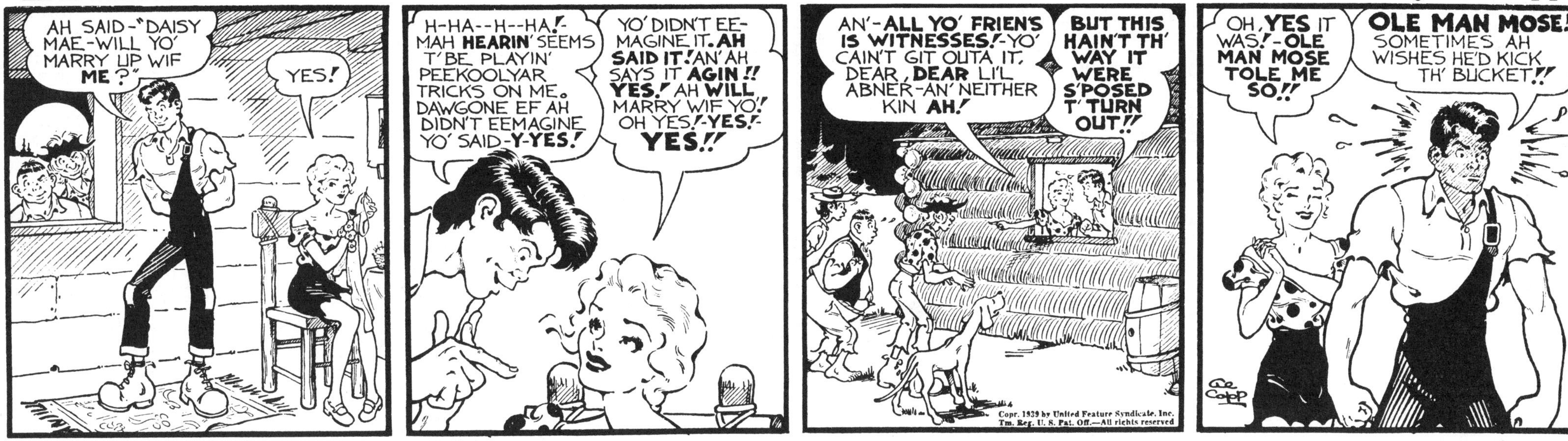
AH SAID-"DAISY MAE-WILL YO' MARRY UP WIF **ME**?"
YES!
H-HA--H--HA!-MAH **HEARIN'** SEEMS T' BE PLAYIN' PEEKOOLYAR TRICKS ON ME. DAWGONE EF AH DIDN'T EEMAGINE YO' SAID-**Y-YES!**
YO' DIDN'T EE-MAGINE IT.-**AH SAID IT!** AN' AH SAYS IT **AGIN!! YES!** AH **WILL** MARRY WIF YO'! OH YES!-**YES!**-**YES!!**
AN'-**ALL YO' FRIEN'S IS WITNESSES!**-YO' CAIN'T GIT OUTA IT, DEAR, **DEAR** LI'L ABNER-AN' NEITHER KIN **AH!**
BUT THIS HAIN'T TH' WAY IT WERE S'POSED T' TURN OUT!!
Copr. 1939 by United Feature Syndicate, Inc. Tm. Reg. U. S. Pat. Off.—All rights reserved
OH, **YES** IT WAS!-**OLE MAN MOSE TOLE ME SO!!**
OLE MAN MOSE!-SOMETIMES AH WISHES HE'D KICK TH' BUCKET!!

LI'L ABNER A Slave of Love! By Al Capp

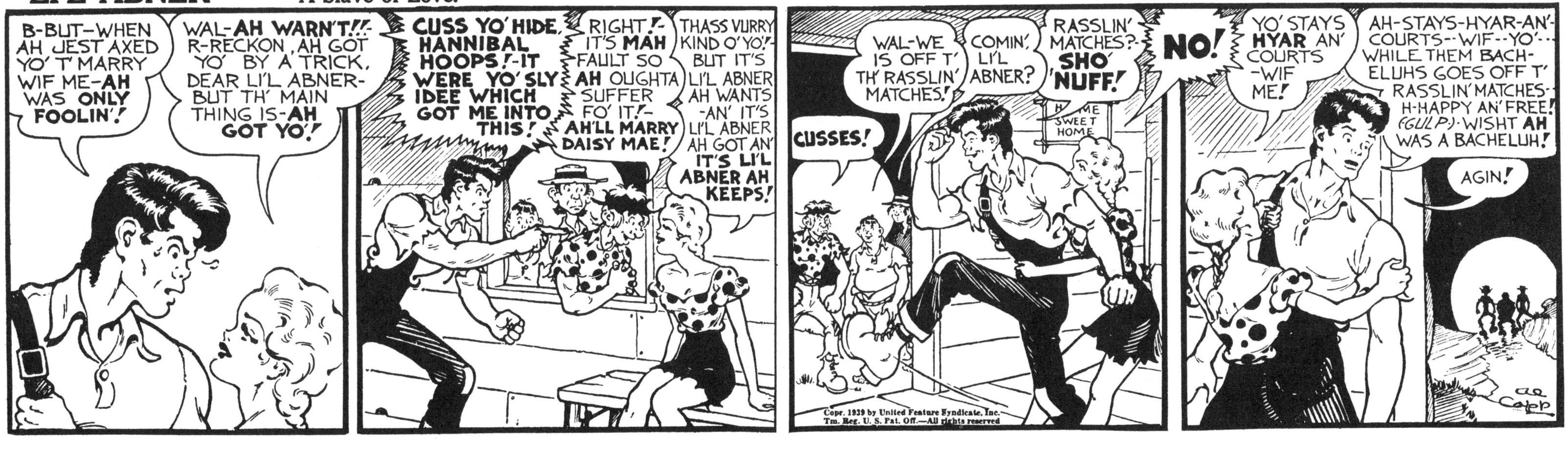
B-BUT-WHEN AH JEST AXED YO' T' MARRY WIF ME-**AH** WAS **ONLY FOOLIN'!**
WAL-**AH WARN'T!!**-R-RECKON, AH GOT YO' BY A TRICK, DEAR LI'L ABNER-BUT TH' MAIN THING IS-**AH GOT YO'!**
CUSS YO' HIDE, HANNIBAL HOOPS!-IT WERE YO' SLY IDEE WHICH GOT ME INTO THIS!
RIGHT!-IT'S **MAH** FAULT SO **AH** OUGHTA SUFFER FO' IT!-**AH'LL MARRY DAISY MAE!**
THASS VURRY KIND O' YO'!-BUT IT'S LI'L ABNER AH WANTS -AN' IT'S LI'L ABNER AH GOT AN' **IT'S LI'L ABNER AH KEEPS!**
WAL-WE IS OFF T' TH' RASSLIN' MATCHES!
COMIN', LI'L ABNER?
RASSLIN' MATCHES?-**SHO' 'NUFF!**
CUSSES!
HOME SWEET HOME
Copr. 1939 by United Feature Syndicate, Inc. Tm. Reg. U. S. Pat. Off.—All rights reserved
NO!
YO' STAYS **HYAR** AN' COURTS -WIF ME!
AH-STAYS-HYAR-AN'-COURTS--WIF--YO'--WHILE THEM BACH-ELUHS GOES OFF T' RASSLIN' MATCHES--H-HAPPY AN' FREE! (GULP.)-WISHT **AH** WAS A BACHELUH!
AGIN!

LI'L ABNER Mystery Man! **By Al Capp**

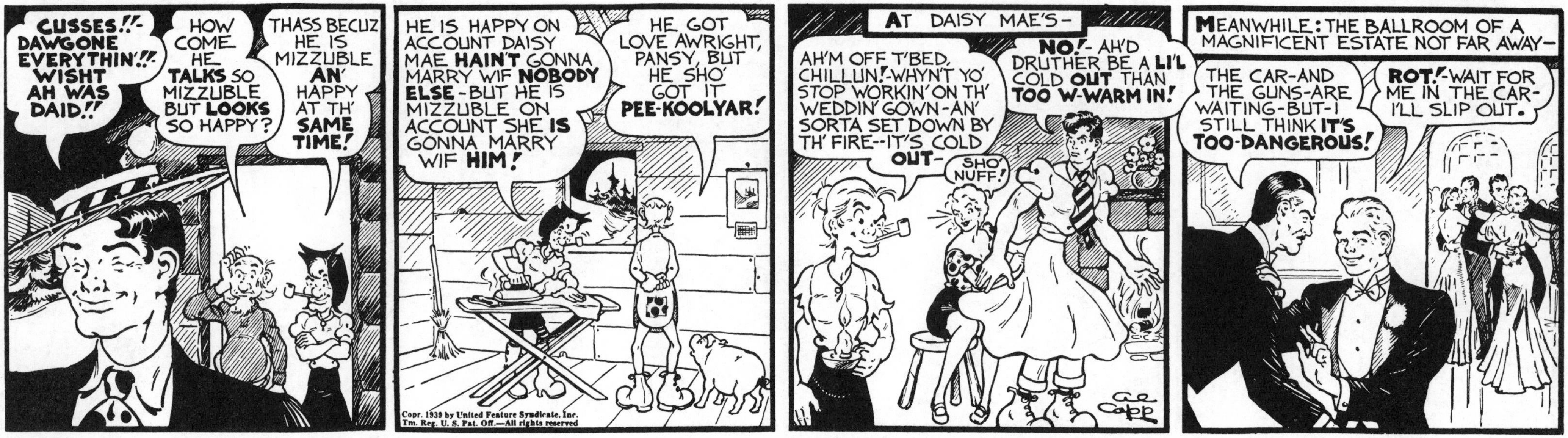

CUSSES!!-DAWGONE EVERYTHIN'!!! WISHT AH WAS DAID!!
HOW COME HE TALKS SO MIZZUBLE BUT LOOKS SO HAPPY?
THASS BECUZ HE IS MIZZUBLE AN' HAPPY AT TH' SAME TIME!
HE IS HAPPY ON ACCOUNT DAISY MAE HAIN'T GONNA MARRY WIF NOBODY ELSE-BUT HE IS MIZZUBLE ON ACCOUNT SHE IS GONNA MARRY WIF HIM!
HE GOT LOVE AWRIGHT, PANSY, BUT HE SHO' GOT IT PEE-KOOLYAR!
Copr. 1939 by United Feature Syndicate, Inc. Tm. Reg. U. S. Pat. Off.—All rights reserved
AT DAISY MAE'S-
AH'M OFF T'BED, CHILLUN!-WHYN'T YO' STOP WORKIN' ON TH' WEDDIN' GOWN-AN' SORTA SET DOWN BY TH' FIRE--IT'S COLD OUT-
SHO' NUFF!
NO!-AH'D DRUTHER BE A LI'L COLD OUT THAN TOO W-WARM IN!
AL CAPP
MEANWHILE: THE BALLROOM OF A MAGNIFICENT ESTATE NOT FAR AWAY-
THE CAR-AND THE GUNS-ARE WAITING-BUT-I STILL THINK IT'S TOO-DANGEROUS!
ROT!-WAIT FOR ME IN THE CAR-I'LL SLIP OUT.

LI'L ABNER Be Careful **By Al Capp**

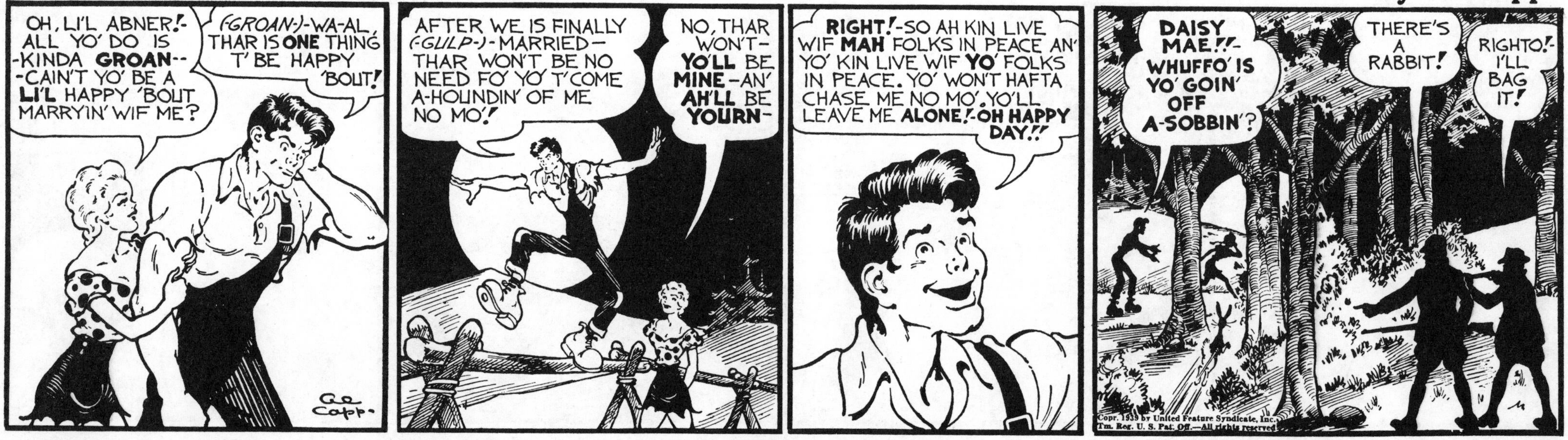

OH, LI'L ABNER!-ALL YO' DO IS -KINDA GROAN-- -CAIN'T YO' BE A LI'L HAPPY 'BOUT MARRYIN' WIF ME?
(-GROAN-)-WA-AL, THAR IS ONE THING T' BE HAPPY 'BOUT!
AL CAPP
AFTER WE IS FINALLY (-GULP-)-MARRIED-THAR WON'T BE NO NEED FO' YO' T'COME A-HOUNDIN' OF ME NO MO'!
NO, THAR WON'T-YO'LL BE MINE-AN' AH'LL BE YOURN-
RIGHT!-SO AH KIN LIVE WIF MAH FOLKS IN PEACE AN' YO' KIN LIVE WIF YO' FOLKS IN PEACE. YO' WON'T HAFTA CHASE ME NO MO'. YO'LL LEAVE ME ALONE!-OH HAPPY DAY!!
DAISY MAE!!-WHUFFO' IS YO' GOIN' OFF A-SOBBIN'?
THERE'S A RABBIT!
RIGHTO!-I'LL BAG IT!
Copr. 1939 by United Feature Syndicate, Inc. Tm. Reg. U. S. Pat. Off.—All rights reserved

LI'L ABNER Abner Forgets Himself! By Al Capp

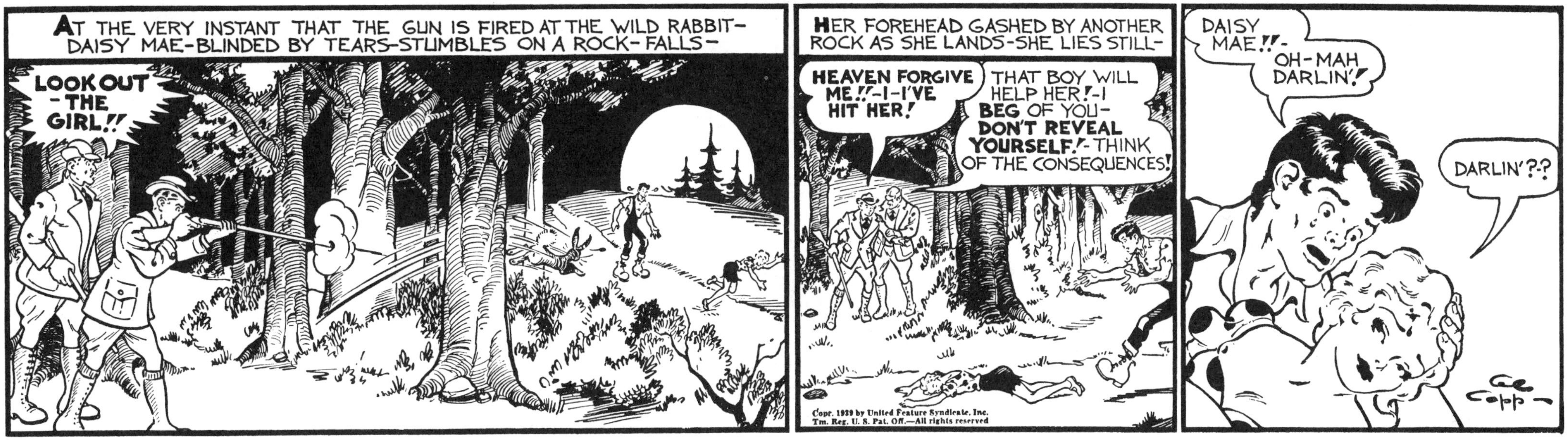
AT THE VERY INSTANT THAT THE GUN IS FIRED AT THE WILD RABBIT-DAISY MAE-BLINDED BY TEARS-STUMBLES ON A ROCK-FALLS-
LOOK OUT -THE GIRL!!
HER FOREHEAD GASHED BY ANOTHER ROCK AS SHE LANDS-SHE LIES STILL-
HEAVEN FORGIVE ME!!-I-I'VE HIT HER!
THAT BOY WILL HELP HER!-I BEG OF YOU-DON'T REVEAL YOURSELF!-THINK OF THE CONSEQUENCES!
Copr. 1939 by United Feature Syndicate, Inc. Tm. Reg. U. S. Pat. Off.—All rights reserved
DAISY MAE!!-
OH-MAH DARLIN'!
DARLIN'?-?
Al Capp

LI'L ABNER Love Hain't On His Side By Al Capp

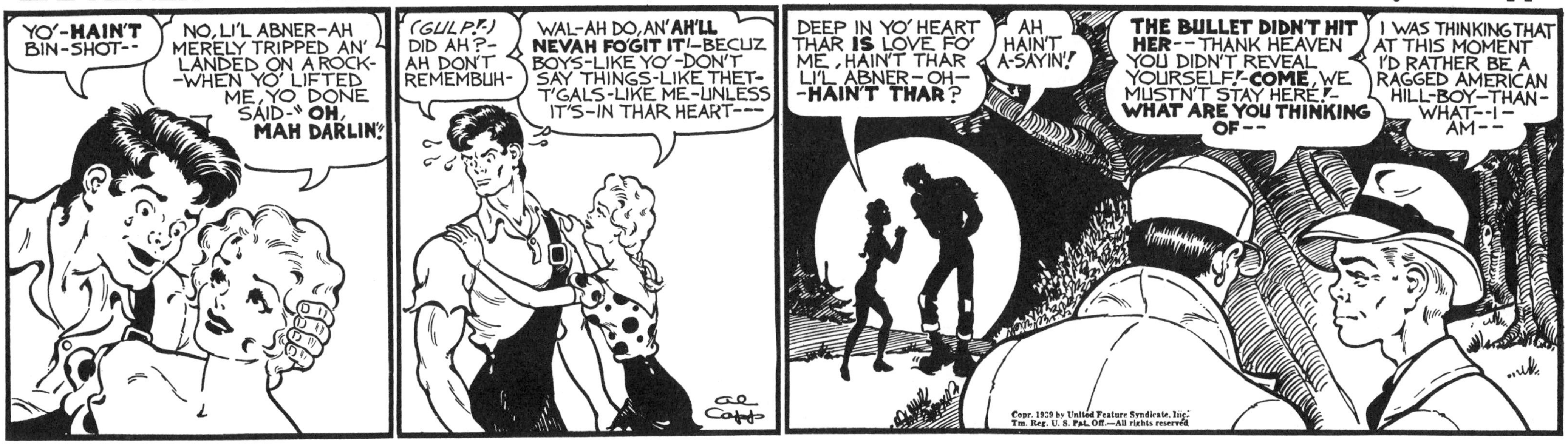
YO'-HAIN'T BIN-SHOT--
NO, LI'L ABNER-AH MERELY TRIPPED AN' LANDED ON A ROCK--WHEN YO' LIFTED ME, YO DONE SAID-"OH, MAH DARLIN'!"
(GULP!-) DID AH?-AH DON'T REMEMBUH-
WAL-AH DO, AN' AH'LL NEVAH FO'GIT IT!-BECUZ BOYS-LIKE YO'-DON'T SAY THINGS-LIKE THET-T'GALS-LIKE ME-UNLESS IT'S-IN THAR HEART---
Al Capp
DEEP IN YO' HEART THAR IS LOVE FO' ME, HAIN'T THAR LI'L ABNER-OH--HAIN'T THAR?
AH HAIN'T A-SAYIN'!
THE BULLET DIDN'T HIT HER--THANK HEAVEN YOU DIDN'T REVEAL YOURSELF!-COME, WE MUSTN'T STAY HERE!-WHAT ARE YOU THINKING OF--
I WAS THINKING THAT AT THIS MOMENT I'D RATHER BE A RAGGED AMERICAN HILL-BOY-THAN-WHAT--I-AM--
Copr. 1939 by United Feature Syndicate, Inc. Tm. Reg. U. S. Pat. Off.—All rights reserved

LI'L ABNER Oh Unhappy Day! By Al Capp

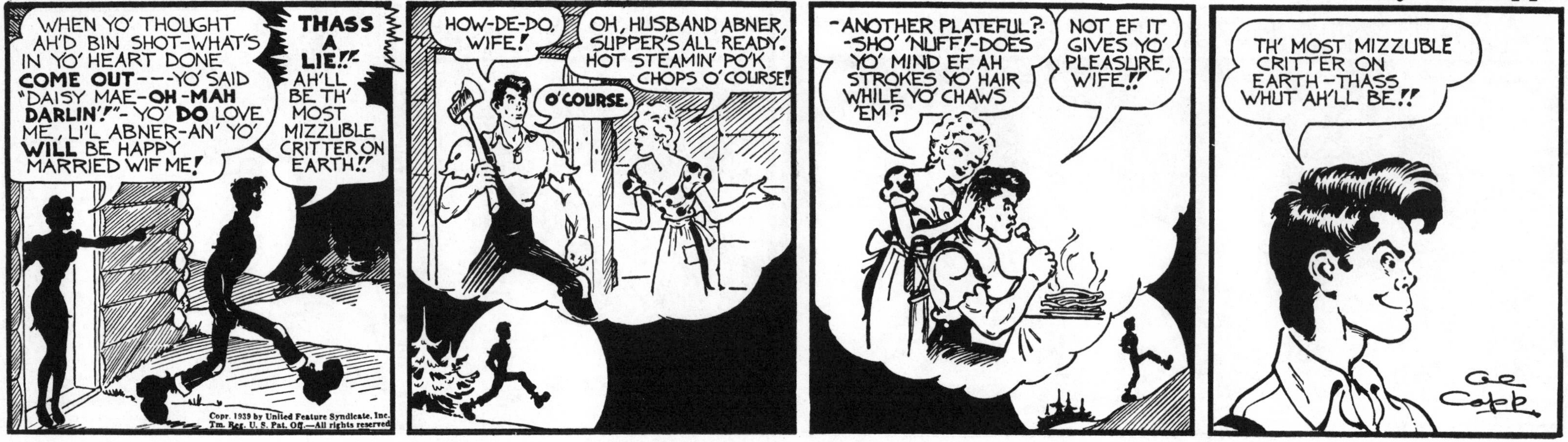

WHEN YO' THOUGHT AH'D BIN SHOT-WHAT'S IN YO' HEART DONE **COME OUT**---YO' SAID "DAISY MAE-**OH-MAH DARLIN'!**"- YO' **DO** LOVE ME, LI'L ABNER-AN' YO' **WILL** BE HAPPY MARRIED WIF ME!
THASS A LIE!!- AH'LL BE TH' MOST MIZZUBLE CRITTER ON EARTH!!
HOW-DE-DO, WIFE!
OH, HUSBAND ABNER, SUPPER'S ALL READY. HOT STEAMIN' PO'K CHOPS O' COURSE!
O' COURSE.
-ANOTHER PLATEFUL?- -SHO' 'NUFF!-DOES YO' MIND EF AH STROKES YO' HAIR WHILE YO' CHAWS 'EM?
NOT EF IT GIVES YO' PLEASURE, WIFE!!
TH' MOST MIZZUBLE CRITTER ON EARTH-THASS WHUT AH'LL BE!!
Copr. 1939 by United Feature Syndicate, Inc. Tm. Reg. U. S. Pat. Off.—All rights reserved

LI'L ABNER Fireside Chat! By Al Capp

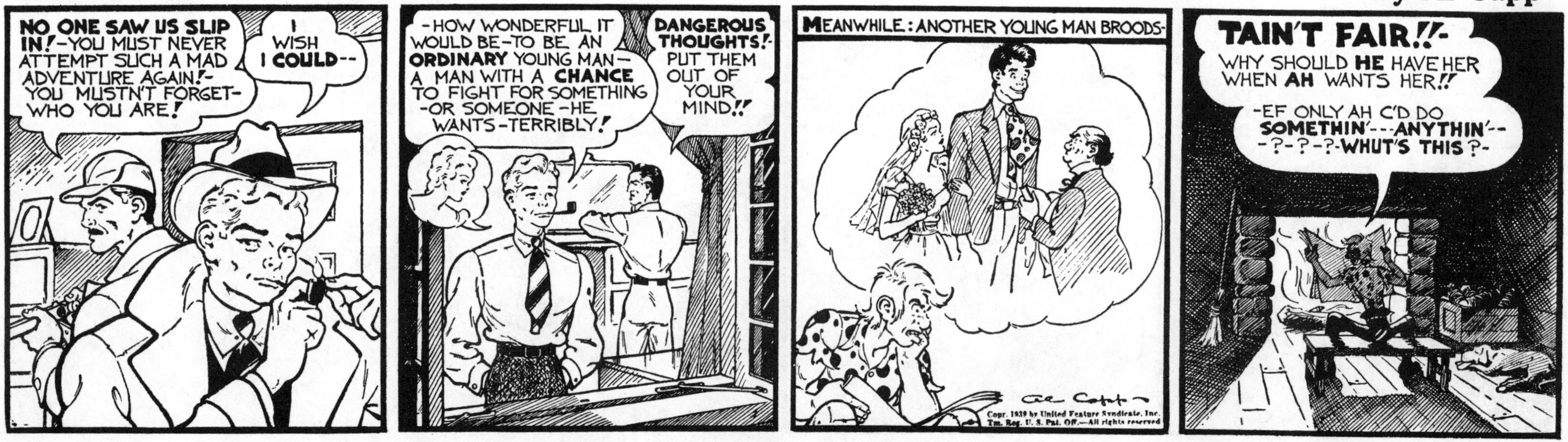

NO ONE SAW US SLIP IN!-YOU MUST NEVER ATTEMPT SUCH A MAD ADVENTURE AGAIN!- YOU MUSTN'T FORGET-WHO YOU ARE!
I WISH I **COULD**--
-HOW WONDERFUL IT WOULD BE-TO BE AN **ORDINARY** YOUNG MAN-A MAN WITH A **CHANCE** TO FIGHT FOR SOMETHING -OR SOMEONE-HE WANTS-TERRIBLY!
DANGEROUS THOUGHTS!- PUT THEM OUT OF YOUR MIND!!
MEANWHILE: ANOTHER YOUNG MAN BROODS-
TAIN'T FAIR!!-
WHY SHOULD **HE** HAVE HER WHEN **AH** WANTS HER!!
-EF ONLY AH C'D DO **SOMETHIN'**---**ANYTHIN'**-- -?-?-?-**WHUT'S THIS**?-
Copr. 1939 by United Feature Syndicate, Inc. Tm. Reg. U. S. Pat. Off.—All rights reserved

LI'L ABNER

Hannibal Hoops Rides Again!

By Al Capp

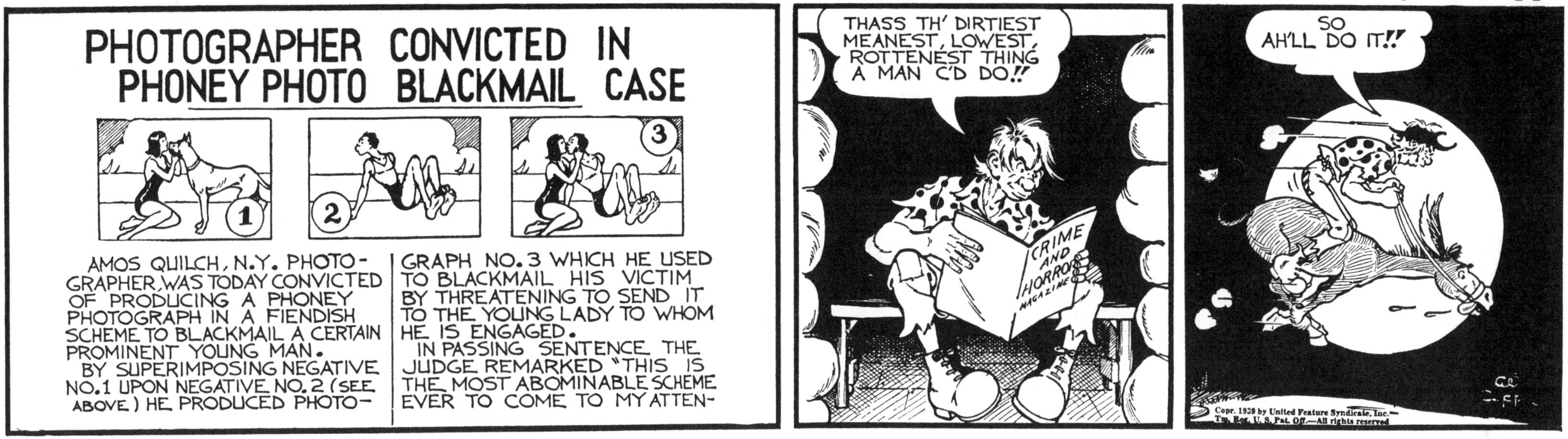

PHOTOGRAPHER CONVICTED IN PHONEY PHOTO BLACKMAIL CASE
1
2
3
AMOS QUILCH, N.Y. PHOTOGRAPHER, WAS TODAY CONVICTED OF PRODUCING A PHONEY PHOTOGRAPH IN A FIENDISH SCHEME TO BLACKMAIL A CERTAIN PROMINENT YOUNG MAN.
BY SUPERIMPOSING NEGATIVE NO.1 UPON NEGATIVE NO.2 (SEE ABOVE) HE PRODUCED PHOTOGRAPH NO.3 WHICH HE USED TO BLACKMAIL HIS VICTIM BY THREATENING TO SEND IT TO THE YOUNG LADY TO WHOM HE IS ENGAGED.
IN PASSING SENTENCE THE JUDGE REMARKED "THIS IS THE MOST ABOMINABLE SCHEME EVER TO COME TO MY ATTEN-
THASS TH' DIRTIEST MEANEST, LOWEST, ROTTENEST THING A MAN C'D DO!!
CRIME AND HORROR MAGAZINE
SO AH'LL DO IT!!
Copr. 1939 by United Feature Syndicate, Inc.— Tm. Reg. U. S. Pat. Off.—All rights reserved

LI'L ABNER

A Gentleman of the Old School!

By Al Capp

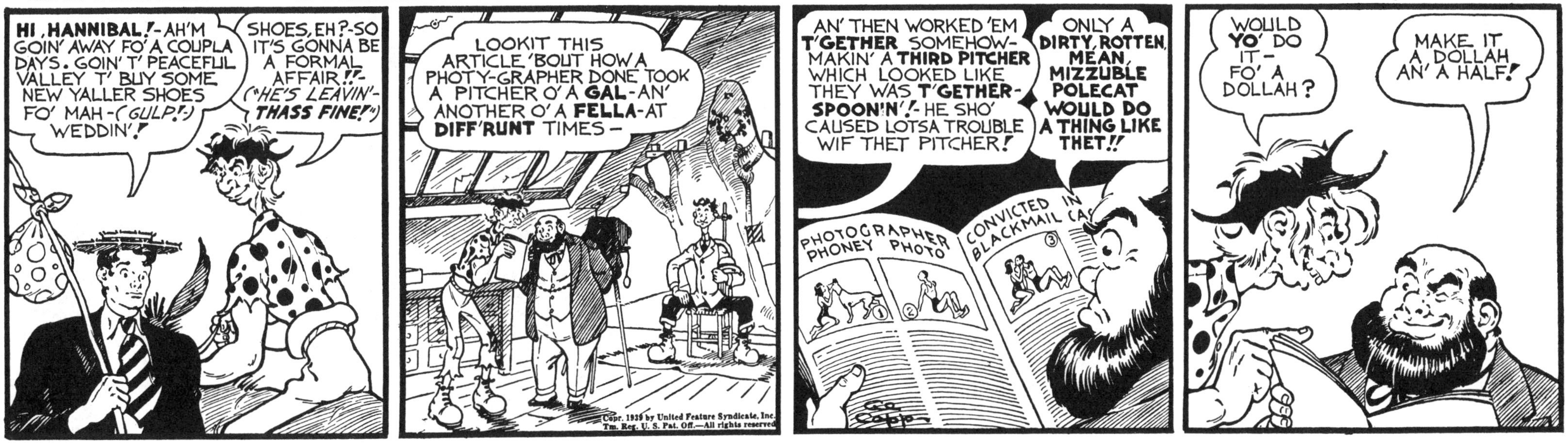

HI, HANNIBAL!-AH'M GOIN' AWAY FO' A COUPLA DAYS. GOIN' T' PEACEFUL VALLEY T' BUY SOME NEW YALLER SHOES FO' MAH-(GULP!-) WEDDIN'!
SHOES, EH?-SO IT'S GONNA BE A FORMAL AFFAIR!!-("HE'S LEAVIN'-THASS FINE!")
LOOKIT THIS ARTICLE 'BOUT HOW A PHOTY-GRAPHER DONE TOOK A PITCHER O' A GAL-AN' ANOTHER O' A FELLA-AT DIFF'RUNT TIMES-
Copr. 1939 by United Feature Syndicate, Inc. Tm. Reg. U. S. Pat. Off.—All rights reserved
AN' THEN WORKED 'EM T'GETHER SOMEHOW-MAKIN' A THIRD PITCHER WHICH LOOKED LIKE THEY WAS T'GETHER-SPOON'N'!-HE SHO' CAUSED LOTSA TROUBLE WIF THET PITCHER!
ONLY A DIRTY, ROTTEN, MEAN, MIZZUBLE POLECAT WOULD DO A THING LIKE THET!!
PHOTOGRAPHER PHONEY PHOTO
CONVICTED IN BLACKMAIL CA
WOULD YO' DO IT-FO' A DOLLAH?
MAKE IT A DOLLAH AN' A HALF!

LI'L ABNER The Man in the Case By Al Capp

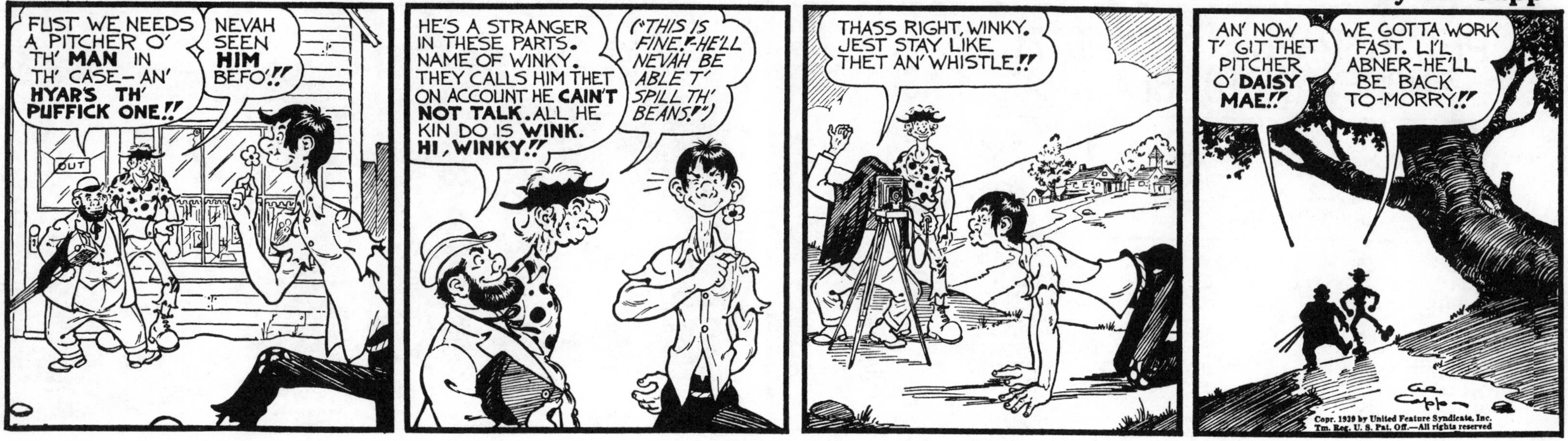

FUST WE NEEDS A PITCHER O' TH' MAN IN TH' CASE–AN' HYAR'S TH' PUFFICK ONE.!!
NEVAH SEEN HIM BEFO'.!!
OUT
HE'S A STRANGER IN THESE PARTS. NAME OF WINKY. THEY CALLS HIM THET ON ACCOUNT HE CAIN'T NOT TALK. ALL HE KIN DO IS WINK. HI, WINKY.!!
("THIS IS FINE.!–HE'LL NEVAH BE ABLE T' SPILL TH' BEANS!")
THASS RIGHT, WINKY. JEST STAY LIKE THET AN' WHISTLE.!!
AN' NOW T' GIT THET PITCHER O' DAISY MAE.!!
WE GOTTA WORK FAST. LI'L ABNER–HE'LL BE BACK TO-MORRY.!!
Al Capp
Copr. 1939 by United Feature Syndicate, Inc.
Tm. Reg. U. S. Pat. Off.—All rights reserved

LI'L ABNER Fiends At Work! By Al Capp

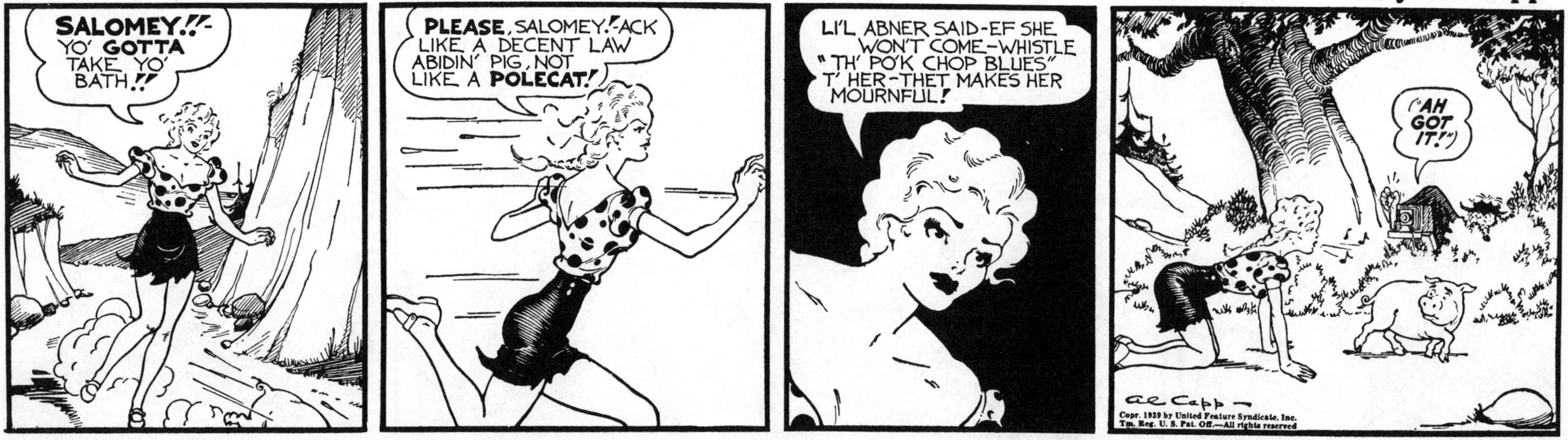

SALOMEY.!!– YO' GOTTA TAKE YO' BATH.!!
PLEASE, SALOMEY.!–ACK LIKE A DECENT LAW ABIDIN' PIG, NOT LIKE A POLECAT!
LI'L ABNER SAID–EF SHE WON'T COME–WHISTLE "TH' PO'K CHOP BLUES" T' HER–THET MAKES HER MOURNFUL!
("AH GOT IT!")
Al Capp
Copr. 1939 by United Feature Syndicate, Inc.
Tm. Reg. U. S. Pat. Off.—All rights reserved

LI'L ABNER The Camera Doesn't Lie! By Al Capp

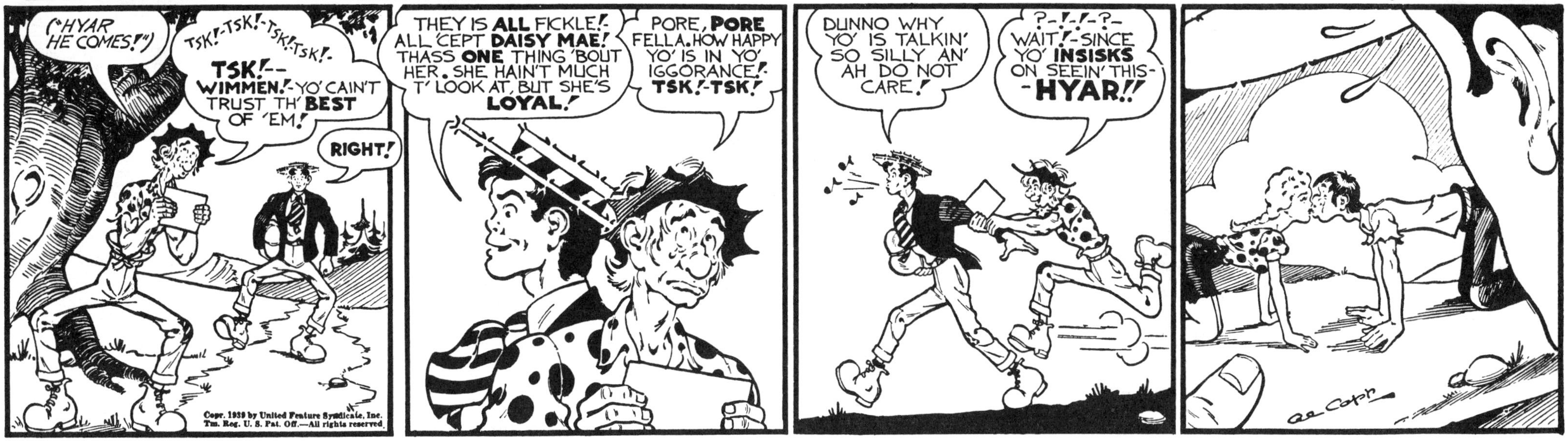
("HYAR HE COMES!")
TSK!-TSK!-TSK!-TSK!- TSK!-- WIMMEN!-YO' CAIN'T TRUST TH' BEST OF 'EM!
RIGHT!
Copr. 1939 by United Feature Syndicate, Inc. Tm. Reg. U. S. Pat. Off.—All rights reserved
THEY IS ALL FICKLE!-ALL 'CEPT DAISY MAE! THASS ONE THING 'BOUT HER. SHE HAIN'T MUCH T' LOOK AT, BUT SHE'S LOYAL!
PORE, PORE FELLA. HOW HAPPY YO' IS IN YO' IGGORANCE!- TSK!-TSK!
DUNNO WHY YO' IS TALKIN' SO SILLY AN' AH DO NOT CARE!
?-!-!-?- WAIT!-SINCE YO' INSISKS ON SEEIN' THIS- -HYAR!!

LI'L ABNER Laugh, Clown, Laugh! By Al Capp

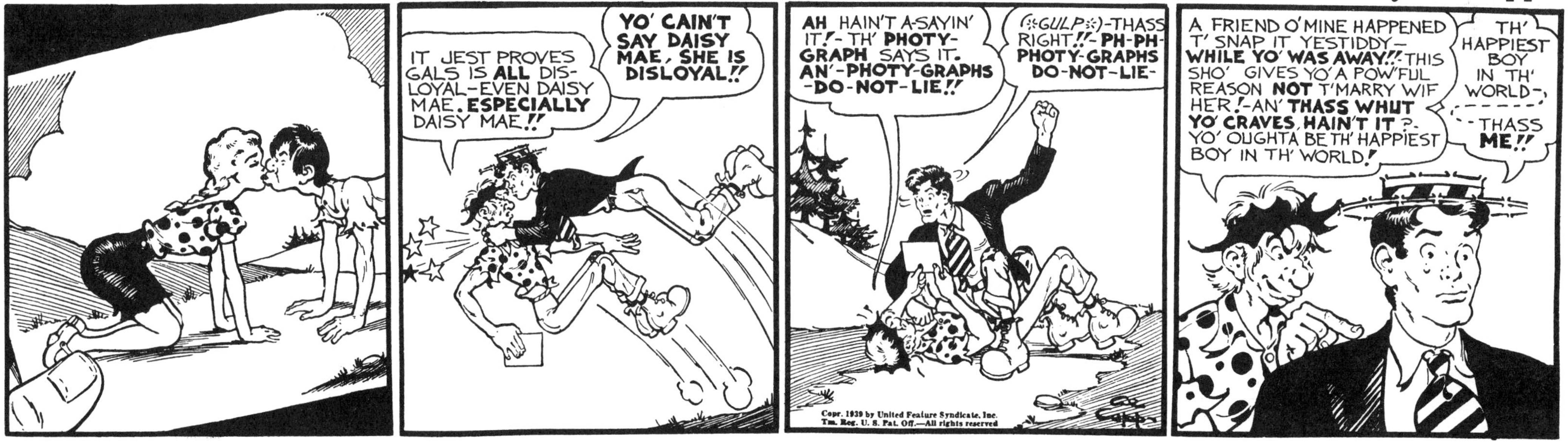
IT JEST PROVES GALS IS ALL DIS-LOYAL-EVEN DAISY MAE. ESPECIALLY DAISY MAE!!
YO' CAIN'T SAY DAISY MAE, SHE IS DISLOYAL!!
AH HAIN'T A-SAYIN' IT!- TH' PHOTY-GRAPH SAYS IT. AN'-PHOTY-GRAPHS -DO-NOT-LIE!!
(GULP)-THASS RIGHT!!-PH-PH-PHOTY-GRAPHS DO-NOT-LIE-
Copr. 1939 by United Feature Syndicate, Inc. Tm. Reg. U. S. Pat. Off.—All rights reserved
A FRIEND O'MINE HAPPENED T' SNAP IT YESTIDDY- WHILE YO' WAS AWAY!! THIS SHO' GIVES YO' A POW'FUL REASON NOT T'MARRY WIF HER!-AN' THASS WHUT YO' CRAVES, HAIN'T IT?- YO' OUGHTA BE TH' HAPPIEST BOY IN TH' WORLD!
TH' HAPPIEST BOY IN TH' WORLD-, - - - - - THASS ME!!

LI'L ABNER He Won't Talk **By Al Capp**

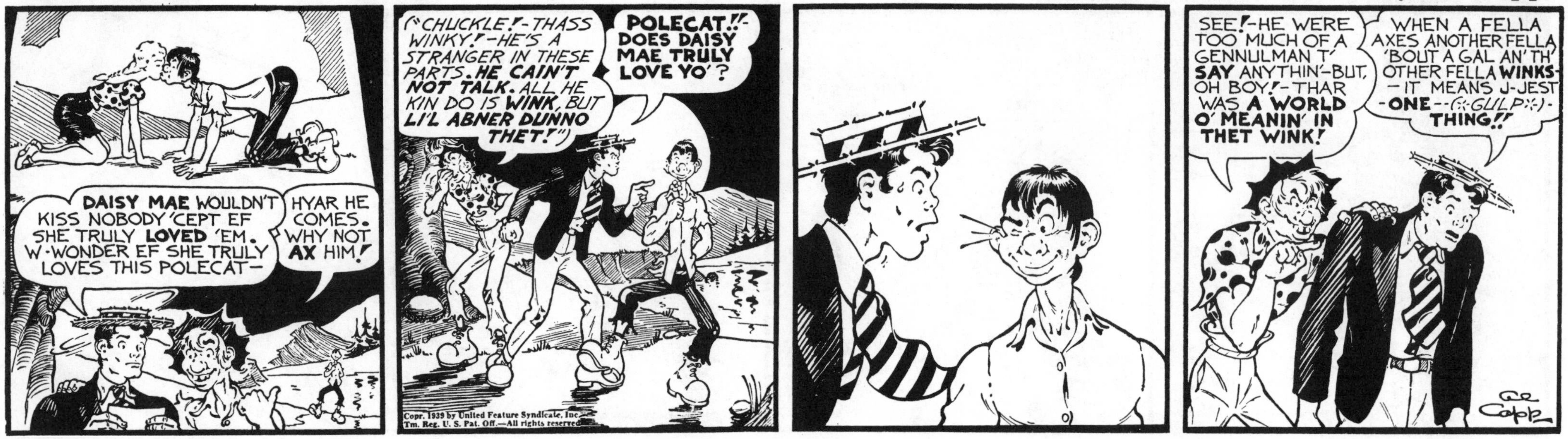

DAISY MAE WOULDN'T KISS NOBODY 'CEPT EF SHE TRULY LOVED 'EM. W-WONDER EF SHE TRULY LOVES THIS POLECAT—
HYAR HE COMES. WHY NOT AX HIM!
(" CHUCKLE!-THASS WINKY!-HE'S A STRANGER IN THESE PARTS. HE CAIN'T NOT TALK. ALL HE KIN DO IS WINK, BUT LI'L ABNER DUNNO THET!")
POLECAT!!-DOES DAISY MAE TRULY LOVE YO'?
Copr. 1939 by United Feature Syndicate, Inc. Tm. Reg. U. S. Pat. Off.—All rights reserved
SEE!-HE WERE TOO MUCH OF A GENNULMAN T' SAY ANYTHIN'-BUT, OH BOY!-THAR WAS A WORLD O' MEANIN' IN THET WINK!
WHEN A FELLA AXES ANOTHER FELLA 'BOUT A GAL AN' TH' OTHER FELLA WINKS—IT MEANS J-JEST -ONE--(GULP)-THING!!
Al Capp

LI'L ABNER Hannibal the Horrible **By Al Capp**

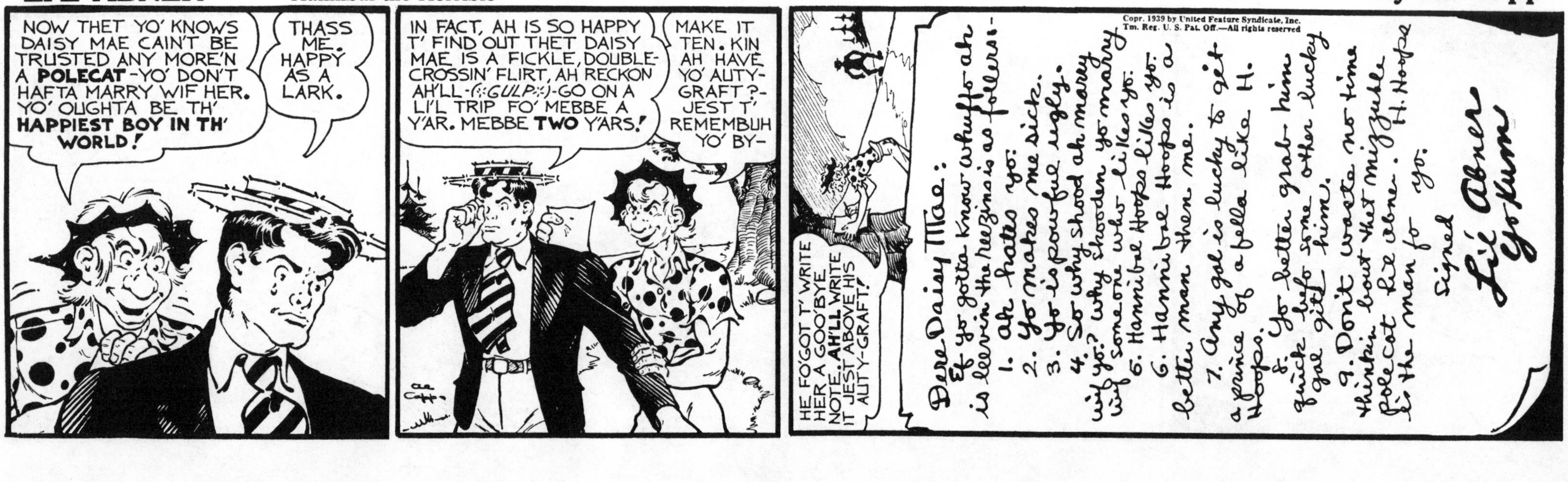

NOW THET YO' KNOWS DAISY MAE CAIN'T BE TRUSTED ANY MORE'N A POLECAT-YO' DON'T HAFTA MARRY WIF HER. YO' OUGHTA BE TH' HAPPIEST BOY IN TH' WORLD!
THASS ME. HAPPY AS A LARK.
Al Capp
IN FACT, AH IS SO HAPPY T' FIND OUT THET DAISY MAE IS A FICKLE, DOUBLE-CROSSIN' FLIRT, AH RECKON AH'LL-(GULP)-GO ON A LI'L TRIP FO' MEBBE A Y'AR. MEBBE TWO Y'ARS!
MAKE IT TEN. KIN AH HAVE YO' AUTY-GRAFT?-JEST T' REMEMBUH YO' BY-
HE FO'GOT T' WRITE HER A GOO'BYE NOTE. AH'LL WRITE IT JEST ABOVE HIS AUTY-GRAFT!
Copr. 1939 by United Feature Syndicate, Inc. Tm. Reg. U. S. Pat. Off.—All rights reserved
Dere Daisy Mae:
Ef yo gotta know whuffo ah is leavin the reezins is as follers:-
1. ah hates yo.
2. Yo makes me sick.
3. Yo is powful ugly.
4. So why shood ah marry wif yo? why shooden yo marry wif someone who likes yo:
5. Hannibal Hoops likes yo.
6. Hannibal Hoops is a better man then me.
7. Any gal is lucky to get a prince of a fella like H. Hoops.
8. Yo better grab him quick befo some other lucky gal gits him.
9. Don't waste no time thinkin bout that mizzuble polecat Li'l abner. H. Hoops is the man fo yo.
signed Li'l Abner Yokum

LI'L ABNER Hain't It a Small world? By Al Capp

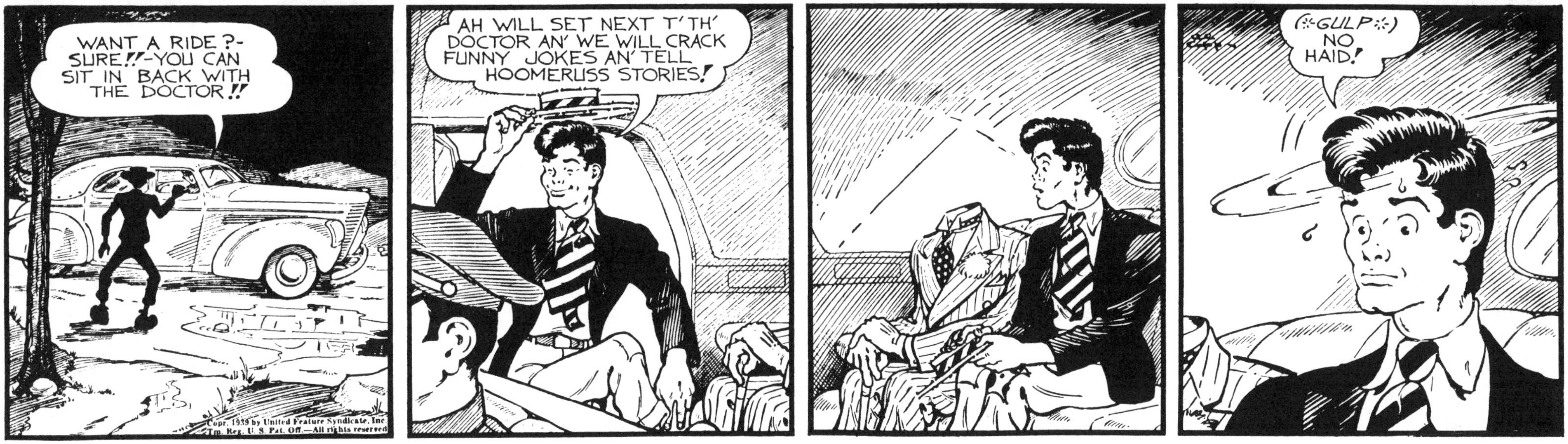
WANT A RIDE?- SURE!!-YOU CAN SIT IN BACK WITH THE DOCTOR!!
Copr. 1939 by United Feature Syndicate, Inc. Tm. Reg. U. S. Pat. Off.—All rights reserved
AH WILL SET NEXT T' TH' DOCTOR AN' WE WILL CRACK FUNNY JOKES AN' TELL HOOMERUSS STORIES!
(GULP) NO HAID!

LI'L ABNER Go 'Way From My Door! By Al Capp

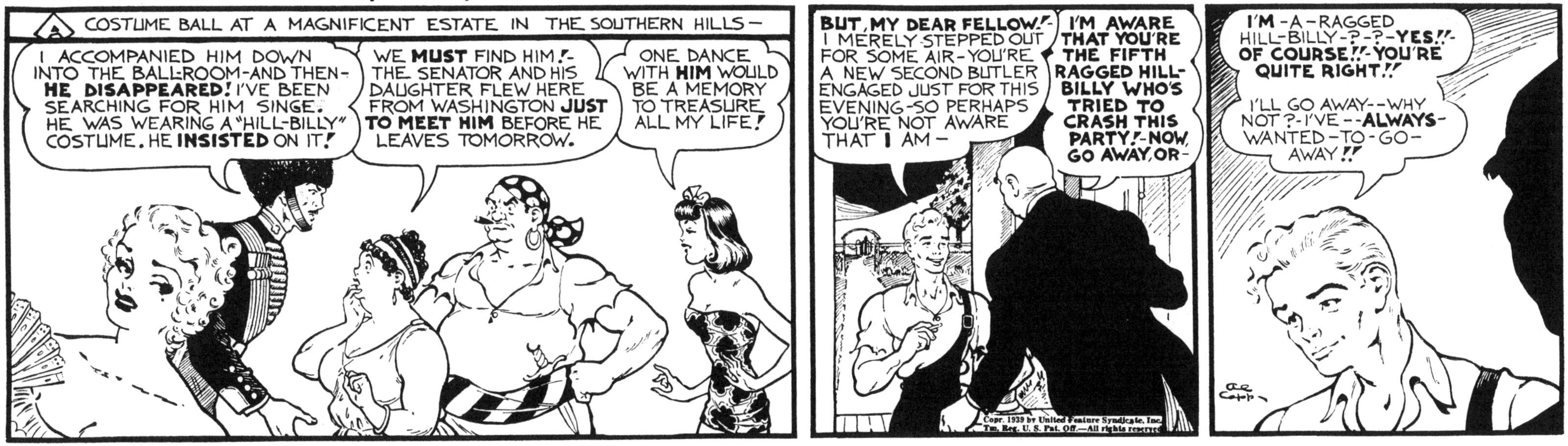
COSTUME BALL AT A MAGNIFICENT ESTATE IN THE SOUTHERN HILLS—
I ACCOMPANIED HIM DOWN INTO THE BALL-ROOM-AND THEN- **HE DISAPPEARED!** I'VE BEEN SEARCHING FOR HIM SINCE. HE WAS WEARING A "HILL-BILLY" COSTUME. HE **INSISTED** ON IT!
WE **MUST** FIND HIM!- THE SENATOR AND HIS DAUGHTER FLEW HERE FROM WASHINGTON **JUST TO MEET HIM** BEFORE HE LEAVES TOMORROW.
ONE DANCE WITH **HIM** WOULD BE A MEMORY TO TREASURE ALL MY LIFE!
BUT, MY DEAR FELLOW!- I MERELY STEPPED OUT FOR SOME AIR-YOU'RE A NEW SECOND BUTLER ENGAGED JUST FOR THIS EVENING-SO PERHAPS YOU'RE NOT AWARE THAT **I** AM—
I'M AWARE THAT YOU'RE THE FIFTH RAGGED HILL-BILLY WHO'S TRIED TO CRASH THIS PARTY!-NOW, GO AWAY, OR-
Copr. 1939 by United Feature Syndicate, Inc. Tm. Reg. U. S. Pat. Off.—All rights reserved
I'M-A-RAGGED HILL-BILLY-?-?-**YES!**- **OF COURSE!!-YOU'RE QUITE RIGHT!!**
I'LL GO AWAY--WHY NOT?-I'VE--**ALWAYS**-WANTED-TO-GO-AWAY!!

LI'L ABNER — She Doesn't Live Here Any More! — By Al Capp

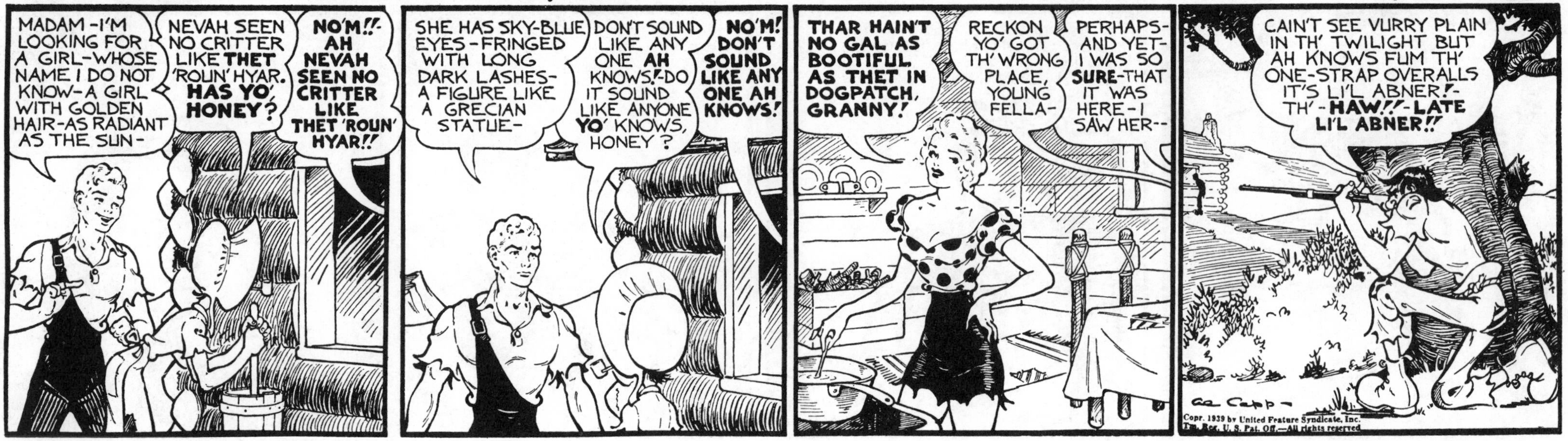
MADAM-I'M LOOKING FOR A GIRL-WHOSE NAME I DO NOT KNOW-A GIRL WITH GOLDEN HAIR-AS RADIANT AS THE SUN-
NEVAH SEEN NO CRITTER LIKE THET 'ROUN' HYAR. HAS YO', HONEY?
NO'M!!- AH NEVAH SEEN NO CRITTER LIKE THET 'ROUN' HYAR!!
SHE HAS SKY-BLUE EYES-FRINGED WITH LONG DARK LASHES-A FIGURE LIKE A GRECIAN STATUE-
DON'T SOUND LIKE ANY ONE AH KNOWS!-DO IT SOUND LIKE ANYONE YO' KNOWS, HONEY?
NO'M! DON'T SOUND LIKE ANY ONE AH KNOWS!
THAR HAIN'T NO GAL AS BOOTIFUL AS THET IN DOGPATCH, GRANNY!
RECKON YO' GOT TH' WRONG PLACE, YOUNG FELLA-
PERHAPS-AND YET-I WAS SO SURE-THAT IT WAS HERE-I SAW HER--
CAIN'T SEE VURRY PLAIN IN TH' TWILIGHT BUT AH KNOWS FUM TH' ONE-STRAP OVERALLS IT'S LI'L ABNER!-TH'-HAW!!-LATE LI'L ABNER!!
Al Capp
Copr. 1939 by United Feature Syndicate, Inc. Tm. Reg. U. S. Pat. Off.—All rights reserved

LI'L ABNER — Ribber, Stay 'Way Fum Mah Door! — By Al Capp

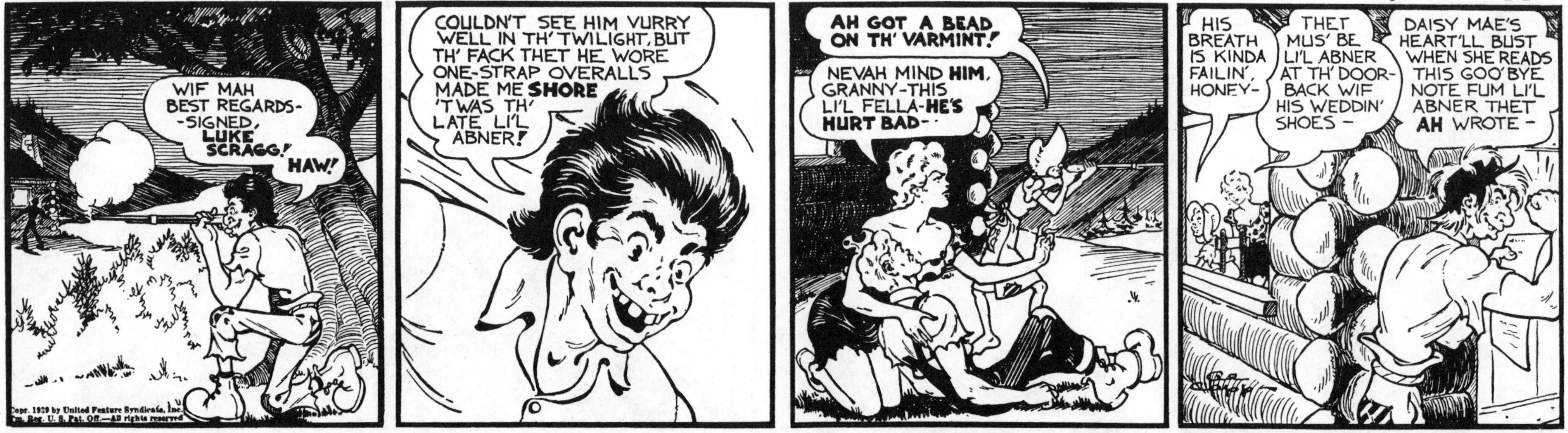
WIF MAH BEST REGARDS--SIGNED, LUKE SCRAGG! HAW!
Copr. 1939 by United Feature Syndicate, Inc. Tm. Reg. U. S. Pat. Off.—All rights reserved
COULDN'T SEE HIM VURRY WELL IN TH' TWILIGHT, BUT TH' FACK THET HE WORE ONE-STRAP OVERALLS MADE ME SHORE 'TWAS TH' LATE LI'L ABNER!
AH GOT A BEAD ON TH' VARMINT!
NEVAH MIND HIM, GRANNY-THIS LI'L FELLA-HE'S HURT BAD--
HIS BREATH IS KINDA FAILIN', HONEY-
THET MUS' BE LI'L ABNER AT TH' DOOR-BACK WIF HIS WEDDIN' SHOES -
DAISY MAE'S HEART'LL BUST WHEN SHE READS THIS GOO'BYE NOTE FUM LI'L ABNER THET AH WROTE -

LI'L ABNER Hannibal's Plot By Al Capp

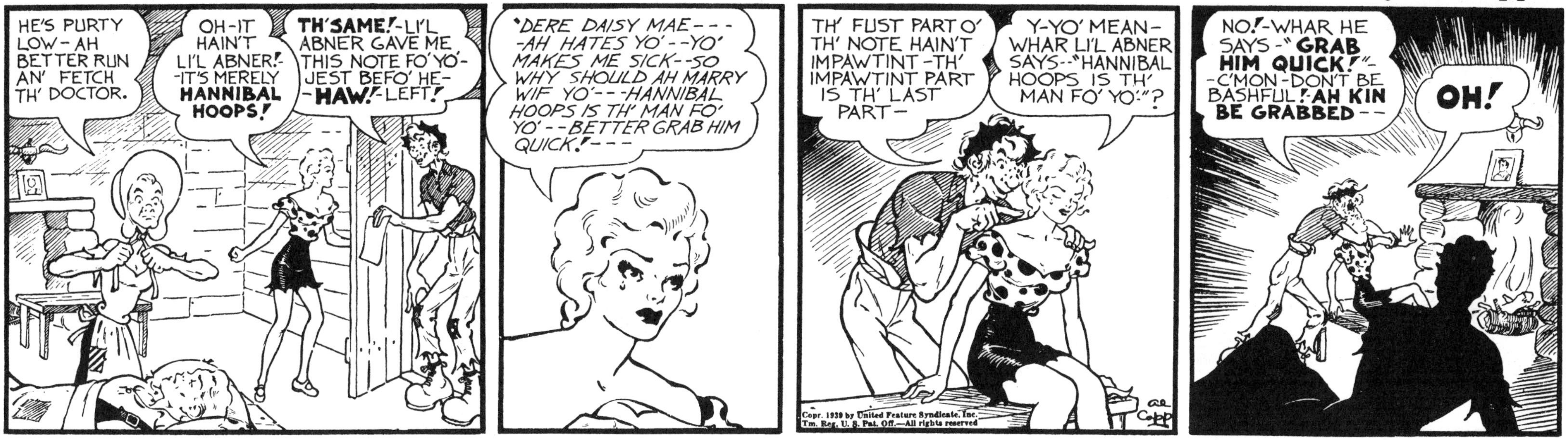

HE'S PURTY LOW-AH BETTER RUN AN' FETCH TH' DOCTOR.
OH-IT HAIN'T LI'L ABNER!-IT'S MERELY HANNIBAL HOOPS!
TH'SAME!-LI'L ABNER GAVE ME THIS NOTE FO' YO'-JEST BEFO' HE--HAW!-LEFT!
"DERE DAISY MAE----AH HATES YO'--YO' MAKES ME SICK--SO WHY SHOULD AH MARRY WIF YO'---HANNIBAL HOOPS IS TH' MAN FO' YO'--BETTER GRAB HIM QUICK!---
TH' FUST PART O' TH' NOTE HAIN'T IMPAWTINT-TH' IMPAWTINT PART IS TH' LAST PART-
Y-YO' MEAN-WHAR LI'L ABNER SAYS--"HANNIBAL HOOPS IS TH' MAN FO' YO'"?
Copr. 1939 by United Feature Syndicate, Inc. Tm. Reg. U. S. Pat. Off.—All rights reserved
NO!-WHAR HE SAYS-"GRAB HIM QUICK!"--C'MON-DON'T BE BASHFUL!-AH KIN BE GRABBED--
OH!

LI'L ABNER The Lion and the Mouse! By Al Capp

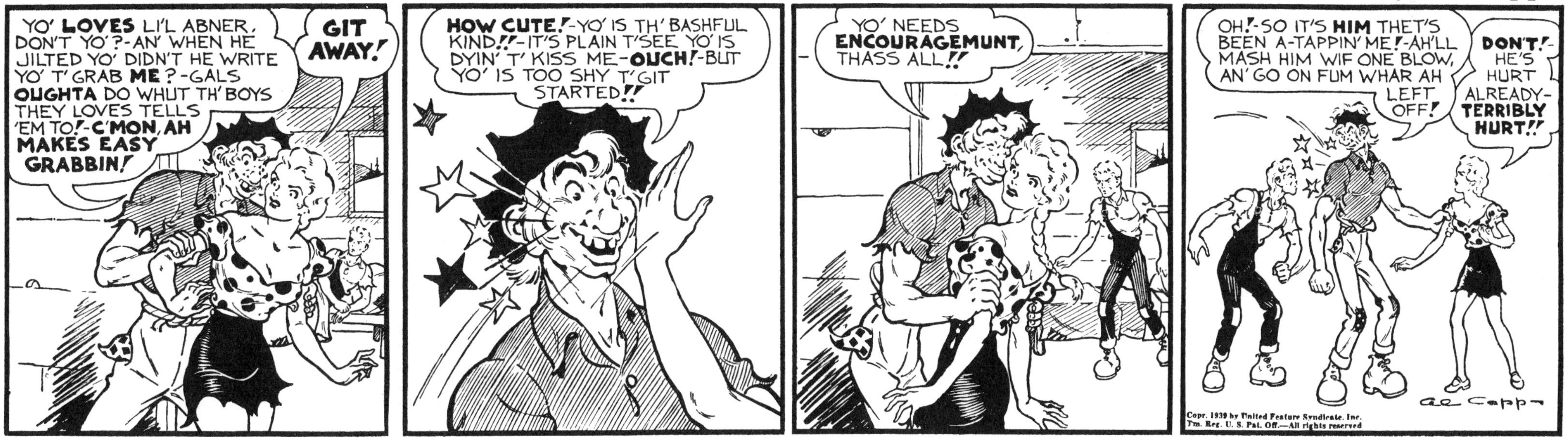

YO' LOVES LI'L ABNER, DON'T YO'?-AN' WHEN HE JILTED YO' DIDN'T HE WRITE YO' T' GRAB ME?-GALS OUGHTA DO WHUT TH' BOYS THEY LOVES TELLS 'EM TO!-C'MON, AH MAKES EASY GRABBIN!
GIT AWAY!
HOW CUTE!-YO' IS TH' BASHFUL KIND!!-IT'S PLAIN T'SEE YO' IS DYIN' T' KISS ME-OUCH!-BUT YO' IS TOO SHY T'GIT STARTED!!
YO' NEEDS ENCOURAGEMUNT, THASS ALL!!
OH!-SO IT'S HIM THET'S BEEN A-TAPPIN' ME!-AH'LL MASH HIM WIF ONE BLOW, AN' GO ON FUM WHAR AH LEFT OFF!
DON'T!-HE'S HURT ALREADY-TERRIBLY HURT!!
Copr. 1939 by United Feature Syndicate, Inc. Tm. Reg. U. S. Pat. Off.—All rights reserved

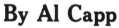

LI'L ABNER Girl of My Dreams

By Al Capp

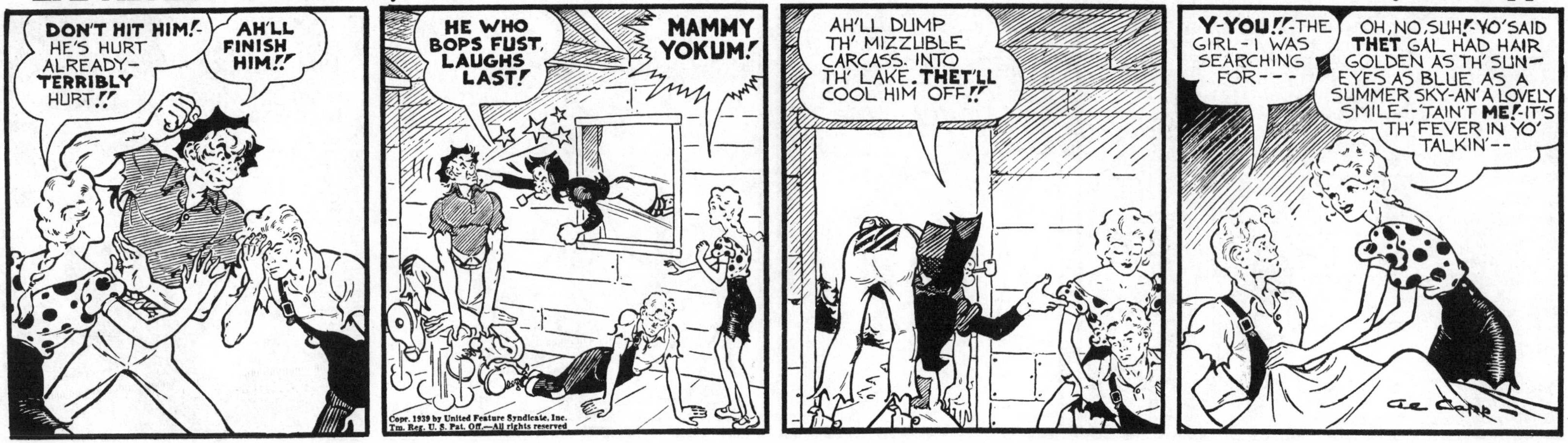
DON'T HIT HIM!- HE'S HURT ALREADY- TERRIBLY HURT!!
AH'LL FINISH HIM!!
HE WHO BOPS FUST, LAUGHS LAST!
MAMMY YOKUM!
Copr. 1939 by United Feature Syndicate, Inc. Tm. Reg. U. S. Pat. Off.—All rights reserved
AH'LL DUMP TH' MIZZUBLE CARCASS. INTO TH' LAKE. THET'LL COOL HIM OFF!!
Y-YOU!!-THE GIRL-I WAS SEARCHING FOR---
OH, NO, SUH!-YO' SAID THET GAL HAD HAIR GOLDEN AS TH' SUN-EYES AS BLUE AS A SUMMER SKY-AN' A LOVELY SMILE--'TAIN'T ME!-IT'S TH' FEVER IN YO' TALKIN'--
Al Capp

LI'L ABNER She Is Now Allergic To Abner!

By Al Capp

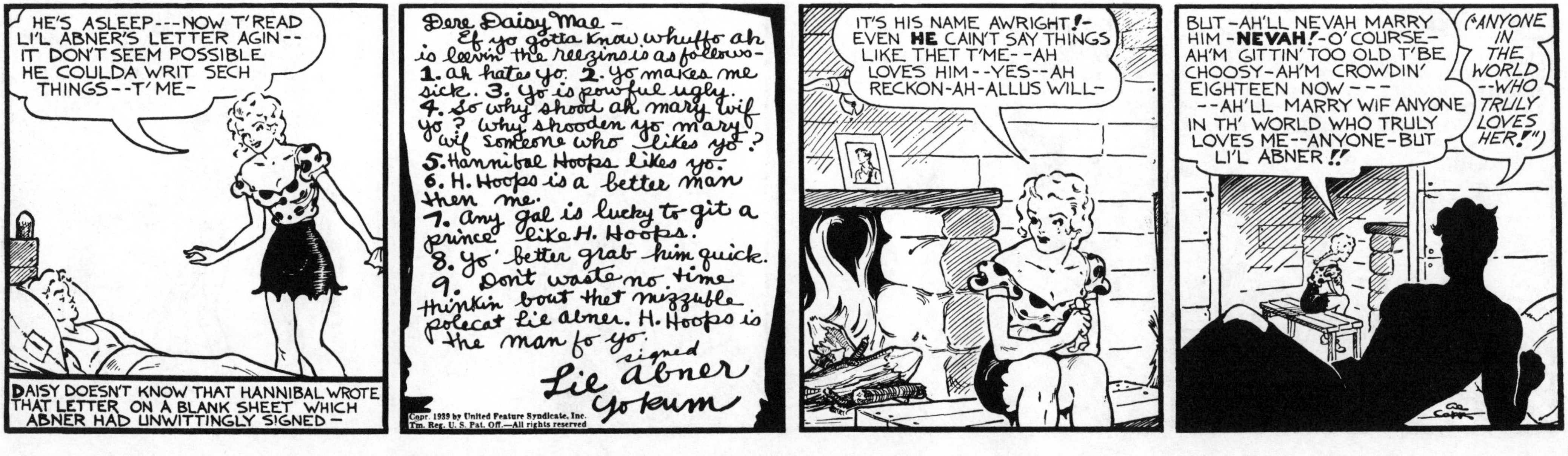
HE'S ASLEEP---NOW T'READ LI'L ABNER'S LETTER AGIN-- IT DON'T SEEM POSSIBLE HE COULDA WRIT SECH THINGS--T'ME-
DAISY DOESN'T KNOW THAT HANNIBAL WROTE THAT LETTER ON A BLANK SHEET WHICH ABNER HAD UNWITTINGLY SIGNED-
Dere Daisy Mae -
Ef yo gotta know whuffo ah is leevin the reezins is as follows-
1. ah hates yo. 2. yo makes me sick. 3. yo is powful ugly.
4. so why shood ah mary wif yo? why shooden yo mary wif someone who likes yo?
5. Hannibal Hoops likes yo.
6. H. Hoops is a better man then me.
7. Any gal is lucky to git a prince like H. Hoops.
8. Yo' better grab him quick.
9. Don't waste no time thinkin bout thet mizzuble polecat Lil abner. H. Hoops is the man fo yo.
signed Lil abner Yokum
Copr. 1939 by United Feature Syndicate, Inc. Tm. Reg. U. S. Pat. Off.—All rights reserved
IT'S HIS NAME AWRIGHT!- EVEN HE CAIN'T SAY THINGS LIKE THET T'ME--AH LOVES HIM--YES--AH RECKON-AH-ALLUS WILL-
BUT-AH'LL NEVAH MARRY HIM-NEVAH!-O'COURSE-AH'M GITTIN' TOO OLD T'BE CHOOSY-AH'M CROWDIN' EIGHTEEN NOW---
--AH'LL MARRY WIF ANYONE IN TH' WORLD WHO TRULY LOVES ME--ANYONE-BUT LI'L ABNER!!
("ANYONE IN THE WORLD --WHO TRULY LOVES HER!")
Al Capp

LI'L ABNER Henry the Wraith! By Al Capp

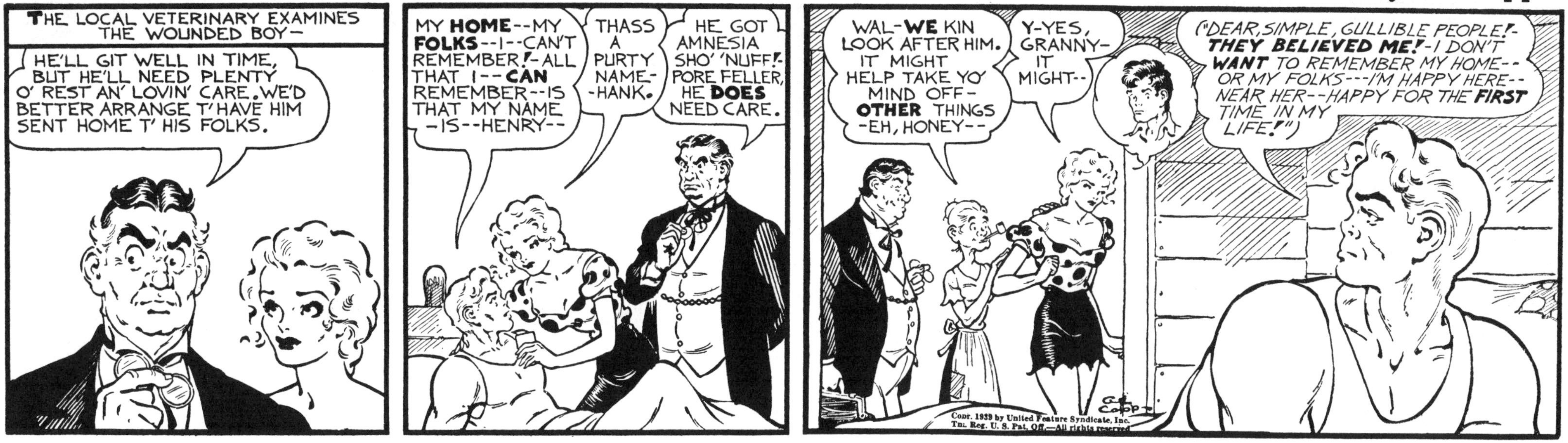
THE LOCAL VETERINARY EXAMINES THE WOUNDED BOY—
HE'LL GIT WELL IN TIME, BUT HE'LL NEED PLENTY O' REST AN' LOVIN' CARE. WE'D BETTER ARRANGE T' HAVE HIM SENT HOME T' HIS FOLKS.
MY HOME--MY FOLKS--I--CAN'T REMEMBER!-ALL THAT I--CAN REMEMBER--IS THAT MY NAME -IS--HENRY--
THASS A PURTY NAME- -HANK.
HE GOT AMNESIA SHO' 'NUFF! PORE FELLER, HE DOES NEED CARE.
WAL-WE KIN LOOK AFTER HIM. IT MIGHT HELP TAKE YO' MIND OFF- OTHER THINGS -EH, HONEY--
Y-YES, GRANNY- IT MIGHT--
("DEAR, SIMPLE, GULLIBLE PEOPLE!- THEY BELIEVED ME!-I DON'T WANT TO REMEMBER MY HOME-- OR MY FOLKS---I'M HAPPY HERE-- NEAR HER--HAPPY FOR THE FIRST TIME IN MY LIFE!")
Copr. 1939 by United Feature Syndicate, Inc. Tm. Reg. U. S. Pat. Off.—All rights reserved

LI'L ABNER That Car Is Here Again By Al Capp

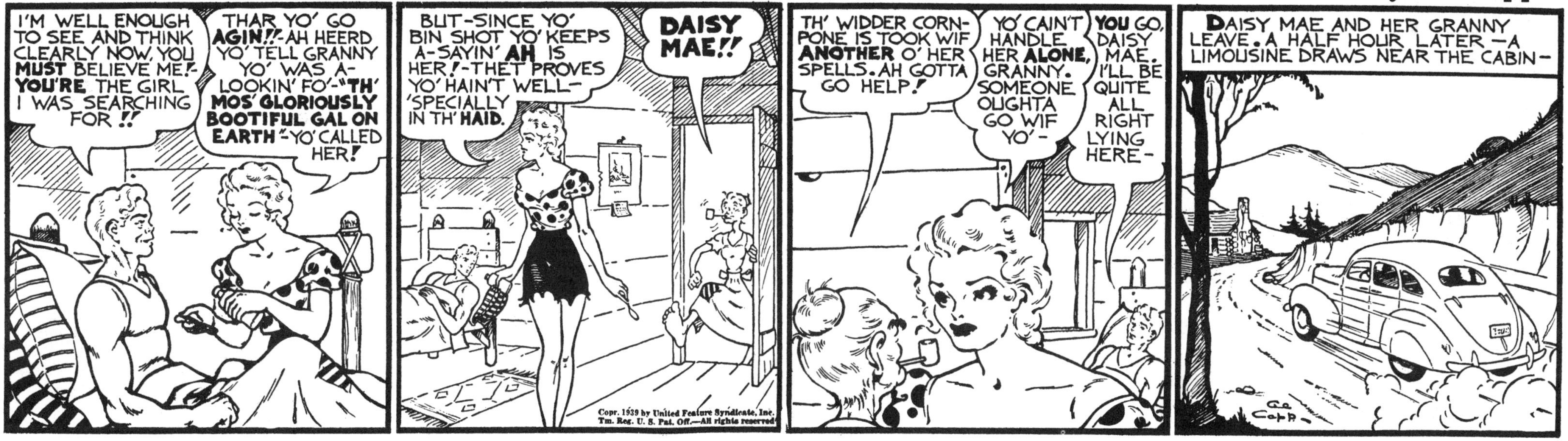
I'M WELL ENOUGH TO SEE AND THINK CLEARLY NOW. YOU MUST BELIEVE ME!- YOU'RE THE GIRL I WAS SEARCHING FOR!!
THAR YO' GO AGIN!!-AH HEERD YO' TELL GRANNY YO' WAS A-LOOKIN' FO'-"TH' MOS' GLORIOUSLY BOOTIFUL GAL ON EARTH"-YO' CALLED HER!
BUT-SINCE YO' BIN SHOT YO' KEEPS A-SAYIN' AH IS HER!-THET PROVES YO' HAIN'T WELL- 'SPECIALLY IN TH' HAID.
DAISY MAE!!
TH' WIDDER CORN-PONE IS TOOK WIF ANOTHER O' HER SPELLS. AH GOTTA GO HELP!
YO' CAIN'T HANDLE HER ALONE, GRANNY. SOMEONE OUGHTA GO WIF YO'-
YOU GO, DAISY MAE. I'LL BE QUITE ALL RIGHT LYING HERE-
DAISY MAE AND HER GRANNY LEAVE. A HALF HOUR LATER—A LIMOUSINE DRAWS NEAR THE CABIN—
Copr. 1939 by United Feature Syndicate, Inc. Tm. Reg. U. S. Pat. Off.—All rights reserved

LI'L ABNER Beauty and the Beast By Al Capp

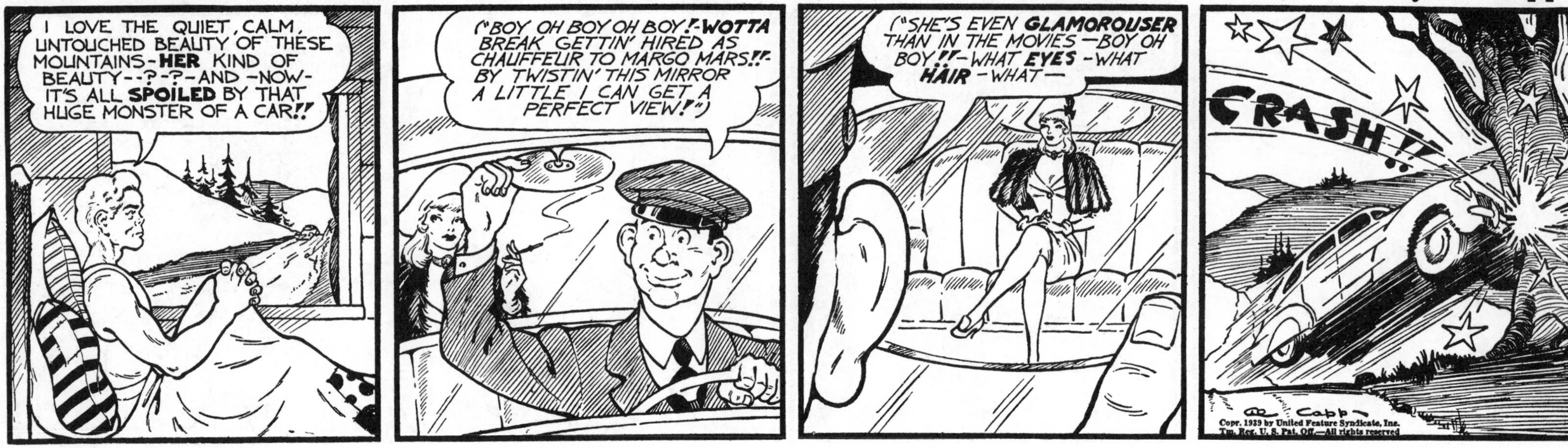
I LOVE THE QUIET, CALM, UNTOUCHED BEAUTY OF THESE MOUNTAINS-HER KIND OF BEAUTY--?-?-AND -NOW- IT'S ALL SPOILED BY THAT HUGE MONSTER OF A CAR!!
("BOY OH BOY OH BOY!-WOTTA BREAK GETTIN' HIRED AS CHAUFFEUR TO MARGO MARS!!- BY TWISTIN' THIS MIRROR A LITTLE I CAN GET A PERFECT VIEW!")
("SHE'S EVEN GLAMOROUSER THAN IN THE MOVIES-BOY OH BOY!!-WHAT EYES-WHAT HAIR-WHAT-
CRASH!!
Copr. 1939 by United Feature Syndicate, Inc. Tm. Reg. U. S. Pat. Off.—All rights reserved

LI'L ABNER It's a Small World! By Al Capp

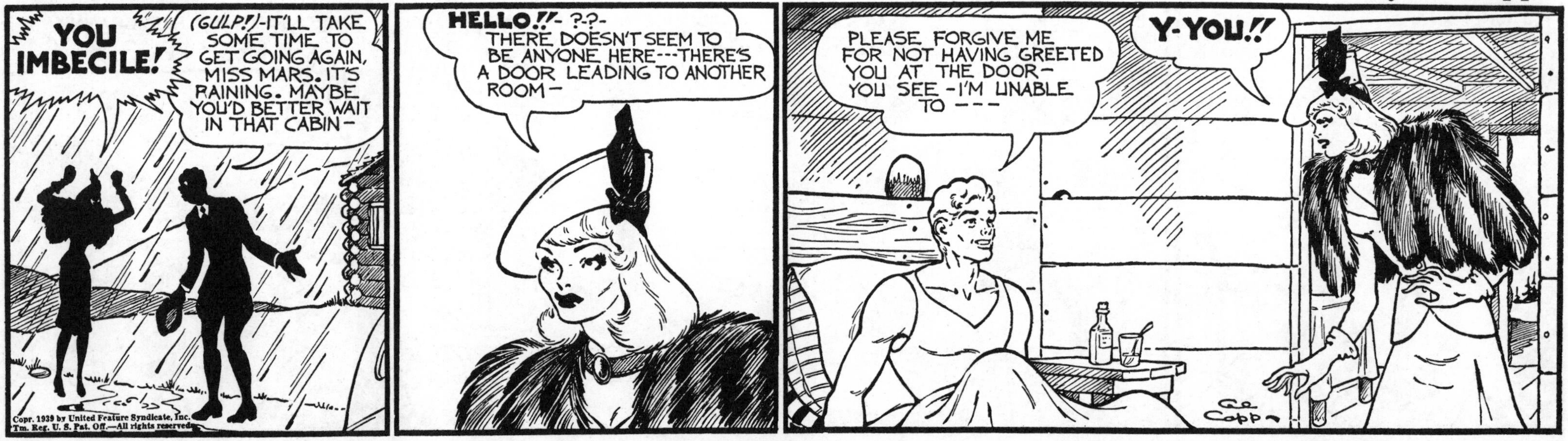
YOU IMBECILE!
(GULP!)-IT'LL TAKE SOME TIME TO GET GOING AGAIN, MISS MARS. IT'S RAINING. MAYBE YOU'D BETTER WAIT IN THAT CABIN-
Copr. 1939 by United Feature Syndicate, Inc. Tm. Reg. U. S. Pat. Off.—All rights reserved
HELLO!!- ?-?- THERE DOESN'T SEEM TO BE ANYONE HERE---THERE'S A DOOR LEADING TO ANOTHER ROOM-
PLEASE FORGIVE ME FOR NOT HAVING GREETED YOU AT THE DOOR- YOU SEE-I'M UNABLE TO---
Y-YOU!!

LI'L ABNER Emergency!! By Al Capp

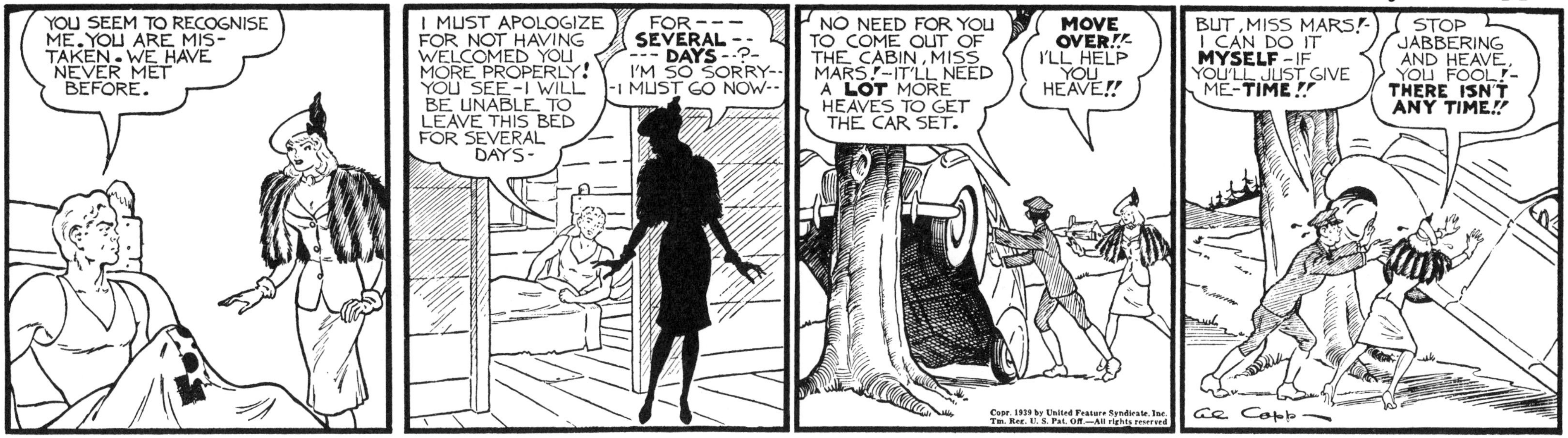
YOU SEEM TO RECOGNISE ME. YOU ARE MISTAKEN. WE HAVE NEVER MET BEFORE.
I MUST APOLOGIZE FOR NOT HAVING WELCOMED YOU MORE PROPERLY! YOU SEE-I WILL BE UNABLE TO LEAVE THIS BED FOR SEVERAL DAYS-
FOR --- SEVERAL -- --- DAYS --?- I'M SO SORRY-- -I MUST GO NOW--
NO NEED FOR YOU TO COME OUT OF THE CABIN, MISS MARS!-IT'LL NEED A LOT MORE HEAVES TO GET THE CAR SET.
MOVE OVER!!- I'LL HELP YOU HEAVE!!
BUT, MISS MARS!- I CAN DO IT MYSELF -IF YOU'LL JUST GIVE ME-TIME!!
STOP JABBERING AND HEAVE, YOU FOOL!- THERE ISN'T ANY TIME!!
Copr. 1939 by United Feature Syndicate, Inc. Tm. Reg. U. S. Pat. Off.—All rights reserved
Al Capp

LI'L ABNER Who Is This Him? By Al Capp

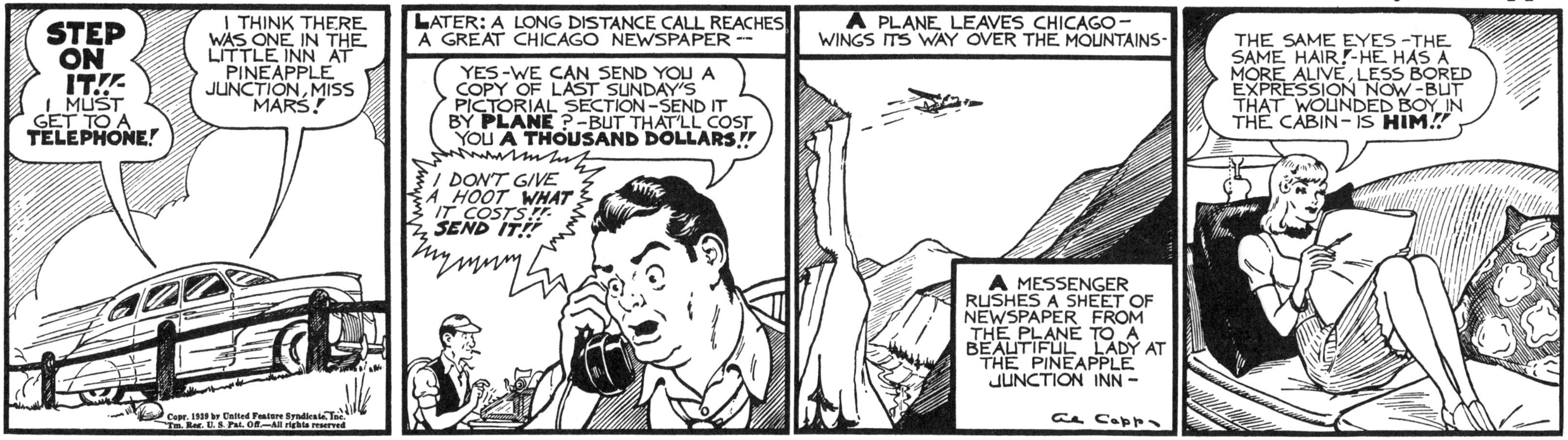
STEP ON IT!!- I MUST GET TO A TELEPHONE!
I THINK THERE WAS ONE IN THE LITTLE INN AT PINEAPPLE JUNCTION, MISS MARS!
Copr. 1939 by United Feature Syndicate, Inc. Tm. Reg. U. S. Pat. Off.—All rights reserved
LATER: A LONG DISTANCE CALL REACHES A GREAT CHICAGO NEWSPAPER --
YES-WE CAN SEND YOU A COPY OF LAST SUNDAY'S PICTORIAL SECTION-SEND IT BY PLANE ?-BUT THAT'LL COST YOU A THOUSAND DOLLARS!!
I DON'T GIVE A HOOT WHAT IT COSTS!!- SEND IT!!
A PLANE LEAVES CHICAGO- WINGS ITS WAY OVER THE MOUNTAINS-
A MESSENGER RUSHES A SHEET OF NEWSPAPER FROM THE PLANE TO A BEAUTIFUL LADY AT THE PINEAPPLE JUNCTION INN-
Al Capp
THE SAME EYES -THE SAME HAIR!-HE HAS A MORE ALIVE, LESS BORED EXPRESSION NOW-BUT THAT WOUNDED BOY IN THE CABIN- IS HIM!!

LI'L ABNER   My Reverie   By Al Capp

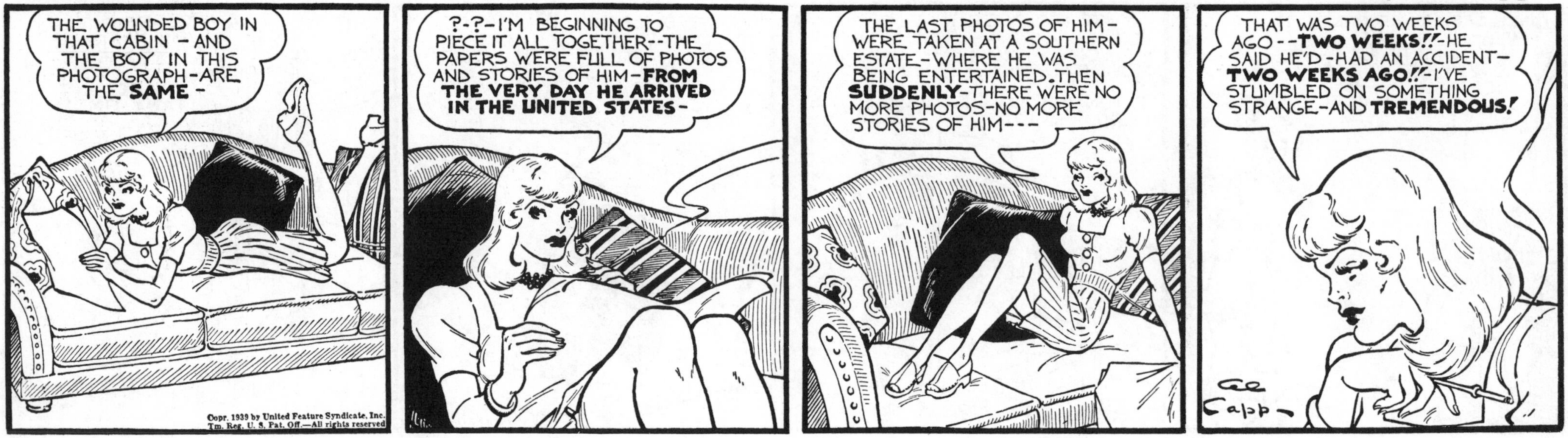

THE WOUNDED BOY IN THAT CABIN - AND THE BOY IN THIS PHOTOGRAPH - ARE THE **SAME** -
Copr. 1939 by United Feature Syndicate, Inc. Tm. Reg. U. S. Pat. Off.—All rights reserved
?-?- I'M BEGINNING TO PIECE IT ALL TOGETHER - - THE PAPERS WERE FULL OF PHOTOS AND STORIES OF HIM - **FROM THE VERY DAY HE ARRIVED IN THE UNITED STATES** -
THE LAST PHOTOS OF HIM - WERE TAKEN AT A SOUTHERN ESTATE - WHERE HE WAS BEING ENTERTAINED. THEN **SUDDENLY** - THERE WERE NO MORE PHOTOS - NO MORE STORIES OF HIM - - -
THAT WAS TWO WEEKS AGO - - **TWO WEEKS!!** - HE SAID HE'D - HAD AN ACCIDENT - **TWO WEEKS AGO!!** - I'VE STUMBLED ON SOMETHING STRANGE - AND **TREMENDOUS!**
Al Capp

LI'L ABNER   A More Sympathetic Role   By Al Capp

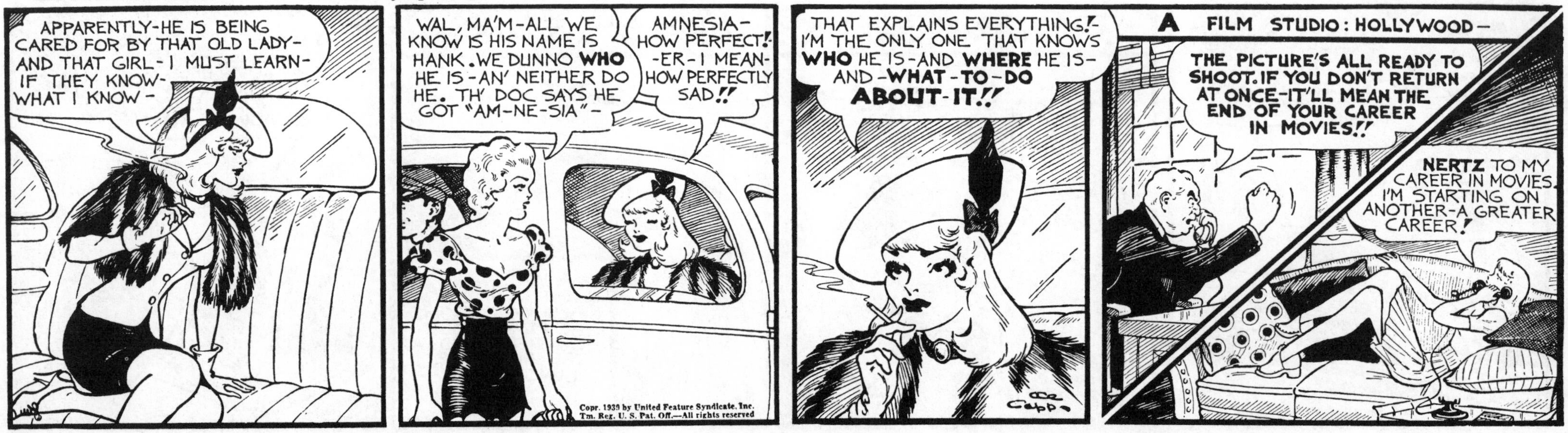

APPARENTLY - HE IS BEING CARED FOR BY THAT OLD LADY - AND THAT GIRL - I MUST LEARN - IF THEY KNOW - WHAT I KNOW -
WAL, MA'M - ALL WE KNOW IS HIS NAME IS HANK. WE DUNNO **WHO** HE IS - AN' NEITHER DO HE. TH' DOC SAYS HE GOT "AM-NE-SIA" -
AMNESIA - HOW PERFECT! - ER - I MEAN - HOW PERFECTLY SAD!!
Copr. 1939 by United Feature Syndicate, Inc. Tm. Reg. U. S. Pat. Off.—All rights reserved
THAT EXPLAINS EVERYTHING! - I'M THE ONLY ONE THAT KNOWS **WHO** HE IS - AND **WHERE** HE IS - AND - **WHAT - TO - DO ABOUT - IT!!**
Al Capp
A FILM STUDIO : HOLLYWOOD -
THE PICTURE'S ALL READY TO SHOOT. IF YOU DON'T RETURN AT ONCE - IT'LL MEAN THE END OF YOUR CAREER IN MOVIES!!
NERTZ TO MY CAREER IN MOVIES. I'M STARTING ON ANOTHER - A GREATER CAREER!

LI'L ABNER

Beware of Blondes Bringing Gifts!

By Al Capp

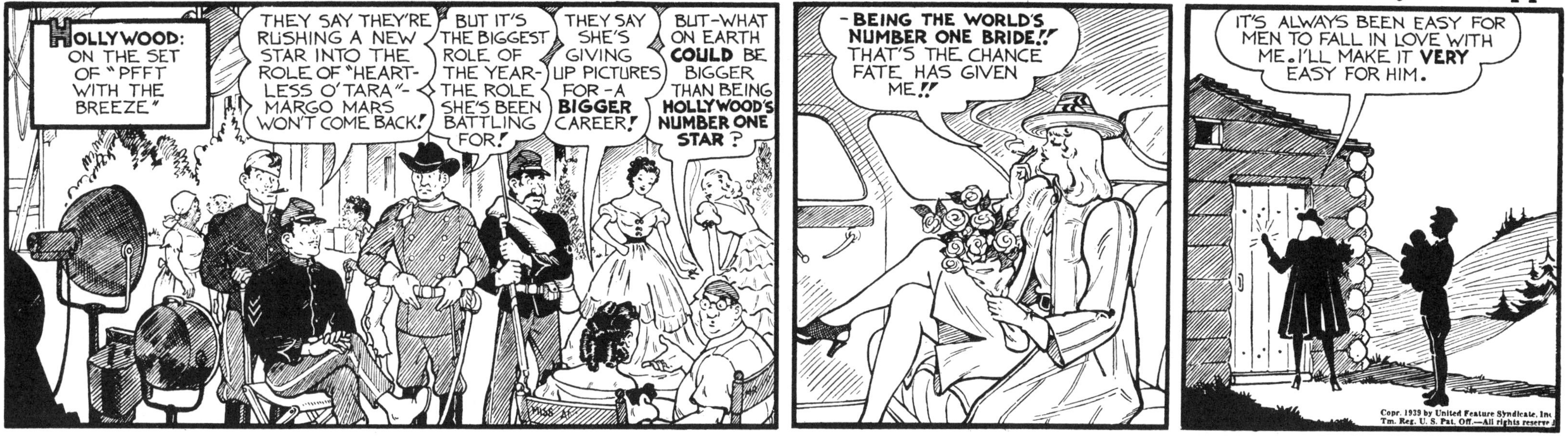
HOLLYWOOD: ON THE SET OF "PFFT WITH THE BREEZE"
THEY SAY THEY'RE RUSHING A NEW STAR INTO THE ROLE OF "HEART-LESS O'TARA"- MARGO MARS WON'T COME BACK!
BUT IT'S THE BIGGEST ROLE OF THE YEAR- THE ROLE SHE'S BEEN BATTLING FOR!
THEY SAY SHE'S GIVING UP PICTURES FOR-A BIGGER CAREER!
BUT-WHAT ON EARTH COULD BE BIGGER THAN BEING HOLLYWOOD'S NUMBER ONE STAR?
-BEING THE WORLD'S NUMBER ONE BRIDE!! THAT'S THE CHANCE FATE HAS GIVEN ME!!
IT'S ALWAYS BEEN EASY FOR MEN TO FALL IN LOVE WITH ME. I'LL MAKE IT VERY EASY FOR HIM.
Copr. 1939 by United Feature Syndicate, Inc. Tm. Reg. U. S. Pat. Off.—All rights reserved

LI'L ABNER

Margo Is In Reverse!

By Al Capp

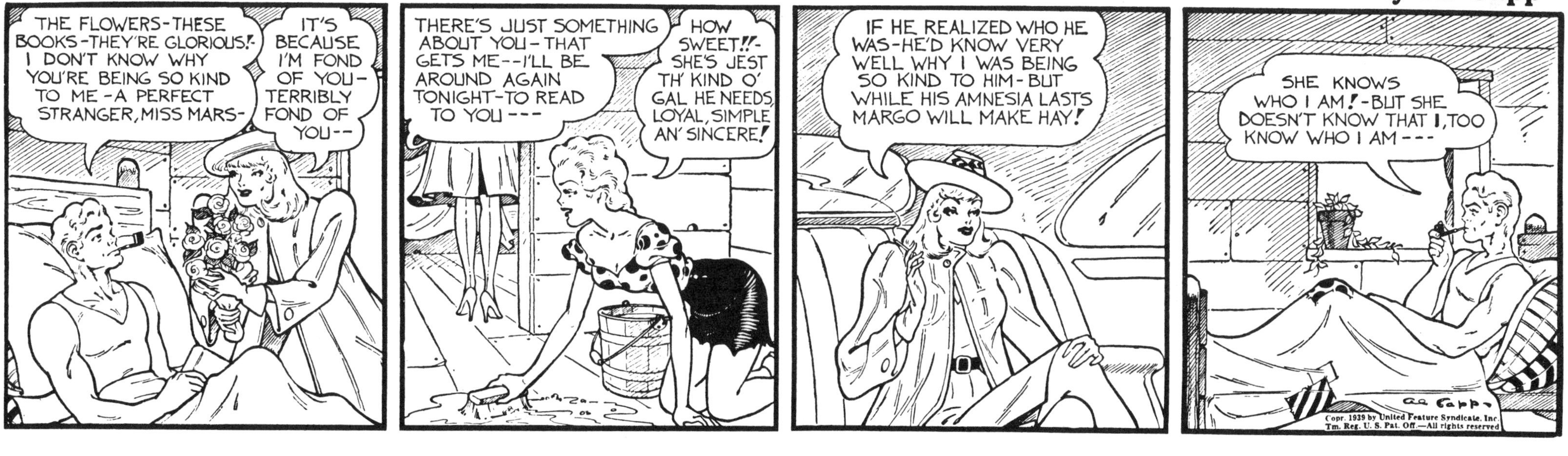
THE FLOWERS-THESE BOOKS-THEY'RE GLORIOUS!- I DON'T KNOW WHY YOU'RE BEING SO KIND TO ME-A PERFECT STRANGER, MISS MARS-
IT'S BECAUSE I'M FOND OF YOU- TERRIBLY FOND OF YOU--
THERE'S JUST SOMETHING ABOUT YOU-THAT GETS ME--I'LL BE AROUND AGAIN TONIGHT-TO READ TO YOU---
HOW SWEET!!- SHE'S JEST TH' KIND O' GAL HE NEEDS, LOYAL, SIMPLE AN' SINCERE!
IF HE REALIZED WHO HE WAS-HE'D KNOW VERY WELL WHY I WAS BEING SO KIND TO HIM-BUT WHILE HIS AMNESIA LASTS MARGO WILL MAKE HAY!
SHE KNOWS WHO I AM!-BUT SHE DOESN'T KNOW THAT I, TOO KNOW WHO I AM---
Al Capp
Copr. 1939 by United Feature Syndicate, Inc. Tm. Reg. U. S. Pat. Off.—All rights reserved

LI'L ABNER A Quiet Reverie By Al Capp

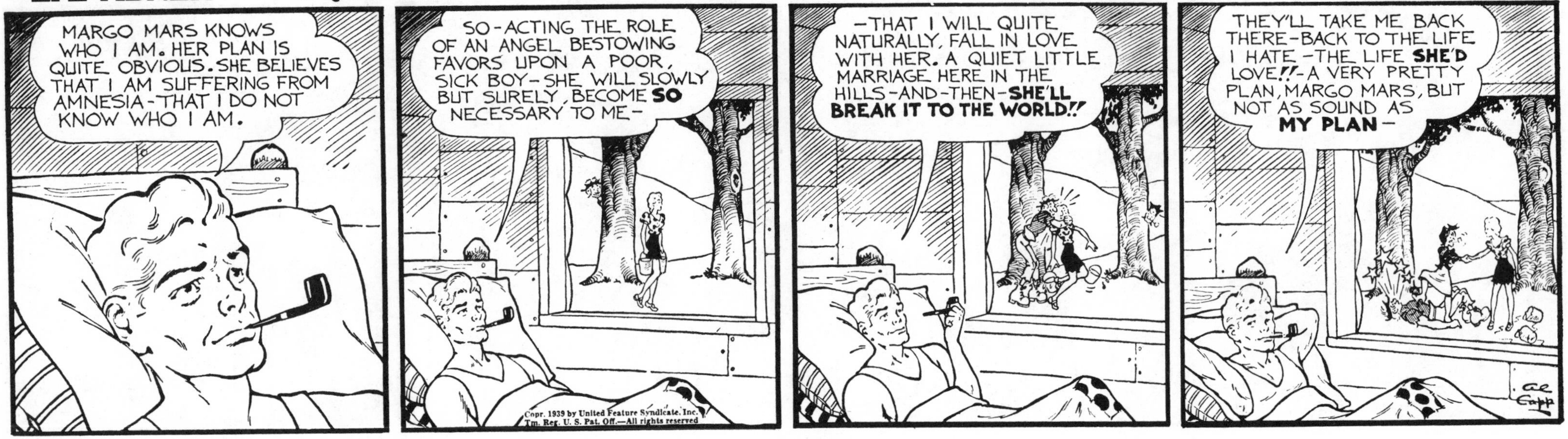

MARGO MARS KNOWS WHO I AM. HER PLAN IS QUITE OBVIOUS. SHE BELIEVES THAT I AM SUFFERING FROM AMNESIA-THAT I DO NOT KNOW WHO I AM.
SO-ACTING THE ROLE OF AN ANGEL BESTOWING FAVORS UPON A POOR, SICK BOY-SHE WILL SLOWLY BUT SURELY, BECOME **SO** NECESSARY TO ME-
Copr. 1939 by United Feature Syndicate, Inc. Tm. Reg. U. S. Pat. Off.—All rights reserved
-THAT I WILL QUITE NATURALLY, FALL IN LOVE WITH HER. A QUIET LITTLE MARRIAGE HERE IN THE HILLS-AND-THEN-**SHE'LL BREAK IT TO THE WORLD!!**
THEY'LL TAKE ME BACK THERE-BACK TO THE LIFE I HATE-THE LIFE **SHE'D** LOVE!!-A VERY PRETTY PLAN, MARGO MARS, BUT NOT AS SOUND AS **MY PLAN**-
Al Capp

LI'L ABNER Daisy May Or May Not By Al Capp

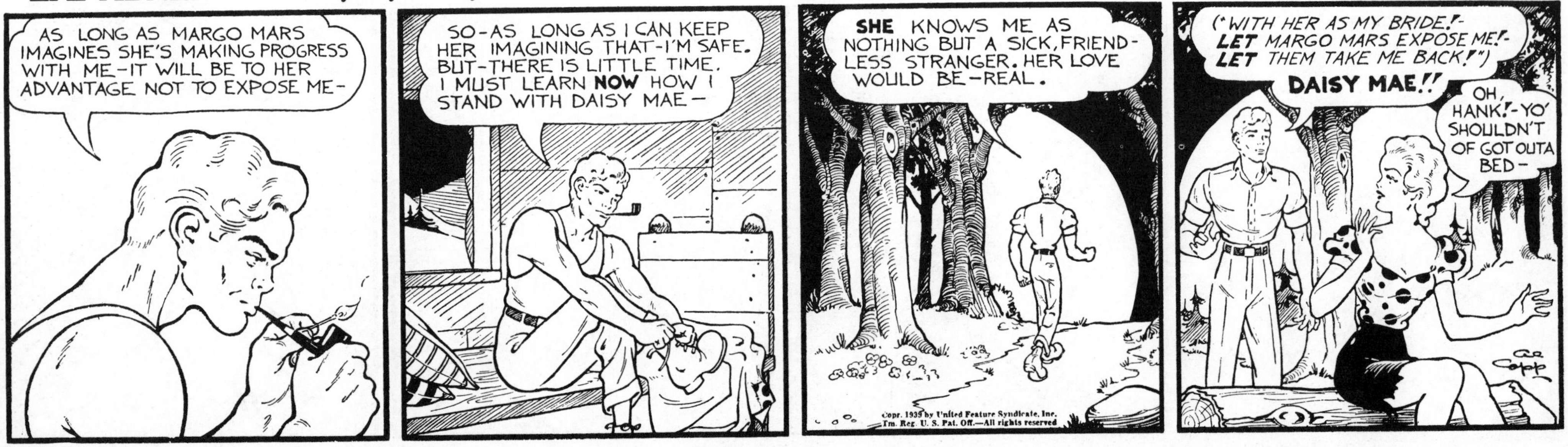

AS LONG AS MARGO MARS IMAGINES SHE'S MAKING PROGRESS WITH ME-IT WILL BE TO HER ADVANTAGE NOT TO EXPOSE ME-
SO-AS LONG AS I CAN KEEP HER IMAGINING THAT-I'M SAFE. BUT-THERE IS LITTLE TIME. I MUST LEARN **NOW** HOW I STAND WITH DAISY MAE-
SHE KNOWS ME AS NOTHING BUT A SICK, FRIENDLESS STRANGER. HER LOVE WOULD BE-REAL.
Copr. 1939 by United Feature Syndicate, Inc. Tm. Reg. U. S. Pat. Off.—All rights reserved
(*"WITH HER AS MY BRIDE!-* ***LET*** *MARGO MARS EXPOSE ME!-* ***LET*** *THEM TAKE ME BACK!"*)
DAISY MAE!!
OH, HANK!-YO' SHOULDN'T OF GOT OUTA BED-
Al Capp

LI'L ABNER — She Still Has the Dog — By Al Capp

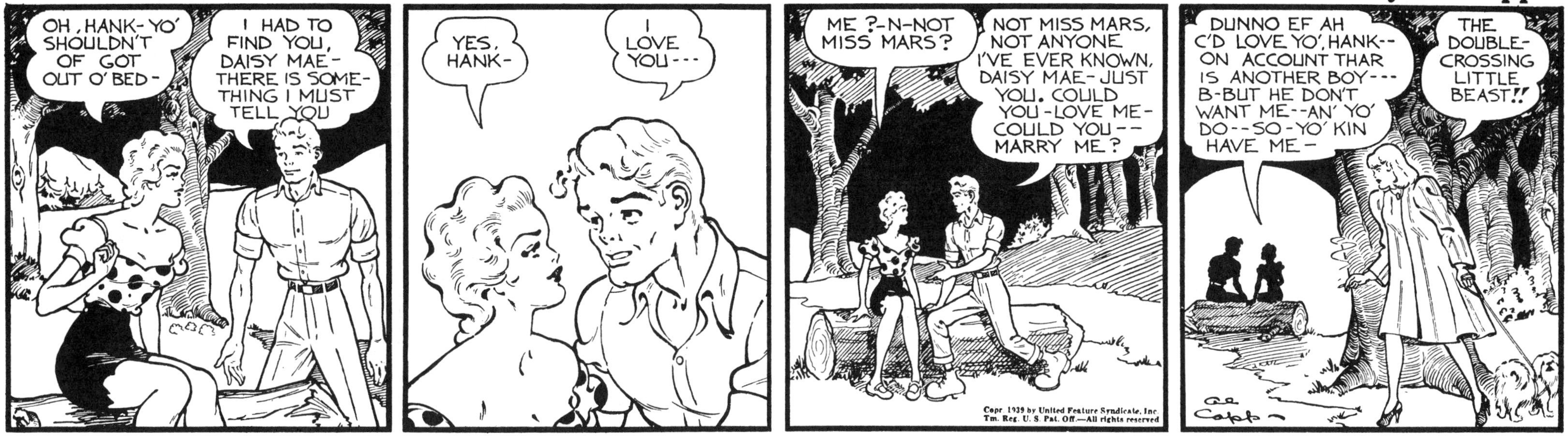
OH, HANK-YO' SHOULDN'T OF GOT OUT O' BED-
I HAD TO FIND YOU, DAISY MAE- THERE IS SOMETHING I MUST TELL YOU
YES, HANK-
I LOVE YOU---
ME ?-N-NOT MISS MARS?
NOT MISS MARS, NOT ANYONE I'VE EVER KNOWN, DAISY MAE-JUST YOU. COULD YOU-LOVE ME-COULD YOU--MARRY ME?
Copr. 1939 by United Feature Syndicate, Inc. Tm. Reg. U. S. Pat. Off.—All rights reserved
DUNNO EF AH C'D LOVE YO', HANK--ON ACCOUNT THAR IS ANOTHER BOY---B-BUT HE DON'T WANT ME--AN' YO' DO--SO-YO' KIN HAVE ME-
THE DOUBLE-CROSSING LITTLE BEAST!!
Al Capp

LI'L ABNER — The Sweetest Story Ever Told — By Al Capp

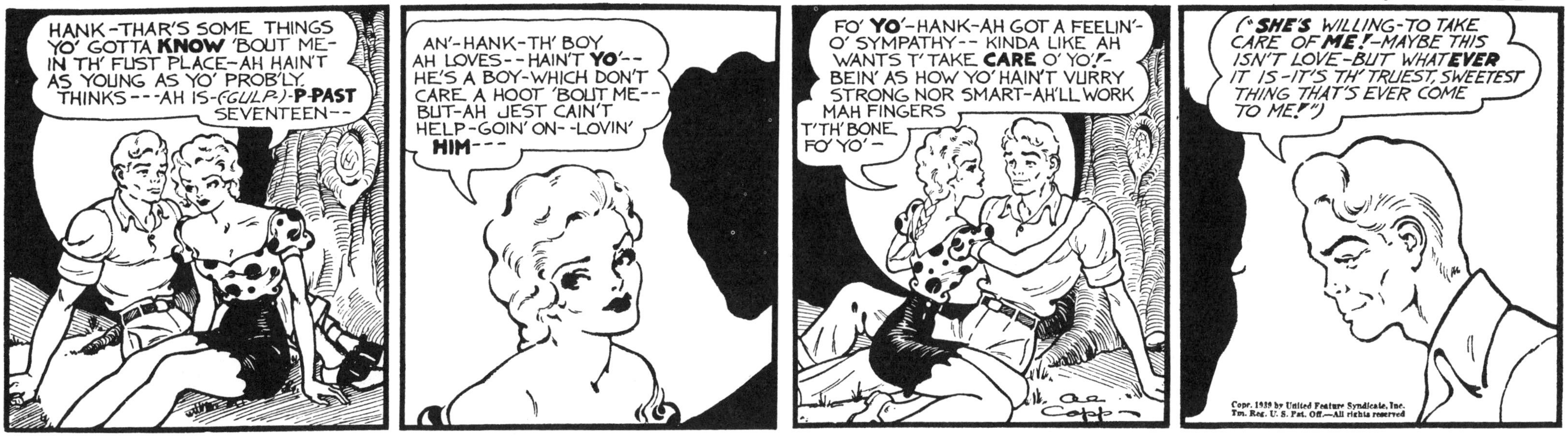
HANK-THAR'S SOME THINGS YO' GOTTA KNOW 'BOUT ME-IN TH' FUST PLACE-AH HAIN'T AS YOUNG AS YO' PROB'LY THINKS---AH IS-(GULP)-P-PAST SEVENTEEN--
AN'-HANK-TH' BOY AH LOVES--HAIN'T YO'--HE'S A BOY-WHICH DON'T CARE A HOOT 'BOUT ME--BUT-AH JEST CAIN'T HELP-GOIN' ON--LOVIN' HIM---
FO' YO'-HANK-AH GOT A FEELIN'-O' SYMPATHY-- KINDA LIKE AH WANTS T' TAKE CARE O' YO'!-BEIN' AS HOW YO' HAIN'T VURRY STRONG NOR SMART-AH'LL WORK MAH FINGERS T'TH' BONE FO' YO'-
Al Capp
("SHE'S WILLING-TO TAKE CARE OF ME!-MAYBE THIS ISN'T LOVE-BUT WHATEVER IT IS-IT'S TH' TRUEST, SWEETEST THING THAT'S EVER COME TO ME!")
Copr. 1939 by United Feature Syndicate, Inc. Tm. Reg. U. S. Pat. Off.—All rights reserved

LI'L ABNER The International Situation Is Critical By Al Capp

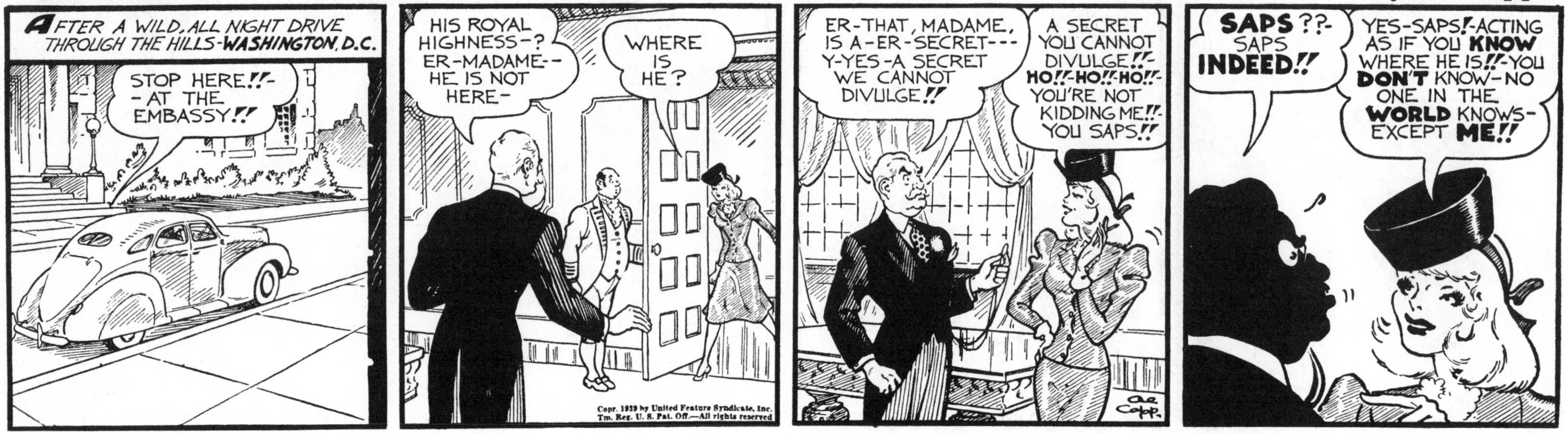
AFTER A WILD, ALL NIGHT DRIVE THROUGH THE HILLS-WASHINGTON, D.C.
STOP HERE!!- -AT THE EMBASSY!!
HIS ROYAL HIGHNESS-? ER-MADAME- -HE IS NOT HERE-
WHERE IS HE?
ER-THAT, MADAME, IS A-ER-SECRET--- Y-YES-A SECRET WE CANNOT DIVULGE!!
A SECRET YOU CANNOT DIVULGE!!- HO!!-HO!!-HO!!- YOU'RE NOT KIDDING ME!!- YOU SAPS!!
SAPS??- SAPS INDEED!!
YES-SAPS!-ACTING AS IF YOU KNOW WHERE HE IS!!-YOU DON'T KNOW-NO ONE IN THE WORLD KNOWS-EXCEPT ME!!
Copr. 1939 by United Feature Syndicate, Inc. Tm. Reg. U. S. Pat. Off.—All rights reserved

LI'L ABNER The Informer By Al Capp

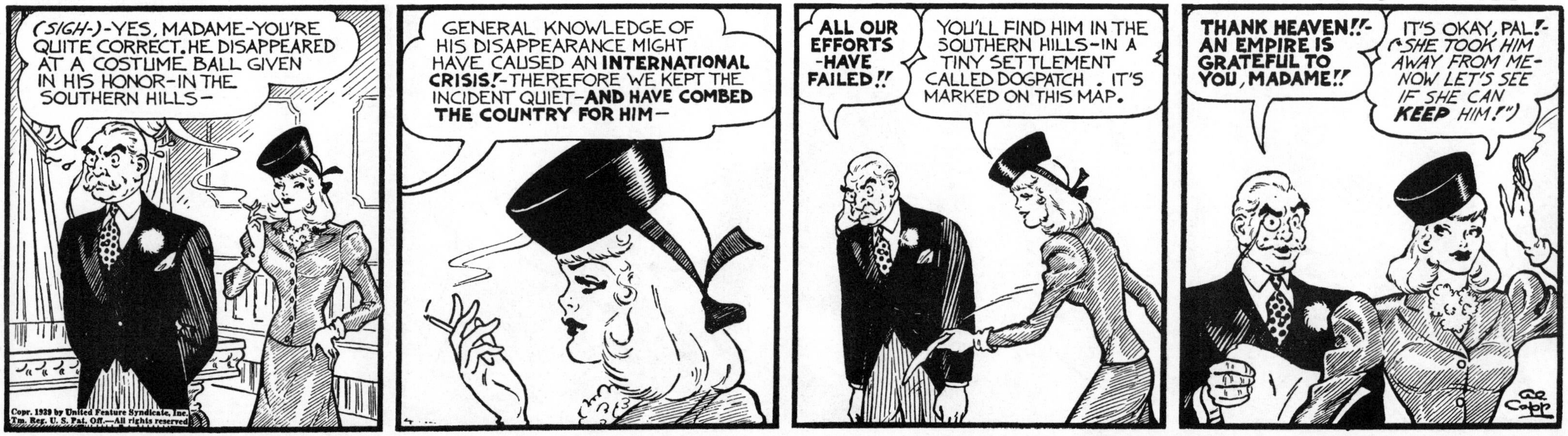
(SIGH-)-YES, MADAME-YOU'RE QUITE CORRECT. HE DISAPPEARED AT A COSTUME BALL GIVEN IN HIS HONOR-IN THE SOUTHERN HILLS-
GENERAL KNOWLEDGE OF HIS DISAPPEARANCE MIGHT HAVE CAUSED AN INTERNATIONAL CRISIS!-THEREFORE WE KEPT THE INCIDENT QUIET-AND HAVE COMBED THE COUNTRY FOR HIM-
ALL OUR EFFORTS -HAVE FAILED!!
YOU'LL FIND HIM IN THE SOUTHERN HILLS-IN A TINY SETTLEMENT CALLED DOGPATCH. IT'S MARKED ON THIS MAP.
THANK HEAVEN!!- AN EMPIRE IS GRATEFUL TO YOU, MADAME!!
IT'S OKAY, PAL!- ("SHE TOOK HIM AWAY FROM ME- NOW LET'S SEE IF SHE CAN KEEP HIM!")
Copr. 1939 by United Feature Syndicate, Inc. Tm. Reg. U. S. Pat. Off.—All rights reserved

LI'L ABNER Find Marryin' Sam! **By Al Capp**

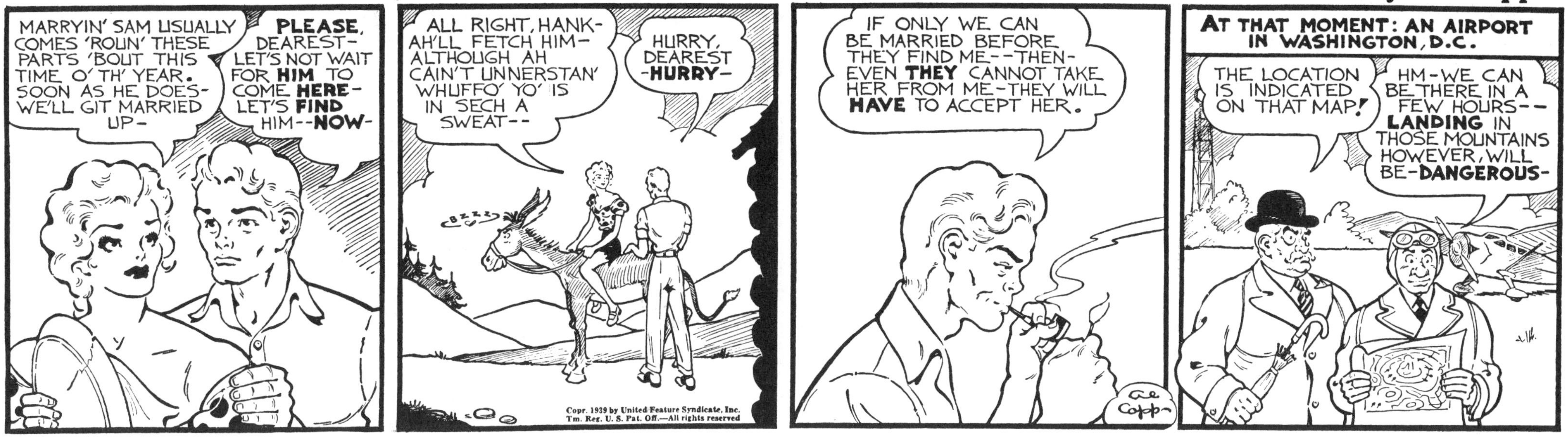
MARRYIN' SAM USUALLY COMES 'ROUN' THESE PARTS 'BOUT THIS TIME O' TH' YEAR. SOON AS HE DOES-WE'LL GIT MARRIED UP-
PLEASE, DEAREST- LET'S NOT WAIT FOR HIM TO COME HERE- LET'S FIND HIM--NOW-
ALL RIGHT, HANK- AH'LL FETCH HIM- ALTHOUGH AH CAIN'T UNNERSTAN' WHUFFO' YO' IS IN SECH A SWEAT--
HURRY, DEAREST -HURRY-
Copr. 1939 by United Feature Syndicate, Inc. Tm. Reg. U. S. Pat. Off.—All rights reserved
IF ONLY WE CAN BE MARRIED BEFORE THEY FIND ME--THEN-EVEN THEY CANNOT TAKE HER FROM ME-THEY WILL HAVE TO ACCEPT HER.
AL CAPP
AT THAT MOMENT: AN AIRPORT IN WASHINGTON, D.C.
THE LOCATION IS INDICATED ON THAT MAP!
HM-WE CAN BE THERE IN A FEW HOURS--LANDING IN THOSE MOUNTAINS HOWEVER, WILL BE-DANGEROUS-

LI'L ABNER Three Hearts In (Gulp) Time **By Al Capp**

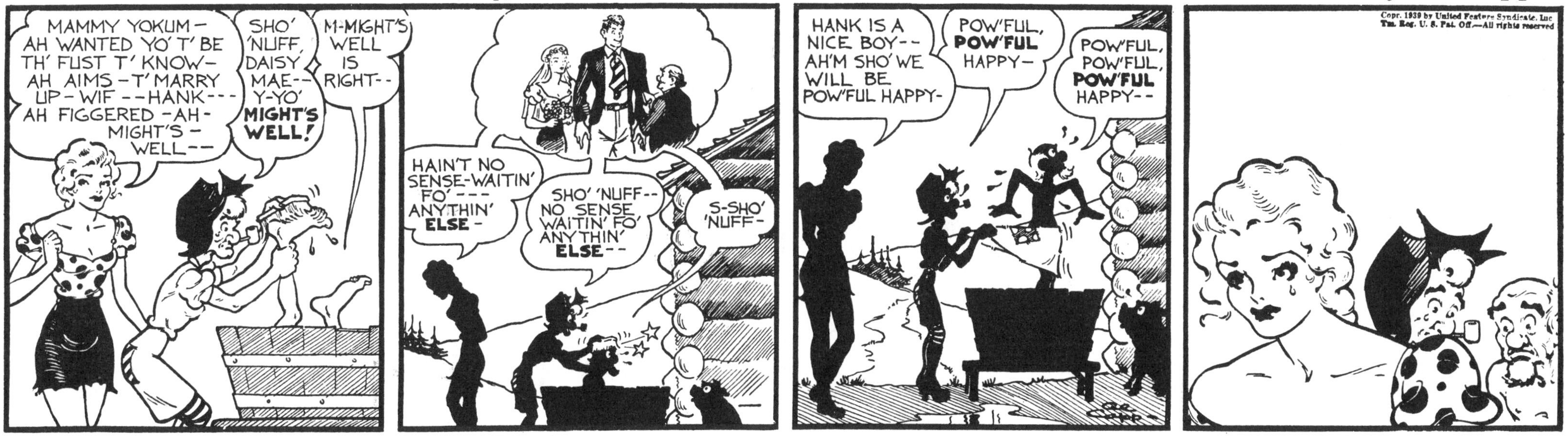
MAMMY YOKUM-AH WANTED YO' T' BE TH' FUST T' KNOW-AH AIMS-T' MARRY UP-WIF--HANK---AH FIGGERED-AH-MIGHT'S-WELL--
SHO' 'NUFF, DAISY MAE--Y-YO' MIGHT'S WELL!
M-MIGHT'S WELL IS RIGHT--
HAIN'T NO SENSE-WAITIN' FO'--- ANYTHIN' ELSE-
SHO' 'NUFF-- NO SENSE WAITIN' FO' ANYTHIN' ELSE--
S-SHO' 'NUFF-
HANK IS A NICE BOY--AH'M SHO' WE WILL BE POW'FUL HAPPY-
POW'FUL, POW'FUL HAPPY-
POW'FUL, POW'FUL, POW'FUL HAPPY--
AL CAPP
Copr. 1939 by United Feature Syndicate, Inc Tm. Reg. U. S. Pat. Off.—All rights reserved

LI'L ABNER Mountain Justice! By Al Capp

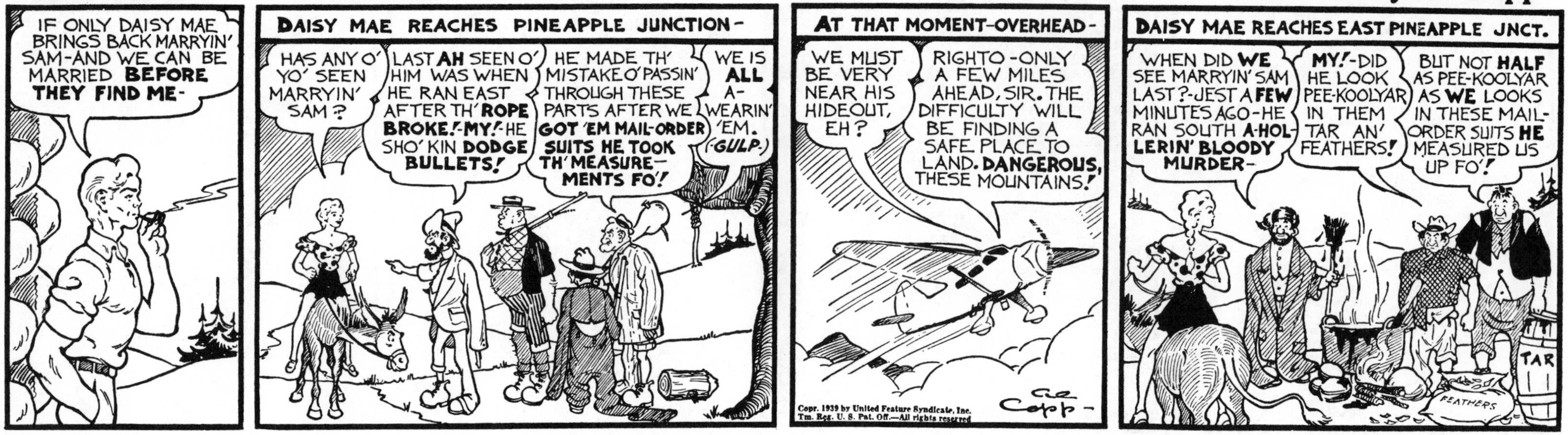

IF ONLY DAISY MAE BRINGS BACK MARRYIN' SAM-AND WE CAN BE MARRIED BEFORE THEY FIND ME-
DAISY MAE REACHES PINEAPPLE JUNCTION-
HAS ANY O' YO' SEEN MARRYIN' SAM?
LAST AH SEEN O' HIM WAS WHEN HE RAN EAST AFTER TH' ROPE BROKE!-MY!-HE SHO' KIN DODGE BULLETS!
HE MADE TH' MISTAKE O' PASSIN' THROUGH THESE PARTS AFTER WE GOT 'EM MAIL-ORDER SUITS HE TOOK TH' MEASURE-MENTS FO'!
WE IS ALL A-WEARIN' 'EM. (-GULP.)
AT THAT MOMENT-OVERHEAD-
WE MUST BE VERY NEAR HIS HIDEOUT, EH?
RIGHTO-ONLY A FEW MILES AHEAD, SIR. THE DIFFICULTY WILL BE FINDING A SAFE PLACE TO LAND. DANGEROUS, THESE MOUNTAINS!
Copr. 1939 by United Feature Syndicate, Inc. Tm. Reg. U. S. Pat. Off.—All rights reserved
Al Capp
DAISY MAE REACHES EAST PINEAPPLE JNCT.
WHEN DID WE SEE MARRYIN' SAM LAST?-JEST A FEW MINUTES AGO-HE RAN SOUTH A-HOL-LERIN' BLOODY MURDER-
MY!-DID HE LOOK PEE-KOOLYAR IN THEM TAR AN' FEATHERS!
BUT NOT HALF AS PEE-KOOLYAR AS WE LOOKS IN THESE MAIL-ORDER SUITS HE MEASURED US UP FO'!
TAR
FEATHERS

LI'L ABNER Wings Over Dogpatch By Al Capp

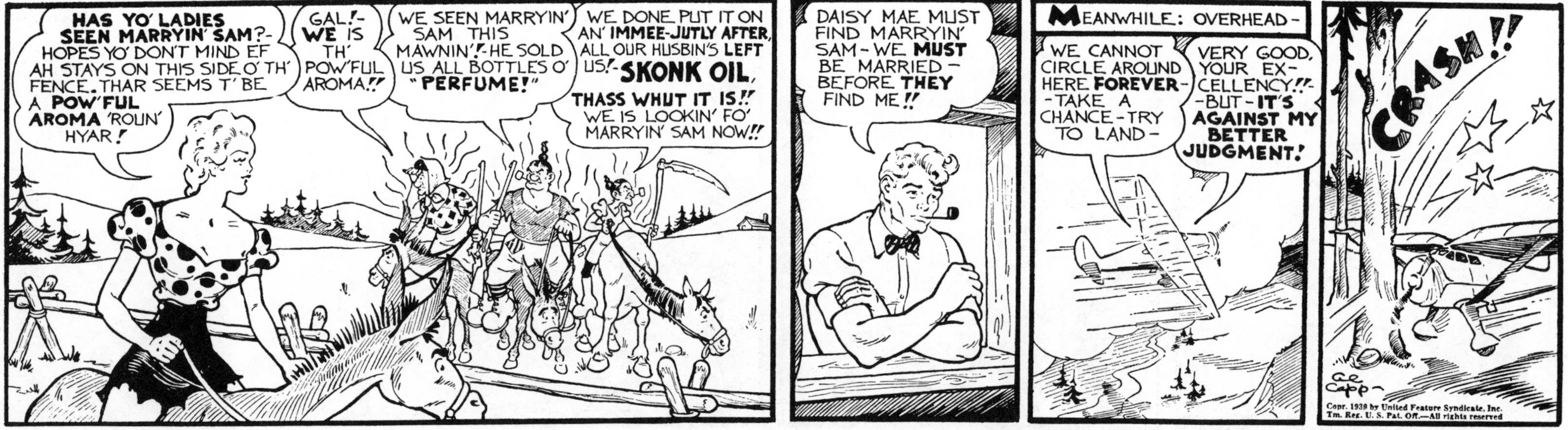

HAS YO' LADIES SEEN MARRYIN' SAM?-HOPES YO' DON'T MIND EF AH STAYS ON THIS SIDE O' TH' FENCE. THAR SEEMS T' BE A POW'FUL AROMA 'ROUN' HYAR!
GAL!-WE IS TH' POW'FUL AROMA!!
WE SEEN MARRYIN' SAM THIS MAWNIN'!-HE SOLD US ALL BOTTLES O' "PERFUME!"
WE DONE PUT IT ON AN' IMMEE-JUTLY AFTER, ALL OUR HUSBIN'S LEFT US!-SKONK OIL, THASS WHUT IT IS!! WE IS LOOKIN' FO' MARRYIN' SAM NOW!!
DAISY MAE MUST FIND MARRYIN' SAM-WE MUST BE MARRIED-BEFORE THEY FIND ME!!
MEANWHILE: OVERHEAD-
WE CANNOT CIRCLE AROUND HERE FOREVER--TAKE A CHANCE-TRY TO LAND-
VERY GOOD, YOUR EX-CELLENCY!!--BUT-IT'S AGAINST MY BETTER JUDGMENT!
CRASH!!
Al Capp
Copr. 1939 by United Feature Syndicate, Inc. Tm. Reg. U. S. Pat. Off.—All rights reserved

LI'L ABNER A Fake From the Lake By Al Capp

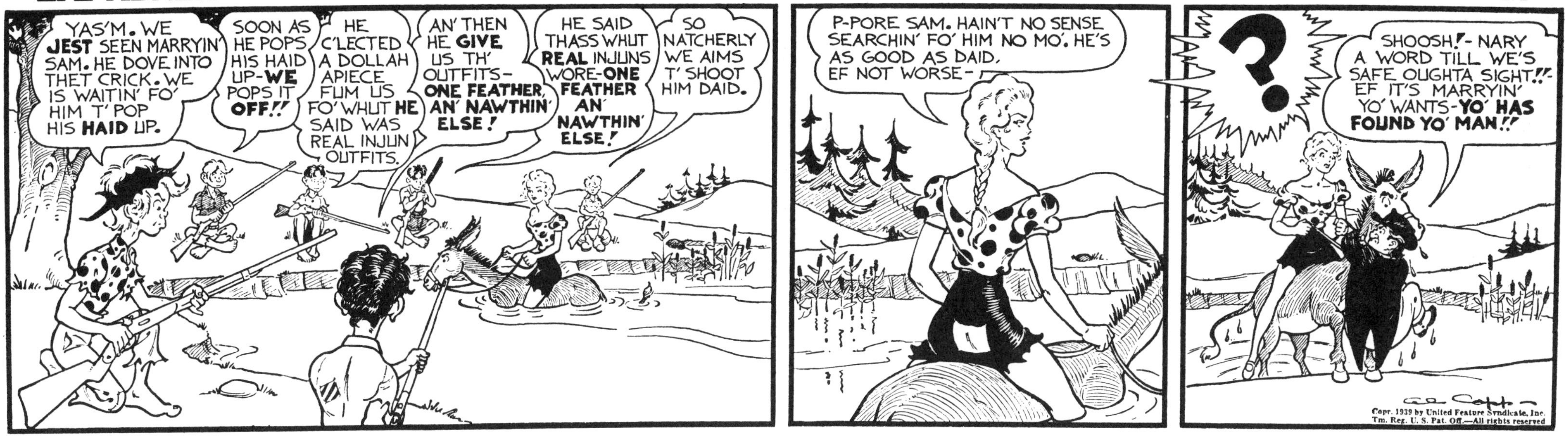

YAS'M. WE JEST SEEN MARRYIN' SAM. HE DOVE INTO THET CRICK. WE IS WAITIN' FO' HIM T' POP HIS HAID UP.
SOON AS HE POPS HIS HAID UP-WE POPS IT OFF!!
HE C'LECTED A DOLLAH APIECE FUM US FO' WHUT HE SAID WAS REAL INJUN OUTFITS.
AN' THEN HE GIVE US TH' OUTFITS-ONE FEATHER AN' NAWTHIN' ELSE!
HE SAID THASS WHUT REAL INJUNS WORE-ONE FEATHER AN' NAWTHIN' ELSE!
SO NATCHERLY WE AIMS T' SHOOT HIM DAID.
P-PORE SAM. HAIN'T NO SENSE SEARCHIN' FO' HIM NO MO'. HE'S AS GOOD AS DAID, EF NOT WORSE-
?
SHOOSH!- NARY A WORD TILL WE'S SAFE OUGHTA SIGHT!!- EF IT'S MARRYIN' YO' WANTS-YO' HAS FOUND YO' MAN!!
Copr. 1939 by United Feature Syndicate, Inc. Tm. Reg. U. S. Pat. Off.—All rights reserved

LI'L ABNER Three's A Crowd By Al Capp

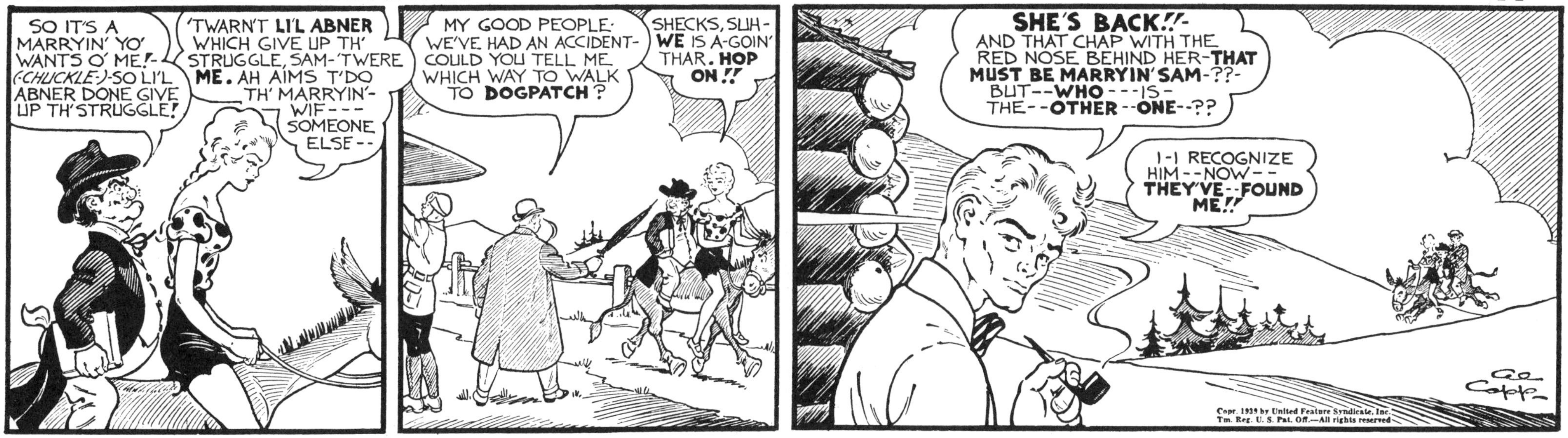

SO IT'S A MARRYIN' YO' WANTS O' ME!-(CHUCKLE)-SO LI'L ABNER DONE GIVE UP TH' STRUGGLE!
'TWARN'T LI'L ABNER WHICH GIVE UP TH' STRUGGLE, SAM-'TWERE ME. AH AIMS T'DO TH' MARRYIN'-WIF--- SOMEONE ELSE--
MY GOOD PEOPLE-WE'VE HAD AN ACCIDENT-COULD YOU TELL ME WHICH WAY TO WALK TO DOGPATCH?
SHECKS, SUH-WE IS A-GOIN' THAR. HOP ON!!
SHE'S BACK!!- AND THAT CHAP WITH THE RED NOSE BEHIND HER-THAT MUST BE MARRYIN' SAM-??- BUT--WHO---IS-THE--OTHER--ONE--??
I-I RECOGNIZE HIM--NOW--THEY'VE--FOUND ME!!
Copr. 1939 by United Feature Syndicate, Inc. Tm. Reg. U. S. Pat. Off.—All rights reserved

LI'L ABNER Long Live the King By Al Capp

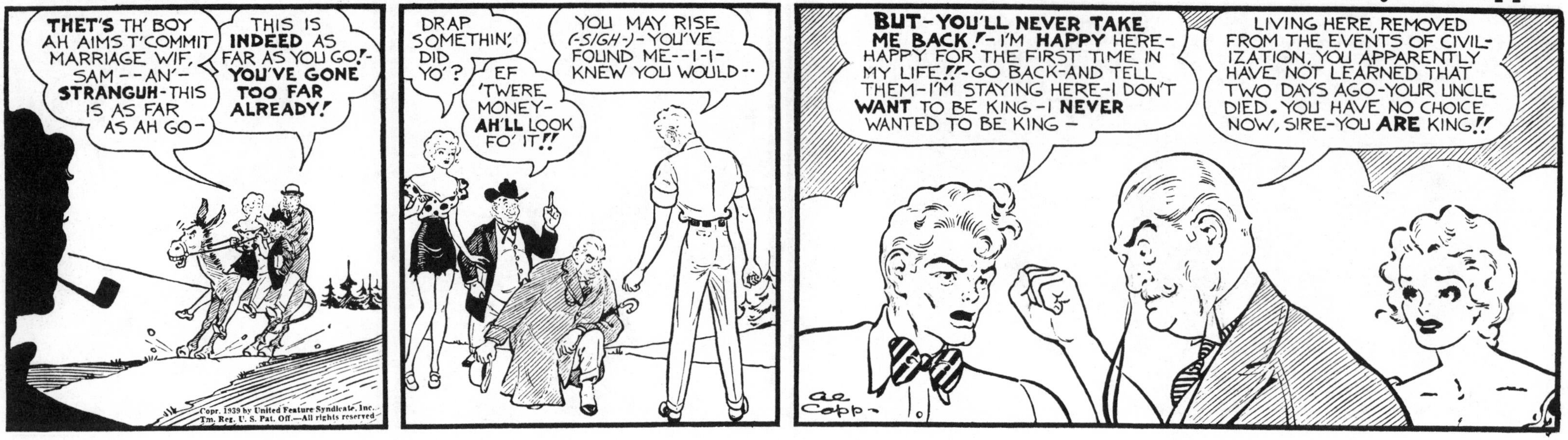

THET'S TH' BOY AH AIMS T'COMMIT MARRIAGE WIF, SAM - - AN' - STRANGUH - THIS IS AS FAR AS AH GO -
THIS IS INDEED AS FAR AS YOU GO! - YOU'VE GONE TOO FAR ALREADY!
Copr. 1939 by United Feature Syndicate, Inc. Tm. Reg. U. S. Pat. Off.—All rights reserved
DRAP SOMETHIN', DID YO'?
EF 'TWERE MONEY- AH'LL LOOK FO' IT!!
YOU MAY RISE (-SIGH-) - YOU'VE FOUND ME - - I - I - KNEW YOU WOULD - -
BUT - YOU'LL NEVER TAKE ME BACK! - I'M HAPPY HERE - HAPPY FOR THE FIRST TIME IN MY LIFE!! - GO BACK - AND TELL THEM - I'M STAYING HERE - I DON'T WANT TO BE KING - I NEVER WANTED TO BE KING -
LIVING HERE, REMOVED FROM THE EVENTS OF CIVILIZATION, YOU APPARENTLY HAVE NOT LEARNED THAT TWO DAYS AGO - YOUR UNCLE DIED. YOU HAVE NO CHOICE NOW, SIRE - YOU ARE KING!!
AL CAPP

LI'L ABNER His Majesty Speaks By Al Capp

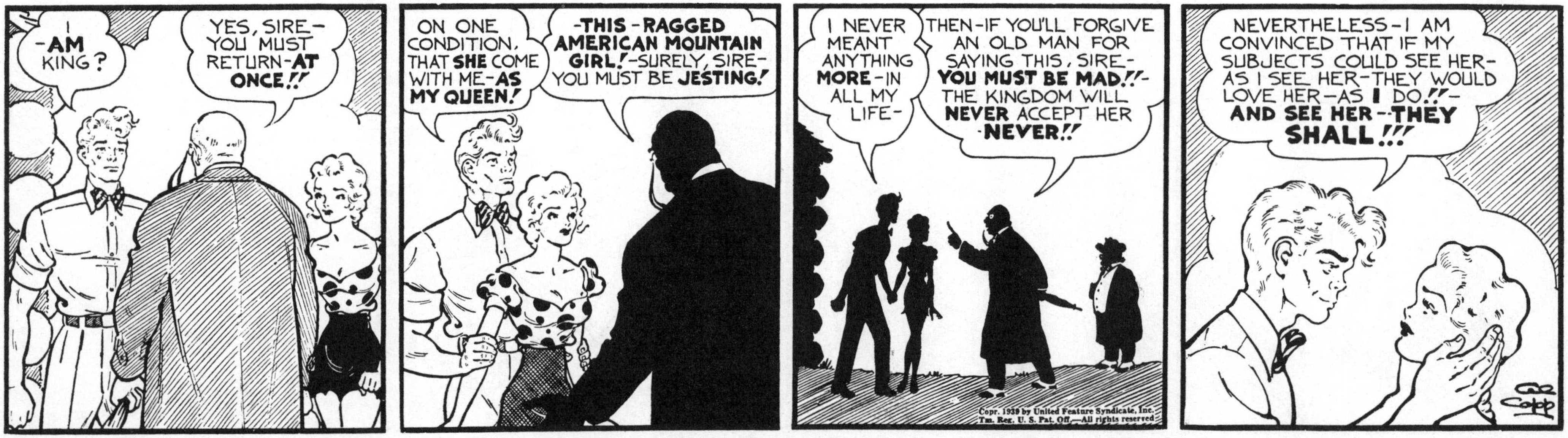

I - AM KING?
YES, SIRE - YOU MUST RETURN - AT ONCE!!
ON ONE CONDITION, THAT SHE COME WITH ME - AS MY QUEEN!
- THIS - RAGGED AMERICAN MOUNTAIN GIRL! - SURELY, SIRE - YOU MUST BE JESTING!
I NEVER MEANT ANYTHING MORE - IN ALL MY LIFE -
THEN - IF YOU'LL FORGIVE AN OLD MAN FOR SAYING THIS, SIRE - YOU MUST BE MAD!! - THE KINGDOM WILL NEVER ACCEPT HER - NEVER!!
Copr. 1939 by United Feature Syndicate, Inc. Tm. Reg. U. S. Pat. Off.—All rights reserved
NEVERTHELESS - I AM CONVINCED THAT IF MY SUBJECTS COULD SEE HER - AS I SEE HER - THEY WOULD LOVE HER - AS I DO!! - AND SEE HER - - THEY SHALL!!!
AL CAPP

LI'L ABNER — Will Love Conquer All? — By Al Capp

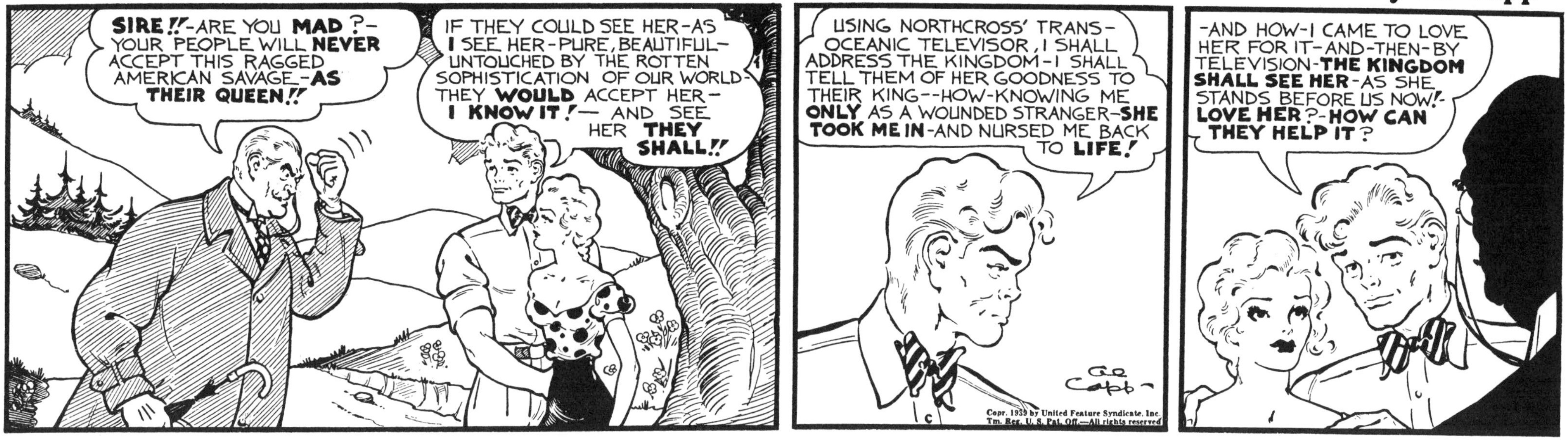
SIRE!!-ARE YOU MAD?-YOUR PEOPLE WILL NEVER ACCEPT THIS RAGGED AMERICAN SAVAGE-AS THEIR QUEEN!!
IF THEY COULD SEE HER-AS I SEE HER-PURE, BEAUTIFUL-UNTOUCHED BY THE ROTTEN SOPHISTICATION OF OUR WORLD-THEY WOULD ACCEPT HER-I KNOW IT!- AND SEE HER THEY SHALL!!
USING NORTHCROSS' TRANS-OCEANIC TELEVISOR, I SHALL ADDRESS THE KINGDOM-I SHALL TELL THEM OF HER GOODNESS TO THEIR KING--HOW-KNOWING ME ONLY AS A WOUNDED STRANGER-SHE TOOK ME IN-AND NURSED ME BACK TO LIFE!
Al Capp
Copr. 1939 by United Feature Syndicate, Inc. Tm. Reg. U. S. Pat. Off.—All rights reserved
-AND HOW-I CAME TO LOVE HER FOR IT-AND-THEN-BY TELEVISION-THE KINGDOM SHALL SEE HER-AS SHE STANDS BEFORE US NOW!-LOVE HER?-HOW CAN THEY HELP IT?

LI'L ABNER — Them That Wants, Gits — By Al Capp

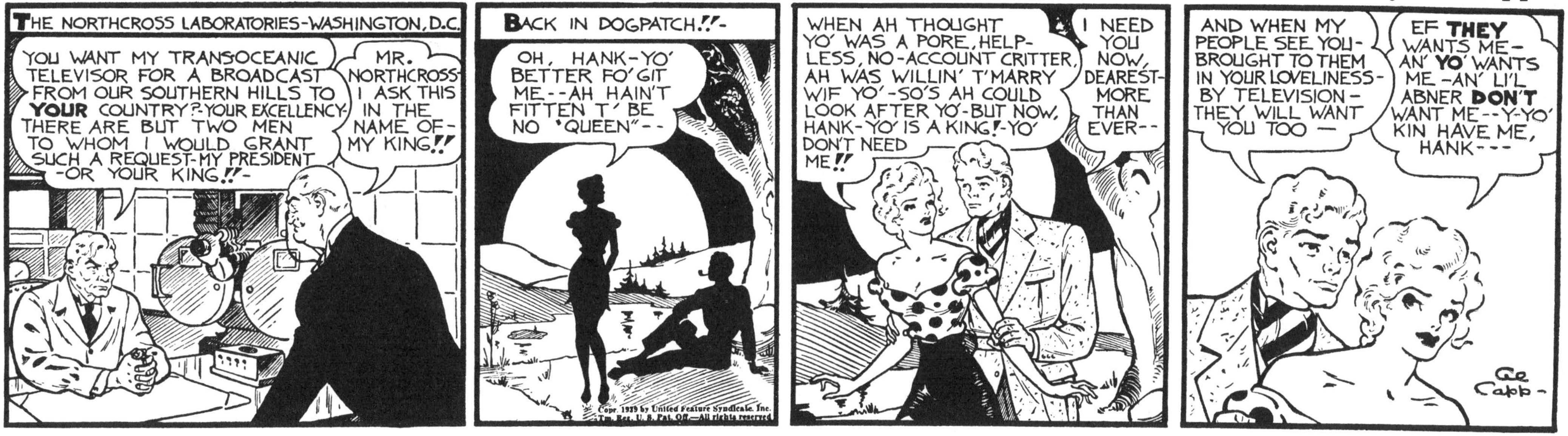
THE NORTHCROSS LABORATORIES-WASHINGTON, D.C.
YOU WANT MY TRANSOCEANIC TELEVISOR FOR A BROADCAST FROM OUR SOUTHERN HILLS TO YOUR COUNTRY?-YOUR EXCELLENCY-THERE ARE BUT TWO MEN TO WHOM I WOULD GRANT SUCH A REQUEST-MY PRESIDENT -OR YOUR KING!!-
MR. NORTHCROSS-I ASK THIS IN THE NAME OF MY KING!!
BACK IN DOGPATCH!!-
OH, HANK-YO' BETTER FO'GIT ME--AH HAIN'T FITTEN T' BE NO "QUEEN"--
Copr. 1939 by United Feature Syndicate, Inc. Tm. Reg. U. S. Pat. Off.—All rights reserved
WHEN AH THOUGHT YO' WAS A PORE, HELP-LESS, NO-ACCOUNT CRITTER, AH WAS WILLIN' T'MARRY WIF YO'-SO'S AH COULD LOOK AFTER YO'-BUT NOW, HANK-YO' IS A KING!-YO' DON'T NEED ME!!
I NEED YOU NOW, DEAREST-MORE THAN EVER--
AND WHEN MY PEOPLE SEE YOU-BROUGHT TO THEM IN YOUR LOVELINESS-BY TELEVISION-THEY WILL WANT YOU TOO-
EF THEY WANTS ME-AN' YO' WANTS ME-AN' LI'L ABNER DON'T WANT ME--Y-YO' KIN HAVE ME, HANK---
Al Capp

LI'L ABNER It's A Small World By Al Capp

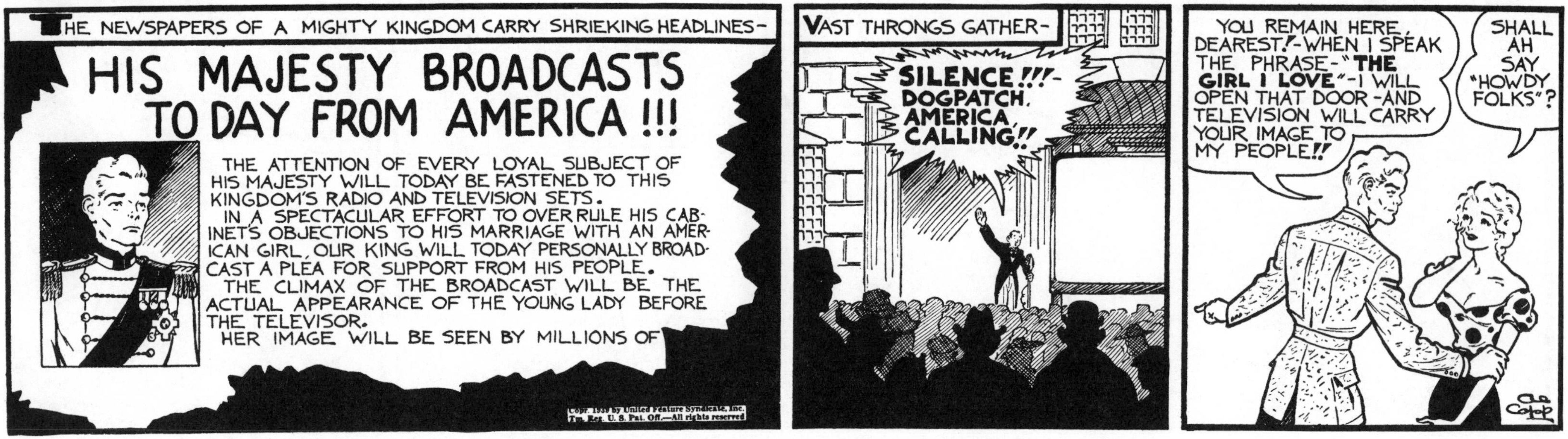
THE NEWSPAPERS OF A MIGHTY KINGDOM CARRY SHRIEKING HEADLINES-
HIS MAJESTY BROADCASTS TO DAY FROM AMERICA !!!
THE ATTENTION OF EVERY LOYAL SUBJECT OF HIS MAJESTY WILL TODAY BE FASTENED TO THIS KINGDOM'S RADIO AND TELEVISION SETS.
IN A SPECTACULAR EFFORT TO OVERRULE HIS CABINET'S OBJECTIONS TO HIS MARRIAGE WITH AN AMERICAN GIRL, OUR KING WILL TODAY PERSONALLY BROADCAST A PLEA FOR SUPPORT FROM HIS PEOPLE.
THE CLIMAX OF THE BROADCAST WILL BE THE ACTUAL APPEARANCE OF THE YOUNG LADY BEFORE THE TELEVISOR.
HER IMAGE WILL BE SEEN BY MILLIONS OF
Copr. 1939 by United Feature Syndicate, Inc. Tm. Reg. U. S. Pat. Off.—All rights reserved
VAST THRONGS GATHER-
SILENCE!!!- DOGPATCH, AMERICA CALLING!!
YOU REMAIN HERE, DEAREST!-WHEN I SPEAK THE PHRASE-"THE GIRL I LOVE"-I WILL OPEN THAT DOOR-AND TELEVISION WILL CARRY YOUR IMAGE TO MY PEOPLE!!
SHALL AH SAY "HOWDY FOLKS"?

LI'L ABNER Hail the Queen! By Al Capp

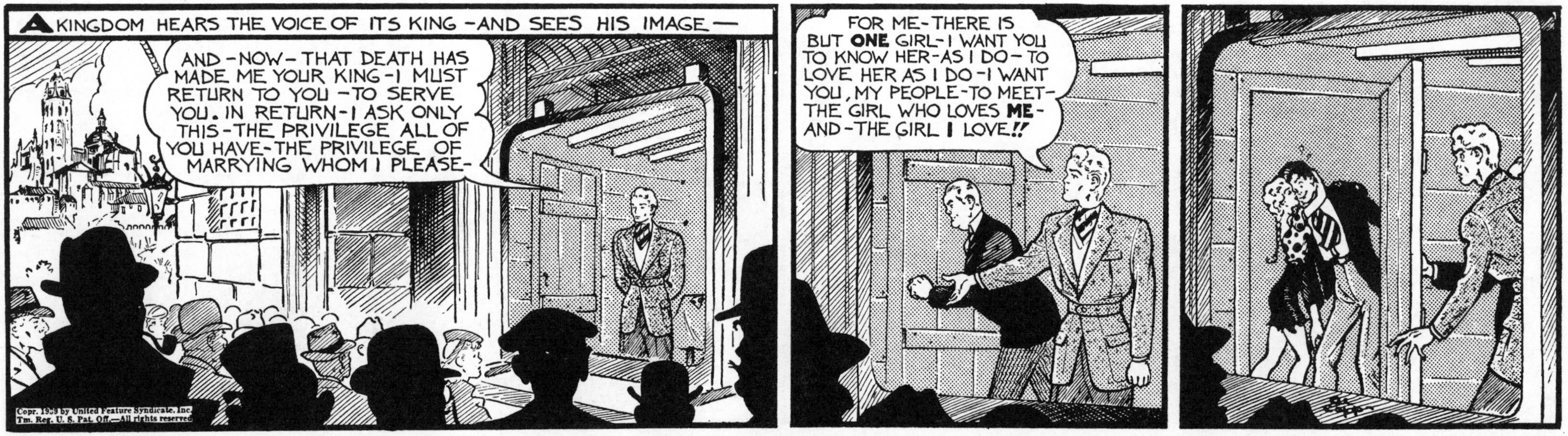
A KINGDOM HEARS THE VOICE OF ITS KING -AND SEES HIS IMAGE—
AND-NOW-THAT DEATH HAS MADE ME YOUR KING-I MUST RETURN TO YOU-TO SERVE YOU. IN RETURN-I ASK ONLY THIS-THE PRIVILEGE ALL OF YOU HAVE-THE PRIVILEGE OF MARRYING WHOM I PLEASE-
Copr. 1939 by United Feature Syndicate, Inc. Tm. Reg. U. S. Pat. Off.—All rights reserved
FOR ME-THERE IS BUT ONE GIRL-I WANT YOU TO KNOW HER-AS I DO-TO LOVE HER AS I DO-I WANT YOU, MY PEOPLE-TO MEET-THE GIRL WHO LOVES ME-AND-THE GIRL I LOVE!!

LI'L ABNER Long Live the King By Al Capp

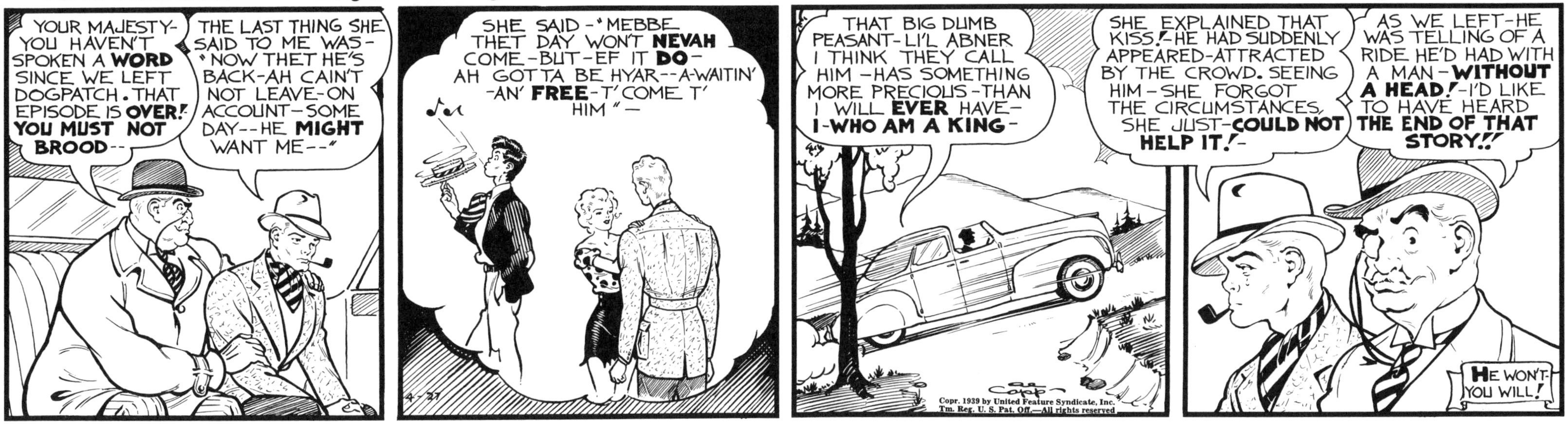

YOUR MAJESTY- YOU HAVEN'T SPOKEN A **WORD** SINCE WE LEFT DOGPATCH. THAT EPISODE IS **OVER!** **YOU MUST NOT BROOD**--
THE LAST THING SHE SAID TO ME WAS- "NOW THET HE'S BACK-AH CAIN'T NOT LEAVE-ON ACCOUNT-SOME DAY--HE **MIGHT** WANT ME--"
SHE SAID-"MEBBE THET DAY WON'T **NEVAH** COME-BUT-EF IT **DO**- AH GOTTA BE HYAR--A-WAITIN' -AN' **FREE**-T' COME T' HIM"-
4-27
THAT BIG DUMB PEASANT-LI'L ABNER I THINK THEY CALL HIM -HAS SOMETHING MORE PRECIOUS-THAN I WILL **EVER** HAVE- **I-WHO AM A KING**-
Copr. 1939 by United Feature Syndicate, Inc. Tm. Reg. U. S. Pat. Off.—All rights reserved
SHE EXPLAINED THAT KISS!-HE HAD SUDDENLY APPEARED-ATTRACTED BY THE CROWD. SEEING HIM-SHE FORGOT THE CIRCUMSTANCES, SHE JUST-**COULD NOT HELP IT!**-
AS WE LEFT-HE WAS TELLING OF A RIDE HE'D HAD WITH A MAN-**WITHOUT A HEAD!**-I'D LIKE TO HAVE HEARD **THE END OF THAT STORY!!**
HE WON'T- YOU WILL!

LI'L ABNER What a Sit-che-ay-shun By Al Capp

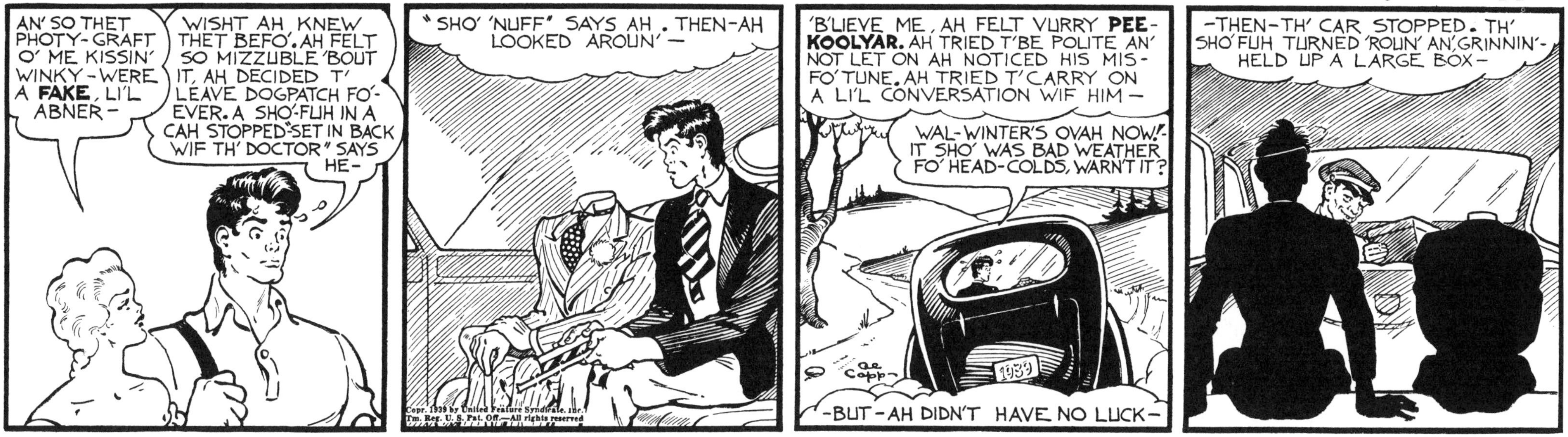

AN' SO THET PHOTY-GRAFT O' ME KISSIN' WINKY-WERE A **FAKE**, LI'L ABNER-
WISHT AH KNEW THET BEFO'. AH FELT SO MIZZUBLE 'BOUT IT, AH DECIDED T' LEAVE DOGPATCH FO'-EVER. A SHO'-FUH IN A CAH STOPPED-SET IN BACK WIF TH' DOCTOR" SAYS HE-
"SHO' 'NUFF" SAYS AH. THEN-AH LOOKED AROUN'-
Copr. 1939 by United Feature Syndicate, Inc. Tm. Reg. U. S. Pat. Off.—All rights reserved
'B'LIEVE ME, AH FELT VURRY **PEE-KOOLYAR.** AH TRIED T'BE POLITE AN' NOT LET ON AH NOTICED HIS MIS-FO'TUNE. AH TRIED T'CARRY ON A LI'L CONVERSATION WIF HIM-
WAL-WINTER'S OVAH NOW!- IT SHO' WAS BAD WEATHER FO' HEAD-COLDS, WARN'T IT?
1939
-BUT-AH DIDN'T HAVE NO LUCK-
-THEN-TH' CAR STOPPED. TH' SHO'FUH TURNED 'ROUN' AN' GRINNIN'-HELD UP A LARGE BOX-

LI'L ABNER — A Confoozing Problum — By Al Capp

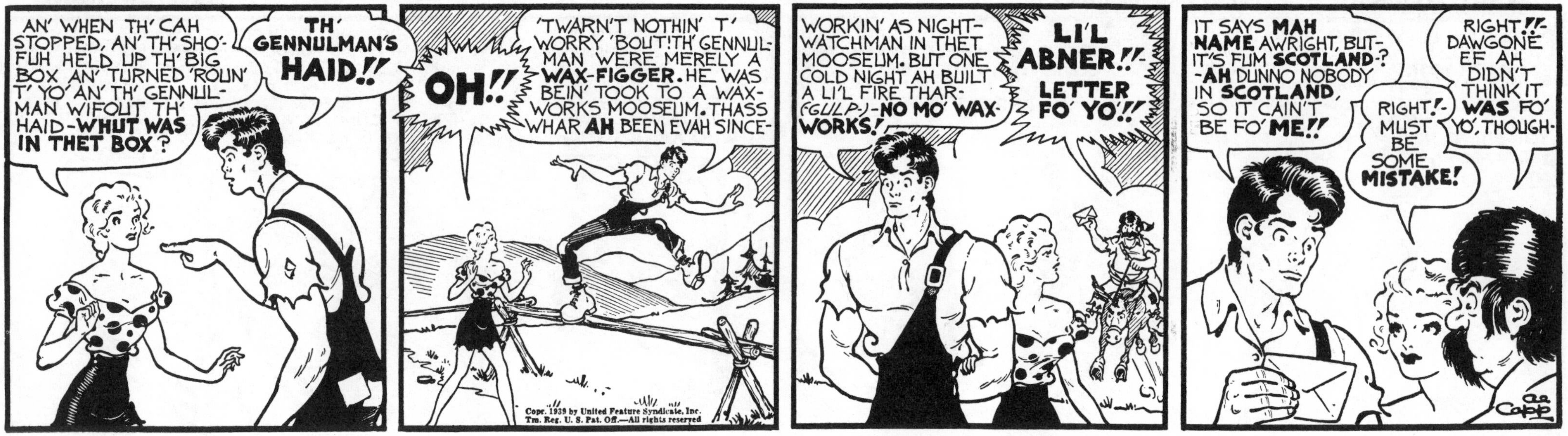
AN' WHEN TH' CAH STOPPED, AN' TH' SHO'-FUH HELD UP TH' BIG BOX AN' TURNED 'ROUN' T' YO' AN' TH' GENNULMAN WIFOUT TH' HAID-WHUT WAS IN THET BOX?
TH' GENNULMAN'S HAID!!
OH!!
'TWARN'T NOTHIN' T' WORRY 'BOUT! TH' GENNULMAN WERE MERELY A WAX-FIGGER. HE WAS BEIN' TOOK TO A WAX-WORKS MOOSEUM. THASS WHAR AH BEEN EVAH SINCE-
Copr. 1939 by United Feature Syndicate, Inc. Tm. Reg. U. S. Pat. Off.—All rights reserved
WORKIN' AS NIGHT-WATCHMAN IN THET MOOSEUM. BUT ONE COLD NIGHT AH BUILT A LI'L FIRE THAR-(GULP-)-NO MO' WAX-WORKS!
LI'L ABNER!!- LETTER FO' YO'!!
IT SAYS MAH NAME AWRIGHT, BUT-IT'S FUM SCOTLAND-? -AH DUNNO NOBODY IN SCOTLAND, SO IT CAIN'T BE FO' ME!!
RIGHT!- MUST BE SOME MISTAKE!
RIGHT!!- DAWGONE EF AH DIDN'T THINK IT WAS FO' YO', THOUGH-

LI'L ABNER — And So to Bed— — By Al Capp

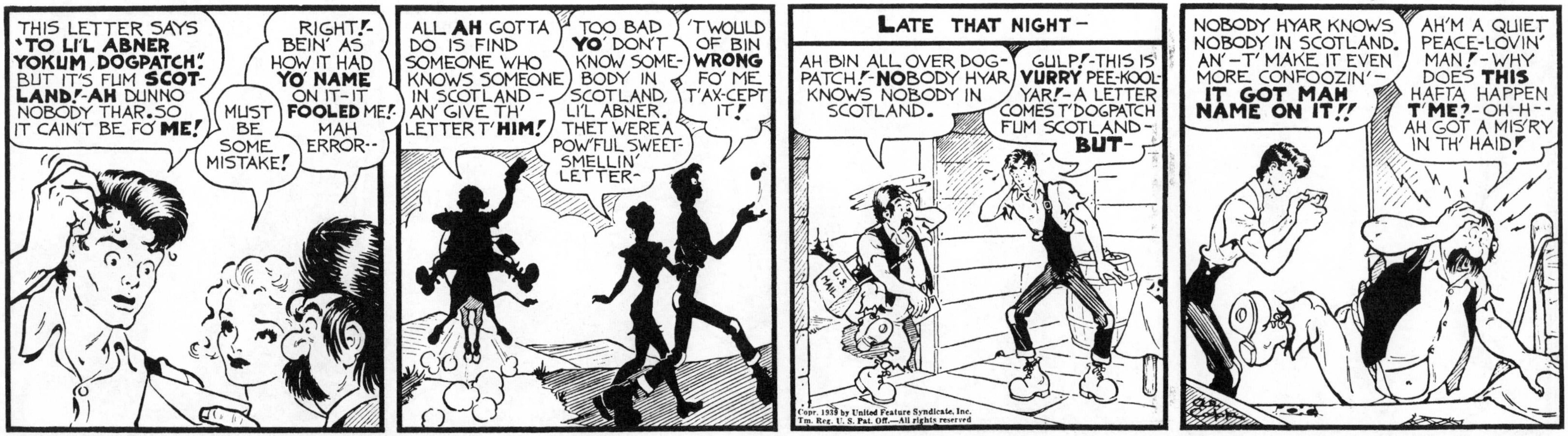
THIS LETTER SAYS "TO LI'L ABNER YOKUM, DOGPATCH." BUT IT'S FUM SCOTLAND!-AH DUNNO NOBODY THAR. SO IT CAIN'T BE FO' ME!
MUST BE SOME MISTAKE!
RIGHT!- BEIN' AS HOW IT HAD YO' NAME ON IT-IT FOOLED ME!- MAH ERROR--
ALL AH GOTTA DO IS FIND SOMEONE WHO KNOWS SOMEONE IN SCOTLAND - AN' GIVE TH' LETTER T' HIM!
TOO BAD YO' DON'T KNOW SOMEBODY IN SCOTLAND, LI'L ABNER. THET WERE A POW'FUL SWEET-SMELLIN' LETTER-
'TWOULD OF BIN WRONG FO' ME T'AX-CEPT IT!
LATE THAT NIGHT-
AH BIN ALL OVER DOGPATCH!-NOBODY HYAR KNOWS NOBODY IN SCOTLAND.
GULP!-THIS IS VURRY PEE-KOOLYAR!-A LETTER COMES T'DOGPATCH FUM SCOTLAND-BUT-
U.S. MAIL
Copr. 1939 by United Feature Syndicate, Inc. Tm. Reg. U. S. Pat. Off.—All rights reserved
NOBODY HYAR KNOWS NOBODY IN SCOTLAND. AN'-T' MAKE IT EVEN MORE CONFOOZIN'- IT GOT MAH NAME ON IT!!
AH'M A QUIET PEACE-LOVIN' MAN!-WHY DOES THIS HAFTA HAPPEN T'ME?-OH-H-- AH GOT A MIS'RY IN TH' HAID!

LI'L ABNER
And So to Bed—Part Two
By Al Capp

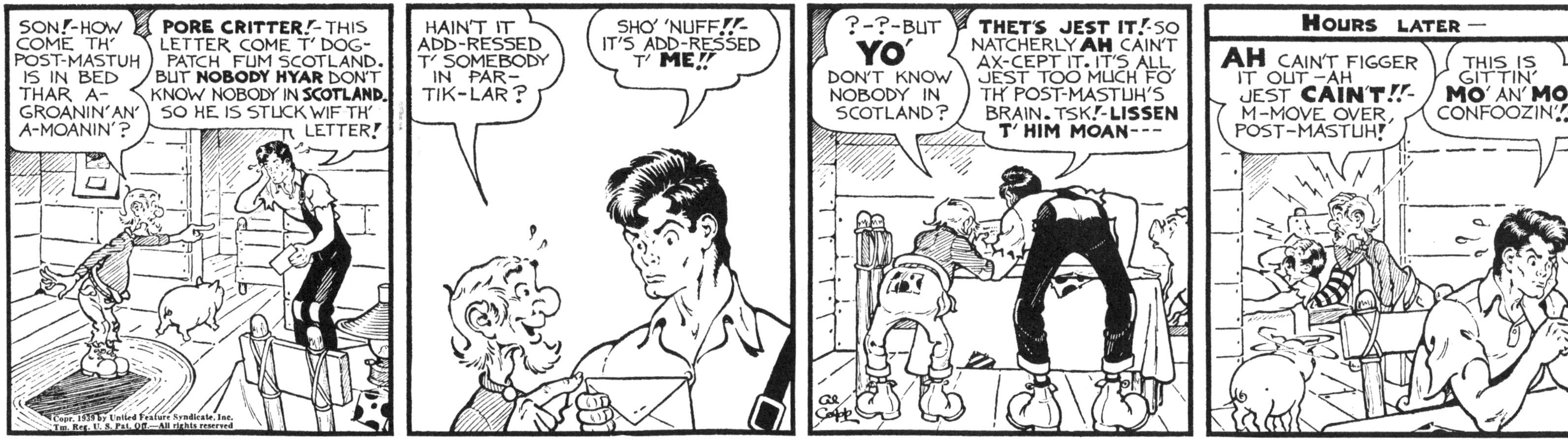
SON!-HOW COME TH' POST-MASTUH IS IN BED THAR A-GROANIN' AN' A-MOANIN'?
PORE CRITTER!-THIS LETTER COME T' DOG-PATCH FUM SCOTLAND. BUT NOBODY HYAR DON'T KNOW NOBODY IN SCOTLAND. SO HE IS STUCK WIF TH' LETTER!
HAIN'T IT ADD-RESSED T' SOMEBODY IN PAR-TIK-LAR?
SHO' 'NUFF!!-IT'S ADD-RESSED T' ME!!
?-?-BUT YO' DON'T KNOW NOBODY IN SCOTLAND?
THET'S JEST IT!-SO NATCHERLY AH CAIN'T AX-CEPT IT. IT'S ALL JEST TOO MUCH FO' TH' POST-MASTUH'S BRAIN. TSK!-LISSEN T' HIM MOAN---
HOURS LATER—
AH CAIN'T FIGGER IT OUT-AH JEST CAIN'T!!-M-MOVE OVER, POST-MASTUH!
THIS IS GITTIN' MO' AN' MO' CONFOOZIN'!!
Copr. 1939 by United Feature Syndicate, Inc. Tm. Reg. U. S. Pat. Off.—All rights reserved

LI'L ABNER
And So to Bed—Part Three
By Al Capp

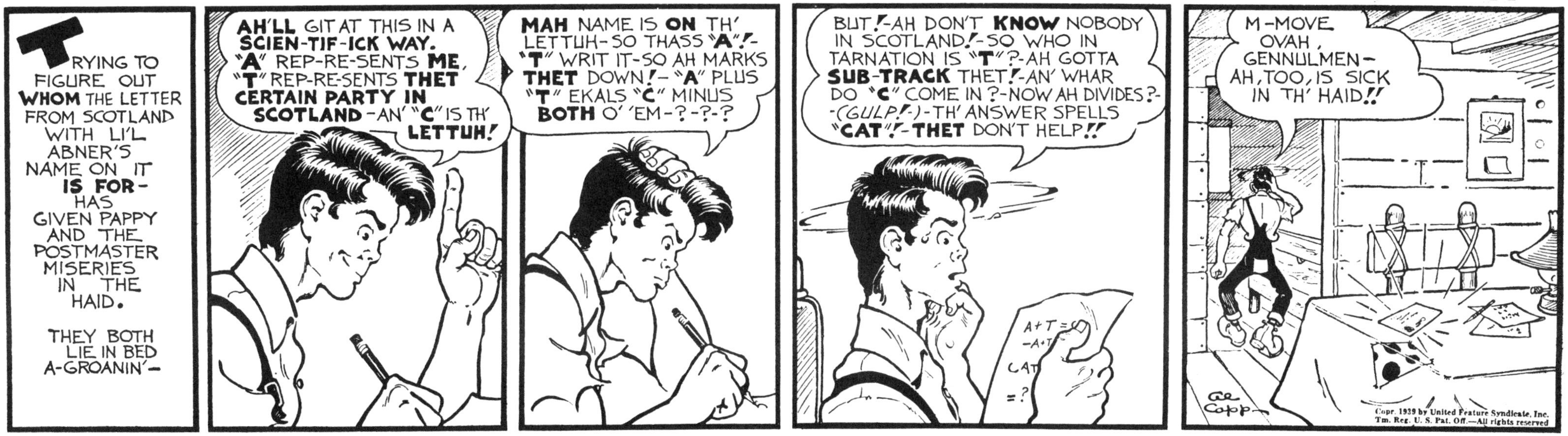
TRYING TO FIGURE OUT WHOM THE LETTER FROM SCOTLAND WITH LI'L ABNER'S NAME ON IT IS FOR-HAS GIVEN PAPPY AND THE POSTMASTER MISERIES IN THE HAID.
THEY BOTH LIE IN BED A-GROANIN'-
AH'LL GIT AT THIS IN A SCIEN-TIF-ICK WAY. "A" REP-RE-SENTS ME, "T" REP-RE-SENTS THET CERTAIN PARTY IN SCOTLAND-AN' "C" IS TH' LETTUH!
MAH NAME IS ON TH' LETTUH-SO THASS "A"!-"T" WRIT IT-SO AH MARKS THET DOWN!-"A" PLUS "T" EKALS "C" MINUS BOTH O' 'EM-?-?-?
BUT!-AH DON'T KNOW NOBODY IN SCOTLAND!-SO WHO IN TARNATION IS "T"?-AH GOTTA SUB-TRACK THET!-AN' WHAR DO "C" COME IN?-NOW AH DIVIDES?-(GULP!-)-TH' ANSWER SPELLS "CAT"!-THET DON'T HELP!!
M-MOVE OVAH, GENNULMEN-AH, TOO, IS SICK IN TH' HAID!!
Copr. 1939 by United Feature Syndicate, Inc. Tm. Reg. U. S. Pat. Off.—All rights reserved

LI'L ABNER   Fo' th' Rest o' Yo' Natcheral Life?   By Al Capp

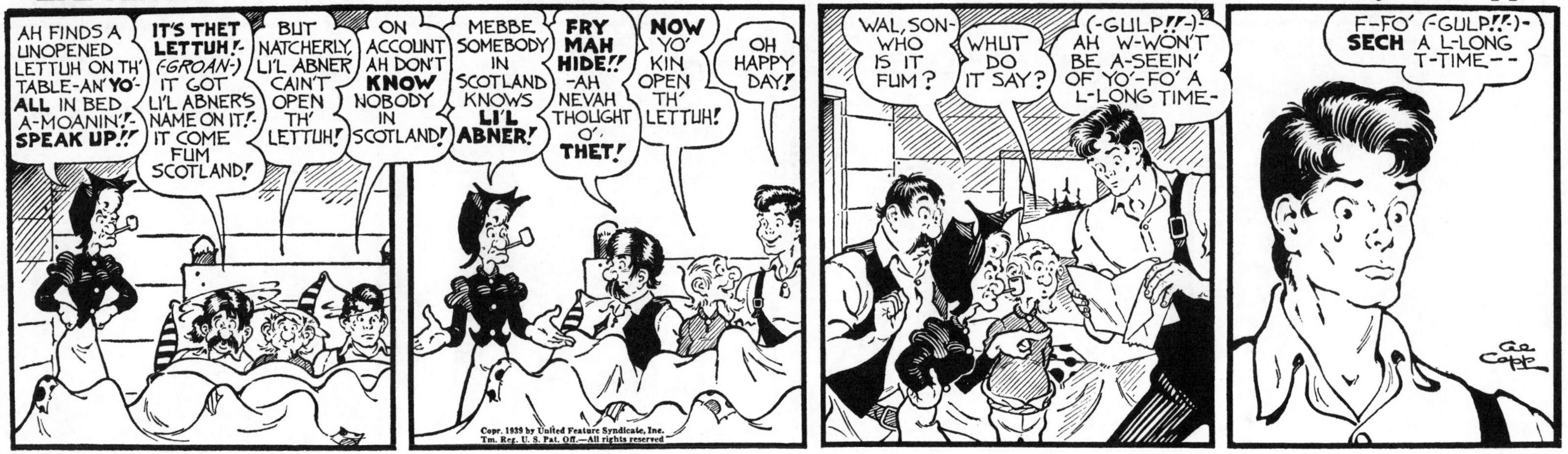

AH FINDS A UNOPENED LETTUH ON TH' TABLE-AN' **YO'-ALL** IN BED A-MOANIN'!- **SPEAK UP!!**
IT'S THET LETTUH!- (-GROAN-) IT GOT LI'L ABNER'S NAME ON IT!- IT COME FUM SCOTLAND!
BUT NATCHERLY, LI'L ABNER CAIN'T OPEN TH' LETTUH!
ON ACCOUNT AH DON'T **KNOW** NOBODY IN SCOTLAND!
MEBBE SOMEBODY IN SCOTLAND KNOWS **LI'L ABNER!**
FRY MAH HIDE!! -AH NEVAH THOUGHT O' **THET!**
NOW YO' KIN OPEN TH' LETTUH!
OH HAPPY DAY!
Copr. 1939 by United Feature Syndicate, Inc. Tm. Reg. U. S. Pat. Off.—All rights reserved
WAL, SON- WHO IS IT FUM?
WHUT DO IT SAY?
(-GULP!!-)- AH W-WON'T BE A-SEEIN' OF YO'-FO' A L-LONG TIME-
F-FO' (-GULP!!-)- **SECH** A L-LONG T-TIME--
Al Capp

LI'L ABNER   The Moors, Toujours the Moors—   By Al Capp

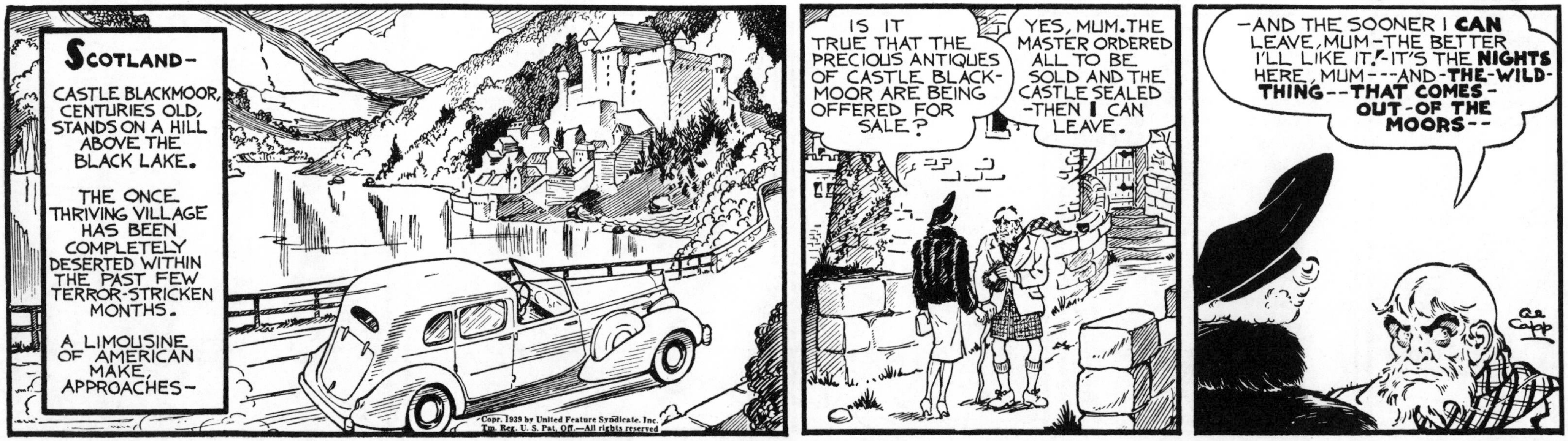

SCOTLAND-
CASTLE BLACKMOOR, CENTURIES OLD, STANDS ON A HILL ABOVE THE BLACK LAKE.
THE ONCE THRIVING VILLAGE HAS BEEN COMPLETELY DESERTED WITHIN THE PAST FEW TERROR-STRICKEN MONTHS.
A LIMOUSINE OF AMERICAN MAKE, APPROACHES-
Copr. 1939 by United Feature Syndicate, Inc. Tm. Reg. U. S. Pat. Off.—All rights reserved
IS IT TRUE THAT THE PRECIOUS ANTIQUES OF CASTLE BLACK-MOOR ARE BEING OFFERED FOR SALE?
YES, MUM. THE MASTER ORDERED ALL TO BE SOLD AND THE CASTLE SEALED -THEN **I** CAN LEAVE.
-AND THE SOONER **I CAN** LEAVE, MUM-THE BETTER I'LL LIKE IT!-IT'S THE **NIGHTS** HERE, MUM---AND-**THE-WILD-THING--THAT COMES-OUT-OF THE MOORS**--
Al Capp

LI'L ABNER — Animal, Vegetable or Mineral? — By Al Capp

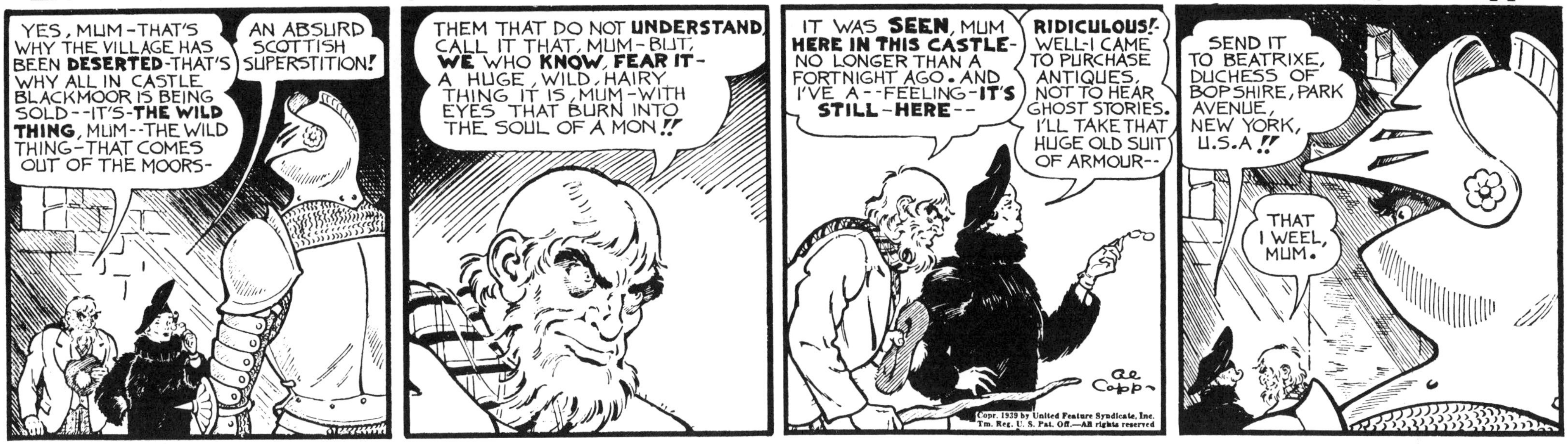
YES, MUM-THAT'S WHY THE VILLAGE HAS BEEN **DESERTED**-THAT'S WHY ALL IN CASTLE BLACKMOOR IS BEING SOLD--IT'S-**THE WILD THING**, MUM--THE WILD THING-THAT COMES OUT OF THE MOORS-
AN ABSURD SCOTTISH SUPERSTITION!
THEM THAT DO NOT **UNDERSTAND** CALL IT THAT, MUM-BUT, **WE** WHO **KNOW**, **FEAR IT**-A HUGE, WILD, HAIRY THING IT IS, MUM-WITH EYES THAT BURN INTO THE SOUL OF A MON!!
IT WAS **SEEN**, MUM **HERE IN THIS CASTLE**-NO LONGER THAN A FORTNIGHT AGO. AND I'VE A--FEELING-**IT'S STILL-HERE**--
RIDICULOUS!-WELL-I CAME TO PURCHASE ANTIQUES, NOT TO HEAR GHOST STORIES. I'LL TAKE THAT HUGE OLD SUIT OF ARMOUR--
Al Capp
Copr. 1939 by United Feature Syndicate, Inc. Tm. Reg. U. S. Pat. Off.—All rights reserved
SEND IT TO BEATRIXE, DUCHESS OF BOPSHIRE, PARK AVENUE, NEW YORK, U.S.A!!
THAT I WEEL, MUM.

LI'L ABNER — It Takes the High Road — By Al Capp

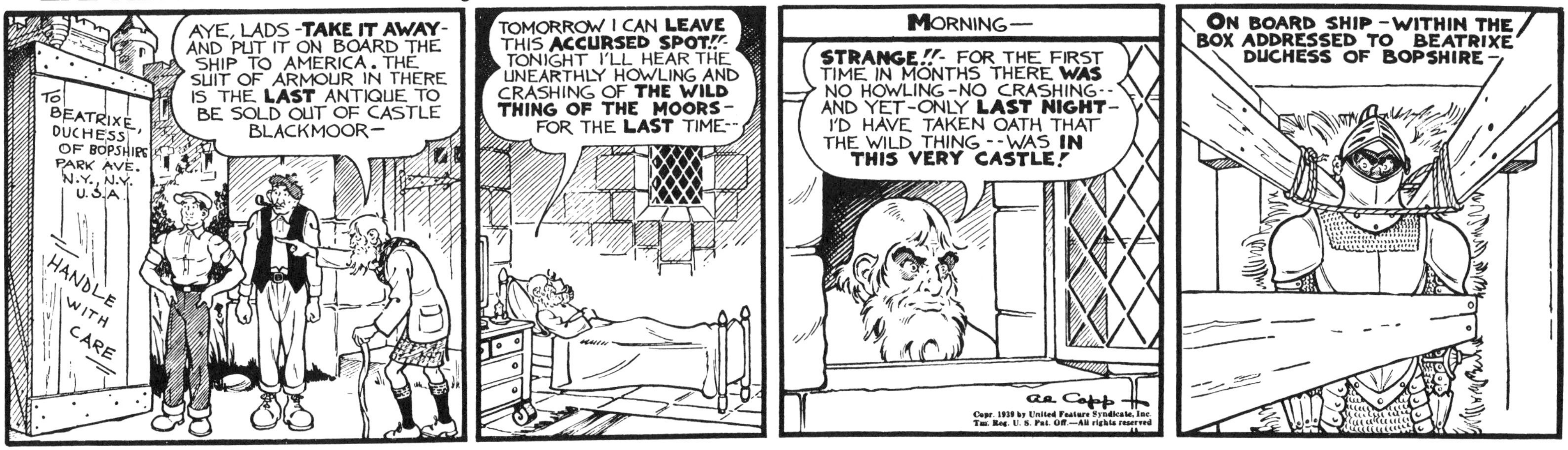
TO BEATRIXE, DUCHESS OF BOPSHIRE PARK AVE. N.Y., N.Y. U.S.A
HANDLE WITH CARE
AYE, LADS-**TAKE IT AWAY**-AND PUT IT ON BOARD THE SHIP TO AMERICA. THE SUIT OF ARMOUR IN THERE IS THE **LAST** ANTIQUE TO BE SOLD OUT OF CASTLE BLACKMOOR-
TOMORROW I CAN **LEAVE** THIS **ACCURSED SPOT!!**-TONIGHT I'LL HEAR THE UNEARTHLY HOWLING AND CRASHING OF **THE WILD THING OF THE MOORS**-FOR THE **LAST** TIME--
MORNING—
STRANGE!!- FOR THE FIRST TIME IN MONTHS THERE **WAS** NO HOWLING-NO CRASHING--AND YET-ONLY **LAST NIGHT**-I'D HAVE TAKEN OATH THAT THE WILD THING--WAS **IN THIS VERY CASTLE!**
Al Capp
Copr. 1939 by United Feature Syndicate, Inc. Tm. Reg. U. S. Pat. Off.—All rights reserved
ON BOARD SHIP-WITHIN THE BOX ADDRESSED TO BEATRIXE DUCHESS OF BOPSHIRE-

LI'L ABNER A Gentleman of the Old School By Al Capp

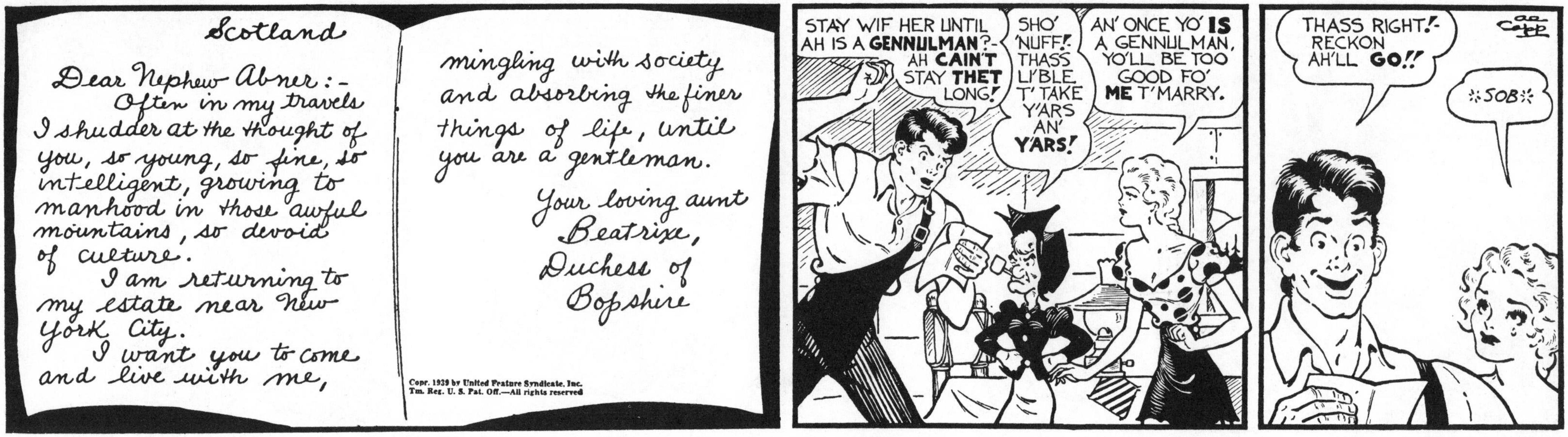
Scotland
Dear Nephew Abner:- Often in my travels I shudder at the thought of you, so young, so fine, so intelligent, growing to manhood in those awful mountains, so devoid of culture.
I am returning to my estate near New York City.
I want you to come and live with me, mingling with society and absorbing the finer things of life, until you are a gentleman.
Your loving aunt Beatrixe, Duchess of Bopshire
Copr. 1939 by United Feature Syndicate, Inc. Tm. Reg. U. S. Pat. Off.—All rights reserved
STAY WIF HER UNTIL AH IS A **GENNULMAN**?- AH **CAIN'T** STAY **THET** LONG!
SHO' 'NUFF! THASS LI'BLE T' TAKE Y'ARS AN' **Y'ARS!**
AN' ONCE YO' **IS** A GENNULMAN, YO'LL BE TOO GOOD FO' **ME** T'MARRY.
THASS RIGHT!- RECKON AH'LL **GO!!**
SOB

LI'L ABNER An Ideal Location By Al Capp

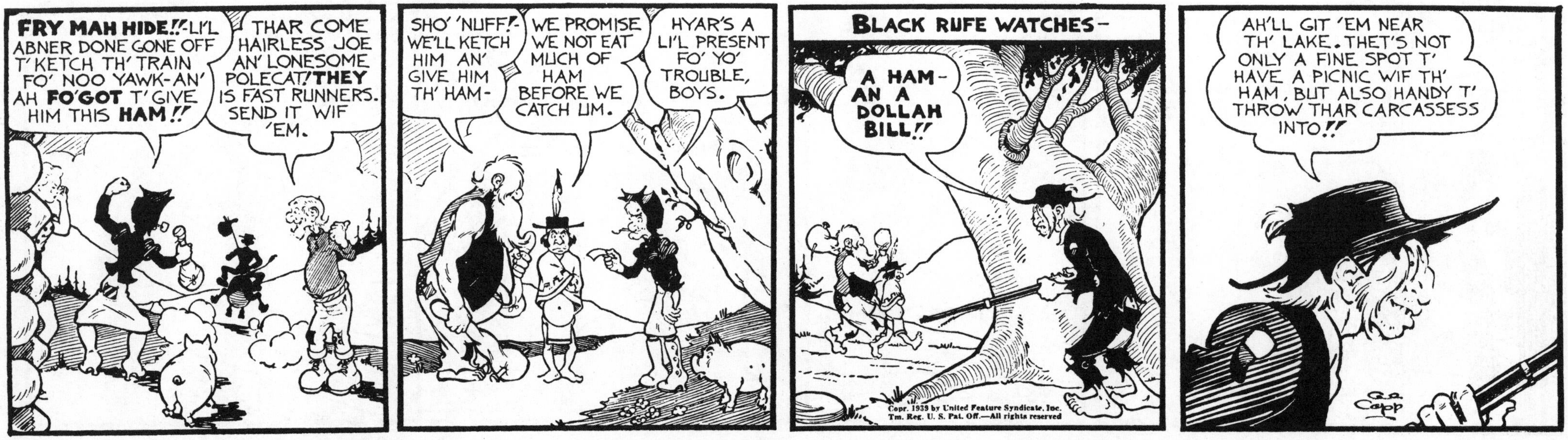
FRY MAH HIDE!!-LI'L ABNER DONE GONE OFF T'KETCH TH' TRAIN FO' NOO YAWK-AN' AH **FO'GOT** T'GIVE HIM THIS **HAM!!**
THAR COME HAIRLESS JOE AN' LONESOME POLECAT! **THEY** IS FAST RUNNERS. SEND IT WIF 'EM.
SHO' 'NUFF!- WE'LL KETCH HIM AN' GIVE HIM TH' HAM-
WE PROMISE WE NOT EAT MUCH OF HAM BEFORE WE CATCH UM.
HYAR'S A LI'L PRESENT FO' YO' TROUBLE, BOYS.
BLACK RUFE WATCHES-
A HAM- AN A DOLLAH BILL!!
Copr. 1939 by United Feature Syndicate, Inc. Tm. Reg. U. S. Pat. Off.—All rights reserved
AH'LL GIT 'EM NEAR TH' LAKE. THET'S NOT ONLY A FINE SPOT T' HAVE A PICNIC WIF TH' HAM, BUT ALSO HANDY T' THROW THAR CARCASSESS INTO!!

LI'L ABNER   Death Takes No Holiday   By Al Capp

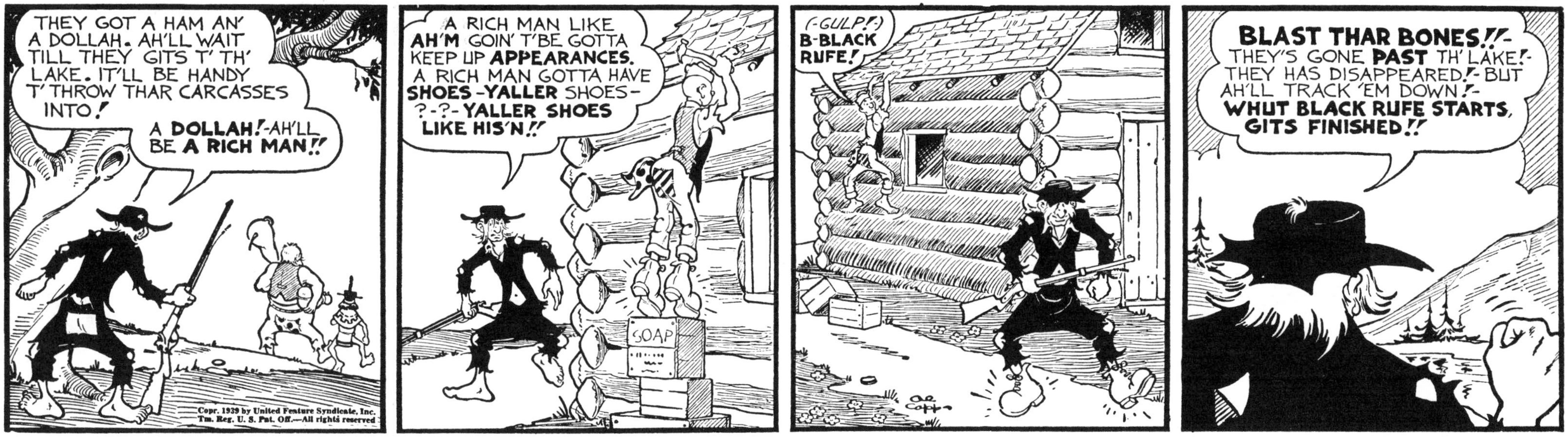
THEY GOT A HAM AN' A DOLLAH. AH'LL WAIT TILL THEY GITS T' TH' LAKE. IT'LL BE HANDY T' THROW THAR CARCASSES INTO!
A DOLLAH!-AH'LL BE A RICH MAN!!
Copr. 1939 by United Feature Syndicate, Inc. Tm. Reg. U. S. Pat. Off.—All rights reserved
A RICH MAN LIKE AH'M GOIN' T'BE GOTTA KEEP UP APPEARANCES. A RICH MAN GOTTA HAVE SHOES-YALLER SHOES- ?-?-YALLER SHOES LIKE HIS'N!!
SOAP
(-GULP!-) B-BLACK RUFE!
BLAST THAR BONES!!-THEY'S GONE PAST TH' LAKE!-THEY HAS DISAPPEARED!-BUT AH'LL TRACK 'EM DOWN!-WHUT BLACK RUFE STARTS, GITS FINISHED!!

LI'L ABNER   Maybe It's a Fire Sale!   By Al Capp

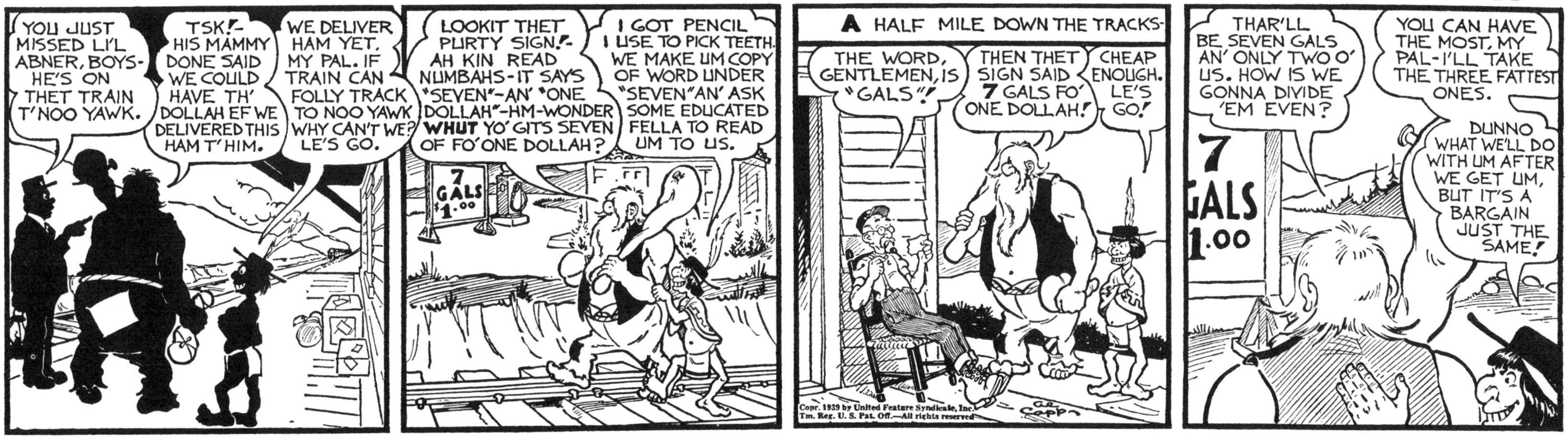
YOU JUST MISSED LI'L ABNER, BOYS-HE'S ON THET TRAIN T'NOO YAWK.
TSK!-HIS MAMMY DONE SAID WE COULD HAVE TH' DOLLAH EF WE DELIVERED THIS HAM T'HIM.
WE DELIVER HAM YET, MY PAL. IF TRAIN CAN FOLLY TRACK TO NOO YAWK WHY CAN'T WE? LE'S GO.
LOOKIT THET PURTY SIGN!-AH KIN READ NUMBAHS-IT SAYS "SEVEN"-AN' "ONE DOLLAH"-HM-WONDER WHUT YO' GITS SEVEN OF FO' ONE DOLLAH?
I GOT PENCIL I USE TO PICK TEETH. WE MAKE UM COPY OF WORD UNDER "SEVEN" AN' ASK SOME EDUCATED FELLA TO READ UM TO US.
7 GALS $1.00
A HALF MILE DOWN THE TRACKS-
THE WORD, GENTLEMEN, IS "GALS"!
THEN THET SIGN SAID 7 GALS FO' ONE DOLLAH!
CHEAP ENOUGH. LE'S GO!
Copr. 1939 by United Feature Syndicate, Inc. Tm. Reg. U. S. Pat. Off.—All rights reserved
THAR'LL BE SEVEN GALS AN' ONLY TWO O' US. HOW IS WE GONNA DIVIDE 'EM EVEN?
YOU CAN HAVE THE MOST, MY PAL-I'LL TAKE THE THREE FATTEST ONES.
DUNNO WHAT WE'LL DO WITH UM AFTER WE GET UM, BUT IT'S A BARGAIN JUST THE SAME!

LI'L ABNER The Villain Still Pursues 'Em By Al Capp

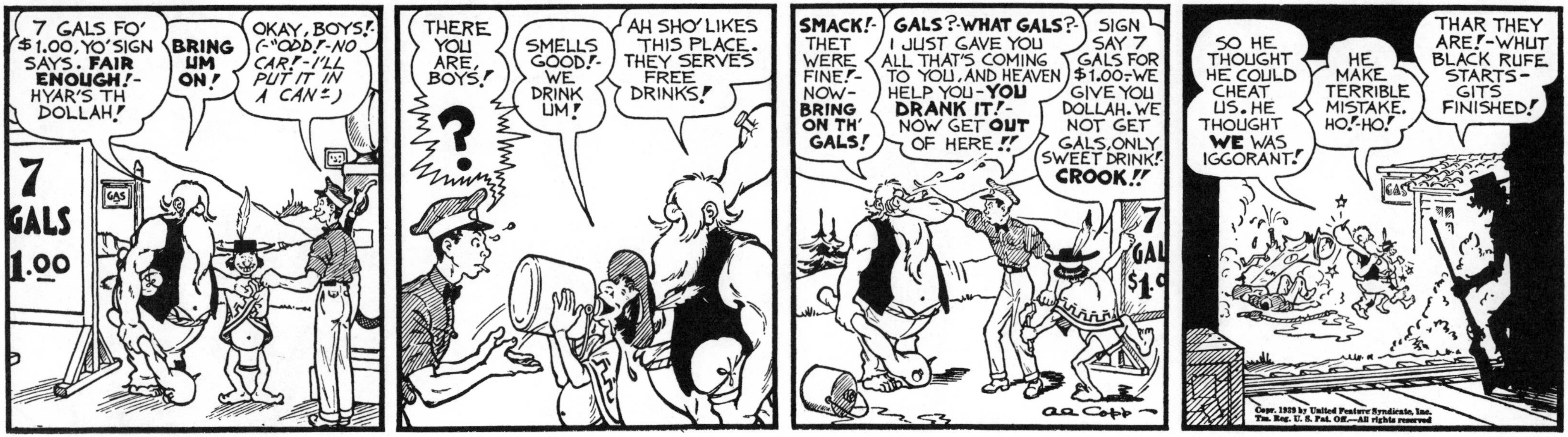

7 GALS FO' $1.00, YO' SIGN SAYS. FAIR ENOUGH!- HYAR'S TH DOLLAH!
BRING UM ON!
OKAY, BOYS!- (-"ODD!-NO CAR!-I'LL PUT IT IN A CAN"-)
7 GALS 1.00
GAS
THERE YOU ARE, BOYS!
?
SMELLS GOOD!- WE DRINK UM!
AH SHO' LIKES THIS PLACE. THEY SERVES FREE DRINKS!
SMACK!- THET WERE FINE!- NOW- BRING ON TH' GALS!
GALS?-WHAT GALS?- I JUST GAVE YOU ALL THAT'S COMING TO YOU, AND HEAVEN HELP YOU-YOU DRANK IT!- NOW GET OUT OF HERE!!
SIGN SAY 7 GALS FOR $1.00-WE GIVE YOU DOLLAH. WE NOT GET GALS, ONLY SWEET DRINK!- CROOK!!
SO HE THOUGHT HE COULD CHEAT US. HE THOUGHT WE WAS IGGORANT!
HE MAKE TERRIBLE MISTAKE. HO!-HO!
THAR THEY ARE!-WHUT BLACK RUFE STARTS- GITS FINISHED!
Copr. 1939 by United Feature Syndicate, Inc. Tm. Reg. U. S. Pat. Off.—All rights reserved

LI'L ABNER One-Track Minds By Al Capp

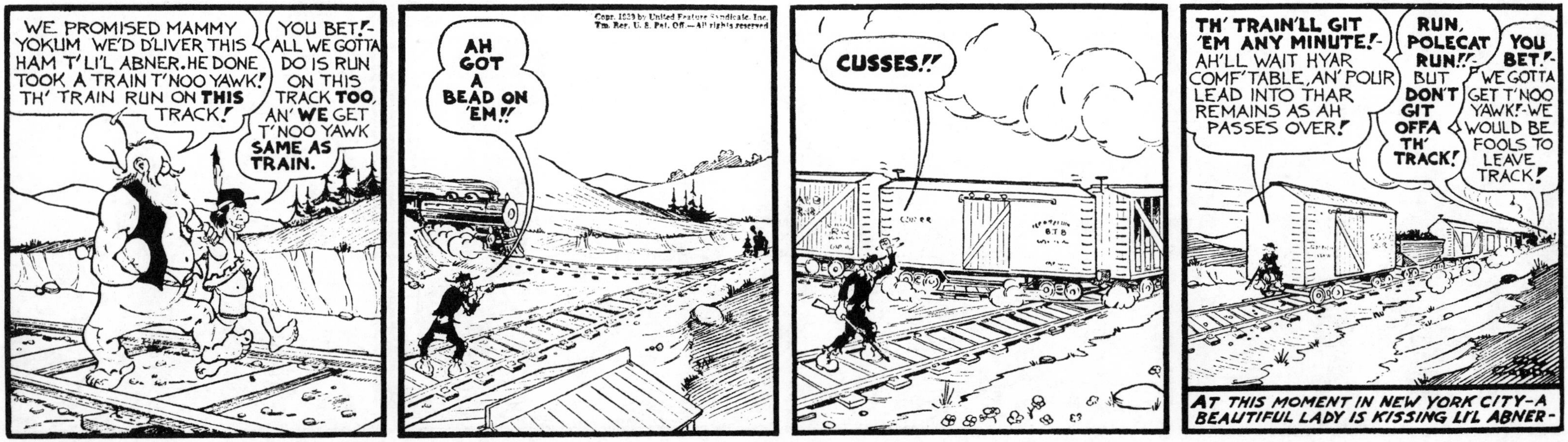

WE PROMISED MAMMY YOKUM WE'D D'LIVER THIS HAM T' LI'L ABNER. HE DONE TOOK A TRAIN T'NOO YAWK! TH' TRAIN RUN ON THIS TRACK!
YOU BET!- ALL WE GOTTA DO IS RUN ON THIS TRACK TOO, AN' WE GET T'NOO YAWK SAME AS TRAIN.
Copr. 1939 by United Feature Syndicate, Inc. Tm. Reg. U. S. Pat. Off.—All rights reserved
AH GOT A BEAD ON 'EM!!
CUSSES!!
TH' TRAIN'LL GIT 'EM ANY MINUTE!- AH'LL WAIT HYAR COMF'TABLE, AN' POUR LEAD INTO THAR REMAINS AS AH PASSES OVER!
RUN, POLECAT RUN!!- BUT DON'T GIT OFFA TH' TRACK!
YOU BET!- WE GOTTA GET T'NOO YAWK!- WE WOULD BE FOOLS TO LEAVE TRACK!
AT THIS MOMENT IN NEW YORK CITY-A BEAUTIFUL LADY IS KISSING LI'L ABNER-

LI'L ABNER The Way of the Transgressor By Al Capp

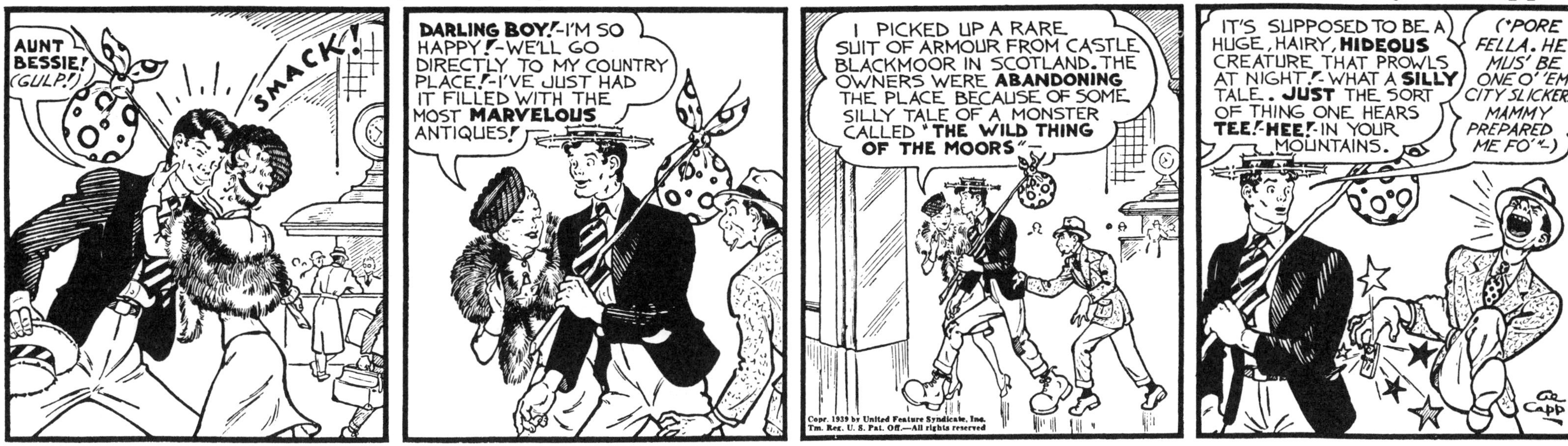
AUNT BESSIE! (GULP!)
SMACK!
DARLING BOY!-I'M SO HAPPY!-WE'LL GO DIRECTLY TO MY COUNTRY PLACE!-I'VE JUST HAD IT FILLED WITH THE MOST MARVELOUS ANTIQUES!
I PICKED UP A RARE SUIT OF ARMOUR FROM CASTLE BLACKMOOR IN SCOTLAND. THE OWNERS WERE ABANDONING THE PLACE BECAUSE OF SOME SILLY TALE OF A MONSTER CALLED "THE WILD THING OF THE MOORS"-
Copr. 1939 by United Feature Syndicate, Inc. Tm. Reg. U. S. Pat. Off.—All rights reserved
IT'S SUPPOSED TO BE A HUGE, HAIRY, HIDEOUS CREATURE THAT PROWLS AT NIGHT!-WHAT A SILLY TALE. JUST THE SORT OF THING ONE HEARS TEE!-HEE!-IN YOUR MOUNTAINS.
("PORE FELLA. HE MUS' BE ONE O' 'EM CITY SLICKERS MAMMY PREPARED ME FO'"-)
AL CAPP

LI'L ABNER The Upworthy Boys?? By Al Capp

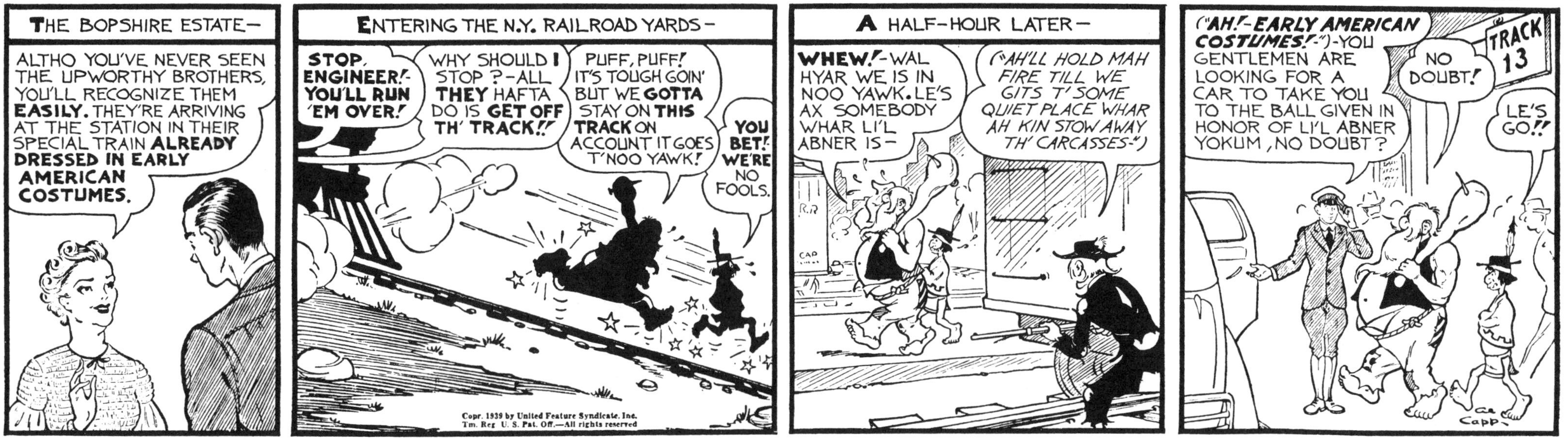
THE BOPSHIRE ESTATE-
ALTHO YOU'VE NEVER SEEN THE UPWORTHY BROTHERS, YOU'LL RECOGNIZE THEM EASILY. THEY'RE ARRIVING AT THE STATION IN THEIR SPECIAL TRAIN ALREADY DRESSED IN EARLY AMERICAN COSTUMES.
ENTERING THE N.Y. RAILROAD YARDS-
STOP, ENGINEER!-YOU'LL RUN 'EM OVER!
WHY SHOULD I STOP?-ALL THEY HAFTA DO IS GET OFF TH' TRACK!!
PUFF, PUFF! IT'S TOUGH GOIN' BUT WE GOTTA STAY ON THIS TRACK ON ACCOUNT IT GOES T'NOO YAWK!
YOU BET!-WE'RE NO FOOLS.
Copr. 1939 by United Feature Syndicate, Inc. Tm. Reg. U. S. Pat. Off.—All rights reserved
A HALF-HOUR LATER-
WHEW!-WAL HYAR WE IS IN NOO YAWK. LE'S AX SOMEBODY WHAR LI'L ABNER IS-
("AH'LL HOLD MAH FIRE TILL WE GITS T' SOME QUIET PLACE WHAR AH KIN STOW AWAY TH' CARCASSES-")
("AH!-EARLY AMERICAN COSTUMES!-")-YOU GENTLEMEN ARE LOOKING FOR A CAR TO TAKE YOU TO THE BALL GIVEN IN HONOR OF LI'L ABNER YOKUM, NO DOUBT?
TRACK 13
NO DOUBT!
LE'S GO!!
AL CAPP

LI'L ABNER They're a Dime a Dozen By Al Capp

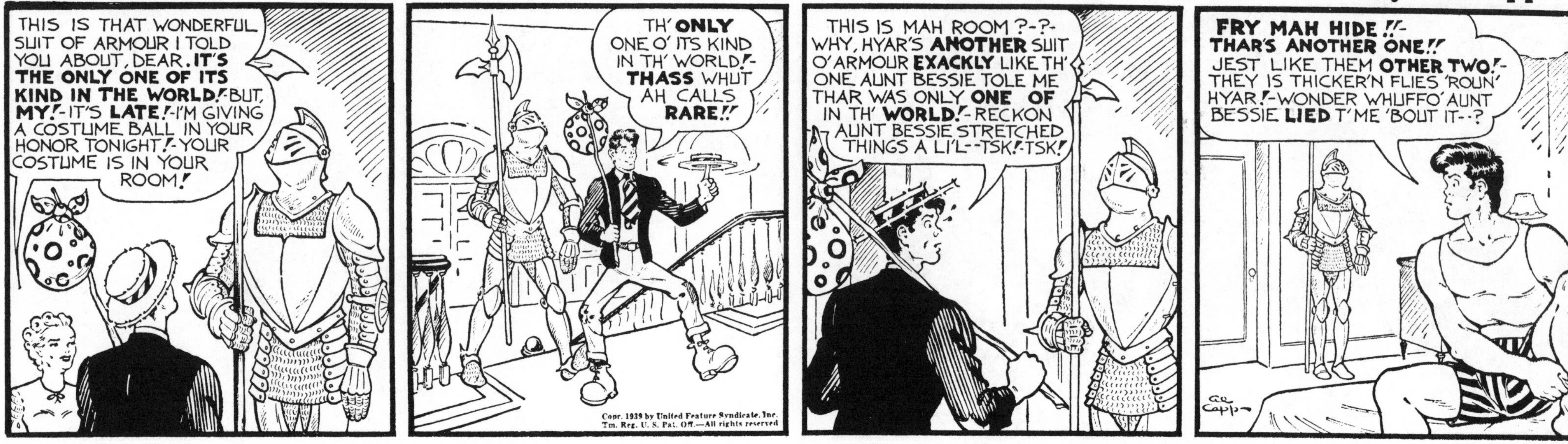
THIS IS THAT WONDERFUL SUIT OF ARMOUR I TOLD YOU ABOUT, DEAR. IT'S THE ONLY ONE OF ITS KIND IN THE WORLD!-BUT, MY!-IT'S LATE!-I'M GIVING A COSTUME BALL IN YOUR HONOR TONIGHT!-YOUR COSTUME IS IN YOUR ROOM!
TH' ONLY ONE O' ITS KIND IN TH' WORLD!-THASS WHUT AH CALLS RARE!!
Copr. 1939 by United Feature Syndicate, Inc. Tm. Reg. U. S. Pat. Off.—All rights reserved
THIS IS MAH ROOM?-?- WHY, HYAR'S ANOTHER SUIT O'ARMOUR EXACKLY LIKE TH' ONE AUNT BESSIE TOLE ME THAR WAS ONLY ONE OF IN TH' WORLD!-RECKON AUNT BESSIE STRETCHED THINGS A LI'L--TSK!-TSK!
FRY MAH HIDE!!- THAR'S ANOTHER ONE!! JEST LIKE THEM OTHER TWO!- THEY IS THICKER'N FLIES 'ROUN' HYAR!-WONDER WHUFFO' AUNT BESSIE LIED T'ME 'BOUT IT--?
Al Capp

LI'L ABNER Knight Wind By Al Capp

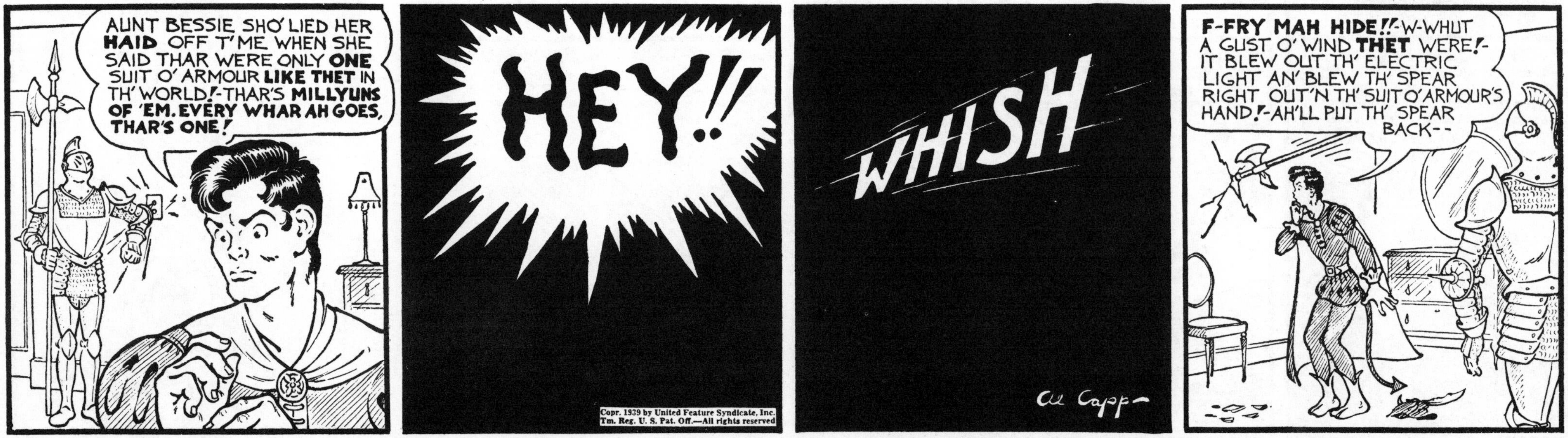
AUNT BESSIE SHO' LIED HER HAID OFF T'ME WHEN SHE SAID THAR WERE ONLY ONE SUIT O' ARMOUR LIKE THET IN TH' WORLD!-THAR'S MILLYUNS OF 'EM. EVERY WHAR AH GOES, THAR'S ONE!
HEY!!
Copr. 1939 by United Feature Syndicate, Inc. Tm. Reg. U. S. Pat. Off.—All rights reserved
WHISH
Al Capp
F-FRY MAH HIDE!!-W-WHUT A GUST O' WIND THET WERE!- IT BLEW OUT TH' ELECTRIC LIGHT AN' BLEW TH' SPEAR RIGHT OUT'N TH' SUIT O'ARMOUR'S HAND!-AH'LL PUT TH' SPEAR BACK--

LI'L ABNER The Way of a Lad With a Lass! By Al Capp

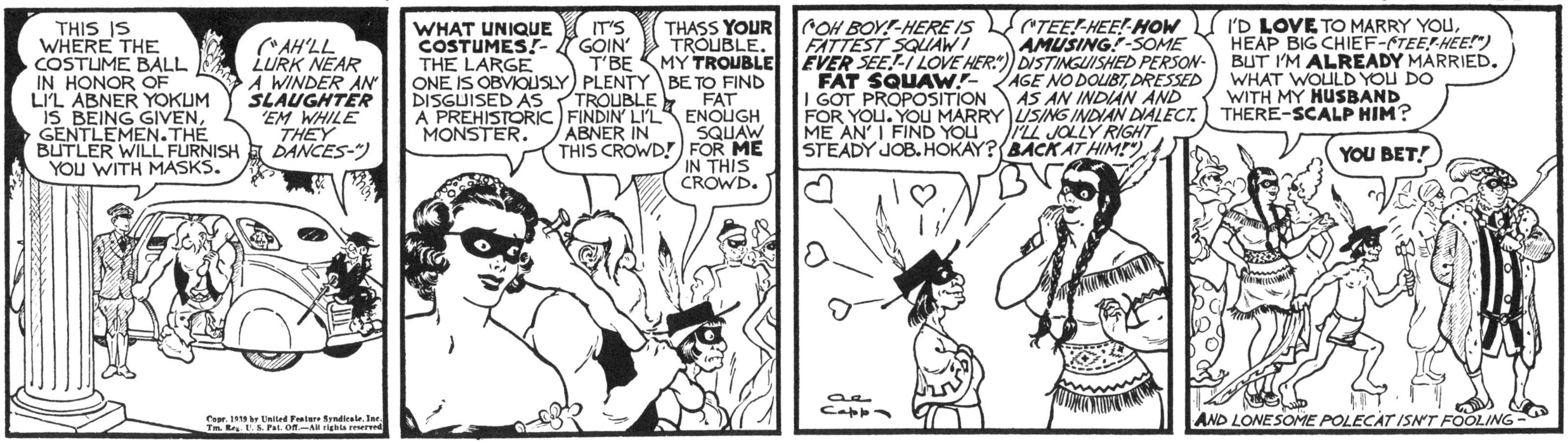
THIS IS WHERE THE COSTUME BALL IN HONOR OF LI'L ABNER YOKUM IS BEING GIVEN, GENTLEMEN. THE BUTLER WILL FURNISH YOU WITH MASKS.
("AH'LL LURK NEAR A WINDER AN' SLAUGHTER 'EM WHILE THEY DANCES-")
Copr. 1939 by United Feature Syndicate, Inc. Tm. Reg. U. S. Pat. Off.—All rights reserved
WHAT UNIQUE COSTUMES!- THE LARGE ONE IS OBVIOUSLY DISGUISED AS A PREHISTORIC MONSTER.
IT'S GOIN' T'BE PLENTY TROUBLE FINDIN' LI'L ABNER IN THIS CROWD!
THASS YOUR TROUBLE. MY TROUBLE BE TO FIND FAT ENOUGH SQUAW FOR ME IN THIS CROWD.
("OH BOY!-HERE IS FATTEST SQUAW I EVER SEE!-I LOVE HER.") FAT SQUAW!- I GOT PROPOSITION FOR YOU. YOU MARRY ME AN' I FIND YOU STEADY JOB. HOKAY?
("TEE!-HEE!-HOW AMUSING!-SOME DISTINGUISHED PERSONAGE NO DOUBT, DRESSED AS AN INDIAN AND USING INDIAN DIALECT. I'LL JOLLY RIGHT BACK AT HIM!")
I'D LOVE TO MARRY YOU, HEAP BIG CHIEF-("TEE!-HEE!") BUT I'M ALREADY MARRIED. WHAT WOULD YOU DO WITH MY HUSBAND THERE-SCALP HIM?
YOU BET!
AND LONESOME POLECAT ISN'T FOOLING-

LI'L ABNER Greater Love Hath No Man! By Al Capp

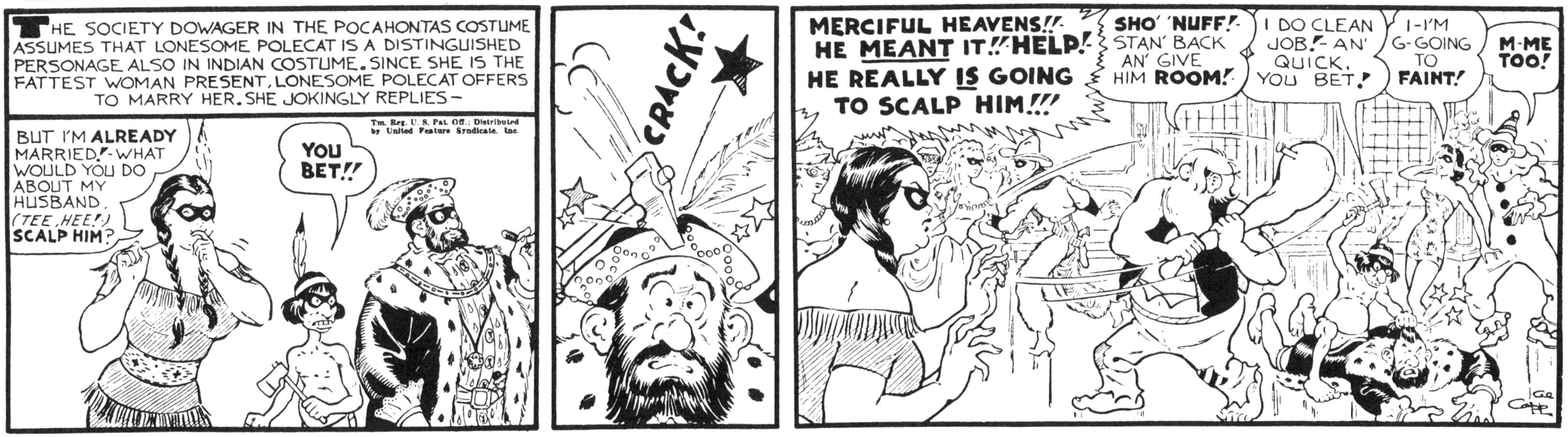
THE SOCIETY DOWAGER IN THE POCAHONTAS COSTUME ASSUMES THAT LONESOME POLECAT IS A DISTINGUISHED PERSONAGE ALSO IN INDIAN COSTUME. SINCE SHE IS THE FATTEST WOMAN PRESENT, LONESOME POLECAT OFFERS TO MARRY HER. SHE JOKINGLY REPLIES-
Tm. Reg. U. S. Pat. Off.; Distributed by United Feature Syndicate, Inc.
BUT I'M ALREADY MARRIED!-WHAT WOULD YOU DO ABOUT MY HUSBAND. (TEE, HEE!) SCALP HIM?
YOU BET!!
CRACK!
MERCIFUL HEAVENS!!- HE MEANT IT!!-HELP!- HE REALLY IS GOING TO SCALP HIM!!!
SHO' 'NUFF!- STAN' BACK AN' GIVE HIM ROOM!
I DO CLEAN JOB!- AN' QUICK, YOU BET!
I-I'M G-GOING TO FAINT!
M-ME TOO!

LI'L ABNER It's a Small World By Al Capp

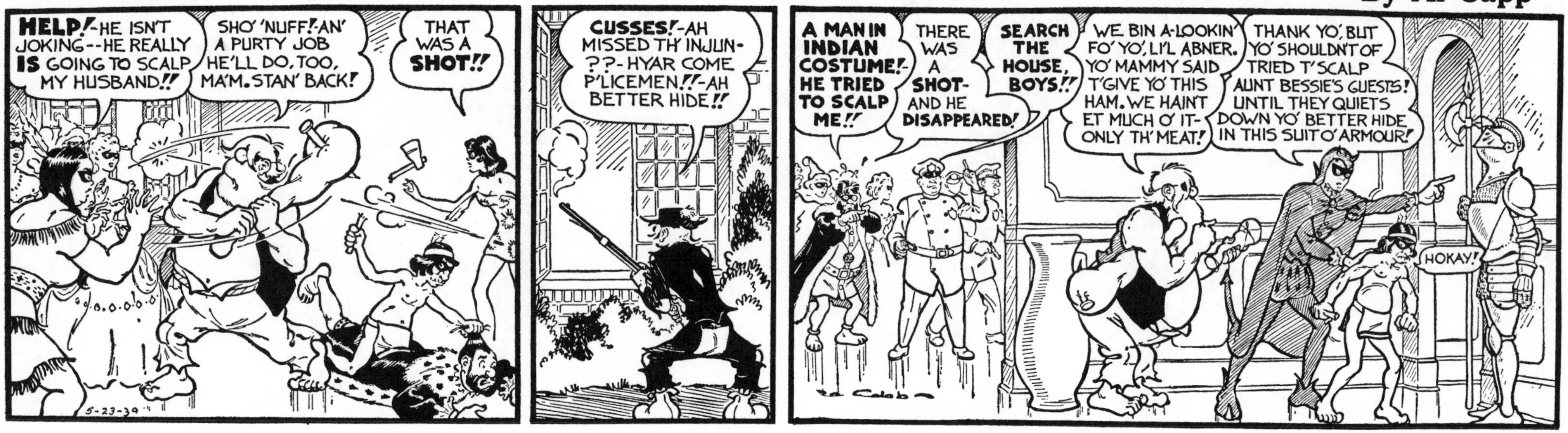
HELP!-HE ISN'T JOKING--HE REALLY IS GOING TO SCALP MY HUSBAND!!
SHO' 'NUFF!-AN' A PURTY JOB HE'LL DO, TOO, MA'M. STAN' BACK!
THAT WAS A SHOT!!
5-23-39
CUSSES!-AH MISSED TH' INJUN-??-HYAR COME P'LICEMEN!!-AH BETTER HIDE!!
A MAN IN INDIAN COSTUME!-HE TRIED TO SCALP ME!!
THERE WAS A SHOT-AND HE DISAPPEARED!
SEARCH THE HOUSE, BOYS!!
WE BIN A-LOOKIN' FO' YO', LI'L ABNER. YO' MAMMY SAID T'GIVE YO' THIS HAM. WE HAINT ET MUCH O' IT-ONLY TH' MEAT!
THANK YO', BUT YO' SHOULDN'T OF TRIED T'SCALP AUNT BESSIE'S GUESTS! UNTIL THEY QUIETS DOWN YO' BETTER HIDE IN THIS SUIT O' ARMOUR!
HOKAY!

LI'L ABNER Just the Tonic He Needs! By Al Capp

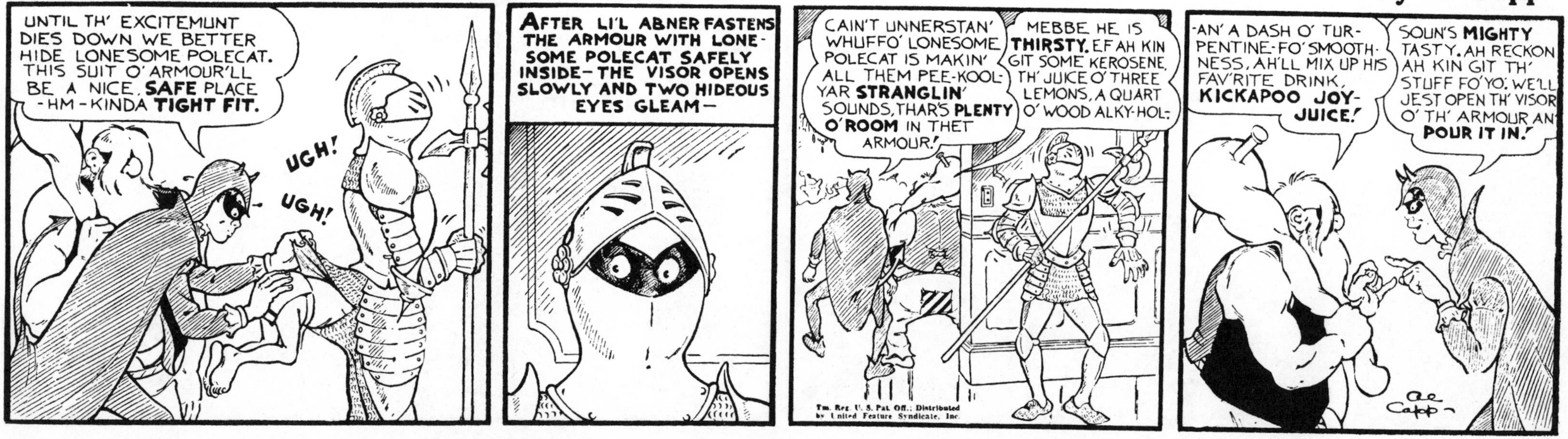
UNTIL TH' EXCITEMUNT DIES DOWN WE BETTER HIDE LONESOME POLECAT. THIS SUIT O' ARMOUR'LL BE A NICE, SAFE PLACE -HM-KINDA TIGHT FIT.
UGH!
UGH!
AFTER LI'L ABNER FASTENS THE ARMOUR WITH LONESOME POLECAT SAFELY INSIDE-THE VISOR OPENS SLOWLY AND TWO HIDEOUS EYES GLEAM-
CAIN'T UNNERSTAN' WHUFFO' LONESOME POLECAT IS MAKIN' ALL THEM PEE-KOOL-YAR STRANGLIN' SOUNDS, THAR'S PLENTY O' ROOM IN THET ARMOUR!
MEBBE HE IS THIRSTY. EF AH KIN GIT SOME KEROSENE, TH' JUICE O' THREE LEMONS, A QUART O' WOOD ALKY-HOL-
Tm. Reg. U. S. Pat. Off.; Distributed by United Feature Syndicate, Inc.
-AN' A DASH O' TURPENTINE-FO' SMOOTHNESS, AH'LL MIX UP HIS FAV'RITE DRINK, KICKAPOO JOY-JUICE!
SOUN'S MIGHTY TASTY. AH RECKON AH KIN GIT TH' STUFF FO' YO'. WE'LL JEST OPEN TH' VISOR O' TH' ARMOUR AN' POUR IT IN!
Al Capp

LI'L ABNER — A Kickapoo Kickup! — By Al Capp

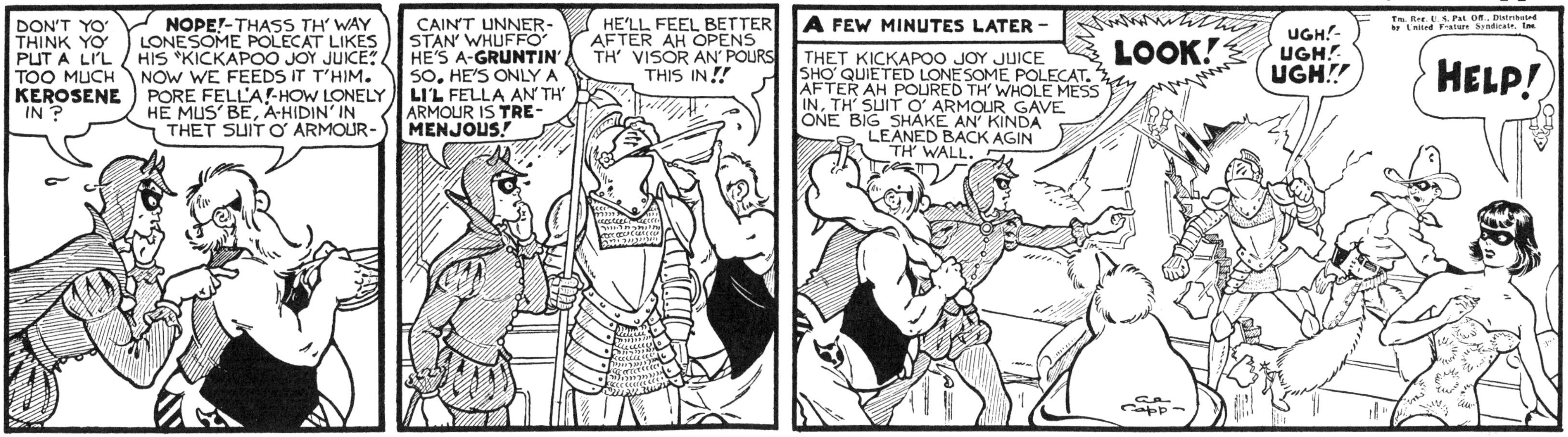

DON'T YO' THINK YO' PUT A LI'L TOO MUCH KEROSENE IN ?
NOPE!-THASS TH' WAY LONESOME POLECAT LIKES HIS "KICKAPOO JOY JUICE." NOW WE FEEDS IT T'HIM. PORE FELL'A!-HOW LONELY HE MUS' BE, A-HIDIN' IN THET SUIT O' ARMOUR-
CAIN'T UNNERSTAN' WHUFFO' HE'S A-GRUNTIN' SO. HE'S ONLY A LI'L FELLA AN' TH' ARMOUR IS TRE-MENJOUS!
HE'LL FEEL BETTER AFTER AH OPENS TH' VISOR AN' POURS THIS IN!!
A FEW MINUTES LATER -
THET KICKAPOO JOY JUICE SHO' QUIETED LONESOME POLECAT. AFTER AH POURED TH' WHOLE MESS IN, TH' SUIT O' ARMOUR GAVE ONE BIG SHAKE AN' KINDA LEANED BACK AGIN TH' WALL.
LOOK!
UGH!- UGH!- UGH!!
HELP!
Tm. Reg. U. S. Pat. Off., Distributed by United Feature Syndicate, Inc.

LI'L ABNER — Easier Said Than Done! — By Al Capp

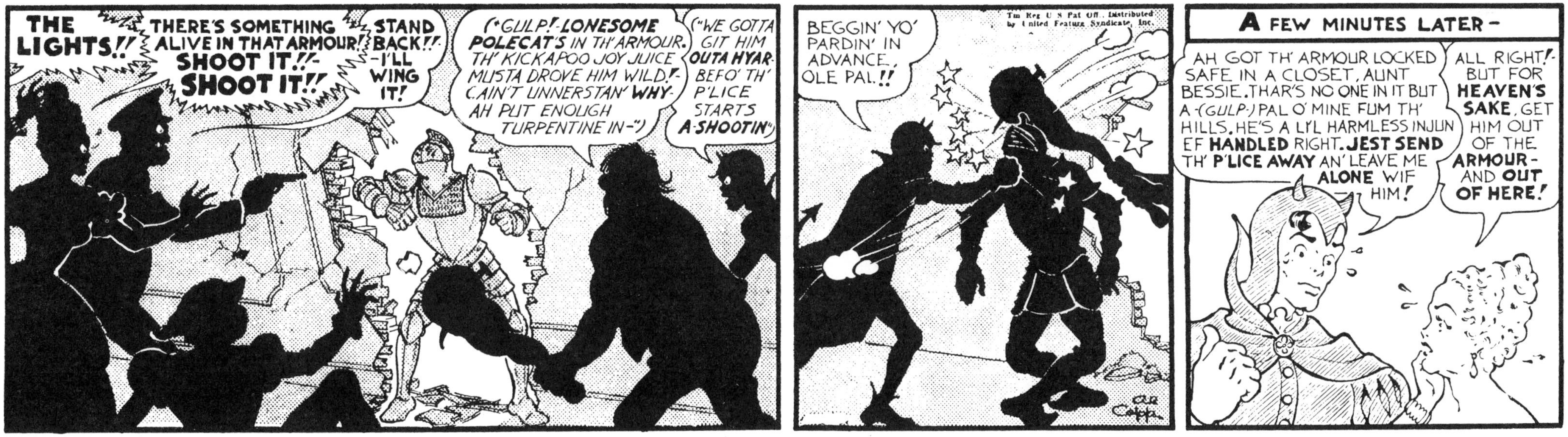

THE LIGHTS!!
THERE'S SOMETHING ALIVE IN THAT ARMOUR! SHOOT IT!!- SHOOT IT!!
STAND BACK!!- I'LL WING IT!
(*GULP!-LONESOME POLECAT'S IN TH' ARMOUR. TH' KICKAPOO JOY JUICE MUSTA DROVE HIM WILD!- CAIN'T UNNERSTAN' WHY- AH PUT ENOUGH TURPENTINE IN-*)
("WE GOTTA GIT HIM OUTA HYAR- BEFO' TH' P'LICE STARTS A-SHOOTIN")
BEGGIN' YO' PARDIN' IN ADVANCE, OLE PAL.!!
Tm Reg U S Pat Off. Distributed by United Feature Syndicate, Inc.
A FEW MINUTES LATER -
AH GOT TH' ARMOUR LOCKED SAFE IN A CLOSET, AUNT BESSIE. THAR'S NO ONE IN IT BUT A-(GULP-) PAL O' MINE FUM TH' HILLS. HE'S A LI'L HARMLESS INJUN EF HANDLED RIGHT. JEST SEND TH' P'LICE AWAY AN' LEAVE ME ALONE WIF HIM!
ALL RIGHT!- BUT FOR HEAVEN'S SAKE, GET HIM OUT OF THE ARMOUR- AND OUT OF HERE!

LI'L ABNER   Where Is Lonesome Polecat?   By Al Capp

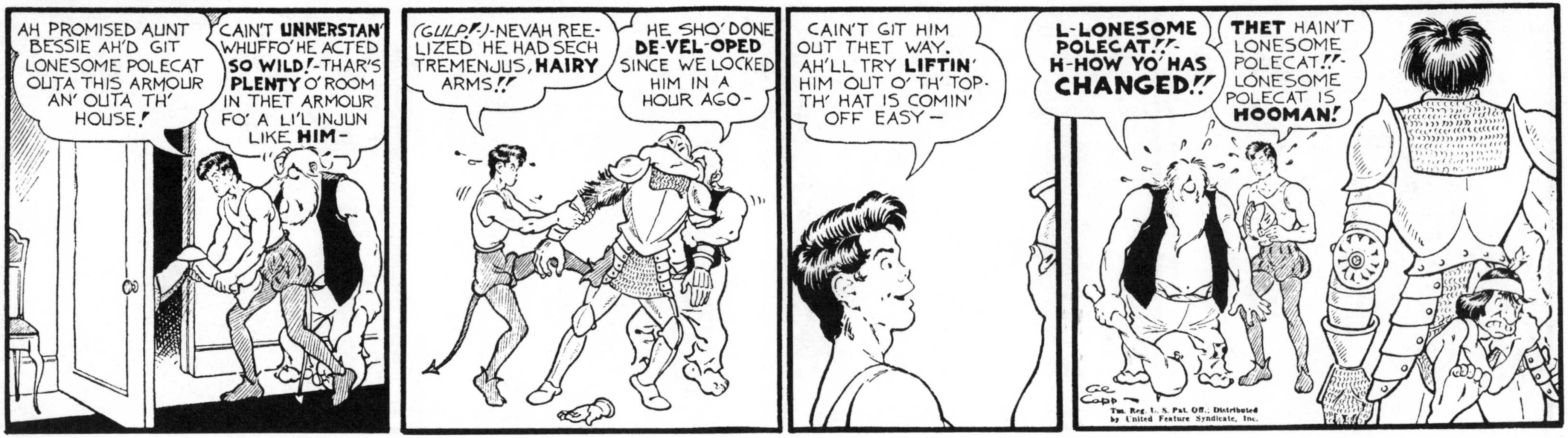
AH PROMISED AUNT BESSIE AH'D GIT LONESOME POLECAT OUTA THIS ARMOUR AN' OUTA TH' HOUSE!
CAIN'T UNNERSTAN' WHUFFO' HE ACTED SO WILD!-THAR'S PLENTY O' ROOM IN THET ARMOUR FO' A LI'L INJUN LIKE HIM-
(GULP!-)-NEVAH REE-LIZED HE HAD SECH TREMENJUS, HAIRY ARMS!!
HE SHO' DONE DE-VEL-OPED SINCE WE LOCKED HIM IN A HOUR AGO-
CAIN'T GIT HIM OUT THET WAY. AH'LL TRY LIFTIN' HIM OUT O' TH' TOP. TH' HAT IS COMIN' OFF EASY-
L-LONESOME POLECAT!!- H-HOW YO' HAS CHANGED!!
THET HAIN'T LONESOME POLECAT!!- LONESOME POLECAT IS HOOMAN!
Tm. Reg. U. S. Pat. Off.; Distributed by United Feature Syndicate, Inc.

LI'L ABNER   Swing Yo' Partner   By Al Capp

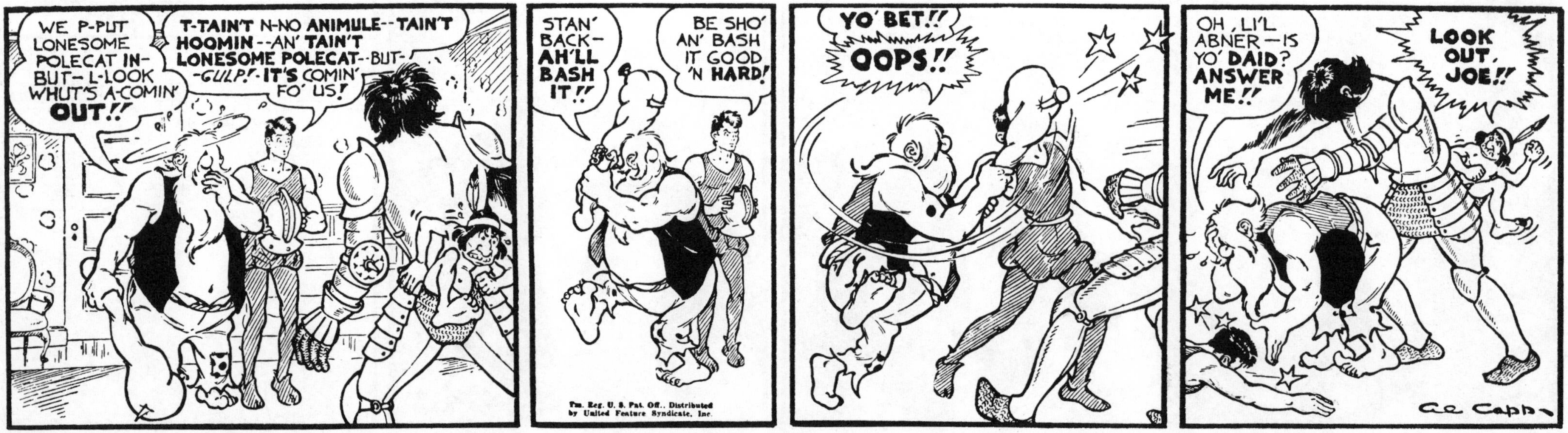
WE P-PUT LONESOME POLECAT IN-BUT-L-LOOK WHUT'S A-COMIN' OUT!!
T-TAIN'T N-NO ANIMULE--TAIN'T HOOMIN--AN' TAIN'T LONESOME POLECAT--BUT--GULP!-IT'S COMIN' FO' US!
STAN' BACK-AH'LL BASH IT!!
BE SHO' AN' BASH IT GOOD 'N HARD!
Tm. Reg. U. S. Pat. Off., Distributed by United Feature Syndicate, Inc.
YO' BET!!
OOPS!!
OH, LI'L ABNER-IS YO' DAID? ANSWER ME!!
LOOK OUT, JOE!!

LI'L ABNER — The Sly Thing of the Moors! — By Al Capp

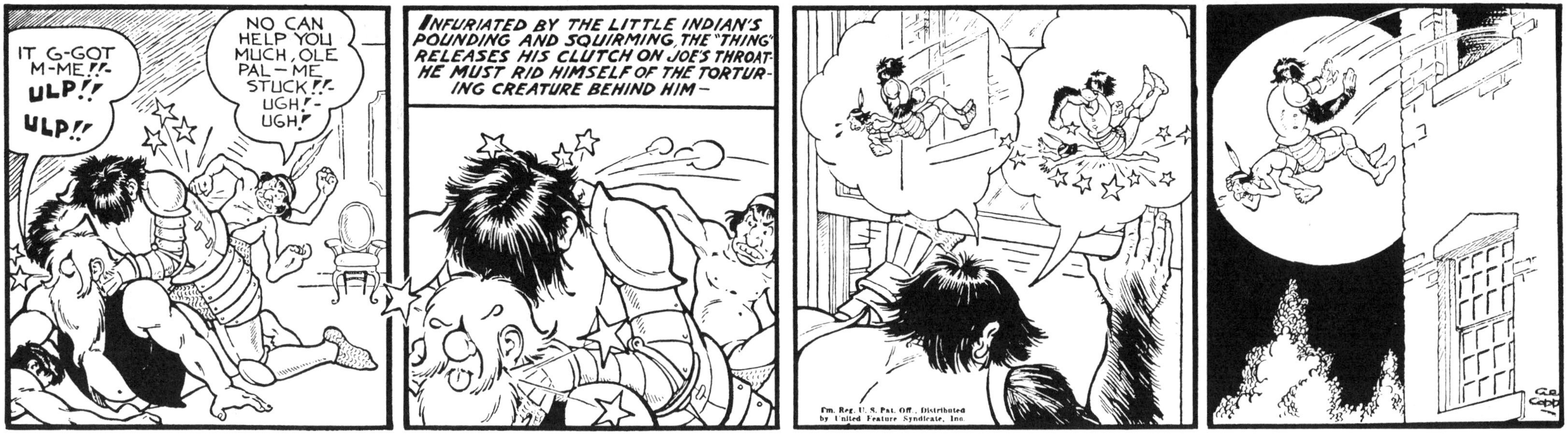
IT G-GOT M-ME!!- ULP!! ULP!!
NO CAN HELP YOU MUCH, OLE PAL—ME STUCK!!- UGH!- UGH!
INFURIATED BY THE LITTLE INDIAN'S POUNDING AND SQUIRMING, THE "THING" RELEASES HIS CLUTCH ON JOE'S THROAT- HE MUST RID HIMSELF OF THE TORTURING CREATURE BEHIND HIM—
Tm. Reg. U. S. Pat. Off., Distributed by United Feature Syndicate, Inc.

LI'L ABNER — Black Rufe Bites the Dust! — By Al Capp

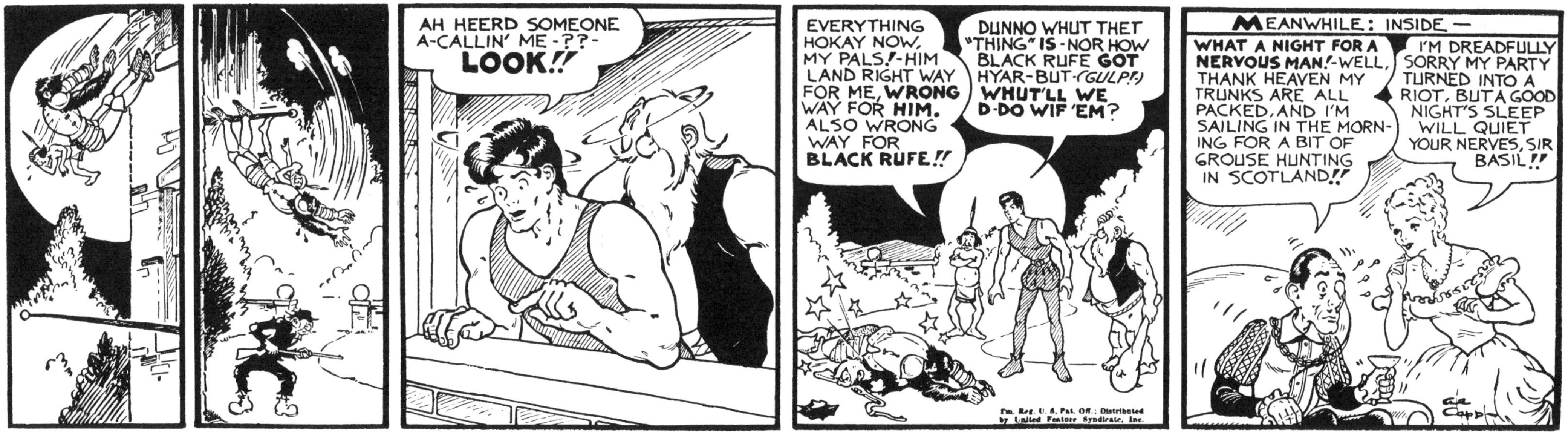
AH HEERD SOMEONE A-CALLIN' ME-??- LOOK!!
EVERYTHING HOKAY NOW, MY PALS!-HIM LAND RIGHT WAY FOR ME, WRONG WAY FOR HIM. ALSO WRONG WAY FOR BLACK RUFE!!
DUNNO WHUT THET "THING" IS-NOR HOW BLACK RUFE GOT HYAR-BUT-(GULP!) WHUT'LL WE D-DO WIF 'EM?
Tm. Reg. U. S. Pat. Off.; Distributed by United Feature Syndicate, Inc.
MEANWHILE: INSIDE—
WHAT A NIGHT FOR A NERVOUS MAN!-WELL, THANK HEAVEN MY TRUNKS ARE ALL PACKED, AND I'M SAILING IN THE MORNING FOR A BIT OF GROUSE HUNTING IN SCOTLAND!!
I'M DREADFULLY SORRY MY PARTY TURNED INTO A RIOT, BUT A GOOD NIGHT'S SLEEP WILL QUIET YOUR NERVES, SIR BASIL!!

LI'L ABNER Night Visitors By Al Capp

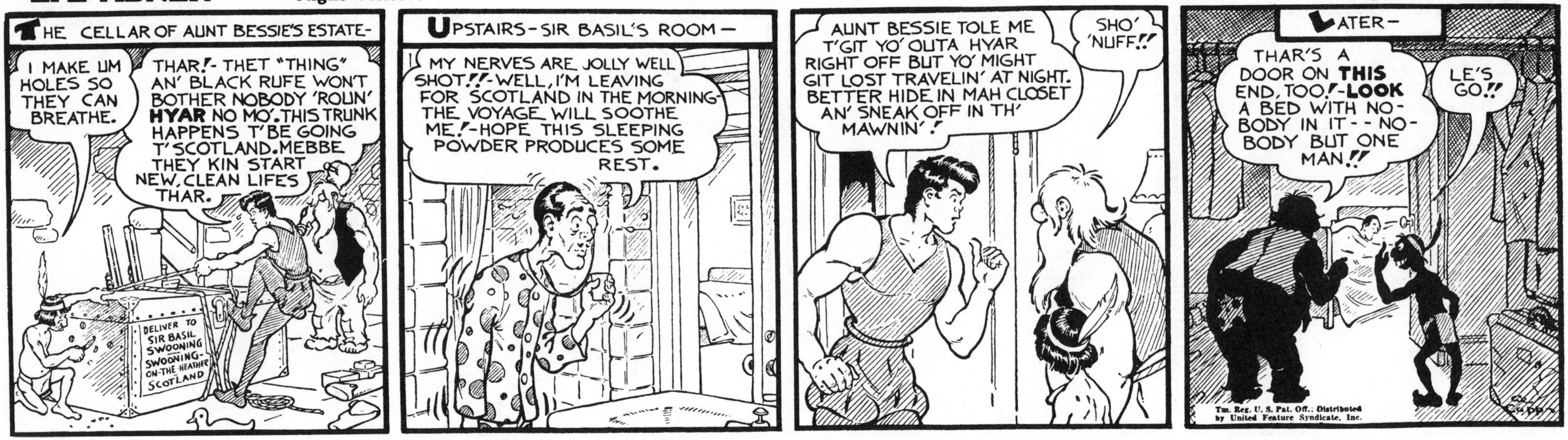
THE CELLAR OF AUNT BESSIE'S ESTATE-
I MAKE UM HOLES SO THEY CAN BREATHE.
THAR!- THET "THING" AN' BLACK RUFE WON'T BOTHER NOBODY 'ROUN' HYAR NO MO'. THIS TRUNK HAPPENS T'BE GOING T'SCOTLAND. MEBBE THEY KIN START NEW, CLEAN LIFES THAR.
DELIVER TO SIR BASIL SWOONING SWOONING-ON-THE-HEATHER SCOTLAND
UPSTAIRS-SIR BASIL'S ROOM-
MY NERVES ARE JOLLY WELL SHOT!!-WELL, I'M LEAVING FOR SCOTLAND IN THE MORNING-THE VOYAGE WILL SOOTHE ME!-HOPE THIS SLEEPING POWDER PRODUCES SOME REST.
AUNT BESSIE TOLE ME T'GIT YO' OUTA HYAR RIGHT OFF BUT YO' MIGHT GIT LOST TRAVELIN' AT NIGHT. BETTER HIDE IN MAH CLOSET AN' SNEAK OFF IN TH' MAWNIN'!
SHO' 'NUFF!!
LATER-
THAR'S A DOOR ON THIS END, TOO!-LOOK A BED WITH NO-BODY IN IT--NO-BODY BUT ONE MAN!!
LE'S GO!!
Tm. Reg. U. S. Pat. Off.; Distributed by United Feature Syndicate, Inc.

LI'L ABNER Dogpatch Lullaby By Al Capp

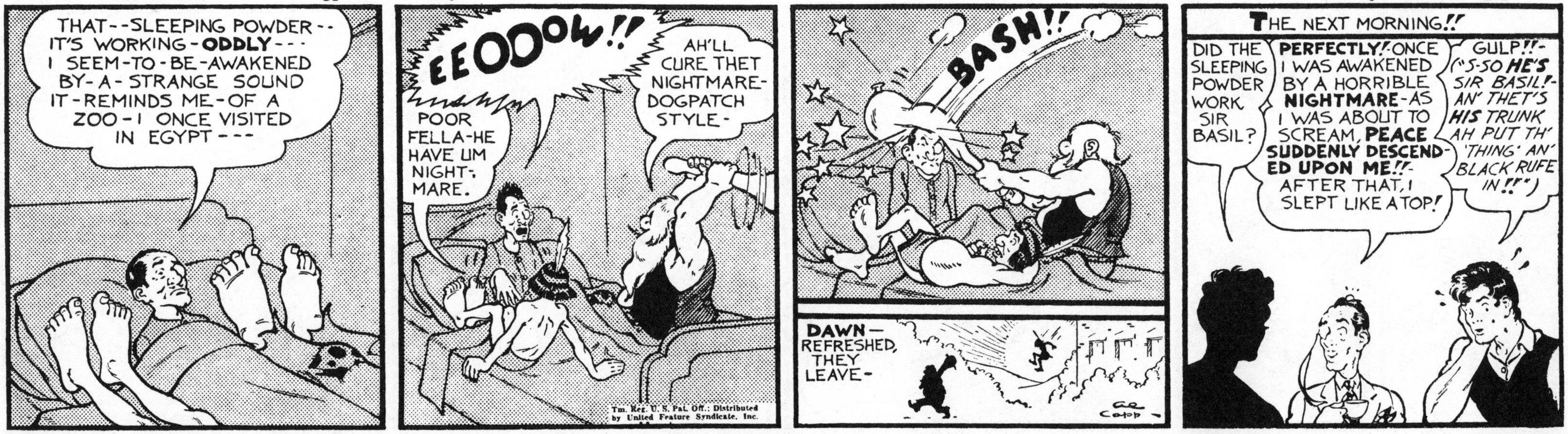
THAT--SLEEPING POWDER--IT'S WORKING-ODDLY---I SEEM-TO-BE-AWAKENED BY-A-STRANGE SOUND IT-REMINDS ME-OF A ZOO-I ONCE VISITED IN EGYPT---
EEOOOW!!
POOR FELLA-HE HAVE UM NIGHT-MARE.
AH'LL CURE THET NIGHTMARE-DOGPATCH STYLE-
Tm. Reg. U. S. Pat. Off.; Distributed by United Feature Syndicate, Inc.
BASH!!
DAWN-REFRESHED, THEY LEAVE-
THE NEXT MORNING!!
DID THE SLEEPING POWDER WORK, SIR BASIL?
PERFECTLY!-ONCE I WAS AWAKENED BY A HORRIBLE NIGHTMARE-AS I WAS ABOUT TO SCREAM, PEACE SUDDENLY DESCENDED UPON ME!!- AFTER THAT, I SLEPT LIKE A TOP!
GULP!!-("S-SO HE'S SIR BASIL!- AN' THET'S HIS TRUNK AH PUT TH' 'THING' AN' BLACK RUFE IN!!")

LI'L ABNER Cafe Society

By Al Capp

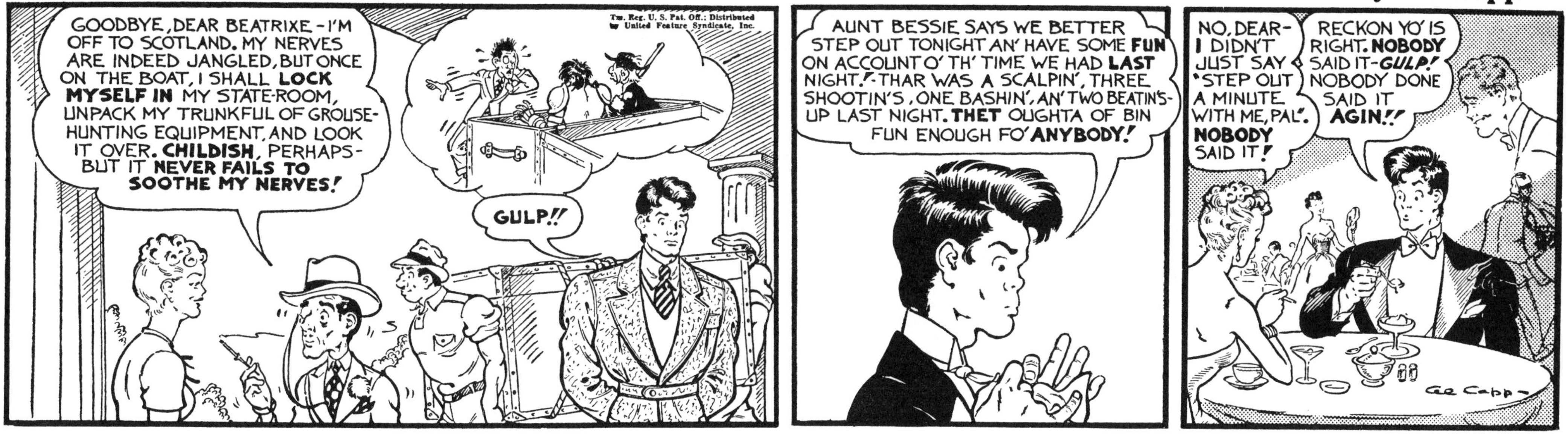

Tm. Reg. U. S. Pat. Off.: Distributed by United Feature Syndicate, Inc.
GOODBYE, DEAR BEATRIXE - I'M OFF TO SCOTLAND. MY NERVES ARE INDEED JANGLED, BUT ONCE ON THE BOAT, I SHALL **LOCK MYSELF IN** MY STATE-ROOM, UNPACK MY TRUNKFUL OF GROUSE-HUNTING EQUIPMENT, AND LOOK IT OVER. **CHILDISH**, PERHAPS- BUT IT **NEVER FAILS TO SOOTHE MY NERVES!**
GULP!!
AUNT BESSIE SAYS WE BETTER STEP OUT TONIGHT AN' HAVE SOME **FUN** ON ACCOUNT O' TH' TIME WE HAD **LAST** NIGHT!-THAR WAS A SCALPIN', THREE SHOOTIN'S, ONE BASHIN', AN' TWO BEATIN'S-UP LAST NIGHT. **THET** OUGHTA OF BIN FUN ENOUGH FO' **ANYBODY!**
NO, DEAR- **I** DIDN'T JUST SAY "STEP OUT A MINUTE WITH ME, PAL". **NOBODY** SAID IT!
RECKON YO' IS RIGHT. **NOBODY** SAID IT-**GULP!** NOBODY DONE SAID IT **AGIN!!**

LI'L ABNER Did Yo' Evah See a Dream Walking?

By Al Capp

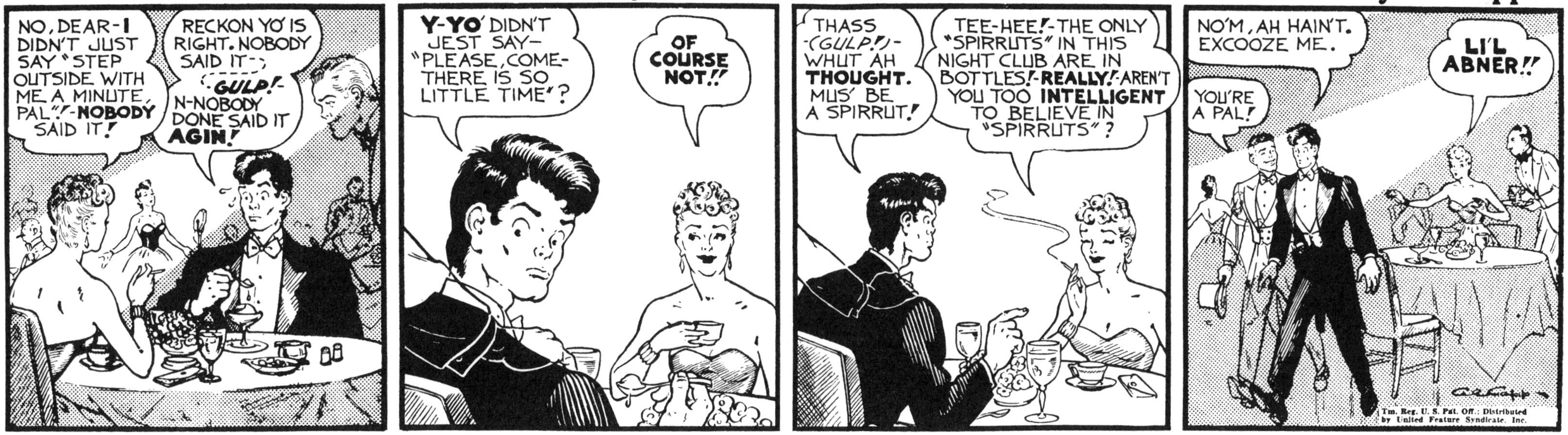

NO, DEAR- **I** DIDN'T JUST SAY "STEP OUTSIDE WITH ME A MINUTE, PAL"!-**NOBODY** SAID IT!
RECKON YO' IS RIGHT. NOBODY SAID IT-- **GULP!**- N-NOBODY DONE SAID IT **AGIN!**
Y-YO' DIDN'T JEST SAY- "PLEASE, COME- THERE IS SO LITTLE TIME"?
OF COURSE NOT!!
THASS -(GULP!)- WHUT AH **THOUGHT.** MUS' BE A SPIRRUT!
TEE-HEE!-THE ONLY "SPIRRUTS" IN THIS NIGHT CLUB ARE IN BOTTLES!-**REALLY!**-AREN'T YOU TOO **INTELLIGENT** TO BELIEVE IN "SPIRRUTS"?
NO'M, AH HAIN'T. EXCOOZE ME.
YOU'RE A PAL!
LI'L ABNER!!
Tm. Reg. U. S. Pat. Off.: Distributed by United Feature Syndicate, Inc.

LI'L ABNER That's the Spirit, Li'l Abner! By Al Capp

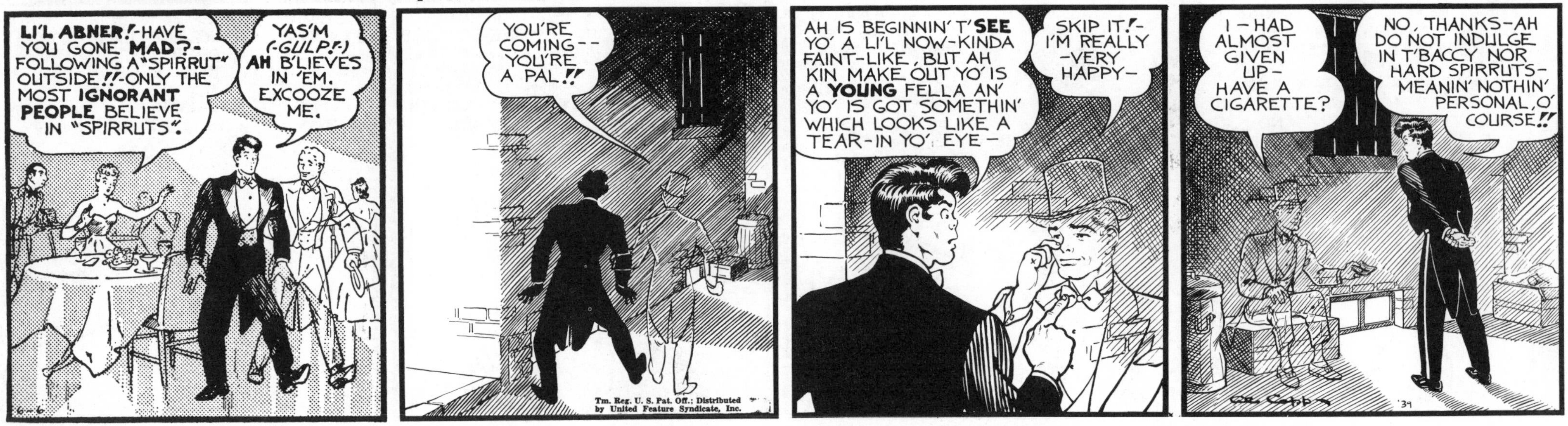
LI'L ABNER!-HAVE YOU GONE MAD?- FOLLOWING A "SPIRRUT" OUTSIDE!!-ONLY THE MOST IGNORANT PEOPLE BELIEVE IN "SPIRRUTS".
YAS'M (-GULP!-) AH B'LIEVES IN 'EM. EXCOOZE ME.
6-6
YOU'RE COMING-- YOU'RE A PAL!!
Tm. Reg. U. S. Pat. Off.; Distributed by United Feature Syndicate, Inc.
AH IS BEGINNIN' T' SEE YO' A LI'L NOW-KINDA FAINT-LIKE, BUT AH KIN MAKE OUT YO' IS A YOUNG FELLA AN' YO' IS GOT SOMETHIN' WHICH LOOKS LIKE A TEAR-IN YO' EYE-
SKIP IT!- I'M REALLY -VERY HAPPY-
I-HAD ALMOST GIVEN UP- HAVE A CIGARETTE?
NO, THANKS-AH DO NOT INDULGE IN T'BACCY NOR HARD SPIRRUTS- MEANIN' NOTHIN' PERSONAL, O' COURSE!!
Al Capp
'39

LI'L ABNER Contact!!! By Al Capp

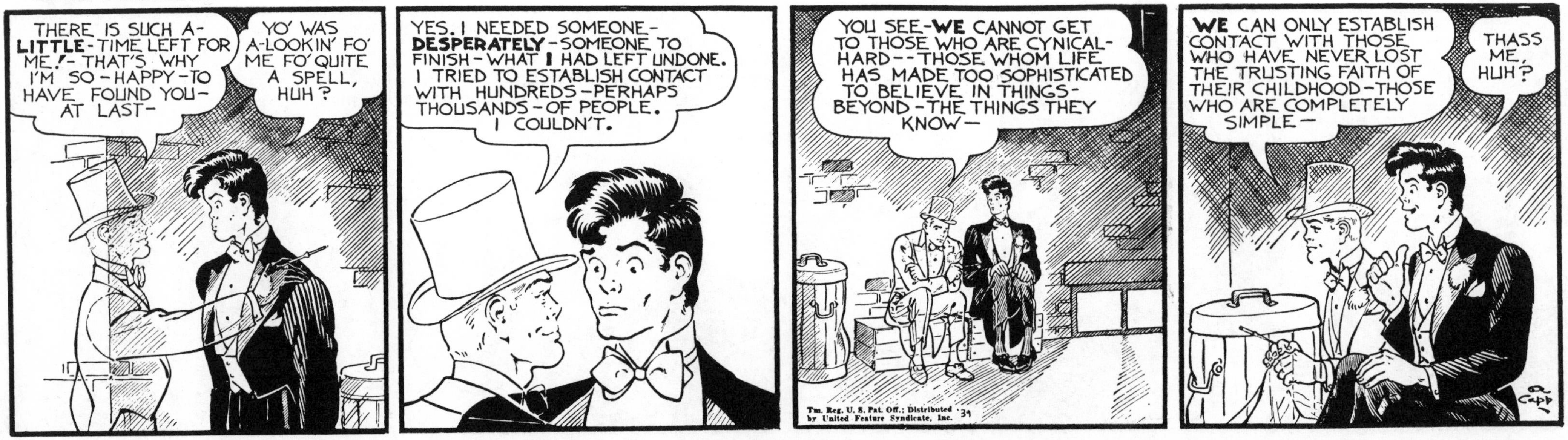
THERE IS SUCH A- LITTLE-TIME LEFT FOR ME!- THAT'S WHY I'M SO-HAPPY-TO HAVE FOUND YOU- AT LAST-
YO' WAS A-LOOKIN' FO' ME FO' QUITE A SPELL, HUH?
YES. I NEEDED SOMEONE- DESPERATELY-SOMEONE TO FINISH-WHAT I HAD LEFT UNDONE. I TRIED TO ESTABLISH CONTACT WITH HUNDREDS-PERHAPS THOUSANDS-OF PEOPLE. I COULDN'T.
YOU SEE-WE CANNOT GET TO THOSE WHO ARE CYNICAL- HARD--THOSE WHOM LIFE HAS MADE TOO SOPHISTICATED TO BELIEVE IN THINGS- BEYOND-THE THINGS THEY KNOW-
Tm. Reg. U. S. Pat. Off.; Distributed by United Feature Syndicate, Inc. '39
WE CAN ONLY ESTABLISH CONTACT WITH THOSE WHO HAVE NEVER LOST THE TRUSTING FAITH OF THEIR CHILDHOOD-THOSE WHO ARE COMPLETELY SIMPLE-
THASS ME, HUH?
A. Capp

LI'L ABNER It's a Small World, Haint It? By Al Capp

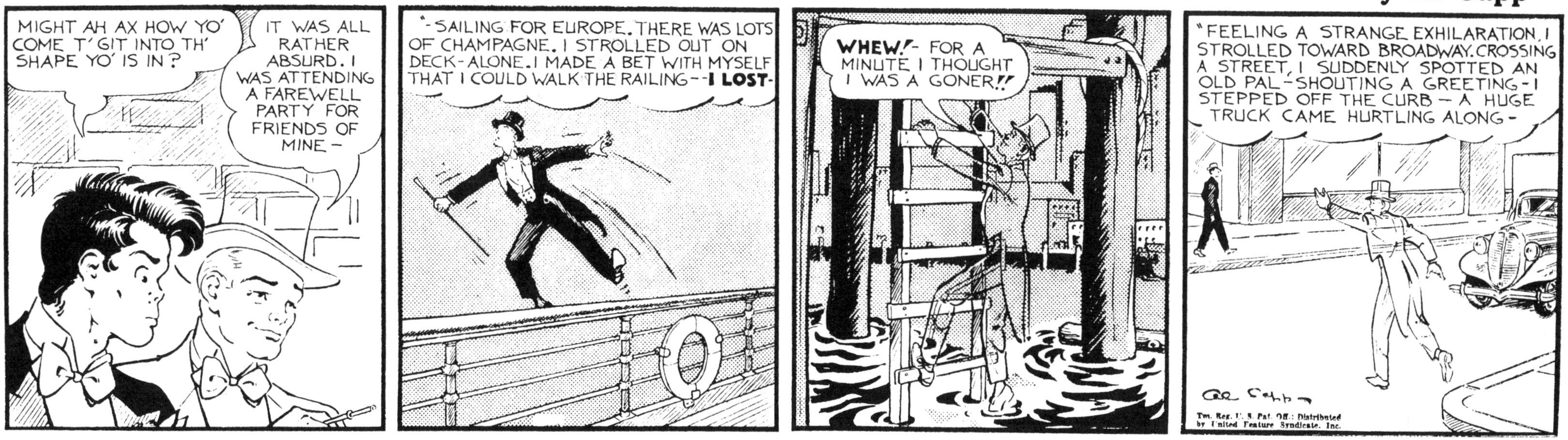
MIGHT AH AX HOW YO' COME T' GIT INTO TH' SHAPE YO' IS IN?
IT WAS ALL RATHER ABSURD. I WAS ATTENDING A FAREWELL PARTY FOR FRIENDS OF MINE –
"–SAILING FOR EUROPE. THERE WAS LOTS OF CHAMPAGNE. I STROLLED OUT ON DECK–ALONE. I MADE A BET WITH MYSELF THAT I COULD WALK THE RAILING – – **I LOST**–
WHEW!– FOR A MINUTE I THOUGHT I WAS A GONER!!
"FEELING A STRANGE EXHILARATION, I STROLLED TOWARD BROADWAY. CROSSING A STREET, I SUDDENLY SPOTTED AN OLD PAL–SHOUTING A GREETING–I STEPPED OFF THE CURB – A HUGE TRUCK CAME HURTLING ALONG–
Tm. Reg. U. S. Pat. Off.: Distributed by United Feature Syndicate, Inc.

LI'L ABNER The Invisible Pan! By Al Capp

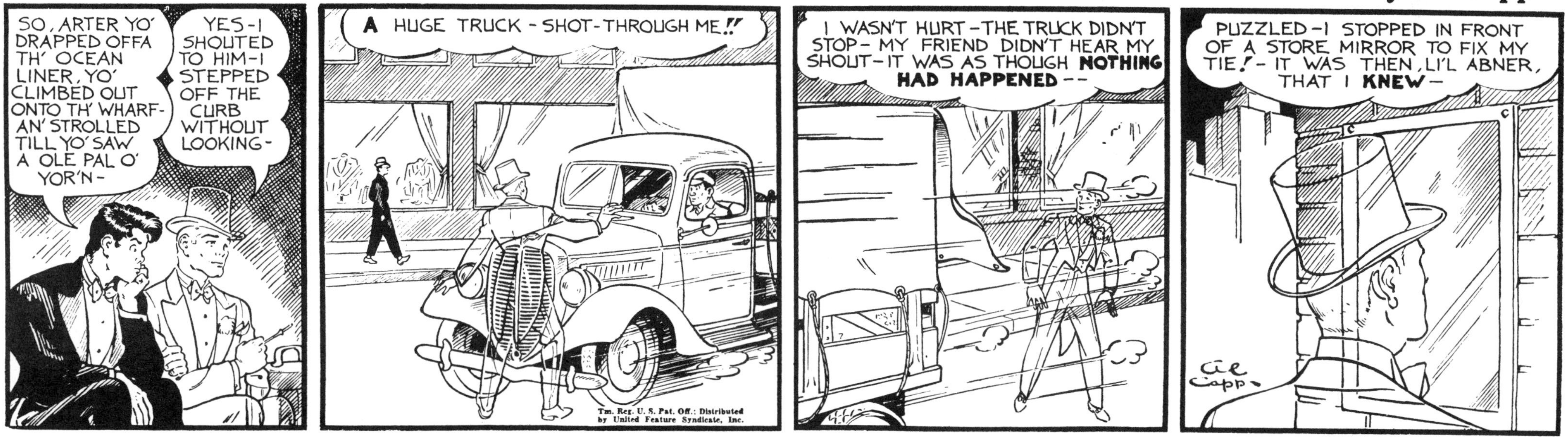
SO, ARTER YO' DRAPPED OFFA TH' OCEAN LINER, YO' CLIMBED OUT ONTO TH' WHARF- AN' STROLLED TILL YO' SAW A OLE PAL O' YOR'N–
YES–I SHOUTED TO HIM–I STEPPED OFF THE CURB WITHOUT LOOKING–
A HUGE TRUCK – SHOT – THROUGH ME!!
I WASN'T HURT – THE TRUCK DIDN'T STOP – MY FRIEND DIDN'T HEAR MY SHOUT – IT WAS AS THOUGH **NOTHING HAD HAPPENED** – –
PUZZLED – I STOPPED IN FRONT OF A STORE MIRROR TO FIX MY TIE! – IT WAS THEN, LI'L ABNER, THAT I **KNEW**–
Tm. Reg. U. S. Pat. Off.: Distributed by United Feature Syndicate, Inc.

LI'L ABNER This Is Where He Comes In— By Al Capp

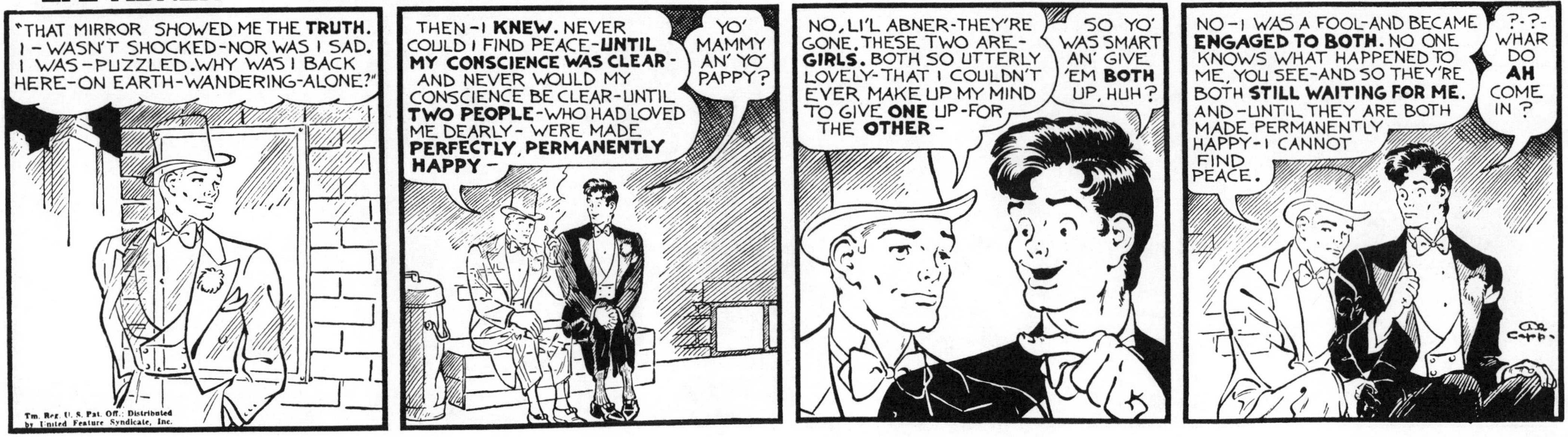
"THAT MIRROR SHOWED ME THE **TRUTH**. I-WASN'T SHOCKED-NOR WAS I SAD. I WAS-PUZZLED. WHY WAS I BACK HERE-ON EARTH-WANDERING-ALONE?"
Tm. Reg. U. S. Pat. Off.; Distributed by United Feature Syndicate, Inc.
THEN-I **KNEW**. NEVER COULD I FIND PEACE-**UNTIL MY CONSCIENCE WAS CLEAR**-AND NEVER WOULD MY CONSCIENCE BE CLEAR-UNTIL **TWO PEOPLE**-WHO HAD LOVED ME DEARLY-WERE MADE **PERFECTLY, PERMANENTLY HAPPY**-
YO' MAMMY AN' YO' PAPPY?
NO, LI'L ABNER-THEY'RE GONE. THESE TWO ARE-**GIRLS**. BOTH SO UTTERLY LOVELY-THAT I COULDN'T EVER MAKE UP MY MIND TO GIVE **ONE** UP-FOR THE **OTHER**-
SO YO' WAS SMART AN' GIVE 'EM **BOTH** UP, HUH?
NO-I WAS A FOOL-AND BECAME **ENGAGED TO BOTH**. NO ONE KNOWS WHAT HAPPENED TO ME, YOU SEE-AND SO THEY'RE BOTH **STILL WAITING FOR ME**. AND-UNTIL THEY ARE BOTH MADE PERMANENTLY HAPPY-I CANNOT FIND PEACE.
?-?-WHAR DO **AH** COME IN?
Al Capp

LI'L ABNER Linda Lou's in Mourning! By Al Capp

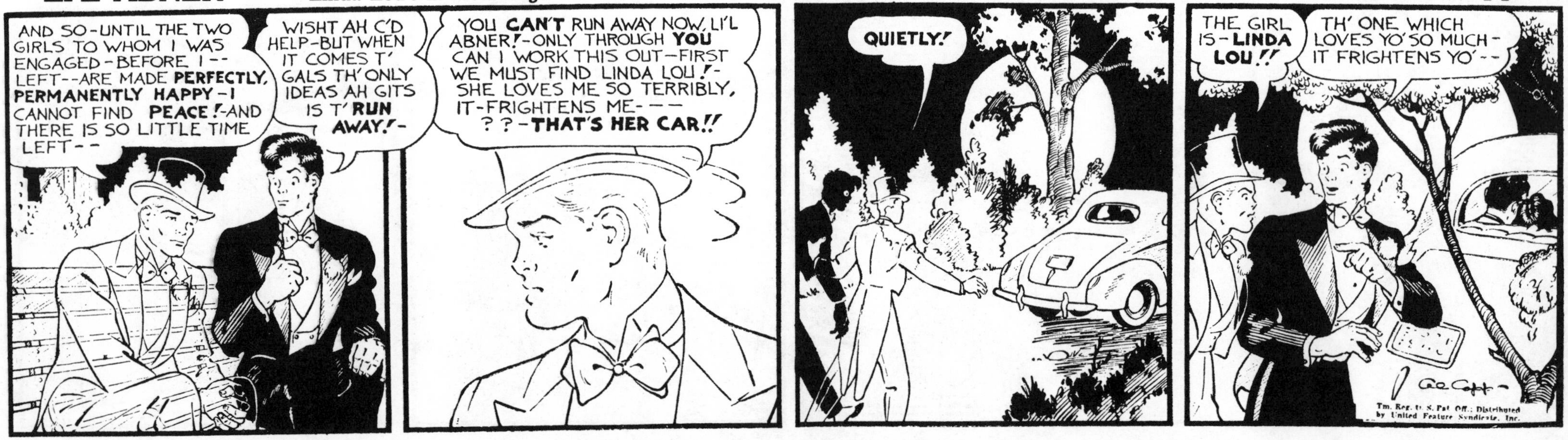
AND SO-UNTIL THE TWO GIRLS TO WHOM I WAS ENGAGED-BEFORE I--LEFT--ARE MADE **PERFECTLY, PERMANENTLY HAPPY**-I CANNOT FIND **PEACE**!-AND THERE IS SO LITTLE TIME LEFT--
WISHT AH C'D HELP-BUT WHEN IT COMES T' GALS TH' ONLY IDEAS AH GITS IS T' **RUN AWAY**!-
YOU **CAN'T** RUN AWAY NOW, LI'L ABNER!-ONLY THROUGH **YOU** CAN I WORK THIS OUT-FIRST WE MUST FIND LINDA LOU!-SHE LOVES ME SO TERRIBLY, IT-FRIGHTENS ME---
??-**THAT'S HER CAR!!**
QUIETLY!
THE GIRL IS-**LINDA LOU!!**
TH' ONE WHICH LOVES YO' SO MUCH-IT FRIGHTENS YO'--
Al Capp
Tm. Reg. U. S. Pat. Off.; Distributed by United Feature Syndicate, Inc.

LI'L ABNER — Love Is Where You Find It! — By Al Capp

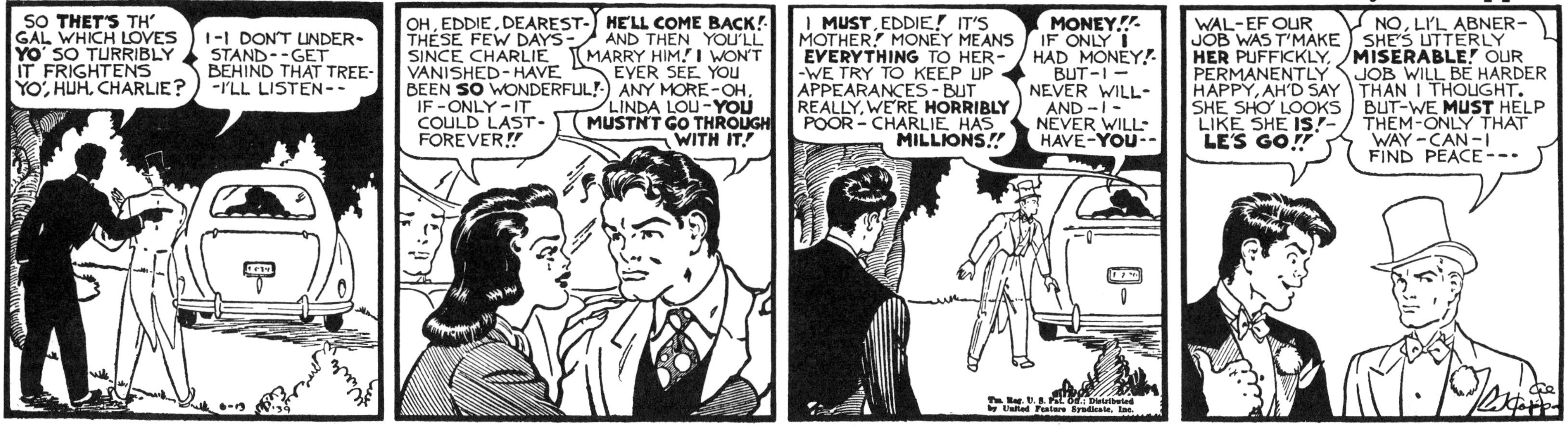
SO THET'S TH' GAL WHICH LOVES YO' SO TURRIBLY IT FRIGHTENS YO', HUH, CHARLIE?
I-I DON'T UNDERSTAND--GET BEHIND THAT TREE--I'LL LISTEN--
OH, EDDIE, DEAREST-THESE FEW DAYS-SINCE CHARLIE VANISHED-HAVE BEEN SO WONDERFUL!-IF-ONLY-IT COULD LAST-FOREVER!!
HE'LL COME BACK!-AND THEN YOU'LL MARRY HIM! I WON'T EVER SEE YOU ANY MORE-OH, LINDA LOU-YOU MUSTN'T GO THROUGH WITH IT!
I MUST, EDDIE! IT'S MOTHER! MONEY MEANS EVERYTHING TO HER--WE TRY TO KEEP UP APPEARANCES-BUT REALLY, WE'RE HORRIBLY POOR-CHARLIE HAS MILLIONS!!
MONEY!!-IF ONLY I HAD MONEY!-BUT-I-NEVER WILL-AND-I-NEVER WILL-HAVE-YOU--
Tm. Reg. U. S. Pat. Off.; Distributed by United Feature Syndicate, Inc.
WAL-EF OUR JOB WAS T'MAKE HER PUFFICKLY PERMANENTLY HAPPY, AH'D SAY SHE SHO' LOOKS LIKE SHE IS!-LE'S GO!!
NO, LI'L ABNER-SHE'S UTTERLY MISERABLE! OUR JOB WILL BE HARDER THAN I THOUGHT. BUT-WE MUST HELP THEM-ONLY THAT WAY-CAN-I FIND PEACE---

LI'L ABNER — Love Is on His Side! — By Al Capp

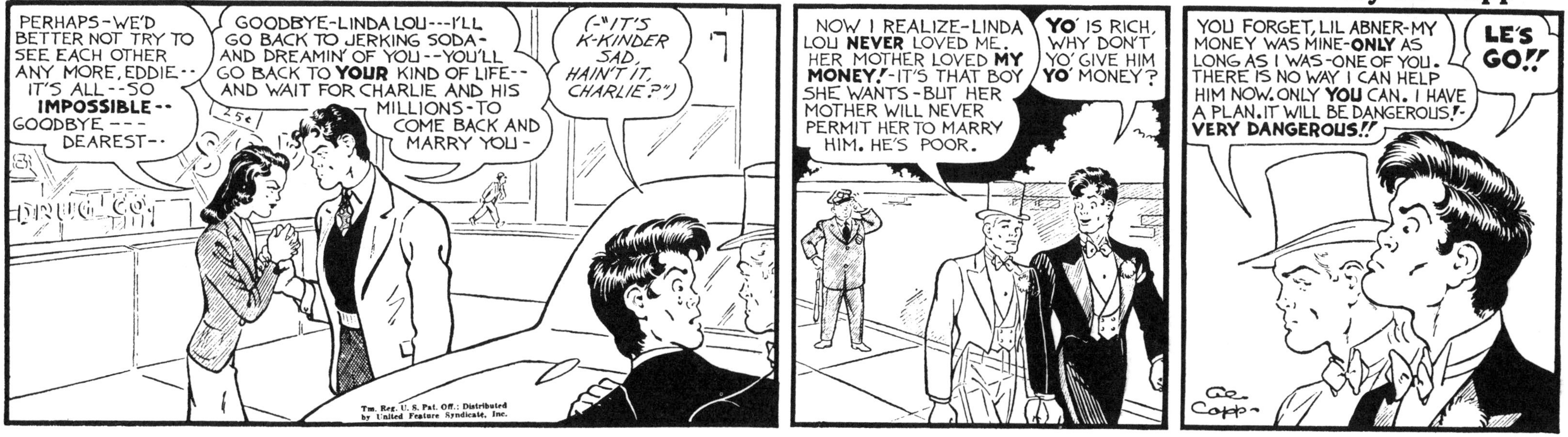
PERHAPS-WE'D BETTER NOT TRY TO SEE EACH OTHER ANY MORE, EDDIE--IT'S ALL--SO IMPOSSIBLE--GOODBYE---DEAREST--
GOODBYE-LINDA LOU---I'LL GO BACK TO JERKING SODA-AND DREAMIN' OF YOU--YOU'LL GO BACK TO YOUR KIND OF LIFE--AND WAIT FOR CHARLIE AND HIS MILLIONS-TO COME BACK AND MARRY YOU-
(-"IT'S K-KINDER SAD, HAIN'T IT, CHARLIE?")
DRUG CO
Tm. Reg. U. S. Pat. Off.; Distributed by United Feature Syndicate, Inc.
NOW I REALIZE-LINDA LOU NEVER LOVED ME. HER MOTHER LOVED MY MONEY!-IT'S THAT BOY SHE WANTS-BUT HER MOTHER WILL NEVER PERMIT HER TO MARRY HIM. HE'S POOR.
YO' IS RICH, WHY DON'T YO' GIVE HIM YO' MONEY?
YOU FORGET, LIL ABNER-MY MONEY WAS MINE-ONLY AS LONG AS I WAS-ONE OF YOU. THERE IS NO WAY I CAN HELP HIM NOW. ONLY YOU CAN. I HAVE A PLAN. IT WILL BE DANGEROUS!-VERY DANGEROUS!!
LE'S GO!!

LI'L ABNER Coming Thru the Windows By Al Capp

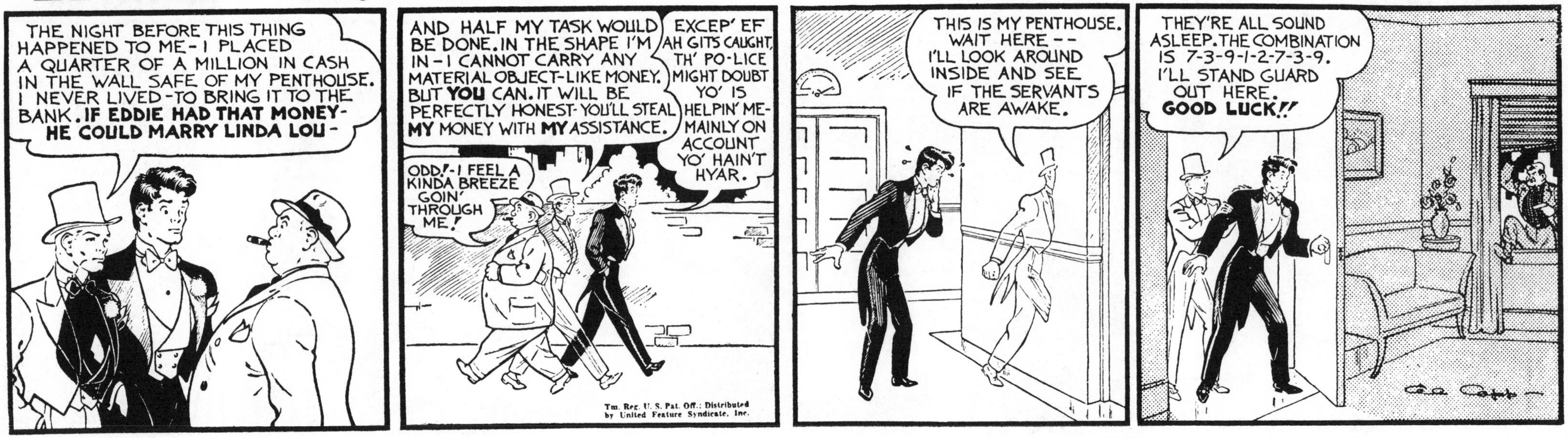

THE NIGHT BEFORE THIS THING HAPPENED TO ME - I PLACED A QUARTER OF A MILLION IN CASH IN THE WALL SAFE OF MY PENTHOUSE. I NEVER LIVED - TO BRING IT TO THE BANK. IF EDDIE HAD THAT MONEY - HE COULD MARRY LINDA LOU -
AND HALF MY TASK WOULD BE DONE. IN THE SHAPE I'M IN - I CANNOT CARRY ANY MATERIAL OBJECT - LIKE MONEY. BUT YOU CAN. IT WILL BE PERFECTLY HONEST - YOU'LL STEAL MY MONEY WITH MY ASSISTANCE.
EXCEP' EF AH GITS CAUGHT, TH' PO-LICE MIGHT DOUBT YO' IS HELPIN' ME - MAINLY ON ACCOUNT YO' HAIN'T HYAR.
ODD!- I FEEL A KINDA BREEZE GOIN' THROUGH ME!
Tm. Reg. U. S. Pat. Off.: Distributed by United Feature Syndicate, Inc.
THIS IS MY PENTHOUSE. WAIT HERE - - I'LL LOOK AROUND INSIDE AND SEE IF THE SERVANTS ARE AWAKE.
THEY'RE ALL SOUND ASLEEP. THE COMBINATION IS 7-3-9-1-2-7-3-9. I'LL STAND GUARD OUT HERE. GOOD LUCK!!
Al Capp

LI'L ABNER It Takes All Kinds of People! By Al Capp

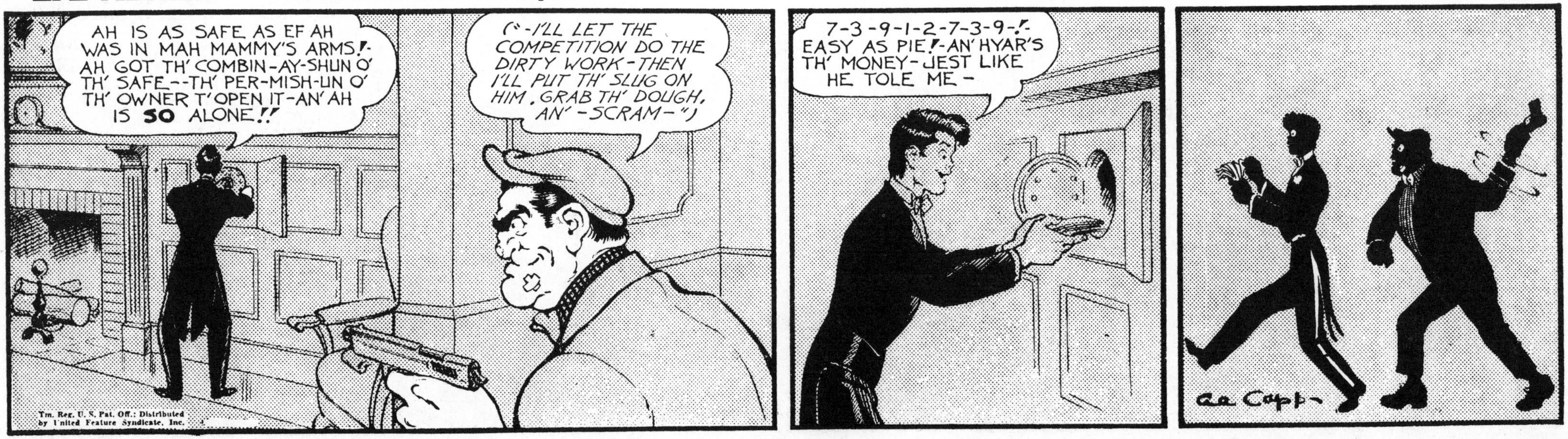

AH IS AS SAFE AS EF AH WAS IN MAH MAMMY'S ARMS!- AH GOT TH' COMBIN-AY-SHUN O' TH' SAFE - - TH' PER-MISH-UN O' TH' OWNER T' OPEN IT - AN' AH IS SO ALONE!!
("- I'LL LET THE COMPETITION DO THE DIRTY WORK - THEN I'LL PUT TH' SLUG ON HIM, GRAB TH' DOUGH, AN' - SCRAM - ")
Tm. Reg. U. S. Pat. Off.: Distributed by United Feature Syndicate, Inc.
7-3-9-1-2-7-3-9-!- EASY AS PIE!- AN' HYAR'S TH' MONEY - JEST LIKE HE TOLE ME -
Al Capp

LI'L ABNER And There Is So Little Time! By Al Capp

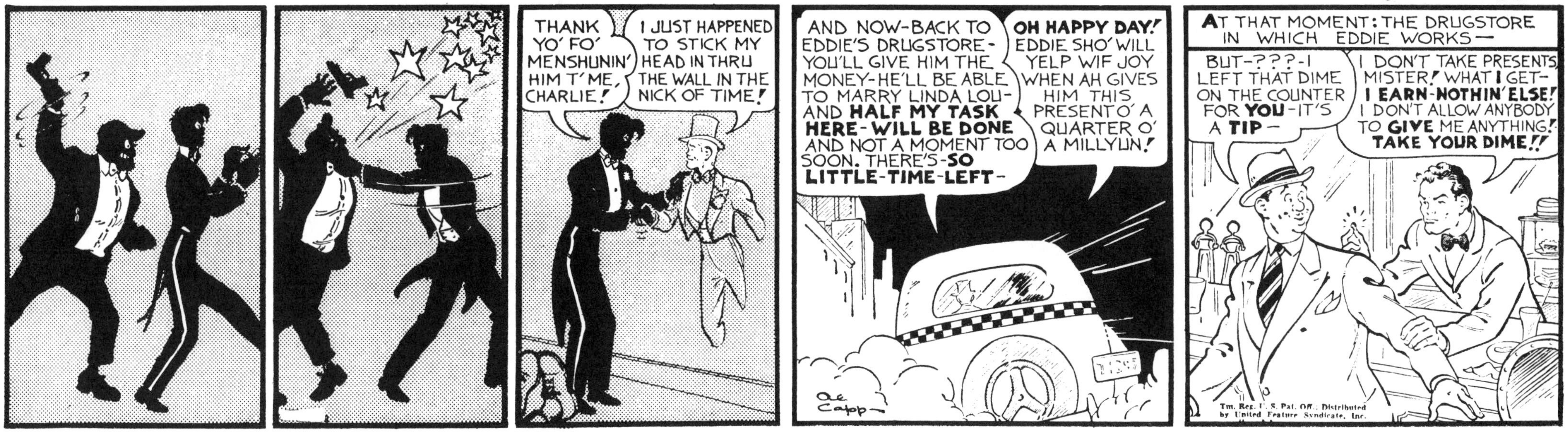

THANK YO' FO' MENSHUNIN' HIM T'ME, CHARLIE!
I JUST HAPPENED TO STICK MY HEAD IN THRU THE WALL IN THE NICK OF TIME!
AND NOW-BACK TO EDDIE'S DRUGSTORE-YOU'LL GIVE HIM THE MONEY-HE'LL BE ABLE TO MARRY LINDA LOU-AND **HALF MY TASK HERE-WILL BE DONE** AND NOT A MOMENT TOO SOON. THERE'S-**SO LITTLE-TIME-LEFT**-
OH HAPPY DAY! EDDIE SHO' WILL YELP WIF JOY WHEN AH GIVES HIM THIS PRESENT O' A QUARTER O' A MILLYUN!
Al Capp
AT THAT MOMENT: THE DRUGSTORE IN WHICH EDDIE WORKS—
BUT-???-I LEFT THAT DIME ON THE COUNTER FOR **YOU**-IT'S A **TIP**—
I DON'T TAKE PRESENTS, MISTER! WHAT **I** GET-**I EARN-NOTHIN' ELSE!** I DON'T ALLOW ANYBODY TO **GIVE** ME ANYTHING!-**TAKE YOUR DIME!!**
Tm. Reg. U. S. Pat. Off.; Distributed by United Feature Syndicate, Inc.

LI'L ABNER Come the Dawn! By Al Capp

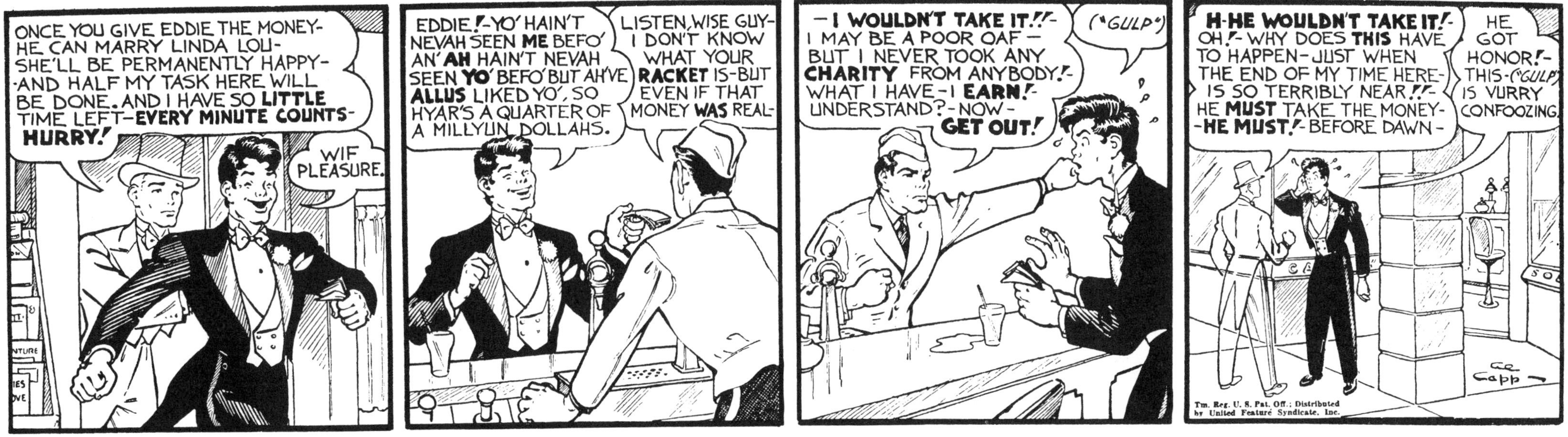

ONCE YOU GIVE EDDIE THE MONEY-HE CAN MARRY LINDA LOU-SHE'LL BE PERMANENTLY HAPPY--AND HALF MY TASK HERE WILL BE DONE. AND I HAVE SO **LITTLE** TIME LEFT-**EVERY MINUTE COUNTS-HURRY!**
WIF PLEASURE.
EDDIE!-YO' HAIN'T NEVAH SEEN **ME** BEFO' AN' **AH** HAIN'T NEVAH SEEN **YO'** BEFO' BUT AH'VE **ALLUS** LIKED YO', SO HYAR'S A QUARTER OF A MILLYUN DOLLAHS.
LISTEN, WISE GUY-I DON'T KNOW WHAT YOUR **RACKET** IS-BUT EVEN IF THAT MONEY **WAS** REAL-
-**I WOULDN'T TAKE IT!!**-I MAY BE A POOR OAF—BUT I NEVER TOOK ANY **CHARITY** FROM ANYBODY!-WHAT I HAVE-I **EARN!**-UNDERSTAND?-NOW-**GET OUT!**
("GULP")
H-HE WOULDN'T TAKE IT!-OH!-WHY DOES **THIS** HAVE TO HAPPEN-JUST WHEN THE END OF MY TIME HERE-IS SO TERRIBLY NEAR!!-HE **MUST** TAKE THE MONEY--**HE MUST!**-BEFORE DAWN-
HE GOT HONOR!-THIS-("GULP") IS VURRY CONFOOZING.
Al Capp
Tm. Reg. U. S. Pat. Off.; Distributed by United Feature Syndicate, Inc.

LI'L ABNER We Expect the Worst! By Al Capp

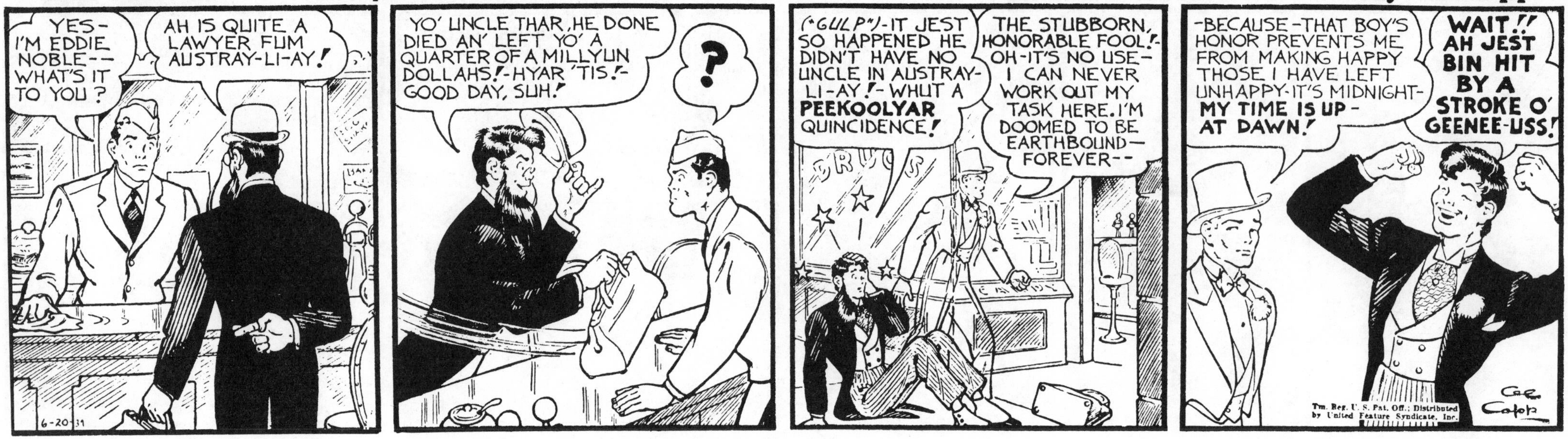
YES- I'M EDDIE NOBLE-- WHAT'S IT TO YOU?
AH IS QUITE A LAWYER FUM AUSTRAY-LI-AY!
YO' UNCLE THAR, HE DONE DIED AN' LEFT YO' A QUARTER OF A MILLYUN DOLLAHS!-HYAR 'TIS!- GOOD DAY, SUH!
?
("GULP")-IT JEST SO HAPPENED HE DIDN'T HAVE NO UNCLE IN AUSTRAY-LI-AY!- WHUT A PEEKOOLYAR QUINCIDENCE!
THE STUBBORN, HONORABLE FOOL!- OH-IT'S NO USE- I CAN NEVER WORK OUT MY TASK HERE. I'M DOOMED TO BE EARTHBOUND- FOREVER--
-BECAUSE-THAT BOY'S HONOR PREVENTS ME FROM MAKING HAPPY THOSE I HAVE LEFT UNHAPPY-IT'S MIDNIGHT- MY TIME IS UP- AT DAWN!
WAIT!! AH JEST BIN HIT BY A STROKE O' GEENEE-USS!
Tm. Reg. U. S. Pat. Off.; Distributed by United Feature Syndicate, Inc.

LI'L ABNER The Con Man! By Al Capp

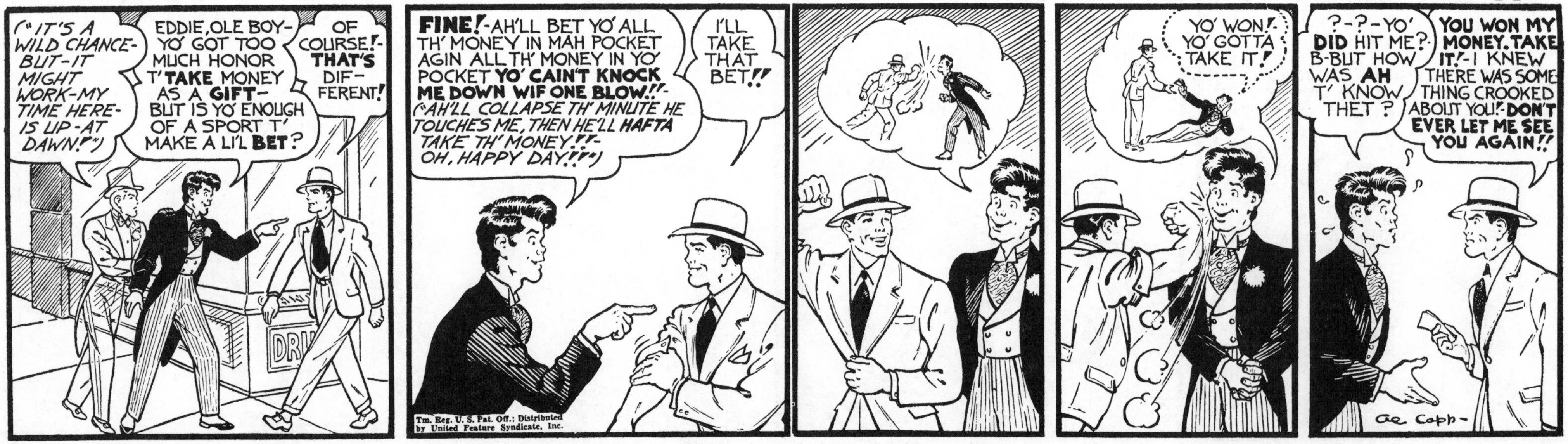
("IT'S A WILD CHANCE- BUT-IT MIGHT WORK-MY TIME HERE IS UP-AT DAWN!")
EDDIE, OLE BOY- YO' GOT TOO MUCH HONOR T' TAKE MONEY AS A GIFT- BUT IS YO' ENOUGH OF A SPORT T' MAKE A LI'L BET?
OF COURSE!- THAT'S DIF-FERENT!
FINE!-AH'LL BET YO' ALL TH' MONEY IN MAH POCKET AGIN ALL TH' MONEY IN YO' POCKET YO' CAIN'T KNOCK ME DOWN WIF ONE BLOW!!- ("AH'LL COLLAPSE TH' MINUTE HE TOUCHES ME, THEN HE'LL HAFTA TAKE TH' MONEY!!- OH, HAPPY DAY!!")
I'LL TAKE THAT BET!!
Tm. Reg. U. S. Pat. Off.; Distributed by United Feature Syndicate, Inc.
YO' WON!- YO' GOTTA TAKE IT!
?-?-YO' DID HIT ME?- B-BUT HOW WAS AH T' KNOW THET?
YOU WON MY MONEY. TAKE IT!-I KNEW THERE WAS SOMETHING CROOKED ABOUT YOU!- DON'T EVER LET ME SEE YOU AGAIN!!

LI'L ABNER Fry His Hide! By Al Capp

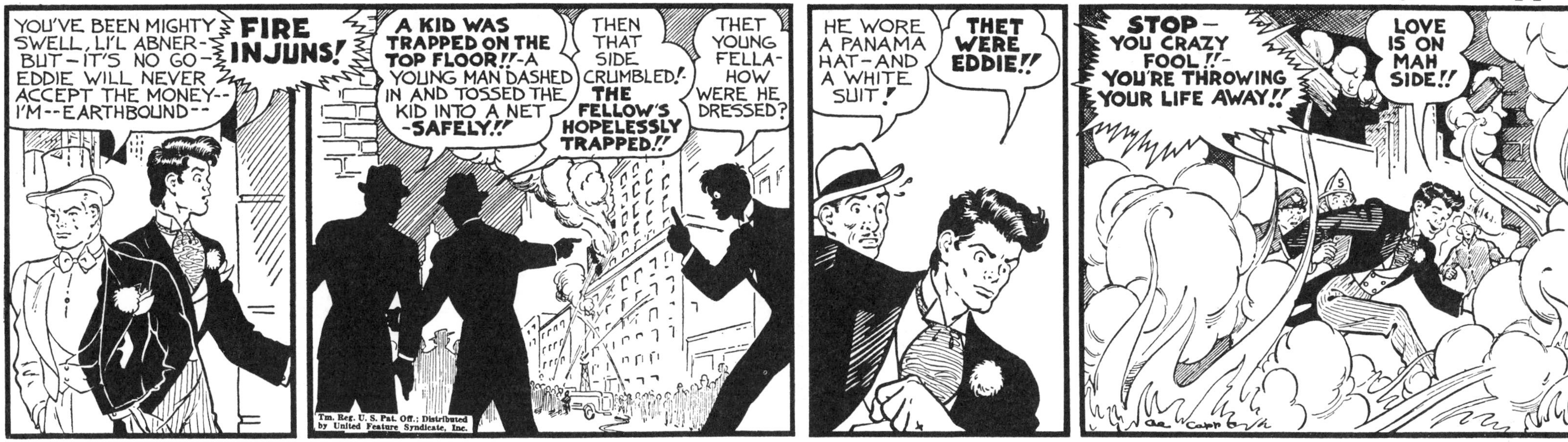
YOU'VE BEEN MIGHTY SWELL, LI'L ABNER- BUT-IT'S NO GO- EDDIE WILL NEVER ACCEPT THE MONEY-- I'M--EARTHBOUND--
FIRE INJUNS!
A KID WAS TRAPPED ON THE TOP FLOOR!!-A YOUNG MAN DASHED IN AND TOSSED THE KID INTO A NET -SAFELY!!
THEN THAT SIDE CRUMBLED!- THE FELLOW'S HOPELESSLY TRAPPED!!
THET YOUNG FELLA- HOW WERE HE DRESSED?
Tm. Reg. U. S. Pat. Off.; Distributed by United Feature Syndicate, Inc.
HE WORE A PANAMA HAT-AND A WHITE SUIT!
THET WERE EDDIE!!
STOP- YOU CRAZY FOOL!!- YOU'RE THROWING YOUR LIFE AWAY!!
LOVE IS ON MAH SIDE!!

LI'L ABNER Cash and Carry By Al Capp

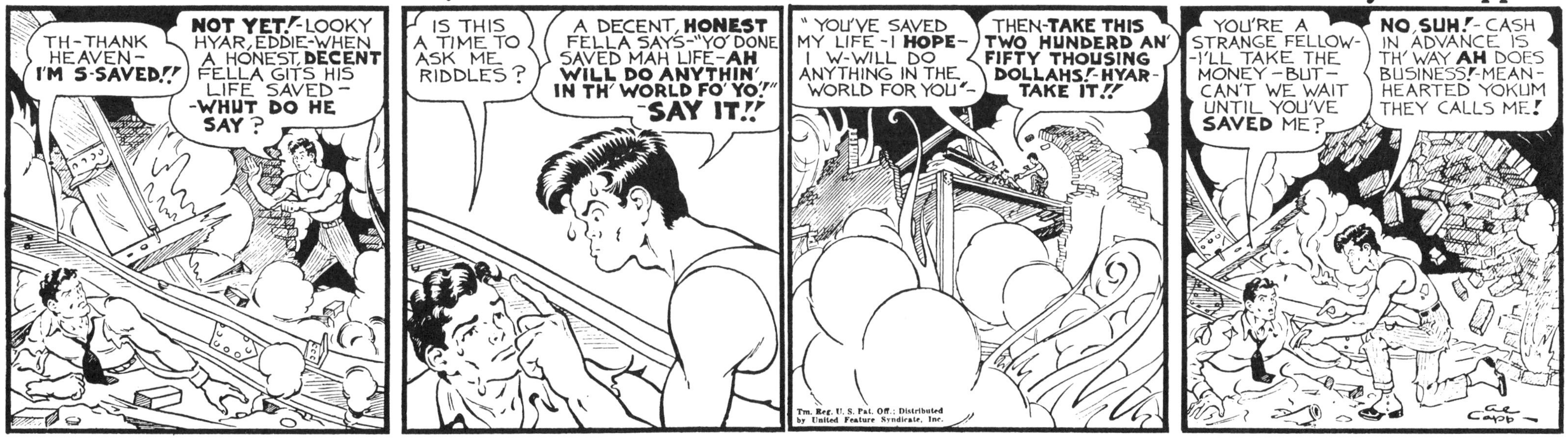
TH-THANK HEAVEN- I'M S-SAVED!!
NOT YET!-LOOKY HYAR, EDDIE-WHEN A HONEST, DECENT FELLA GITS HIS LIFE SAVED- -WHUT DO HE SAY?
IS THIS A TIME TO ASK ME RIDDLES?
A DECENT, HONEST FELLA SAYS-"YO' DONE SAVED MAH LIFE-AH WILL DO ANYTHIN' IN TH' WORLD FO' YO'!" -SAY IT!!
"YOU'VE SAVED MY LIFE-I HOPE- I W-WILL DO ANYTHING IN THE WORLD FOR YOU"-
THEN-TAKE THIS TWO HUNDERD AN' FIFTY THOUSING DOLLAHS!-HYAR- TAKE IT!!
Tm. Reg. U. S. Pat. Off.; Distributed by United Feature Syndicate, Inc.
YOU'RE A STRANGE FELLOW- -I'LL TAKE THE MONEY-BUT- CAN'T WE WAIT UNTIL YOU'VE SAVED ME?
NO, SUH!-CASH IN ADVANCE IS TH' WAY AH DOES BUSINESS!-MEAN-HEARTED YOKUM THEY CALLS ME!

LI'L ABNER Wrong-Way Yokum By Al Capp

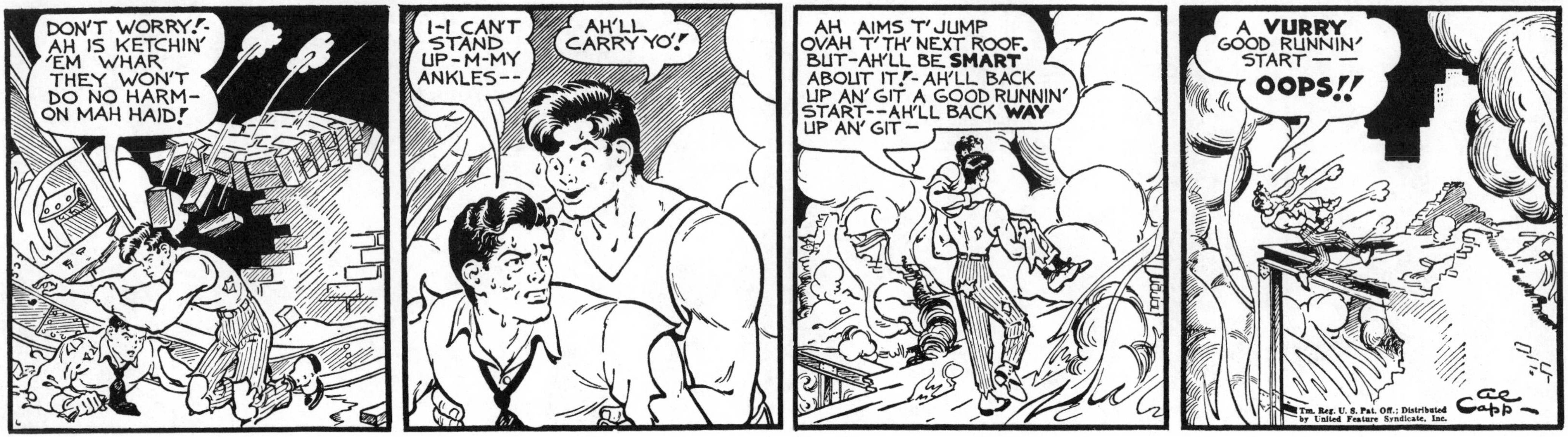
DON'T WORRY!-AH IS KETCHIN' 'EM WHAR THEY WON'T DO NO HARM-ON MAH HAID!
I-I CAN'T STAND UP-M-MY ANKLES--
AH'LL CARRY YO'!
AH AIMS T' JUMP OVAH T' TH' NEXT ROOF. BUT-AH'LL BE SMART ABOUT IT!-AH'LL BACK UP AN' GIT A GOOD RUNNIN' START--AH'LL BACK WAY UP AN' GIT -
A VURRY GOOD RUNNIN' START — —
OOPS!!
Tm. Reg. U. S. Pat. Off.; Distributed by United Feature Syndicate, Inc.
Al Capp

LI'L ABNER Thirty Years—Skiddoo!!! By Al Capp

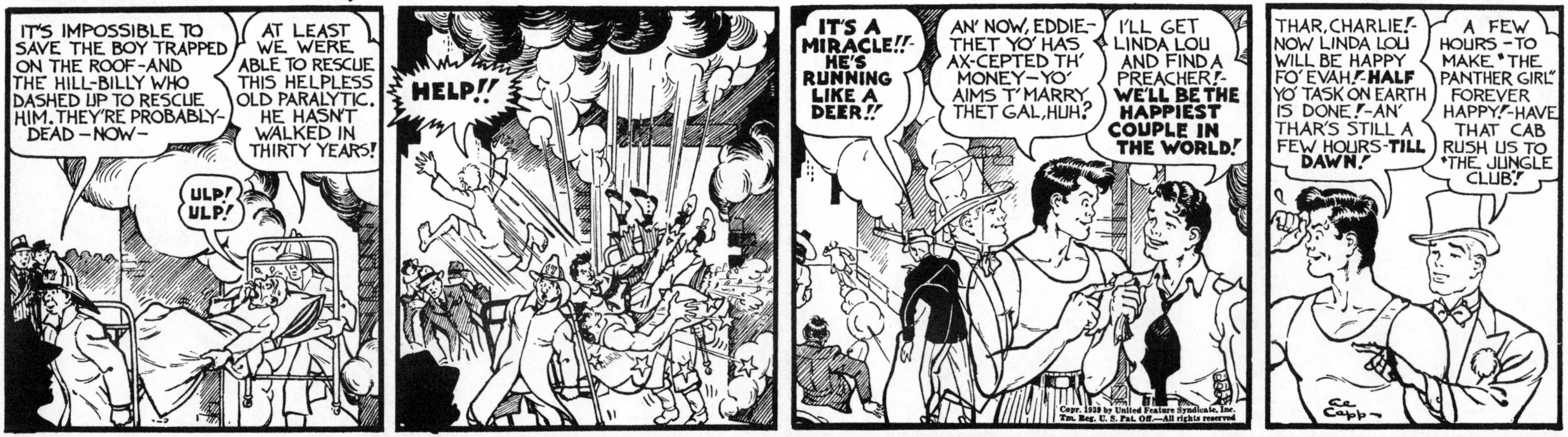
IT'S IMPOSSIBLE TO SAVE THE BOY TRAPPED ON THE ROOF-AND THE HILL-BILLY WHO DASHED UP TO RESCUE HIM. THEY'RE PROBABLY-DEAD-NOW-
AT LEAST WE WERE ABLE TO RESCUE THIS HELPLESS OLD PARALYTIC. HE HASN'T WALKED IN THIRTY YEARS!
ULP! ULP!
HELP!!
IT'S A MIRACLE!!-HE'S RUNNING LIKE A DEER!!
AN' NOW, EDDIE-THET YO' HAS AX-CEPTED TH' MONEY-YO' AIMS T' MARRY THET GAL, HUH?
I'LL GET LINDA LOU AND FIND A PREACHER!-WE'LL BE THE HAPPIEST COUPLE IN THE WORLD!
Copr. 1939 by United Feature Syndicate, Inc. Tm. Reg. U. S. Pat. Off.—All rights reserved
THAR, CHARLIE!-NOW LINDA LOU WILL BE HAPPY FO' EVAH!-HALF YO' TASK ON EARTH IS DONE!-AN' THAR'S STILL A FEW HOURS-TILL DAWN!
A FEW HOURS-TO MAKE "THE PANTHER GIRL" FOREVER HAPPY!-HAVE THAT CAB RUSH US TO "THE JUNGLE CLUB"!
Al Capp

LI'L ABNER An Old Flame Never Dies By Al Capp

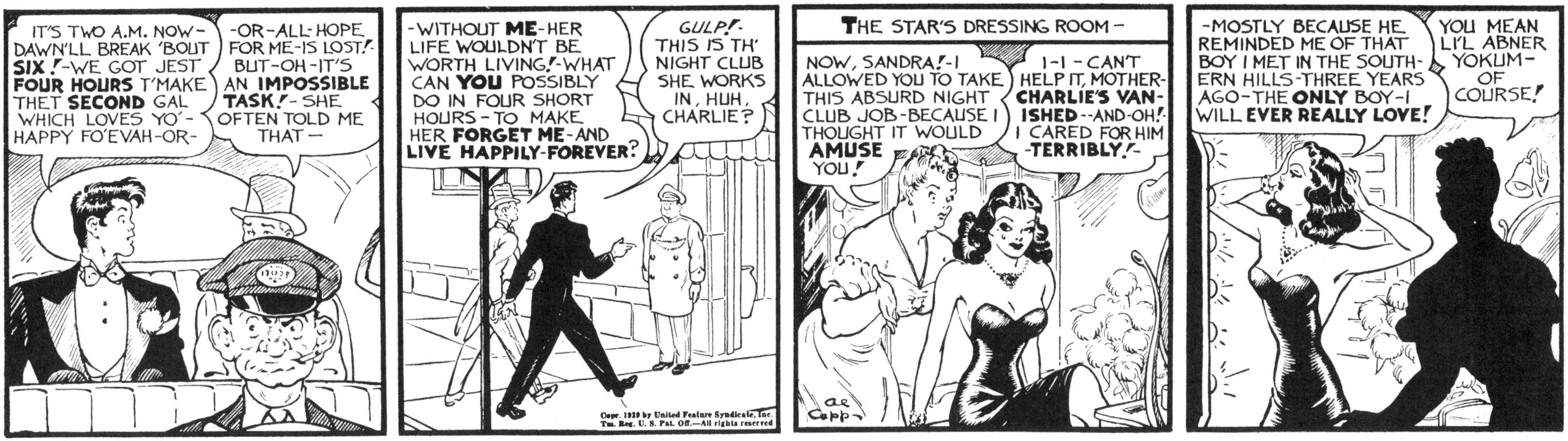
IT'S TWO A.M. NOW-DAWN'LL BREAK 'BOUT SIX!-WE GOT JEST FOUR HOURS T'MAKE THET SECOND GAL WHICH LOVES YO'-HAPPY FO'EVAH-OR-
-OR-ALL-HOPE FOR ME-IS LOST!-BUT-OH-IT'S AN IMPOSSIBLE TASK!-SHE OFTEN TOLD ME THAT-
-WITHOUT ME-HER LIFE WOULDN'T BE WORTH LIVING!-WHAT CAN YOU POSSIBLY DO IN FOUR SHORT HOURS-TO MAKE HER FORGET ME-AND LIVE HAPPILY-FOREVER?
GULP!-THIS IS TH' NIGHT CLUB SHE WORKS IN, HUH, CHARLIE?
Copr. 1939 by United Feature Syndicate, Inc. Tm. Reg. U. S. Pat. Off.—All rights reserved
THE STAR'S DRESSING ROOM-
NOW, SANDRA!-I ALLOWED YOU TO TAKE THIS ABSURD NIGHT CLUB JOB-BECAUSE I THOUGHT IT WOULD AMUSE YOU!
I-I-CAN'T HELP IT, MOTHER-CHARLIE'S VANISHED--AND-OH!-I CARED FOR HIM -TERRIBLY!-
Al Capp
-MOSTLY BECAUSE HE REMINDED ME OF THAT BOY I MET IN THE SOUTHERN HILLS-THREE YEARS AGO-THE ONLY BOY-I WILL EVER REALLY LOVE!
YOU MEAN LI'L ABNER YOKUM-OF COURSE!

LI'L ABNER Rancid Romance! By Al Capp

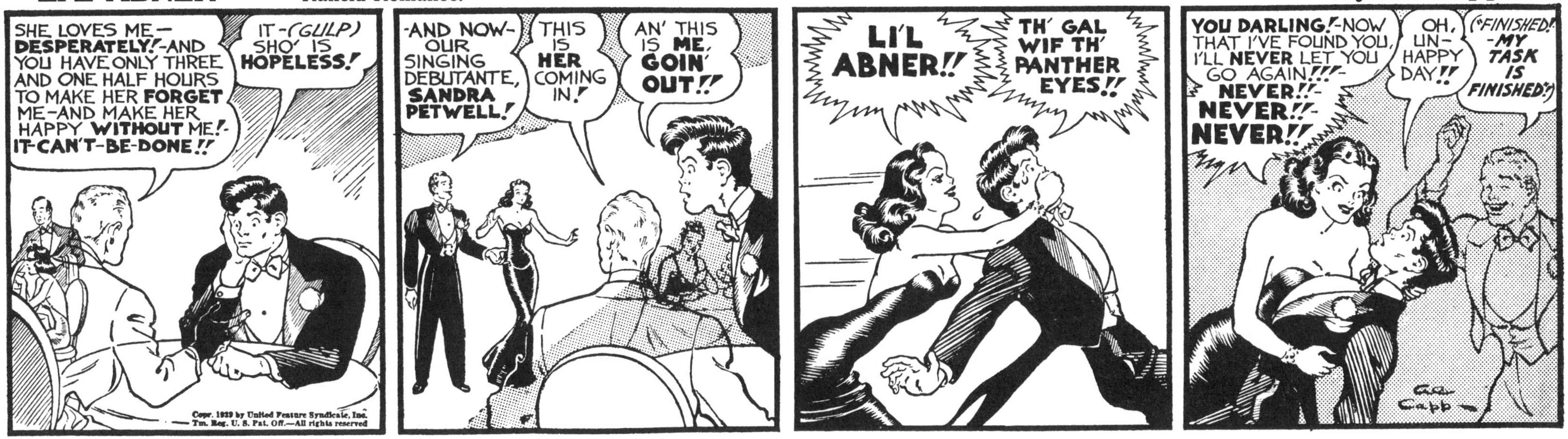
SHE LOVES ME-DESPERATELY!-AND YOU HAVE ONLY THREE AND ONE HALF HOURS TO MAKE HER FORGET ME-AND MAKE HER HAPPY WITHOUT ME!-IT-CAN'T-BE-DONE!!
IT-(GULP) SHO' IS HOPELESS!
Copr. 1939 by United Feature Syndicate, Inc. Tm. Reg. U. S. Pat. Off.—All rights reserved
-AND NOW-OUR SINGING DEBUTANTE, SANDRA PETWELL!
THIS IS HER COMING IN!
AN' THIS IS ME, GOIN' OUT!!
LI'L ABNER!!
TH' GAL WIF TH' PANTHER EYES!!
YOU DARLING!-NOW THAT I'VE FOUND YOU, I'LL NEVER LET YOU GO AGAIN!!!-NEVER!!-NEVER!!-NEVER!!
OH, UN-HAPPY DAY!!
(*FINISHED!-MY TASK IS FINISHED*!)
Al Capp

LI'L ABNER The Parting of the Ways— By Al Capp

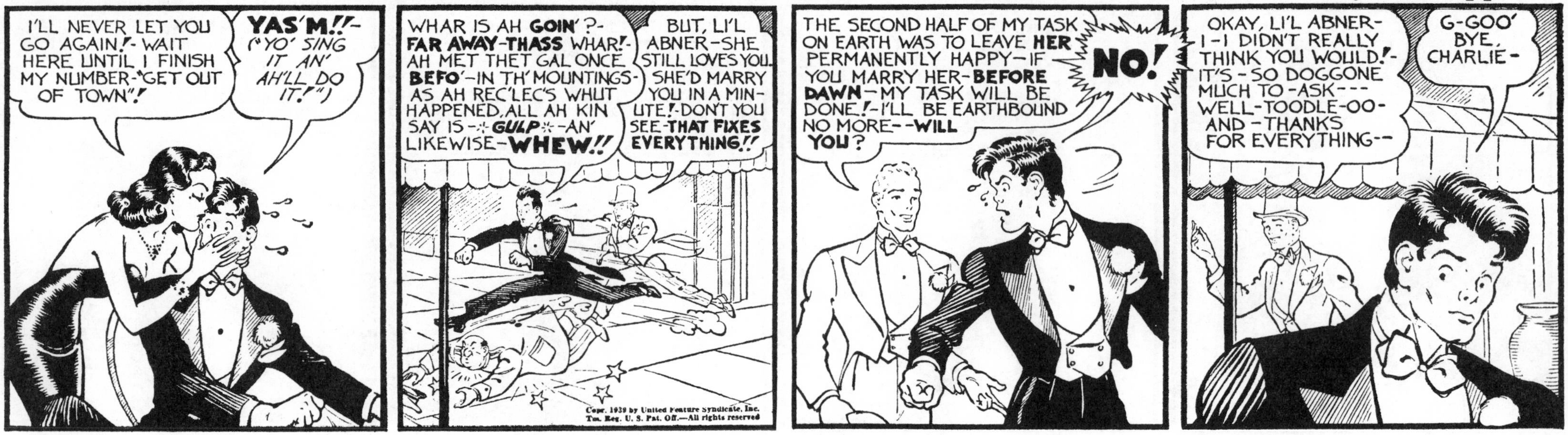

I'LL NEVER LET YOU GO AGAIN!- WAIT HERE UNTIL I FINISH MY NUMBER-"GET OUT OF TOWN"!
YAS'M!!- ("YO' SING IT AN' AH'LL DO IT!")
WHAR IS AH GOIN'?- FAR AWAY-THASS WHAR!- AH MET THET GAL ONCE BEFO'-IN TH' MOUNTINGS- AS AH REC'LEC'S WHUT HAPPENED, ALL AH KIN SAY IS -*GULP*-AN' LIKEWISE-WHEW!!
BUT, LI'L ABNER-SHE STILL LOVES YOU. SHE'D MARRY YOU IN A MIN-UTE!-DON'T YOU SEE-THAT FIXES EVERYTHING!!
Copr. 1939 by United Feature Syndicate, Inc. Tm. Reg. U. S. Pat. Off.—All rights reserved
THE SECOND HALF OF MY TASK ON EARTH WAS TO LEAVE HER PERMANENTLY HAPPY-IF YOU MARRY HER-BEFORE DAWN-MY TASK WILL BE DONE!-I'LL BE EARTHBOUND NO MORE--WILL YOU?
NO!
OKAY, LI'L ABNER- I-I DIDN'T REALLY THINK YOU WOULD!- IT'S-SO DOGGONE MUCH TO-ASK--- WELL-TOODLE-OO- AND-THANKS FOR EVERYTHING--
G-GOO' BYE, CHARLIE-

LI'L ABNER Li'l White Lie By Al Capp

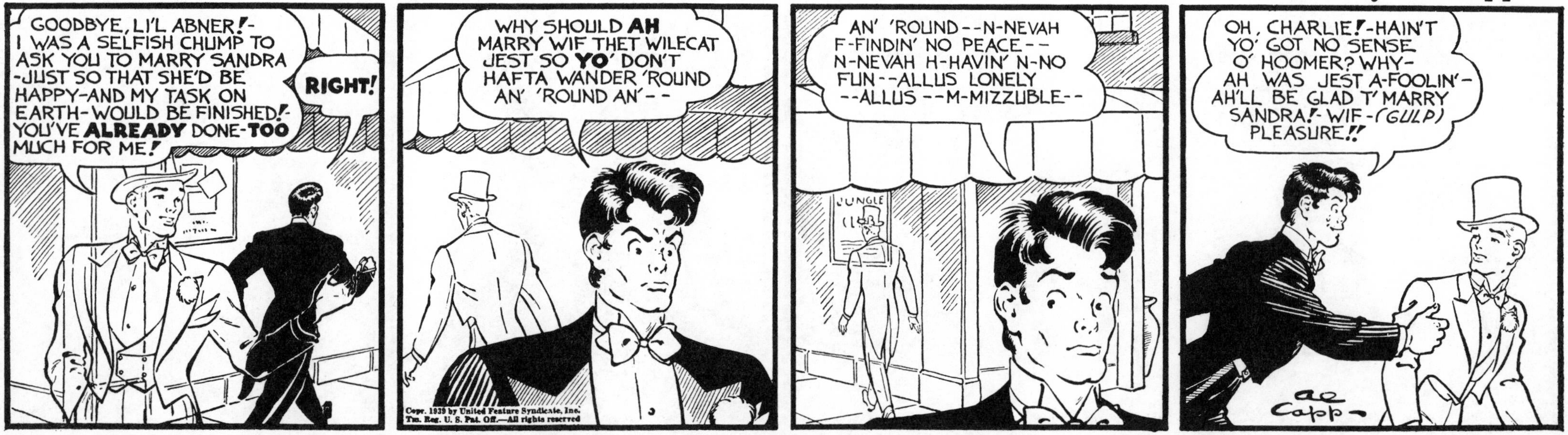

GOODBYE, LI'L ABNER!- I WAS A SELFISH CHUMP TO ASK YOU TO MARRY SANDRA -JUST SO THAT SHE'D BE HAPPY-AND MY TASK ON EARTH-WOULD BE FINISHED!- YOU'VE ALREADY DONE-TOO MUCH FOR ME!
RIGHT!
WHY SHOULD AH MARRY WIF THET WILECAT JEST SO YO' DON'T HAFTA WANDER 'ROUND AN' 'ROUND AN'--
Copr. 1939 by United Feature Syndicate, Inc. Tm. Reg. U. S. Pat. Off.—All rights reserved
AN' 'ROUND--N-NEVAH F-FINDIN' NO PEACE-- N-NEVAH H-HAVIN' N-NO FUN--ALLUS LONELY --ALLUS--M-MIZZUBLE--
JUNGLE CLUB
OH, CHARLIE!-HAIN'T YO' GOT NO SENSE O' HOOMER? WHY- AH WAS JEST A-FOOLIN'- AH'LL BE GLAD T' MARRY SANDRA!- WIF-(GULP) PLEASURE!!
al capp

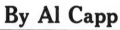

LI'L ABNER Boy Meets Girl! By Al Capp

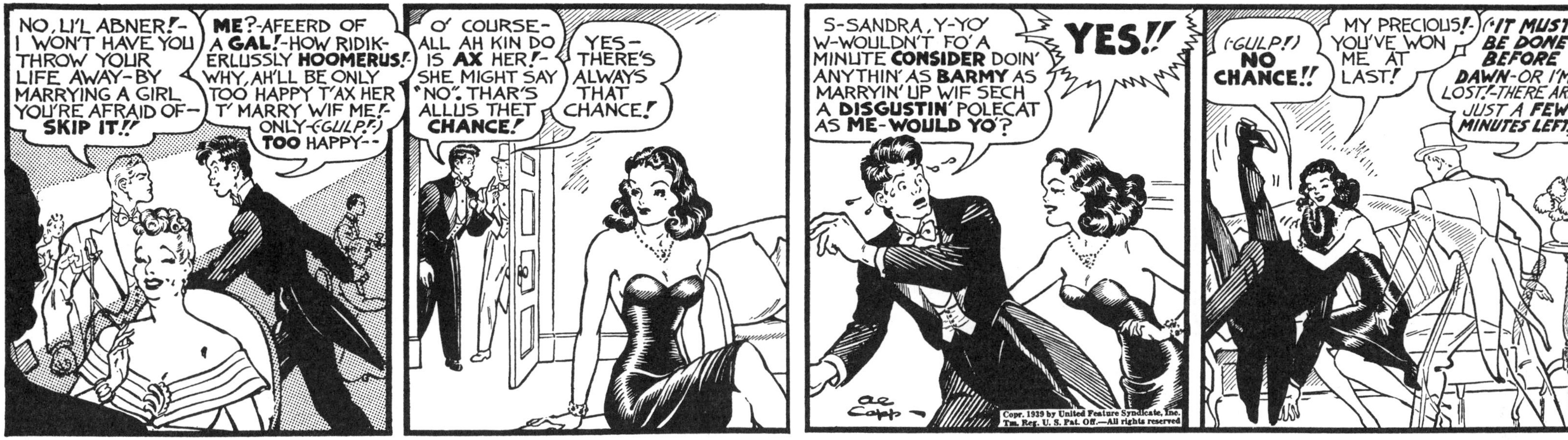
NO, LI'L ABNER!- I WON'T HAVE YOU THROW YOUR LIFE AWAY-BY MARRYING A GIRL YOU'RE AFRAID OF- SKIP IT!!
ME?-AFEERD OF A GAL!-HOW RIDIKERLUSSLY HOOMERUS!- WHY, AH'LL BE ONLY TOO HAPPY T'AX HER T' MARRY WIF ME!- ONLY-(-GULP!-) TOO HAPPY--
O' COURSE- ALL AH KIN DO IS AX HER!- SHE MIGHT SAY "NO". THAR'S ALLUS THET CHANCE!
YES- THERE'S ALWAYS THAT CHANCE!
S-SANDRA, Y-YO' W-WOULDN'T FO' A MINUTE CONSIDER DOIN' ANYTHIN' AS BARMY AS MARRYIN' UP WIF SECH A DISGUSTIN' POLECAT AS ME-WOULD YO'?
YES!!
Copr. 1939 by United Feature Syndicate, Inc. Tm. Reg. U. S. Pat. Off.—All rights reserved
(-GULP!-) NO CHANCE!!
MY PRECIOUS!- YOU'VE WON ME AT LAST!
("IT MUST BE DONE BEFORE DAWN-OR I'M LOST!-THERE ARE JUST A FEW MINUTES LEFT.")

LI'L ABNER A Lamb to the Slaughter!! By Al Capp

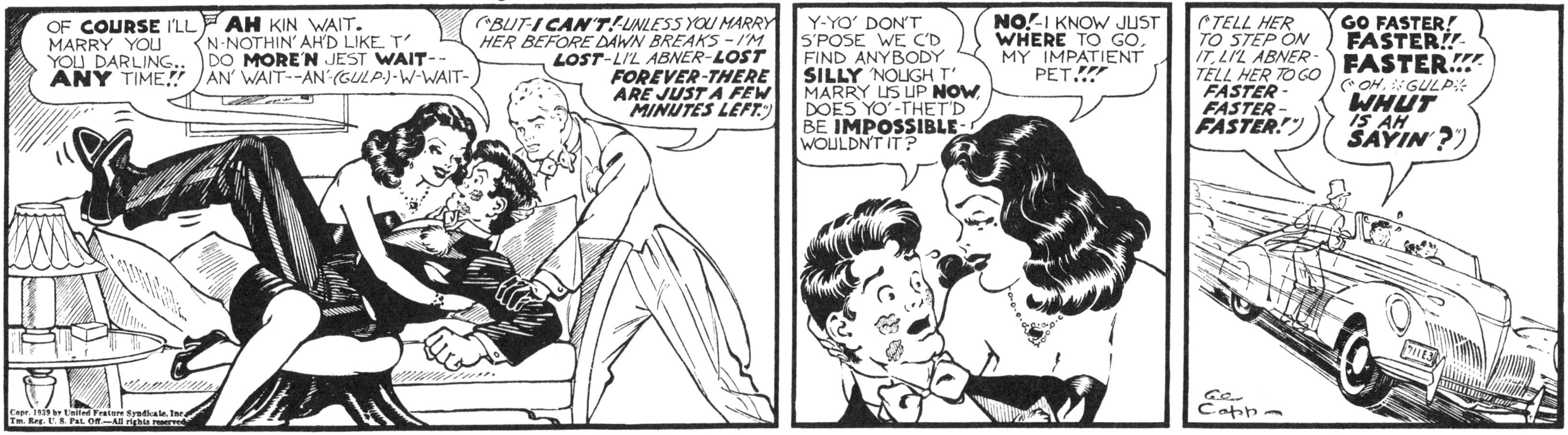
OF COURSE I'LL MARRY YOU YOU DARLING.. ANY TIME!!
AH KIN WAIT. N-NOTHIN' AH'D LIKE T' DO MORE'N JEST WAIT-- AN' WAIT--AN'-(GULP-)-W-WAIT-
("BUT-I CAN'T!-UNLESS YOU MARRY HER BEFORE DAWN BREAKS-I'M LOST-LI'L ABNER-LOST FOREVER-THERE ARE JUST A FEW MINUTES LEFT.")
Copr. 1939 by United Feature Syndicate, Inc. Tm. Reg. U. S. Pat. Off.—All rights reserved
Y-YO' DON'T S'POSE WE C'D FIND ANYBODY SILLY 'NOUGH T' MARRY US UP NOW, DOES YO'-THET'D BE IMPOSSIBLE- WOULDN'T IT?
NO!-I KNOW JUST WHERE TO GO, MY IMPATIENT PET!!!
("TELL HER TO STEP ON IT, LI'L ABNER- TELL HER TO GO FASTER- FASTER- FASTER!")
GO FASTER! FASTER!!- FASTER!!!
("OH, GULP WHUT IS AH SAYIN'?")

LI'L ABNER Comes the Dawn!! By Al Capp

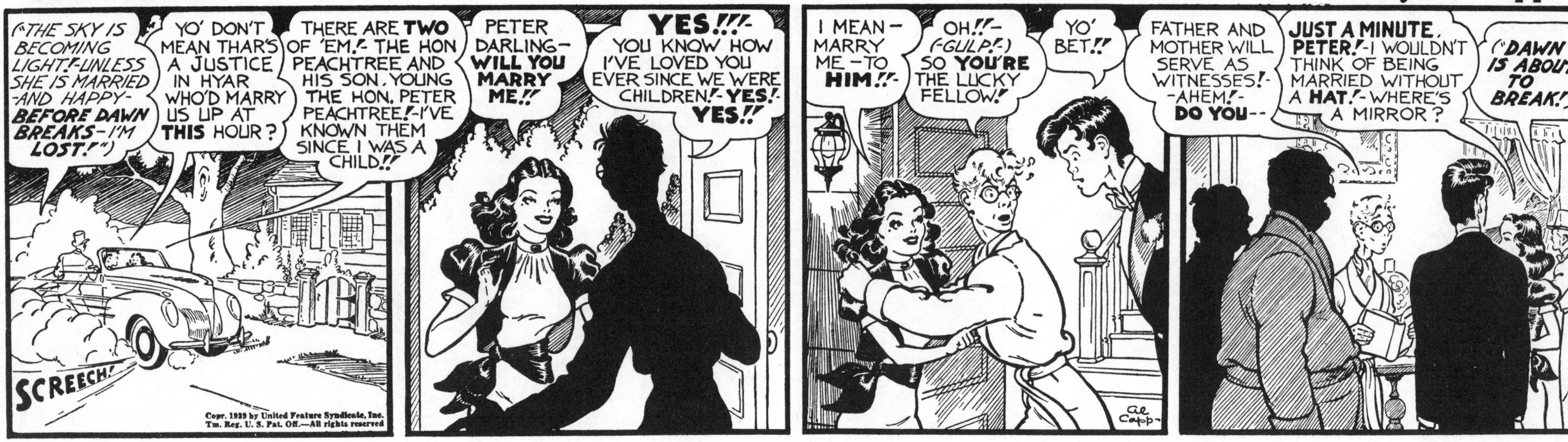
("THE SKY IS BECOMING LIGHT!-UNLESS SHE IS MARRIED -AND HAPPY- BEFORE DAWN BREAKS-I'M LOST!")
YO' DON'T MEAN THAR'S A JUSTICE IN HYAR WHO'D MARRY US UP AT THIS HOUR?
THERE ARE TWO OF 'EM!- THE HON PEACHTREE AND HIS SON. YOUNG THE HON. PETER PEACHTREE!-I'VE KNOWN THEM SINCE I WAS A CHILD!!
SCREECH!
Copr. 1939 by United Feature Syndicate, Inc. Tm. Reg. U. S. Pat. Off.—All rights reserved
PETER DARLING- WILL YOU MARRY ME!!
YES!!!- YOU KNOW HOW I'VE LOVED YOU EVER SINCE WE WERE CHILDREN!-YES!- YES!!
I MEAN- MARRY ME-TO HIM!!-
OH!!- (-GULP!-) SO YOU'RE THE LUCKY FELLOW!
YO' BET!!
FATHER AND MOTHER WILL SERVE AS WITNESSES!- -AHEM!- DO YOU--
JUST A MINUTE, PETER!-I WOULDN'T THINK OF BEING MARRIED WITHOUT A HAT!-WHERE'S A MIRROR?
("DAWN IS ABOUT TO BREAK!")

LI'L ABNER Sandra Gets the Bird By Al Capp

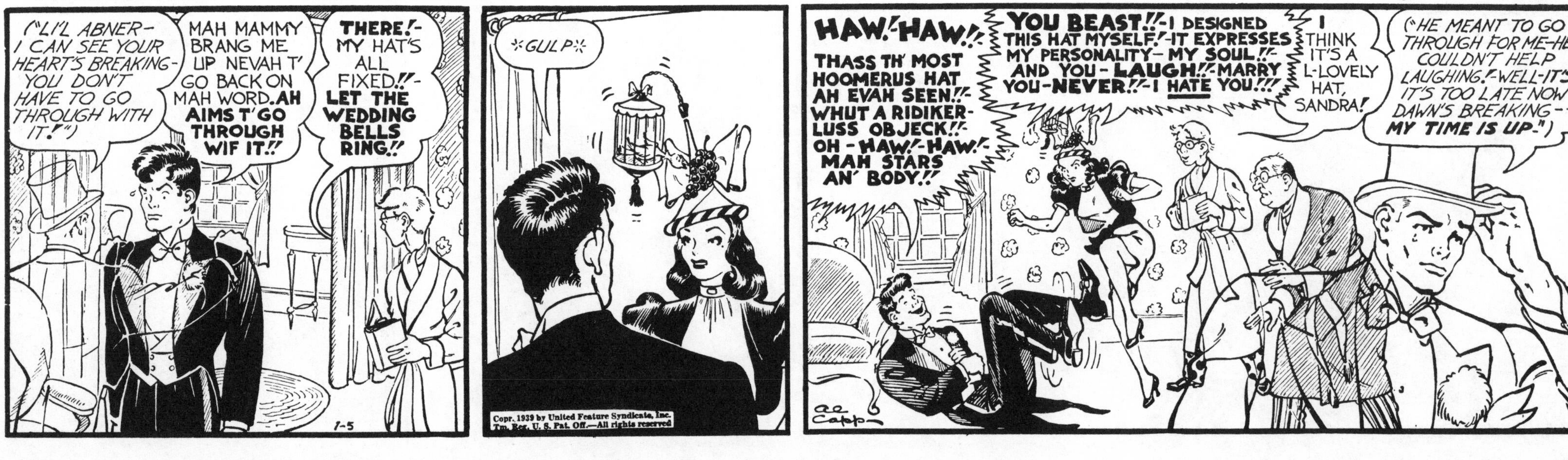
("LI'L ABNER- I CAN SEE YOUR HEART'S BREAKING- YOU DON'T HAVE TO GO THROUGH WITH IT!")
MAH MAMMY BRANG ME UP NEVAH T' GO BACK ON MAH WORD. AH AIMS T' GO THROUGH WIF IT!!
THERE!- MY HAT'S ALL FIXED!!- LET THE WEDDING BELLS RING!!
1-5
GULP
Copr. 1939 by United Feature Syndicate, Inc. Tm. Reg. U. S. Pat. Off.—All rights reserved
HAW!-HAW!! THASS TH' MOST HOOMERUS HAT AH EVAH SEEN!!- WHUT A RIDIKER-LUSS OBJECK!!- OH-HAW!-HAW!- MAH STARS AN' BODY!!
YOU BEAST!!-I DESIGNED THIS HAT MYSELF!-IT EXPRESSES MY PERSONALITY- MY SOUL!!- AND YOU- LAUGH!!-MARRY YOU-NEVER!!-I HATE YOU!!!
I THINK IT'S A L-LOVELY HAT, SANDRA!
("HE MEANT TO GO THROUGH FOR ME-HE COULDN'T HELP LAUGHING!-WELL-IT'S IT'S TOO LATE NOW- DAWN'S BREAKING-- MY TIME IS UP.")

LI'L ABNER The Ghost Goes West By Al Capp

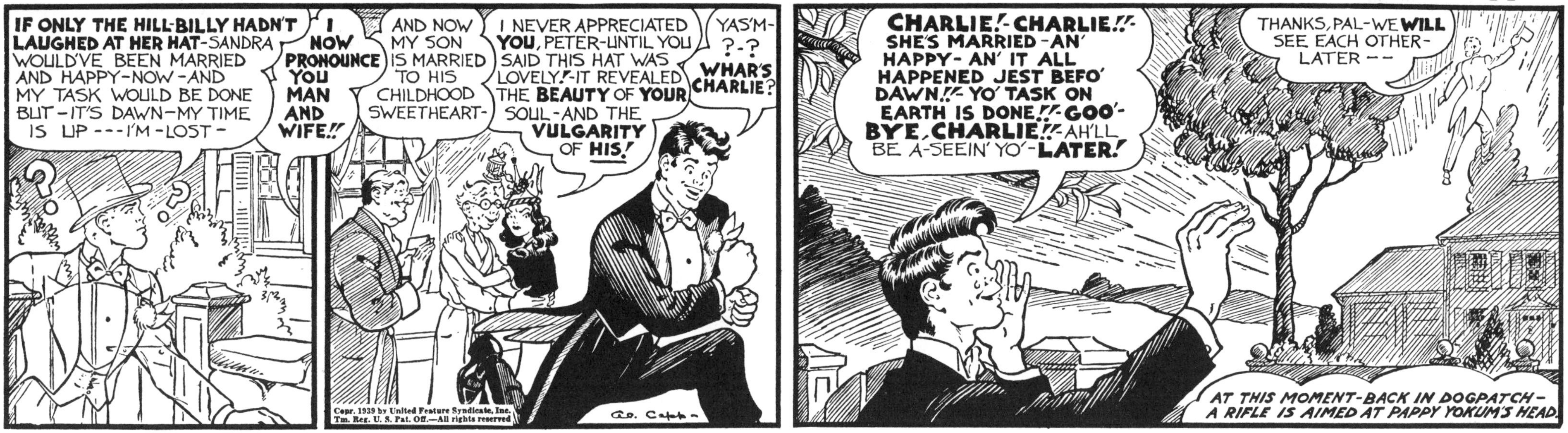

IF ONLY THE HILL-BILLY HADN'T LAUGHED AT HER HAT-SANDRA WOULD'VE BEEN MARRIED AND HAPPY-NOW-AND MY TASK WOULD BE DONE BUT-IT'S DAWN-MY TIME IS UP---I'M-LOST-
I NOW PRONOUNCE YOU MAN AND WIFE.!!
AND NOW MY SON IS MARRIED TO HIS CHILDHOOD SWEETHEART-
I NEVER APPRECIATED YOU, PETER-UNTIL YOU SAID THIS HAT WAS LOVELY.!-IT REVEALED THE BEAUTY OF YOUR SOUL-AND THE VULGARITY OF HIS!
YAS'M-?-? WHAR'S CHARLIE?
Copr. 1939 by United Feature Syndicate, Inc. Tm. Reg. U. S. Pat. Off.—All rights reserved
CHARLIE!-CHARLIE!!-SHE'S MARRIED-AN' HAPPY-AN' IT ALL HAPPENED JEST BEFO' DAWN.!!-YO' TASK ON EARTH IS DONE.!!-GOO'-BYE, CHARLIE!!-AH'LL BE A-SEEIN' YO'-LATER!
THANKS, PAL-WE WILL SEE EACH OTHER-LATER--
AT THIS MOMENT-BACK IN DOGPATCH-A RIFLE IS AIMED AT PAPPY YOKUM'S HEAD.

LI'L ABNER Welcome, Stranger By Al Capp

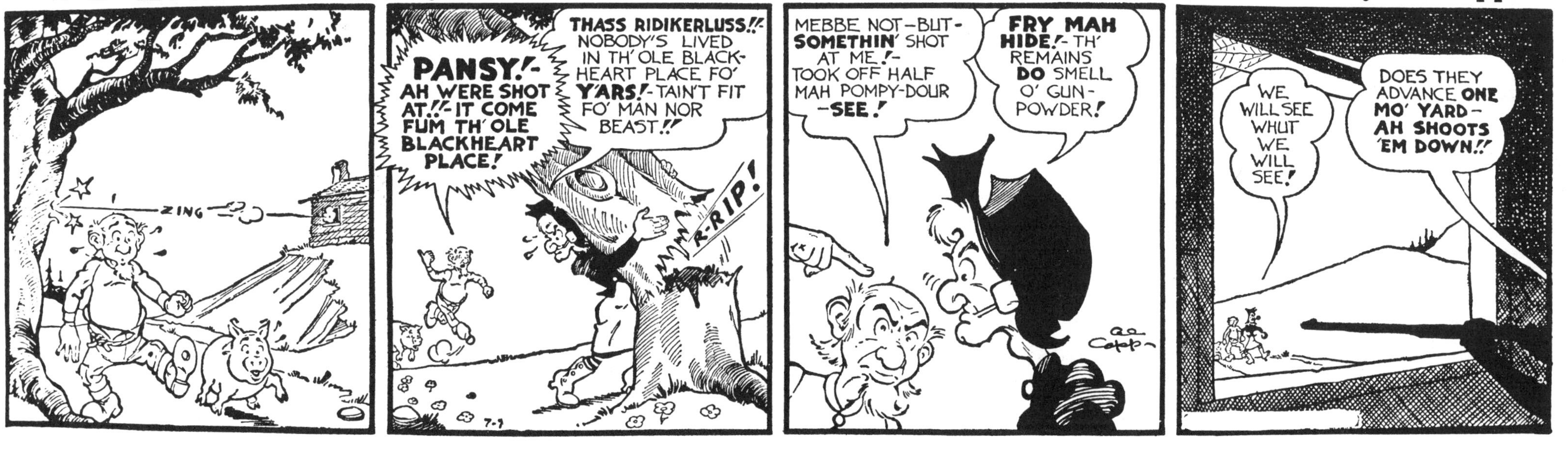

ZING
PANSY!-AH WERE SHOT AT.!!-IT COME FUM TH' OLE BLACKHEART PLACE!
THASS RIDIKERLUSS!!-NOBODY'S LIVED IN TH' OLE BLACK-HEART PLACE FO' Y'ARS!-TAIN'T FIT FO' MAN NOR BEAST.!!
R-RIP!
MEBBE NOT-BUT-SOMETHIN' SHOT AT ME.!-TOOK OFF HALF MAH POMPY-DOUR-SEE.!
FRY MAH HIDE.!-TH' REMAINS DO SMELL O' GUN-POWDER!
WE WILL SEE WHUT WE WILL SEE!
DOES THEY ADVANCE ONE MO' YARD-AH SHOOTS 'EM DOWN.!!

LI'L ABNER — If It's Not One Yokum It's Another — By Al Capp

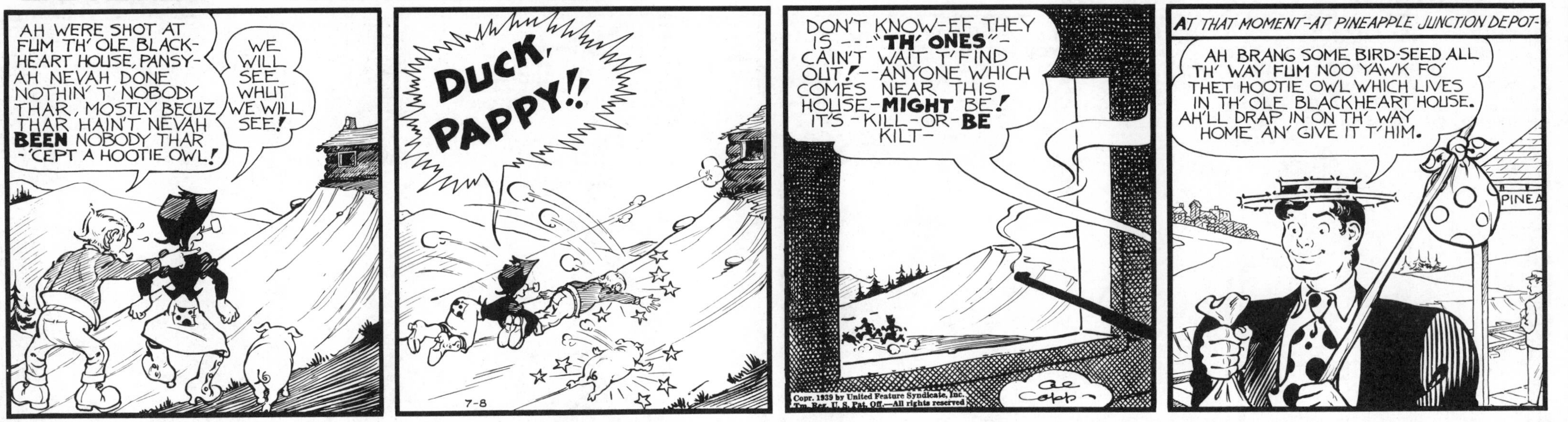
AH WERE SHOT AT FUM TH' OLE BLACK-HEART HOUSE, PANSY-AH NEVAH DONE NOTHIN' T' NOBODY THAR, MOSTLY BECUZ THAR HAIN'T NEVAH BEEN NOBODY THAR -'CEPT A HOOTIE OWL!
WE WILL SEE WHUT WE WILL SEE!
DUCK, PAPPY!!
7-8
DON'T KNOW-EF THEY IS ---"TH' ONES"- CAIN'T WAIT T'FIND OUT!--ANYONE WHICH COMES NEAR THIS HOUSE-MIGHT BE! IT'S -KILL-OR-BE KILT-
Copr. 1939 by United Feature Syndicate, Inc. Tm. Reg. U. S. Pat. Off.—All rights reserved
AL CAPP
AT THAT MOMENT-AT PINEAPPLE JUNCTION DEPOT-
AH BRANG SOME BIRD-SEED ALL TH' WAY FUM NOO YAWK FO' THET HOOTIE OWL WHICH LIVES IN TH' OLE BLACKHEART HOUSE. AH'LL DRAP IN ON TH' WAY HOME AN' GIVE IT T'HIM.
PINEA

LI'L ABNER — Like a Lamb to the Slaughter — By Al Capp

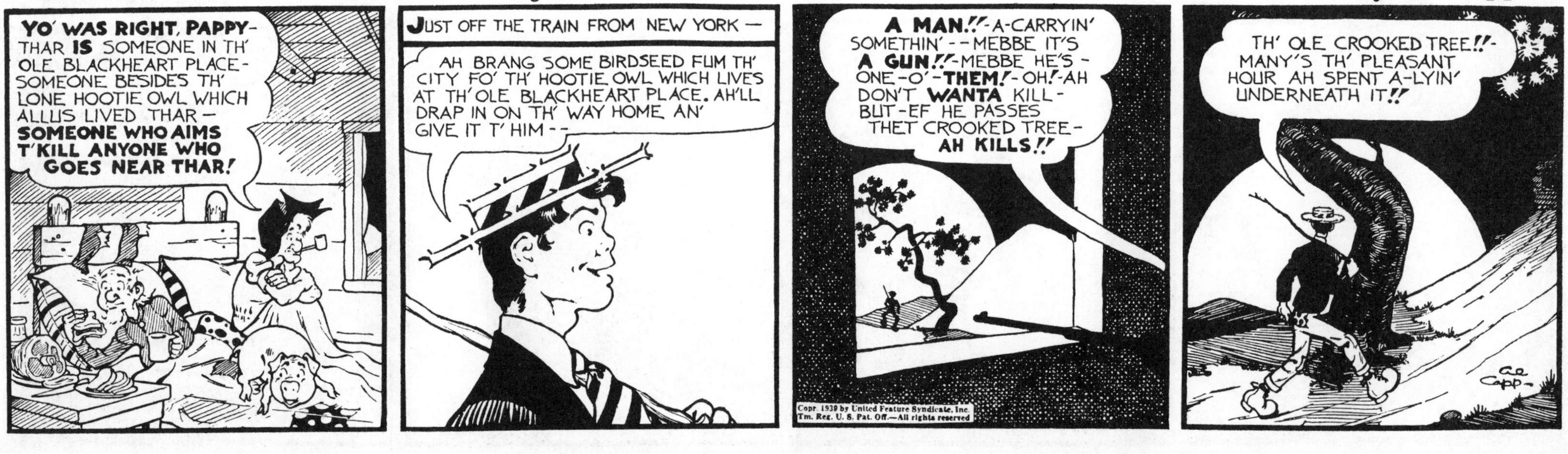
YO' WAS RIGHT, PAPPY- THAR IS SOMEONE IN TH' OLE BLACKHEART PLACE- SOMEONE BESIDES TH' LONE HOOTIE OWL WHICH ALLUS LIVED THAR- SOMEONE WHO AIMS T'KILL ANYONE WHO GOES NEAR THAR!
JUST OFF THE TRAIN FROM NEW YORK —
AH BRANG SOME BIRDSEED FUM TH' CITY FO' TH' HOOTIE OWL WHICH LIVES AT TH' OLE BLACKHEART PLACE. AH'LL DRAP IN ON TH' WAY HOME AN' GIVE IT T' HIM--
A MAN!!-A-CARRYIN' SOMETHIN'--MEBBE IT'S A GUN!!-MEBBE HE'S - ONE-O'-THEM!-OH!-AH DON'T WANTA KILL- BUT-EF HE PASSES THET CROOKED TREE- AH KILLS!!
Copr. 1939 by United Feature Syndicate, Inc. Tm. Reg. U. S. Pat. Off.—All rights reserved
TH' OLE CROOKED TREE!!- MANY'S TH' PLEASANT HOUR AH SPENT A-LYIN' UNDERNEATH IT!!
AL CAPP

LI'L ABNER Different Worlds By Al Capp

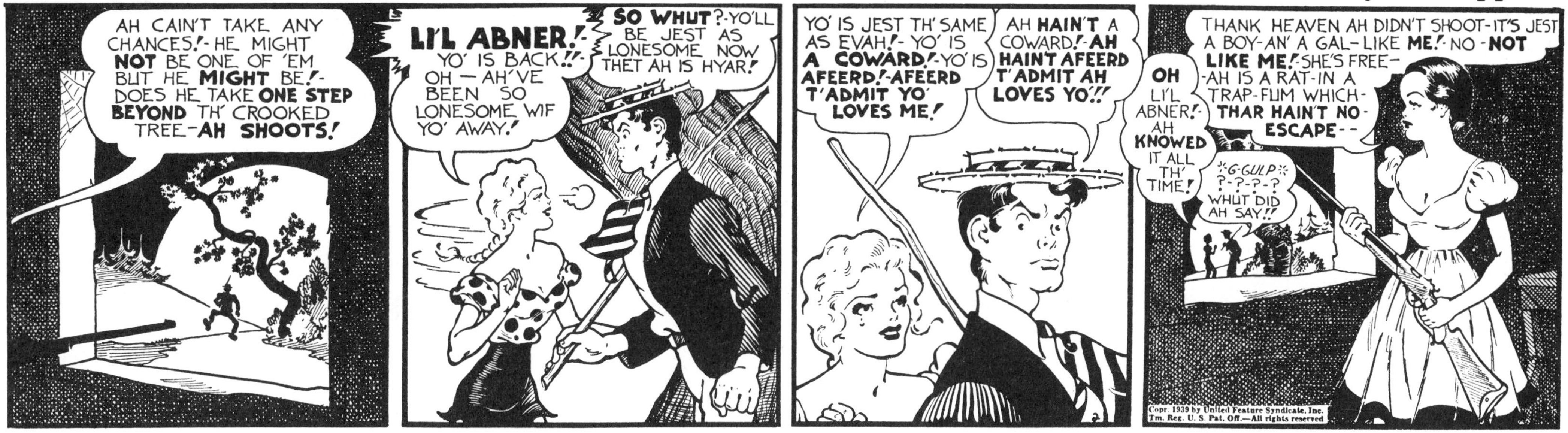

AH CAIN'T TAKE ANY CHANCES!-HE MIGHT NOT BE ONE OF 'EM BUT HE MIGHT BE!-DOES HE TAKE ONE STEP BEYOND TH' CROOKED TREE-AH SHOOTS!
LI'L ABNER!-YO' IS BACK!!-OH—AH'VE BEEN SO LONESOME WIF YO' AWAY!
SO WHUT?-YO'LL BE JEST AS LONESOME NOW THET AH IS HYAR!
YO' IS JEST TH' SAME AS EVAH!-YO' IS A COWARD!-YO' IS AFEERD!-AFEERD T'ADMIT YO' LOVES ME!
AH HAIN'T A COWARD!-AH HAIN'T AFEERD T'ADMIT AH LOVES YO'!!
OH LI'L ABNER!-AH KNOWED IT ALL TH' TIME!
G-GULP ?-?-?-? WHUT DID AH SAY!!
THANK HEAVEN AH DIDN'T SHOOT-IT'S JEST A BOY-AN' A GAL-LIKE ME!-NO-NOT LIKE ME!-SHE'S FREE--AH IS A RAT-IN A TRAP-FUM WHICH-THAR HAIN'T NO-ESCAPE--
Copr. 1939 by United Feature Syndicate, Inc. Tm. Reg. U. S. Pat. Off.—All rights reserved

LI'L ABNER A Rendezvous With Death! By Al Capp

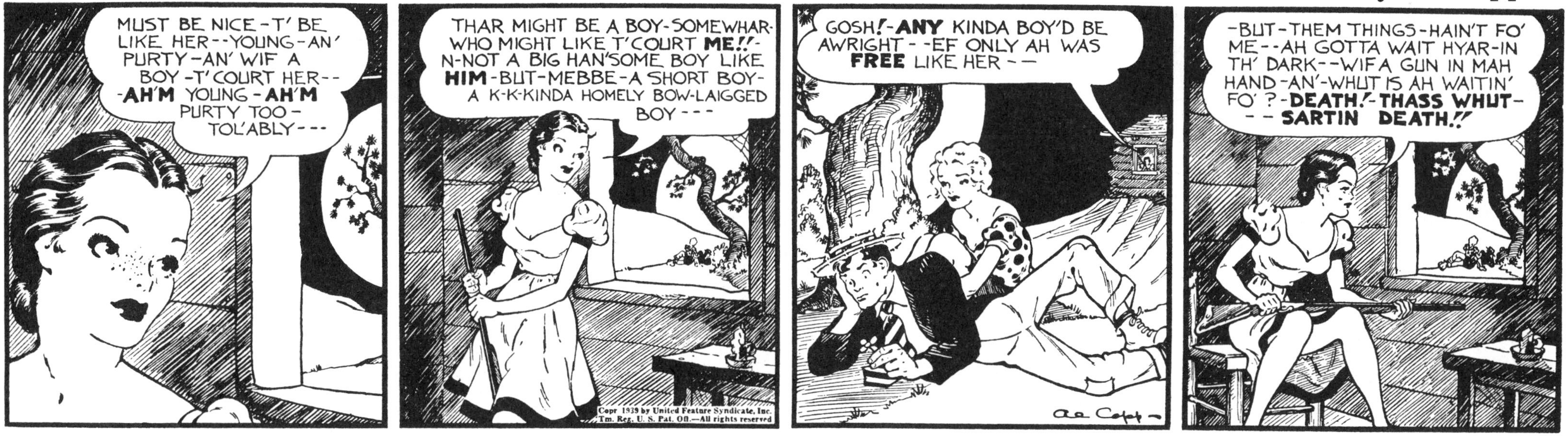

MUST BE NICE-T' BE LIKE HER--YOUNG-AN' PURTY-AN' WIF A BOY-T' COURT HER---AH'M YOUNG-AH'M PURTY TOO-TOL'ABLY---
THAR MIGHT BE A BOY-SOMEWHAR-WHO MIGHT LIKE T'COURT ME!!-N-NOT A BIG HAN'SOME BOY LIKE HIM-BUT-MEBBE-A SHORT BOY-A K-K-KINDA HOMELY BOW-LAIGGED BOY---
Copr. 1939 by United Feature Syndicate, Inc. Tm. Reg. U. S. Pat. Off.—All rights reserved
GOSH!-ANY KINDA BOY'D BE AWRIGHT--EF ONLY AH WAS FREE LIKE HER--
-BUT-THEM THINGS-HAIN'T FO' ME--AH GOTTA WAIT HYAR-IN TH' DARK--WIF A GUN IN MAH HAND-AN'-WHUT IS AH WAITIN' FO'?-DEATH!-THASS WHUT---SARTIN DEATH!!

LI'L ABNER A Lover of the Old School By Al Capp

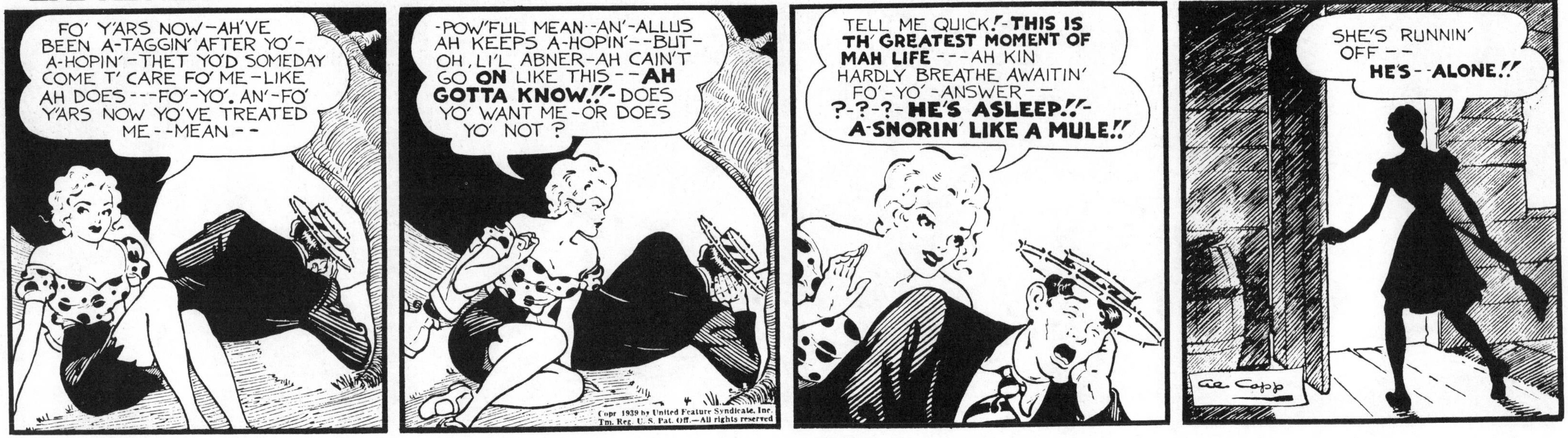

FO' Y'ARS NOW–AH'VE BEEN A-TAGGIN' AFTER YO'– A-HOPIN'–THET YO'D SOMEDAY COME T' CARE FO' ME–LIKE AH DOES---FO'-YO'. AN'-FO' Y'ARS NOW YO'VE TREATED ME--MEAN--
-POW'FUL MEAN--AN'-ALLUS AH KEEPS A-HOPIN'--BUT–OH, LI'L ABNER–AH CAIN'T GO ON LIKE THIS--AH GOTTA KNOW.!!-DOES YO' WANT ME–OR DOES YO' NOT ?
Copr. 1939 by United Feature Syndicate, Inc. Tm. Reg. U. S. Pat. Off.—All rights reserved
TELL ME QUICK!-THIS IS TH' GREATEST MOMENT OF MAH LIFE---AH KIN HARDLY BREATHE AWAITIN' FO'-YO'-ANSWER--
?-?-?-HE'S ASLEEP.!!- A-SNORIN' LIKE A MULE.!!
SHE'S RUNNIN' OFF--
HE'S--ALONE.!!

LI'L ABNER Could Be By Al Capp

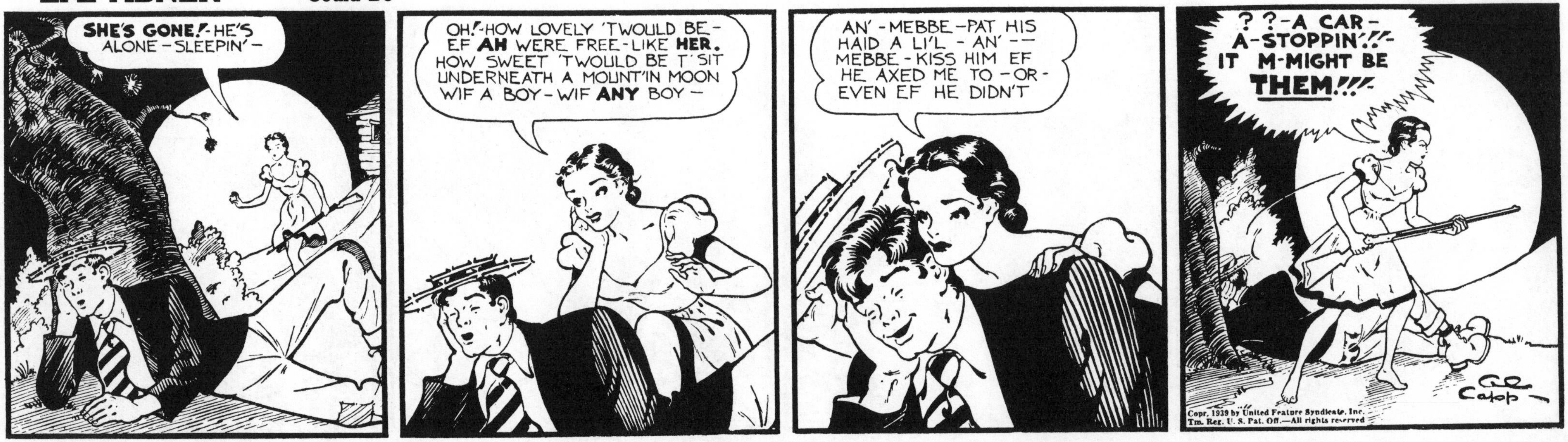

SHE'S GONE!-HE'S ALONE–SLEEPIN'–
OH!-HOW LOVELY 'TWOULD BE–EF AH WERE FREE-LIKE HER. HOW SWEET 'TWOULD BE T' SIT UNDERNEATH A MOUNT'IN MOON WIF A BOY–WIF ANY BOY–
AN'-MEBBE–PAT HIS HAID A LI'L–AN'-- MEBBE–KISS HIM EF HE AXED ME TO–OR–EVEN EF HE DIDN'T
??–A CAR– A-STOPPIN'.!!- IT M-MIGHT BE THEM!!!
Copr. 1939 by United Feature Syndicate, Inc. Tm. Reg. U. S. Pat. Off.—All rights reserved

LI'L ABNER A Bad Brake for Li'l Abner **By Al Capp**

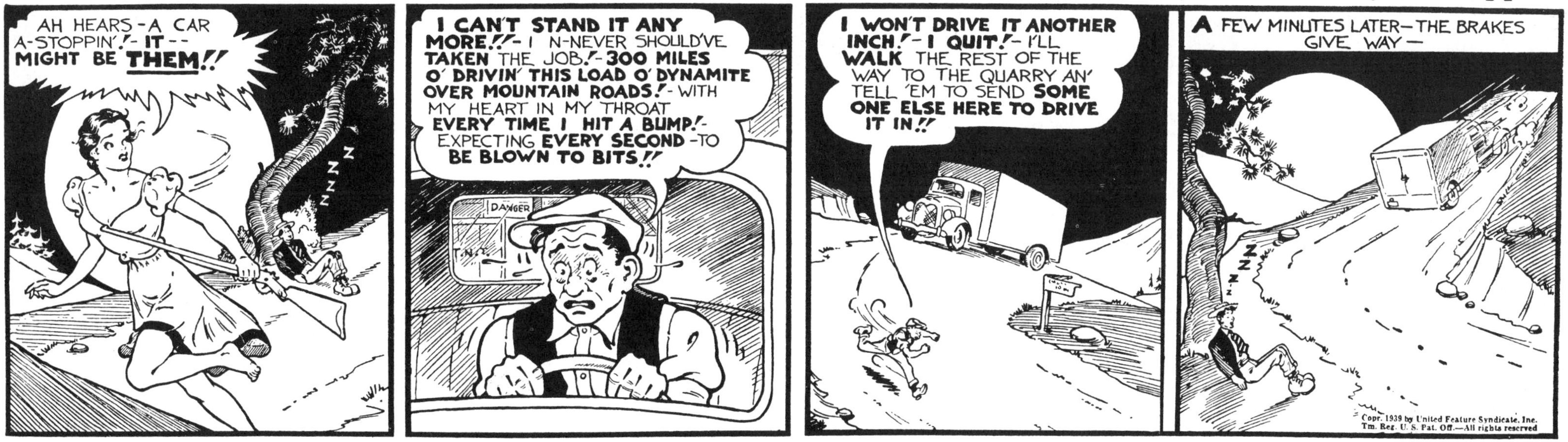

AH HEARS-A CAR A-STOPPIN'!- IT -- MIGHT BE THEM!!
Z Z Z Z
I CAN'T STAND IT ANY MORE!!- I N-NEVER SHOULD'VE TAKEN THE JOB!-300 MILES O' DRIVIN' THIS LOAD O' DYNAMITE OVER MOUNTAIN ROADS!- WITH MY HEART IN MY THROAT EVERY TIME I HIT A BUMP!- EXPECTING EVERY SECOND -TO BE BLOWN TO BITS!!
DANGER
T.N.T.
I WON'T DRIVE IT ANOTHER INCH!- I QUIT!- I'LL WALK THE REST OF THE WAY TO THE QUARRY AN' TELL 'EM TO SEND SOME ONE ELSE HERE TO DRIVE IT IN!!
A FEW MINUTES LATER—THE BRAKES GIVE WAY—
Z Z Z
Copr. 1939 by United Feature Syndicate, Inc.
Tm. Reg. U. S. Pat. Off.—All rights reserved

LI'L ABNER The Truck Kissed Him, Too! **By Al Capp**

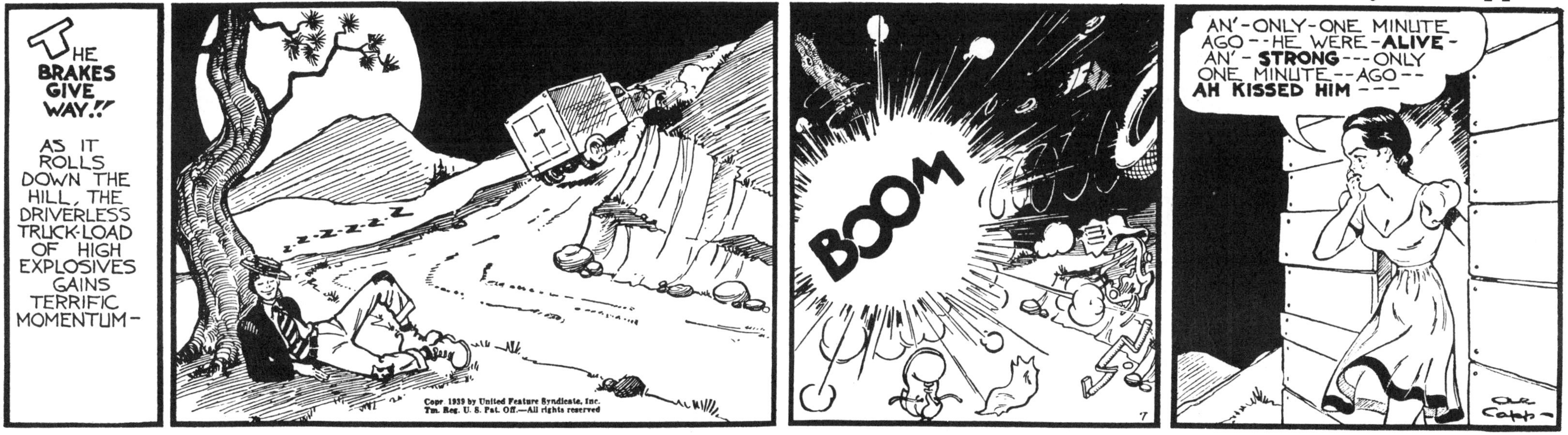

THE BRAKES GIVE WAY!!
AS IT ROLLS DOWN THE HILL, THE DRIVERLESS TRUCK-LOAD OF HIGH EXPLOSIVES GAINS TERRIFIC MOMENTUM-
Z-Z-Z-Z-Z-Z
Copr. 1939 by United Feature Syndicate, Inc.
Tm. Reg. U. S. Pat. Off.—All rights reserved
BOOM
AN'-ONLY-ONE MINUTE AGO--HE WERE-ALIVE-AN'-STRONG---ONLY ONE MINUTE--AGO--AH KISSED HIM---
Al Capp

LI'L ABNER — A Friend in Need! — By Al Capp

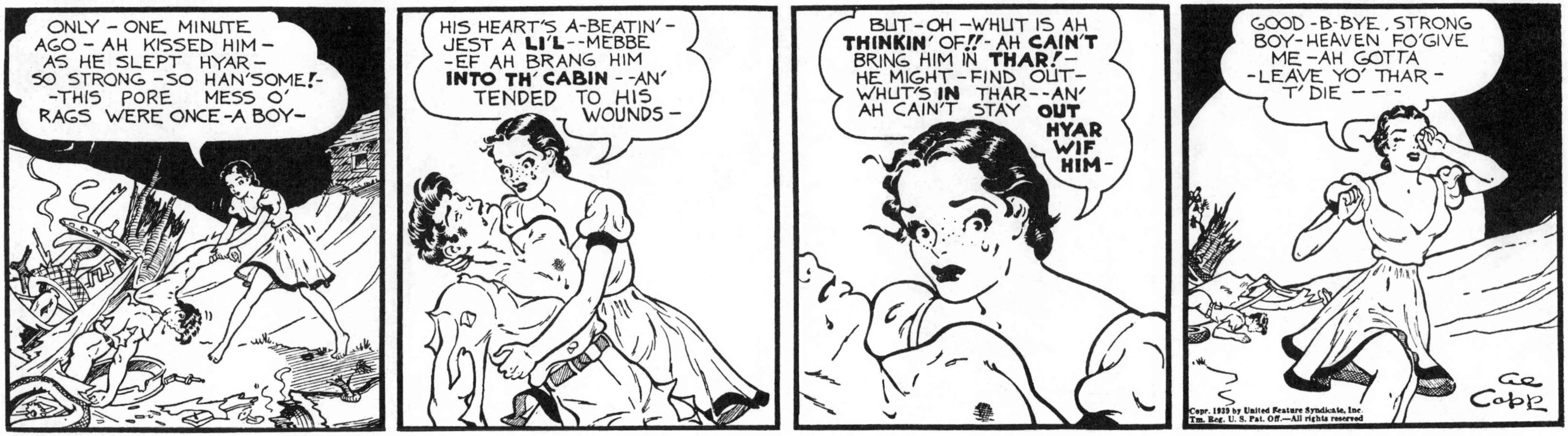

ONLY - ONE MINUTE AGO - AH KISSED HIM - AS HE SLEPT HYAR - SO STRONG - SO HAN'SOME!- -THIS PORE MESS O' RAGS WERE ONCE - A BOY-
HIS HEART'S A-BEATIN' - JEST A **LI'L** - - MEBBE -EF AH BRANG HIM **INTO TH' CABIN** - - AN' TENDED TO HIS WOUNDS -
BUT - OH - WHUT IS AH **THINKIN'** OF!! - AH **CAIN'T** BRING HIM IN **THAR!** - HE MIGHT - FIND OUT - WHUT'S **IN** THAR - - AN' AH CAIN'T STAY **OUT HYAR WIF HIM** -
GOOD - B - BYE, STRONG BOY - HEAVEN FO'GIVE ME - AH GOTTA - LEAVE YO' THAR - T' DIE - - -
Copr. 1939 by United Feature Syndicate, Inc. Tm. Reg. U. S. Pat. Off.—All rights reserved
Al Capp

LI'L ABNER — Luck o' the Yokums! — By Al Capp

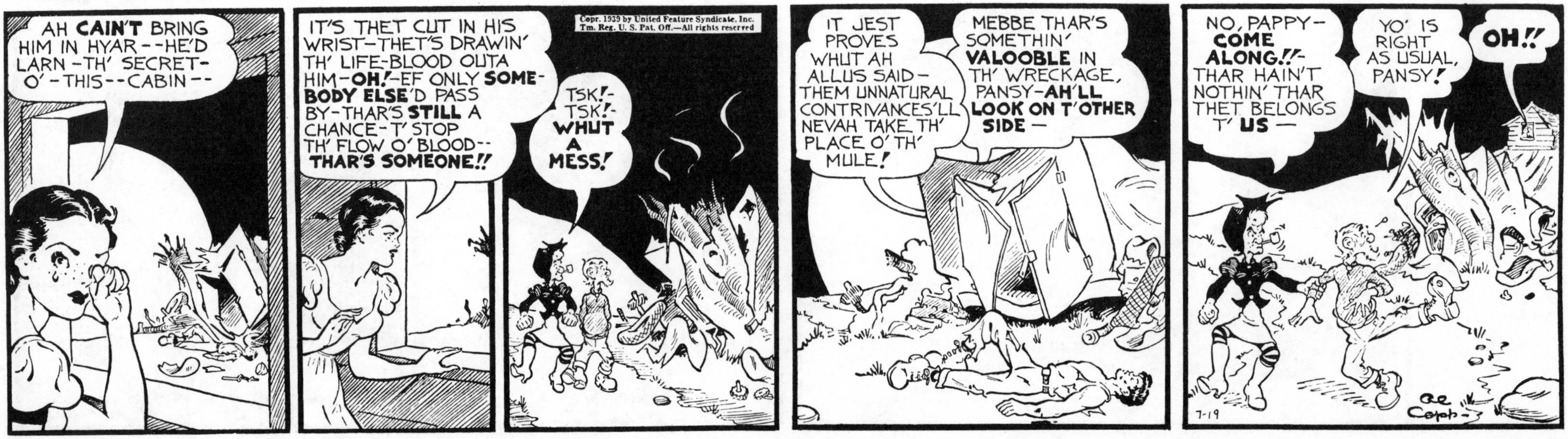

AH **CAIN'T** BRING HIM IN HYAR - - HE'D LARN - TH' SECRET - O' - THIS - - CABIN - -
IT'S THET CUT IN HIS WRIST - THET'S DRAWIN' TH' LIFE-BLOOD OUTA HIM - **OH!** - EF ONLY **SOMEBODY ELSE**'D PASS BY - THAR'S **STILL** A CHANCE - T' STOP TH' FLOW O' BLOOD - - **THAR'S SOMEONE!!**
Copr. 1939 by United Feature Syndicate, Inc. Tm. Reg. U. S. Pat. Off.—All rights reserved
TSK! - TSK! - **WHUT A MESS!**
IT JEST PROVES WHUT AH ALLUS SAID - THEM UNNATURAL CONTRIVANCES'LL NEVAH TAKE TH' PLACE O' TH' MULE!
MEBBE THAR'S SOMETHIN' **VALOOBLE** IN TH' WRECKAGE, PANSY - **AH'LL LOOK ON T'OTHER SIDE** -
NO, PAPPY - **COME ALONG!!** - THAR HAIN'T NOTHIN' THAR THET BELONGS T' **US** -
YO' IS RIGHT AS USUAL, PANSY!
OH!!
7-19
Al Capp

LI'L ABNER Behind That Door!! By Al Capp

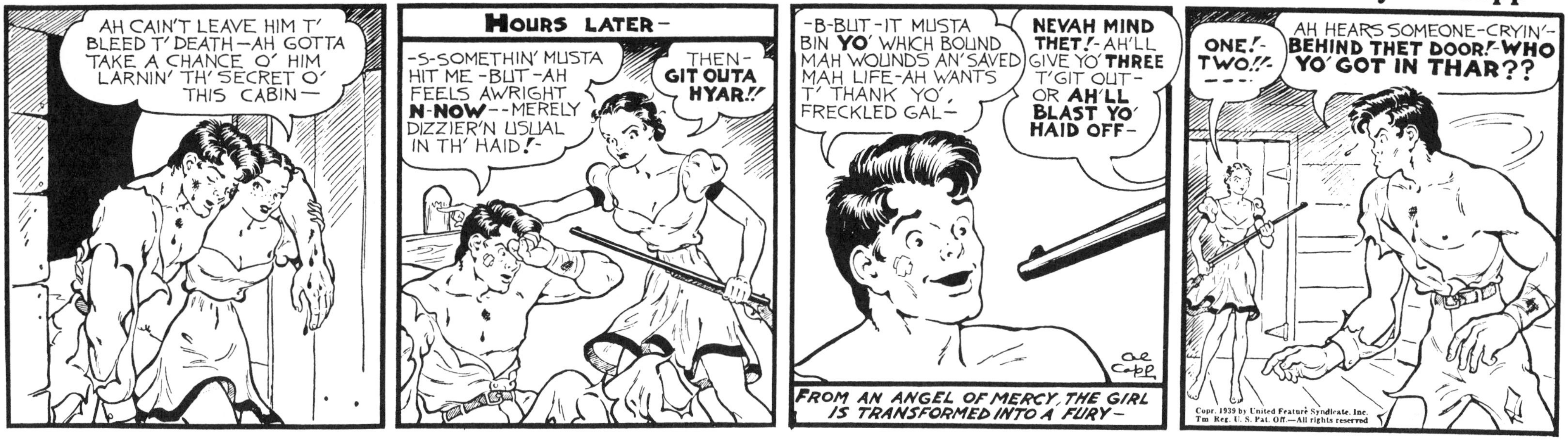

AH CAIN'T LEAVE HIM T' BLEED T' DEATH—AH GOTTA TAKE A CHANCE O' HIM LARNIN' TH' SECRET O' THIS CABIN—
HOURS LATER—
-S-SOMETHIN' MUSTA HIT ME—BUT—AH FEELS AWRIGHT N-NOW—MERELY DIZZIER'N USUAL IN TH' HAID!-
THEN—GIT OUTA HYAR!!
-B-BUT—IT MUSTA BIN YO' WHICH BOUND MAH WOUNDS AN' SAVED MAH LIFE-AH WANTS T' THANK YO', FRECKLED GAL—
NEVAH MIND THET!-AH'LL GIVE YO' THREE T'GIT OUT—OR AH'LL BLAST YO' HAID OFF—
FROM AN ANGEL OF MERCY, THE GIRL IS TRANSFORMED INTO A FURY—
ONE!-TWO!!- ---
AH HEARS SOMEONE—CRYIN'—BEHIND THET DOOR!-WHO YO' GOT IN THAR??
Copr. 1939 by United Feature Syndicate, Inc. Tm Reg. U. S. Pat. Off.—All rights reserved

LI'L ABNER What Do He See? By Al Capp

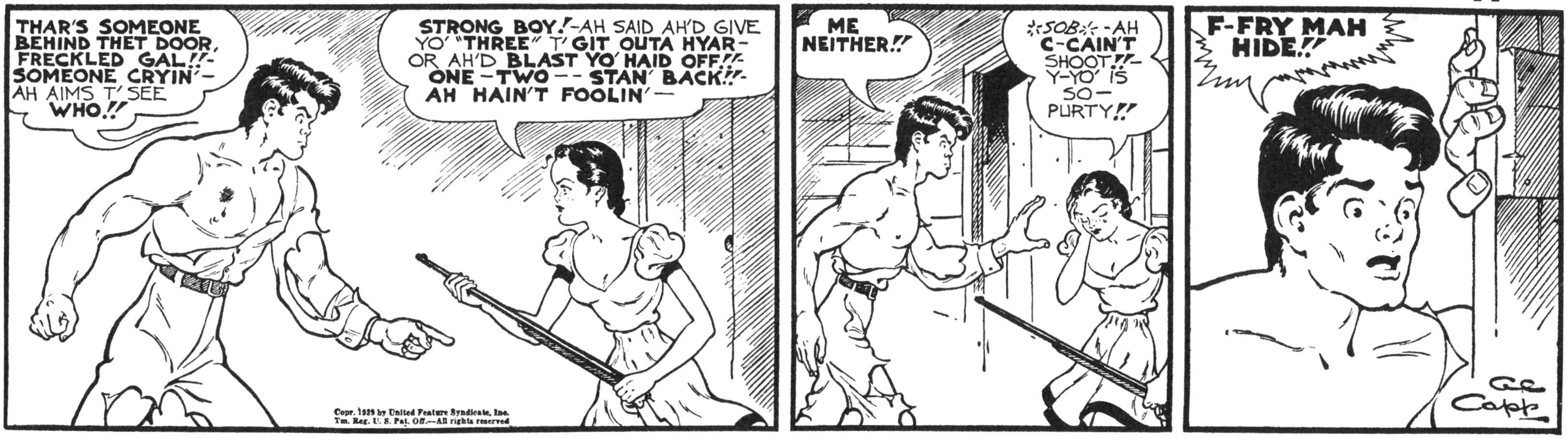

THAR'S SOMEONE BEHIND THET DOOR, FRECKLED GAL!!-SOMEONE CRYIN'—AH AIMS T' SEE WHO!!
STRONG BOY!-AH SAID AH'D GIVE YO' "THREE" T' GIT OUTA HYAR—OR AH'D BLAST YO' HAID OFF!!-ONE—TWO——STAN' BACK!!-AH HAIN'T FOOLIN'—
Copr. 1939 by United Feature Syndicate, Inc. Tm. Reg. U. S. Pat. Off.—All rights reserved
ME NEITHER!!
SOB—AH C-CAIN'T SHOOT!!-Y-YO' IS SO—PURTY!!
F-FRY MAH HIDE!!

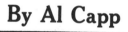

LI'L ABNER Little Man-Child, What Now? By Al Capp

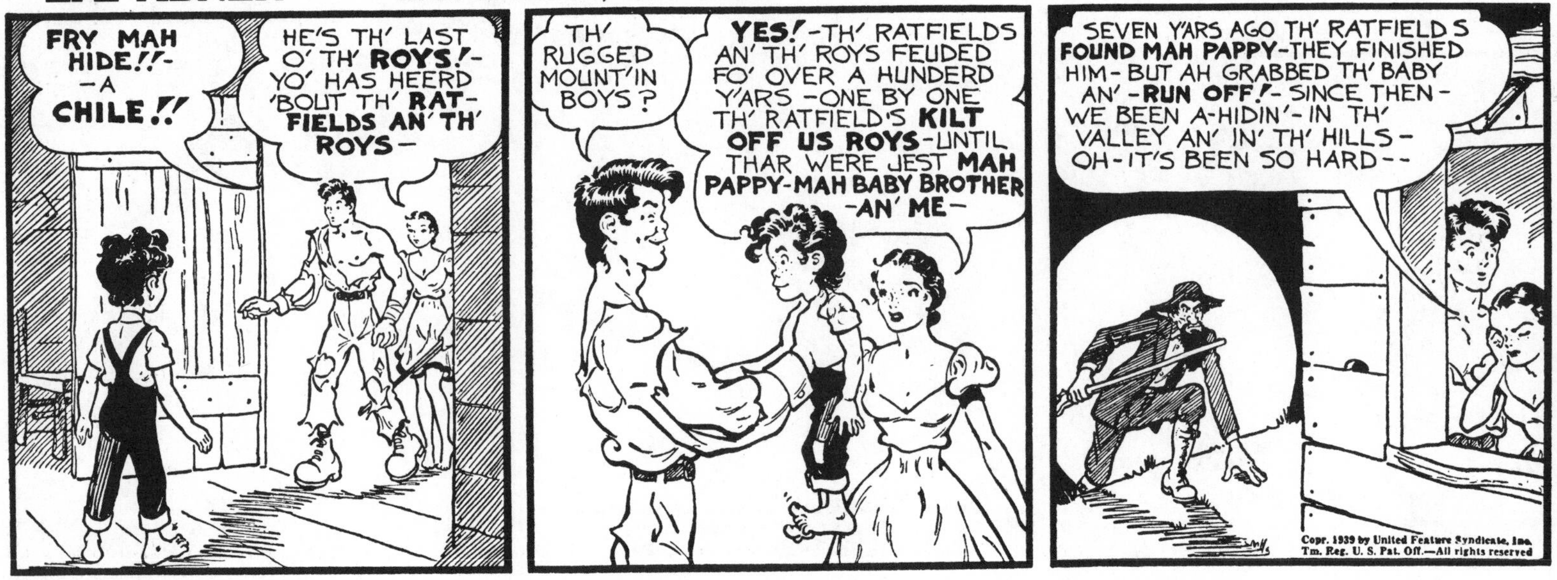
FRY MAH HIDE!!- -A CHILE!!
HE'S TH' LAST O' TH' ROYS!- YO' HAS HEERD 'BOUT TH' RATFIELDS AN' TH' ROYS-
TH' RUGGED MOUNT'IN BOYS?
YES!-TH' RATFIELDS AN' TH' ROYS FEUDED FO' OVER A HUNDERD Y'ARS-ONE BY ONE TH' RATFIELD'S KILT OFF US ROYS-UNTIL THAR WERE JEST MAH PAPPY-MAH BABY BROTHER -AN' ME-
SEVEN Y'ARS AGO TH' RATFIELDS FOUND MAH PAPPY-THEY FINISHED HIM-BUT AH GRABBED TH' BABY AN'-RUN OFF!-SINCE THEN-WE BEEN A-HIDIN'-IN TH' VALLEY AN' IN TH' HILLS-OH-IT'S BEEN SO HARD--
Copr. 1939 by United Feature Syndicate, Inc. Tm. Reg. U. S. Pat. Off.—All rights reserved
BUT-NOW-THEY'S FOUND OUT THAR IS STILL A MAN-CHILD, NAME OF ROY, ALIVE--- THEY'RE AFTER HIM-- AN'-THEY'LL GIT HIM-LIKE-THEY-GOT-ALL O' US---
Al Capp

LI'L ABNER Mammy Knows Best! By Al Capp

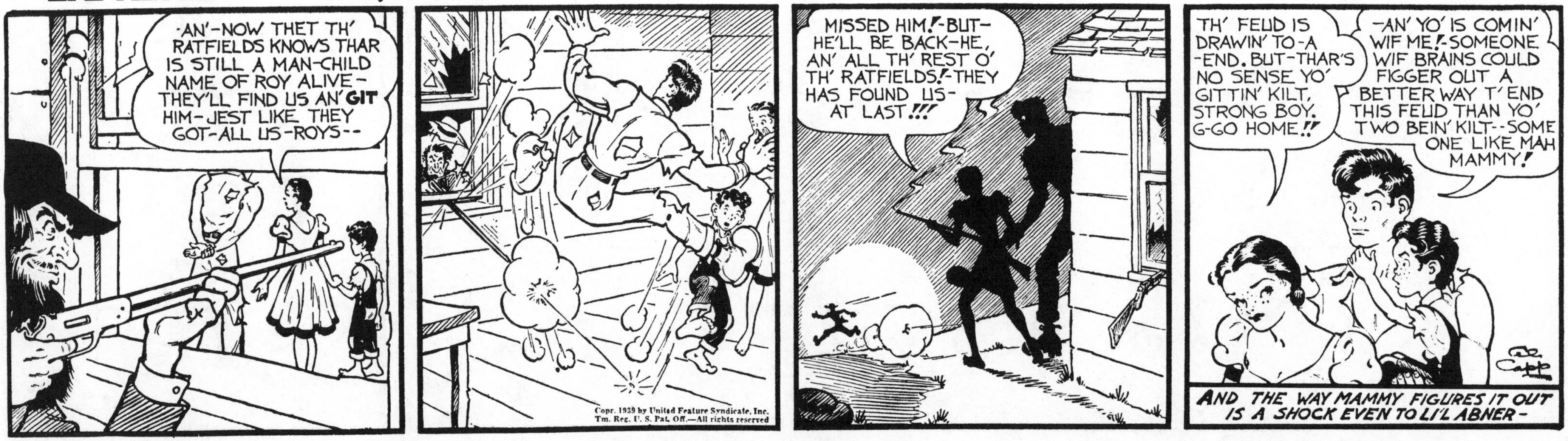
-AN'-NOW THET TH' RATFIELDS KNOWS THAR IS STILL A MAN-CHILD NAME OF ROY ALIVE-THEY'LL FIND US AN' GIT HIM-JEST LIKE THEY GOT-ALL US-ROYS--
Copr. 1939 by United Feature Syndicate, Inc. Tm. Reg. U. S. Pat. Off.—All rights reserved
MISSED HIM!-BUT-HE'LL BE BACK-HE, AN' ALL TH' REST O' TH' RATFIELDS!-THEY HAS FOUND US-AT LAST!!!
TH' FEUD IS DRAWIN' TO-A-END. BUT-THAR'S NO SENSE YO' GITTIN' KILT, STRONG BOY. G-GO HOME!!
-AN' YO' IS COMIN' WIF ME!-SOMEONE WIF BRAINS COULD FIGGER OUT A BETTER WAY T' END THIS FEUD THAN YO' TWO BEIN' KILT--SOME ONE LIKE MAH MAMMY!
Al Capp
AND THE WAY MAMMY FIGURES IT OUT IS A SHOCK EVEN TO LI'L ABNER-

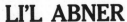

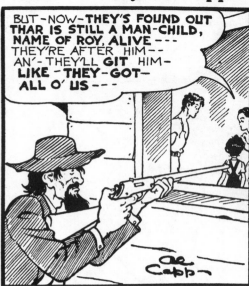

LI'L ABNER

Pappy Is Now th' Last o' th' Yokums

By Al Capp

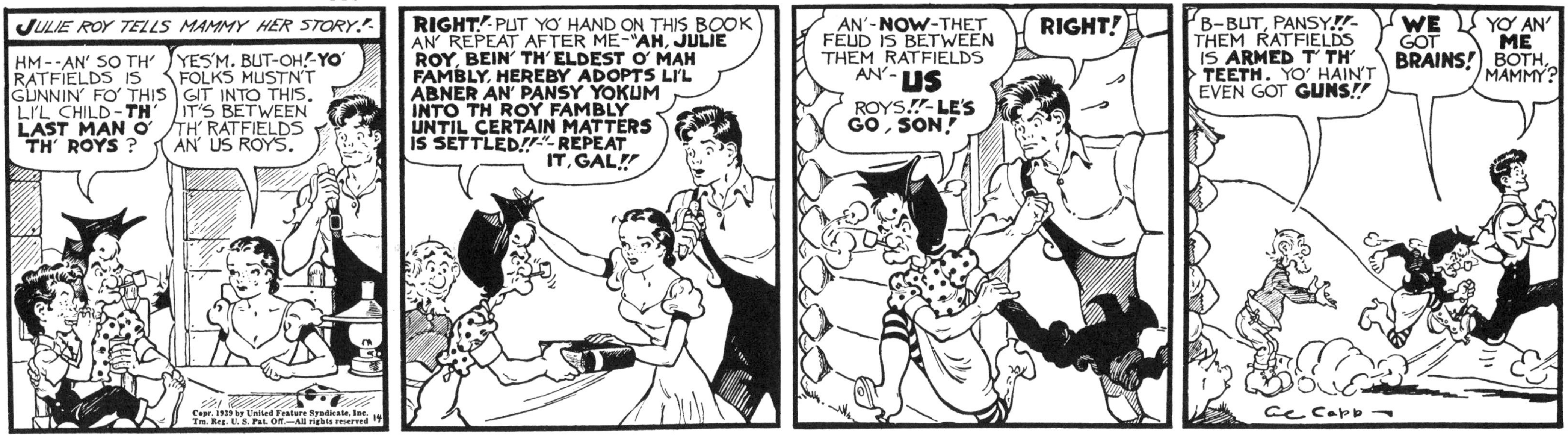
JULIE ROY TELLS MAMMY HER STORY!-
HM--AN' SO TH' RATFIELDS IS GUNNIN' FO' THIS LI'L CHILD-TH' LAST MAN O' TH' ROYS?
YES'M. BUT-OH!-YO' FOLKS MUSTN'T GIT INTO THIS. IT'S BETWEEN TH' RATFIELDS AN' US ROYS.
Copr. 1939 by United Feature Syndicate, Inc. Tm. Reg. U. S. Pat. Off.—All rights reserved
RIGHT!-PUT YO' HAND ON THIS BOOK AN' REPEAT AFTER ME-"AH, JULIE ROY, BEIN' TH' ELDEST O' MAH FAMBLY, HEREBY ADOPTS LI'L ABNER AN' PANSY YOKUM INTO TH ROY FAMBLY UNTIL CERTAIN MATTERS IS SETTLED!!"-REPEAT IT, GAL!!
AN'-NOW-THET FEUD IS BETWEEN THEM RATFIELDS AN'-US ROYS!!-LE'S GO, SON!
RIGHT!
B-BUT, PANSY!!-THEM RATFIELDS IS ARMED T' TH' TEETH. YO' HAIN'T EVEN GOT GUNS!!
WE GOT BRAINS!
YO' AN' ME BOTH, MAMMY?

LI'L ABNER

Thunder Over Dogpatch

By Al Capp

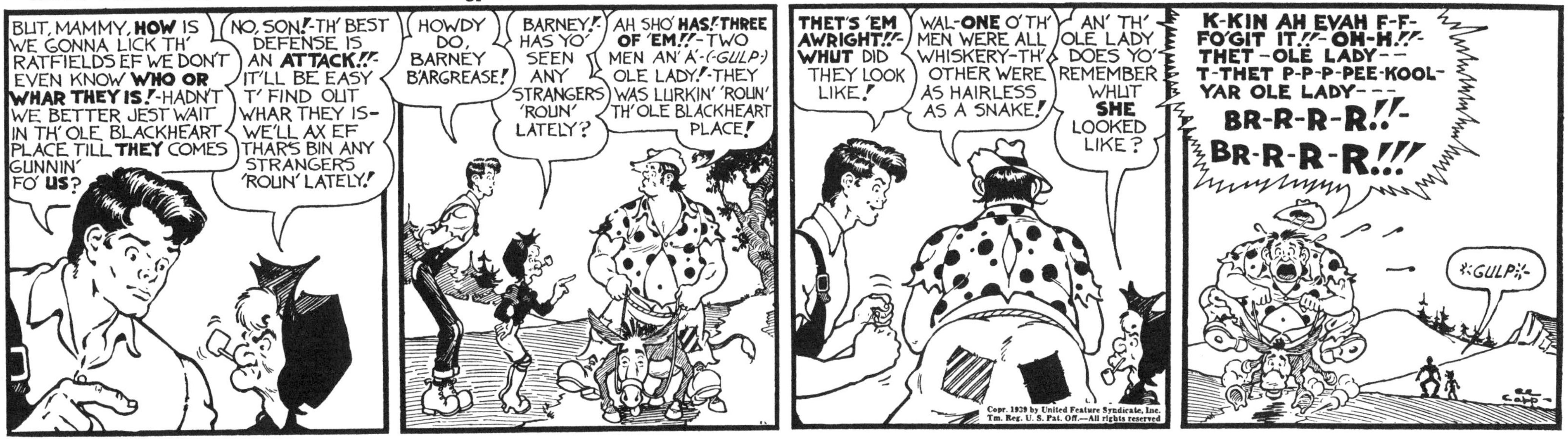
BUT, MAMMY, HOW IS WE GONNA LICK TH' RATFIELDS EF WE DON'T EVEN KNOW WHO OR WHAR THEY IS!-HADN'T WE BETTER JEST WAIT IN TH' OLE BLACKHEART PLACE TILL THEY COMES GUNNIN' FO' US?
NO, SON!-TH' BEST DEFENSE IS AN ATTACK!!-IT'LL BE EASY T' FIND OUT WHAR THEY IS-WE'LL AX EF THAR'S BIN ANY STRANGERS 'ROUN' LATELY!
HOWDY DO, BARNEY B'ARGREASE!
BARNEY!-HAS YO' SEEN ANY STRANGERS 'ROUN' LATELY?
AH SHO' HAS!-THREE OF 'EM!!-TWO MEN AN' A'-(-GULP-) OLE LADY!-THEY WAS LURKIN' 'ROUN' TH' OLE BLACKHEART PLACE!
THET'S 'EM AWRIGHT!!-WHUT DID THEY LOOK LIKE!
WAL-ONE O' TH' MEN WERE ALL WHISKERY-TH' OTHER WERE AS HAIRLESS AS A SNAKE!
AN' TH' OLE LADY DOES YO' REMEMBER WHUT SHE LOOKED LIKE?
Copr. 1939 by United Feature Syndicate, Inc. Tm. Reg. U. S. Pat. Off.—All rights reserved
K-KIN AH EVAH F-F-FO'GIT IT!!-OH-H!!-THET-OLE LADY--T-THET P-P-P-PEE-KOOL-YAR OLE LADY---
BR-R-R-R!!-
BR-R-R-R!!!
GULP

LI'L ABNER

This Just Gives Yo' an Idea!

By Al Capp

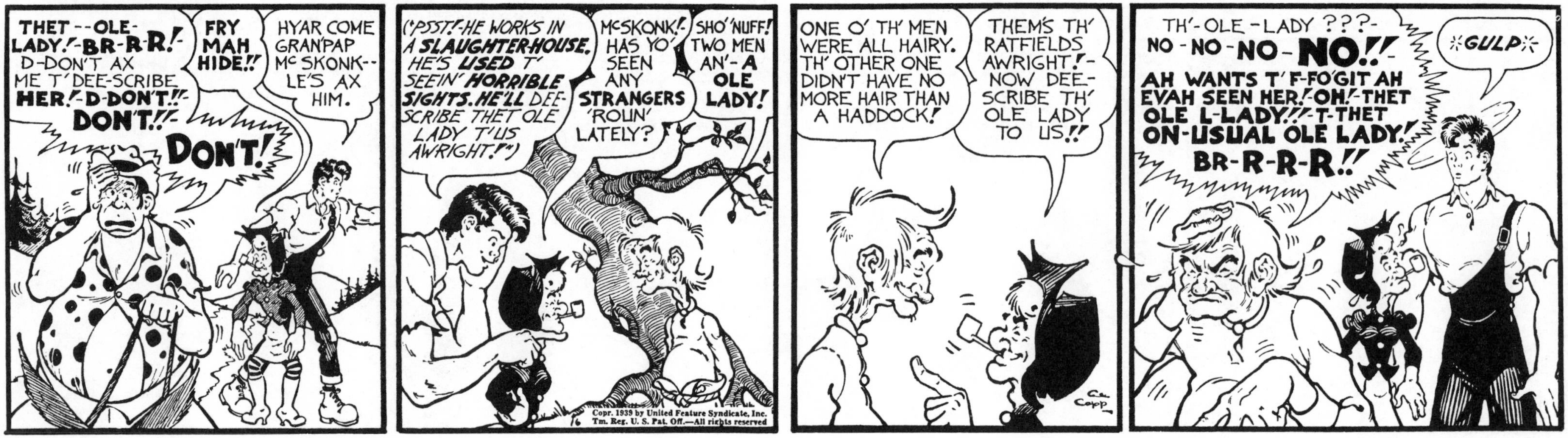
THET--OLE-LADY!-BR-R-R!-D-DON'T AX ME T' DEE-SCRIBE HER!-D-DON'T!!-DON'T!!-
DON'T!
FRY MAH HIDE!!
HYAR COME GRANPAP McSKONK--LE'S AX HIM.
("PSST!-HE WORKS IN A SLAUGHTER-HOUSE. HE'S USED T' SEEIN' HORRIBLE SIGHTS. HE'LL DEE-SCRIBE THET OLE LADY T'US AWRIGHT!")
McSKONK!-HAS YO' SEEN ANY STRANGERS 'ROUN' LATELY?
SHO' NUFF! TWO MEN AN'-A OLE LADY!
Copr. 1939 by United Feature Syndicate, Inc. Tm. Reg. U. S. Pat. Off.—All rights reserved
ONE O' TH' MEN WERE ALL HAIRY. TH' OTHER ONE DIDN'T HAVE NO MORE HAIR THAN A HADDOCK!
THEM'S TH' RATFIELDS AWRIGHT!-NOW DEE-SCRIBE TH' OLE LADY TO US!!
TH'-OLE-LADY???-NO-NO-NO-NO!!-AH WANTS T' F-FO'GIT AH EVAH SEEN HER!-OH!-THET OLE L-LADY!!!-T-THET ON-USUAL OLE LADY!-BR-R-R-R!!
GULP

LI'L ABNER

Fearless Willie Faints Again!

By Al Capp

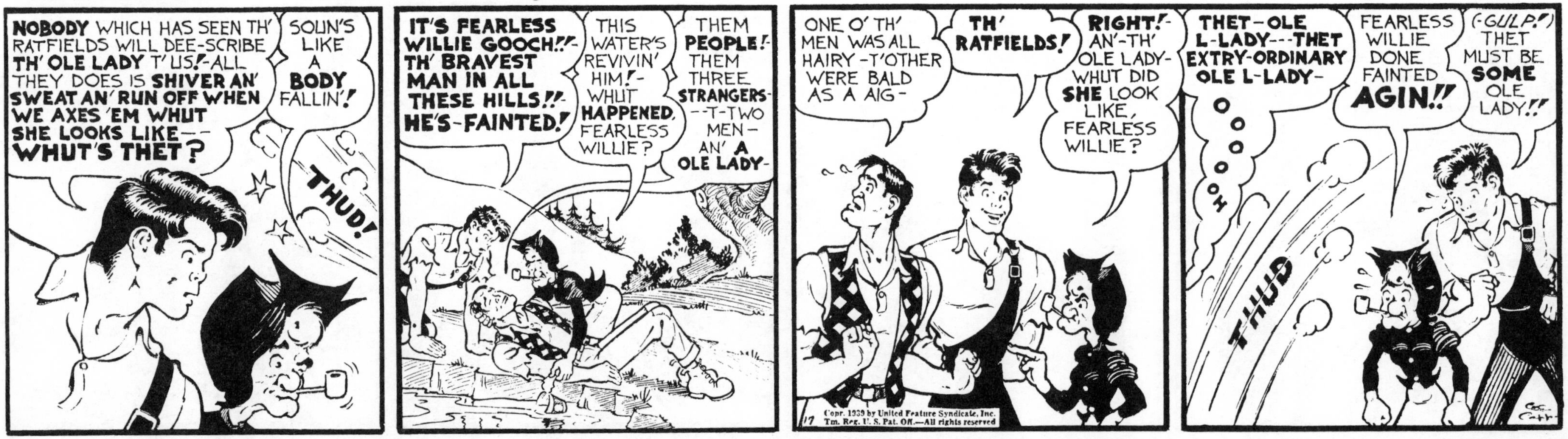
NOBODY WHICH HAS SEEN TH' RATFIELDS WILL DEE-SCRIBE TH' OLE LADY T'US!-ALL THEY DOES IS SHIVER AN' SWEAT AN' RUN OFF WHEN WE AXES 'EM WHUT SHE LOOKS LIKE--WHUT'S THET?
SOUN'S LIKE A BODY FALLIN'!
THUD!
IT'S FEARLESS WILLIE GOOCH!!-TH' BRAVEST MAN IN ALL THESE HILLS!!-HE'S FAINTED!
THIS WATER'S REVIVIN' HIM!-WHUT HAPPENED, FEARLESS WILLIE?
THEM PEOPLE!-THEM THREE STRANGERS--T-TWO MEN-AN' A OLE LADY-
ONE O' TH' MEN WAS ALL HAIRY-T'OTHER WERE BALD AS A AIG-
TH' RATFIELDS!
RIGHT!-AN'-TH' OLE LADY-WHUT DID SHE LOOK LIKE, FEARLESS WILLIE?
Copr. 1939 by United Feature Syndicate, Inc. Tm. Reg. U. S. Pat. Off.—All rights reserved
THET-OLE L-LADY---THET EXTRY-ORDINARY OLE L-LADY-
OOOOOH
THUD
FEARLESS WILLIE DONE FAINTED AGIN!!
(-GULP!-) THET MUST BE SOME OLE LADY!!

LI'L ABNER Mose Don't Wanna Kick th' Bucket— By Al Capp

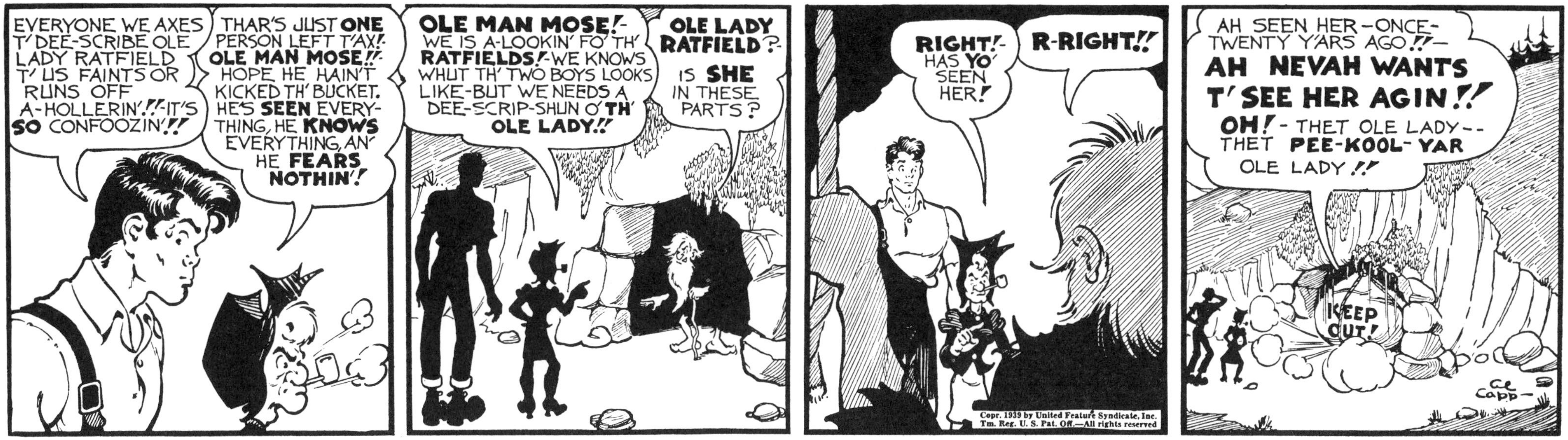

EVERYONE WE AXES T' DEE-SCRIBE OLE LADY RATFIELD T' US FAINTS OR RUNS OFF A-HOLLERIN'!!-IT'S SO CONFOOZIN'!!
THAR'S JUST ONE PERSON LEFT T'AX!- OLE MAN MOSE!!- HOPE HE HAIN'T KICKED TH' BUCKET. HE'S SEEN EVERY-THING, HE KNOWS EVERYTHING, AN' HE FEARS NOTHIN'!
OLE MAN MOSE!- WE IS A-LOOKIN' FO' TH' RATFIELDS!-WE KNOWS WHUT TH' TWO BOYS LOOKS LIKE-BUT WE NEEDS A DEE-SCRIP-SHUN O' TH' OLE LADY!!
OLE LADY RATFIELD?- IS SHE IN THESE PARTS?
RIGHT!- HAS YO' SEEN HER!
R-RIGHT!!
Copr. 1939 by United Feature Syndicate, Inc. Tm. Reg. U. S. Pat. Off.—All rights reserved
AH SEEN HER-ONCE- TWENTY Y'ARS AGO!!— AH NEVAH WANTS T' SEE HER AGIN!! OH!- THET OLE LADY-- THET PEE-KOOL-YAR OLE LADY!!
KEEP OUT!
Al Capp

LI'L ABNER Blood Is Where You Find It! By Al Capp

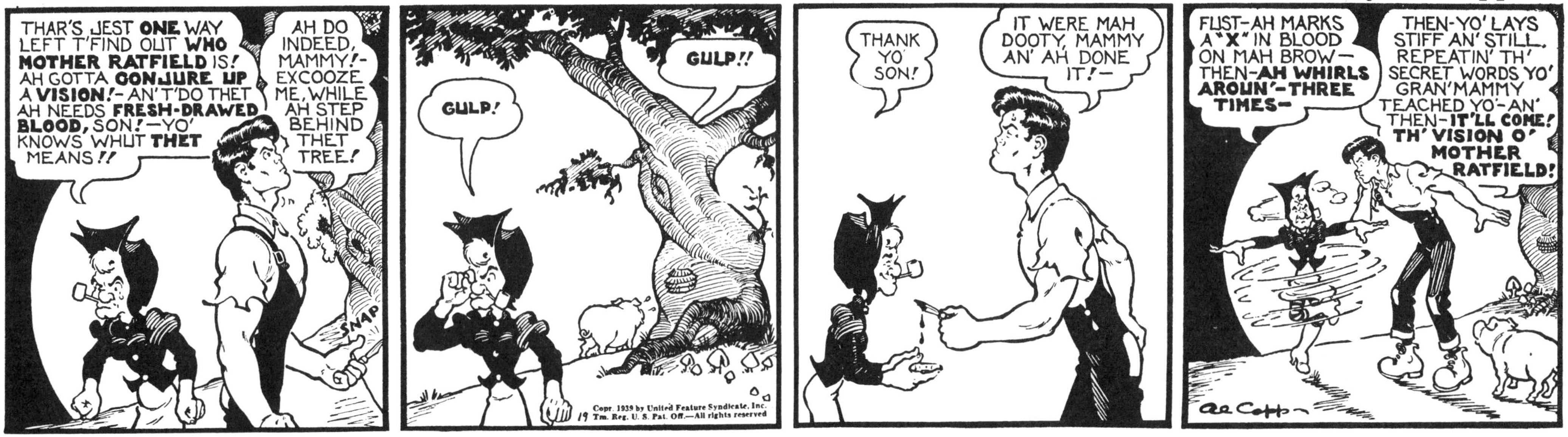

THAR'S JEST ONE WAY LEFT T'FIND OUT WHO MOTHER RATFIELD IS! AH GOTTA CONJURE UP A VISION!- AN' T'DO THET AH NEEDS FRESH-DRAWED BLOOD, SON!-YO' KNOWS WHUT THET MEANS!!
AH DO INDEED, MAMMY!- EXCOOZE ME, WHILE AH STEP BEHIND THET TREE!
SNAP
GULP!
GULP!!
Copr. 1939 by United Feature Syndicate, Inc. Tm. Reg. U. S. Pat. Off.—All rights reserved
THANK YO' SON!
IT WERE MAH DOOTY, MAMMY AN' AH DONE IT!—
FUST-AH MARKS A "X" IN BLOOD ON MAH BROW— THEN-AH WHIRLS AROUN'-THREE TIMES—
THEN-YO' LAYS STIFF AN' STILL, REPEATIN' TH' SECRET WORDS YO' GRAN'MAMMY TEACHED YO'-AN' THEN-IT'LL COME! TH' VISION O' MOTHER RATFIELD!
Al Capp

LI'L ABNER Seein' Ain't Believin'! By Al Capp

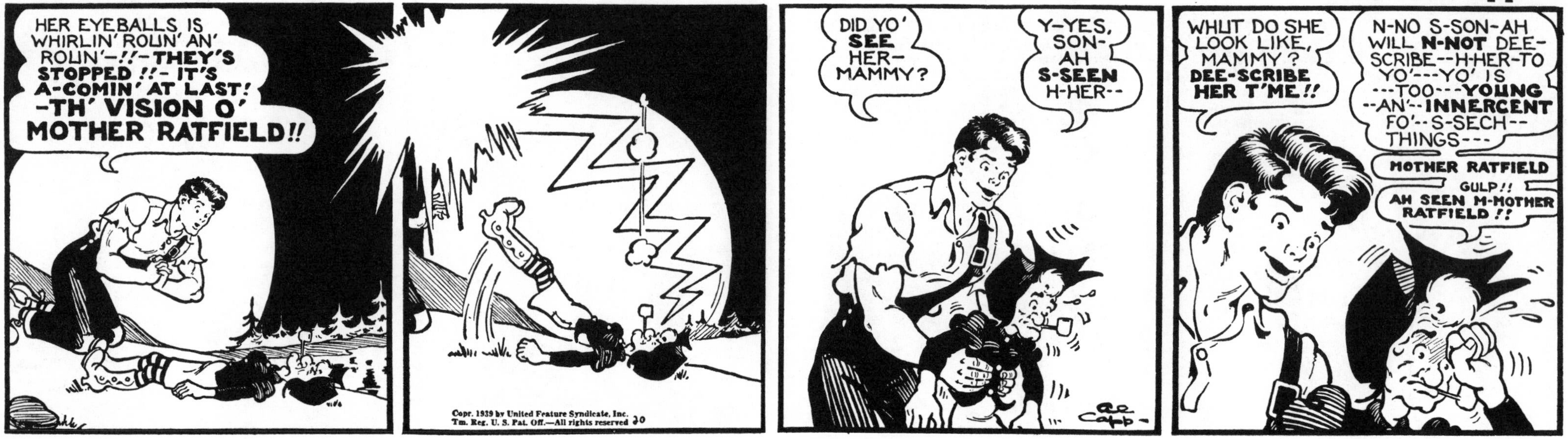
HER EYEBALLS IS WHIRLIN' ROUN' AN' ROUN'-!!-THEY'S STOPPED!!- IT'S A-COMIN' AT LAST! -TH' VISION O' MOTHER RATFIELD!!
Copr. 1939 by United Feature Syndicate, Inc. Tm. Reg. U. S. Pat. Off.—All rights reserved
DID YO' SEE HER-MAMMY?
Y-YES, SON-AH S-SEEN H-HER--
WHUT DO SHE LOOK LIKE, MAMMY? DEE-SCRIBE HER T'ME!!
N-NO S-SON-AH WILL N-NOT DEE-SCRIBE--H-HER-TO YO'---YO' IS ---TOO---YOUNG --AN'--INNERCENT FO'--S-SECH-- THINGS---
MOTHER RATFIELD
GULP!!
AH SEEN M-MOTHER RATFIELD!!

LI'L ABNER Bury Her Not on the Lone Prairie! By Al Capp

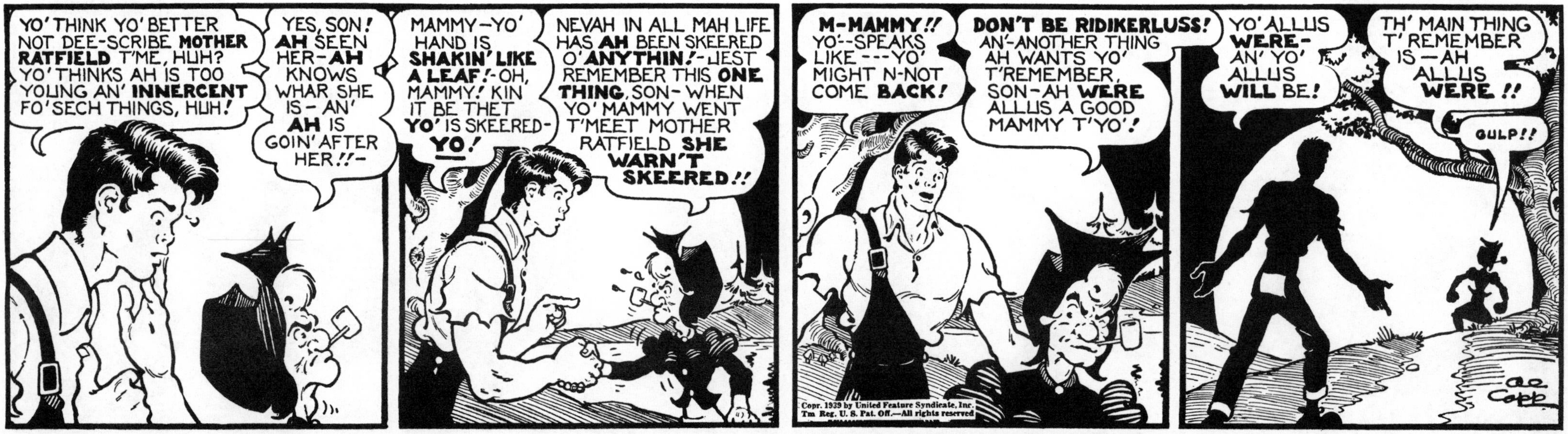
YO' THINK YO' BETTER NOT DEE-SCRIBE MOTHER RATFIELD T'ME, HUH? YO' THINKS AH IS TOO YOUNG AN' INNERCENT FO' SECH THINGS, HUH!
YES, SON! AH SEEN HER-AH KNOWS WHAR SHE IS-AN' AH IS GOIN' AFTER HER!!-
MAMMY-YO' HAND IS SHAKIN' LIKE A LEAF!-OH, MAMMY! KIN IT BE THET YO' IS SKEERED-YO'!
NEVAH IN ALL MAH LIFE HAS AH BEEN SKEERED O'ANYTHIN!-JEST REMEMBER THIS ONE THING, SON-WHEN YO' MAMMY WENT T'MEET MOTHER RATFIELD SHE WARN'T SKEERED!!
M-MAMMY!! YO'--SPEAKS LIKE---YO' MIGHT N-NOT COME BACK!
DON'T BE RIDIKERLUSS! AN'-ANOTHER THING AH WANTS YO' T'REMEMBER, SON-AH WERE ALLUS A GOOD MAMMY T'YO'!
Copr. 1939 by United Feature Syndicate, Inc. Tm Reg. U. S. Pat. Off.—All rights reserved
YO' ALLUS WERE-AN' YO' ALLUS WILL BE!
TH' MAIN THING T' REMEMBER IS-AH ALLUS WERE!!
GULP!!

LI'L ABNER Swing Low, Sweet Chariot! By Al Capp

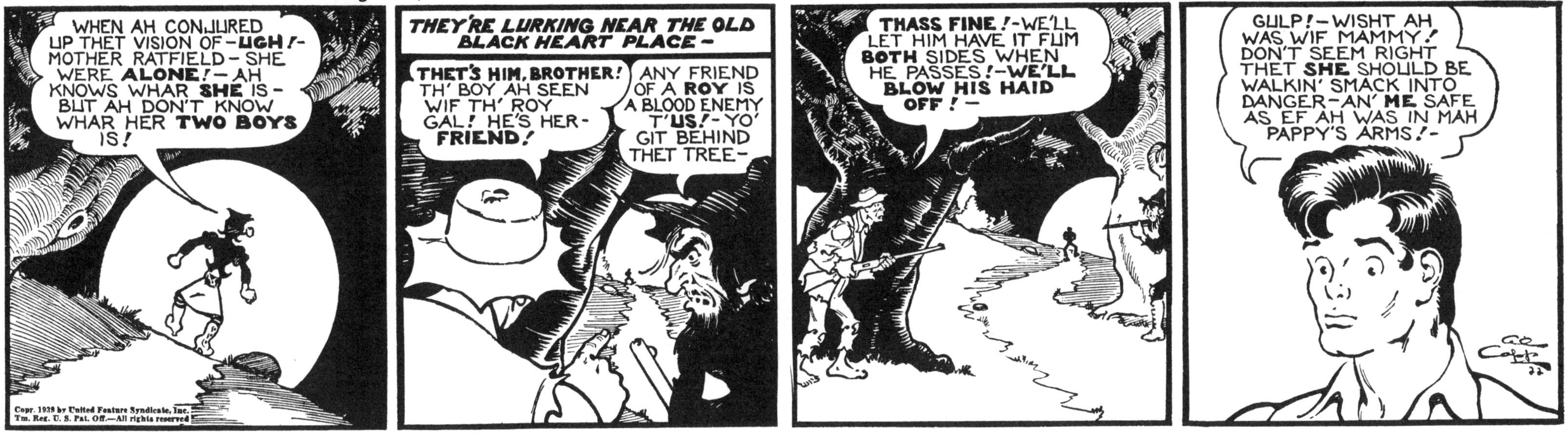
WHEN AH CONJURED UP THET VISION OF-UGH!-MOTHER RATFIELD-SHE WERE ALONE!-AH KNOWS WHAR SHE IS-BUT AH DON'T KNOW WHAR HER TWO BOYS IS!
Copr. 1939 by United Feature Syndicate, Inc. Tm. Reg. U. S. Pat. Off.—All rights reserved
THEY'RE LURKING NEAR THE OLD BLACK HEART PLACE -
THET'S HIM, BROTHER! TH' BOY AH SEEN WIF TH' ROY GAL! HE'S HER-FRIEND!
ANY FRIEND OF A ROY IS A BLOOD ENEMY T'US!-YO' GIT BEHIND THET TREE-
THASS FINE!-WE'LL LET HIM HAVE IT FUM BOTH SIDES WHEN HE PASSES!-WE'LL BLOW HIS HAID OFF!-
GULP!-WISHT AH WAS WIF MAMMY! DON'T SEEM RIGHT THET SHE SHOULD BE WALKIN' SMACK INTO DANGER-AN' ME SAFE AS EF AH WAS IN MAH PAPPY'S ARMS!-
22

LI'L ABNER Abandon All Hope, Yo' Who Enter Thar! By Al Capp

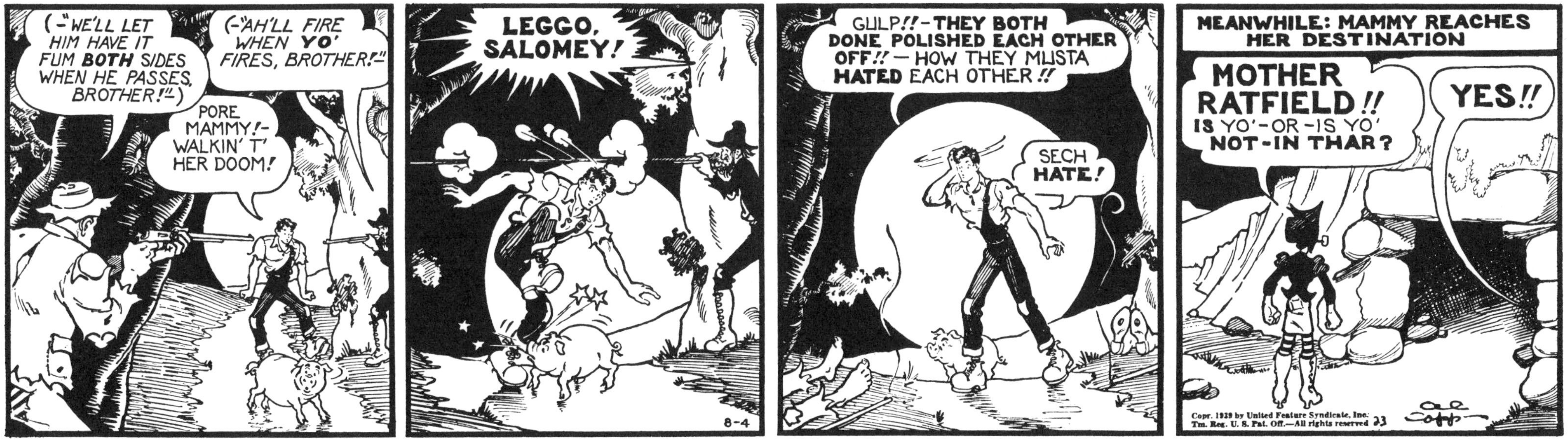
(-"WE'LL LET HIM HAVE IT FUM BOTH SIDES WHEN HE PASSES, BROTHER!"-)
(-"AH'LL FIRE WHEN YO' FIRES, BROTHER!"-
PORE MAMMY!-WALKIN' T' HER DOOM!
LEGGO, SALOMEY!
8-4
GULP!!-THEY BOTH DONE POLISHED EACH OTHER OFF!!-HOW THEY MUSTA HATED EACH OTHER!!
SECH HATE!
MEANWHILE: MAMMY REACHES HER DESTINATION
MOTHER RATFIELD!! IS YO'-OR-IS YO' NOT-IN THAR?
YES!!
Copr. 1939 by United Feature Syndicate, Inc. Tm. Reg. U. S. Pat. Off.—All rights reserved
23

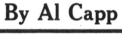

LI'L ABNER Greetings From Mother Ratfield By Al Capp

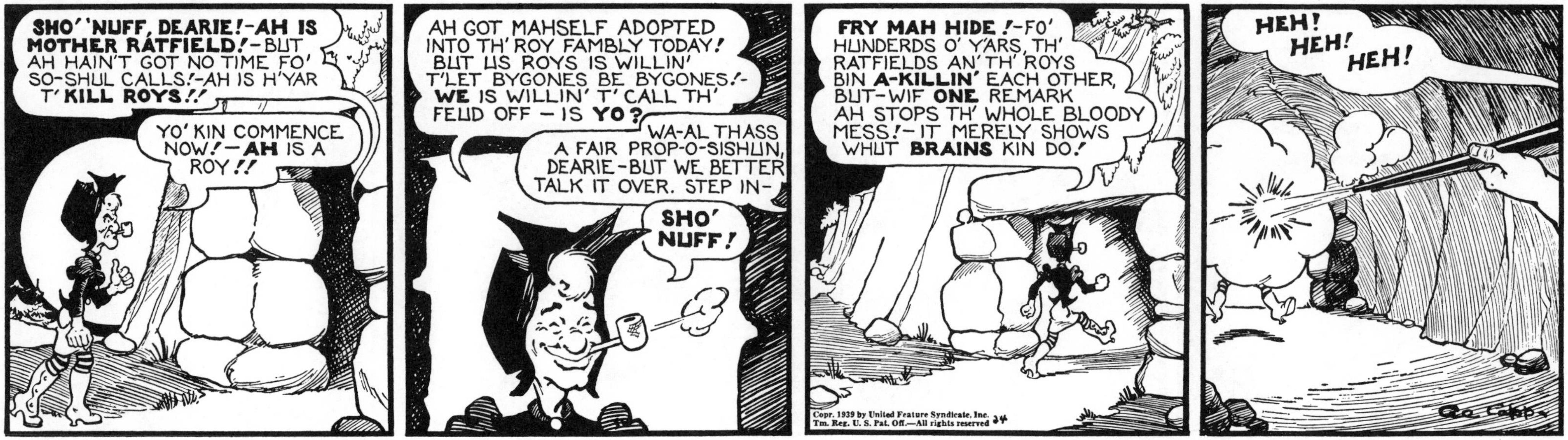

SHO' 'NUFF, DEARIE!-AH IS MOTHER RATFIELD!-BUT AH HAIN'T GOT NO TIME FO' SO-SHUL CALLS!-AH IS H'YAR T' KILL ROYS!!
YO' KIN COMMENCE NOW!-AH IS A ROY!!
AH GOT MAHSELF ADOPTED INTO TH' ROY FAMBLY TODAY! BUT US ROYS IS WILLIN' T'LET BYGONES BE BYGONES!-WE IS WILLIN' T' CALL TH' FEUD OFF - IS YO?
WA-AL THASS A FAIR PROP-O-SISHUN, DEARIE-BUT WE BETTER TALK IT OVER. STEP IN-
SHO' NUFF!
FRY MAH HIDE!-FO' HUNDERDS O' YARS, TH' RATFIELDS AN' TH' ROYS BIN A-KILLIN' EACH OTHER, BUT-WIF ONE REMARK AH STOPS TH' WHOLE BLOODY MESS!-IT MERELY SHOWS WHUT BRAINS KIN DO!
Copr. 1939 by United Feature Syndicate, Inc. Tm. Reg. U. S. Pat. Off.—All rights reserved
HEH! HEH! HEH!

LI'L ABNER Ratfield Rides Again By Al Capp

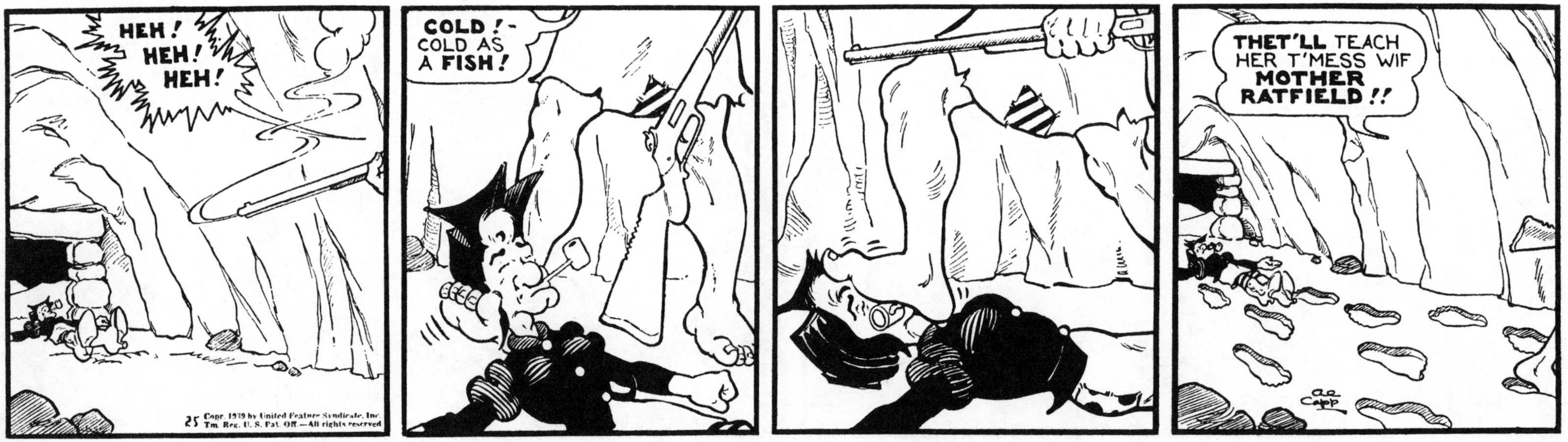

HEH! HEH! HEH!
Copr. 1939 by United Feature Syndicate, Inc. Tm. Reg. U. S. Pat. Off.—All rights reserved
COLD!-COLD AS A FISH!
THET'LL TEACH HER T'MESS WIF MOTHER RATFIELD!!

LI'L ABNER Won't You Come Into My Parlor? By Al Capp

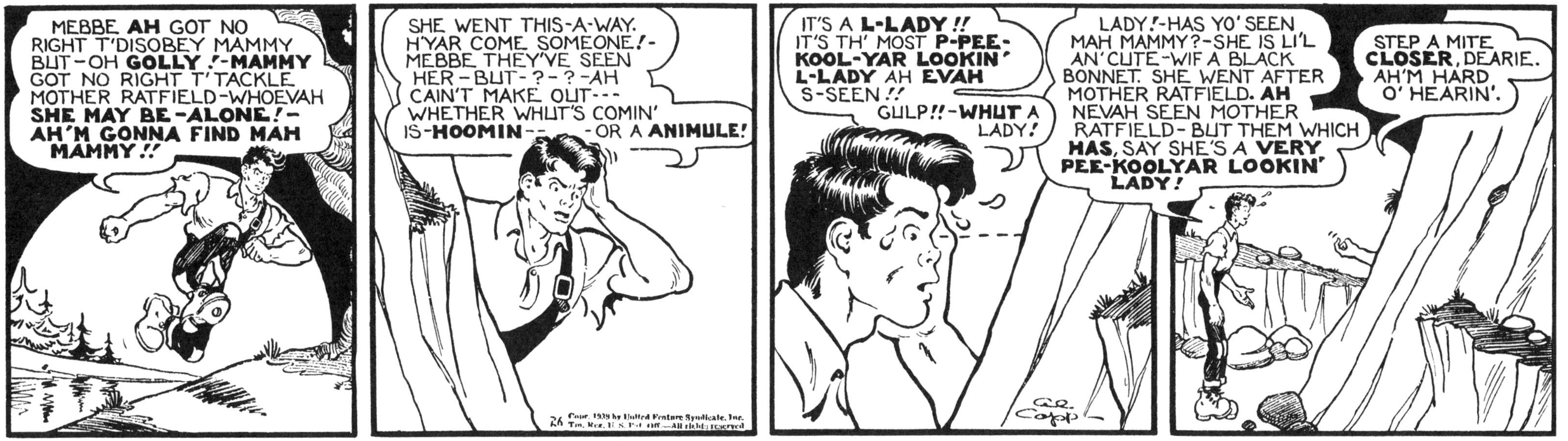
MEBBE **AH** GOT NO RIGHT T'DISOBEY MAMMY BUT-OH **GOLLY** !-**MAMMY** GOT NO RIGHT T'TACKLE MOTHER RATFIELD-WHOEVAH **SHE MAY BE-ALONE!-AH'M GONNA FIND MAH MAMMY!!**
SHE WENT THIS-A-WAY. H'YAR COME SOMEONE!-MEBBE THEY'VE SEEN HER-BUT-?-?-AH CAIN'T MAKE OUT---WHETHER WHUT'S COMIN' IS-**HOOMIN**-- -OR A **ANIMULE!**
26 Copr. 1938 by United Feature Syndicate, Inc. Tm. Reg. U. S. Pat. Off.—All rights reserved
IT'S A **L-LADY!!** IT'S TH' MOST **P-PEE-KOOL-YAR LOOKIN' L-LADY** AH **EVAH** S-SEEN!!
GULP!!-**WHUT** A LADY!
LADY!-HAS YO' SEEN MAH MAMMY?-SHE IS LI'L AN' CUTE-WIF A BLACK BONNET. SHE WENT AFTER MOTHER RATFIELD. **AH** NEVAH SEEN MOTHER RATFIELD-BUT THEM WHICH **HAS**, SAY SHE'S A **VERY PEE-KOOLYAR LOOKIN' LADY!**
STEP A MITE **CLOSER**, DEARIE. AH'M HARD O' HEARIN'.

LI'L ABNER Mother Knows Best! By Al Capp

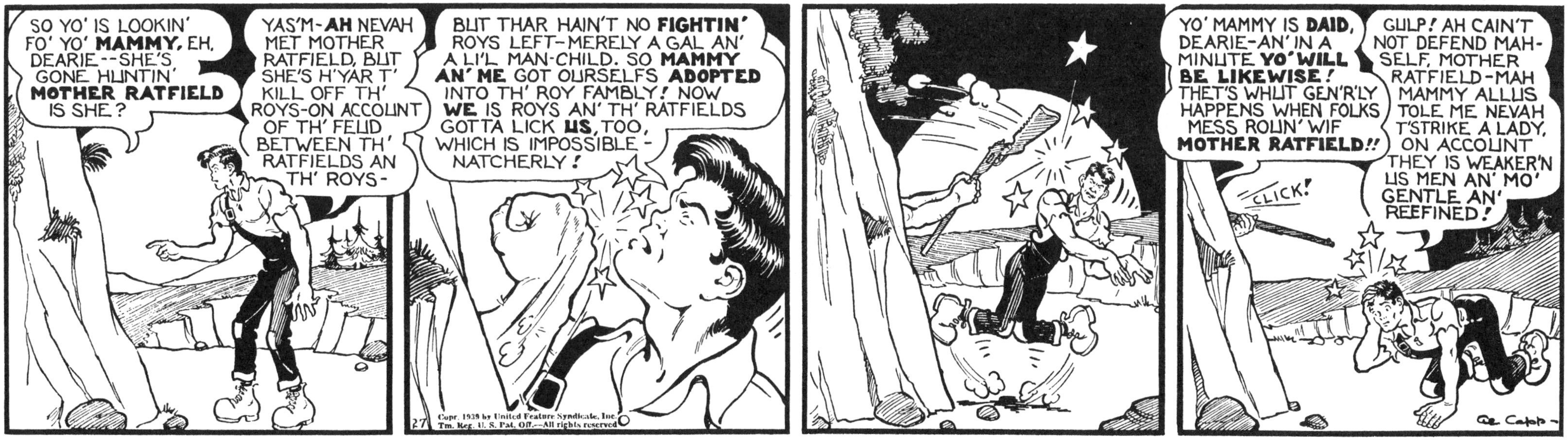
SO YO' IS LOOKIN' FO' YO' **MAMMY**, EH, DEARIE--SHE'S GONE HUNTIN' **MOTHER RATFIELD** IS SHE?
YAS'M-**AH** NEVAH MET MOTHER RATFIELD, BUT SHE'S H'YAR T' KILL OFF TH' ROYS-ON ACCOUNT OF TH' FEUD BETWEEN TH' RATFIELDS AN TH' ROYS-
BUT THAR HAIN'T NO **FIGHTIN'** ROYS LEFT-MERELY A GAL AN' A LI'L MAN-CHILD. SO **MAMMY AN' ME** GOT OURSELFS **ADOPTED** INTO TH' ROY FAMBLY! NOW **WE** IS ROYS AN' TH' RATFIELDS GOTTA LICK **US**, TOO, WHICH IS IMPOSSIBLE-NATCHERLY!
27 Copr. 1938 by United Feature Syndicate, Inc. Tm. Reg. U. S. Pat. Off.—All rights reserved
YO' MAMMY IS **DAID**, DEARIE-AN' IN A MINUTE **YO' WILL BE LIKEWISE!** THET'S WHUT GEN'R'LY HAPPENS WHEN FOLKS MESS ROUN' WIF **MOTHER RATFIELD!!**
GULP! AH CAIN'T NOT DEFEND MAH-SELF, MOTHER RATFIELD-MAH MAMMY ALLUS TOLE ME NEVAH T'STRIKE A LADY, ON ACCOUNT THEY IS WEAKER'N US MEN AN' MO' GENTLE AN' REEFINED!
CLICK!

LI'L ABNER Mother's Day By Al Capp

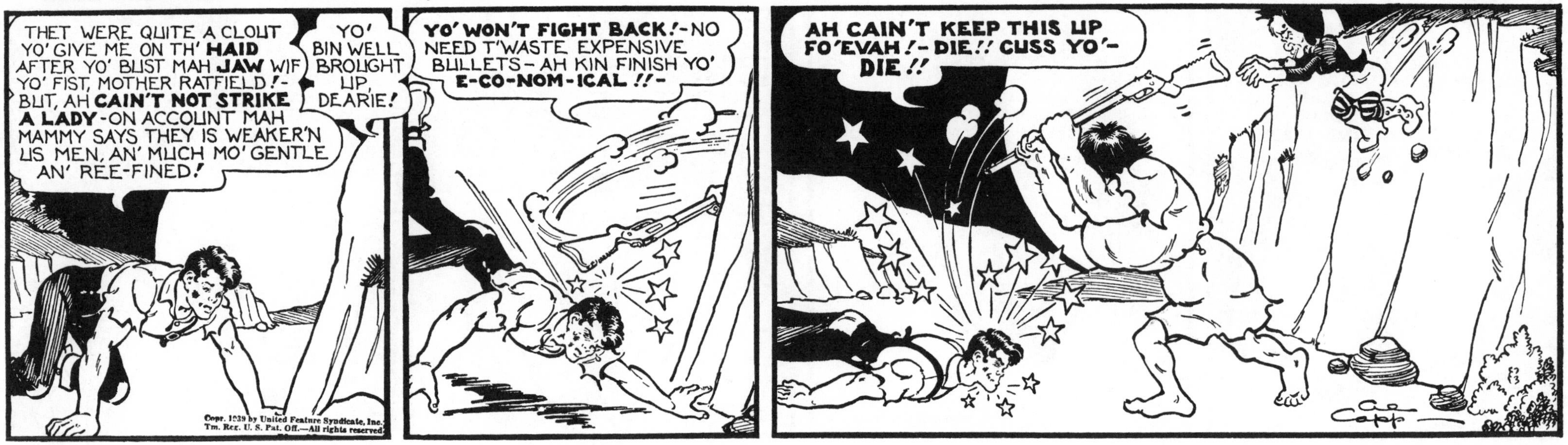

THET WERE QUITE A CLOUT YO' GIVE ME ON TH' **HAID** AFTER YO' BUST MAH **JAW** WIF YO' FIST, MOTHER RATFIELD!- BUT, AH **CAIN'T NOT STRIKE A LADY**-ON ACCOUNT MAH MAMMY SAYS THEY IS WEAKER'N US MEN, AN' MUCH MO' GENTLE AN' REE-FINED!
YO' BIN WELL BROUGHT UP, DEARIE!
Copr. 1939 by United Feature Syndicate, Inc. Tm. Reg. U. S. Pat. Off.—All rights reserved.
YO' WON'T FIGHT BACK!-NO NEED T'WASTE EXPENSIVE BULLETS-AH KIN FINISH YO' **E-CO-NOM-ICAL!!**-
AH CAIN'T KEEP THIS UP FO'EVAH!-DIE!! CUSS YO'-DIE!!
Al Capp

LI'L ABNER Who Opened the Cage? By Al Capp

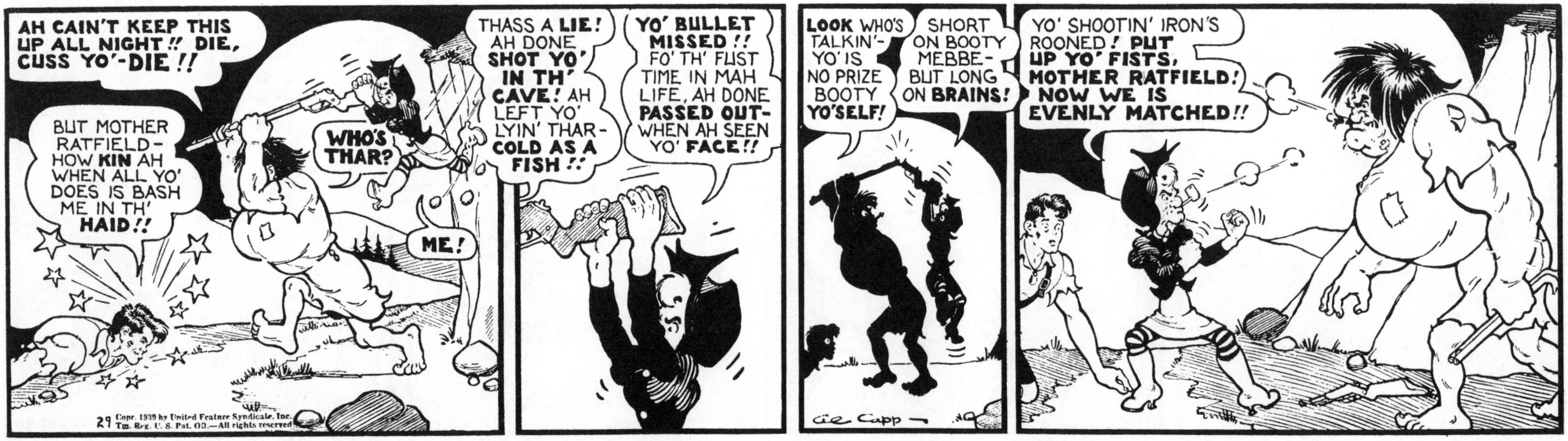

AH CAIN'T KEEP THIS UP ALL NIGHT!! DIE, CUSS YO'-DIE!!
BUT MOTHER RATFIELD- HOW **KIN** AH WHEN ALL YO' DOES IS BASH ME IN TH' **HAID!!**
WHO'S THAR?
ME!
29 Copr. 1939 by United Feature Syndicate, Inc. Tm. Reg. U. S. Pat. Off.—All rights reserved.
THASS A **LIE!** AH DONE **SHOT YO' IN TH' CAVE!** AH LEFT YO' LYIN' THAR- **COLD AS A FISH!!**
YO' BULLET MISSED!! FO' TH' FUST TIME IN MAH LIFE, AH DONE **PASSED OUT**-WHEN AH SEEN YO' **FACE!!**
LOOK WHO'S TALKIN'- YO' IS NO PRIZE BOOTY **YO'SELF!**
SHORT ON BOOTY MEBBE- BUT LONG ON **BRAINS!**
Al Capp
YO' SHOOTIN' IRON'S ROONED! **PUT UP YO' FISTS, MOTHER RATFIELD! NOW WE IS EVENLY MATCHED!!**

LI'L ABNER Just Passing Through By Al Capp

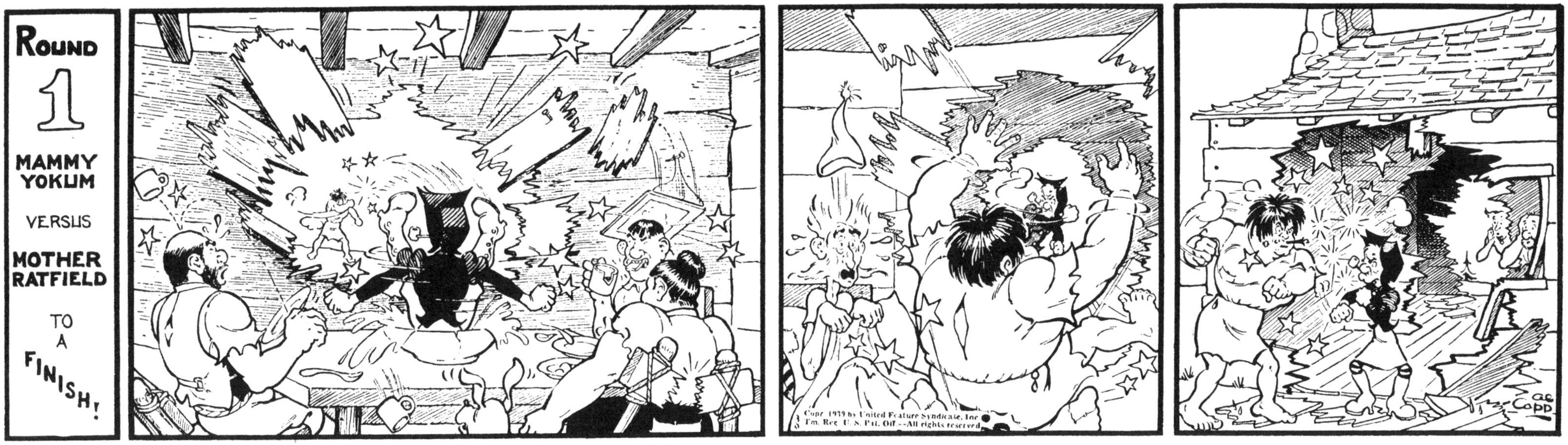

ROUND
1
MAMMY YOKUM
VERSUS
MOTHER RATFIELD
TO A FINISH!
Copr. 1939 by United Feature Syndicate, Inc. Tm. Reg. U.S. Pat. Off.--All rights reserved

LI'L ABNER Where Are You Going, My Pretty Maid? By Al Capp

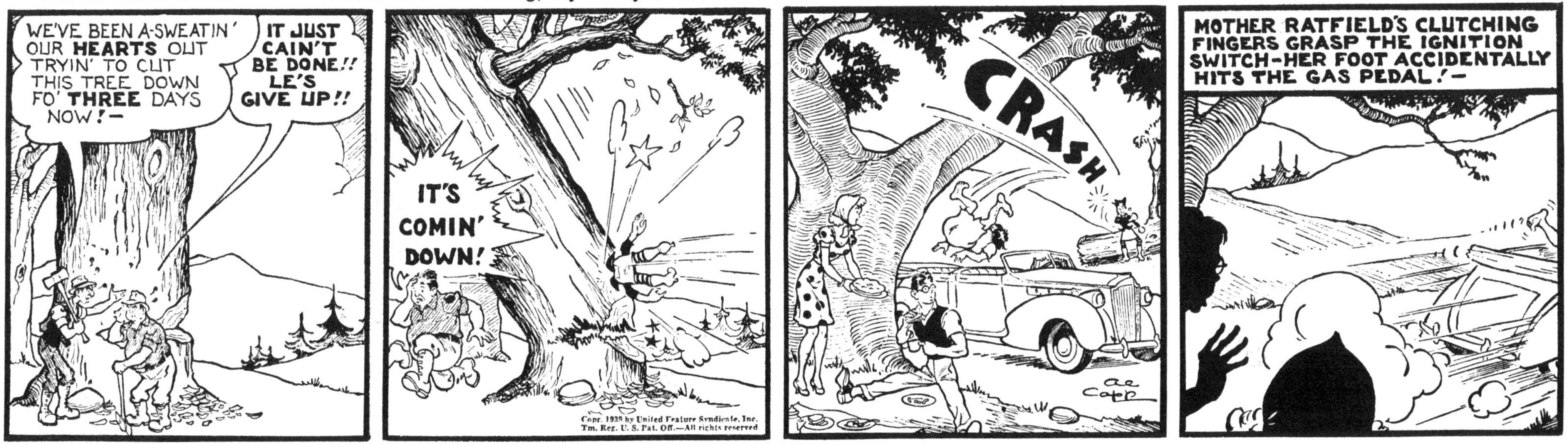

WE'VE BEEN A-SWEATIN' OUR HEARTS OUT TRYIN' TO CUT THIS TREE DOWN FO' THREE DAYS NOW!—
IT JUST CAIN'T BE DONE!! LE'S GIVE UP!!
IT'S COMIN' DOWN!
Copr. 1939 by United Feature Syndicate, Inc. Tm. Reg. U.S. Pat. Off.—All rights reserved
CRASH
MOTHER RATFIELD'S CLUTCHING FINGERS GRASP THE IGNITION SWITCH—HER FOOT ACCIDENTALLY HITS THE GAS PEDAL!—

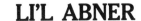

LI'L ABNER They're Off! By Al Capp

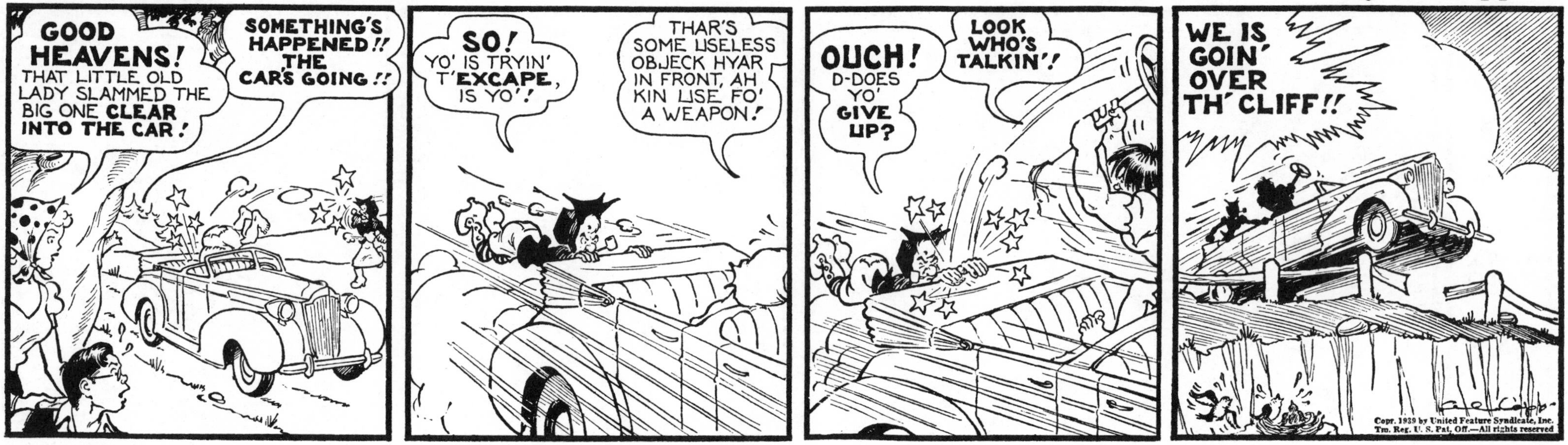
GOOD HEAVENS! THAT LITTLE OLD LADY SLAMMED THE BIG ONE CLEAR INTO THE CAR!
SOMETHING'S HAPPENED!! THE CAR'S GOING!!
SO! YO' IS TRYIN' T'EXCAPE, IS YO'!
THAR'S SOME USELESS OBJECK HYAR IN FRONT, AH KIN USE FO' A WEAPON!
OUCH! D-DOES YO' GIVE UP?
LOOK WHO'S TALKIN'!
WE IS GOIN' OVER TH' CLIFF!!
Copr. 1939 by United Feature Syndicate, Inc. Tm. Reg. U. S. Pat. Off.—All rights reserved

LI'L ABNER On Again, Off Again! By Al Capp

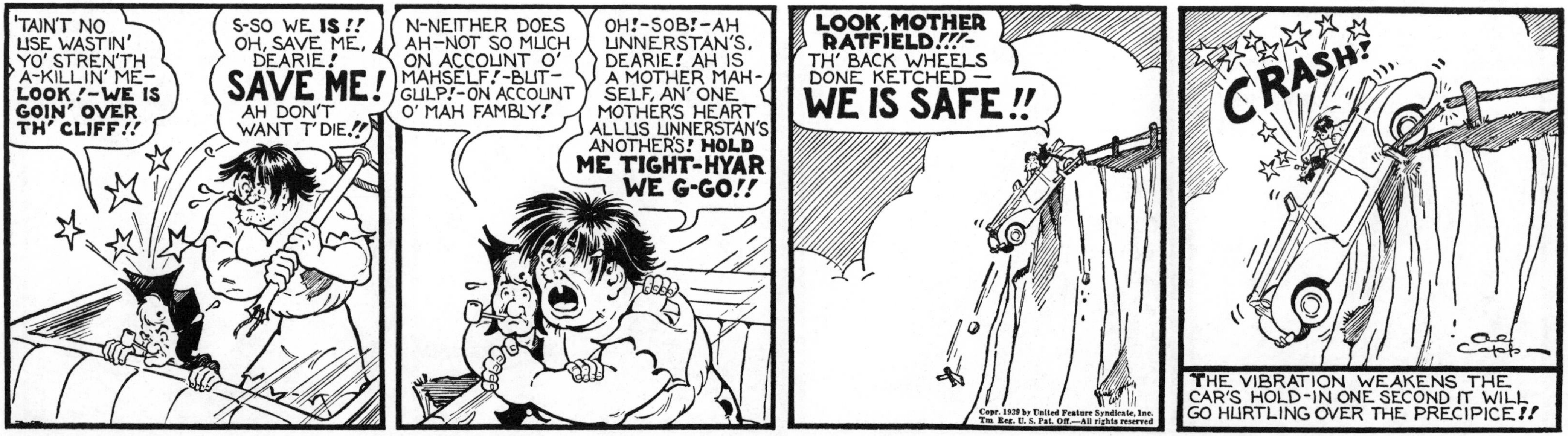
'TAIN'T NO USE WASTIN' YO' STREN'TH A-KILLIN' ME- LOOK!-WE IS GOIN' OVER TH' CLIFF!!
S-SO WE IS!! OH, SAVE ME, DEARIE! SAVE ME! AH DON'T WANT T'DIE!!
N-NEITHER DOES AH-NOT SO MUCH ON ACCOUNT O' MAHSELF!-BUT-GULP!-ON ACCOUNT O' MAH FAMBLY!
OH!-SOB!-AH UNNERSTAN'S, DEARIE! AH IS A MOTHER MAH-SELF, AN' ONE MOTHER'S HEART ALLUS UNNERSTAN'S ANOTHER'S! HOLD ME TIGHT-HYAR WE G-GO!!
LOOK, MOTHER RATFIELD!!!- TH' BACK WHEELS DONE KETCHED — WE IS SAFE!!
Copr. 1939 by United Feature Syndicate, Inc. Tm. Reg. U. S. Pat. Off.—All rights reserved
CRASH!
THE VIBRATION WEAKENS THE CAR'S HOLD-IN ONE SECOND IT WILL GO HURTLING OVER THE PRECIPICE!!

LI'L ABNER Haystack Homicide By Al Capp

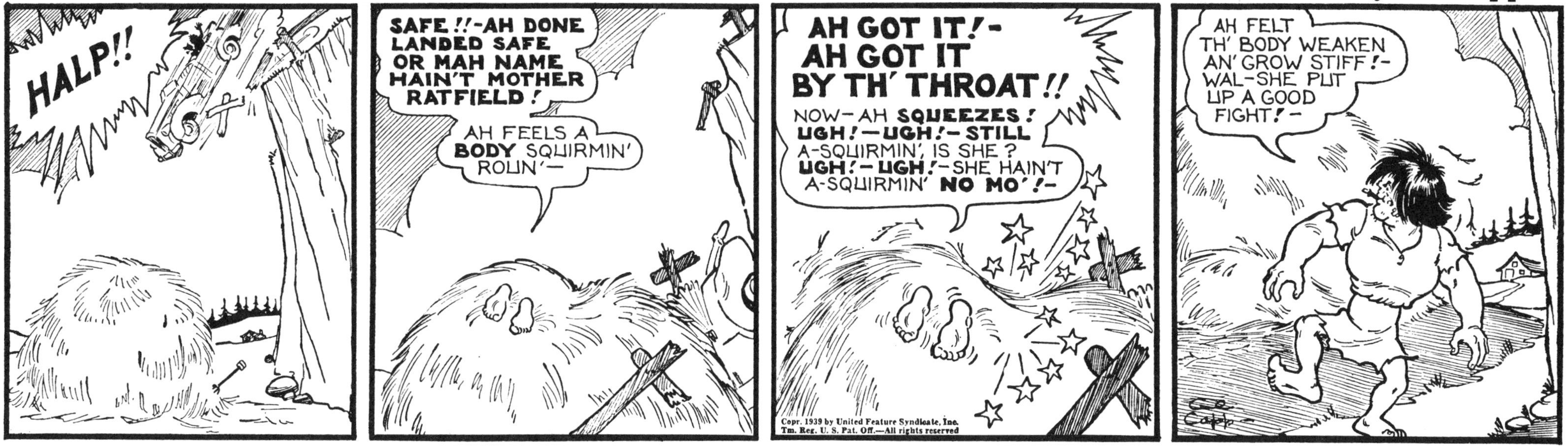
HALP!!
SAFE!!-AH DONE LANDED SAFE OR MAH NAME HAIN'T MOTHER RATFIELD!
AH FEELS A BODY SQUIRMIN' ROUN'—
AH GOT IT!- AH GOT IT BY TH' THROAT!!
NOW-AH SQUEEZES! UGH!—UGH!—STILL A-SQUIRMIN', IS SHE? UGH!—UGH!—SHE HAIN'T A-SQUIRMIN' NO MO'!-
Copr. 1939 by United Feature Syndicate, Inc. Tm. Reg. U. S. Pat. Off.—All rights reserved
AH FELT TH' BODY WEAKEN AN' GROW STIFF!- WAL-SHE PUT UP A GOOD FIGHT!-

LI'L ABNER These Boys Are Really Fight Experts!! By Al Capp

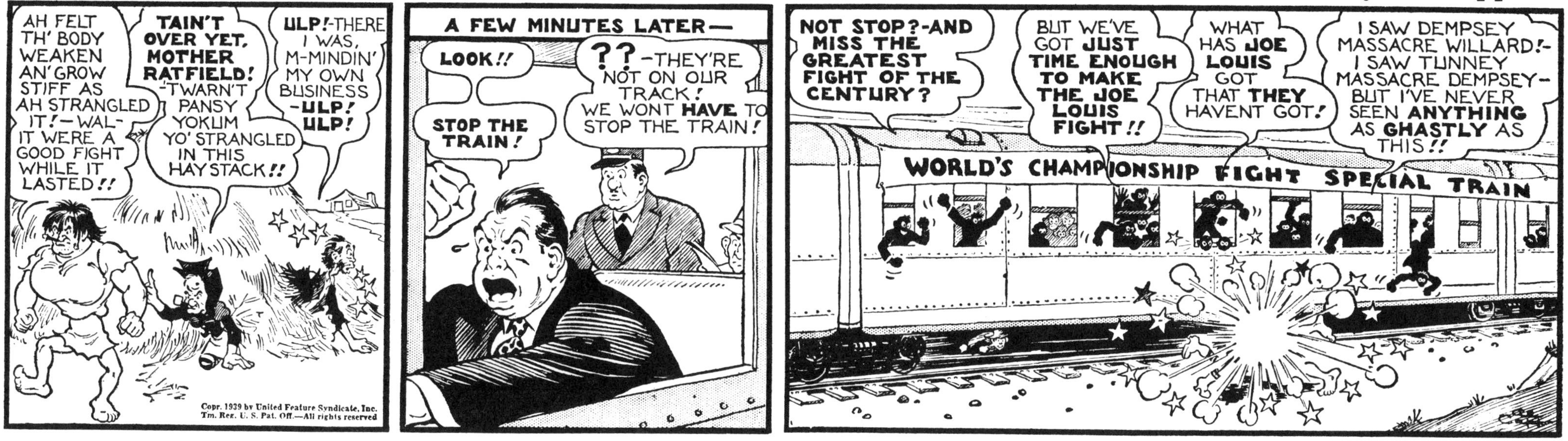
AH FELT TH' BODY WEAKEN AN' GROW STIFF AS AH STRANGLED IT!—WAL- IT WERE A GOOD FIGHT WHILE IT LASTED!!
TAIN'T OVER YET, MOTHER RATFIELD! -TWARN'T PANSY YOKUM YO' STRANGLED IN THIS HAYSTACK!!
ULP!-THERE I WAS, M-MINDIN' MY OWN BUSINESS -ULP! ULP!
Copr. 1939 by United Feature Syndicate, Inc. Tm. Reg. U. S. Pat. Off.—All rights reserved
A FEW MINUTES LATER—
LOOK!!
STOP THE TRAIN!
??-THEY'RE NOT ON OUR TRACK! WE WONT HAVE TO STOP THE TRAIN!
NOT STOP?-AND MISS THE GREATEST FIGHT OF THE CENTURY?
BUT WE'VE GOT JUST TIME ENOUGH TO MAKE THE JOE LOUIS FIGHT!!
WHAT HAS JOE LOUIS GOT THAT THEY HAVENT GOT!
I SAW DEMPSEY MASSACRE WILLARD!- I SAW TUNNEY MASSACRE DEMPSEY- BUT I'VE NEVER SEEN ANYTHING AS GHASTLY AS THIS!!
WORLD'S CHAMPIONSHIP FIGHT SPECIAL TRAIN

LI'L ABNER Murder in the Moonlight! By Al Capp

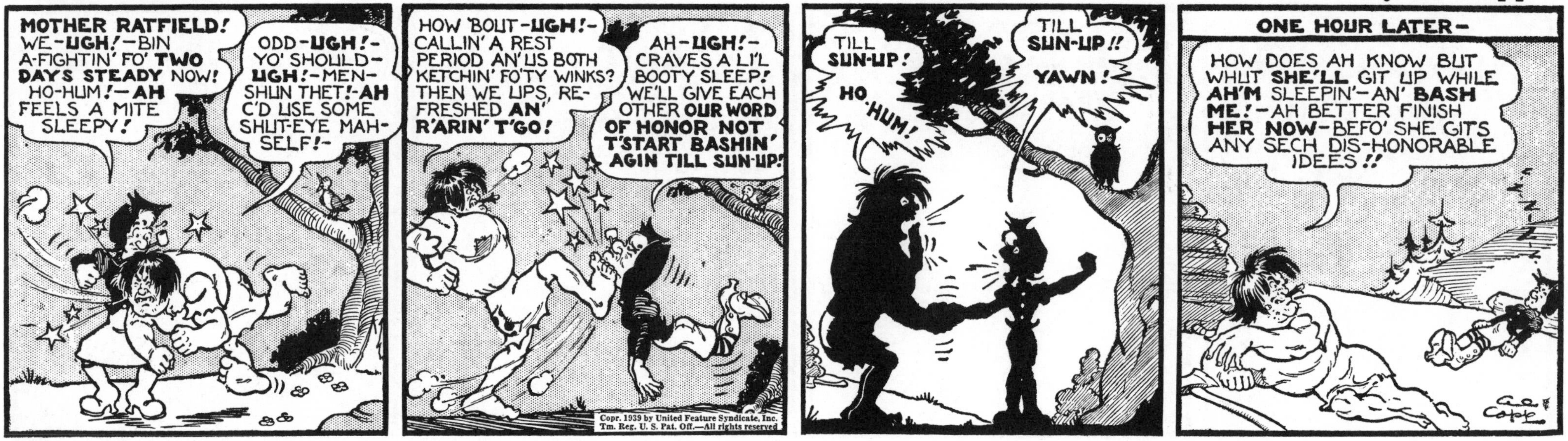

MOTHER RATFIELD! WE-UGH!-BIN A-FIGHTIN' FO' TWO DAYS STEADY NOW! HO-HUM!-AH FEELS A MITE SLEEPY!
ODD-UGH!-YO' SHOULD-UGH!-MEN-SHUN THET!-AH C'D USE SOME SHUT-EYE MAH-SELF!-
HOW 'BOUT-UGH!-CALLIN' A REST PERIOD AN' US BOTH KETCHIN' FO'TY WINKS? THEN WE UPS, RE-FRESHED AN' R'ARIN' T'GO!
AH-UGH!-CRAVES A LI'L BOOTY SLEEP! WE'LL GIVE EACH OTHER OUR WORD OF HONOR NOT T'START BASHIN' AGIN TILL SUN-UP!
Copr. 1939 by United Feature Syndicate, Inc. Tm. Reg. U. S. Pat. Off.—All rights reserved
TILL SUN-UP!
HO-HUM!
TILL SUN-UP!!
YAWN!
ONE HOUR LATER—
HOW DOES AH KNOW BUT WHUT SHE'LL GIT UP WHILE AH'M SLEEPIN'-AN' BASH ME!-AH BETTER FINISH HER NOW-BEFO' SHE GITS ANY SECH DIS-HONORABLE IDEES!!

LI'L ABNER Will Ratfield Ride Again? By Al Capp

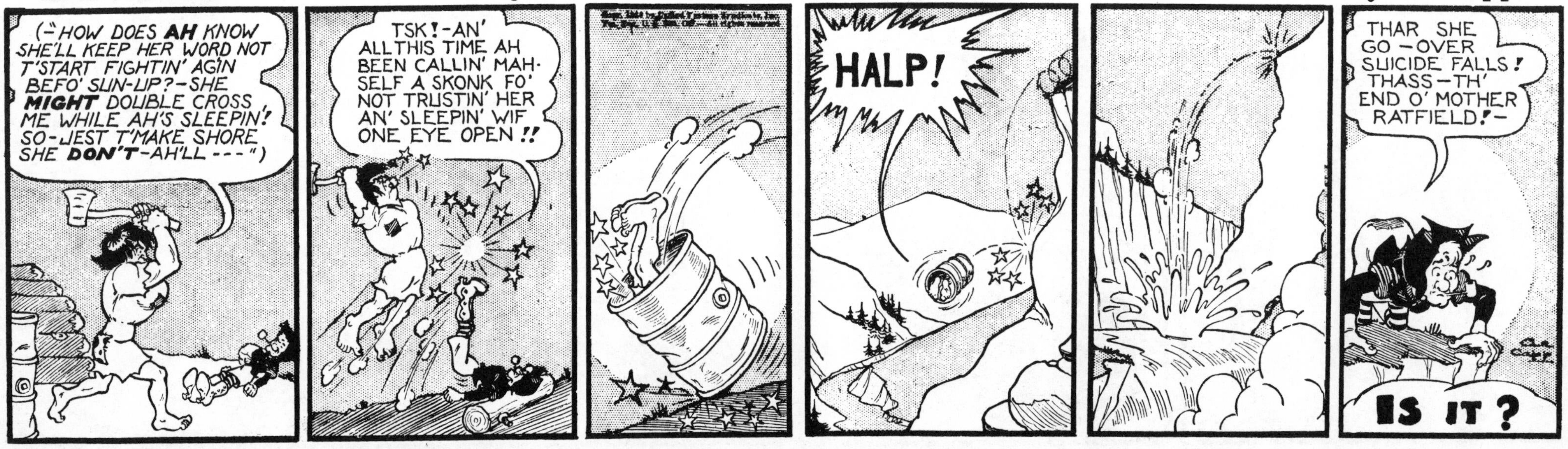

("HOW DOES AH KNOW SHE'LL KEEP HER WORD NOT T'START FIGHTIN' AGIN BEFO' SUN-UP?-SHE MIGHT DOUBLE CROSS ME WHILE AH'S SLEEPIN'! SO-JEST T'MAKE SHORE SHE DON'T-AH'LL ---")
TSK!-AN' ALL THIS TIME AH BEEN CALLIN' MAH-SELF A SKONK FO' NOT TRUSTIN' HER AN' SLEEPIN' WIF ONE EYE OPEN!!
HALP!
THAR SHE GO—OVER SUICIDE FALLS! THASS—TH' END O' MOTHER RATFIELD!—
IS IT?

LI'L ABNER Love Rears Its Fickle Head! By Al Capp

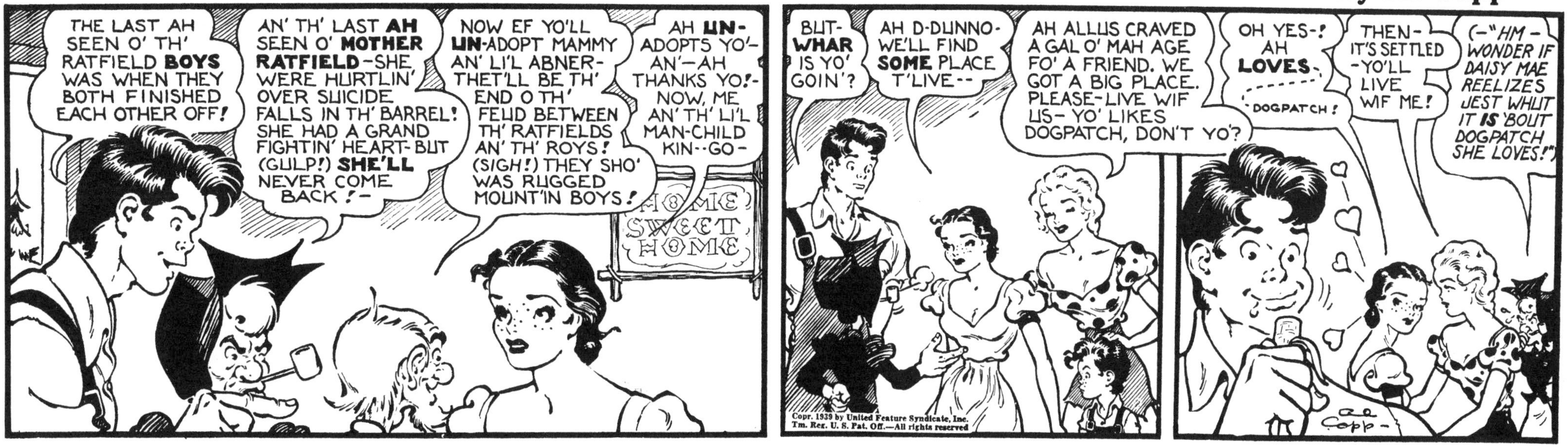
THE LAST AH SEEN O' TH' RATFIELD BOYS WAS WHEN THEY BOTH FINISHED EACH OTHER OFF!
AN' TH' LAST AH SEEN O' MOTHER RATFIELD–SHE WERE HURTLIN' OVER SUICIDE FALLS IN TH' BARREL! SHE HAD A GRAND FIGHTIN' HEART-BUT (GULP!) SHE'LL NEVER COME BACK!–
NOW EF YO'LL UN-ADOPT MAMMY AN' LI'L ABNER-THET'LL BE TH' END O TH' FEUD BETWEEN TH' RATFIELDS AN' TH' ROYS! (SIGH!) THEY SHO' WAS RUGGED MOUNT'IN BOYS!
AH UN-ADOPTS YO'–AN'–AH THANKS YO!–NOW, ME AN' TH' LI'L MAN-CHILD KIN--GO–
HOME SWEET HOME
BUT–WHAR IS YO' GOIN'?
AH D-DUNNO–WE'LL FIND SOME PLACE T'LIVE--
AH ALLUS CRAVED A GAL O' MAH AGE FO' A FRIEND. WE GOT A BIG PLACE. PLEASE–LIVE WIF US–YO' LIKES DOGPATCH, DON'T YO'?
OH YES–! AH LOVES–
DOGPATCH!
THEN–IT'S SETTLED–YO'LL LIVE WIF ME!
(–"HM–WONDER IF DAISY MAE REELIZES JEST WHUT IT IS 'BOUT DOGPATCH SHE LOVES!")
Copr. 1939 by United Feature Syndicate, Inc. Tm. Reg. U. S. Pat. Off.—All rights reserved

LI'L ABNER Th' Finest Young Gennulman By Al Capp

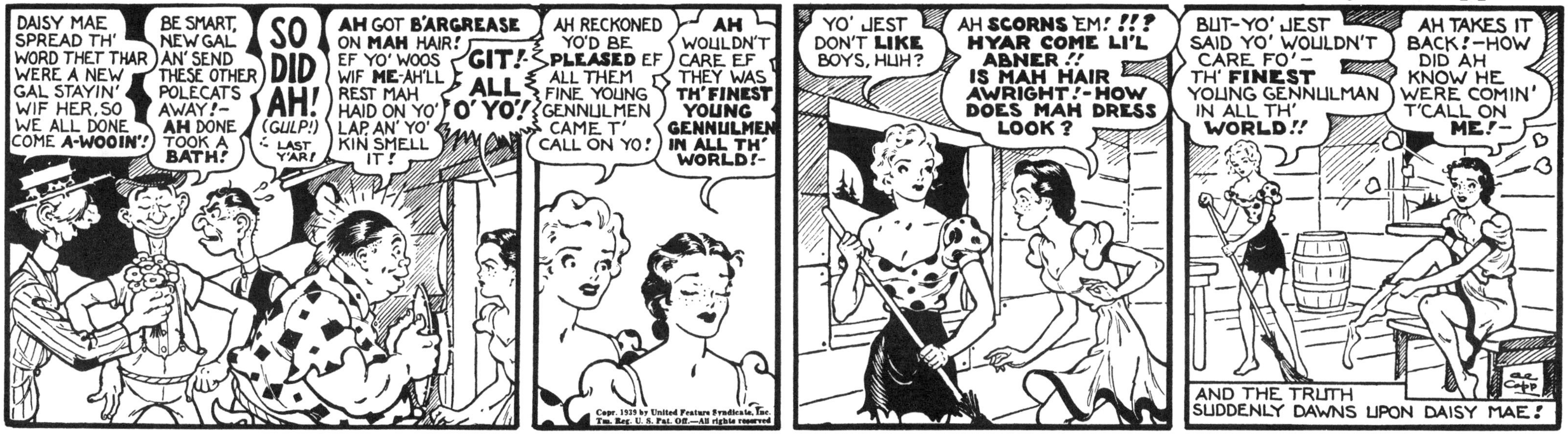
DAISY MAE SPREAD TH' WORD THET THAR WERE A NEW GAL STAYIN' WIF HER, SO WE ALL DONE COME A-WOOIN'!
BE SMART, NEW GAL AN' SEND THESE OTHER POLECATS AWAY!–AH DONE TOOK A BATH!
SO DID AH! (GULP!) LAST Y'AR!
AH GOT B'ARGREASE ON MAH HAIR! EF YO' WOOS WIF ME–AH'LL REST MAH HAID ON YO' LAP AN' YO' KIN SMELL IT!
GIT! ALL O' YO'!
AH RECKONED YO'D BE PLEASED EF ALL THEM FINE YOUNG GENNULMEN CAME T' CALL ON YO'!
AH WOULDN'T CARE EF THEY WAS TH' FINEST YOUNG GENNULMEN IN ALL TH' WORLD!–
Copr. 1939 by United Feature Syndicate, Inc. Tm. Reg. U. S. Pat. Off.—All rights reserved
YO' JEST DON'T LIKE BOYS, HUH?
AH SCORNS 'EM! !!? HYAR COME LI'L ABNER!! IS MAH HAIR AWRIGHT!–HOW DOES MAH DRESS LOOK?
BUT–YO' JEST SAID YO' WOULDN'T CARE FO'–TH' FINEST YOUNG GENNULMAN IN ALL TH' WORLD!!
AH TAKES IT BACK!–HOW DID AH KNOW HE WERE COMIN' T'CALL ON ME!–
AND THE TRUTH SUDDENLY DAWNS UPON DAISY MAE!

LI'L ABNER The Lamp Is Low and So Is Daisy By Al Capp

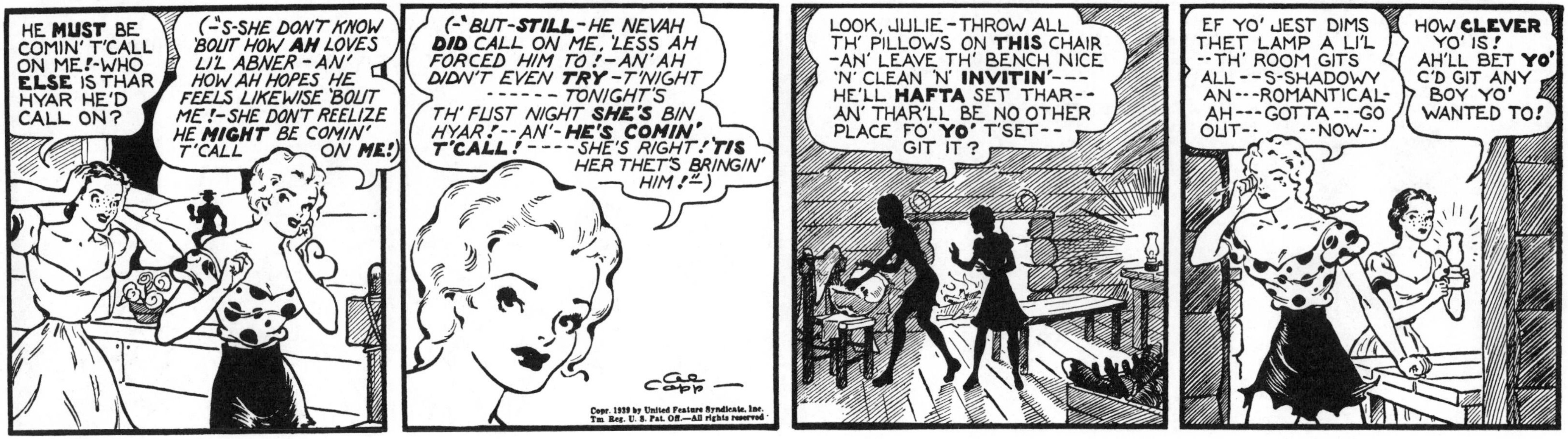
HE MUST BE COMIN' T'CALL ON ME!-WHO ELSE IS THAR HYAR HE'D CALL ON?
(-"S-SHE DON'T KNOW 'BOUT HOW AH LOVES LI'L ABNER - AN' HOW AH HOPES HE FEELS LIKEWISE 'BOUT ME!-SHE DON'T REELIZE HE MIGHT BE COMIN' T'CALL ON ME!)
(-"BUT-STILL-HE NEVAH DID CALL ON ME, 'LESS AH FORCED HIM TO!-AN' AH DIDN'T EVEN TRY-T'NIGHT ------ TONIGHT'S TH' FUST NIGHT SHE'S BIN HYAR!--AN'-HE'S COMIN' T'CALL!----SHE'S RIGHT!'TIS HER THET'S BRINGIN' HIM!")
Al Capp
Copr. 1939 by United Feature Syndicate, Inc. Tm. Reg. U. S. Pat. Off.—All rights reserved
LOOK, JULIE-THROW ALL TH' PILLOWS ON THIS CHAIR -AN' LEAVE TH' BENCH NICE 'N' CLEAN 'N' INVITIN'--- HE'LL HAFTA SET THAR-- AN' THAR'LL BE NO OTHER PLACE FO' YO' T'SET-- GIT IT?
EF YO' JEST DIMS THET LAMP A LI'L --TH' ROOM GITS ALL--S-SHADOWY AN---ROMANTICAL- AH---GOTTA---GO OUT-- --NOW--
HOW CLEVER YO' IS! AH'LL BET YO' C'D GIT ANY BOY YO' WANTED TO!

LI'L ABNER Why Don't They Tell Him These Things? By Al Capp

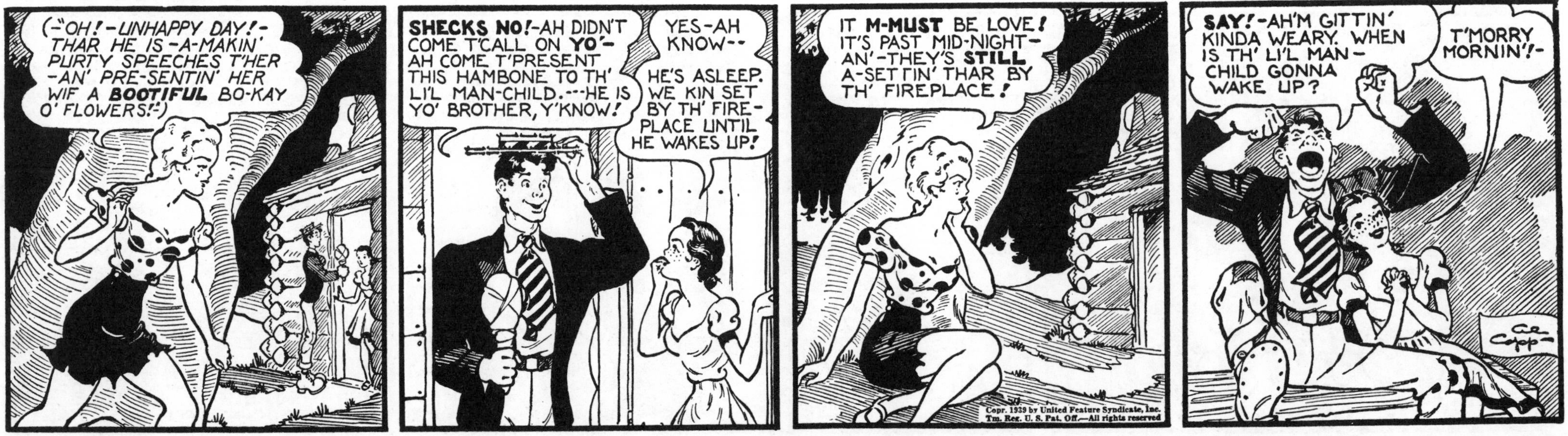
(-"OH!-UNHAPPY DAY!- THAR HE IS-A-MAKIN' PURTY SPEECHES T'HER -AN' PRE-SENTIN' HER WIF A BOOTIFUL BO-KAY O' FLOWERS!")
SHECKS NO!-AH DIDN'T COME T'CALL ON YO'- AH COME T'PRESENT THIS HAMBONE TO TH' LI'L MAN-CHILD.--HE IS YO' BROTHER, Y'KNOW!
YES-AH KNOW--
HE'S ASLEEP. WE KIN SET BY TH' FIRE-PLACE UNTIL HE WAKES UP!
IT M-MUST BE LOVE! IT'S PAST MID-NIGHT- AN'-THEY'S STILL A-SETTIN' THAR BY TH' FIREPLACE!
Copr. 1939 by United Feature Syndicate, Inc. Tm. Reg. U. S. Pat. Off.—All rights reserved
SAY!-AH'M GITTIN' KINDA WEARY. WHEN IS TH' LI'L MAN-CHILD GONNA WAKE UP?
T'MORRY MORNIN'!-
Al Capp

LI'L ABNER The Wolf Trapped! By Al Capp

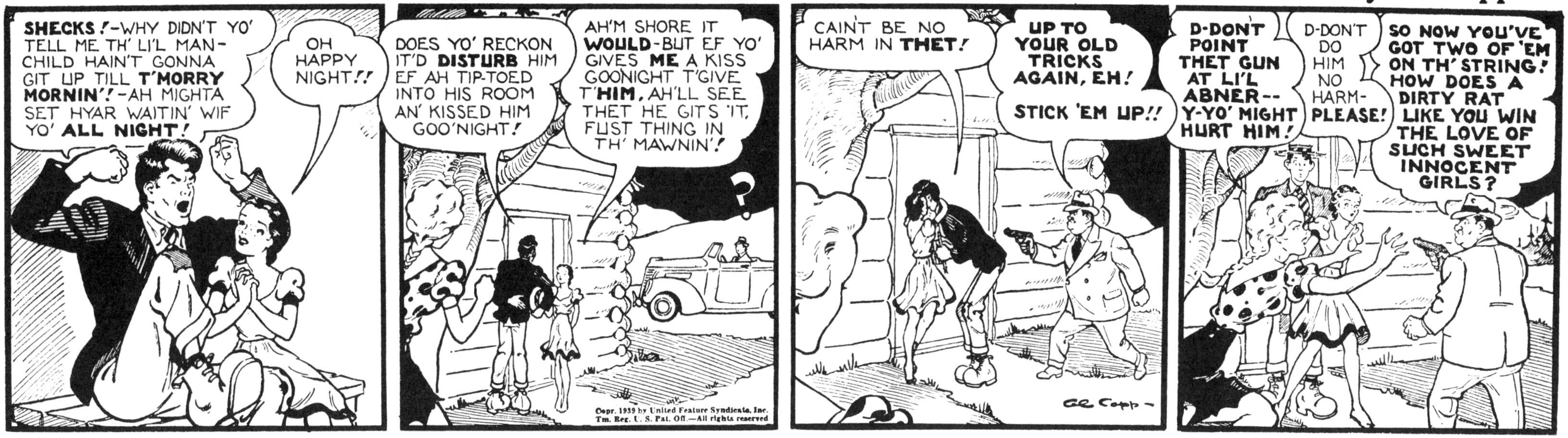

SHECKS!-WHY DIDN'T YO' TELL ME TH' LI'L MAN-CHILD HAIN'T GONNA GIT UP TILL T'MORRY MORNIN'!-AH MIGHTA SET HYAR WAITIN' WIF YO' ALL NIGHT!
OH HAPPY NIGHT!!
DOES YO' RECKON IT'D DISTURB HIM EF AH TIP-TOED INTO HIS ROOM AN' KISSED HIM GOO'NIGHT!
AH'M SHORE IT WOULD-BUT EF YO' GIVES ME A KISS GOONIGHT T'GIVE T'HIM, AH'LL SEE THET HE GITS 'IT, FUST THING IN TH' MAWNIN'!
?
Copr. 1939 by United Feature Syndicate, Inc. Tm. Reg. U. S. Pat. Off.—All rights reserved
CAIN'T BE NO HARM IN THET!
UP TO YOUR OLD TRICKS AGAIN, EH!
STICK 'EM UP!!
Al Capp
D-DON'T POINT THET GUN AT LI'L ABNER-- Y-YO' MIGHT HURT HIM!
D-DON'T DO HIM NO HARM- PLEASE!
SO NOW YOU'VE GOT TWO OF 'EM ON TH' STRING! HOW DOES A DIRTY RAT LIKE YOU WIN THE LOVE OF SUCH SWEET INNOCENT GIRLS?

LI'L ABNER A Hard Man to Fool By Al Capp

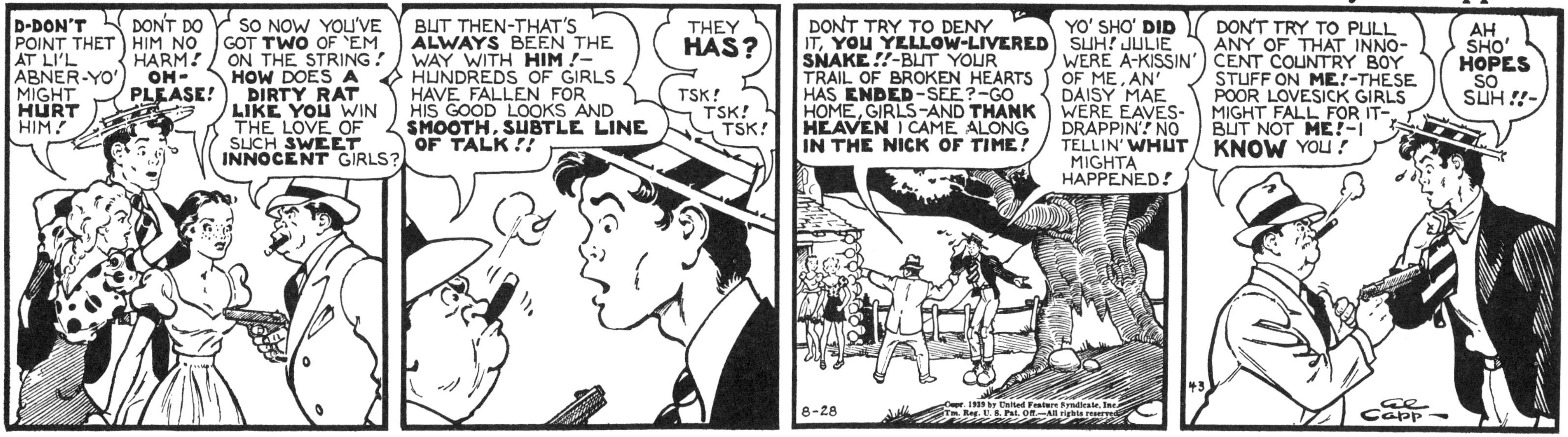

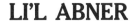

D-DON'T POINT THET AT LI'L ABNER-YO' MIGHT HURT HIM!
DON'T DO HIM NO HARM! OH-PLEASE!
SO NOW YOU'VE GOT TWO OF 'EM ON THE STRING! HOW DOES A DIRTY RAT LIKE YOU WIN THE LOVE OF SUCH SWEET INNOCENT GIRLS?
BUT THEN-THAT'S ALWAYS BEEN THE WAY WITH HIM!-HUNDREDS OF GIRLS HAVE FALLEN FOR HIS GOOD LOOKS AND SMOOTH, SUBTLE LINE OF TALK!!
THEY HAS?
TSK! TSK! TSK!
DON'T TRY TO DENY IT, YOU YELLOW-LIVERED SNAKE!!-BUT YOUR TRAIL OF BROKEN HEARTS HAS ENDED-SEE?-GO HOME, GIRLS-AND THANK HEAVEN I CAME ALONG IN THE NICK OF TIME!
YO' SHO' DID SUH! JULIE WERE A-KISSIN' OF ME, AN' DAISY MAE WERE EAVES-DRAPPIN'! NO TELLIN' WHUT MIGHTA HAPPENED!
8-28
Copr. 1939 by United Feature Syndicate, Inc. Tm. Reg. U. S. Pat. Off.—All rights reserved
DON'T TRY TO PULL ANY OF THAT INNO-CENT COUNTRY BOY STUFF ON ME!-THESE POOR LOVESICK GIRLS MIGHT FALL FOR IT-BUT NOT ME!-I KNOW YOU!
AH SHO' HOPES SO SUH!!-
43
Al Capp

LI'L ABNER The Smart Aleck! By Al Capp

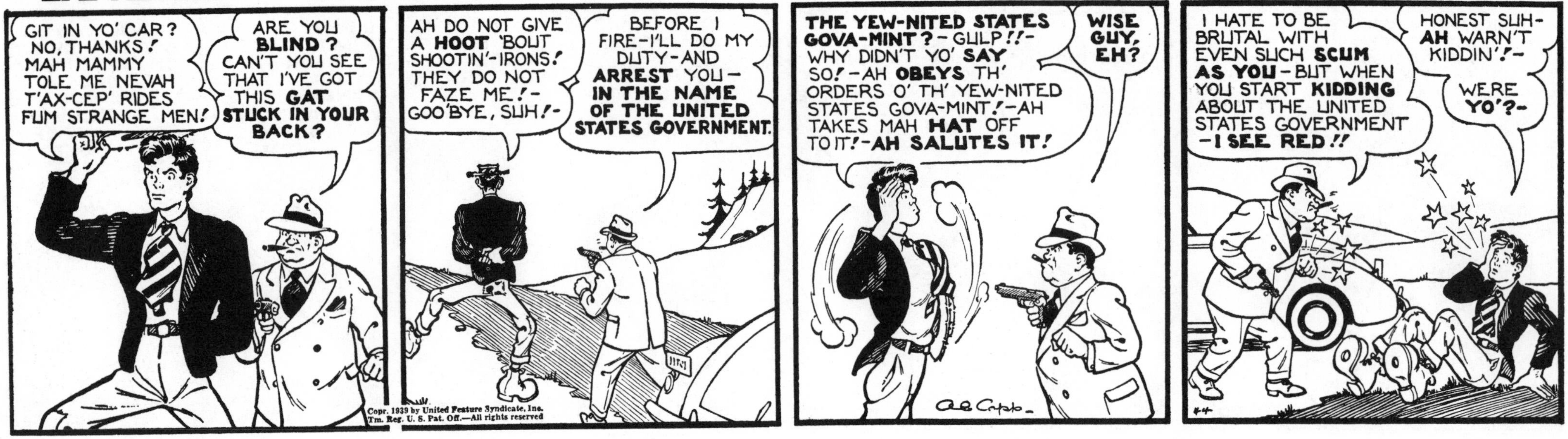
GIT IN YO' CAR? NO, THANKS! MAH MAMMY TOLE ME NEVAH T'AX-CEP' RIDES FUM STRANGE MEN!
ARE YOU BLIND? CAN'T YOU SEE THAT I'VE GOT THIS GAT STUCK IN YOUR BACK?
AH DO NOT GIVE A HOOT 'BOUT SHOOTIN'-IRONS! THEY DO NOT FAZE ME!- GOO'BYE, SUH!-
BEFORE I FIRE-I'LL DO MY DUTY-AND ARREST YOU- IN THE NAME OF THE UNITED STATES GOVERNMENT.
Copr. 1939 by United Feature Syndicate, Inc. Tm. Reg. U. S. Pat. Off.—All rights reserved
THE YEW-NITED STATES GOVA-MINT?-GULP!!- WHY DIDN'T YO' SAY SO!-AH OBEYS TH' ORDERS O' TH' YEW-NITED STATES GOVA-MINT!-AH TAKES MAH HAT OFF TO IT!-AH SALUTES IT!
WISE GUY, EH?
I HATE TO BE BRUTAL WITH EVEN SUCH SCUM AS YOU-BUT WHEN YOU START KIDDING ABOUT THE UNITED STATES GOVERNMENT -I SEE RED!!
HONEST SUH- AH WARN'T KIDDIN'!-
WERE YO'?-

LI'L ABNER The Wages of Cynicism! By Al Capp

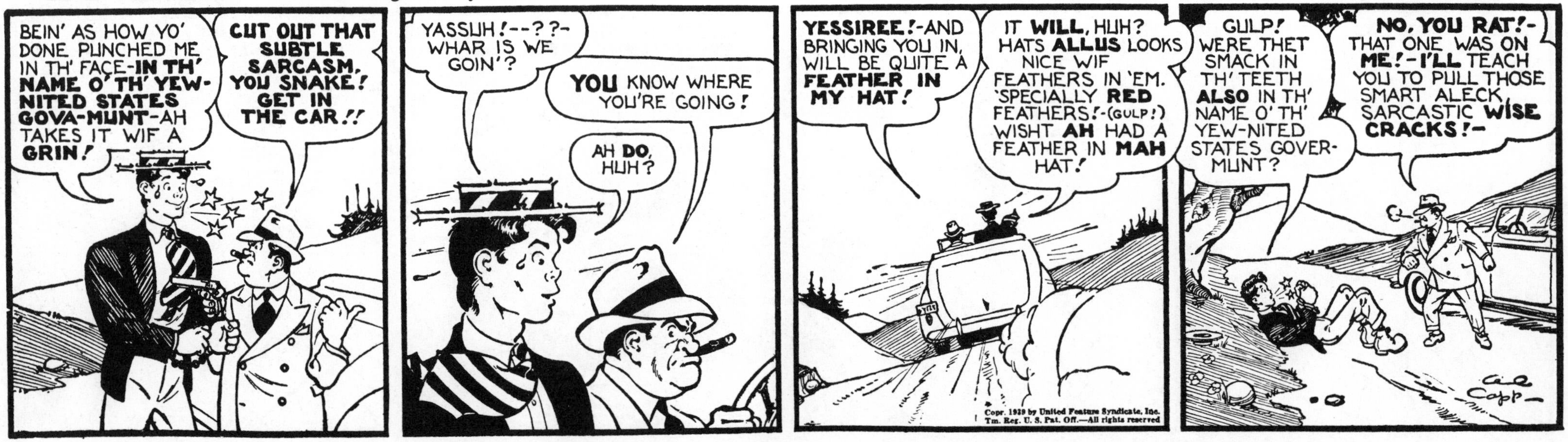
BEIN' AS HOW YO' DONE PUNCHED ME IN TH' FACE-IN TH' NAME O' TH' YEW-NITED STATES GOVA-MUNT-AH TAKES IT WIF A GRIN!
CUT OUT THAT SUBTLE SARCASM, YOU SNAKE! GET IN THE CAR!!
YASSUH!--??- WHAR IS WE GOIN'?
YOU KNOW WHERE YOU'RE GOING!
AH DO, HUH?
YESSIREE!-AND BRINGING YOU IN, WILL BE QUITE A FEATHER IN MY HAT!
IT WILL, HUH? HATS ALLUS LOOKS NICE WIF FEATHERS IN 'EM. 'SPECIALLY RED FEATHERS!-(GULP!) WISHT AH HAD A FEATHER IN MAH HAT!
Copr. 1939 by United Feature Syndicate, Inc. Tm. Reg. U. S. Pat. Off.—All rights reserved
GULP! WERE THET SMACK IN TH' TEETH ALSO IN TH' NAME O' TH' YEW-NITED STATES GOVER-MUNT?
NO, YOU RAT!- THAT ONE WAS ON ME!-I'LL TEACH YOU TO PULL THOSE SMART ALECK, SARCASTIC WISE CRACKS!-

LI'L ABNER Strange Enchantment! By Al Capp

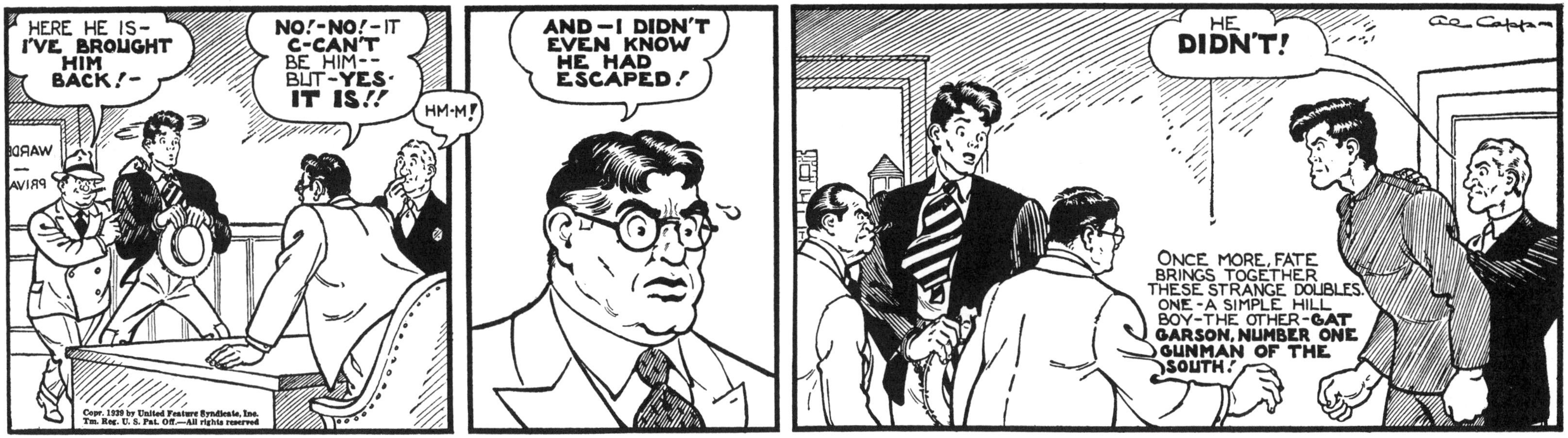

HERE HE IS- I'VE BROUGHT HIM BACK!-
NO!-NO!-IT C-CAN'T BE HIM-- BUT-YES- IT IS!!
HM-M!
Copr. 1939 by United Feature Syndicate, Inc. Tm. Reg. U. S. Pat. Off.—All rights reserved
AND—I DIDN'T EVEN KNOW HE HAD ESCAPED!
HE DIDN'T!
ONCE MORE, FATE BRINGS TOGETHER THESE STRANGE DOUBLES. ONE-A SIMPLE HILL BOY-THE OTHER-GAT GARSON, NUMBER ONE GUNMAN OF THE SOUTH!

LI'L ABNER Yokum Rides Again! By Al Capp

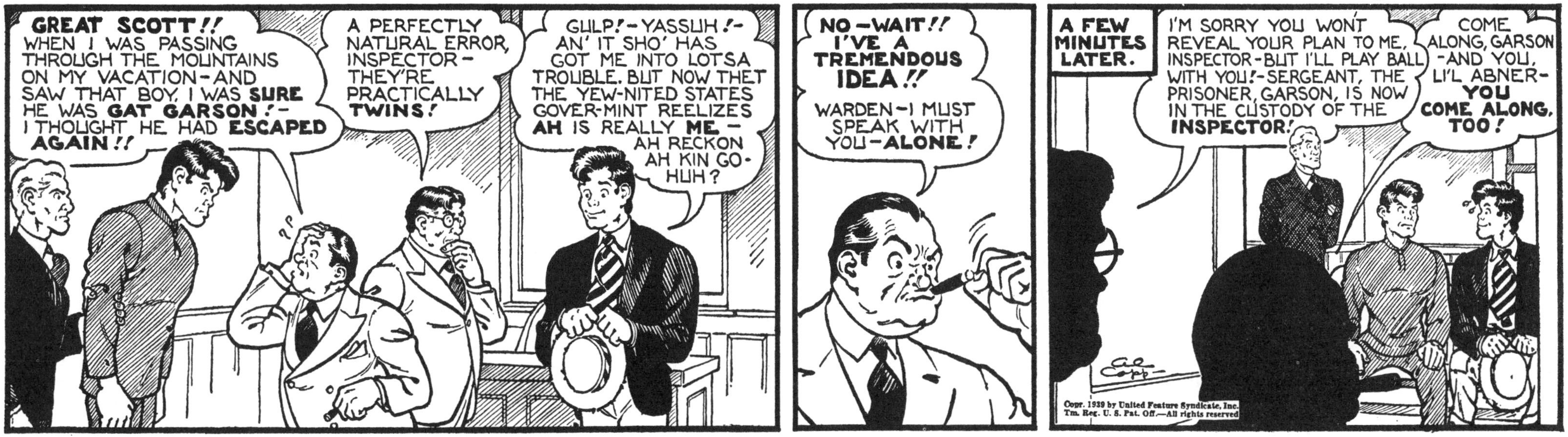

GREAT SCOTT!! WHEN I WAS PASSING THROUGH THE MOUNTAINS ON MY VACATION-AND SAW THAT BOY, I WAS SURE HE WAS GAT GARSON!- I THOUGHT HE HAD ESCAPED AGAIN!!
A PERFECTLY NATURAL ERROR, INSPECTOR- THEY'RE PRACTICALLY TWINS!
GULP!-YASSUH!- AN' IT SHO' HAS GOT ME INTO LOTSA TROUBLE. BUT NOW THET THE YEW-NITED STATES GOVER-MINT REELIZES AH IS REALLY ME- AH RECKON AH KIN GO- HUH?
NO—WAIT!! I'VE A TREMENDOUS IDEA!!
WARDEN—I MUST SPEAK WITH YOU—ALONE!
A FEW MINUTES LATER.
I'M SORRY YOU WON'T REVEAL YOUR PLAN TO ME, INSPECTOR-BUT I'LL PLAY BALL WITH YOU!-SERGEANT, THE PRISONER, GARSON, IS NOW IN THE CUSTODY OF THE INSPECTOR!
COME ALONG, GARSON -AND YOU, LI'L ABNER- YOU COME ALONG, TOO!
Copr. 1939 by United Feature Syndicate, Inc. Tm. Reg. U. S. Pat. Off.—All rights reserved

LI'L ABNER The Wreck of the Desperates By Al Capp

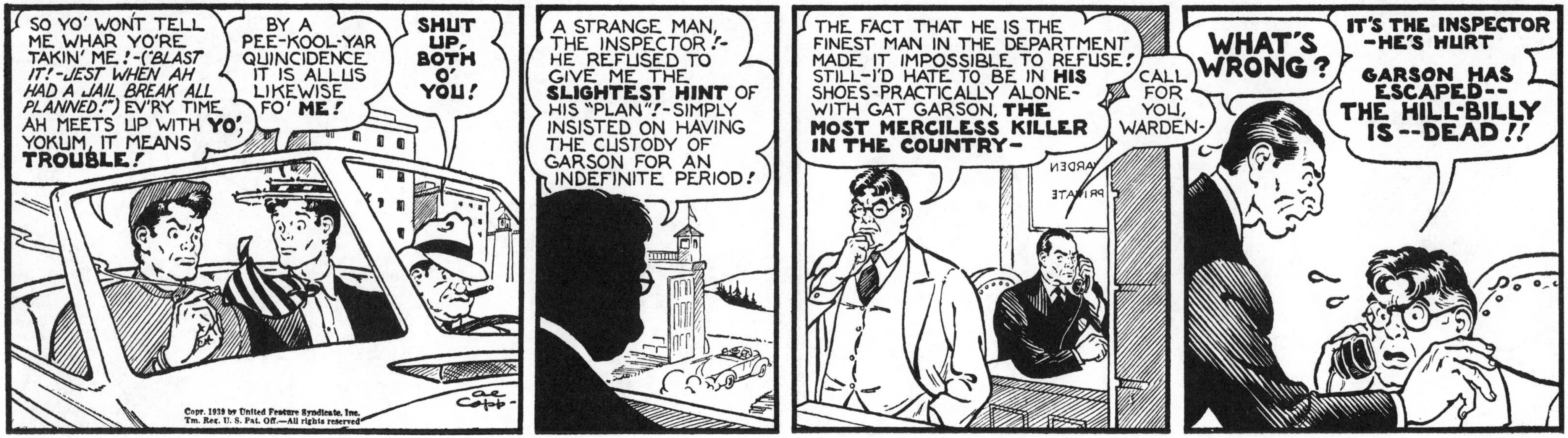

SO YO' WON'T TELL ME WHAR YO'RE TAKIN' ME!-('BLAST IT!-JEST WHEN AH HAD A JAIL BREAK ALL PLANNED!") EV'RY TIME AH MEETS UP WITH YO', YOKUM, IT MEANS TROUBLE!
BY A PEE-KOOL-YAR QUINCIDENCE IT IS ALLUS LIKEWISE FO' ME!
SHUT UP, BOTH O' YOU!
Copr. 1939 by United Feature Syndicate, Inc. Tm. Reg. U. S. Pat. Off.—All rights reserved
A STRANGE MAN, THE INSPECTOR!- HE REFUSED TO GIVE ME THE SLIGHTEST HINT OF HIS "PLAN"!-SIMPLY INSISTED ON HAVING THE CUSTODY OF GARSON FOR AN INDEFINITE PERIOD!
THE FACT THAT HE IS THE FINEST MAN IN THE DEPARTMENT MADE IT IMPOSSIBLE TO REFUSE! STILL-I'D HATE TO BE IN HIS SHOES-PRACTICALLY ALONE-WITH GAT GARSON, THE MOST MERCILESS KILLER IN THE COUNTRY-
CALL FOR YOU, WARDEN-
WHAT'S WRONG?
IT'S THE INSPECTOR -HE'S HURT
GARSON HAS ESCAPED-- THE HILL-BILLY IS --DEAD!!

LI'L ABNER Hevvin-Bound! By Al Capp

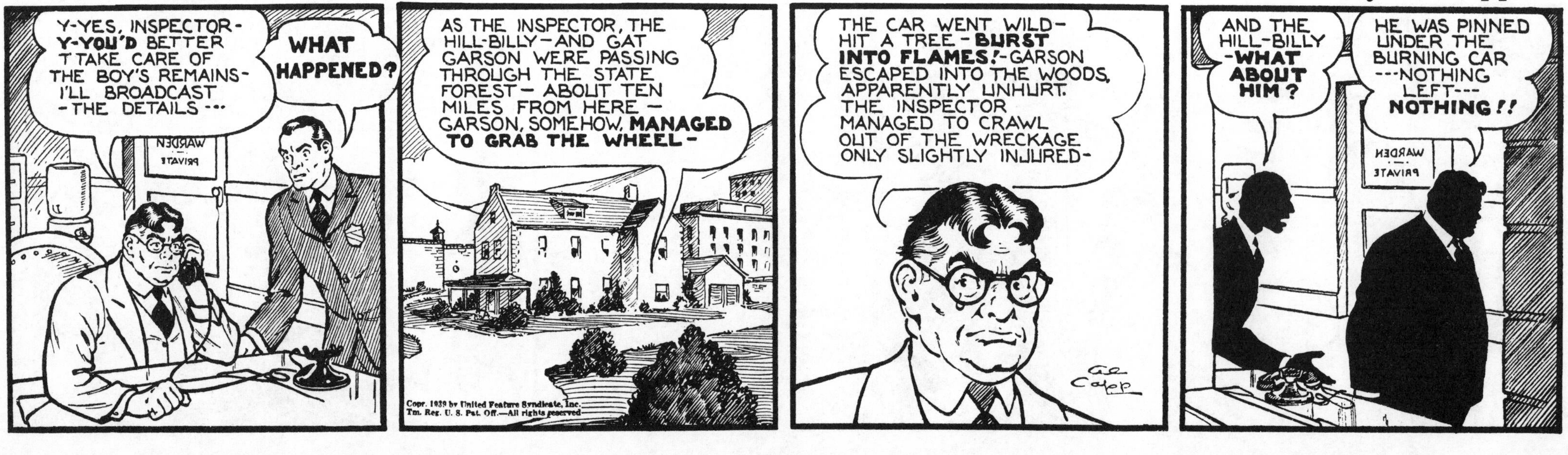

Y-YES, INSPECTOR- Y-YOU'D BETTER T TAKE CARE OF THE BOY'S REMAINS- I'LL BROADCAST -THE DETAILS ---
WHAT HAPPENED?
AS THE INSPECTOR, THE HILL-BILLY—AND GAT GARSON WERE PASSING THROUGH THE STATE FOREST— ABOUT TEN MILES FROM HERE— GARSON, SOMEHOW, MANAGED TO GRAB THE WHEEL-
Copr. 1939 by United Feature Syndicate, Inc. Tm. Reg. U. S. Pat. Off.—All rights reserved
THE CAR WENT WILD- HIT A TREE - BURST INTO FLAMES!-GARSON ESCAPED INTO THE WOODS, APPARENTLY UNHURT. THE INSPECTOR MANAGED TO CRAWL OUT OF THE WRECKAGE ONLY SLIGHTLY INJURED-
AND THE HILL-BILLY -WHAT ABOUT HIM?
HE WAS PINNED UNDER THE BURNING CAR ---NOTHING LEFT--- NOTHING!!

LI'L ABNER — The Hot Seat! — By Al Capp

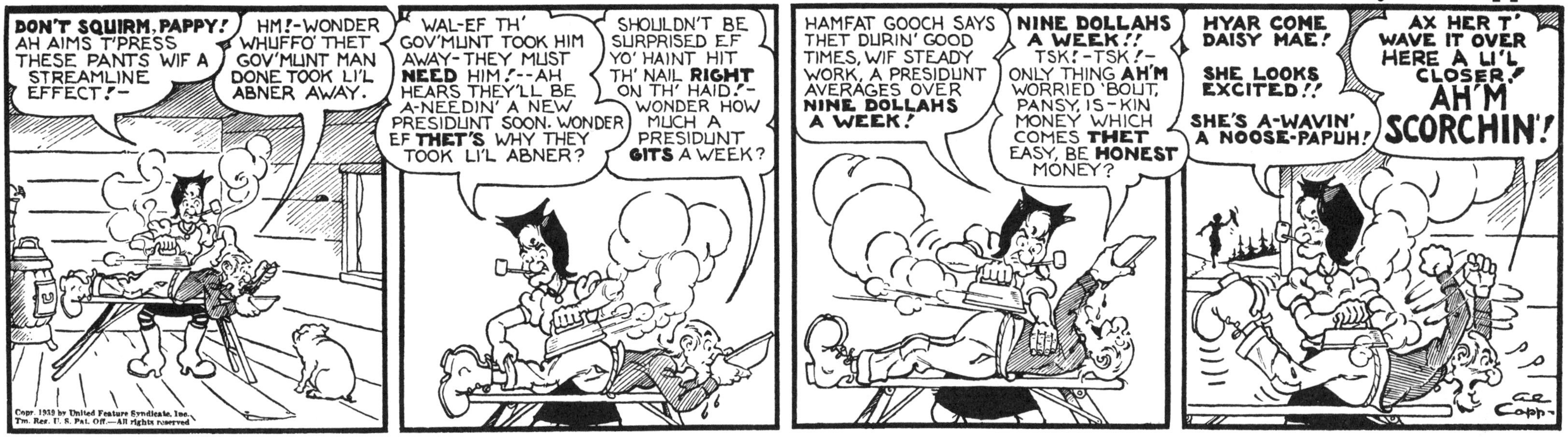
DON'T SQUIRM, PAPPY! AH AIMS T'PRESS THESE PANTS WIF A STREAMLINE EFFECT!-
HM!-WONDER WHUFFO' THET GOV'MUNT MAN DONE TOOK LI'L ABNER AWAY.
Copr. 1939 by United Feature Syndicate, Inc. Tm. Reg. U. S. Pat. Off.—All rights reserved
WAL-EF TH' GOV'MUNT TOOK HIM AWAY-THEY MUST NEED HIM!--AH HEARS THEY'LL BE A-NEEDIN' A NEW PRESIDUNT SOON. WONDER EF THET'S WHY THEY TOOK LI'L ABNER?
SHOULDN'T BE SURPRISED EF YO' HAINT HIT TH' NAIL RIGHT ON TH' HAID!-WONDER HOW MUCH A PRESIDUNT GITS A WEEK?
HAMFAT GOOCH SAYS THET DURIN' GOOD TIMES, WIF STEADY WORK, A PRESIDUNT AVERAGES OVER NINE DOLLAHS A WEEK!
NINE DOLLAHS A WEEK!! TSK!-TSK!-ONLY THING AH'M WORRIED 'BOUT, PANSY, IS-KIN MONEY WHICH COMES THET EASY, BE HONEST MONEY?
HYAR COME DAISY MAE!
SHE LOOKS EXCITED!!
SHE'S A-WAVIN' A NOOSE-PAPUH!
AX HER T' WAVE IT OVER HERE A LI'L CLOSER! AH'M SCORCHIN'!
Al Capp

LI'L ABNER — Yo' Don't Know the Half of It! — By Al Capp

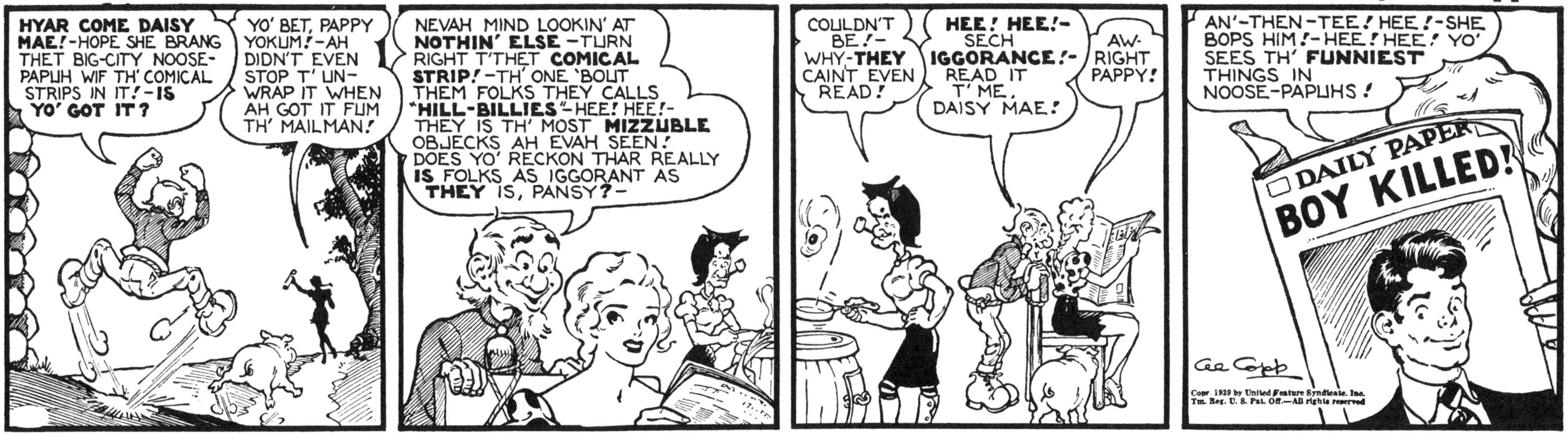
HYAR COME DAISY MAE!-HOPE SHE BRANG THET BIG-CITY NOOSE-PAPUH WIF TH' COMICAL STRIPS IN IT!-IS YO' GOT IT?
YO' BET, PAPPY YOKUM!-AH DIDN'T EVEN STOP T' UN-WRAP IT WHEN AH GOT IT FUM TH' MAILMAN!
NEVAH MIND LOOKIN' AT NOTHIN' ELSE-TURN RIGHT T'THET COMICAL STRIP!-TH' ONE 'BOUT THEM FOLKS THEY CALLS "HILL-BILLIES"-HEE! HEE!-THEY IS TH' MOST MIZZUBLE OBJECKS AH EVAH SEEN! DOES YO' RECKON THAR REALLY IS FOLKS AS IGGORANT AS THEY IS, PANSY?-
COULDN'T BE!-WHY-THEY CAIN'T EVEN READ!
HEE! HEE!-SECH IGGORANCE!-READ IT T' ME, DAISY MAE!
AW-RIGHT PAPPY!
AN'-THEN-TEE! HEE!-SHE BOPS HIM!-HEE! HEE! YO' SEES TH' FUNNIEST THINGS IN NOOSE-PAPUHS!
DAILY PAPER
BOY KILLED!
Al Capp
Copr. 1939 by United Feature Syndicate, Inc. Tm. Reg. U. S. Pat. Off.—All rights reserved

LI'L ABNER — It Brightens Up the Room — By Al Capp

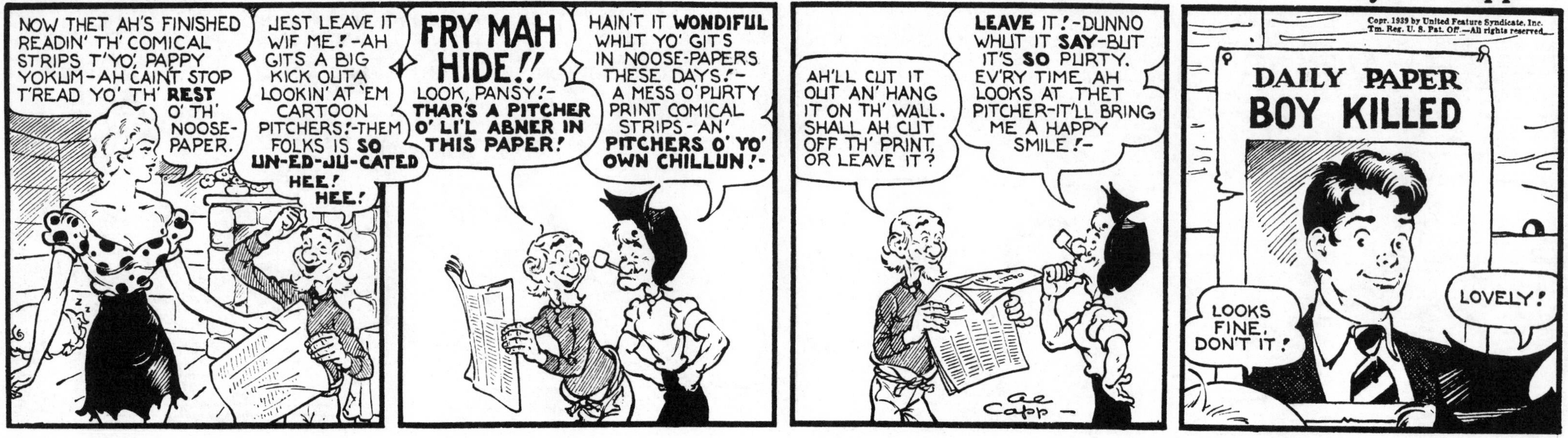
NOW THET AH'S FINISHED READIN' TH' COMICAL STRIPS T'YO', PAPPY YOKUM—AH CAIN'T STOP T'READ YO' TH' **REST** O' TH' NOOSE-PAPER.
JEST LEAVE IT WIF ME!—AH GITS A BIG KICK OUTA LOOKIN' AT 'EM CARTOON PITCHERS!—THEM FOLKS IS **SO UN-ED-JU-CATED**
HEE! HEE!
FRY MAH HIDE!!
LOOK, PANSY!— **THAR'S A PITCHER O' LI'L ABNER IN THIS PAPER!**
HAIN'T IT **WONDIFUL** WHUT YO' GITS IN NOOSE-PAPERS THESE DAYS!— A MESS O' PURTY PRINT COMICAL STRIPS—AN' **PITCHERS O' YO' OWN CHILLUN!**—
AH'LL CUT IT OUT AN' HANG IT ON TH' WALL. SHALL AH CUT OFF TH' PRINT, OR LEAVE IT?
LEAVE IT!—DUNNO WHUT IT **SAY**—BUT IT'S **SO** PURTY. EV'RY TIME AH LOOKS AT THET PITCHER—IT'LL BRING ME A HAPPY SMILE!—
Copr. 1939 by United Feature Syndicate, Inc. Tm. Reg. U. S. Pat. Off.—All rights reserved
DAILY PAPER
BOY KILLED
LOOKS FINE, DON'T IT!
LOVELY!

LI'L ABNER — When Ignorance Was Bliss — By Al Capp

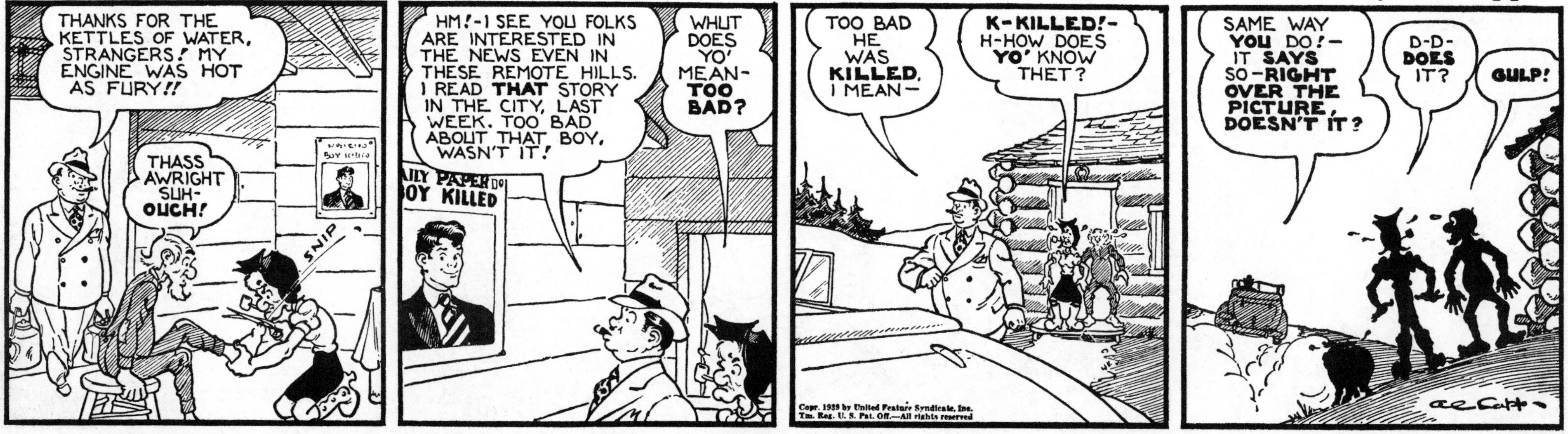
THANKS FOR THE KETTLES OF WATER, STRANGERS! MY ENGINE WAS HOT AS FURY!!
THASS AWRIGHT SUH— **OUCH!**
SNIP
HM!—I SEE YOU FOLKS ARE INTERESTED IN THE NEWS EVEN IN THESE REMOTE HILLS. I READ **THAT** STORY IN THE CITY, LAST WEEK. TOO BAD ABOUT THAT BOY, WASN'T IT!
WHUT DOES YO' MEAN— **TOO BAD?**
TOO BAD HE WAS **KILLED**, I MEAN—
K-KILLED!— H-HOW DOES **YO'** KNOW THET?
Copr. 1939 by United Feature Syndicate, Inc. Tm. Reg. U. S. Pat. Off.—All rights reserved
SAME WAY **YOU** DO!— IT **SAYS** SO—**RIGHT OVER THE PICTURE, DOESN'T IT?**
D-D- **DOES** IT?
GULP!

LI'L ABNER The Corpse Walks Again! By Al Capp

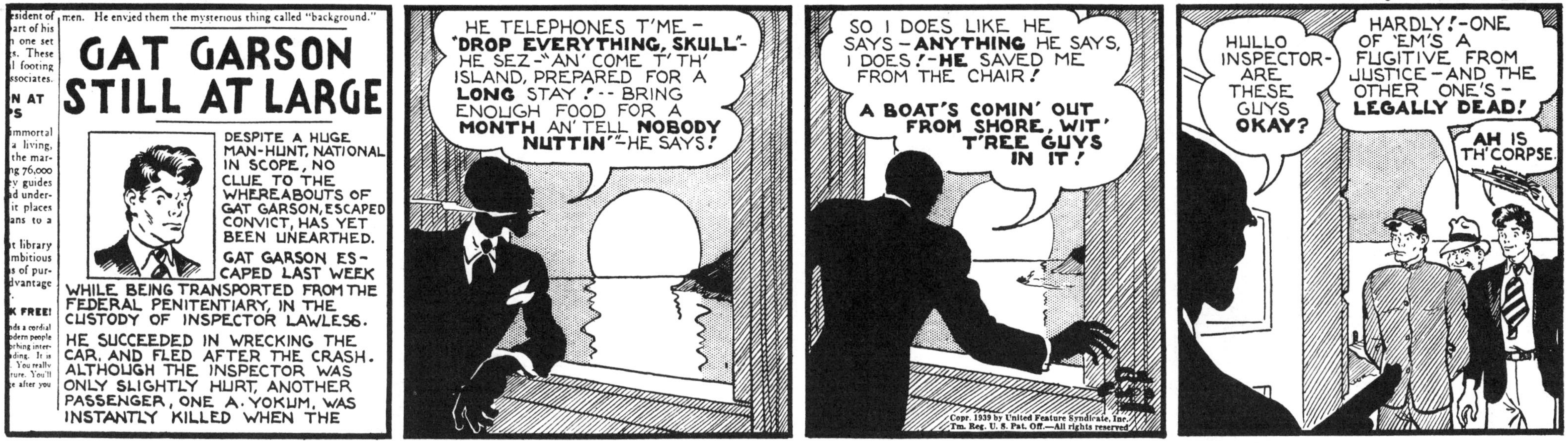

men. He envied them the mysterious thing called "background."
GAT GARSON STILL AT LARGE
DESPITE A HUGE MAN-HUNT, NATIONAL IN SCOPE, NO CLUE TO THE WHEREABOUTS OF GAT GARSON, ESCAPED CONVICT, HAS YET BEEN UNEARTHED.
GAT GARSON ESCAPED LAST WEEK WHILE BEING TRANSPORTED FROM THE FEDERAL PENITENTIARY, IN THE CUSTODY OF INSPECTOR LAWLESS.
HE SUCCEEDED IN WRECKING THE CAR, AND FLED AFTER THE CRASH. ALTHOUGH THE INSPECTOR WAS ONLY SLIGHTLY HURT, ANOTHER PASSENGER, ONE A. YOKUM, WAS INSTANTLY KILLED WHEN THE
HE TELEPHONES T'ME – "DROP EVERYTHING, SKULL" – HE SEZ – "AN' COME T' TH' ISLAND, PREPARED FOR A LONG STAY! -- BRING ENOUGH FOOD FOR A MONTH AN' TELL NOBODY NUTTIN'" – HE SAYS!
SO I DOES LIKE HE SAYS – ANYTHING HE SAYS, I DOES! – HE SAVED ME FROM THE CHAIR!
A BOAT'S COMIN' OUT FROM SHORE, WIT' T'REE GUYS IN IT!
Copr. 1939 by United Feature Syndicate, Inc. Tm. Reg. U. S. Pat. Off.—All rights reserved
HULLO INSPECTOR – ARE THESE GUYS OKAY?
HARDLY! – ONE OF 'EM'S A FUGITIVE FROM JUSTICE – AND THE OTHER ONE'S – LEGALLY DEAD!
AH IS TH' CORPSE.

LI'L ABNER Haunted and Hunted! By Al Capp

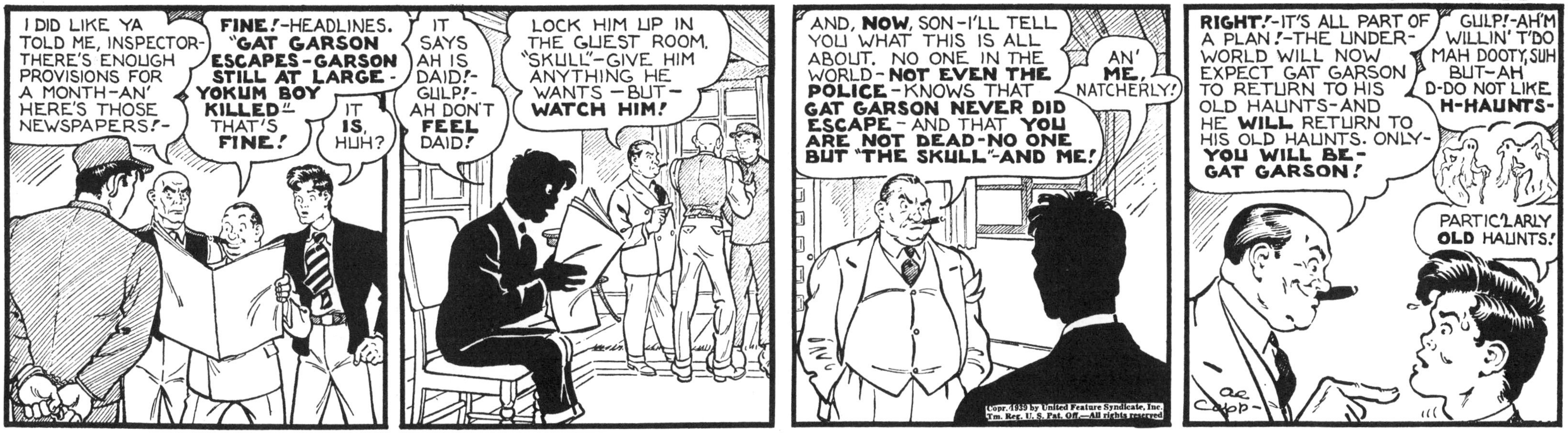

I DID LIKE YA TOLD ME, INSPECTOR – THERE'S ENOUGH PROVISIONS FOR A MONTH – AN' HERE'S THOSE NEWSPAPERS! –
FINE! – HEADLINES. "GAT GARSON ESCAPES – GARSON STILL AT LARGE – YOKUM BOY KILLED" – THAT'S FINE!
IT IS, HUH?
IT SAYS AH IS DAID! – GULP! – AH DON'T FEEL DAID!
LOCK HIM UP IN THE GUEST ROOM, "SKULL" – GIVE HIM ANYTHING HE WANTS – BUT – WATCH HIM!
AND, NOW, SON – I'LL TELL YOU WHAT THIS IS ALL ABOUT. NO ONE IN THE WORLD – NOT EVEN THE POLICE – KNOWS THAT GAT GARSON NEVER DID ESCAPE – AND THAT YOU ARE NOT DEAD – NO ONE BUT "THE SKULL" – AND ME!
AN' ME, NATCHERLY!
Copr. 1939 by United Feature Syndicate, Inc. Tm. Reg. U. S. Pat. Off.—All rights reserved
RIGHT! – IT'S ALL PART OF A PLAN! – THE UNDERWORLD WILL NOW EXPECT GAT GARSON TO RETURN TO HIS OLD HAUNTS – AND HE WILL RETURN TO HIS OLD HAUNTS. ONLY – YOU WILL BE – GAT GARSON!
GULP! – AH'M WILLIN' T'DO MAH DOOTY, SUH BUT – AH D-DO NOT LIKE H-HAUNTS –
PARTIC'LARLY OLD HAUNTS!
al capp

LI'L ABNER Criminals Beware! By Al Capp

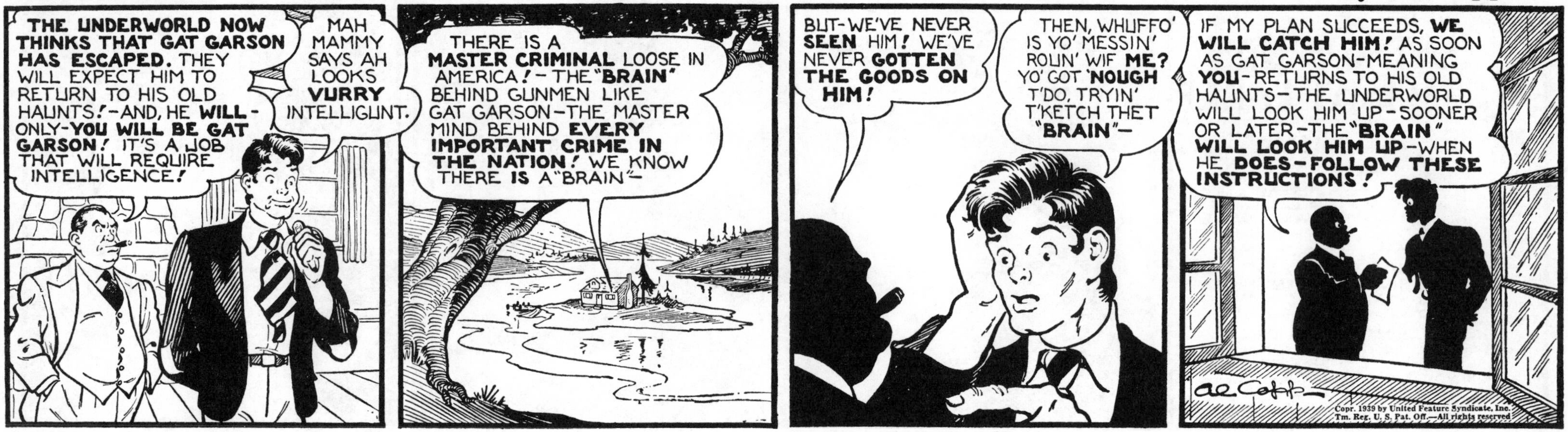
THE UNDERWORLD NOW THINKS THAT GAT GARSON HAS ESCAPED. THEY WILL EXPECT HIM TO RETURN TO HIS OLD HAUNTS!-AND, HE WILL-ONLY-YOU WILL BE GAT GARSON! IT'S A JOB THAT WILL REQUIRE INTELLIGENCE!
MAH MAMMY SAYS AH LOOKS VURRY INTELLIGUNT.
THERE IS A MASTER CRIMINAL LOOSE IN AMERICA!-THE "BRAIN" BEHIND GUNMEN LIKE GAT GARSON-THE MASTER MIND BEHIND EVERY IMPORTANT CRIME IN THE NATION! WE KNOW THERE IS A "BRAIN"-
BUT-WE'VE NEVER SEEN HIM! WE'VE NEVER GOTTEN THE GOODS ON HIM!
THEN, WHUFFO' IS YO' MESSIN' ROUN' WIF ME? YO' GOT 'NOUGH T'DO, TRYIN' T'KETCH THET "BRAIN"-
IF MY PLAN SUCCEEDS, WE WILL CATCH HIM! AS SOON AS GAT GARSON-MEANING YOU-RETURNS TO HIS OLD HAUNTS-THE UNDERWORLD WILL LOOK HIM UP-SOONER OR LATER-THE "BRAIN" WILL LOOK HIM UP-WHEN HE DOES-FOLLOW THESE INSTRUCTIONS!-
Copr. 1939 by United Feature Syndicate, Inc. Tm. Reg. U. S. Pat. Off.—All rights reserved

LI'L ABNER The Girl He Left Behind! By Al Capp

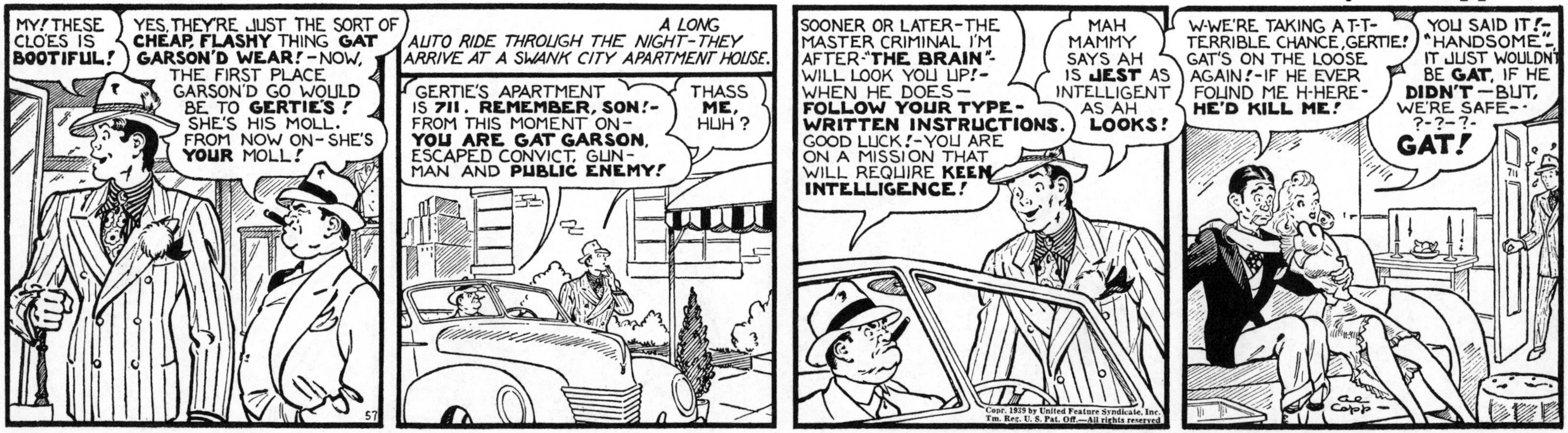
MY! THESE CLO'ES IS BOOTIFUL!
YES, THEY'RE JUST THE SORT OF CHEAP, FLASHY THING GAT GARSON'D WEAR!-NOW, THE FIRST PLACE GARSON'D GO WOULD BE TO GERTIE'S! SHE'S HIS MOLL. FROM NOW ON-SHE'S YOUR MOLL!
A LONG AUTO RIDE THROUGH THE NIGHT-THEY ARRIVE AT A SWANK CITY APARTMENT HOUSE.
GERTIE'S APARTMENT IS 711. REMEMBER, SON!-FROM THIS MOMENT ON-YOU ARE GAT GARSON, ESCAPED CONVICT, GUNMAN AND PUBLIC ENEMY!
THASS ME, HUH?
SOONER OR LATER-THE MASTER CRIMINAL I'M AFTER-"THE BRAIN"-WILL LOOK YOU UP!-WHEN HE DOES-FOLLOW YOUR TYPEWRITTEN INSTRUCTIONS. GOOD LUCK!-YOU ARE ON A MISSION THAT WILL REQUIRE KEEN INTELLIGENCE!
MAH MAMMY SAYS AH IS JEST AS INTELLIGENT AS AH LOOKS!
W-WE'RE TAKING A T-T-TERRIBLE CHANCE, GERTIE! GAT'S ON THE LOOSE AGAIN!-IF HE EVER FOUND ME H-HERE-HE'D KILL ME!
YOU SAID IT!-"HANDSOME"-IT JUST WOULDN'T BE GAT, IF HE DIDN'T-BUT, WE'RE SAFE--?-?-?-GAT!
Copr. 1939 by United Feature Syndicate, Inc. Tm. Reg. U. S. Pat. Off.—All rights reserved

LI'L ABNER — Love Flies Out the Window! — By Al Capp

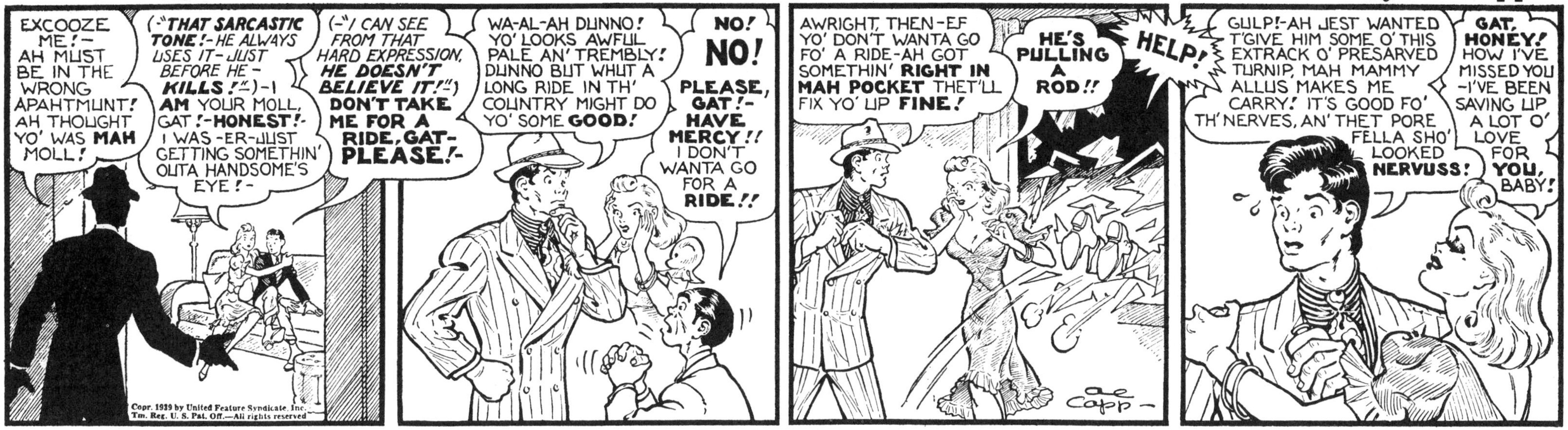
EXCOOZE ME!-AH MUST BE IN THE WRONG APAHTMUNT! AH THOUGHT YO' WAS MAH MOLL!
(-"THAT SARCASTIC TONE!-HE ALWAYS USES IT-JUST BEFORE HE-KILLS!"-)-I AM YOUR MOLL, GAT!-HONEST!-I WAS-ER-JUST GETTING SOMETHIN' OUTA HANDSOME'S EYE!-
(-"I CAN SEE FROM THAT HARD EXPRESSION, HE DOESN'T BELIEVE IT!"-) DON'T TAKE ME FOR A RIDE, GAT-PLEASE!-
Copr. 1939 by United Feature Syndicate, Inc. Tm. Reg. U. S. Pat. Off.—All rights reserved
WA-AL-AH DUNNO! YO' LOOKS AWFUL PALE AN' TREMBLY! DUNNO BUT WHUT A LONG RIDE IN TH' COUNTRY MIGHT DO YO' SOME GOOD!
NO! NO! PLEASE, GAT!-HAVE MERCY!! I DON'T WANTA GO FOR A RIDE!!
AWRIGHT, THEN-EF YO' DON'T WANTA GO FO' A RIDE-AH GOT SOMETHIN' RIGHT IN MAH POCKET THET'LL FIX YO' UP FINE!
HE'S PULLING A ROD!!
HELP!
GULP!-AH JEST WANTED T'GIVE HIM SOME O' THIS EXTRACK O' PRESARVED TURNIP, MAH MAMMY ALLUS MAKES ME CARRY! IT'S GOOD FO' TH' NERVES, AN' THET PORE FELLA SHO' LOOKED NERVUSS!
GAT, HONEY! HOW I'VE MISSED YOU-I'VE BEEN SAVING UP A LOT O' LOVE FOR YOU, BABY!

LI'L ABNER — Gas House Romance! — By Al Capp

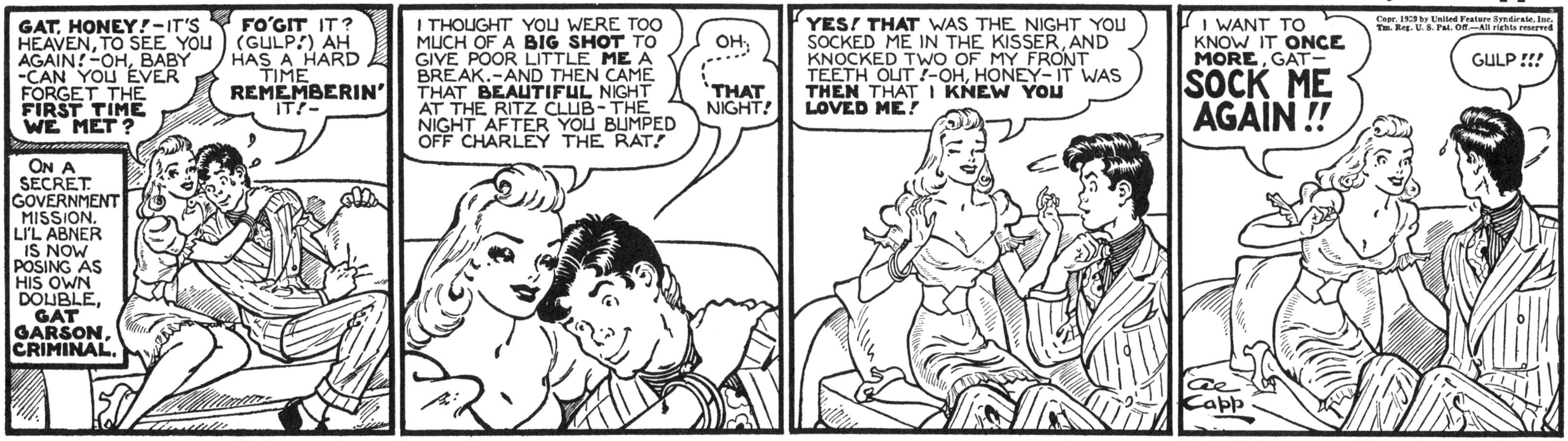
GAT, HONEY!-IT'S HEAVEN, TO SEE YOU AGAIN!-OH, BABY-CAN YOU EVER FORGET THE FIRST TIME WE MET?
FO'GIT IT? (GULP!) AH HAS A HARD TIME REMEMBERIN' IT!-
ON A SECRET GOVERNMENT MISSION, LI'L ABNER IS NOW POSING AS HIS OWN DOUBLE, GAT GARSON, CRIMINAL.
I THOUGHT YOU WERE TOO MUCH OF A BIG SHOT TO GIVE POOR LITTLE ME A BREAK.-AND THEN CAME THAT BEAUTIFUL NIGHT AT THE RITZ CLUB-THE NIGHT AFTER YOU BUMPED OFF CHARLEY THE RAT!
OH,-THAT NIGHT!
YES! THAT WAS THE NIGHT YOU SOCKED ME IN THE KISSER, AND KNOCKED TWO OF MY FRONT TEETH OUT!-OH, HONEY-IT WAS THEN THAT I KNEW YOU LOVED ME!
I WANT TO KNOW IT ONCE MORE, GAT-SOCK ME AGAIN!!
GULP!!!
Copr. 1939 by United Feature Syndicate, Inc. Tm. Reg. U. S. Pat. Off.—All rights reserved

LI'L ABNER Love Jumps Out the Window! By Al Capp

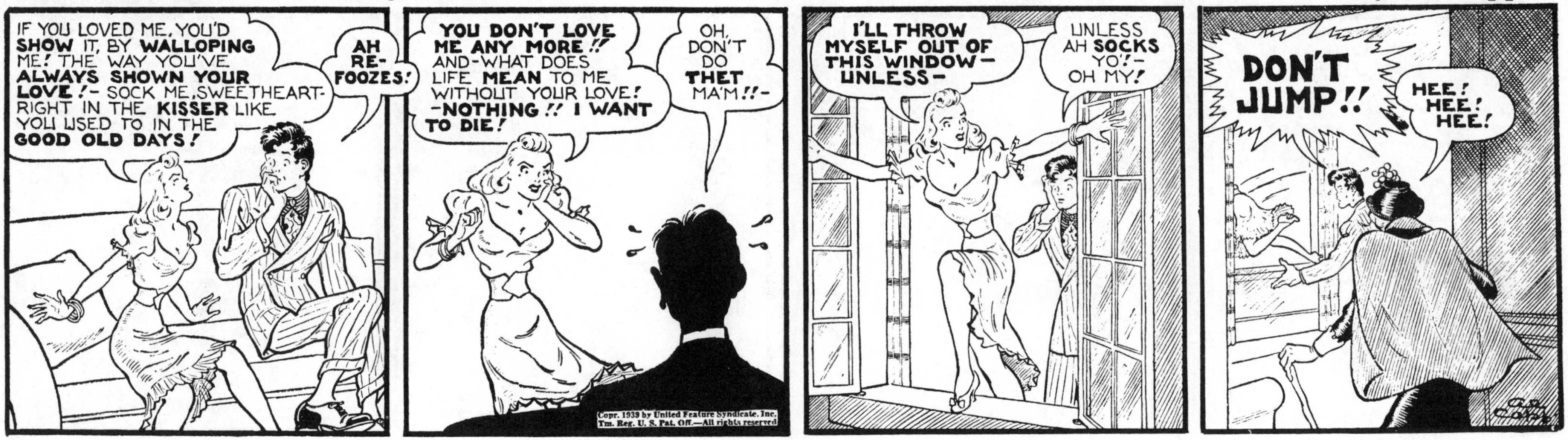

IF YOU LOVED ME, YOU'D SHOW IT, BY WALLOPING ME! THE WAY YOU'VE ALWAYS SHOWN YOUR LOVE!- SOCK ME, SWEETHEART- RIGHT IN THE KISSER LIKE YOU USED TO IN THE GOOD OLD DAYS!
AH RE-FOOZES!
YOU DON'T LOVE ME ANY MORE!! AND-WHAT DOES LIFE MEAN TO ME WITHOUT YOUR LOVE! -NOTHING!! I WANT TO DIE!
OH, DON'T DO THET MA'M!!-
Copr. 1939 by United Feature Syndicate, Inc. Tm. Reg. U. S. Pat. Off.—All rights reserved
I'LL THROW MYSELF OUT OF THIS WINDOW- UNLESS-
UNLESS AH SOCKS YO'!- OH MY!
DON'T JUMP!!
HEE! HEE! HEE!

LI'L ABNER Little Old Lady By Al Capp

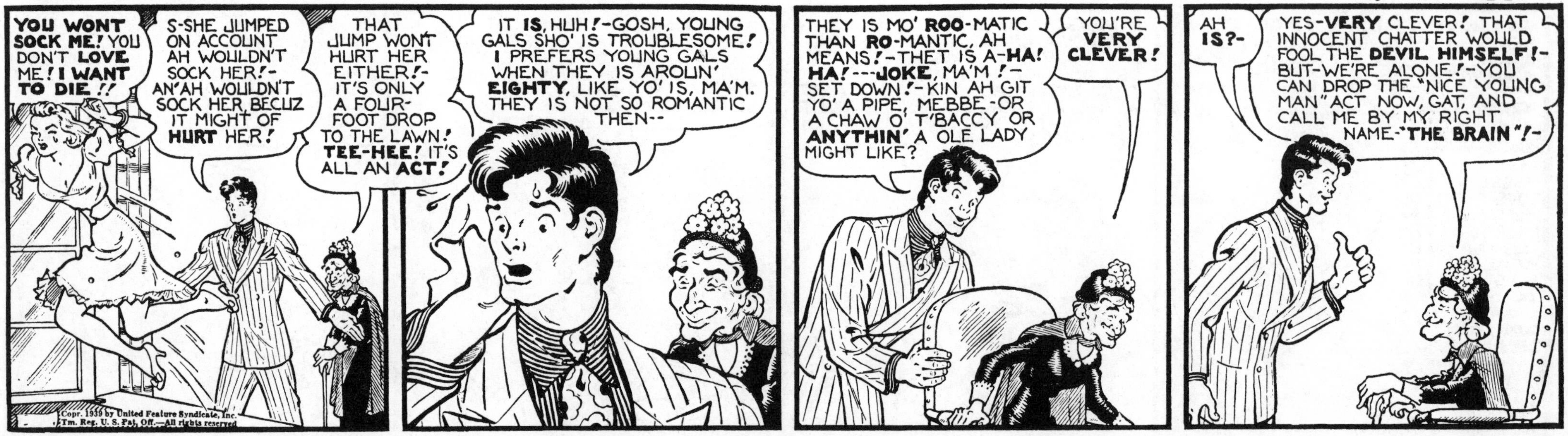

YOU WONT SOCK ME! YOU DON'T LOVE ME! I WANT TO DIE!!
S-SHE JUMPED ON ACCOUNT AH WOULDN'T SOCK HER!- AN'AH WOULDN'T SOCK HER, BECUZ IT MIGHT OF HURT HER!
THAT JUMP WONT HURT HER EITHER!- IT'S ONLY A FOUR-FOOT DROP TO THE LAWN! TEE-HEE! IT'S ALL AN ACT!
Copr. 1939 by United Feature Syndicate, Inc. Tm. Reg. U. S. Pat. Off.—All rights reserved
IT IS, HUH!-GOSH, YOUNG GALS SHO' IS TROUBLESOME! I PREFERS YOUNG GALS WHEN THEY IS AROUN' EIGHTY, LIKE YO' IS, MA'M. THEY IS NOT SO ROMANTIC THEN--
THEY IS MO' ROO-MATIC THAN RO-MANTIC, AH MEANS!-THET IS A-HA! HA!--JOKE, MA'M!- SET DOWN!-KIN AH GIT YO' A PIPE, MEBBE-OR A CHAW O' T'BACCY OR ANYTHIN' A OLE LADY MIGHT LIKE?
YOU'RE VERY CLEVER!
AH IS?-
YES-VERY CLEVER! THAT INNOCENT CHATTER WOULD FOOL THE DEVIL HIMSELF!- BUT-WE'RE ALONE!-YOU CAN DROP THE "NICE YOUNG MAN" ACT NOW, GAT, AND CALL ME BY MY RIGHT NAME-"THE BRAIN"!-

LI'L ABNER — Secret Operative Yokum — By Al Capp

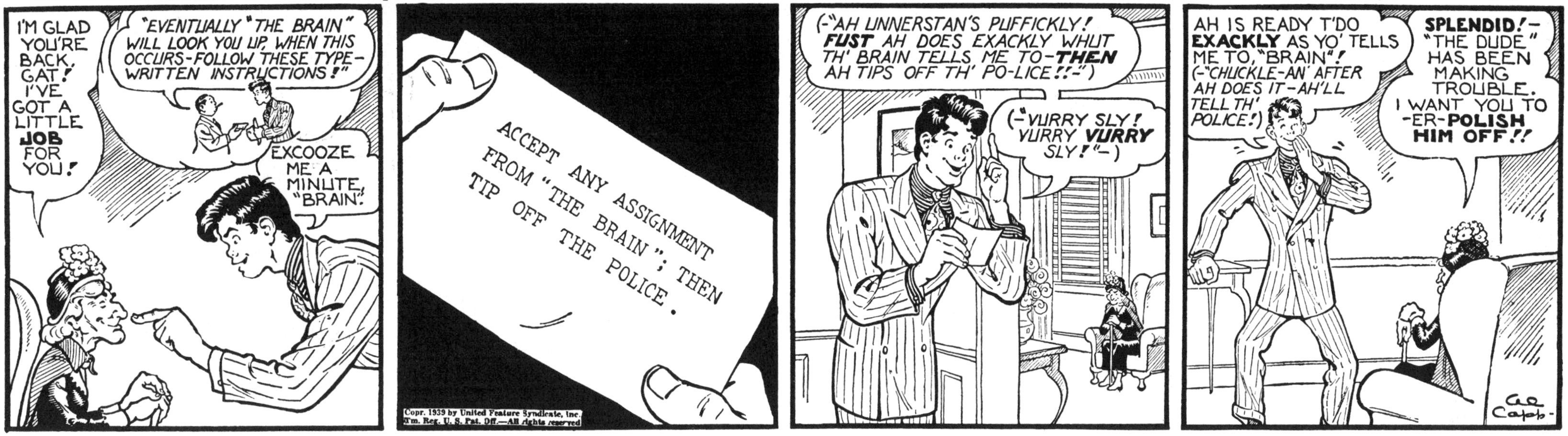

I'M GLAD YOU'RE BACK, GAT! I'VE GOT A LITTLE **JOB** FOR YOU!
"EVENTUALLY "THE BRAIN" WILL LOOK YOU UP, WHEN THIS OCCURS-FOLLOW THESE TYPE-WRITTEN INSTRUCTIONS!"
EXCOOZE ME A MINUTE, "BRAIN"!
ACCEPT ANY ASSIGNMENT FROM "THE BRAIN"; THEN TIP OFF THE POLICE.
Copr. 1939 by United Feature Syndicate, Inc. Tm. Reg. U. S. Pat. Off.—All rights reserved
(-"AH UNNERSTAN'S PUFFICKLY! **FUST** AH DOES EXACKLY WHUT TH' BRAIN TELLS ME TO-**THEN** AH TIPS OFF TH' PO-LICE!!-")
(-"VURRY SLY! VURRY **VURRY** SLY!"-)
AH IS READY T'DO **EXACKLY** AS YO' TELLS ME TO, "BRAIN"! (-"CHUCKLE-AN' AFTER AH DOES IT-AH'LL TELL TH' POLICE!)
SPLENDID!- "THE DUDE" HAS BEEN MAKING TROUBLE. I WANT YOU TO -ER-**POLISH HIM OFF!!**
Al Capp

LI'L ABNER — Crool Is the Name for Yokum! — By Al Capp

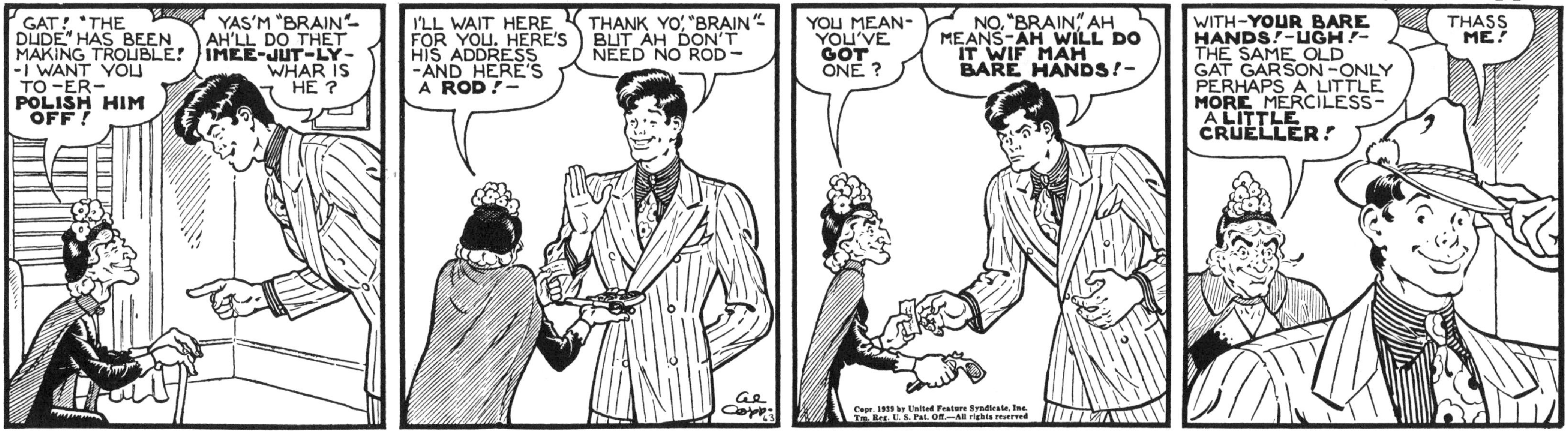

GAT! "THE DUDE" HAS BEEN MAKING TROUBLE! -I WANT YOU TO-ER- **POLISH HIM OFF!**
YAS'M "BRAIN"- AH'LL DO THET **IMEE-JUT-LY**- WHAR IS HE?
I'LL WAIT HERE FOR YOU. HERE'S HIS ADDRESS -AND HERE'S A **ROD!**-
THANK YO', "BRAIN"- BUT AH DON'T NEED NO ROD-
Al Capp
YOU MEAN- YOU'VE **GOT** ONE?
NO, "BRAIN," AH MEANS-**AH WILL DO IT WIF MAH BARE HANDS!**-
Copr. 1939 by United Feature Syndicate, Inc. Tm. Reg. U. S. Pat. Off.—All rights reserved
WITH-**YOUR BARE HANDS!**-**UGH!**- THE SAME OLD GAT GARSON-ONLY PERHAPS A LITTLE **MORE** MERCILESS- A **LITTLE CRUELLER!**
THASS **ME!**

LI'L ABNER Swing Low, Sweet Chariot By Al Capp

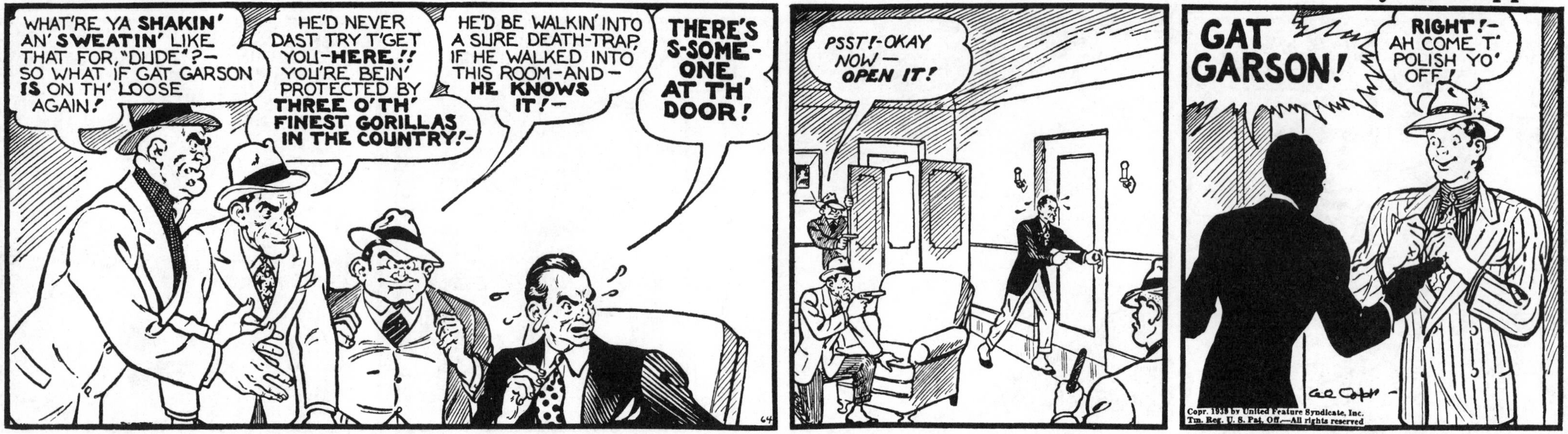
WHAT'RE YA **SHAKIN'** AN' **SWEATIN'** LIKE THAT FOR, "DUDE"?— SO WHAT IF GAT GARSON **IS** ON TH' LOOSE AGAIN!
HE'D NEVER DAST TRY T'GET YOU—**HERE!!** YOU'RE BEIN' PROTECTED BY **THREE O'TH' FINEST GORILLAS IN THE COUNTRY!**—
HE'D BE WALKIN' INTO A SURE DEATH-TRAP IF HE WALKED INTO THIS ROOM—AND—**HE KNOWS IT!**—
THERE'S S-SOME-ONE AT TH' DOOR!
PSST!—OKAY NOW— **OPEN IT!**
GAT GARSON!
RIGHT!— AH COME T' POLISH YO' OFF!
Copr. 1939 by United Feature Syndicate, Inc. Tm. Reg. U. S. Pat. Off.—All rights reserved

LI'L ABNER The Black Deed Done By Al Capp

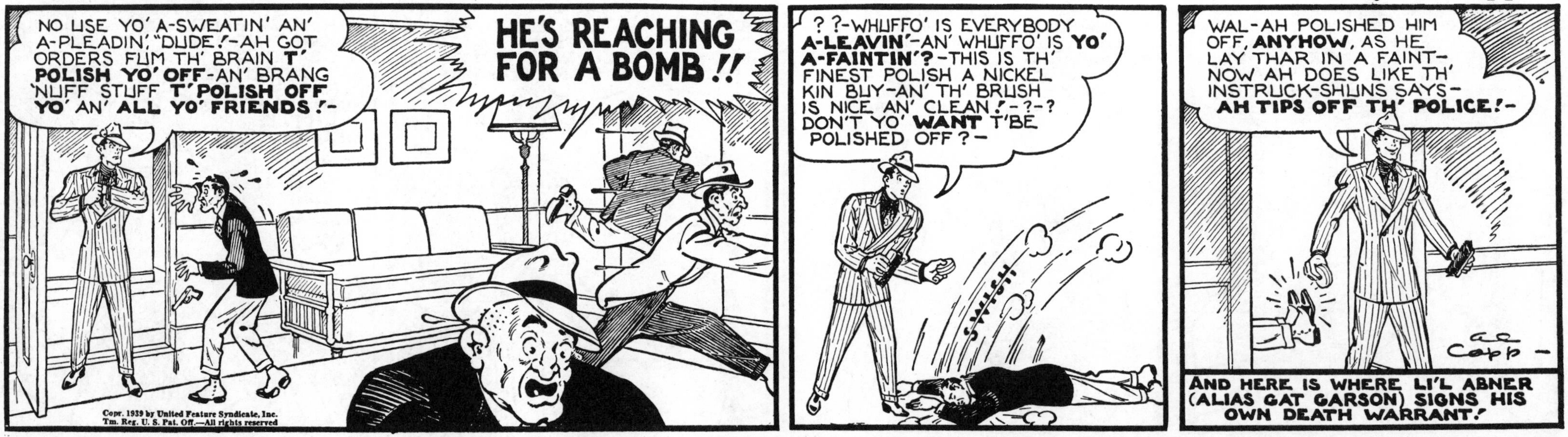
NO USE YO' A-SWEATIN' AN' A-PLEADIN', "DUDE!"—AH GOT ORDERS FUM TH' BRAIN **T' POLISH YO' OFF**—AN' BRANG 'NUFF STUFF **T' POLISH OFF YO'** AN' **ALL YO' FRIENDS!**—
HE'S REACHING FOR A BOMB!!
Copr. 1939 by United Feature Syndicate, Inc. Tm. Reg. U. S. Pat. Off.—All rights reserved
? ?—WHUFFO' IS EVERYBODY **A-LEAVIN'**—AN' WHUFFO' IS **YO' A-FAINTIN'?**—THIS IS TH' FINEST POLISH A NICKEL KIN BUY—AN' TH' BRUSH IS NICE AN' CLEAN!—?—? DON'T YO' **WANT** T'BE POLISHED OFF?—
WAL—AH POLISHED HIM OFF, **ANYHOW**, AS HE LAY THAR IN A FAINT— NOW AH DOES LIKE TH' INSTRUCK-SHUNS SAYS— **AH TIPS OFF TH' POLICE!**—
AND HERE IS WHERE LI'L ABNER (ALIAS GAT GARSON) SIGNS HIS OWN DEATH WARRANT!

LI'L ABNER **Fireside Chat!** By Al Capp

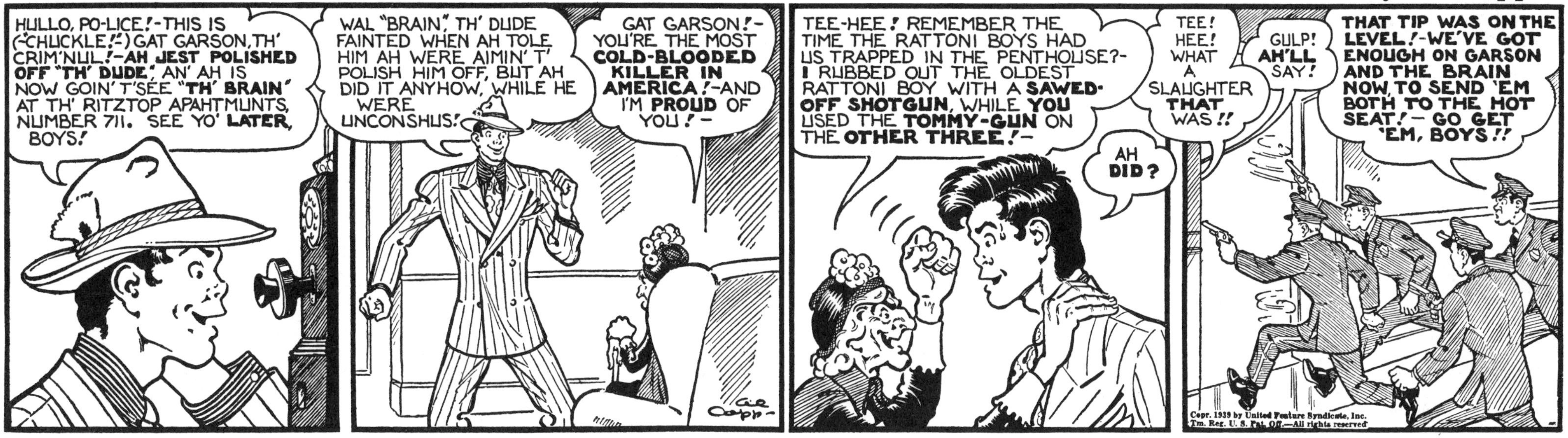

HULLO, PO-LICE!-THIS IS (-CHUCKLE!-) GAT GARSON, TH' CRIM'NUL!-AH JEST POLISHED OFF "TH' DUDE," AN' AH IS NOW GOIN' T'SEE "TH' BRAIN" AT TH' RITZTOP APAHTMUNTS, NUMBER 711. SEE YO' LATER, BOYS!
WAL "BRAIN," TH' DUDE FAINTED WHEN AH TOLE HIM AH WERE AIMIN' T' POLISH HIM OFF, BUT AH DID IT ANYHOW, WHILE HE WERE UNCONSHUS!
GAT GARSON!-YOU'RE THE MOST COLD-BLOODED KILLER IN AMERICA!-AND I'M PROUD OF YOU!-
TEE-HEE! REMEMBER THE TIME THE RATTONI BOYS HAD US TRAPPED IN THE PENTHOUSE?-I RUBBED OUT THE OLDEST RATTONI BOY WITH A SAWED-OFF SHOTGUN, WHILE YOU USED THE TOMMY-GUN ON THE OTHER THREE!-
AH DID?
TEE! HEE! WHAT A SLAUGHTER THAT WAS!!
GULP! AH'LL SAY!
THAT TIP WAS ON THE LEVEL!-WE'VE GOT ENOUGH ON GARSON AND THE BRAIN NOW, TO SEND 'EM BOTH TO THE HOT SEAT!-GO GET 'EM, BOYS!!
Copr. 1939 by United Feature Syndicate, Inc. Tm. Reg. U. S. Pat. Off.—All rights reserved

LI'L ABNER **Oh, Happy Daze!** By Al Capp

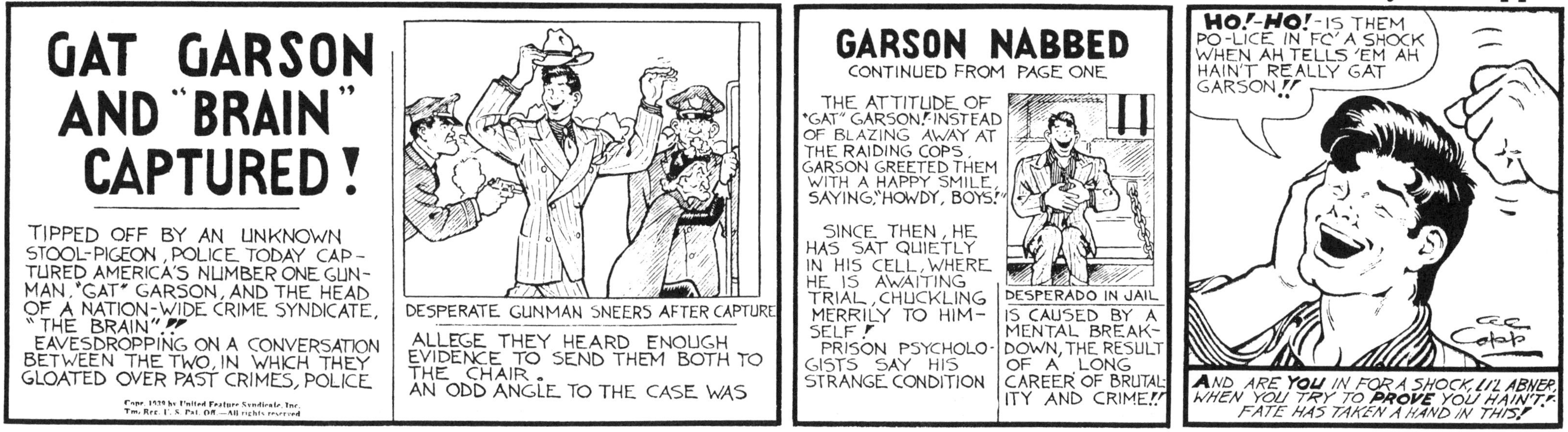

GAT GARSON AND "BRAIN" CAPTURED!
TIPPED OFF BY AN UNKNOWN STOOL-PIGEON, POLICE TODAY CAPTURED AMERICA'S NUMBER ONE GUNMAN, "GAT" GARSON, AND THE HEAD OF A NATION-WIDE CRIME SYNDICATE, "THE BRAIN"!!
EAVESDROPPING ON A CONVERSATION BETWEEN THE TWO, IN WHICH THEY GLOATED OVER PAST CRIMES, POLICE
DESPERATE GUNMAN SNEERS AFTER CAPTURE
ALLEGE THEY HEARD ENOUGH EVIDENCE TO SEND THEM BOTH TO THE CHAIR.
AN ODD ANGLE TO THE CASE WAS
Copr. 1939 by United Feature Syndicate, Inc. Tm. Reg. U. S. Pat. Off.—All rights reserved
GARSON NABBED
CONTINUED FROM PAGE ONE
THE ATTITUDE OF "GAT" GARSON!-INSTEAD OF BLAZING AWAY AT THE RAIDING COPS, GARSON GREETED THEM WITH A HAPPY SMILE, SAYING, "HOWDY, BOYS!"
SINCE THEN, HE HAS SAT QUIETLY IN HIS CELL, WHERE HE IS AWAITING TRIAL, CHUCKLING MERRILY TO HIMSELF!
PRISON PSYCHOLOGISTS SAY HIS STRANGE CONDITION
DESPERADO IN JAIL
IS CAUSED BY A MENTAL BREAKDOWN, THE RESULT OF A LONG CAREER OF BRUTALITY AND CRIME!!
HO!-HO!-IS THEM PO-LICE IN FO' A SHOCK WHEN AH TELLS 'EM AH HAIN'T REALLY GAT GARSON!!
AND ARE YOU IN FOR A SHOCK, LI'L ABNER, WHEN YOU TRY TO PROVE YOU HAIN'T!-FATE HAS TAKEN A HAND IN THIS!

LI'L ABNER Pearly Gates, Open Wide! By Al Capp

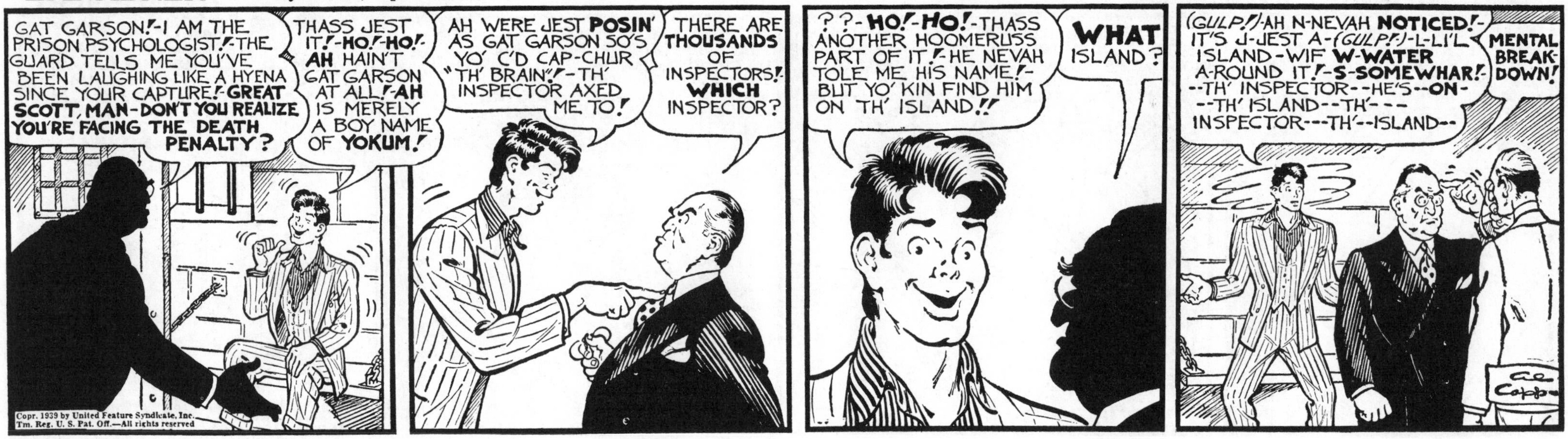
GAT GARSON!-I AM THE PRISON PSYCHOLOGIST!-THE GUARD TELLS ME YOU'VE BEEN LAUGHING LIKE A HYENA SINCE YOUR CAPTURE!-GREAT SCOTT, MAN-DON'T YOU REALIZE YOU'RE FACING THE DEATH PENALTY?
THASS JEST IT!-HO!-HO!-AH HAIN'T GAT GARSON AT ALL!-AH IS MERELY A BOY NAME OF YOKUM!
AH WERE JEST POSIN' AS GAT GARSON SO'S YO' C'D CAP-CHUR "TH' BRAIN"!-TH' INSPECTOR AXED ME TO!
THERE ARE THOUSANDS OF INSPECTORS!-WHICH INSPECTOR?
??-HO!-HO!-THASS ANOTHER HOOMERUSS PART OF IT!-HE NEVAH TOLE ME HIS NAME!-BUT YO' KIN FIND HIM ON TH' ISLAND!!
WHAT ISLAND?
(GULP!!)-AH N-NEVAH NOTICED!-IT'S J-JEST A-(GULP!)-L-LI'L ISLAND-WIF W-WATER A-ROUND IT!-S-SOMEWHAR!--TH' INSPECTOR--HE'S--ON--TH' ISLAND--TH'---INSPECTOR---TH'--ISLAND--
MENTAL BREAK-DOWN!
Copr. 1939 by United Feature Syndicate, Inc. Tm. Reg. U. S. Pat. Off.—All rights reserved

LI'L ABNER That Makes It Suicide! By Al Capp

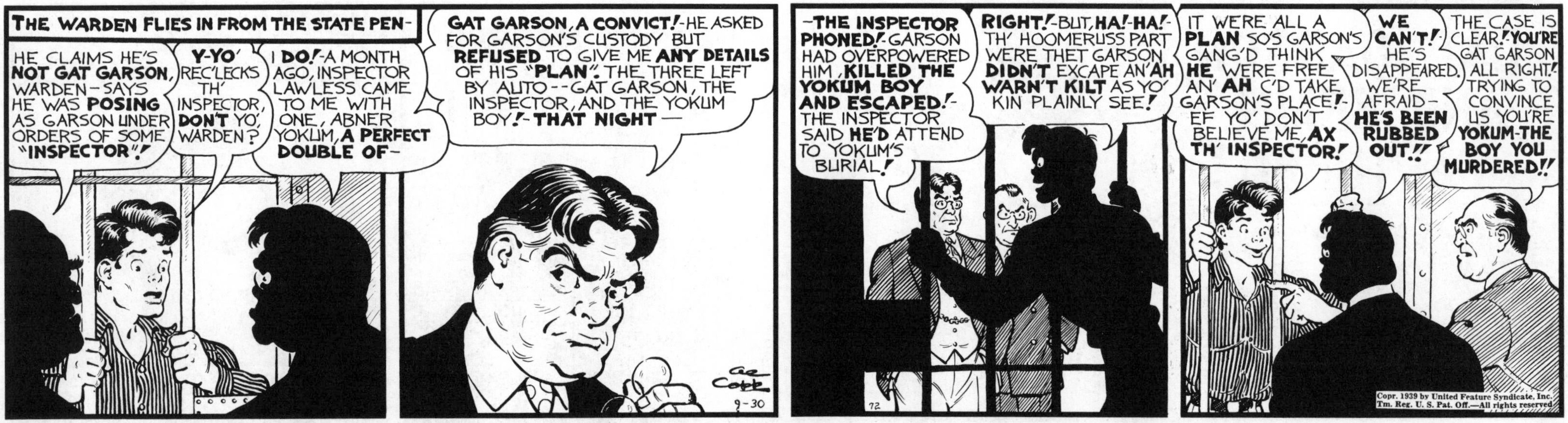
THE WARDEN FLIES IN FROM THE STATE PEN-
HE CLAIMS HE'S NOT GAT GARSON, WARDEN-SAYS HE WAS POSING AS GARSON UNDER ORDERS OF SOME "INSPECTOR"!
Y-YO' REC'LECKS TH' INSPECTOR, DON'T YO', WARDEN?
I DO!-A MONTH AGO, INSPECTOR LAWLESS CAME TO ME WITH ONE, ABNER YOKUM, A PERFECT DOUBLE OF-
GAT GARSON, A CONVICT!-HE ASKED FOR GARSON'S CUSTODY BUT REFUSED TO GIVE ME ANY DETAILS OF HIS "PLAN". THE THREE LEFT BY AUTO--GAT GARSON, THE INSPECTOR, AND THE YOKUM BOY!-THAT NIGHT—
9-30
-THE INSPECTOR PHONED!-GARSON HAD OVERPOWERED HIM, KILLED THE YOKUM BOY AND ESCAPED!-THE INSPECTOR SAID HE'D ATTEND TO YOKUM'S BURIAL!
RIGHT!-BUT, HA!-HA!-TH' HOOMERUSS PART WERE THET GARSON DIDN'T EXCAPE AN' AH WARN'T KILT AS YO' KIN PLAINLY SEE!
IT WERE ALL A PLAN SO'S GARSON'S GANG'D THINK HE WERE FREE AN' AH C'D TAKE GARSON'S PLACE!-EF YO' DON'T BELIEVE ME, AX TH' INSPECTOR!
WE CAN'T!-HE'S DISAPPEARED. WE'RE AFRAID-HE'S BEEN RUBBED OUT!!
THE CASE IS CLEAR!-YOU'RE GAT GARSON ALL RIGHT!-TRYING TO CONVINCE US YOU'RE YOKUM-THE BOY YOU MURDERED!!
Copr. 1939 by United Feature Syndicate, Inc. Tm. Reg. U. S. Pat. Off.—All rights reserved

LI'L ABNER He's a Playboy at Heart! By Al Capp

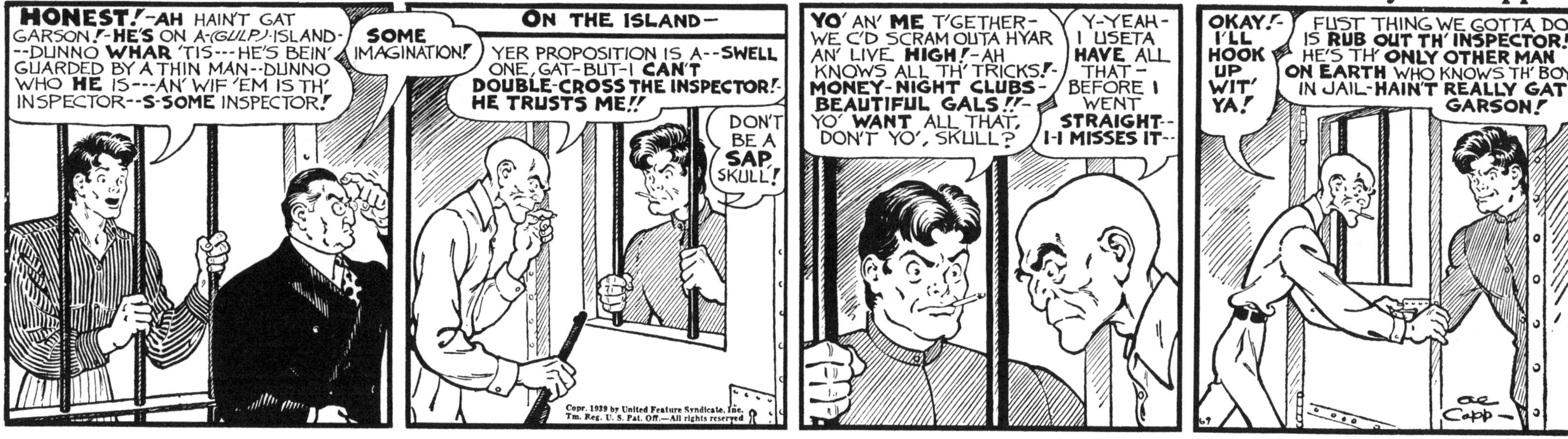
HONEST!-AH HAIN'T GAT GARSON!-HE'S ON A-(GULP)-ISLAND--DUNNO WHAR 'TIS---HE'S BEIN' GUARDED BY A THIN MAN--DUNNO WHO HE IS---AN' WIF 'EM IS TH' INSPECTOR--S-SOME INSPECTOR!
SOME IMAGINATION!
ON THE ISLAND-
YER PROPOSITION IS A--SWELL ONE, GAT-BUT-I CAN'T DOUBLE-CROSS THE INSPECTOR!-HE TRUSTS ME!!
DON'T BE A SAP SKULL!
Copr. 1939 by United Feature Syndicate, Inc. Tm. Reg. U. S. Pat. Off.—All rights reserved
YO' AN' ME T'GETHER-WE C'D SCRAM OUTA HYAR AN' LIVE HIGH!-AH KNOWS ALL TH' TRICKS!-MONEY-NIGHT CLUBS-BEAUTIFUL GALS!!-YO' WANT ALL THAT, DON'T YO', SKULL?
Y-YEAH-I USETA HAVE ALL THAT-BEFORE I WENT STRAIGHT--I-I MISSES IT--
OKAY!-I'LL HOOK UP WIT' YA!
FUST THING WE GOTTA DO IS RUB OUT TH' INSPECTOR!-HE'S TH' ONLY OTHER MAN ON EARTH WHO KNOWS TH' BOY IN JAIL-HAIN'T REALLY GAT GARSON!
Al Capp

LI'L ABNER And Now There Are Two! By Al Capp

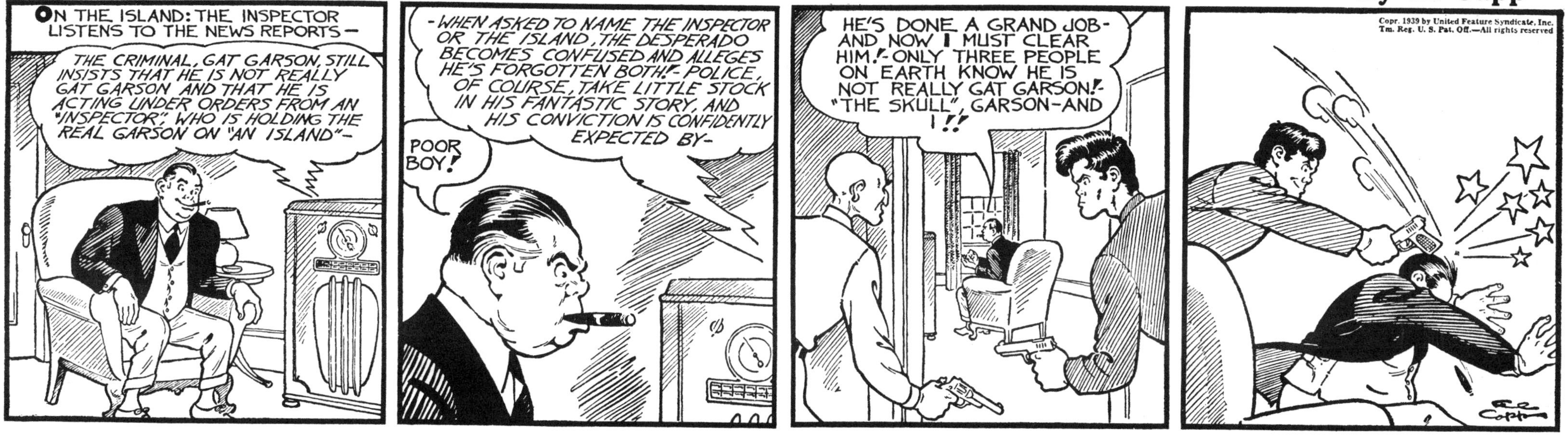
ON THE ISLAND: THE INSPECTOR LISTENS TO THE NEWS REPORTS-
THE CRIMINAL, GAT GARSON, STILL INSISTS THAT HE IS NOT REALLY GAT GARSON AND THAT HE IS ACTING UNDER ORDERS FROM AN "INSPECTOR," WHO IS HOLDING THE REAL GARSON ON "AN ISLAND"-
-WHEN ASKED TO NAME THE INSPECTOR OR THE ISLAND, THE DESPERADO BECOMES CONFUSED AND ALLEGES HE'S FORGOTTEN BOTH!-POLICE, OF COURSE, TAKE LITTLE STOCK IN HIS FANTASTIC STORY, AND HIS CONVICTION IS CONFIDENTLY EXPECTED BY-
POOR BOY!
HE'S DONE A GRAND JOB-AND NOW I MUST CLEAR HIM!-ONLY THREE PEOPLE ON EARTH KNOW HE IS NOT REALLY GAT GARSON!-"THE SKULL", GARSON-AND I!!
Copr. 1939 by United Feature Syndicate, Inc. Tm. Reg. U. S. Pat. Off.—All rights reserved
Al Capp

LI'L ABNER While Home Burns! By Al Capp

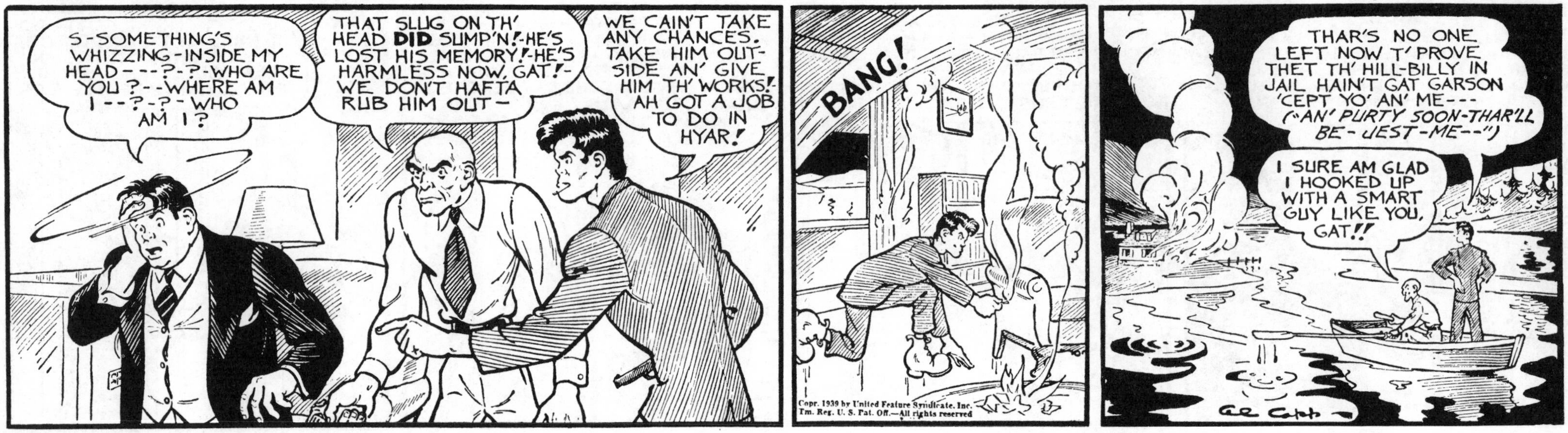

S-SOMETHING'S WHIZZING-INSIDE MY HEAD---?-?-WHO ARE YOU?--WHERE AM I--?-?-WHO AM I?
THAT SLUG ON TH' HEAD DID SUMP'N!-HE'S LOST HIS MEMORY!-HE'S HARMLESS NOW, GAT!-WE DON'T HAFTA RUB HIM OUT-
WE CAIN'T TAKE ANY CHANCES. TAKE HIM OUT-SIDE AN' GIVE HIM TH' WORKS!-AH GOT A JOB TO DO IN HYAR!
BANG!
Copr. 1939 by United Feature Syndicate, Inc. Tm. Reg. U. S. Pat. Off.—All rights reserved
THAR'S NO ONE LEFT NOW T' PROVE THET TH' HILL-BILLY IN JAIL HAIN'T GAT GARSON 'CEPT YO' AN' ME---
("AN' PURTY SOON-THAR'LL BE-JEST-ME--")
I SURE AM GLAD I HOOKED UP WITH A SMART GUY LIKE YOU, GAT!!
Al Capp

LI'L ABNER They're Gonna Fry His Hide! By Al Capp

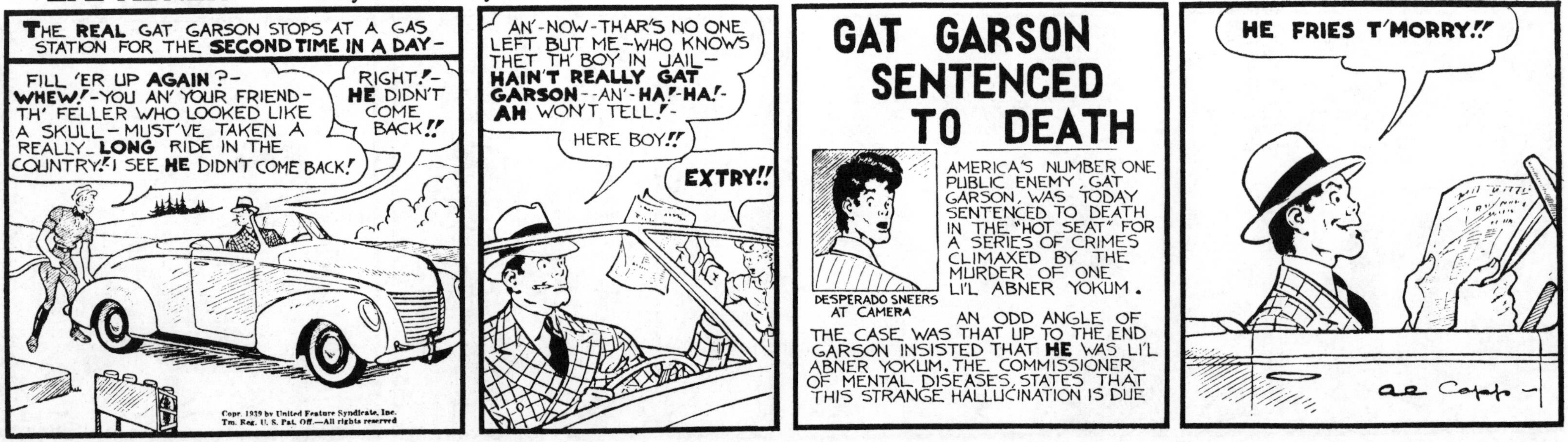

THE REAL GAT GARSON STOPS AT A GAS STATION FOR THE SECOND TIME IN A DAY-
FILL 'ER UP AGAIN?-WHEW!-YOU AN' YOUR FRIEND-TH' FELLER WHO LOOKED LIKE A SKULL-MUST'VE TAKEN A REALLY-LONG RIDE IN THE COUNTRY!-I SEE HE DIDN'T COME BACK!
RIGHT!-HE DIDN'T COME BACK!!
Copr. 1939 by United Feature Syndicate, Inc. Tm. Reg. U. S. Pat. Off.—All rights reserved
AN'-NOW-THAR'S NO ONE LEFT BUT ME-WHO KNOWS THET TH' BOY IN JAIL-HAIN'T REALLY GAT GARSON--AN'-HA!-HA!-AH WON'T TELL!-
HERE BOY!!
EXTRY!!
GAT GARSON SENTENCED TO DEATH
AMERICA'S NUMBER ONE PUBLIC ENEMY, GAT GARSON, WAS TODAY SENTENCED TO DEATH IN THE "HOT SEAT" FOR A SERIES OF CRIMES CLIMAXED BY THE MURDER OF ONE LI'L ABNER YOKUM.
DESPERADO SNEERS AT CAMERA
AN ODD ANGLE OF THE CASE WAS THAT UP TO THE END GARSON INSISTED THAT HE WAS LI'L ABNER YOKUM. THE COMMISSIONER OF MENTAL DISEASES, STATES THAT THIS STRANGE HALLUCINATION IS DUE
HE FRIES T'MORRY!!
Al Capp

LI'L ABNER On With the Show! By Al Capp

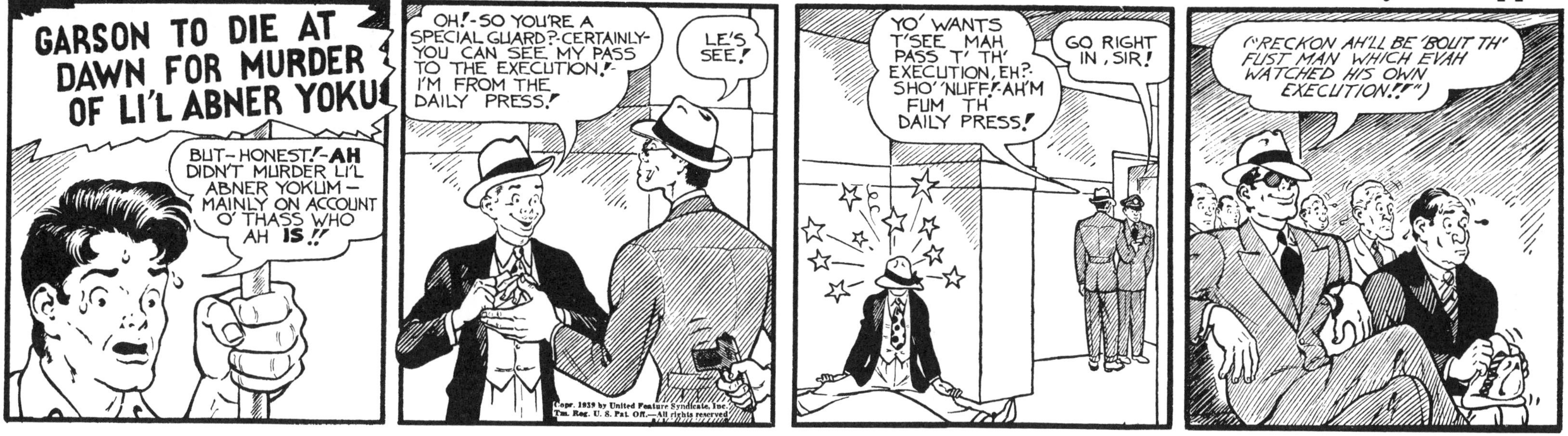
GARSON TO DIE AT DAWN FOR MURDER OF LI'L ABNER YOKU
BUT–HONEST!–AH DIDN'T MURDER LI'L ABNER YOKUM–MAINLY ON ACCOUNT O' THASS WHO AH IS!!
OH!–SO YOU'RE A SPECIAL GUARD?–CERTAINLY–YOU CAN SEE MY PASS TO THE EXECUTION!–I'M FROM THE DAILY PRESS!
LE'S SEE!
Copr. 1939 by United Feature Syndicate, Inc. Tm. Reg. U. S. Pat. Off.—All rights reserved
YO' WANTS T'SEE MAH PASS T' TH' EXECUTION, EH?–SHO' 'NUFF!–AH'M FUM TH' DAILY PRESS!
GO RIGHT IN, SIR!
("RECKON AH'LL BE 'BOUT TH' FUST MAN WHICH EVAH WATCHED HIS OWN EXECUTION!!")

LI'L ABNER Welcome, Stranger! By Al Capp

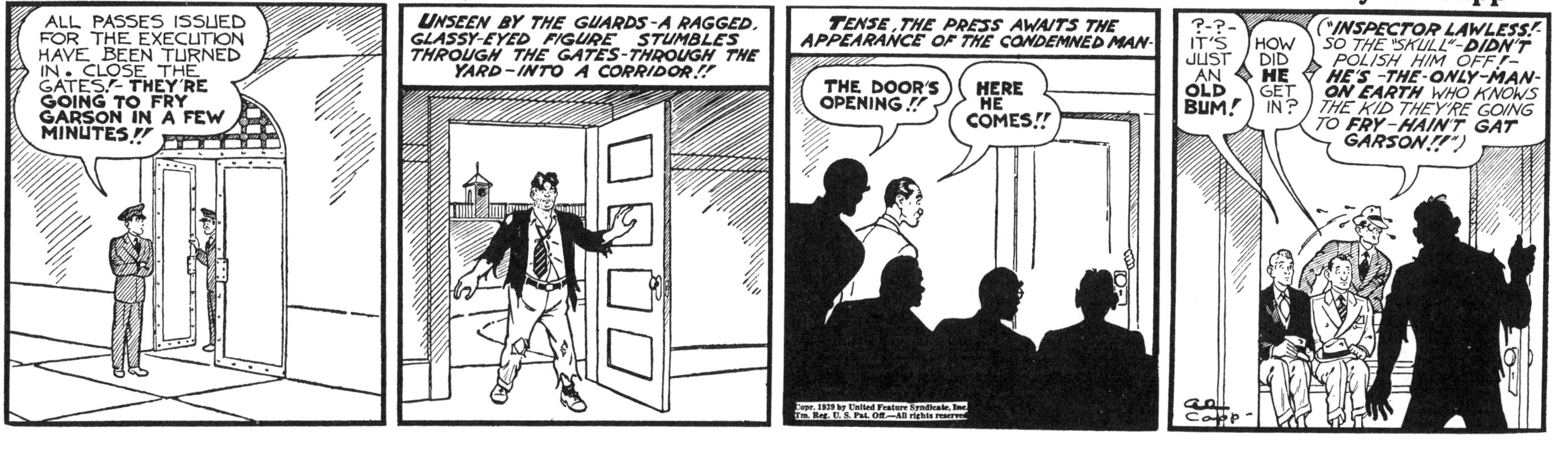
ALL PASSES ISSUED FOR THE EXECUTION HAVE BEEN TURNED IN. CLOSE THE GATES!–THEY'RE GOING TO FRY GARSON IN A FEW MINUTES!!
UNSEEN BY THE GUARDS–A RAGGED, GLASSY-EYED FIGURE STUMBLES THROUGH THE GATES–THROUGH THE YARD–INTO A CORRIDOR!!
TENSE, THE PRESS AWAITS THE APPEARANCE OF THE CONDEMNED MAN–
THE DOOR'S OPENING!!
HERE HE COMES!!
Copr. 1939 by United Feature Syndicate, Inc. Tm. Reg. U. S. Pat. Off.—All rights reserved
?-?-IT'S JUST AN OLD BUM!
HOW DID HE GET IN?
("INSPECTOR LAWLESS!–SO THE "SKULL"–DIDN'T POLISH HIM OFF!–HE'S–THE–ONLY–MAN–ON EARTH WHO KNOWS THE KID THEY'RE GOING TO FRY–HAIN'T GAT GARSON!!")
Al Capp

LI'L ABNER — This is Vurry Confoozin'— — By Al Capp

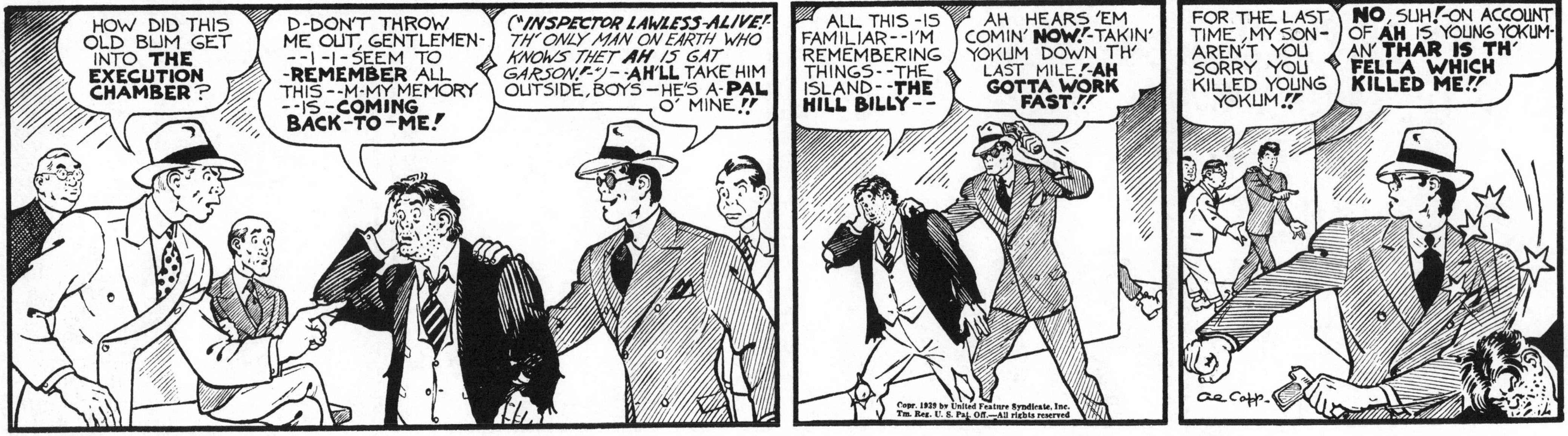

HOW DID THIS OLD BUM GET INTO **THE EXECUTION CHAMBER**?
D-DON'T THROW ME OUT, GENTLEMEN- --I-I-SEEM TO -**REMEMBER** ALL THIS--M-MY MEMORY --IS-**COMING BACK-TO-ME!**
("*INSPECTOR LAWLESS-ALIVE!- TH' ONLY MAN ON EARTH WHO KNOWS THET* **AH** *IS GAT GARSON!*-")--**AH'LL** TAKE HIM OUTSIDE, BOYS—HE'S A-**PAL** O' MINE!!
ALL THIS-IS FAMILIAR--I'M REMEMBERING THINGS--THE ISLAND--**THE HILL BILLY**--
AH HEARS 'EM COMIN' **NOW!**-TAKIN' YOKUM DOWN TH' LAST MILE!-**AH GOTTA WORK FAST!!**
Copr. 1939 by United Feature Syndicate, Inc. Tm. Reg. U. S. Pat. Off.—All rights reserved
FOR THE LAST TIME, MY SON- AREN'T YOU SORRY YOU KILLED YOUNG YOKUM!!
NO, SUH!-ON ACCOUNT OF **AH** IS YOUNG YOKUM- AN' **THAR IS TH' FELLA WHICH KILLED ME!!**
Al Capp

LI'L ABNER — Voice of Experience! — By Al Capp

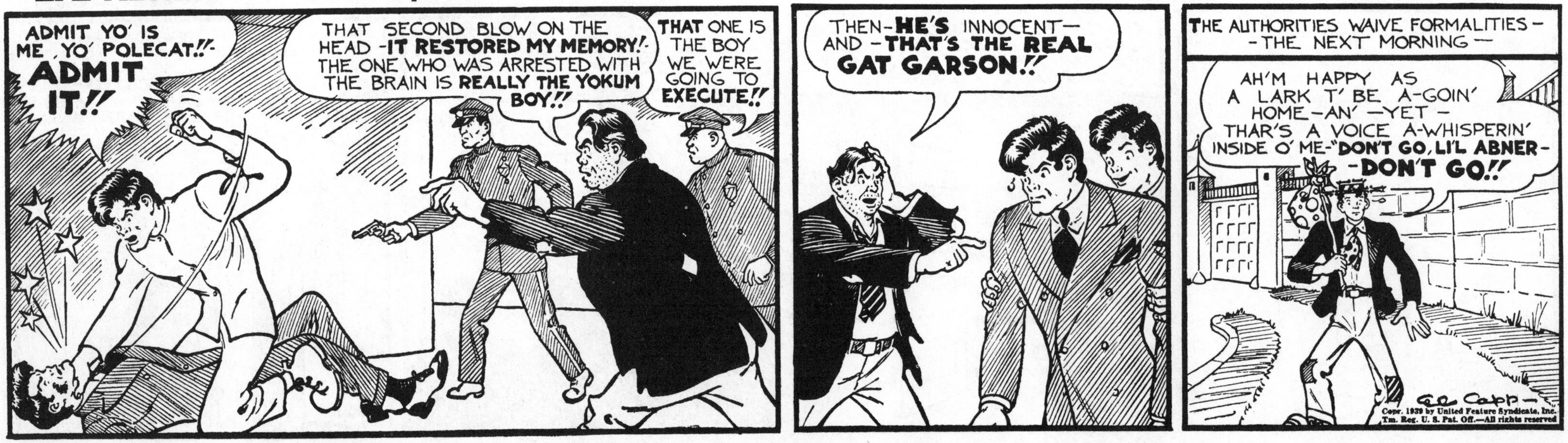

ADMIT YO' IS ME, YO' POLECAT!!- **ADMIT IT!!**
THAT SECOND BLOW ON THE HEAD-**IT RESTORED MY MEMORY!**- THE ONE WHO WAS ARRESTED WITH THE BRAIN IS **REALLY THE YOKUM BOY!!**
THAT ONE IS THE BOY WE WERE GOING TO **EXECUTE!!**
THEN-**HE'S** INNOCENT— AND-**THAT'S THE REAL GAT GARSON!!**
THE AUTHORITIES WAIVE FORMALITIES— -THE NEXT MORNING—
AH'M HAPPY AS A LARK T' BE A-GOIN' HOME-AN'-YET- THAR'S A VOICE A-WHISPERIN' INSIDE O' ME-"**DON'T GO, LI'L ABNER- -DON'T GO!!**"
Al Capp
Copr. 1939 by United Feature Syndicate, Inc. Tm. Reg. U. S. Pat. Off.—All rights reserved

LI'L ABNER Yokums Rush In! By Al Capp

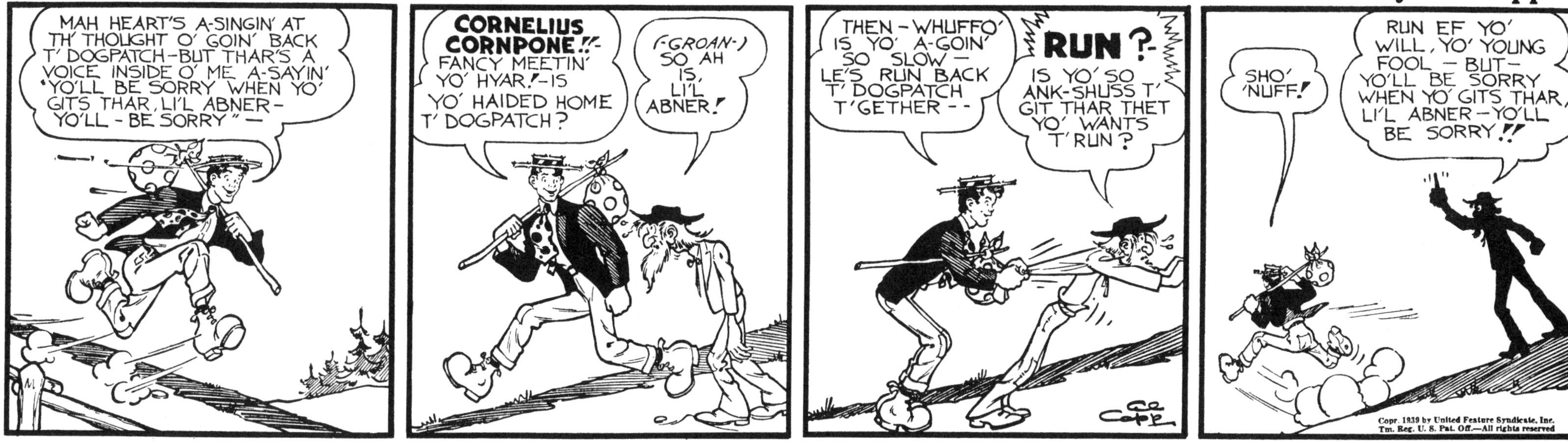

MAH HEART'S A-SINGIN' AT TH' THOUGHT O' GOIN' BACK T' DOGPATCH—BUT THAR'S A VOICE INSIDE O' ME A-SAYIN' "YO'LL BE SORRY WHEN YO' GITS THAR, LI'L ABNER—YO'LL-BE SORRY"—
CORNELIUS CORNPONE!!—FANCY MEETIN' YO' HYAR!—IS YO' HAIDED HOME T' DOGPATCH?
(-GROAN-) SO AH IS, LI'L ABNER!
THEN—WHUFFO' IS YO' A-GOIN' SO SLOW—LE'S RUN BACK T' DOGPATCH T'GETHER— —
RUN?-
IS YO' SO ANK-SHUSS T' GIT THAR THET YO' WANTS T' RUN?
SHO' 'NUFF!
RUN EF YO' WILL, YO' YOUNG FOOL—BUT—YO'LL BE SORRY WHEN YO' GITS THAR, LI'L ABNER—YO'LL BE SORRY!!
Copr. 1939 by United Feature Syndicate, Inc.
Tm. Reg. U. S. Pat. Off.—All rights reserved

LI'L ABNER Get Out of Town! By Al Capp

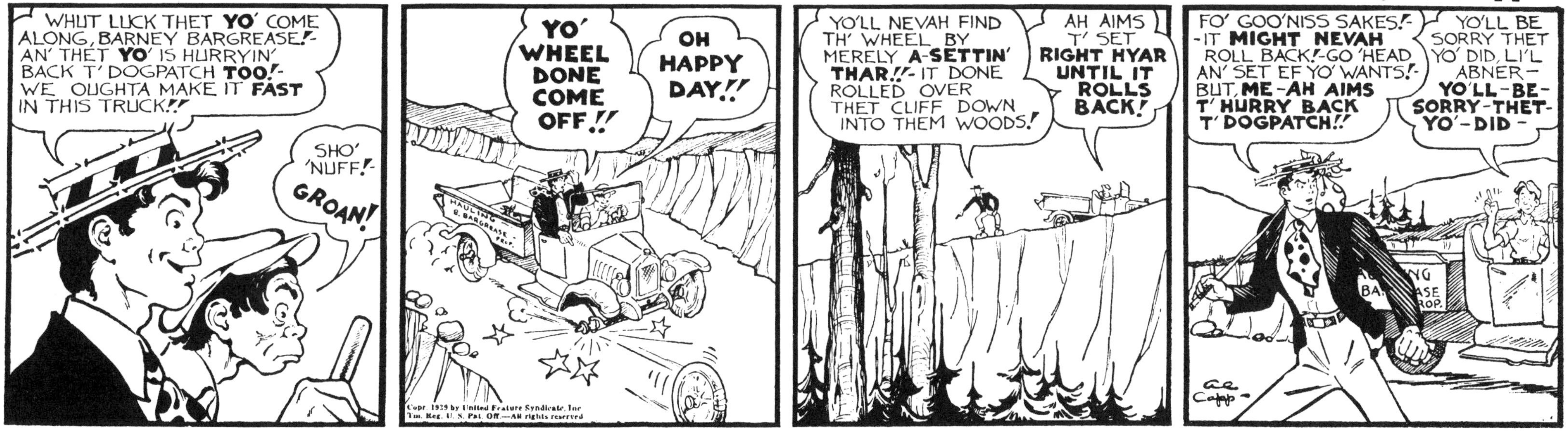

WHUT LUCK THET YO' COME ALONG, BARNEY BARGREASE!—AN' THET YO' IS HURRYIN' BACK T' DOGPATCH TOO!—WE OUGHTA MAKE IT FAST IN THIS TRUCK!!
SHO' 'NUFF!-
GROAN!
YO' WHEEL DONE COME OFF!!
OH HAPPY DAY!!
HAULING B. BARGREASE PROP.
Copr. 1939 by United Feature Syndicate, Inc
Tm. Reg. U. S. Pat. Off.—All rights reserved
YO'LL NEVAH FIND TH' WHEEL BY MERELY A-SETTIN' THAR!!—IT DONE ROLLED OVER THET CLIFF DOWN INTO THEM WOODS!
AH AIMS T' SET RIGHT HYAR UNTIL IT ROLLS BACK!
FO' GOO'NISS SAKES!—IT MIGHT NEVAH ROLL BACK!—GO 'HEAD AN' SET EF YO' WANTS!—BUT, ME-AH AIMS T' HURRY BACK T' DOGPATCH!!
YO'LL BE SORRY THET YO' DID, LI'L ABNER—YO'LL-BE-SORRY-THET-YO'-DID—

LI'L ABNER

This is Very Confoozin'

By Al Capp

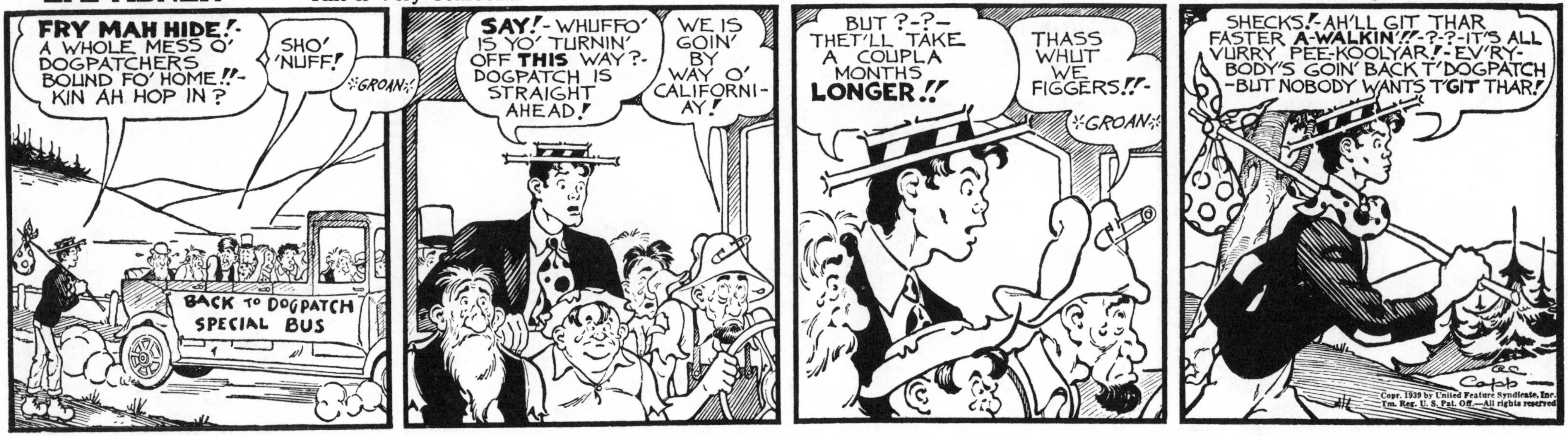
FRY MAH HIDE!- A WHOLE MESS O' DOGPATCHERS BOUND FO' HOME!!- KIN AH HOP IN?
SHO' 'NUFF!
GROAN
BACK TO DOGPATCH SPECIAL BUS
SAY!- WHUFFO' IS YO' TURNIN' OFF THIS WAY?- DOGPATCH IS STRAIGHT AHEAD!
WE IS GOIN' BY WAY O' CALIFORNI-AY!
BUT ?-?- THET'LL TAKE A COUPLA MONTHS LONGER!!
THASS WHUT WE FIGGERS!!-
GROAN
SHECKS!- AH'LL GIT THAR FASTER A-WALKIN'!!-?-?-IT'S ALL VURRY PEE-KOOLYAR!- EV'RY-BODY'S GOIN' BACK T'DOGPATCH -BUT NOBODY WANTS T'GIT THAR!
CAPP
Copr. 1939 by United Feature Syndicate, Inc. Tm. Reg. U. S. Pat. Off.—All rights reserved

LI'L ABNER

Horror Over Dogpatch!

By Al Capp

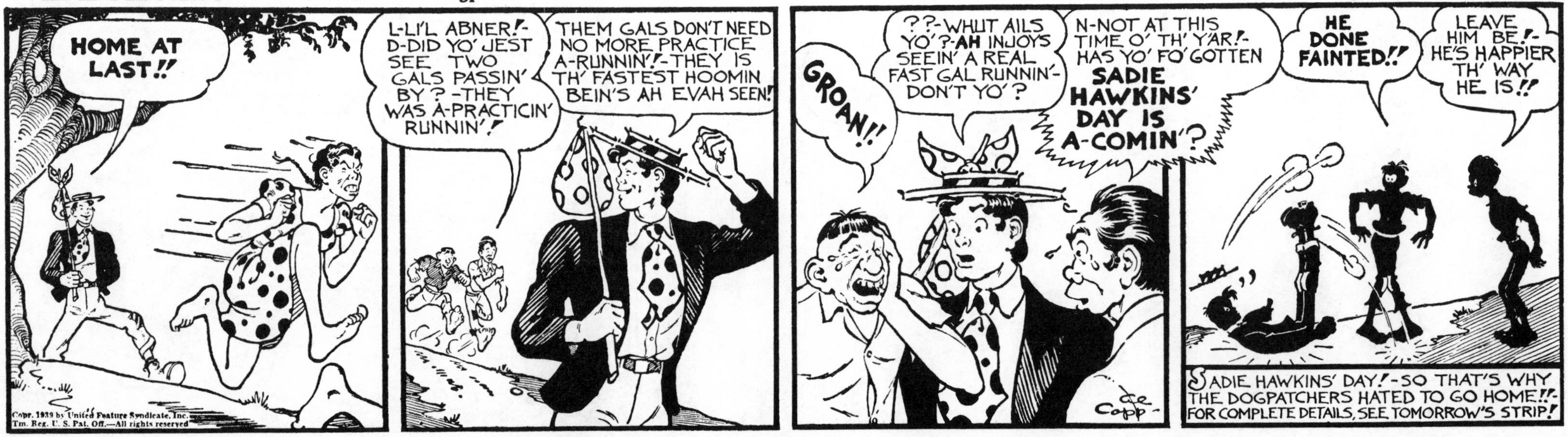
HOME AT LAST!!
L-LI'L ABNER!- D-DID YO' JEST SEE TWO GALS PASSIN' BY? -THEY WAS A-PRACTICIN' RUNNIN'!
THEM GALS DON'T NEED NO MORE PRACTICE A-RUNNIN'!-THEY IS TH' FASTEST HOOMIN BEIN'S AH EVAH SEEN!
GROAN!!
??-WHUT AILS YO'?-AH INJOYS SEEIN' A REAL FAST GAL RUNNIN'- DON'T YO'?
N-NOT AT THIS TIME O' TH' YAR!- HAS YO' FO'GOTTEN SADIE HAWKINS' DAY IS A-COMIN'?
HE DONE FAINTED!!
LEAVE HIM BE!- HE'S HAPPIER TH' WAY HE IS!!
SADIE HAWKINS' DAY!-SO THAT'S WHY THE DOGPATCHERS HATED TO GO HOME!!- FOR COMPLETE DETAILS, SEE TOMORROW'S STRIP!
CAPP
Copr. 1939 by United Feature Syndicate, Inc. Tm. Reg. U. S. Pat. Off.—All rights reserved

LI'L ABNER — The Strange Case of Sadie Hawkins—Part I — By Al Capp

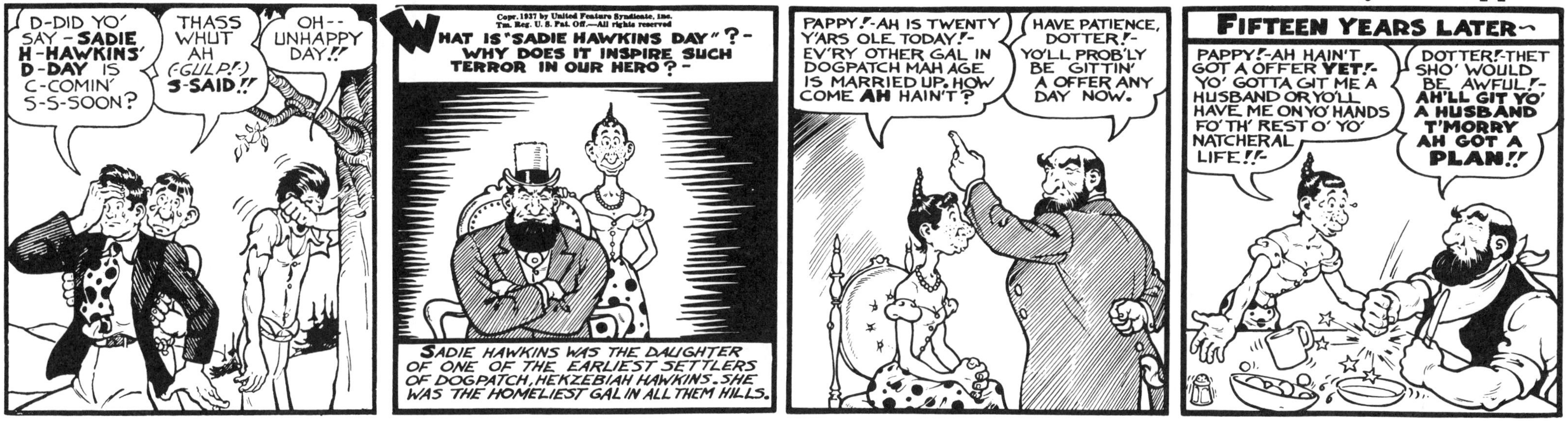

D-DID YO' SAY - SADIE H-HAWKINS' D-DAY IS C-COMIN' S-S-SOON?
THASS WHUT AH (-GULP!-) S-SAID!!
OH-- UNHAPPY DAY!!
Copr. 1937 by United Feature Syndicate, Inc. Tm. Reg. U. S. Pat. Off.—All rights reserved
WHAT IS "SADIE HAWKINS DAY"?- WHY DOES IT INSPIRE SUCH TERROR IN OUR HERO?-
SADIE HAWKINS WAS THE DAUGHTER OF ONE OF THE EARLIEST SETTLERS OF DOGPATCH, HEKZEBIAH HAWKINS. SHE WAS THE HOMELIEST GAL IN ALL THEM HILLS.
PAPPY!-AH IS TWENTY Y'ARS OLE TODAY!- EV'RY OTHER GAL IN DOGPATCH MAH AGE IS MARRIED UP. HOW COME AH HAIN'T?
HAVE PATIENCE, DOTTER!- YO'LL PROB'LY BE GITTIN' A OFFER ANY DAY NOW.
FIFTEEN YEARS LATER—
PAPPY!-AH HAIN'T GOT A OFFER YET!- YO' GOTTA GIT ME A HUSBAND OR YO'LL HAVE ME ON YO' HANDS FO' TH' REST O' YO' NATCHERAL LIFE!!-
DOTTER!-THET SHO' WOULD BE AWFUL!- AH'LL GIT YO' A HUSBAND T'MORRY AH GOT A PLAN!!

LI'L ABNER — The Strange Case of Sadie Hawkins—Part II — By Al Capp

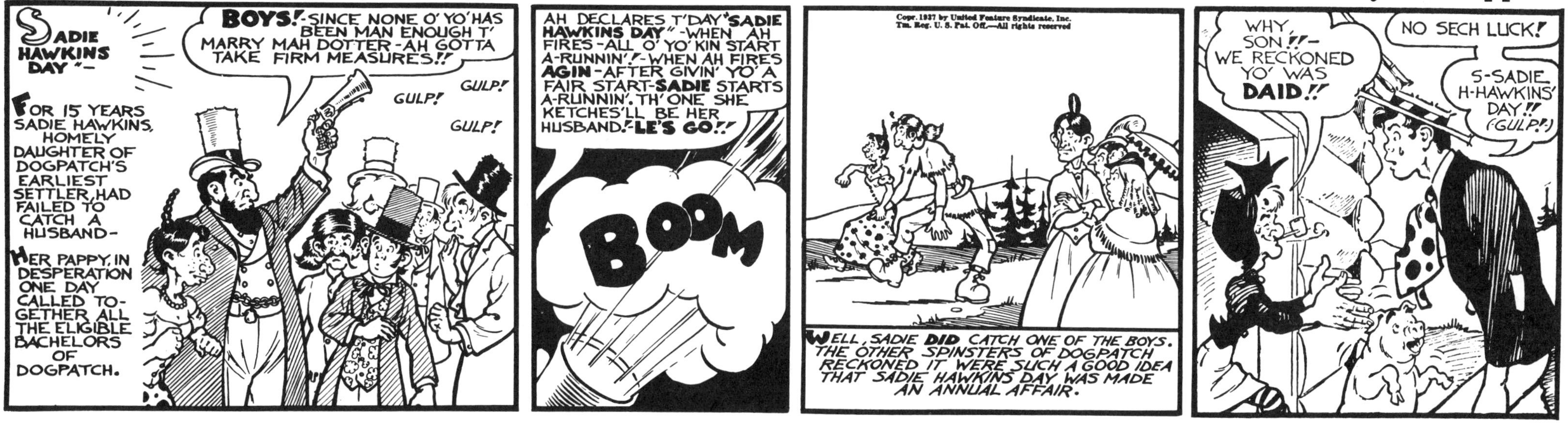

SADIE HAWKINS DAY"-
FOR 15 YEARS SADIE HAWKINS, HOMELY DAUGHTER OF DOGPATCH'S EARLIEST SETTLER, HAD FAILED TO CATCH A HUSBAND-
HER PAPPY, IN DESPERATION ONE DAY CALLED TOGETHER ALL THE ELIGIBLE BACHELORS OF DOGPATCH.
BOYS!-SINCE NONE O' YO' HAS BEEN MAN ENOUGH T' MARRY MAH DOTTER-AH GOTTA TAKE FIRM MEASURES!!
GULP!
GULP!
GULP!
AH DECLARES T'DAY "SADIE HAWKINS DAY"-WHEN AH FIRES-ALL O' YO' KIN START A-RUNNIN'!-WHEN AH FIRES AGIN-AFTER GIVIN' YO' A FAIR START-SADIE STARTS A-RUNNIN'. TH' ONE SHE KETCHES'LL BE HER HUSBAND!-LE'S GO!!
BOOM
Copr. 1937 by United Feature Syndicate, Inc. Tm. Reg. U. S. Pat. Off.—All rights reserved
WELL, SADIE DID CATCH ONE OF THE BOYS. THE OTHER SPINSTERS OF DOGPATCH RECKONED IT WERE SUCH A GOOD IDEA THAT SADIE HAWKINS DAY WAS MADE AN ANNUAL AFFAIR.
WHY, SON!!- WE RECKONED YO' WAS DAID!!
NO SECH LUCK!
S-SADIE H-HAWKINS' DAY!! (-GULP!-)

LI'L ABNER The Future Victims! By Al Capp

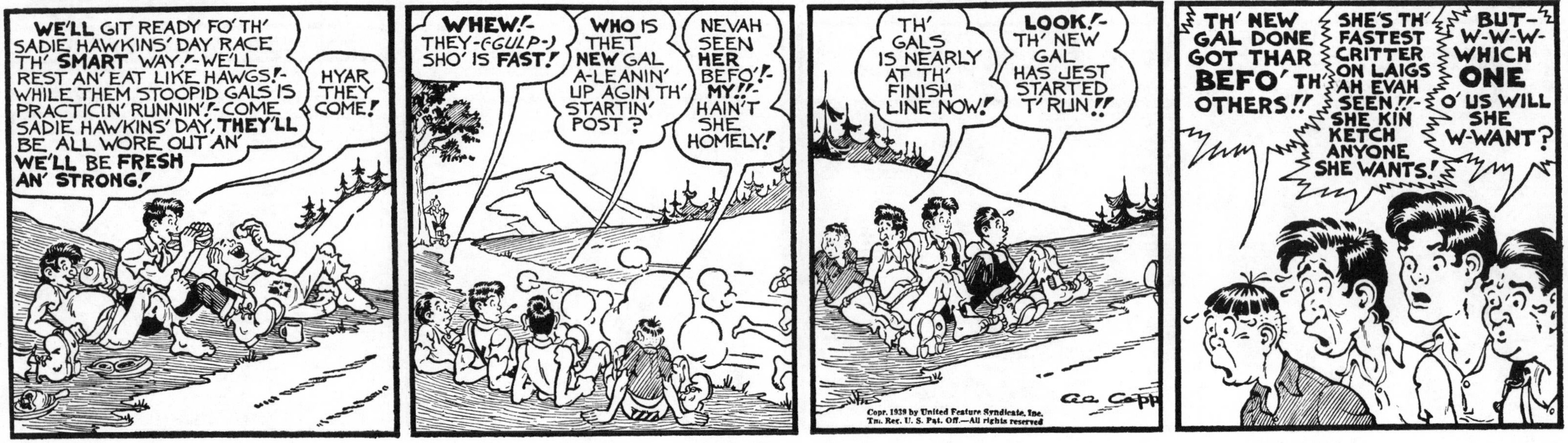

WE'LL GIT READY FO' TH' SADIE HAWKINS' DAY RACE TH' SMART WAY!-WE'LL REST AN' EAT LIKE HAWGS!-WHILE THEM STOOPID GALS IS PRACTICIN' RUNNIN'!-COME SADIE HAWKINS' DAY, THEY'LL BE ALL WORE OUT AN' WE'LL BE FRESH AN' STRONG!
HYAR THEY COME!
WHEW!-THEY-(-GULP-) SHO' IS FAST!
WHO IS THET NEW GAL A-LEANIN' UP AGIN TH' STARTIN' POST?
NEVAH SEEN HER BEFO'!-MY!!-HAIN'T SHE HOMELY!
TH' GALS IS NEARLY AT TH' FINISH LINE NOW!
LOOK!-TH' NEW GAL HAS JEST STARTED T' RUN!!
Copr. 1939 by United Feature Syndicate, Inc. Tm. Reg. U. S. Pat. Off.—All rights reserved
TH' NEW GAL DONE GOT THAR BEFO' TH' OTHERS!!
SHE'S TH' FASTEST CRITTER ON LAIGS AH EVAH SEEN!!-SHE KIN KETCH ANYONE SHE WANTS!
BUT-W-W-W-WHICH ONE O' US WILL SHE W-WANT?

LI'L ABNER The Curse of Beauty! By Al Capp

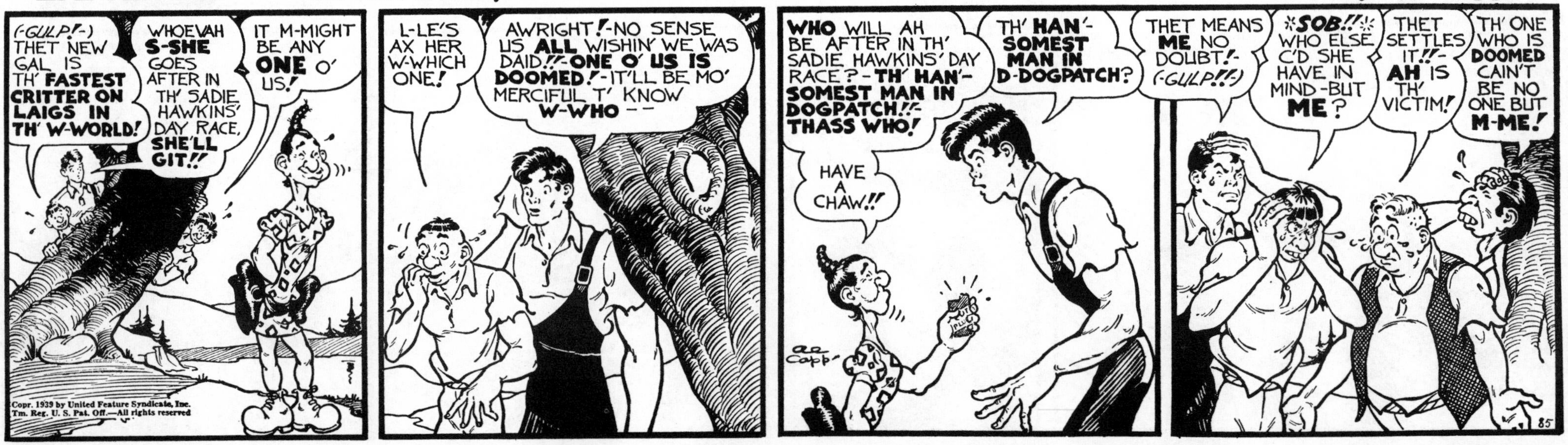

(-GULP!-) THET NEW GAL IS TH' FASTEST CRITTER ON LAIGS IN TH' W-WORLD!
WHOEVAH S-SHE GOES AFTER IN TH' SADIE HAWKINS' DAY RACE, SHE'LL GIT!!
IT M-MIGHT BE ANY ONE O' US!
Copr. 1939 by United Feature Syndicate, Inc. Tm. Reg. U. S. Pat. Off.—All rights reserved
L-LE'S AX HER W-WHICH ONE!
AWRIGHT!-NO SENSE US ALL WISHIN' WE WAS DAID!!-ONE O' US IS DOOMED!-IT'LL BE MO' MERCIFUL T' KNOW W-WHO --
WHO WILL AH BE AFTER IN TH' SADIE HAWKINS' DAY RACE?-TH' HAN'-SOMEST MAN IN DOGPATCH!!-THASS WHO!
HAVE A CHAW!!
TH' HAN'-SOMEST MAN IN D-DOGPATCH?
THET MEANS ME NO DOUBT!-(-GULP!!-)
SOB!! WHO ELSE C'D SHE HAVE IN MIND-BUT ME?
THET SETTLES IT!!-AH IS TH' VICTIM!
TH' ONE WHO IS DOOMED CAIN'T BE NO ONE BUT M-ME!

LI'L ABNER A Hair-Raising Sight! By Al Capp

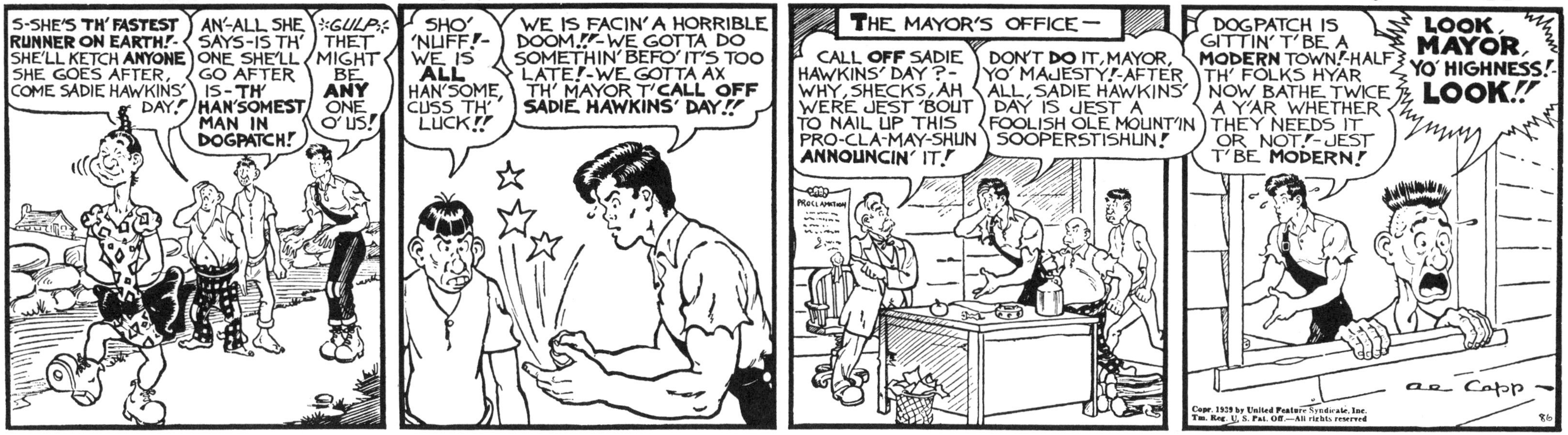

S-SHE'S TH' FASTEST RUNNER ON EARTH!-SHE'LL KETCH ANYONE SHE GOES AFTER, COME SADIE HAWKINS' DAY!
AN'-ALL SHE SAYS-IS TH' ONE SHE'LL GO AFTER IS-TH' HAN'SOMEST MAN IN DOGPATCH!
GULP! THET MIGHT BE ANY ONE O' US!
SHO' 'NUFF!-WE IS ALL HAN'SOME, CUSS TH' LUCK!!
WE IS FACIN' A HORRIBLE DOOM!!-WE GOTTA DO SOMETHIN' BEFO' IT'S TOO LATE!-WE GOTTA AX TH' MAYOR T' CALL OFF SADIE HAWKINS' DAY!!
THE MAYOR'S OFFICE—
CALL OFF SADIE HAWKINS' DAY?-WHY, SHECKS, AH WERE JEST 'BOUT TO NAIL UP THIS PRO-CLA-MAY-SHUN ANNOUNCIN' IT!
PROCLAMATION
DON'T DO IT, MAYOR, YO' MAJESTY!-AFTER ALL, SADIE HAWKINS' DAY IS JEST A FOOLISH OLE MOUNT'IN SOOPERSTISHUN!
DOGPATCH IS GITTIN' T'BE A MODERN TOWN!-HALF TH' FOLKS HYAR NOW BATHE TWICE A Y'AR WHETHER THEY NEEDS IT OR NOT!-JEST T'BE MODERN!
LOOK, MAYOR, YO' HIGHNESS!-LOOK!!
Al Capp
Copr. 1939 by United Feature Syndicate, Inc. Tm. Reg. U. S. Pat. Off.—All rights reserved

LI'L ABNER A Fate Worse Than Death!! By Al Capp

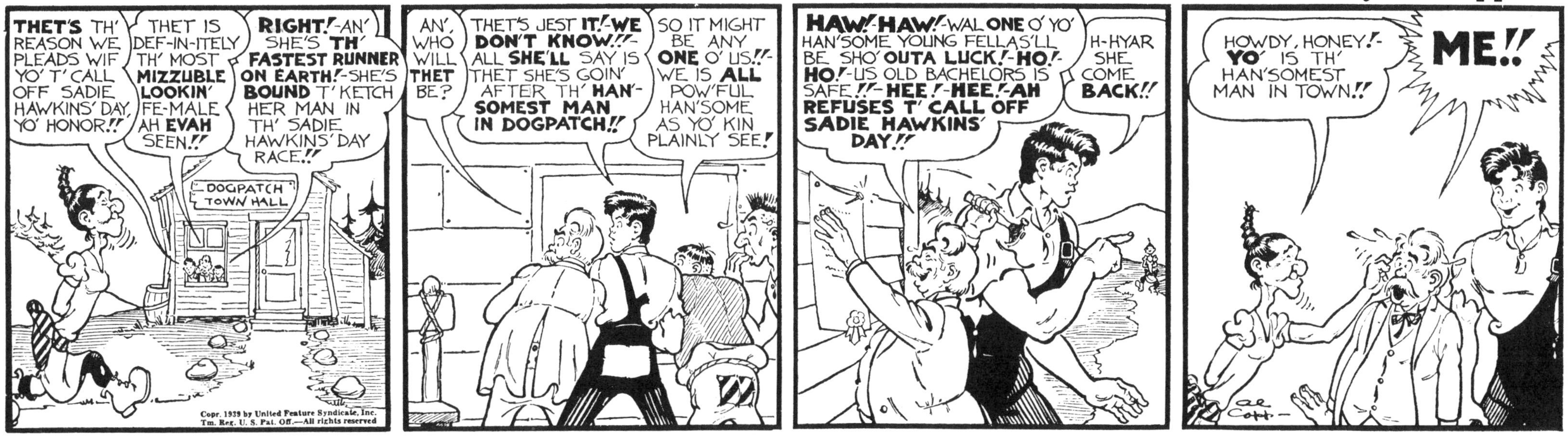

THET'S TH' REASON WE PLEADS WIF YO' T' CALL OFF SADIE HAWKINS' DAY, YO' HONOR!!
THET IS DEF-IN-ITELY TH' MOST MIZZUBLE LOOKIN' FE-MALE AH EVAH SEEN!!
RIGHT!-AN' SHE'S TH' FASTEST RUNNER ON EARTH!-SHE'S BOUND T' KETCH HER MAN IN TH' SADIE HAWKINS' DAY RACE!!
DOGPATCH TOWN HALL
Copr. 1939 by United Feature Syndicate, Inc. Tm. Reg. U. S. Pat. Off.—All rights reserved
AN', WHO WILL THET BE?
THET'S JEST IT!-WE DON'T KNOW!!-ALL SHE'LL SAY IS THET SHE'S GOIN' AFTER TH' HAN-SOMEST MAN IN DOGPATCH!!
SO IT MIGHT BE ANY ONE O' US!!-WE IS ALL POW'FUL HAN'SOME AS YO' KIN PLAINLY SEE!
HAW!-HAW!-WAL ONE O' YO' HAN'SOME YOUNG FELLAS'LL BE SHO' OUTA LUCK!-HO!-HO!-US OLD BACHELORS IS SAFE!!-HEE!-HEE!-AH REFUSES T' CALL OFF SADIE HAWKINS' DAY!!
H-HYAR SHE COME BACK!!
HOWDY, HONEY!-YO' IS TH' HAN'SOMEST MAN IN TOWN!!
ME!!
Al Capp

LI'L ABNER Doomed!! By Al Capp

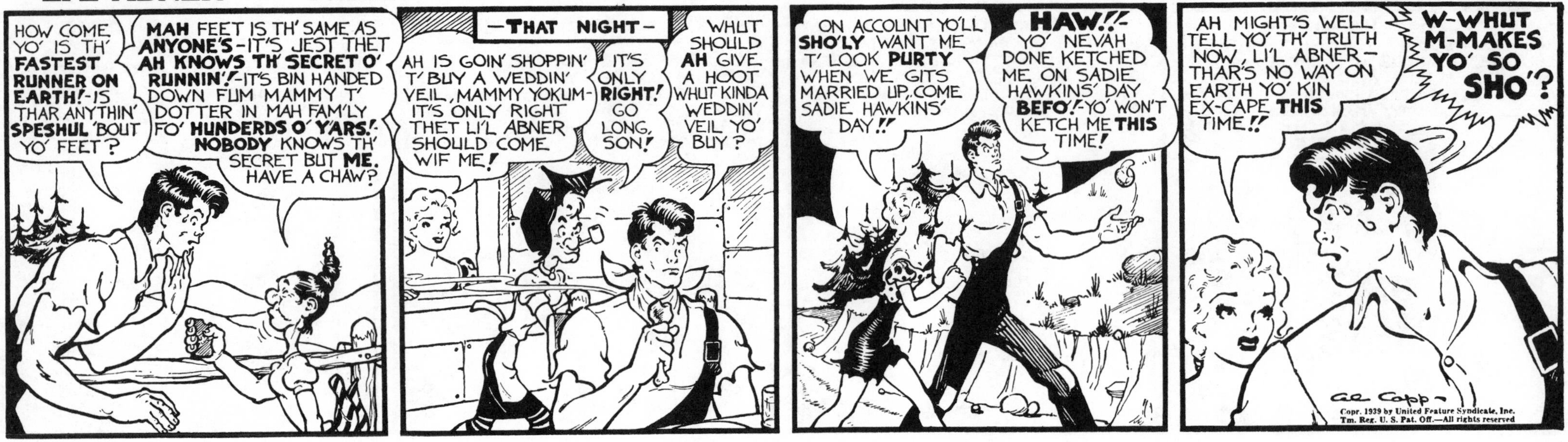
HOW COME YO' IS TH' FASTEST RUNNER ON EARTH!-IS THAR ANYTHIN' SPESHUL 'BOUT YO' FEET?
MAH FEET IS TH' SAME AS ANYONE'S-IT'S JEST THET AH KNOWS TH' SECRET O' RUNNIN'!-IT'S BIN HANDED DOWN FUM MAMMY T' DOTTER IN MAH FAM'LY FO' HUNDERDS O' YARS!- NOBODY KNOWS TH' SECRET BUT ME. HAVE A CHAW?
-THAT NIGHT-
AH IS GOIN' SHOPPIN' T' BUY A WEDDIN' VEIL, MAMMY YOKUM-IT'S ONLY RIGHT THET LI'L ABNER SHOULD COME WIF ME!
IT'S ONLY RIGHT! GO LONG, SON!
WHUT SHOULD AH GIVE A HOOT WHUT KINDA WEDDIN' VEIL YO' BUY?
ON ACCOUNT YO'LL SHO'LY WANT ME T' LOOK PURTY WHEN WE GITS MARRIED UP, COME SADIE HAWKINS' DAY!!
HAW!!- YO' NEVAH DONE KETCHED ME ON SADIE HAWKINS' DAY BEFO'!-YO' WON'T KETCH ME THIS TIME!
AH MIGHT'S WELL TELL YO' TH' TRUTH NOW, LI'L ABNER-THAR'S NO WAY ON EARTH YO' KIN EX-CAPE THIS TIME!!
W-WHUT M-MAKES YO' SO SHO'?
Copr. 1939 by United Feature Syndicate, Inc. Tm. Reg. U. S. Pat. Off.—All rights reserved

LI'L ABNER What's That Behind th' Mulberry Bush? By Al Capp

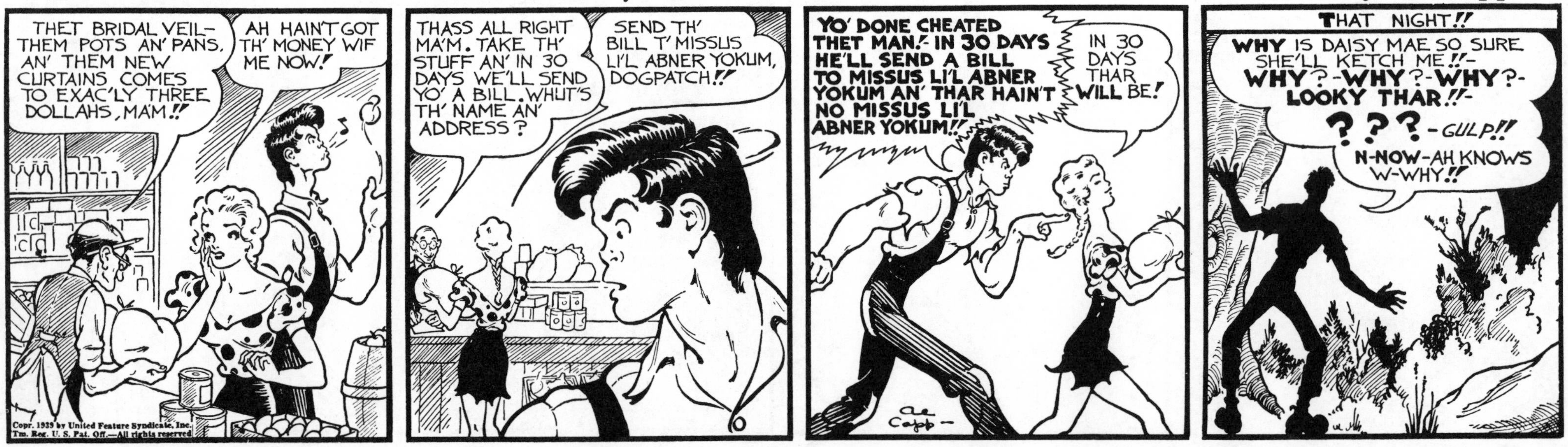
THET BRIDAL VEIL-THEM POTS AN' PANS, AN' THEM NEW CURTAINS COMES TO EXAC'LY THREE DOLLAHS, MA'M!!
AH HAIN'T GOT TH' MONEY WIF ME NOW!
THASS ALL RIGHT MA'M. TAKE TH' STUFF AN' IN 30 DAYS WE'LL SEND YO' A BILL. WHUT'S TH' NAME AN' ADDRESS?
SEND TH' BILL T' MISSUS LI'L ABNER YOKUM, DOGPATCH!!
YO' DONE CHEATED THET MAN!- IN 30 DAYS HE'LL SEND A BILL TO MISSUS LI'L ABNER YOKUM AN' THAR HAIN'T NO MISSUS LI'L ABNER YOKUM!!
IN 30 DAYS THAR WILL BE!
THAT NIGHT!!
WHY IS DAISY MAE SO SURE SHE'LL KETCH ME!!- WHY?-WHY?-WHY?- LOOKY THAR!!-
???-GULP!!
N-NOW-AH KNOWS W-WHY!!
Copr. 1939 by United Feature Syndicate, Inc. Tm. Reg. U. S. Pat. Off.—All rights reserved

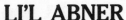

LI'L ABNER The Women! By Al Capp

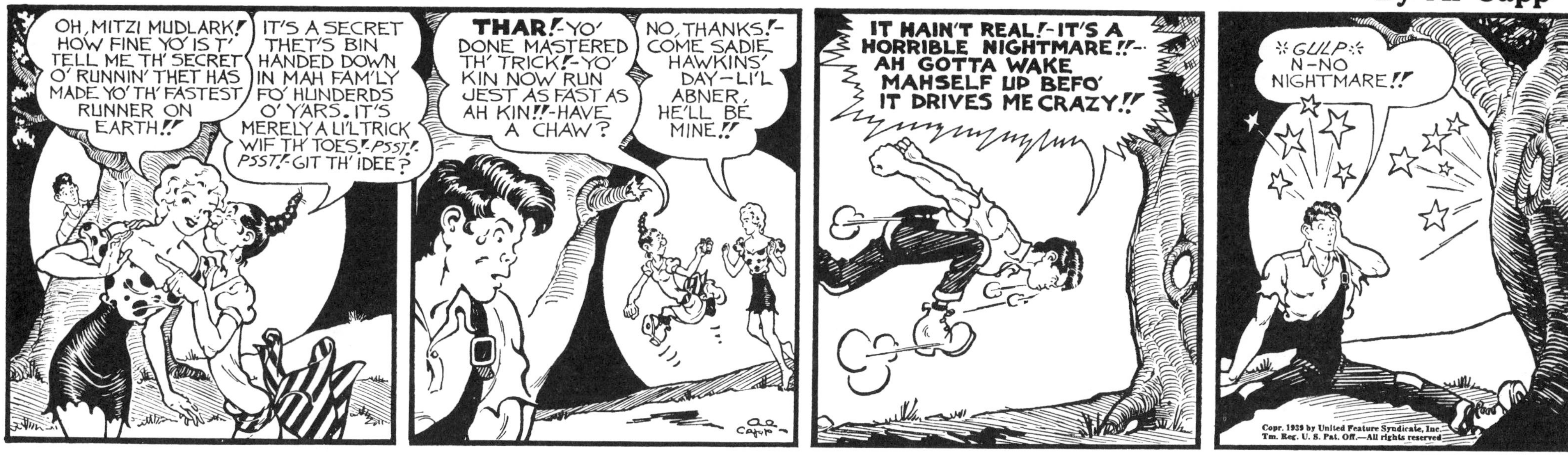

OH, MITZI MUDLARK! HOW FINE YO' IS T' TELL ME TH' SECRET O' RUNNIN' THET HAS MADE YO' TH' FASTEST RUNNER ON EARTH!!
IT'S A SECRET THET'S BIN HANDED DOWN IN MAH FAM'LY FO' HUNDERDS O' YARS. IT'S MERELY A LI'L TRICK WIF TH' TOES!-PSST!-PSST!-GIT TH' IDEE?
THAR!-YO' DONE MASTERED TH' TRICK!-YO' KIN NOW RUN JEST AS FAST AS AH KIN!!-HAVE A CHAW?
NO, THANKS!-COME SADIE HAWKINS' DAY-LI'L ABNER, HE'LL BE MINE!!
IT HAIN'T REAL!-IT'S A HORRIBLE NIGHTMARE!!-AH GOTTA WAKE MAHSELF UP BEFO' IT DRIVES ME CRAZY!!
GULP N-NO NIGHTMARE!!
Copr. 1939 by United Feature Syndicate, Inc. Tm. Reg. U. S. Pat. Off.—All rights reserved

LI'L ABNER Anything Means Anything By Al Capp

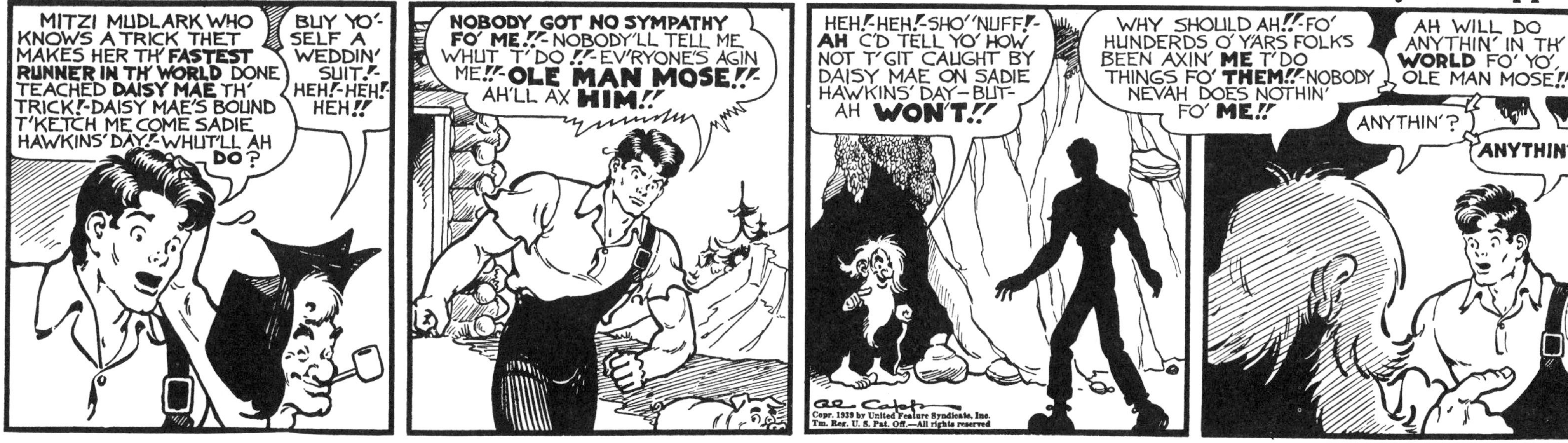

MITZI MUDLARK WHO KNOWS A TRICK THET MAKES HER TH' FASTEST RUNNER IN TH' WORLD DONE TEACHED DAISY MAE TH' TRICK!-DAISY MAE'S BOUND T'KETCH ME COME SADIE HAWKINS' DAY!-WHUT'LL AH DO?
BUY YO'SELF A WEDDIN' SUIT!-HEH!-HEH!-HEH!!
NOBODY GOT NO SYMPATHY FO' ME!!-NOBODY'LL TELL ME WHUT T'DO!!-EV'RYONE'S AGIN ME!!-OLE MAN MOSE!!-AH'LL AX HIM!!
HEH!-HEH!-SHO' 'NUFF!-AH C'D TELL YO' HOW NOT T'GIT CAUGHT BY DAISY MAE ON SADIE HAWKINS' DAY-BUT-AH WON'T!!
WHY SHOULD AH!!-FO' HUNDERDS O' YARS FOLKS BEEN AXIN' ME T'DO THINGS FO' THEM!!-NOBODY NEVAH DOES NOTHIN' FO' ME!!
AH WILL DO ANYTHIN' IN TH' WORLD FO' YO', OLE MAN MOSE!!
ANYTHIN'?
ANYTHIN'!
Copr. 1939 by United Feature Syndicate, Inc. Tm. Reg. U. S. Pat. Off.—All rights reserved

LI'L ABNER The Eagles, They Fly High! By Al Capp

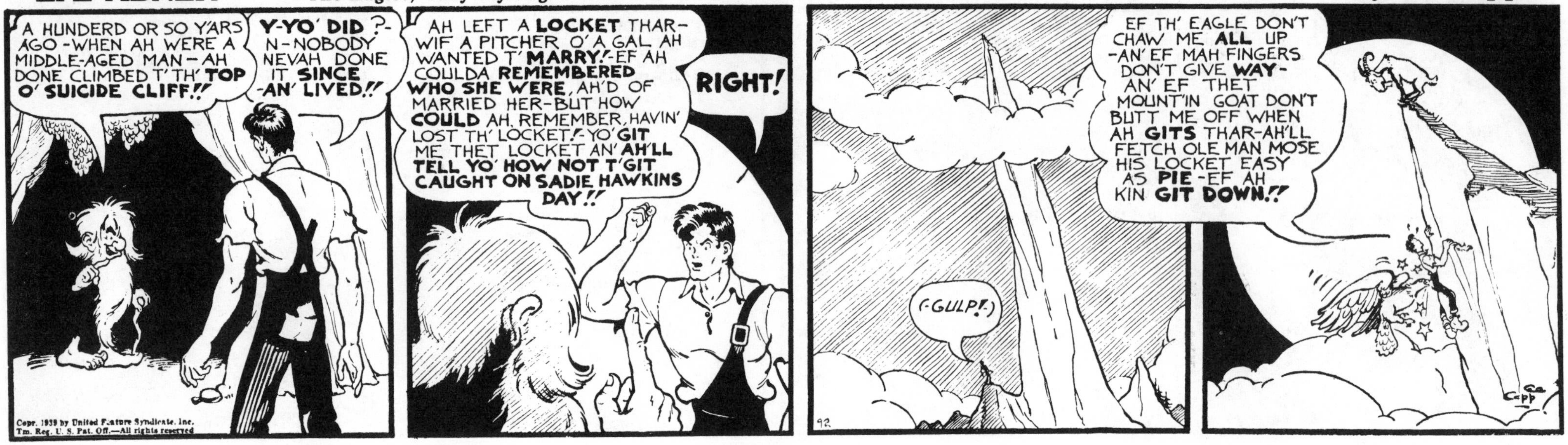
A HUNDERD OR SO Y'ARS AGO - WHEN AH WERE A MIDDLE-AGED MAN - AH DONE CLIMBED T' TH' TOP O' SUICIDE CLIFF!!
Y-YO' DID ?- N-NOBODY NEVAH DONE IT SINCE -AN' LIVED!!
AH LEFT A LOCKET THAR- WIF A PITCHER O' A GAL AH WANTED T' MARRY!- EF AH COULDA REMEMBERED WHO SHE WERE, AH'D OF MARRIED HER-BUT HOW COULD AH REMEMBER, HAVIN' LOST TH' LOCKET!- YO' GIT ME THET LOCKET AN' AH'LL TELL YO' HOW NOT T'GIT CAUGHT ON SADIE HAWKINS DAY!!
RIGHT!
(-GULP!-)
EF TH' EAGLE DON'T CHAW ME ALL UP -AN' EF MAH FINGERS DON'T GIVE WAY- AN' EF THET MOUNT'IN GOAT DON'T BUTT ME OFF WHEN AH GITS THAR-AH'LL FETCH OLE MAN MOSE HIS LOCKET EASY AS PIE-EF AH KIN GIT DOWN!!
Copr. 1939 by United Feature Syndicate, Inc. Tm. Reg. U. S. Pat. Off.—All rights reserved
Capp

LI'L ABNER Yokum Rides Again! By Al Capp

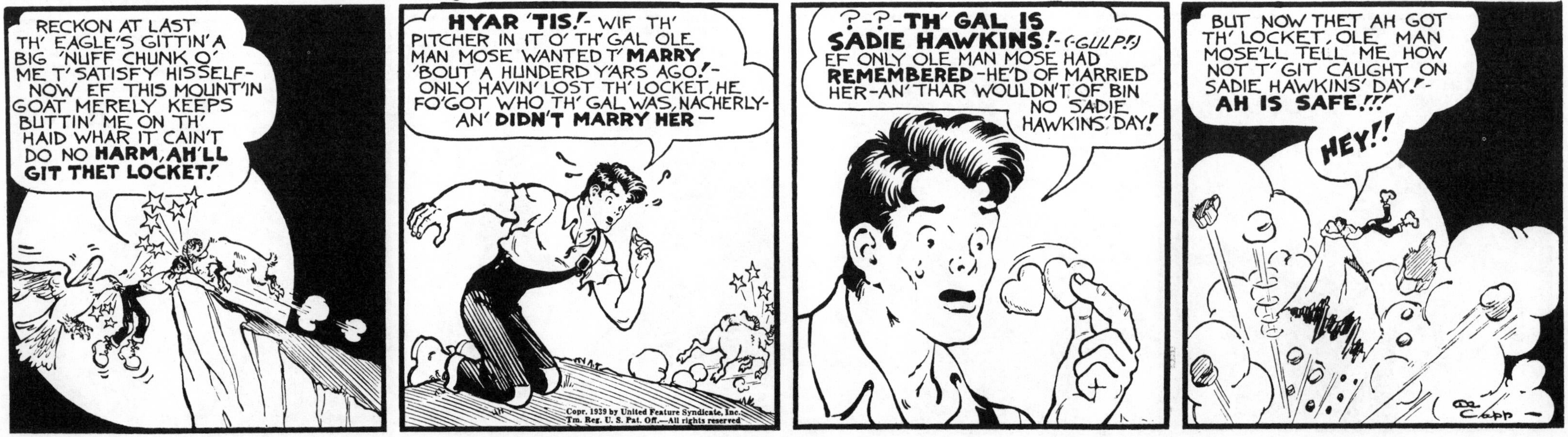
RECKON AT LAST TH' EAGLE'S GITTIN' A BIG 'NUFF CHUNK O' ME T' SATISFY HISSELF- NOW EF THIS MOUNT'IN GOAT MERELY KEEPS BUTTIN' ME ON TH' HAID WHAR IT CAIN'T DO NO HARM, AH'LL GIT THET LOCKET!
HYAR 'TIS!- WIF TH' PITCHER IN IT O' TH' GAL OLE MAN MOSE WANTED T' MARRY 'BOUT A HUNDERD Y'ARS AGO!- ONLY HAVIN' LOST TH' LOCKET, HE FO'GOT WHO TH' GAL WAS, NACHERLY- AN' DIDN'T MARRY HER -
Copr. 1939 by United Feature Syndicate, Inc. Tm. Reg. U. S. Pat. Off.—All rights reserved
?-?-TH' GAL IS SADIE HAWKINS!- (-GULP!-) EF ONLY OLE MAN MOSE HAD REMEMBERED -HE'D OF MARRIED HER-AN' THAR WOULDN'T OF BIN NO SADIE HAWKINS' DAY!
BUT NOW THET AH GOT TH' LOCKET, OLE MAN MOSE'LL TELL ME HOW NOT T' GIT CAUGHT ON SADIE HAWKINS' DAY!- AH IS SAFE!!!
HEY!!
Capp

LI'L ABNER It Looks Bad! By Al Capp

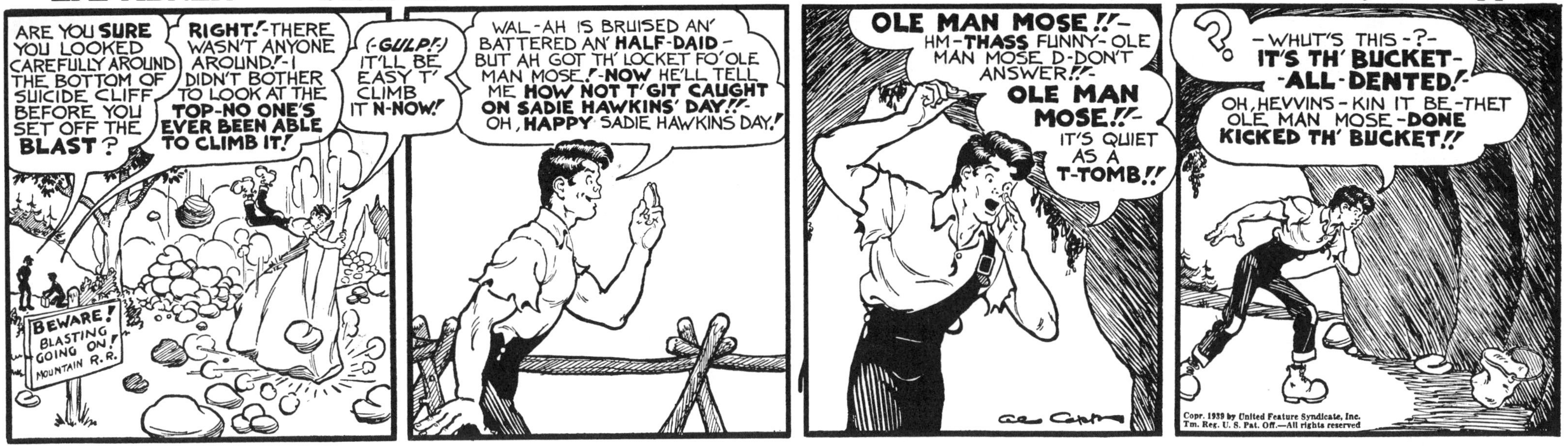

ARE YOU SURE YOU LOOKED CAREFULLY AROUND THE BOTTOM OF SUICIDE CLIFF BEFORE YOU SET OFF THE BLAST ?
RIGHT!-THERE WASN'T ANYONE AROUND!-I DIDN'T BOTHER TO LOOK AT THE TOP-NO ONE'S EVER BEEN ABLE TO CLIMB IT!
(-GULP!-) IT'LL BE EASY T' CLIMB IT N-NOW!
BEWARE! BLASTING GOING ON! MOUNTAIN R.R.
WAL-AH IS BRUISED AN' BATTERED AN' HALF-DAID-BUT AH GOT TH' LOCKET FO' OLE MAN MOSE!-NOW HE'LL TELL ME HOW NOT T' GIT CAUGHT ON SADIE HAWKINS' DAY!!-OH, HAPPY SADIE HAWKINS DAY!
OLE MAN MOSE!!-HM-THASS FUNNY-OLE MAN MOSE D-DON'T ANSWER!!-OLE MAN MOSE!!-IT'S QUIET AS A T-TOMB!!
?
-WHUT'S THIS-?-IT'S TH' BUCKET--ALL-DENTED!-OH, HEVVINS-KIN IT BE-THET OLE MAN MOSE-DONE KICKED TH' BUCKET!!
Copr. 1939 by United Feature Syndicate, Inc. Tm. Reg. U. S. Pat. Off.—All rights reserved

LI'L ABNER He Fears the Worst! By Al Capp

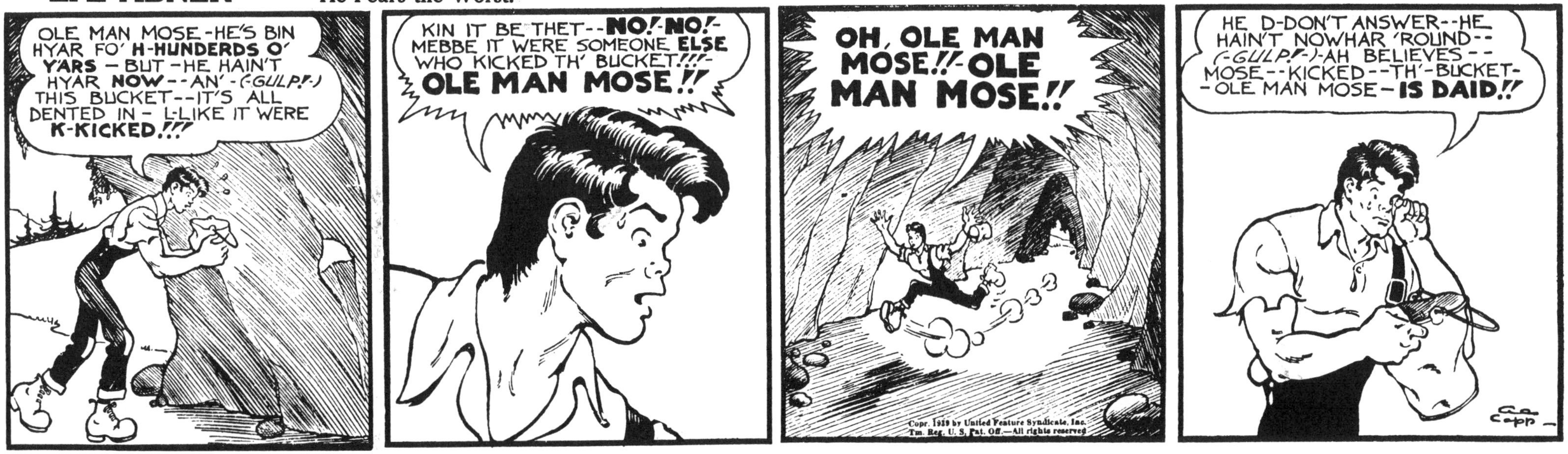

OLE MAN MOSE-HE'S BIN HYAR FO' H-HUNDERDS O' YARS-BUT-HE HAIN'T HYAR NOW--AN'-(-GULP!-) THIS BUCKET--IT'S ALL DENTED IN-L-LIKE IT WERE K-KICKED!!!
KIN IT BE THET--NO!-NO!-MEBBE IT WERE SOMEONE ELSE WHO KICKED TH' BUCKET!!!-OLE MAN MOSE!!
OH, OLE MAN MOSE!!-OLE MAN MOSE!!
Copr. 1939 by United Feature Syndicate, Inc. Tm. Reg. U. S. Pat. Off.—All rights reserved
HE D-DON'T ANSWER--HE HAIN'T NOWHAR 'ROUND--(-GULP!-)-AH BELIEVES--MOSE--KICKED--TH'-BUCKET--OLE MAN MOSE-IS DAID!!

LI'L ABNER Gone With the Wind! By Al Capp

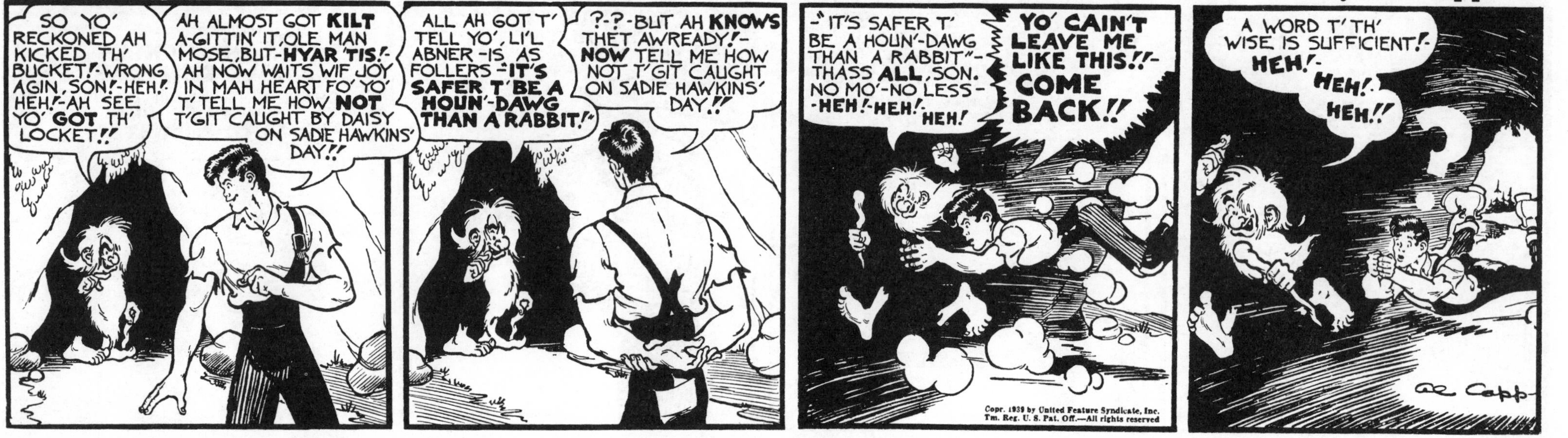
SO YO' RECKONED AH KICKED TH' BUCKET!-WRONG AGIN, SON!-HEH! HEH!-AH SEE YO' GOT TH' LOCKET!!
AH ALMOST GOT KILT A-GITTIN' IT, OLE MAN MOSE, BUT-HYAR 'TIS!-AH NOW WAITS WIF JOY IN MAH HEART FO' YO' T' TELL ME HOW NOT T'GIT CAUGHT BY DAISY ON SADIE HAWKINS' DAY!!
ALL AH GOT T' TELL YO', LI'L ABNER-IS AS FOLLERS-"IT'S SAFER T'BE A HOUN'-DAWG THAN A RABBIT!"
?-?-BUT AH KNOWS THET AWREADY!-NOW TELL ME HOW NOT T'GIT CAUGHT ON SADIE HAWKINS' DAY!!
-"IT'S SAFER T' BE A HOUN'-DAWG THAN A RABBIT"-THASS ALL, SON. NO MO'-NO LESS--HEH!-HEH! HEH!
YO' CAIN'T LEAVE ME LIKE THIS!!-COME BACK!!
A WORD T'TH' WISE IS SUFFICIENT!-HEH!-HEH!-HEH!!
?
Copr. 1939 by United Feature Syndicate, Inc. Tm. Reg. U. S. Pat. Off.—All rights reserved
Al Capp

LI'L ABNER From th' Moufs of Babes! By Al Capp

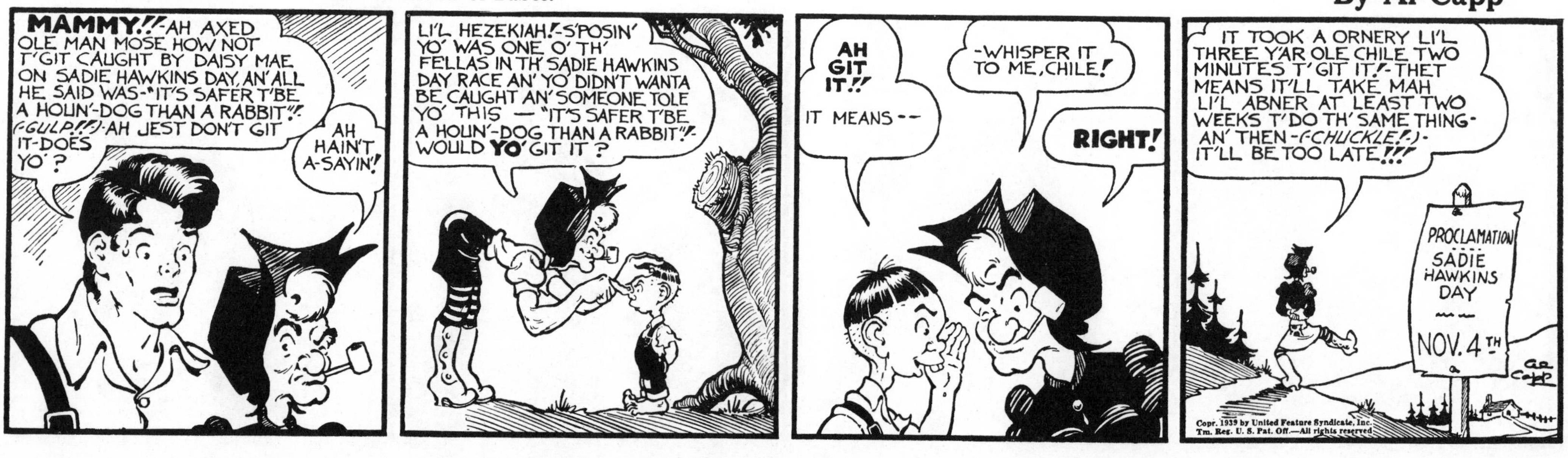
MAMMY!!-AH AXED OLE MAN MOSE HOW NOT T'GIT CAUGHT BY DAISY MAE ON SADIE HAWKINS DAY, AN' ALL HE SAID WAS-"IT'S SAFER T'BE A HOUN'-DOG THAN A RABBIT"!-(-GULP!!-)-AH JEST DON'T GIT IT-DOES YO'?
AH HAIN'T A-SAYIN'!
LI'L HEZEKIAH!-S'POSIN' YO' WAS ONE O' TH' FELLAS IN TH' SADIE HAWKINS DAY RACE AN' YO' DIDN'T WANTA BE CAUGHT AN' SOMEONE TOLE YO' THIS — "IT'S SAFER T'BE A HOUN'-DOG THAN A RABBIT"!-WOULD YO' GIT IT?
AH GIT IT!!
IT MEANS --
-WHISPER IT TO ME, CHILE!
RIGHT!
IT TOOK A ORNERY LI'L THREE Y'AR OLE CHILE TWO MINUTES T'GIT IT!-THET MEANS IT'LL TAKE MAH LI'L ABNER AT LEAST TWO WEEKS T'DO TH' SAME THING-AN' THEN-(-CHUCKLE!-)-IT'LL BE TOO LATE!!!
PROCLAMATION
SADIE HAWKINS DAY
NOV. 4TH
Al Capp
Copr. 1939 by United Feature Syndicate, Inc. Tm. Reg. U. S. Pat. Off.—All rights reserved

LI'L ABNER Cain't Make a Rabbit Stew Fum a Houn'-Dawg! By Al Capp

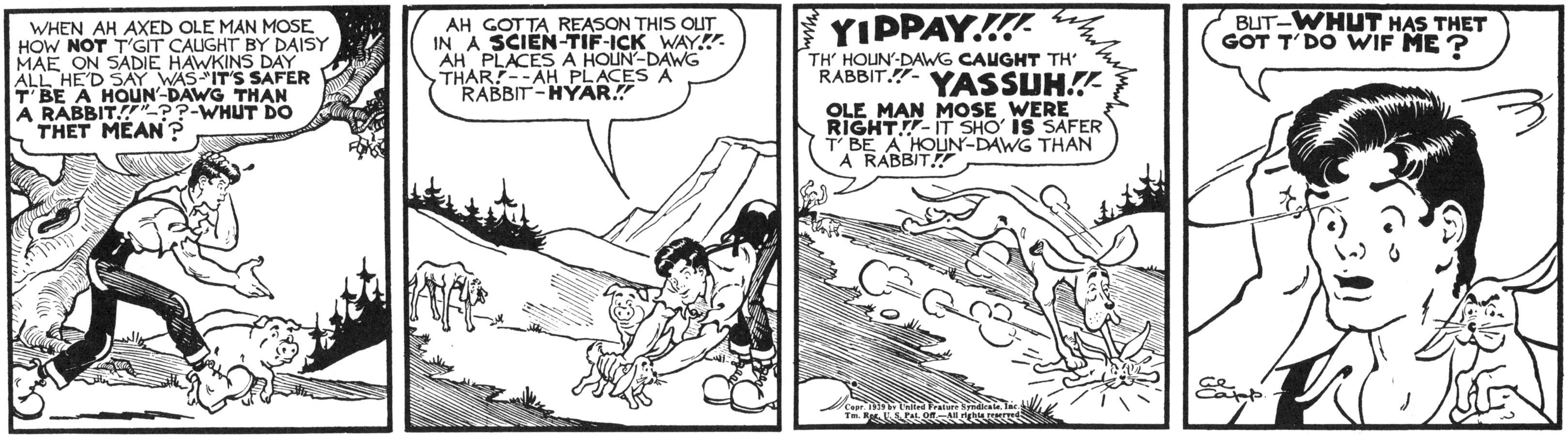
WHEN AH AXED OLE MAN MOSE HOW NOT T'GIT CAUGHT BY DAISY MAE ON SADIE HAWKINS DAY ALL HE'D SAY WAS-"IT'S SAFER T' BE A HOUN'-DAWG THAN A RABBIT!!"-??-WHUT DO THET MEAN?
AH GOTTA REASON THIS OUT IN A SCIEN-TIF-ICK WAY!!-AH PLACES A HOUN'-DAWG THAR!--AH PLACES A RABBIT-HYAR!!
YIPPAY!!!-
TH' HOUN'-DAWG CAUGHT TH' RABBIT!!-YASSUH!!-OLE MAN MOSE WERE RIGHT!!-IT SHO' IS SAFER T' BE A HOUN'-DAWG THAN A RABBIT!!
Copr. 1939 by United Feature Syndicate, Inc. Tm. Reg. U. S. Pat. Off.—All rights reserved
BUT-WHUT HAS THET GOT T' DO WIF ME?
AL CAPP

LI'L ABNER Just Before the Battle, Mother! By Al Capp

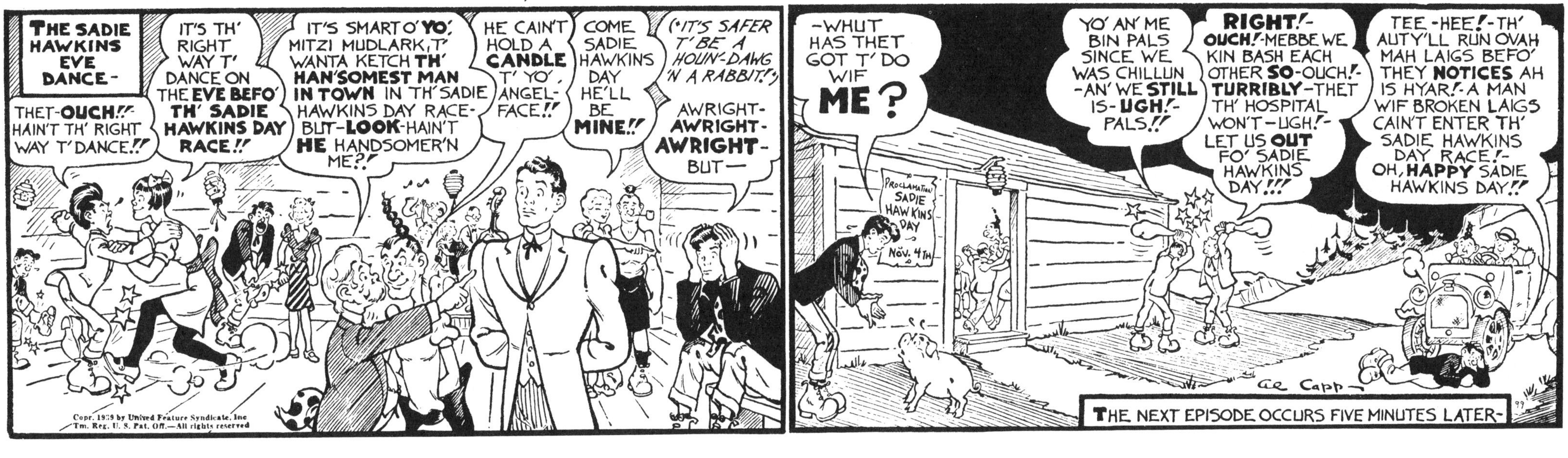
THE SADIE HAWKINS EVE DANCE-
THET-OUCH!!-HAIN'T TH' RIGHT WAY T' DANCE!!
IT'S TH' RIGHT WAY T' DANCE ON THE EVE BEFO' TH' SADIE HAWKINS DAY RACE!!
IT'S SMART O' YO', MITZI MUDLARK, T' WANTA KETCH TH' HAN'SOMEST MAN IN TOWN IN TH' SADIE HAWKINS DAY RACE-BUT-LOOK-HAIN'T HE HANDSOMER'N ME?!
HE CAIN'T HOLD A CANDLE T' YO', ANGEL-FACE!!
COME SADIE HAWKINS DAY HE'LL BE MINE!!
("IT'S SAFER T' BE A HOUN'-DAWG 'N A RABBIT!")
AWRIGHT-AWRIGHT-AWRIGHT-BUT—
Copr. 1939 by United Feature Syndicate, Inc Tm. Reg. U. S. Pat. Off.—All rights reserved
-WHUT HAS THET GOT T' DO WIF ME?
PROCLAMATION SADIE HAWKINS DAY NOV. 4TH
YO' AN' ME BIN PALS SINCE WE WAS CHILLUN -AN' WE STILL IS-UGH!-PALS!!
RIGHT!-OUCH!-MEBBE WE KIN BASH EACH OTHER SO-OUCH!-TURRIBLY-THET TH' HOSPITAL WON'T-UGH!-LET US OUT FO' SADIE HAWKINS DAY!!!
TEE-HEE!-TH' AUTY'LL RUN OVAH MAH LAIGS BEFO' THEY NOTICES AH IS HYAR!-A MAN WIF BROKEN LAIGS CAIN'T ENTER TH' SADIE HAWKINS DAY RACE!-OH, HAPPY SADIE HAWKINS DAY!!
AL CAPP
THE NEXT EPISODE OCCURS FIVE MINUTES LATER-

LI'L ABNER

An Apple a Day Keeps Sadie Hawkins Away!

By Al Capp

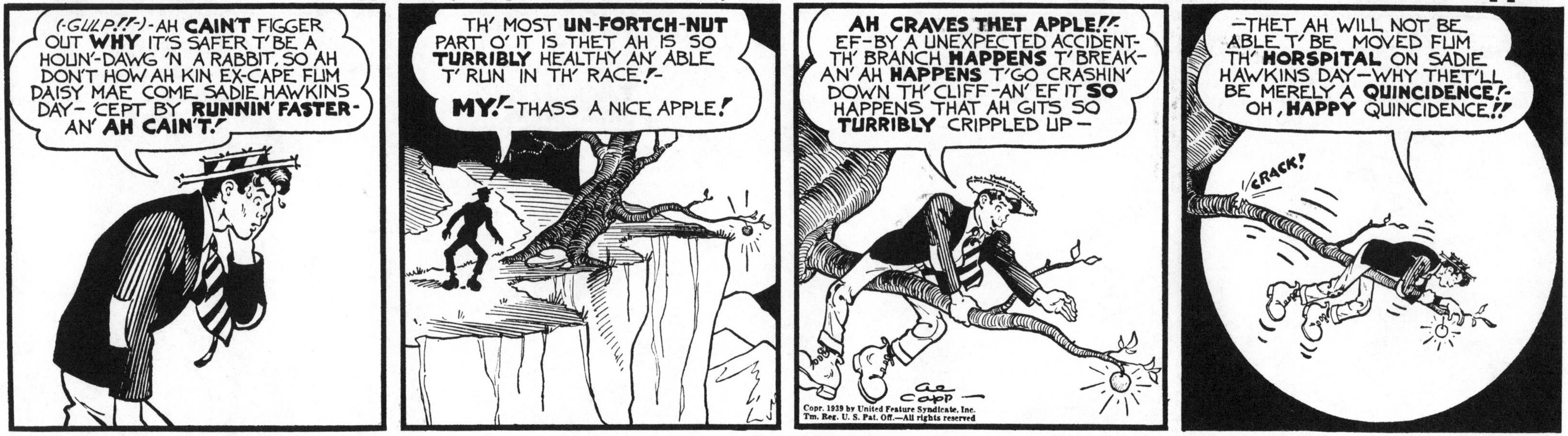
(-GULP!!-)-AH CAIN'T FIGGER OUT WHY IT'S SAFER T'BE A HOUN'-DAWG 'N A RABBIT, SO AH DON'T HOW AH KIN EX-CAPE FUM DAISY MAE COME SADIE HAWKINS DAY-'CEPT BY RUNNIN' FASTER-AN' AH CAIN'T!
TH' MOST UN-FORTCH-NUT PART O' IT IS THET AH IS SO TURRIBLY HEALTHY AN' ABLE T' RUN IN TH' RACE!- MY!-THASS A NICE APPLE!
AH CRAVES THET APPLE!!-EF-BY A UNEXPECTED ACCIDENT-TH' BRANCH HAPPENS T' BREAK-AN' AH HAPPENS T'GO CRASHIN' DOWN TH' CLIFF-AN' EF IT SO HAPPENS THAT AH GITS SO TURRIBLY CRIPPLED UP-
Copr. 1939 by United Feature Syndicate, Inc. Tm. Reg. U. S. Pat. Off.—All rights reserved
-THET AH WILL NOT BE ABLE T' BE MOVED FUM TH' HORSPITAL ON SADIE HAWKINS DAY-WHY THET'LL BE MERELY A QUINCIDENCE!-OH, HAPPY QUINCIDENCE!!
CRACK!

LI'L ABNER

Daisy's Fatal Error

By Al Capp

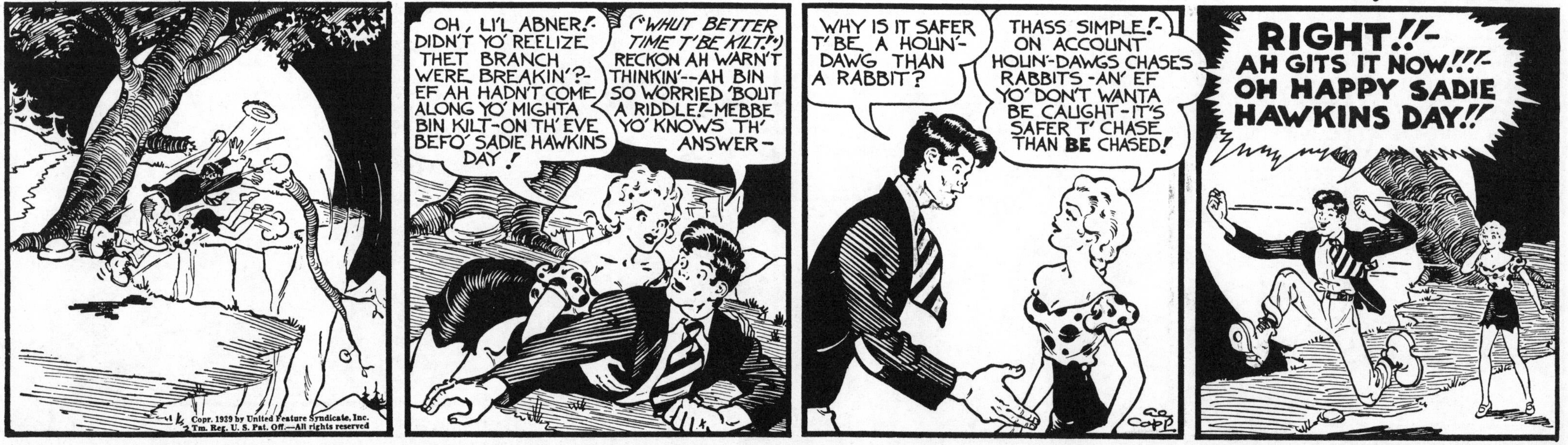
Copr. 1939 by United Feature Syndicate, Inc. Tm. Reg. U. S. Pat. Off.—All rights reserved
OH, LI'L ABNER!-DIDN'T YO' REELIZE THET BRANCH WERE BREAKIN'?-EF AH HADN'T COME ALONG YO' MIGHTA BIN KILT-ON TH' EVE BEFO' SADIE HAWKINS DAY!
("WHUT BETTER TIME T'BE KILT!") RECKON AH WARN'T THINKIN'--AH BIN SO WORRIED 'BOUT A RIDDLE!-MEBBE YO' KNOWS TH' ANSWER-
WHY IS IT SAFER T' BE A HOUN'-DAWG THAN A RABBIT?
THASS SIMPLE!-ON ACCOUNT HOUN'-DAWGS CHASES RABBITS-AN' EF YO' DON'T WANTA BE CAUGHT-IT'S SAFER T' CHASE THAN BE CHASED!
RIGHT!!-AH GITS IT NOW!!!-OH HAPPY SADIE HAWKINS DAY!!

LI'L ABNER Comes Love By Al Capp

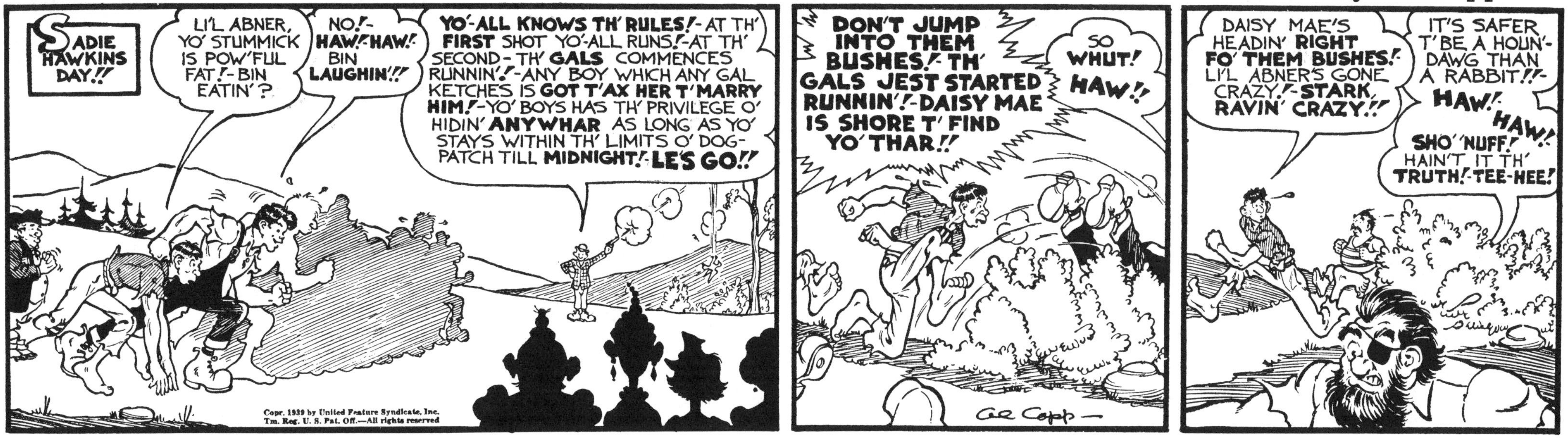

SADIE HAWKINS DAY!!
LI'L ABNER, YO' STUMMICK IS POW'FUL FAT!-BIN EATIN'?
NO!-HAW!-HAW!-BIN LAUGHIN'!!
YO'-ALL KNOWS TH' RULES!-AT TH' FIRST SHOT YO'-ALL RUNS!-AT TH' SECOND-TH' GALS COMMENCES RUNNIN'!-ANY BOY WHICH ANY GAL KETCHES IS GOT T'AX HER T'MARRY HIM!-YO' BOYS HAS TH' PRIVILEGE O' HIDIN' ANYWHAR AS LONG AS YO' STAYS WITHIN TH' LIMITS O' DOGPATCH TILL MIDNIGHT!-LE'S GO!!
Copr. 1939 by United Feature Syndicate, Inc. Tm. Reg. U. S. Pat. Off.—All rights reserved
DON'T JUMP INTO THEM BUSHES!-TH' GALS JEST STARTED RUNNIN'!-DAISY MAE IS SHORE T' FIND YO' THAR!!
SO WHUT! HAW!!
Al Capp
DAISY MAE'S HEADIN' RIGHT FO' THEM BUSHES!-LI'L ABNER'S GONE CRAZY!-STARK, RAVIN' CRAZY!!
IT'S SAFER T' BE A HOUN'-DAWG THAN A RABBIT!!-HAW!-HAW!!
SHO' 'NUFF!-HAIN'T IT TH' TRUTH!-TEE-HEE!

LI'L ABNER The Helpless Hand! By Al Capp

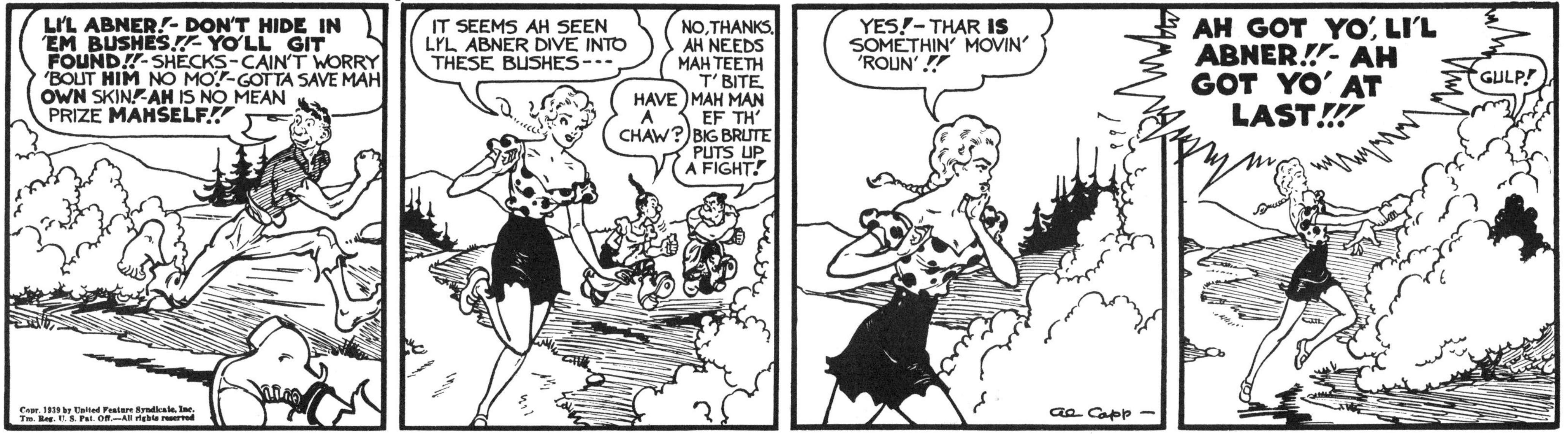

LI'L ABNER!-DON'T HIDE IN 'EM BUSHES!!-YO'LL GIT FOUND!!-SHECKS-CAIN'T WORRY 'BOUT HIM NO MO'!-GOTTA SAVE MAH OWN SKIN!-AH IS NO MEAN PRIZE MAHSELF!!
Copr. 1939 by United Feature Syndicate, Inc. Tm. Reg. U. S. Pat. Off.—All rights reserved
IT SEEMS AH SEEN LI'L ABNER DIVE INTO THESE BUSHES---
HAVE A CHAW?
NO, THANKS. AH NEEDS MAH TEETH T' BITE MAH MAN EF TH' BIG BRUTE PUTS UP A FIGHT!
YES!-THAR IS SOMETHIN' MOVIN' 'ROUN'!!
Al Capp
AH GOT YO', LI'L ABNER!!-AH GOT YO' AT LAST!!!
GULP!

LI'L ABNER It's Safer T' Be a Houn'-Dawg Than a Rabbit! By Al Capp

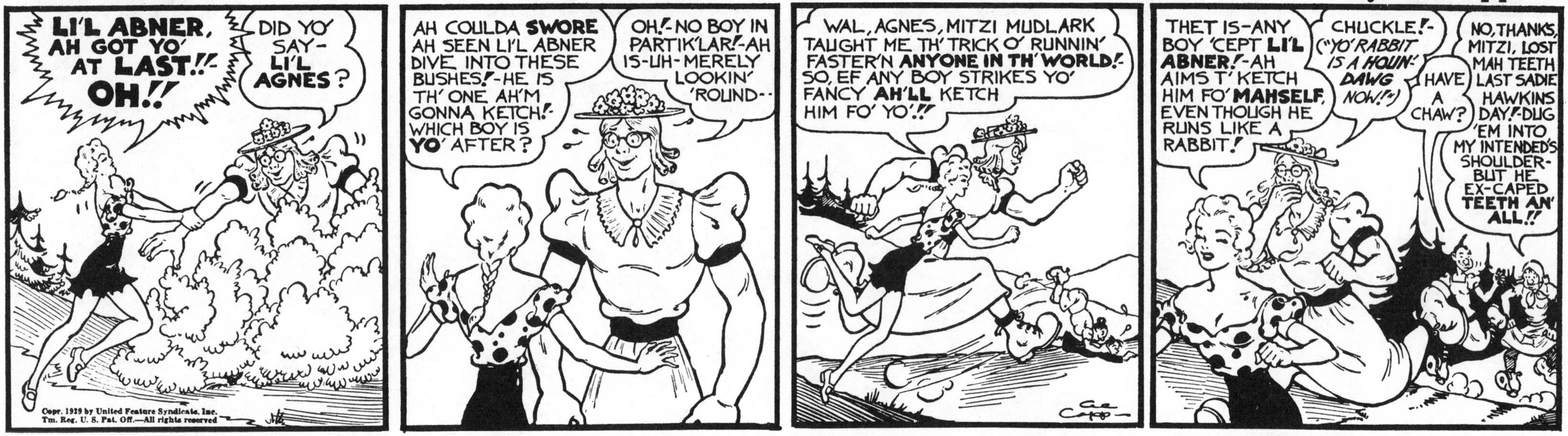

LI'L ABNER, AH GOT YO' AT LAST!!- OH!!
DID YO' SAY- LI'L AGNES?
Copr. 1939 by United Feature Syndicate, Inc. Tm. Reg. U. S. Pat. Off.—All rights reserved
AH COULDA SWORE AH SEEN LI'L ABNER DIVE INTO THESE BUSHES!-HE IS TH' ONE AH'M GONNA KETCH!-WHICH BOY IS YO' AFTER?
OH!-NO BOY IN PARTIK'LAR!-AH IS-UH-MERELY LOOKIN' 'ROUND--
WAL, AGNES, MITZI MUDLARK TAUGHT ME TH' TRICK O' RUNNIN' FASTER'N ANYONE IN TH' WORLD!-SO, EF ANY BOY STRIKES YO' FANCY AH'LL KETCH HIM FO' YO'!!
THET IS-ANY BOY 'CEPT LI'L ABNER!-AH AIMS T' KETCH HIM FO' MAHSELF, EVEN THOUGH HE RUNS LIKE A RABBIT!
CHUCKLE!-("YO' RABBIT IS A HOUN'-DAWG NOW!")
HAVE A CHAW?
NO, THANKS, MITZI, LOST MAH TEETH LAST SADIE HAWKINS DAY!-DUG 'EM INTO MY INTENDED'S SHOULDER-BUT HE EX-CAPED TEETH AN' ALL!!

LI'L ABNER To the Brave Belong the Fair! By Al Capp

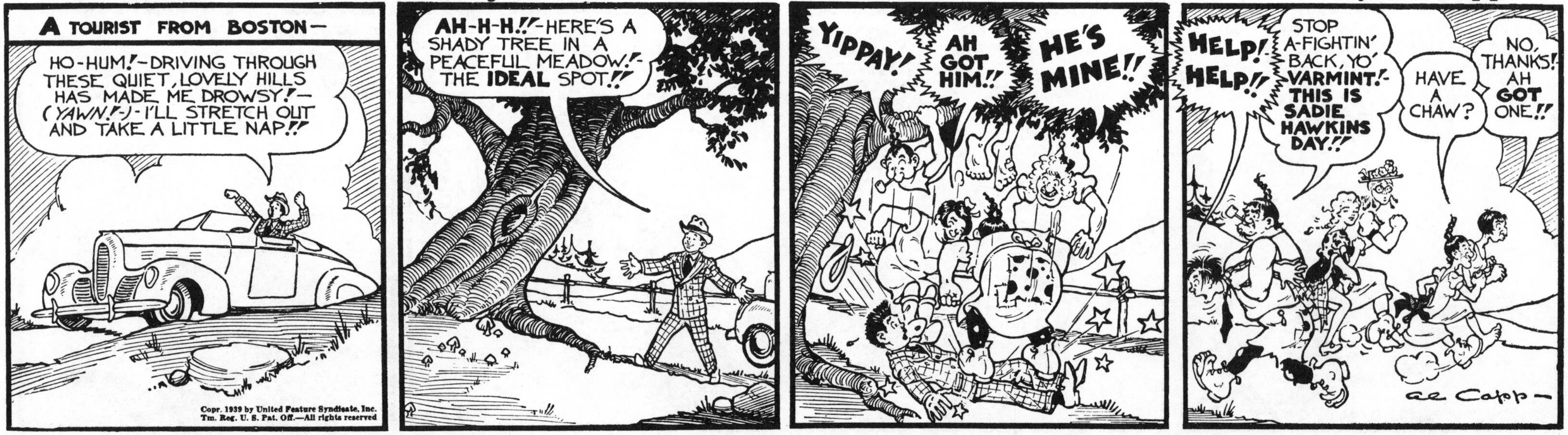

A TOURIST FROM BOSTON—
HO-HUM!-DRIVING THROUGH THESE QUIET, LOVELY HILLS HAS MADE ME DROWSY!-(YAWN!-)-I'LL STRETCH OUT AND TAKE A LITTLE NAP!!
Copr. 1939 by United Feature Syndicate, Inc. Tm. Reg. U. S. Pat. Off.—All rights reserved
AH-H-H!!-HERE'S A SHADY TREE IN A PEACEFUL MEADOW!-THE IDEAL SPOT!!
YIPPAY!
AH GOT HIM!!
HE'S MINE!!
HELP! HELP!!
STOP A-FIGHTIN' BACK, YO' VARMINT!-THIS IS SADIE HAWKINS DAY!!
HAVE A CHAW?
NO, THANKS! AH GOT ONE!!

LI'L ABNER All's Not Fish That Flies! By Al Capp

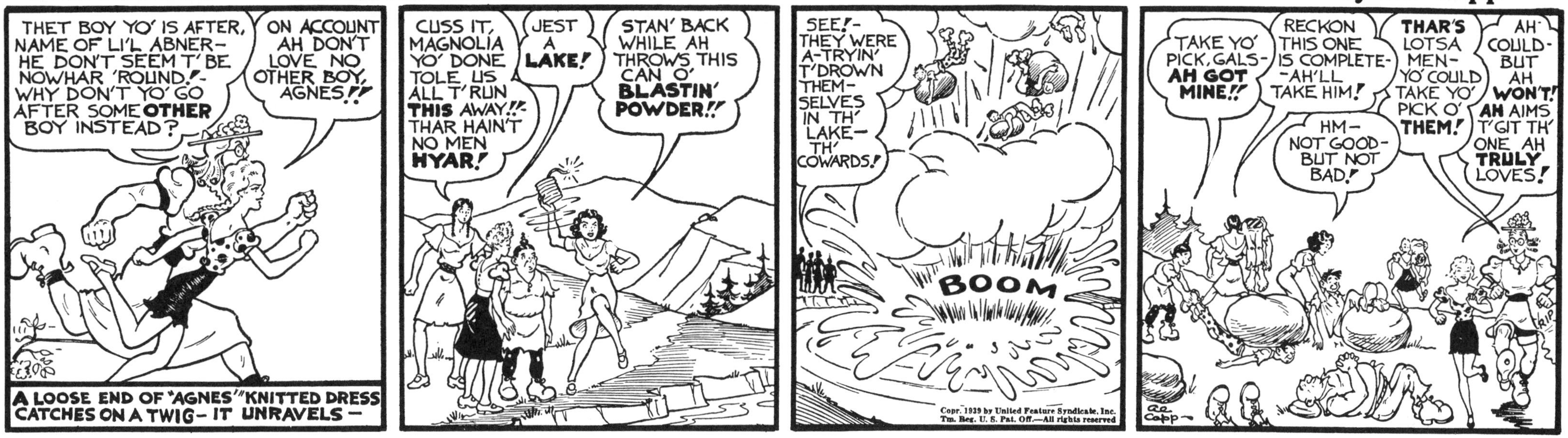

THET BOY YO' IS AFTER, NAME OF LI'L ABNER- HE DON'T SEEM T' BE NOWHAR 'ROUND!- WHY DON'T YO' GO AFTER SOME **OTHER** BOY INSTEAD?
ON ACCOUNT AH DON'T LOVE NO OTHER BOY, AGNES!!
A LOOSE END OF "AGNES'" KNITTED DRESS CATCHES ON A TWIG- IT UNRAVELS-
CUSS IT, MAGNOLIA YO' DONE TOLE US ALL T' RUN **THIS** AWAY!!- THAR HAIN'T NO MEN **HYAR!**
JEST A **LAKE!**
STAN' BACK WHILE AH THROWS THIS CAN O' **BLASTIN' POWDER!!**
SEE!- THEY WERE A-TRYIN' T'DROWN THEM-SELVES IN TH' LAKE- TH' COWARDS!
BOOM
Copr. 1939 by United Feature Syndicate, Inc. Tm. Reg. U. S. Pat. Off.—All rights reserved
TAKE YO' PICK, GALS- **AH GOT MINE!!**
RECKON THIS ONE IS COMPLETE- -AH'LL TAKE HIM!
HM- NOT GOOD- BUT NOT BAD!
THAR'S LOTSA MEN- YO' COULD TAKE YO' PICK O' **THEM!**
AH COULD- BUT AH **WON'T! AH** AIMS T'GIT TH' ONE AH **TRULY** LOVES!
RIP
Al Capp

LI'L ABNER The Truth Exposed! By Al Capp

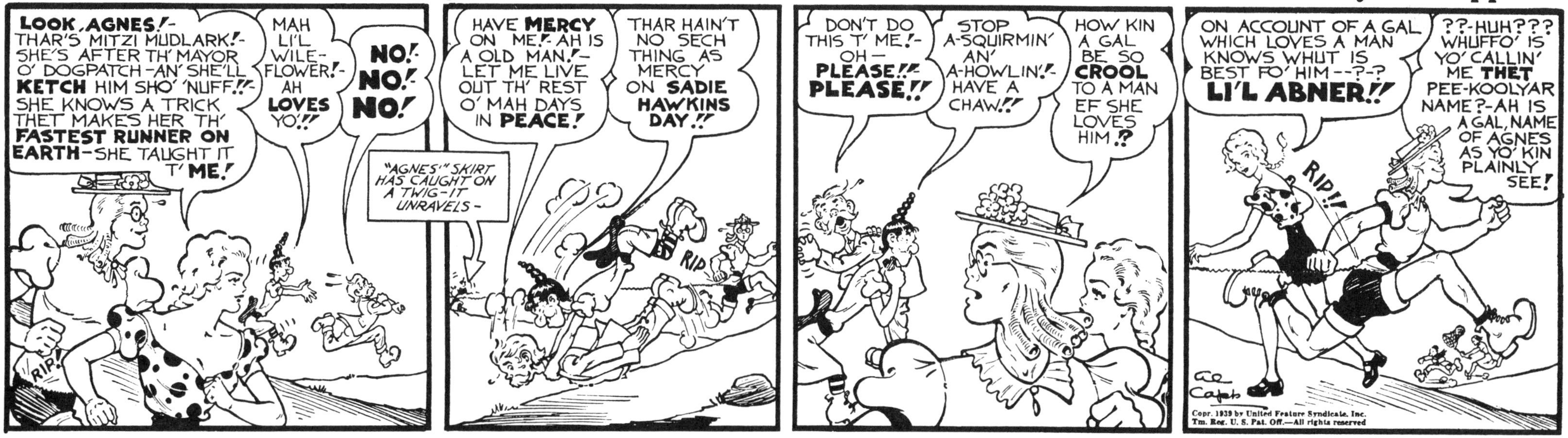

LOOK, AGNES!- THAR'S MITZI MUDLARK!- SHE'S AFTER TH' MAYOR O' DOGPATCH -AN' SHE'LL **KETCH** HIM SHO' 'NUFF!!- SHE KNOWS A TRICK THET MAKES HER TH' **FASTEST RUNNER ON EARTH**-SHE TAUGHT IT T' **ME!**
MAH LI'L WILE-FLOWER!- AH **LOVES** YO'!!
NO!- NO!- NO!
RIP!
"AGNES'" SKIRT HAS CAUGHT ON A TWIG-IT UNRAVELS-
HAVE **MERCY** ON ME!- AH IS A OLD MAN!- LET ME LIVE OUT TH' REST O' MAH DAYS IN **PEACE!**
THAR HAIN'T NO SECH THING AS MERCY ON **SADIE HAWKINS DAY!!**
RIP
DON'T DO THIS T' ME!- OH- **PLEASE!!- PLEASE!!**
STOP A-SQUIRMIN' AN' A-HOWLIN'!- HAVE A CHAW!!
HOW KIN A GAL BE SO **CROOL** TO A MAN EF SHE LOVES HIM?
ON ACCOUNT OF A GAL WHICH LOVES A MAN KNOWS WHUT IS BEST FO' HIM--?-? **LI'L ABNER!!**
??-HUH??? WHUFFO' IS YO' CALLIN' ME **THET** PEE-KOOLYAR NAME?-AH IS A GAL, NAME OF AGNES AS YO' KIN PLAINLY SEE!
RIP!!
Al Capp
Copr. 1939 by United Feature Syndicate, Inc. Tm. Reg. U. S. Pat. Off.—All rights reserved

LI'L ABNER Wal, Fry His Hide! By Al Capp

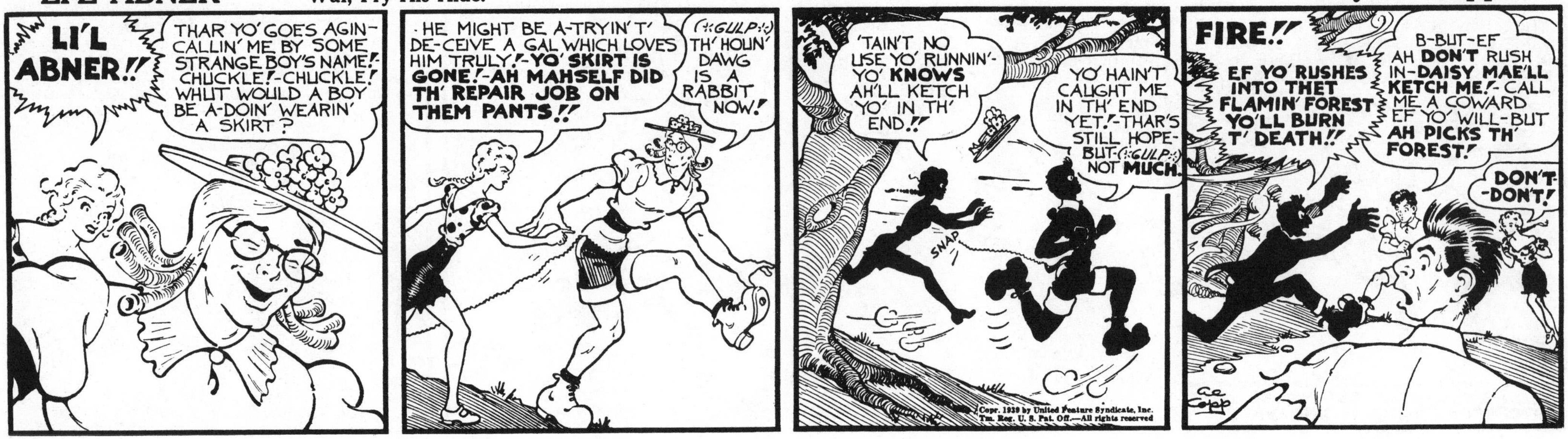
LI'L ABNER!!
THAR YO' GOES AGIN-CALLIN' ME BY SOME STRANGE BOY'S NAME!-CHUCKLE!-CHUCKLE! WHUT WOULD A BOY BE A-DOIN' WEARIN' A SKIRT?
HE MIGHT BE A-TRYIN' T' DE-CEIVE A GAL WHICH LOVES HIM TRULY!-YO' SKIRT IS GONE!-AH MAHSELF DID TH' REPAIR JOB ON THEM PANTS!!
(GULP) TH' HOUN' DAWG IS A RABBIT NOW!
'TAIN'T NO USE YO' RUNNIN'-YO' KNOWS AH'LL KETCH YO' IN TH' END!!
SNAP
YO' HAIN'T CAUGHT ME IN TH' END YET!-THAR'S STILL HOPE-BUT-(GULP) NOT MUCH
Copr. 1939 by United Feature Syndicate, Inc. Tm. Reg. U. S. Pat. Off.—All rights reserved
FIRE!!
EF YO' RUSHES INTO THET FLAMIN' FOREST YO'LL BURN T' DEATH!!
B-BUT-EF AH DON'T RUSH IN-DAISY MAE'LL KETCH ME!-CALL ME A COWARD EF YO' WILL-BUT AH PICKS TH' FOREST!
DON'T-DON'T!
CAPP

LI'L ABNER A Hot Time in the Ole Town Tonight By Al Capp

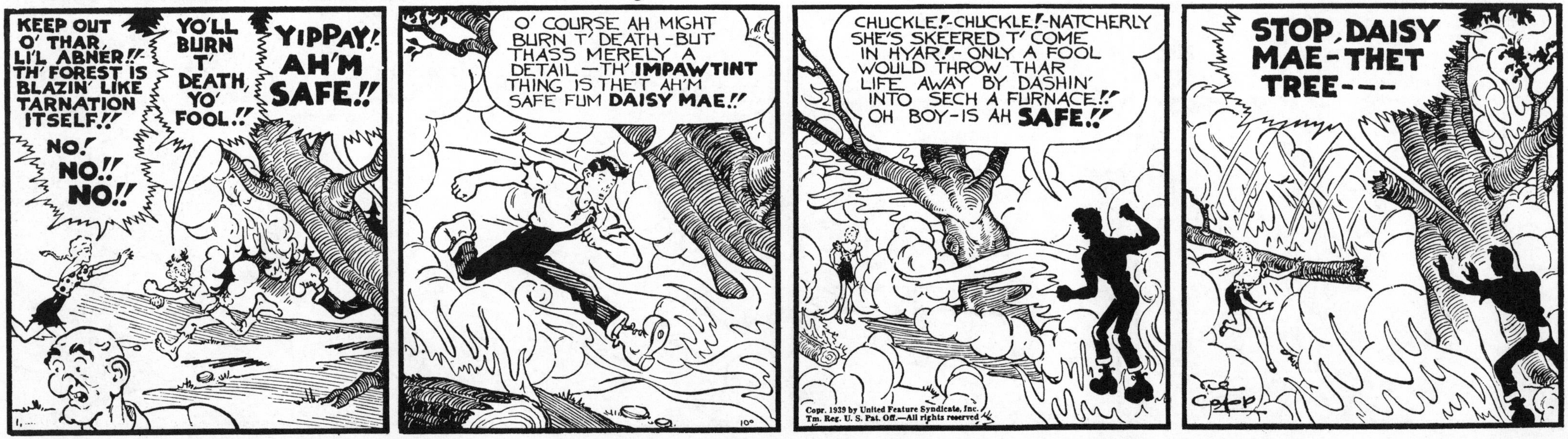
KEEP OUT O' THAR, LI'L ABNER!!-TH' FOREST IS BLAZIN' LIKE TARNATION ITSELF!!
YO'LL BURN T' DEATH, YO' FOOL!!
YIPPAY!-AH'M SAFE!!
NO! NO!! NO!!
O' COURSE AH MIGHT BURN T' DEATH-BUT THASS MERELY A DETAIL-TH' IMPAWTINT THING IS THET AH'M SAFE FUM DAISY MAE!!
CHUCKLE!-CHUCKLE!-NATCHERLY SHE'S SKEERED T' COME IN HYAR!-ONLY A FOOL WOULD THROW THAR LIFE AWAY BY DASHIN' INTO SECH A FURNACE!! OH BOY-IS AH SAFE!!
Copr. 1939 by United Feature Syndicate, Inc. Tm. Reg. U. S. Pat. Off.—All rights reserved
STOP, DAISY MAE-THET TREE---
CAPP

LI'L ABNER The Law of Sadie Hawkins Day! By Al Capp

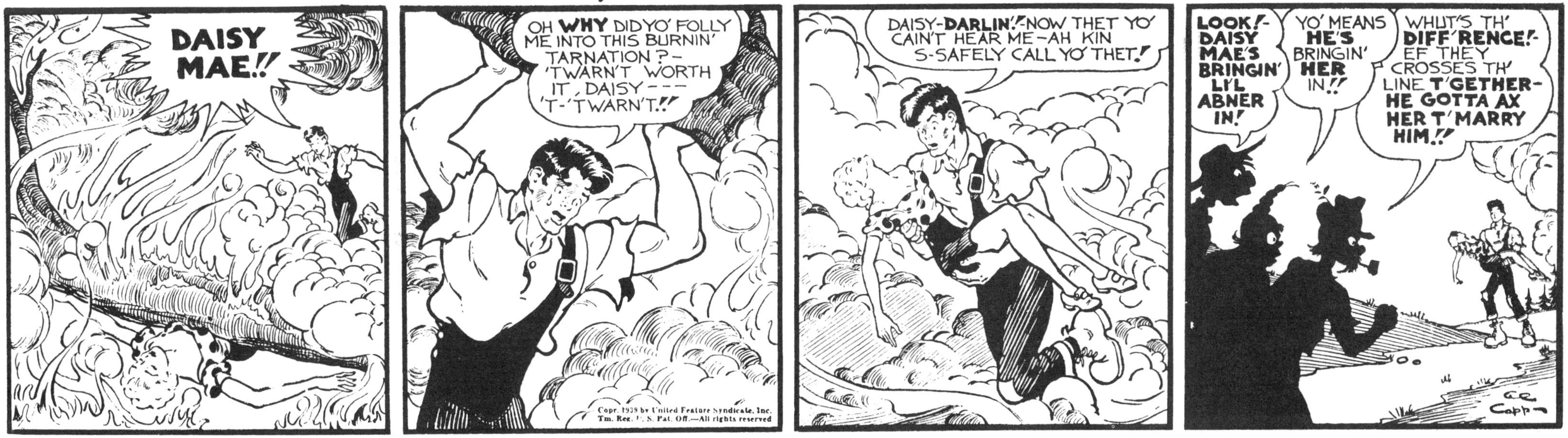
DAISY MAE.!!
OH WHY DID YO' FOLLY ME INTO THIS BURNIN' TARNATION?- 'TWARN'T WORTH IT, DAISY--- 'T-'TWARN'T.!!
Copr. 1939 by United Feature Syndicate, Inc. Tm. Reg. U. S. Pat. Off.—All rights reserved
DAISY-DARLIN'!-NOW THET YO' CAIN'T HEAR ME-AH KIN S-SAFELY CALL YO' THET!
LOOK!-DAISY MAE'S BRINGIN' LI'L ABNER IN!
YO' MEANS HE'S BRINGIN' HER IN!!
WHUT'S TH' DIFF'RENCE!-EF THEY CROSSES TH' LINE T'GETHER-HE GOTTA AX HER T'MARRY HIM.!!
Capp

LI'L ABNER Marryin' Sam Rides Again By Al Capp

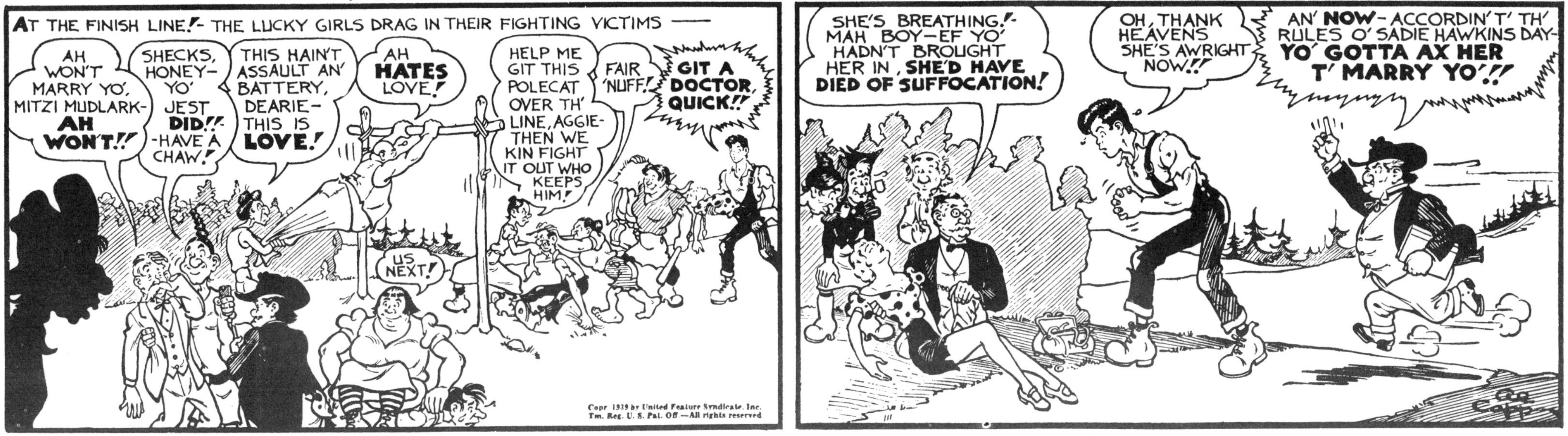
AT THE FINISH LINE!- THE LUCKY GIRLS DRAG IN THEIR FIGHTING VICTIMS ——
AH WON'T MARRY YO', MITZI MUDLARK-AH WON'T!!
SHECKS, HONEY-YO' JEST DID!!-HAVE A CHAW!
THIS HAIN'T ASSAULT AN' BATTERY, DEARIE-THIS IS LOVE!
AH HATES LOVE!
HELP ME GIT THIS POLECAT OVER TH' LINE, AGGIE-THEN WE KIN FIGHT IT OUT WHO KEEPS HIM!
FAIR 'NUFF!
GIT A DOCTOR, QUICK!!
US NEXT!
Copr. 1939 by United Feature Syndicate, Inc. Tm. Reg. U. S. Pat. Off.—All rights reserved
SHE'S BREATHING!-MAH BOY-EF YO' HADN'T BROUGHT HER IN, SHE'D HAVE DIED OF SUFFOCATION!
OH, THANK HEAVENS SHE'S AWRIGHT NOW!!
AN' NOW-ACCORDIN' T' TH' RULES O' SADIE HAWKINS DAY-YO' GOTTA AX HER T' MARRY YO'!!
Capp

LI'L ABNER To the Victim Belongs the Spoiled! **By Al Capp**

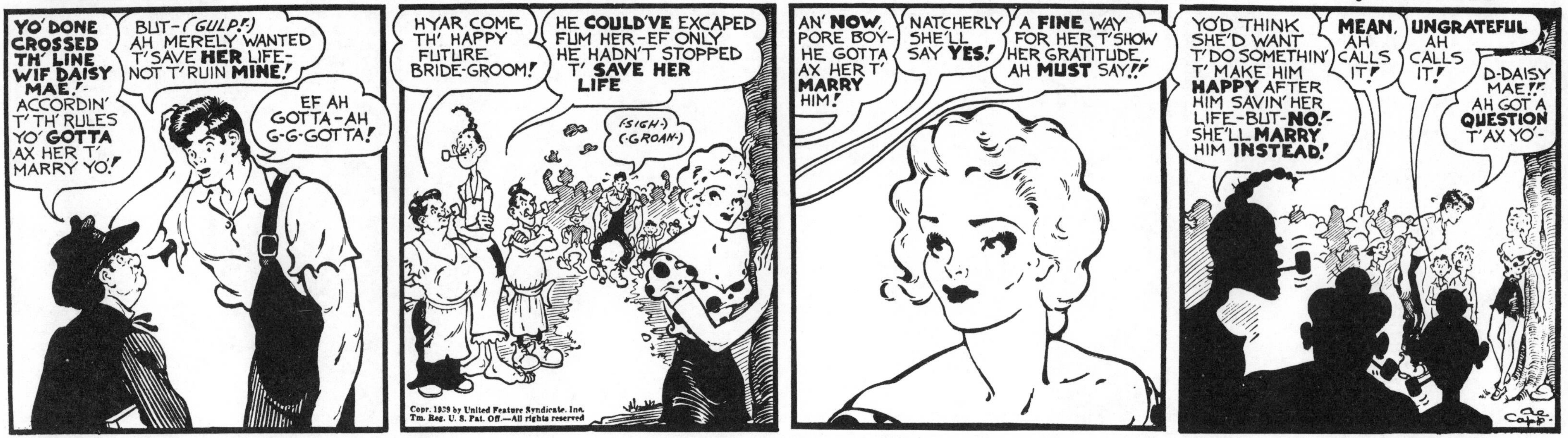

YO' DONE CROSSED TH' LINE WIF DAISY MAE!- ACCORDIN' T' TH' RULES YO' GOTTA AX HER T' MARRY YO'!
BUT-(GULP!-) AH MERELY WANTED T' SAVE HER LIFE- NOT T' RUIN MINE!
EF AH GOTTA-AH G-G-GOTTA!
HYAR COME TH' HAPPY FUTURE BRIDE-GROOM!
HE COULD'VE EXCAPED FUM HER-EF ONLY HE HADN'T STOPPED T' SAVE HER LIFE
(-SIGH-) (-GROAN-)
Copr. 1939 by United Feature Syndicate, Inc. Tm. Reg. U. S. Pat. Off.—All rights reserved
AN' NOW, PORE BOY- HE GOTTA AX HER T' MARRY HIM!
NATCHERLY SHE'LL SAY YES!
A FINE WAY FOR HER T'SHOW HER GRATITUDE, AH MUST SAY!!
YO'D THINK SHE'D WANT T'DO SOMETHIN' T' MAKE HIM HAPPY AFTER HIM SAVIN' HER LIFE-BUT-NO!- SHE'LL MARRY HIM INSTEAD!
MEAN, AH CALLS IT!
UNGRATEFUL AH CALLS IT!
D-DAISY MAE!!- AH GOT A QUESTION T'AX YO'-
Al Capp

LI'L ABNER Thanks for the Memory! **By Al Capp**

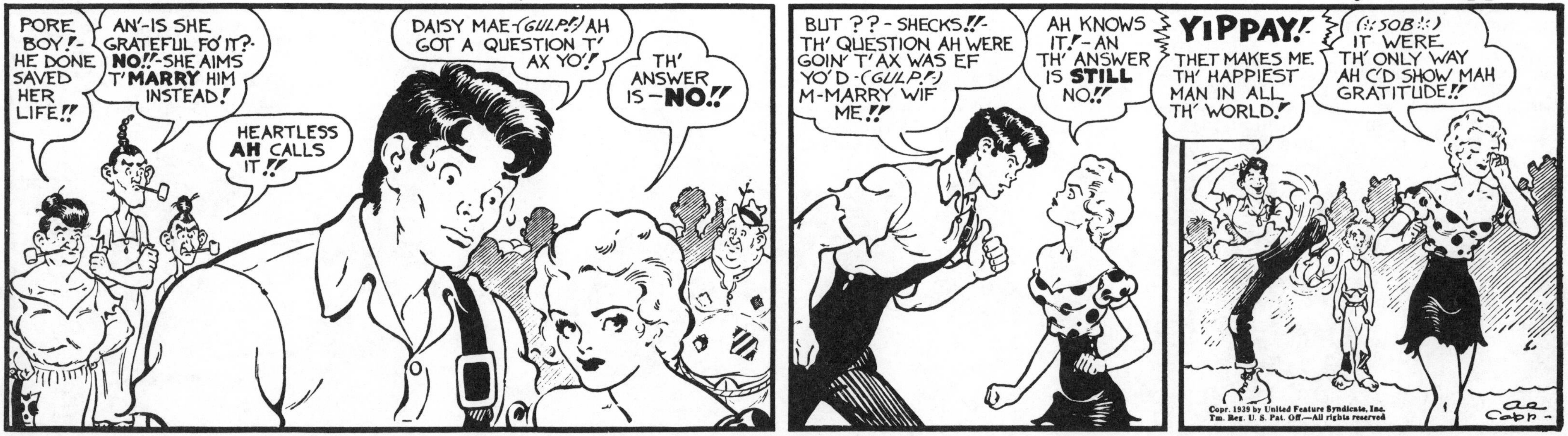

PORE BOY!- HE DONE SAVED HER LIFE!!
AN'-IS SHE GRATEFUL FO' IT?- NO!!-SHE AIMS T' MARRY HIM INSTEAD!
HEARTLESS AH CALLS IT!!
DAISY MAE-(GULP!-) AH GOT A QUESTION T' AX YO'!
TH' ANSWER IS—NO!!
BUT ??- SHECKS!!- TH' QUESTION AH WERE GOIN' T'AX WAS EF YO'D-(GULP!-) M-MARRY WIF ME!!
AH KNOWS IT!-AN TH' ANSWER IS STILL NO!!
YIPPAY!! THET MAKES ME TH' HAPPIEST MAN IN ALL TH' WORLD!
(SOB) IT WERE TH' ONLY WAY AH C'D SHOW MAH GRATITUDE!!
Copr. 1939 by United Feature Syndicate, Inc. Tm. Reg. U. S. Pat. Off.—All rights reserved
Al Capp

LI'L ABNER In the Bag! By Al Capp

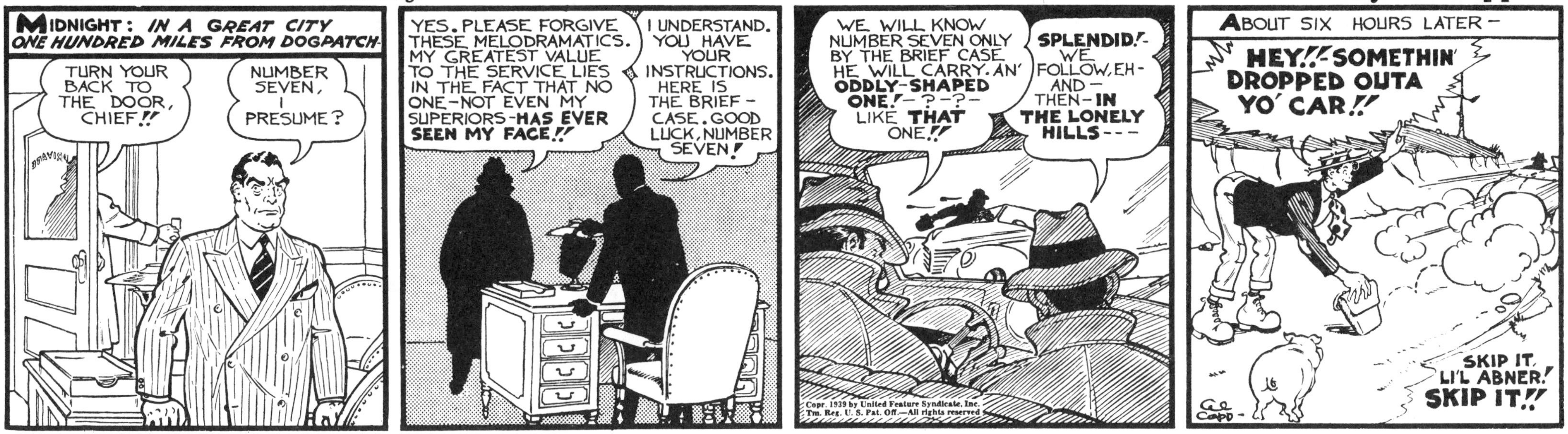

MIDNIGHT: IN A GREAT CITY ONE HUNDRED MILES FROM DOGPATCH-
TURN YOUR BACK TO THE DOOR, CHIEF!!
NUMBER SEVEN, I PRESUME?
YES. PLEASE FORGIVE THESE MELODRAMATICS. MY GREATEST VALUE TO THE SERVICE LIES IN THE FACT THAT NO ONE-NOT EVEN MY SUPERIORS-HAS EVER SEEN MY FACE!!
I UNDERSTAND. YOU HAVE YOUR INSTRUCTIONS. HERE IS THE BRIEF-CASE. GOOD LUCK, NUMBER SEVEN!
WE WILL KNOW NUMBER SEVEN ONLY BY THE BRIEF CASE HE WILL CARRY. AN' ODDLY-SHAPED ONE!-?-?- LIKE THAT ONE!!
SPLENDID!- WE FOLLOW, EH- AND- THEN-IN THE LONELY HILLS---
Copr. 1939 by United Feature Syndicate, Inc. Tm. Reg. U. S. Pat. Off.—All rights reserved
ABOUT SIX HOURS LATER-
HEY!!-SOMETHIN' DROPPED OUTA YO' CAR!!
SKIP IT, LI'L ABNER! SKIP IT!!

LI'L ABNER Lucky Seven! By Al Capp

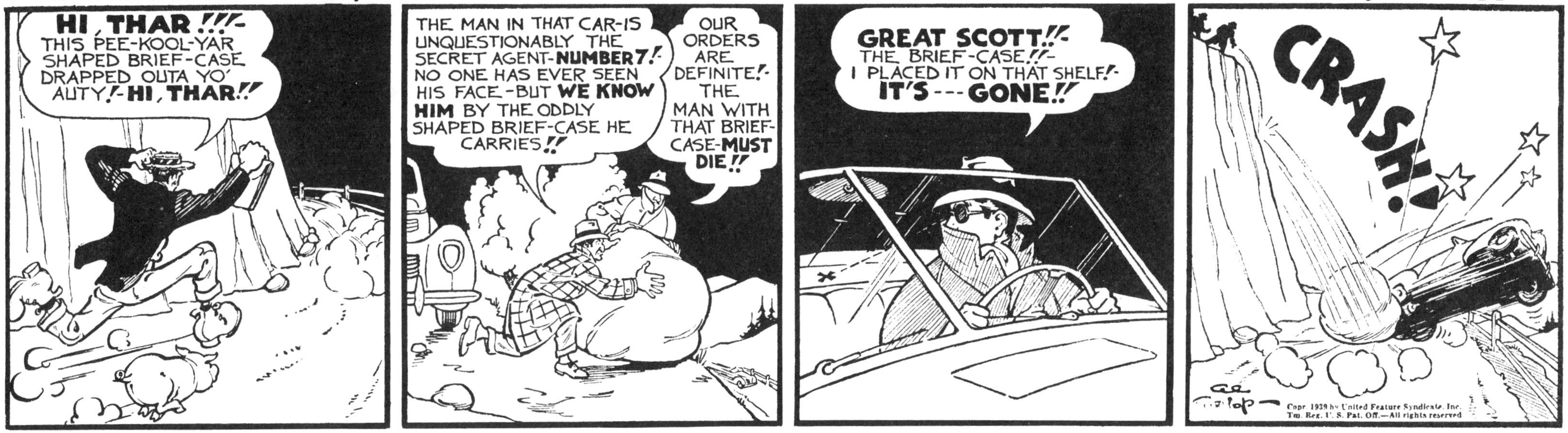

HI, THAR!!!- THIS PEE-KOOL-YAR SHAPED BRIEF-CASE DRAPPED OUTA YO' AUTY!-HI, THAR!!
THE MAN IN THAT CAR-IS UNQUESTIONABLY THE SECRET AGENT-NUMBER 7!- NO ONE HAS EVER SEEN HIS FACE-BUT WE KNOW HIM BY THE ODDLY SHAPED BRIEF-CASE HE CARRIES!!
OUR ORDERS ARE DEFINITE!- THE MAN WITH THAT BRIEF-CASE-MUST DIE!!
GREAT SCOTT!!- THE BRIEF-CASE!!- I PLACED IT ON THAT SHELF!- IT'S---GONE!!
CRASH!
Copr. 1939 by United Feature Syndicate, Inc. Tm. Reg. U. S. Pat. Off.—All rights reserved

LI'L ABNER Salomey Knows Best **By Al Capp**

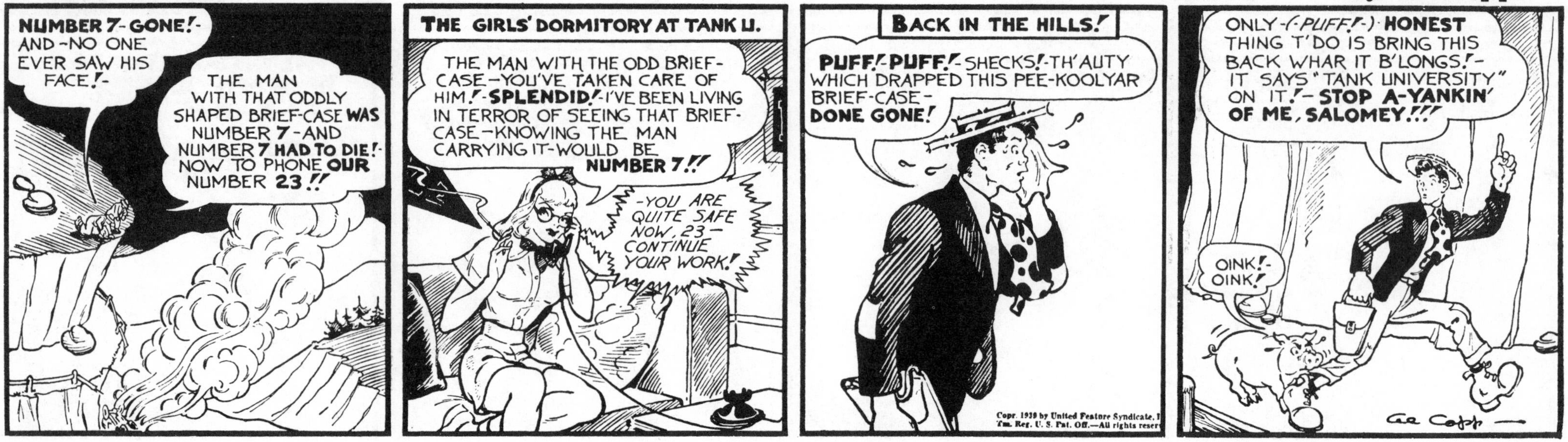

NUMBER 7-GONE!-AND-NO ONE EVER SAW HIS FACE!-
THE MAN WITH THAT ODDLY SHAPED BRIEF-CASE WAS NUMBER 7-AND NUMBER 7 HAD TO DIE!-NOW TO PHONE OUR NUMBER 23!!
THE GIRLS' DORMITORY AT TANK U.
THE MAN WITH THE ODD BRIEF-CASE-YOU'VE TAKEN CARE OF HIM!-SPLENDID!-I'VE BEEN LIVING IN TERROR OF SEEING THAT BRIEF-CASE-KNOWING THE MAN CARRYING IT-WOULD BE NUMBER 7!!
-YOU ARE QUITE SAFE NOW, 23-CONTINUE YOUR WORK!
BACK IN THE HILLS!
PUFF!-PUFF!-SHECKS!-TH' AUTY WHICH DRAPPED THIS PEE-KOOLYAR BRIEF-CASE-DONE GONE!
Copr. 1939 by United Feature Syndicate, I
Tm. Reg. U. S. Pat. Off.—All rights reserv
ONLY-(-PUFF!-)-HONEST THING T'DO IS BRING THIS BACK WHAR IT B'LONGS!-IT SAYS "TANK UNIVERSITY" ON IT!-STOP A-YANKIN' OF ME, SALOMEY!!!
OINK!-OINK!
Al Capp

LI'L ABNER Turn Back, Son—Turn Back! **By Al Capp**

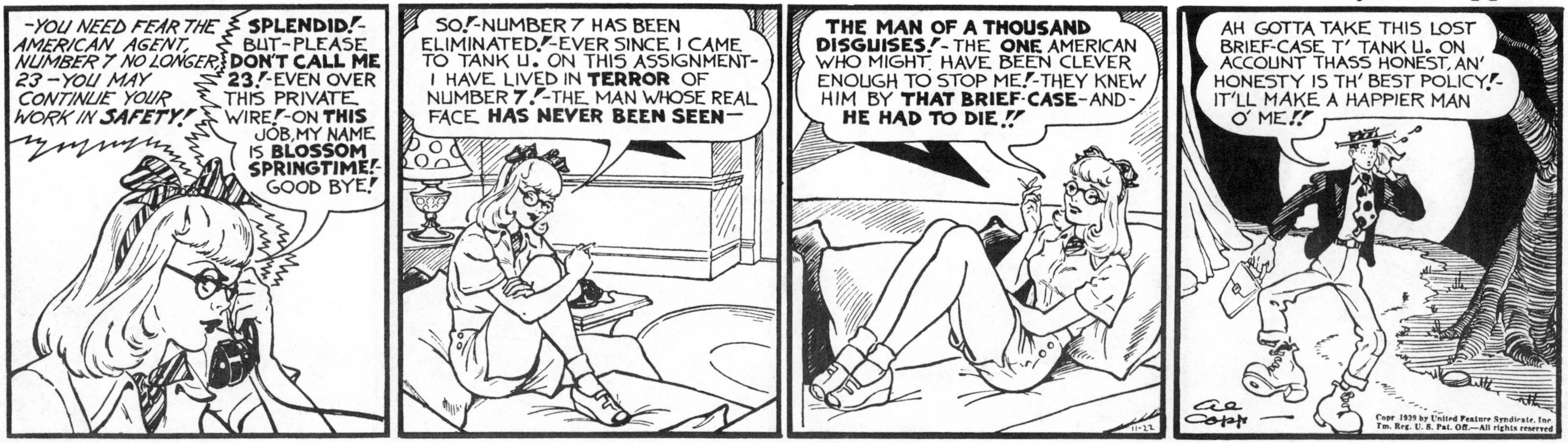

-YOU NEED FEAR THE AMERICAN AGENT, NUMBER 7 NO LONGER, 23-YOU MAY CONTINUE YOUR WORK IN SAFETY!
SPLENDID!-BUT-PLEASE DON'T CALL ME 23!-EVEN OVER THIS PRIVATE WIRE!-ON THIS JOB, MY NAME IS BLOSSOM SPRINGTIME!-GOOD BYE!
SO!-NUMBER 7 HAS BEEN ELIMINATED!-EVER SINCE I CAME TO TANK U. ON THIS ASSIGNMENT-I HAVE LIVED IN TERROR OF NUMBER 7!-THE MAN WHOSE REAL FACE HAS NEVER BEEN SEEN-
THE MAN OF A THOUSAND DISGUISES!-THE ONE AMERICAN WHO MIGHT HAVE BEEN CLEVER ENOUGH TO STOP ME!-THEY KNEW HIM BY THAT BRIEF-CASE-AND-HE HAD TO DIE!!
11-22
AH GOTTA TAKE THIS LOST BRIEF-CASE T' TANK U. ON ACCOUNT THASS HONEST, AN' HONESTY IS TH' BEST POLICY!-IT'LL MAKE A HAPPIER MAN O' ME!!
Al Capp
Copr 1939 by United Feature Syndicate, Inc
Tm. Reg. U. S. Pat. Off.—All rights reserved

LI'L ABNER Greetings, Brain! By Al Capp

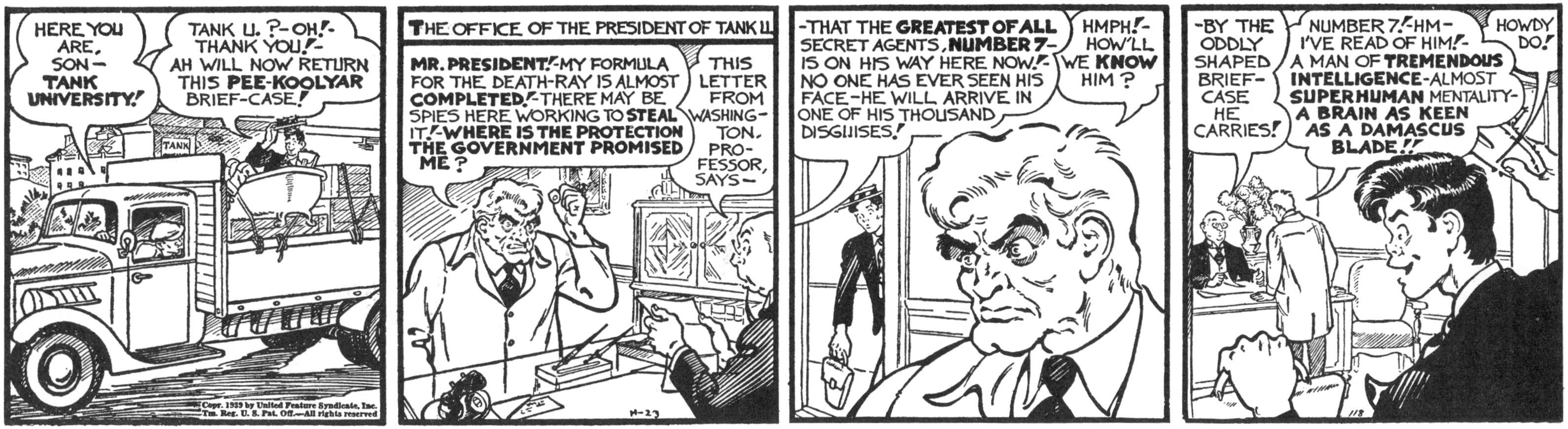
HERE YOU ARE, SON - TANK UNIVERSITY!
TANK U.?-OH!-THANK YOU!-AH WILL NOW RETURN THIS PEE-KOOLYAR BRIEF-CASE!
TANK
Copr. 1939 by United Feature Syndicate, Inc. Tm. Reg. U. S. Pat. Off.—All rights reserved
THE OFFICE OF THE PRESIDENT OF TANK U.
MR. PRESIDENT!-MY FORMULA FOR THE DEATH-RAY IS ALMOST COMPLETED!-THERE MAY BE SPIES HERE WORKING TO STEAL IT!-WHERE IS THE PROTECTION THE GOVERNMENT PROMISED ME?
THIS LETTER FROM WASHINGTON, PROFESSOR, SAYS-
-THAT THE GREATEST OF ALL SECRET AGENTS, NUMBER 7-IS ON HIS WAY HERE NOW!-NO ONE HAS EVER SEEN HIS FACE-HE WILL ARRIVE IN ONE OF HIS THOUSAND DISGUISES!
HMPH!-HOW'LL WE KNOW HIM?
-BY THE ODDLY SHAPED BRIEF-CASE HE CARRIES!
NUMBER 7!-HM-I'VE READ OF HIM!-A MAN OF TREMENDOUS INTELLIGENCE-ALMOST SUPERHUMAN MENTALITY-A BRAIN AS KEEN AS A DAMASCUS BLADE!!
HOWDY DO!

LI'L ABNER Ain't Nature Wonderful! By Al Capp

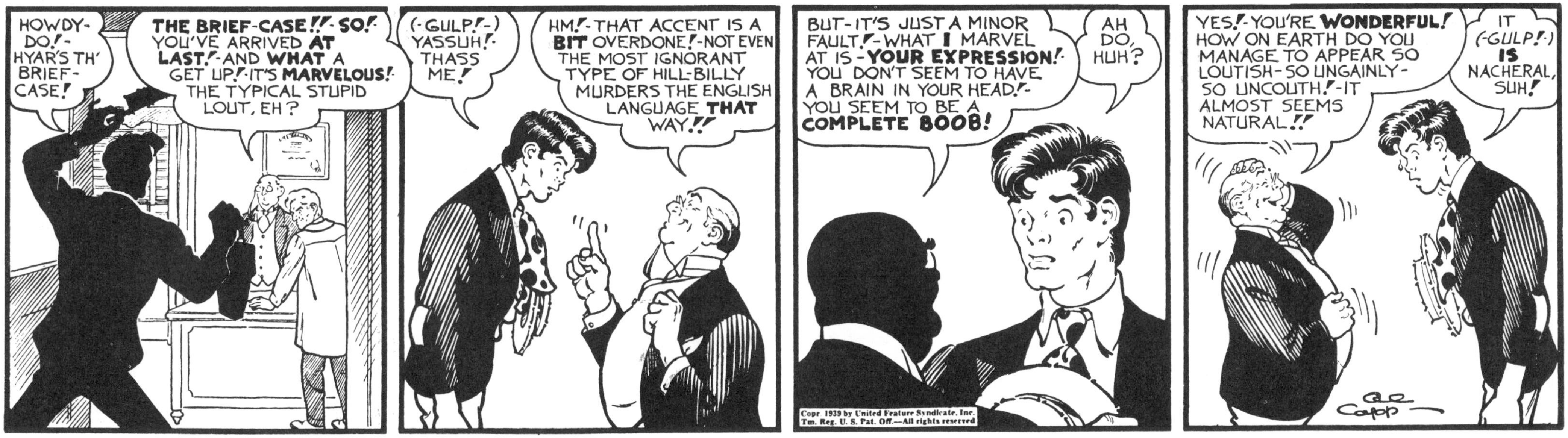
HOWDY-DO!-HYAR'S TH' BRIEF-CASE!
THE BRIEF-CASE!!-SO!-YOU'VE ARRIVED AT LAST!-AND WHAT A GET UP!-IT'S MARVELOUS!-THE TYPICAL STUPID LOUT, EH?
(-GULP!-) YASSUH!-THASS ME!
HM!-THAT ACCENT IS A BIT OVERDONE!-NOT EVEN THE MOST IGNORANT TYPE OF HILL-BILLY MURDERS THE ENGLISH LANGUAGE THAT WAY!!
BUT-IT'S JUST A MINOR FAULT!-WHAT I MARVEL AT IS-YOUR EXPRESSION!-YOU DON'T SEEM TO HAVE A BRAIN IN YOUR HEAD!-YOU SEEM TO BE A COMPLETE BOOB!
AH DO, HUH?
Copr. 1939 by United Feature Syndicate, Inc. Tm. Reg. U. S. Pat. Off.—All rights reserved
YES!-YOU'RE WONDERFUL!-HOW ON EARTH DO YOU MANAGE TO APPEAR SO LOUTISH-SO UNGAINLY-SO UNCOUTH!-IT ALMOST SEEMS NATURAL!!
IT (-GULP!-) IS NACHERAL, SUH!
Al Capp

LI'L ABNER Thass Diff'runt! By Al Capp

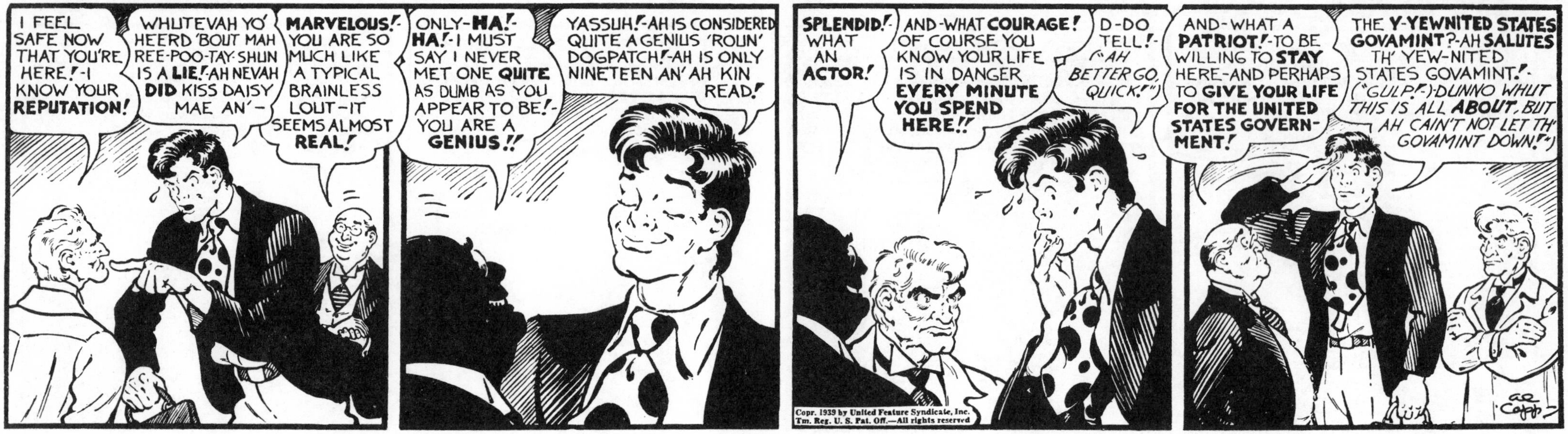

I FEEL SAFE NOW THAT YOU'RE HERE!-I KNOW YOUR REPUTATION!
WHUTEVAH YO' HEERD 'BOUT MAH REE-POO-TAY-SHUN IS A LIE!-AH NEVAH DID KISS DAISY MAE AN'-
MARVELOUS!-YOU ARE SO MUCH LIKE A TYPICAL BRAINLESS LOUT-IT SEEMS ALMOST REAL!
ONLY-HA!-HA!-I MUST SAY I NEVER MET ONE QUITE AS DUMB AS YOU APPEAR TO BE!-YOU ARE A GENIUS!!
YASSUH!-AH IS CONSIDERED QUITE A GENIUS 'ROUN' DOGPATCH!-AH IS ONLY NINETEEN AN' AH KIN READ!
SPLENDID!-WHAT AN ACTOR!
AND-WHAT COURAGE! OF COURSE YOU KNOW YOUR LIFE IS IN DANGER EVERY MINUTE YOU SPEND HERE!!
D-DO TELL!-("AH BETTER GO, QUICK!")
AND-WHAT A PATRIOT!-TO BE WILLING TO STAY HERE-AND PERHAPS TO GIVE YOUR LIFE FOR THE UNITED STATES GOVERNMENT!
THE Y-YEWNITED STATES GOVAMINT?-AH SALUTES TH' YEW-NITED STATES GOVAMINT!-("GULP!-)-DUNNO WHUT THIS IS ALL ABOUT, BUT AH CAIN'T NOT LET TH' GOVAMINT DOWN!")
Copr. 1939 by United Feature Syndicate, Inc. Tm. Reg. U. S. Pat. Off.—All rights reserved

LI'L ABNER The Same Thing Everyone's Laughing At—! By Al Capp

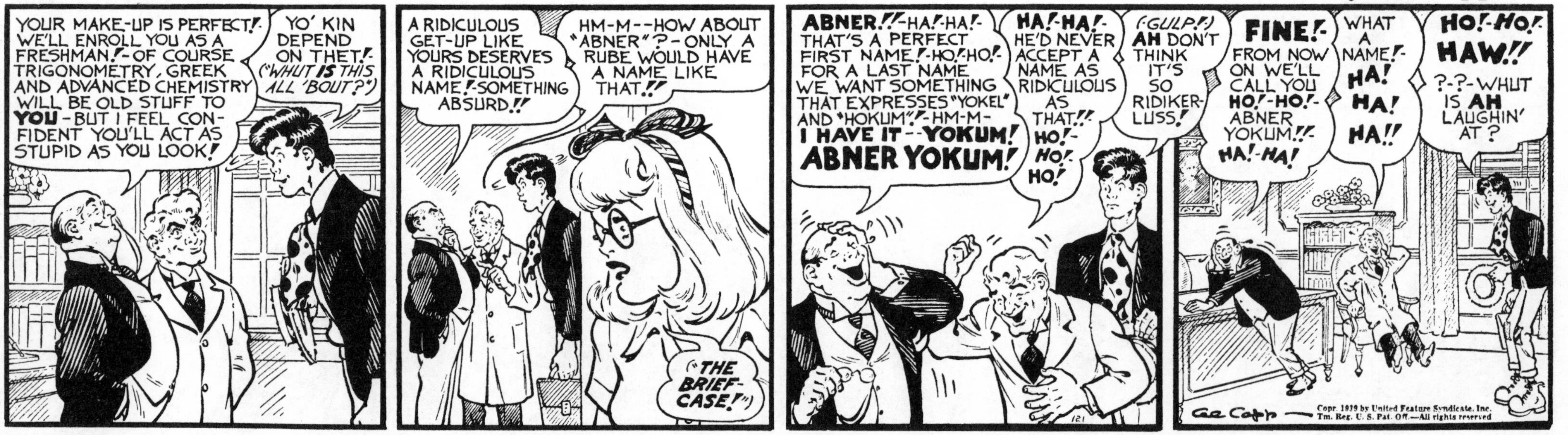

YOUR MAKE-UP IS PERFECT!-WE'LL ENROLL YOU AS A FRESHMAN!-OF COURSE TRIGONOMETRY, GREEK AND ADVANCED CHEMISTRY WILL BE OLD STUFF TO YOU-BUT I FEEL CONFIDENT YOU'LL ACT AS STUPID AS YOU LOOK!
YO' KIN DEPEND ON THET!-("WHUT IS THIS ALL 'BOUT?")
A RIDICULOUS GET-UP LIKE YOURS DESERVES A RIDICULOUS NAME!-SOMETHING ABSURD!!
HM-M--HOW ABOUT "ABNER"?-ONLY A RUBE WOULD HAVE A NAME LIKE THAT!!
("THE BRIEF-CASE!")
ABNER!!-HA!-HA!-THAT'S A PERFECT FIRST NAME!-HO!-HO!-FOR A LAST NAME WE WANT SOMETHING THAT EXPRESSES "YOKEL" AND "HOKUM"!-HM-M-I HAVE IT--YOKUM! ABNER YOKUM!
HA!-HA!-HE'D NEVER ACCEPT A NAME AS RIDICULOUS AS THAT!!-HO!-HO!-HO!
(GULP!) AH DON'T THINK IT'S SO RIDIKERLUSS!
FINE!-FROM NOW ON WE'LL CALL YOU HO!-HO!-ABNER YOKUM!!-HA!-HA!
WHAT A NAME!-HA! HA! HA!!
HO!-HO!-HAW!!
?-?-WHUT IS AH LAUGHIN' AT?
Copr. 1939 by United Feature Syndicate, Inc. Tm. Reg. U. S. Pat. Off.—All rights reserved

LI'L ABNER The Brief Case of the Briefcase! By Al Capp

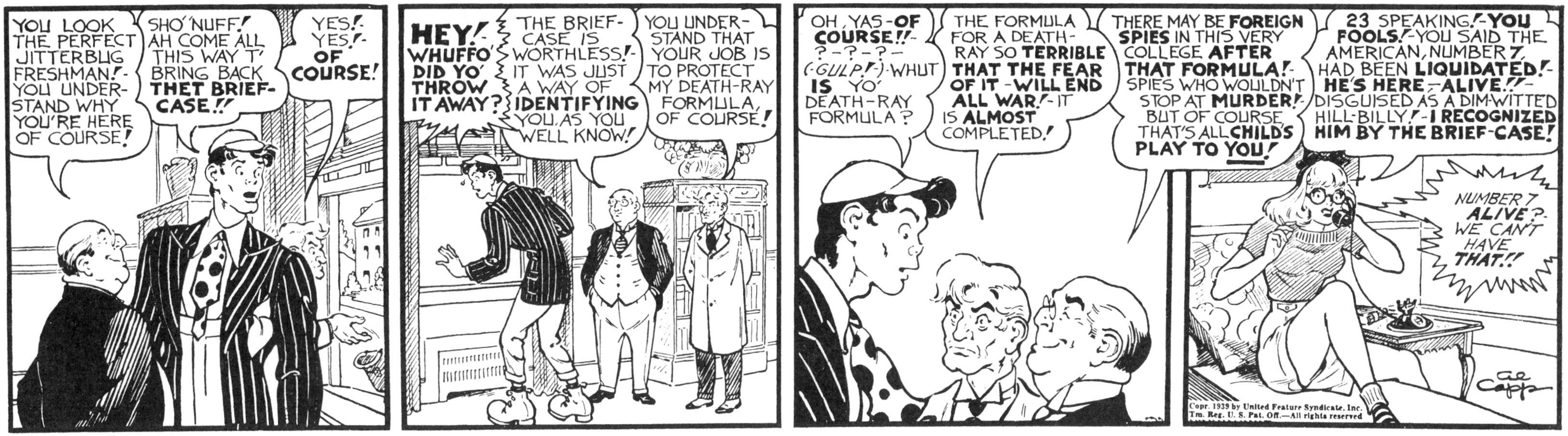
YOU LOOK THE PERFECT JITTERBUG FRESHMAN!- YOU UNDERSTAND WHY YOU'RE HERE OF COURSE!
SHO' NUFF! AH COME ALL THIS WAY T' BRING BACK THET BRIEF-CASE!!
YES!- YES!- OF COURSE!
HEY!- WHUFFO' DID YO' THROW IT AWAY?
THE BRIEF-CASE IS WORTHLESS!- IT WAS JUST A WAY OF IDENTIFYING YOU AS YOU WELL KNOW!
YOU UNDERSTAND THAT YOUR JOB IS TO PROTECT MY DEATH-RAY FORMULA, OF COURSE!
OH, YAS-OF COURSE!!- ?-?-?- (-GULP!-) WHUT IS YO' DEATH-RAY FORMULA?
THE FORMULA FOR A DEATH-RAY SO TERRIBLE THAT THE FEAR OF IT -WILL END ALL WAR!- IT IS ALMOST COMPLETED!
THERE MAY BE FOREIGN SPIES IN THIS VERY COLLEGE AFTER THAT FORMULA!- SPIES WHO WOULDN'T STOP AT MURDER!- BUT OF COURSE THAT'S ALL CHILD'S PLAY TO YOU!
23 SPEAKING!- YOU FOOLS!- YOU SAID THE AMERICAN, NUMBER 7, HAD BEEN LIQUIDATED!- HE'S HERE - ALIVE!!- DISGUISED AS A DIM-WITTED HILL-BILLY!- I RECOGNIZED HIM BY THE BRIEF-CASE!
NUMBER 7 ALIVE?- WE CAN'T HAVE THAT!!
Al Capp
Copr. 1939 by United Feature Syndicate, Inc. Tm. Reg. U. S. Pat. Off.—All rights reserved

LI'L ABNER Confoozed About His Repootayshun! By Al Capp

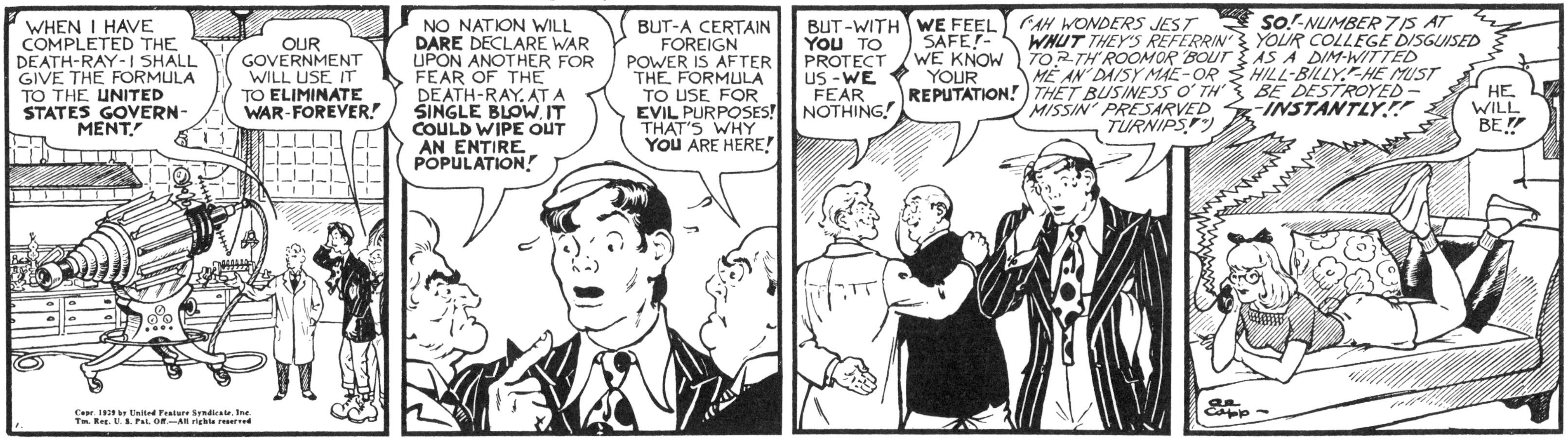
WHEN I HAVE COMPLETED THE DEATH-RAY- I SHALL GIVE THE FORMULA TO THE UNITED STATES GOVERNMENT!
OUR GOVERNMENT WILL USE IT TO ELIMINATE WAR-FOREVER!
Copr. 1939 by United Feature Syndicate, Inc. Tm. Reg. U. S. Pat. Off.—All rights reserved
NO NATION WILL DARE DECLARE WAR UPON ANOTHER FOR FEAR OF THE DEATH-RAY. AT A SINGLE BLOW, IT COULD WIPE OUT AN ENTIRE POPULATION!
BUT-A CERTAIN FOREIGN POWER IS AFTER THE FORMULA TO USE FOR EVIL PURPOSES! THAT'S WHY YOU ARE HERE!
BUT-WITH YOU TO PROTECT US-WE FEAR NOTHING!
WE FEEL SAFE!- WE KNOW YOUR REPUTATION!
("AH WONDERS JEST WHUT THEY'S REFERRIN' TO?-TH' ROOMOR 'BOUT ME AN' DAISY MAE-OR THET BUSINESS O' TH' MISSIN' PRESARVED TURNIPS?")
SO!- NUMBER 7 IS AT YOUR COLLEGE DISGUISED AS A DIM-WITTED HILL-BILLY!- HE MUST BE DESTROYED- -INSTANTLY!!
HE WILL BE!!
Al Capp

LI'L ABNER The Rah-Rah Boys! By Al Capp

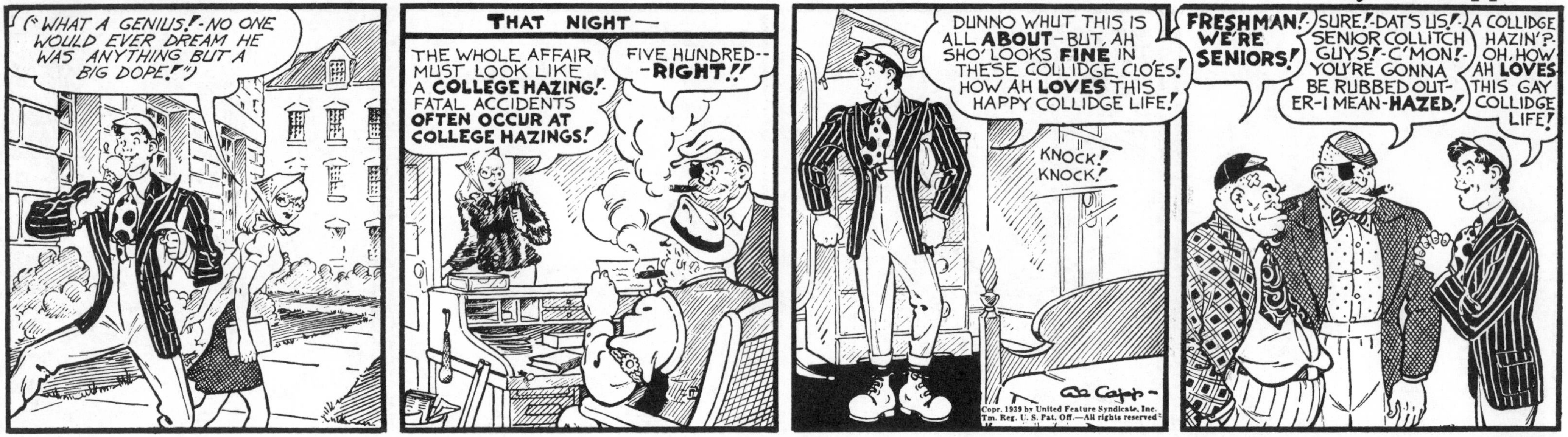
("WHAT A GENIUS!-NO ONE WOULD EVER DREAM HE WAS ANYTHING BUT A BIG DOPE!")
THAT NIGHT—
THE WHOLE AFFAIR MUST LOOK LIKE A COLLEGE HAZING!-FATAL ACCIDENTS OFTEN OCCUR AT COLLEGE HAZINGS!
FIVE HUNDRED--RIGHT!!
DUNNO WHUT THIS IS ALL ABOUT-BUT, AH SHO' LOOKS FINE IN THESE COLLIDGE CLO'ES! HOW AH LOVES THIS HAPPY COLLIDGE LIFE!
KNOCK! KNOCK!
Copr. 1939 by United Feature Syndicate, Inc. Tm. Reg. U. S. Pat. Off.—All rights reserved
FRESHMAN!-WE'RE SENIORS!
SURE!-DAT'S US!-SENIOR COLLITCH GUYS!-C'MON!-YOU'RE GONNA BE RUBBED OUT-ER-I MEAN-HAZED!
A COLLIDGE HAZIN'?-OH, HOW AH LOVES THIS GAY COLLIDGE LIFE!

LI'L ABNER His College Daze By Al Capp

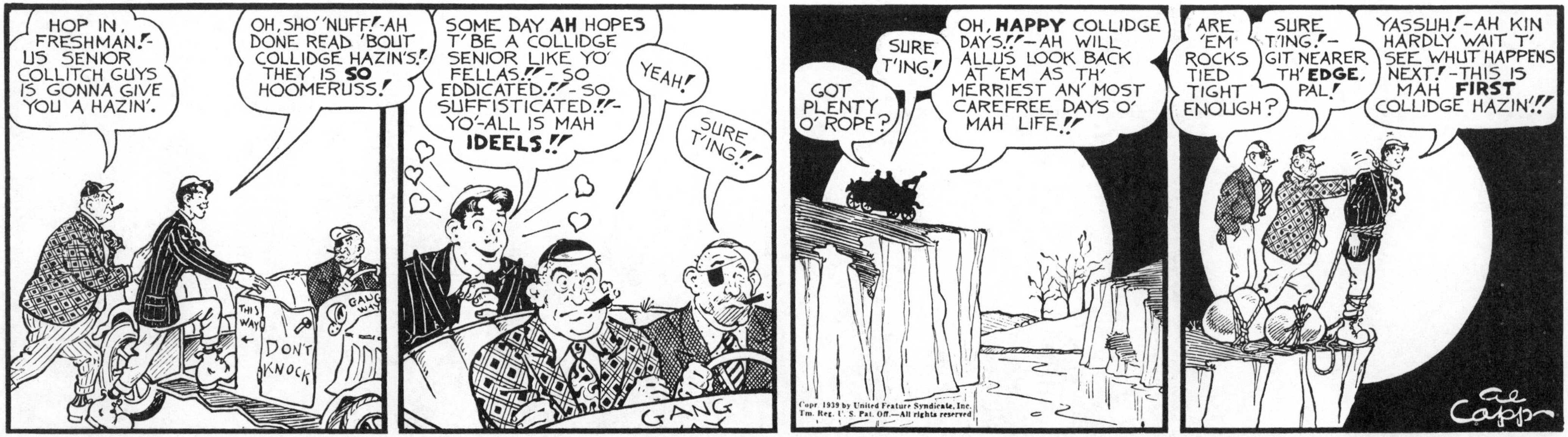
HOP IN, FRESHMAN!-US SENIOR COLLITCH GUYS IS GONNA GIVE YOU A HAZIN'.
OH, SHO' 'NUFF!-AH DONE READ 'BOUT COLLIDGE HAZIN'S!-THEY IS SO HOOMERUSS!
THIS WAY
DON'T KNOCK
SOME DAY AH HOPES T' BE A COLLIDGE SENIOR LIKE YO' FELLAS!!-SO EDDICATED!!-SO SUFFISTICATED!!-YO'-ALL IS MAH IDEELS!!
YEAH!
SURE T'ING!!
GOT PLENTY O' ROPE?
SURE T'ING!
OH, HAPPY COLLIDGE DAYS!!-AH WILL ALLUS LOOK BACK AT 'EM AS TH' MERRIEST AN' MOST CAREFREE DAYS O' MAH LIFE!!
Copr 1939 by United Feature Syndicate, Inc. Tm. Reg. U. S. Pat. Off.—All rights reserved
ARE 'EM ROCKS TIED TIGHT ENOUGH?
SURE T'ING!-GIT NEARER TH' EDGE, PAL!
YASSUH!-AH KIN HARDLY WAIT T' SEE WHUT HAPPENS NEXT!-THIS IS MAH FIRST COLLIDGE HAZIN'!!

LI'L ABNER — Follow the Leader! — By Al Capp

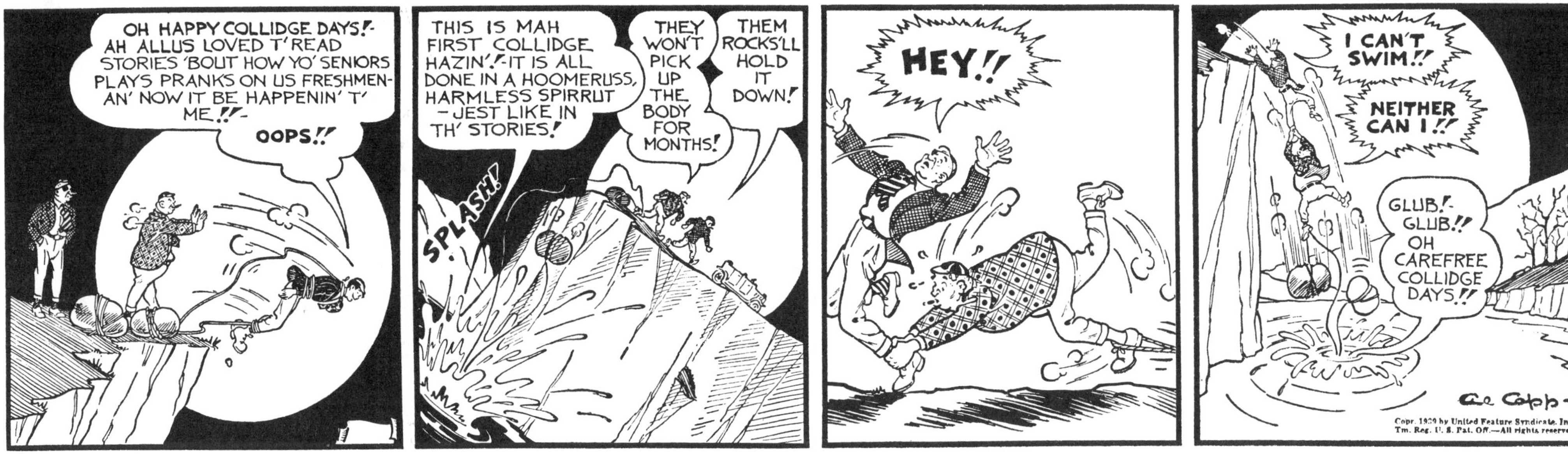
OH HAPPY COLLIDGE DAYS!- AH ALLUS LOVED T' READ STORIES 'BOUT HOW YO' SENIORS PLAYS PRANKS ON US FRESHMEN- AN' NOW IT BE HAPPENIN' T' ME!!-
OOPS!!
SPLASH!
THIS IS MAH FIRST COLLIDGE HAZIN'!-IT IS ALL DONE IN A HOOMERUSS, HARMLESS SPIRRUT -JEST LIKE IN TH' STORIES!
THEY WON'T PICK UP THE BODY FOR MONTHS!
THEM ROCKS'LL HOLD IT DOWN!
HEY!!
I CAN'T SWIM!!
NEITHER CAN I!!
GLUB!- GLUB!! OH CAREFREE COLLIDGE DAYS!!
Al Capp
Copr. 1939 by United Feature Syndicate, Inc.
Tm. Reg. U. S. Pat. Off.—All rights reserved

LI'L ABNER — In Davy Jones' Locker — By Al Capp

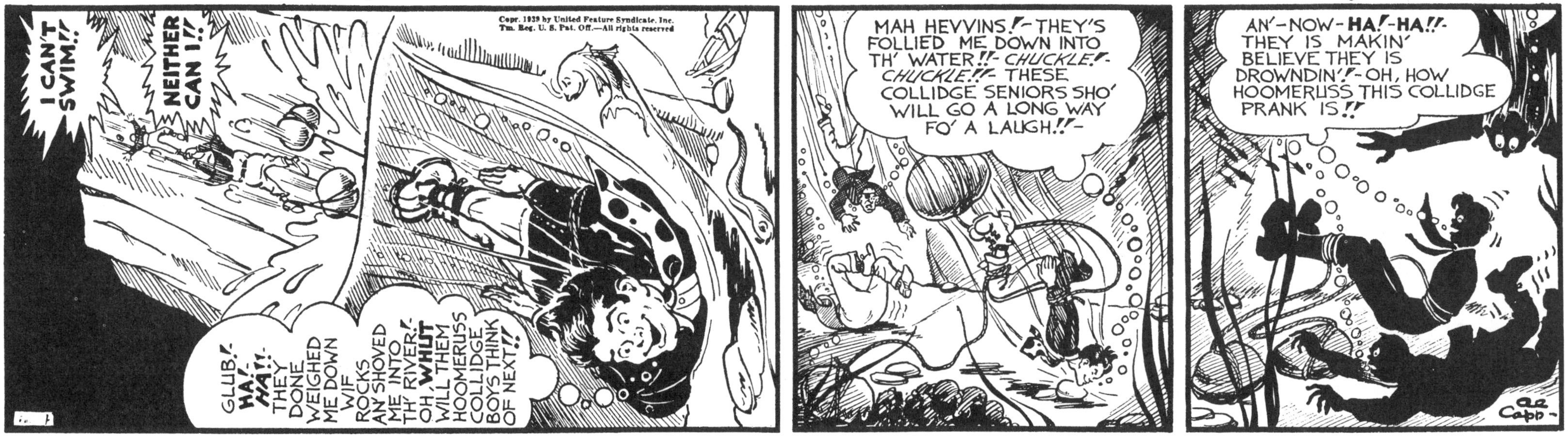
Copr. 1939 by United Feature Syndicate, Inc.
Tm. Reg. U. S. Pat. Off.—All rights reserved
I CAN'T SWIM!!
NEITHER CAN I!!
GLUB!-HA!-HA!!-THEY DONE WEIGHED ME DOWN WIF ROCKS AN' SHOVED ME INTO TH' RIVER!-OH, WHUT WILL THEM HOOMERUSS COLLIDGE BOYS THINK OF NEXT!!
MAH HEVVINS!-THEY'S FOLLIED ME DOWN INTO TH' WATER!!-CHUCKLE!-CHUCKLE!!-THESE COLLIDGE SENIORS SHO' WILL GO A LONG WAY FO' A LAUGH!!-
AN'-NOW-HA!-HA!!-THEY IS MAKIN' BELIEVE THEY IS DROWNDIN'!-OH, HOW HOOMERUSS THIS COLLIDGE PRANK IS!!
Al Capp

LI'L ABNER Who Told Him? By Al Capp

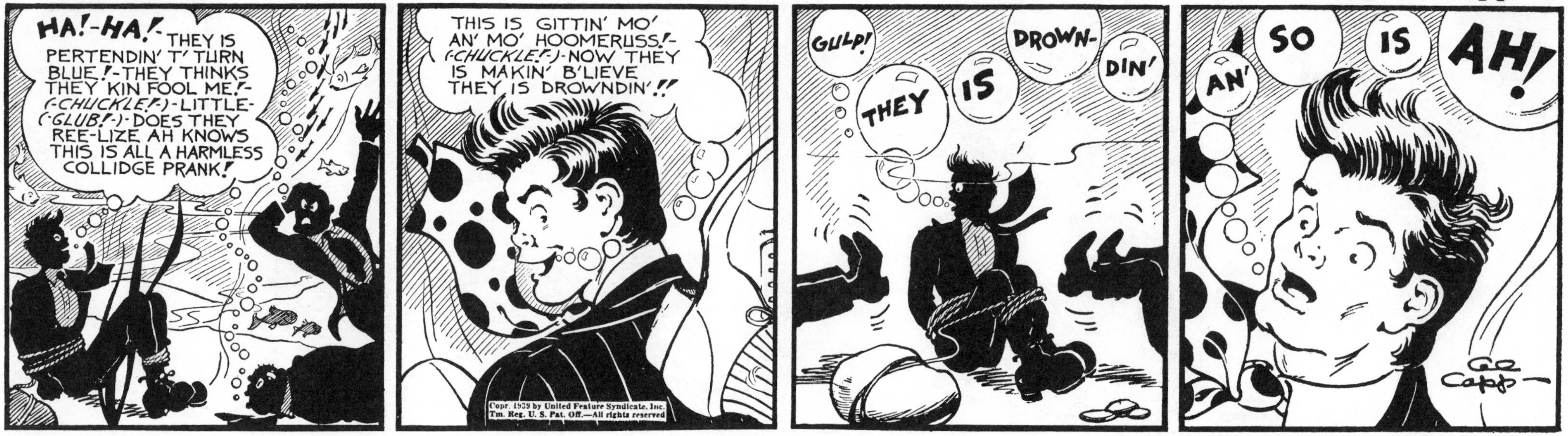

HA!-HA!-THEY IS PERTENDIN' T' TURN BLUE!-THEY THINKS THEY KIN FOOL ME!-(-CHUCKLE!-)-LITTLE-(-GLUB!-)-DOES THEY REE-LIZE AH KNOWS THIS IS ALL A HARMLESS COLLIDGE PRANK!
THIS IS GITTIN' MO' AN' MO' HOOMERUSS!-(-CHUCKLE!-)-NOW THEY IS MAKIN' B'LIEVE THEY IS DROWNDIN'!!
Copr. 1939 by United Feature Syndicate, Inc. Tm. Reg. U. S. Pat. Off.—All rights reserved
GULP!
THEY
IS
DROWN-
DIN'
AN'
SO
IS
AH!
Al Capp

LI'L ABNER Professor—Beware! By Al Capp

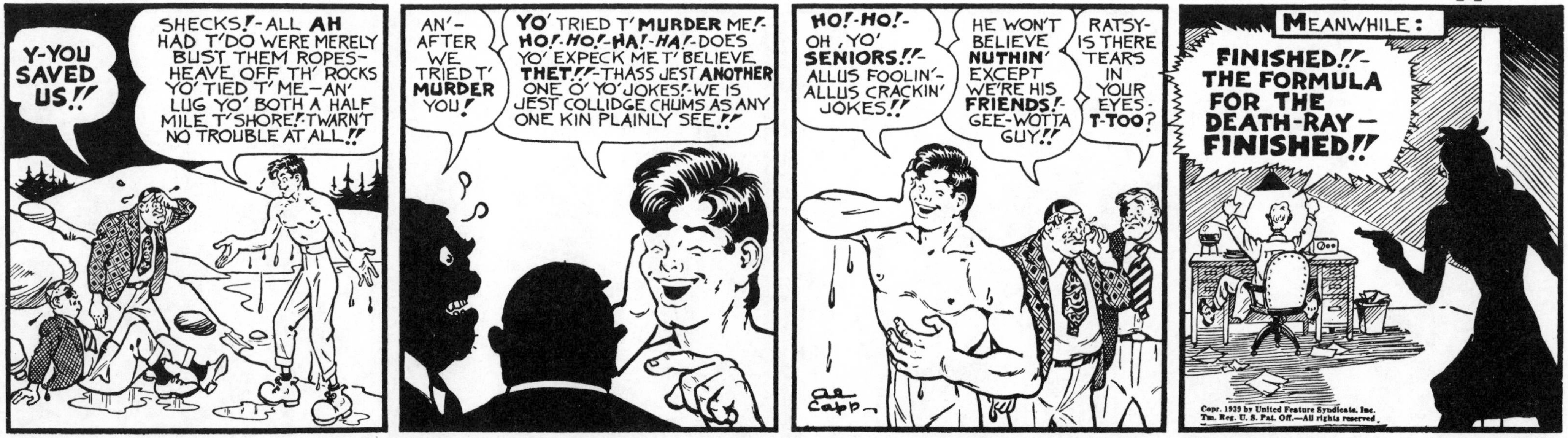

Y-YOU SAVED US!!
SHECKS!-ALL AH HAD T'DO WERE MERELY BUST THEM ROPES-HEAVE OFF TH' ROCKS YO' TIED T' ME-AN' LUG YO' BOTH A HALF MILE T'SHORE!-TWARN'T NO TROUBLE AT ALL!!
AN'-AFTER WE TRIED T' MURDER YOU!
YO' TRIED T' MURDER ME!-HO!-HO!-HA!-HA!-DOES YO' EXPECK ME T' BELIEVE THET!!-THASS JEST ANOTHER ONE O' YO' JOKES!-WE IS JEST COLLIDGE CHUMS AS ANY ONE KIN PLAINLY SEE!!
HO!-HO!-OH, YO' SENIORS!!-ALLUS FOOLIN'-ALLUS CRACKIN' JOKES!!
HE WON'T BELIEVE NUTHIN' EXCEPT WE'RE HIS FRIENDS!-GEE-WOTTA GUY!!
RATSY-IS THERE TEARS IN YOUR EYES-T-TOO?
Al Capp
MEANWHILE:
FINISHED!!-THE FORMULA FOR THE DEATH-RAY-FINISHED!!
Copr. 1939 by United Feature Syndicate, Inc. Tm. Reg. U. S. Pat. Off.—All rights reserved

LI'L ABNER He Is All Brain! By Al Capp

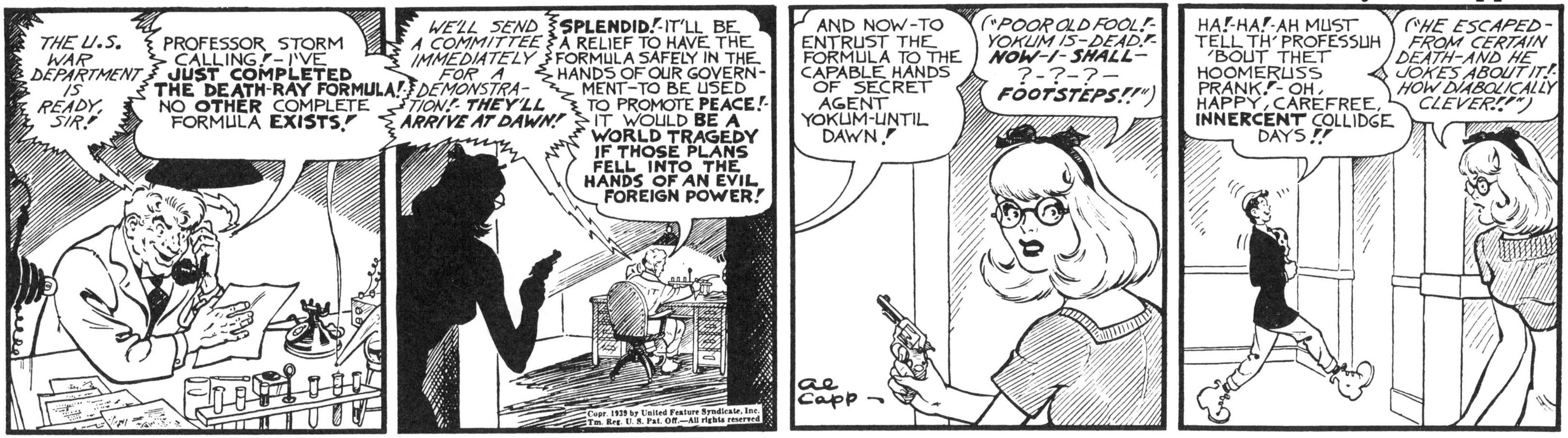
THE U.S. WAR DEPARTMENT IS READY, SIR!
PROFESSOR STORM CALLING!-I'VE JUST COMPLETED THE DEATH-RAY FORMULA!-NO OTHER COMPLETE FORMULA EXISTS!
WE'LL SEND A COMMITTEE IMMEDIATELY FOR A DEMONSTRATION!-THEY'LL ARRIVE AT DAWN!
SPLENDID!-IT'LL BE A RELIEF TO HAVE THE FORMULA SAFELY IN THE HANDS OF OUR GOVERNMENT-TO BE USED TO PROMOTE PEACE!-IT WOULD BE A WORLD TRAGEDY IF THOSE PLANS FELL INTO THE HANDS OF AN EVIL FOREIGN POWER!
Copr. 1939 by United Feature Syndicate, Inc. Tm. Reg. U. S. Pat. Off.—All rights reserved
AND NOW-TO ENTRUST THE FORMULA TO THE CAPABLE HANDS OF SECRET AGENT YOKUM-UNTIL DAWN!
("POOR OLD FOOL!-YOKUM IS-DEAD!-NOW-I-SHALL-?-?-?-FOOTSTEPS!!")
AL CAPP
HA!-HA!-AH MUST TELL TH' PROFESSUH 'BOUT THET HOOMERUSS PRANK!-OH, HAPPY, CAREFREE, INNERCENT COLLIDGE DAYS!!
("HE ESCAPED-FROM CERTAIN DEATH-AND HE JOKES ABOUT IT!-HOW DIABOLICALLY CLEVER!!")

LI'L ABNER Wrong Distance Calling! By Al Capp

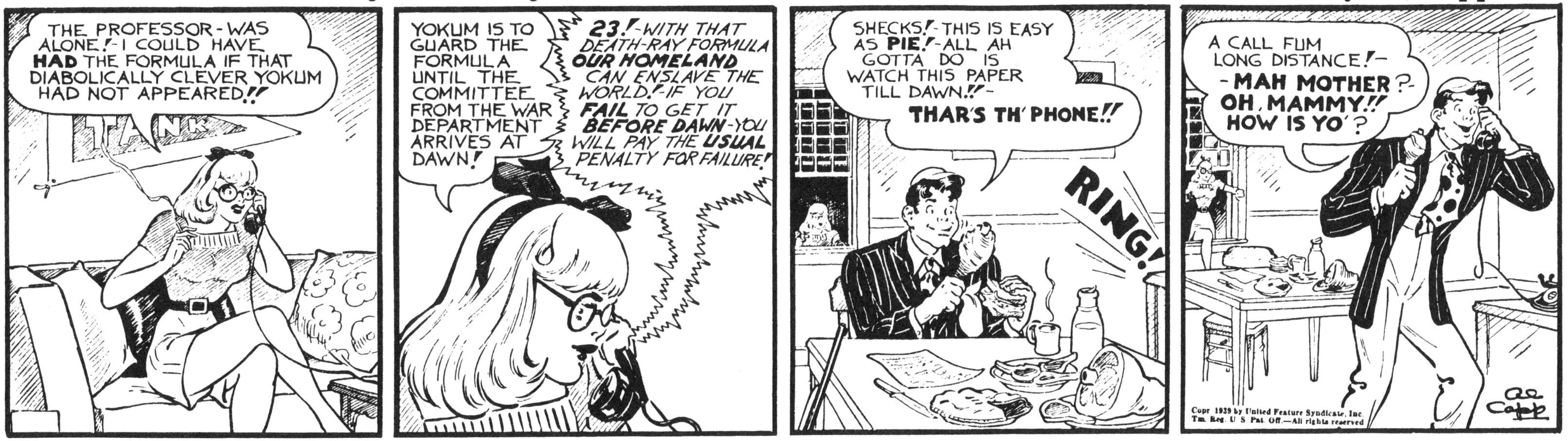
THE PROFESSOR-WAS ALONE!-I COULD HAVE HAD THE FORMULA IF THAT DIABOLICALLY CLEVER YOKUM HAD NOT APPEARED!!
TANK
YOKUM IS TO GUARD THE FORMULA UNTIL THE COMMITTEE FROM THE WAR DEPARTMENT ARRIVES AT DAWN!
23!-WITH THAT DEATH-RAY FORMULA OUR HOMELAND CAN ENSLAVE THE WORLD!-IF YOU FAIL TO GET IT BEFORE DAWN-YOU WILL PAY THE USUAL PENALTY FOR FAILURE!
SHECKS!-THIS IS EASY AS PIE!-ALL AH GOTTA DO IS WATCH THIS PAPER TILL DAWN!!-
THAR'S TH' PHONE!!
RING!
A CALL FUM LONG DISTANCE!-
-MAH MOTHER?-OH, MAMMY!! HOW IS YO'?
Copr. 1939 by United Feature Syndicate, Inc. Tm. Reg. U S Pat. Off.—All rights reserved
AL CAPP

LI'L ABNER X Marks the Spot! By Al Capp

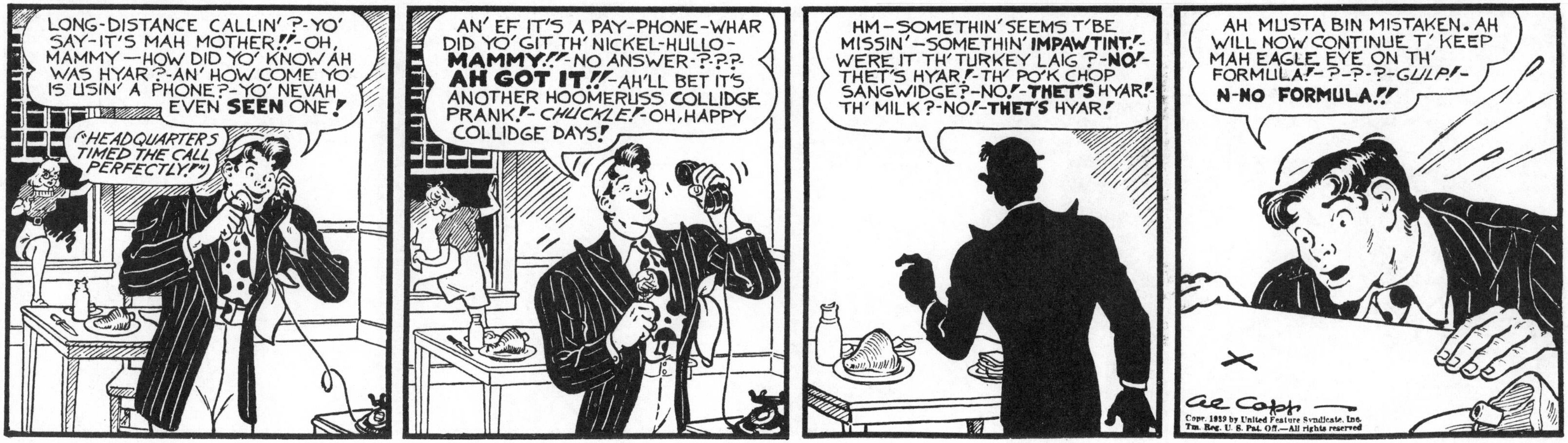
LONG-DISTANCE CALLIN'?-YO' SAY-IT'S MAH MOTHER!!-OH, MAMMY—HOW DID YO' KNOW AH WAS HYAR?-AN' HOW COME YO' IS USIN' A PHONE?-YO' NEVAH EVEN SEEN ONE!
("HEADQUARTERS TIMED THE CALL PERFECTLY!")
AN' EF IT'S A PAY-PHONE-WHAR DID YO' GIT TH' NICKEL-HULLO-MAMMY!!-NO ANSWER-?-?-?-AH GOT IT!!-AH'LL BET IT'S ANOTHER HOOMERUSS COLLIDGE PRANK!-CHUCKLE!-OH, HAPPY COLLIDGE DAYS!
HM—SOMETHIN' SEEMS T'BE MISSIN'—SOMETHIN' IMPAWTINT!-WERE IT TH' TURKEY LAIG?-NO!-THET'S HYAR!-TH' PO'K CHOP SANGWIDGE?-NO!-THET'S HYAR!-TH' MILK?-NO!-THET'S HYAR!
AH MUSTA BIN MISTAKEN. AH WILL NOW CONTINUE T' KEEP MAH EAGLE EYE ON TH' FORMULA!-?-?-?-GULP!-N-NO FORMULA!!
X
Al Capp
Copr. 1939 by United Feature Syndicate, Inc. Tm. Reg. U. S. Pat. Off.—All rights reserved

LI'L ABNER Oh, Professor, How Could You! By Al Capp

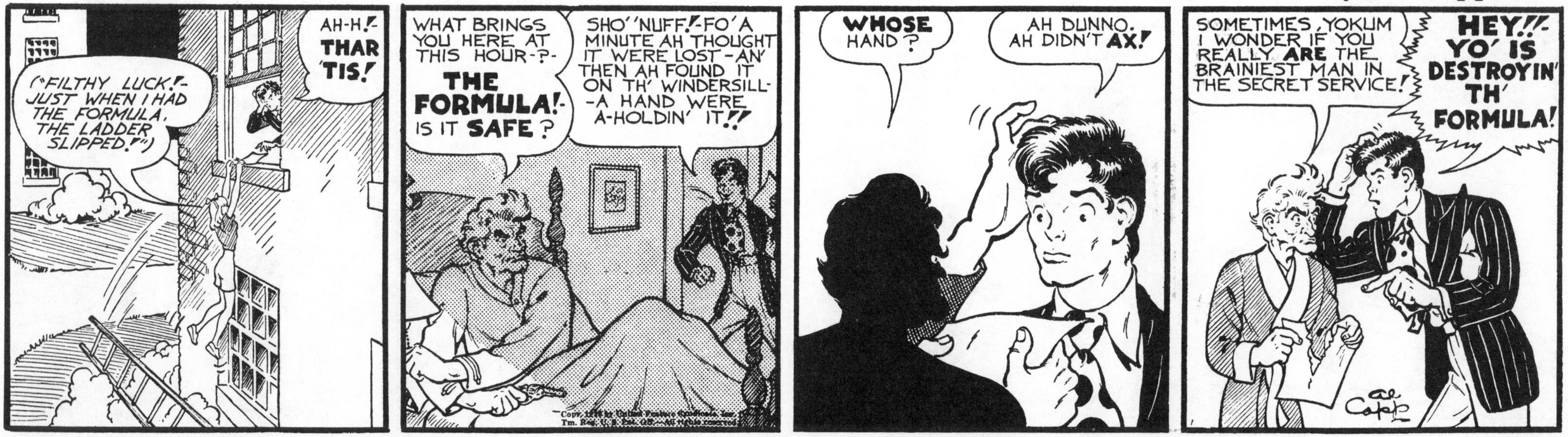
("FILTHY LUCK!-JUST WHEN I HAD THE FORMULA, THE LADDER SLIPPED!")
AH-H!-THAR 'TIS!
WHAT BRINGS YOU HERE AT THIS HOUR-?-THE FORMULA!-IS IT SAFE?
SHO' 'NUFF!-FO' A MINUTE AH THOUGHT IT WERE LOST-AN' THEN AH FOUND IT ON TH' WINDERSILL--A HAND WERE A-HOLDIN' IT!!
WHOSE HAND?
AH DUNNO. AH DIDN'T AX!
SOMETIMES, YOKUM I WONDER IF YOU REALLY ARE THE BRAINIEST MAN IN THE SECRET SERVICE!
HEY!!-YO' IS DESTROYIN' TH' FORMULA!
Al Capp

LI'L ABNER Dawn Look Now! By Al Capp

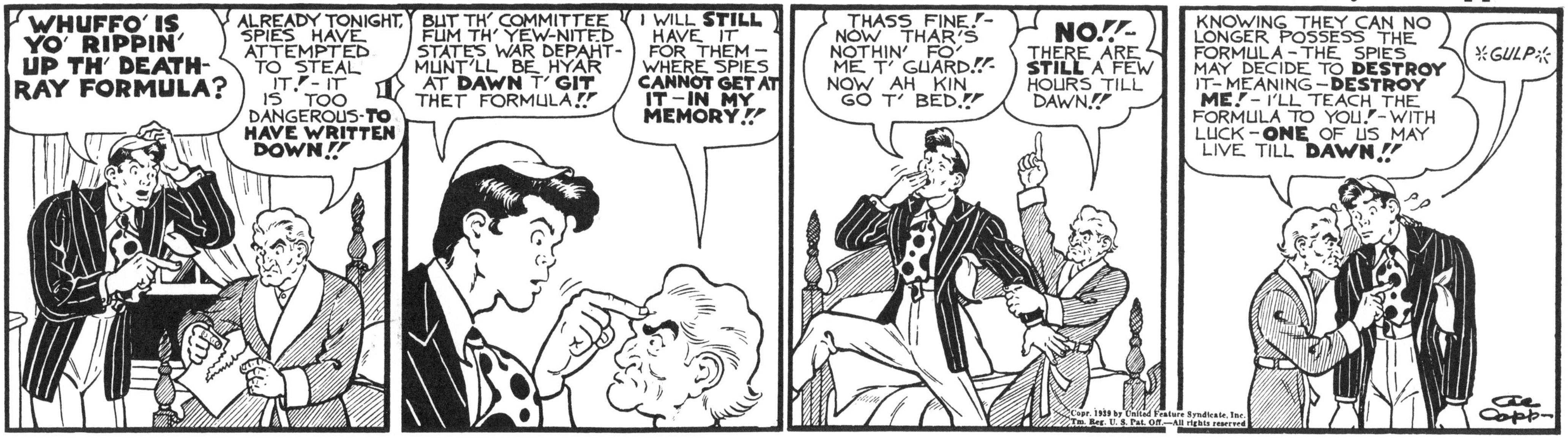

WHUFFO' IS YO' RIPPIN' UP TH' DEATH-RAY FORMULA?
ALREADY TONIGHT, SPIES HAVE ATTEMPTED TO STEAL IT!'- IT IS TOO DANGEROUS-TO HAVE WRITTEN DOWN!!'
BUT TH' COMMITTEE FUM TH' YEW-NITED STATES WAR DEPAHT-MUNT'LL BE HYAR AT DAWN T' GIT THET FORMULA!!'
I WILL STILL HAVE IT FOR THEM - WHERE SPIES CANNOT GET AT IT - IN MY MEMORY!!'
THASS FINE!'- NOW THAR'S NOTHIN' FO' ME T' GUARD!!'- NOW AH KIN GO T' BED!!'
NO!!'- THERE ARE STILL A FEW HOURS TILL DAWN!!'
Copr. 1939 by United Feature Syndicate, Inc. Tm. Reg. U. S. Pat. Off.—All rights reserved
KNOWING THEY CAN NO LONGER POSSESS THE FORMULA - THE SPIES MAY DECIDE TO DESTROY IT - MEANING - DESTROY ME!' - I'LL TEACH THE FORMULA TO YOU!'- WITH LUCK - ONE OF US MAY LIVE TILL DAWN!!'
GULP

LI'L ABNER The Professor Has Two Lives to Give! By Al Capp

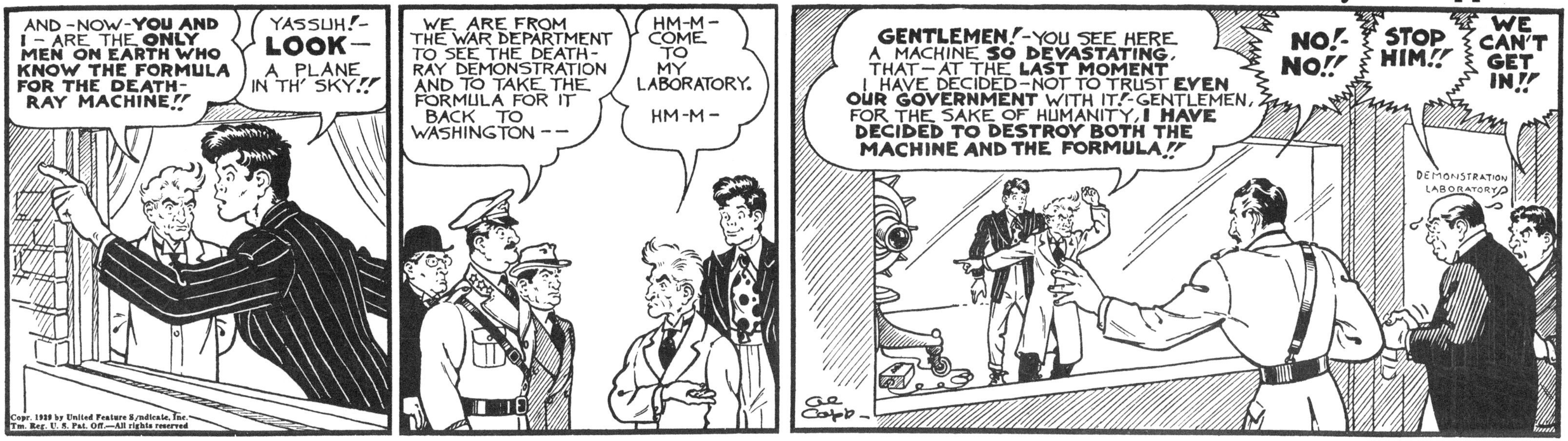

AND - NOW - YOU AND I - ARE THE ONLY MEN ON EARTH WHO KNOW THE FORMULA FOR THE DEATH-RAY MACHINE!!'
YASSUH!'- LOOK - A PLANE IN TH' SKY!!'
Copr. 1939 by United Feature Syndicate, Inc. Tm. Reg. U. S. Pat. Off.—All rights reserved
WE ARE FROM THE WAR DEPARTMENT TO SEE THE DEATH-RAY DEMONSTRATION AND TO TAKE THE FORMULA FOR IT BACK TO WASHINGTON --
HM-M - COME TO MY LABORATORY.
HM-M -
GENTLEMEN!'- YOU SEE HERE A MACHINE SO DEVASTATING, THAT - AT THE LAST MOMENT I HAVE DECIDED - NOT TO TRUST EVEN OUR GOVERNMENT WITH IT!'- GENTLEMEN, FOR THE SAKE OF HUMANITY, I HAVE DECIDED TO DESTROY BOTH THE MACHINE AND THE FORMULA!!'
NO!'- NO!!'
STOP HIM!!'
WE CAN'T GET IN!!'
DEMONSTRATION LABORATORY

LI'L ABNER Hold Your Hats, Boys! By Al Capp

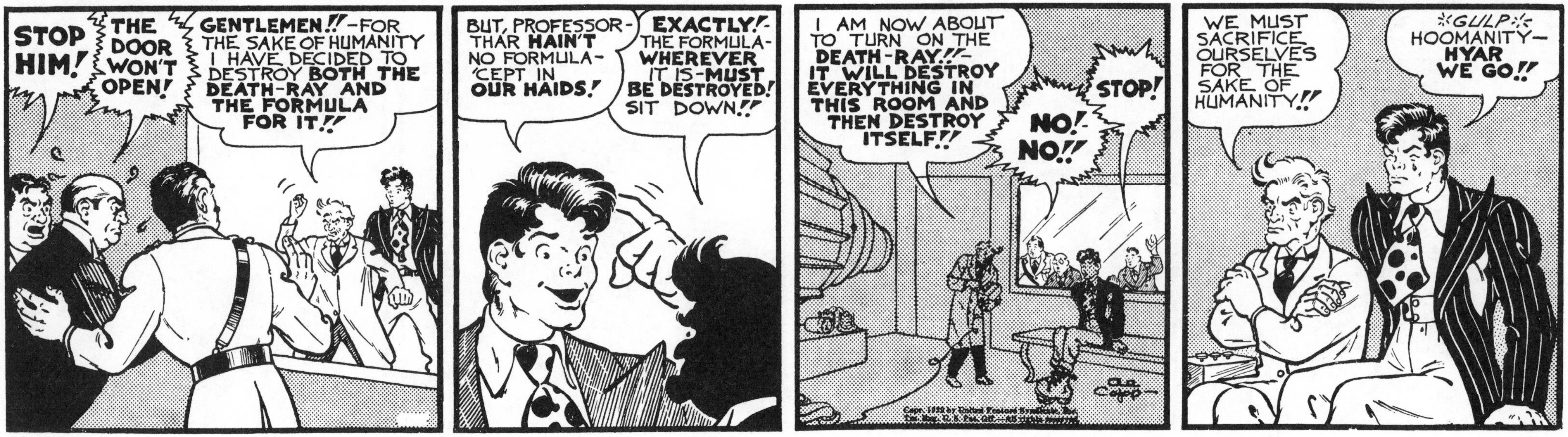
STOP HIM!
THE DOOR WON'T OPEN!
GENTLEMEN!!-FOR THE SAKE OF HUMANITY I HAVE DECIDED TO DESTROY BOTH THE DEATH-RAY AND THE FORMULA FOR IT!!
BUT, PROFESSOR-THAR HAIN'T NO FORMULA-'CEPT IN OUR HAIDS!
EXACTLY!-THE FORMULA-WHEREVER IT IS-MUST BE DESTROYED! SIT DOWN!!
I AM NOW ABOUT TO TURN ON THE DEATH-RAY!!-IT WILL DESTROY EVERYTHING IN THIS ROOM AND THEN DESTROY ITSELF!!
NO!-NO!!
STOP!
WE MUST SACRIFICE OURSELVES FOR THE SAKE OF HUMANITY!!
GULP HOOMANITY-HYAR WE GO!!

LI'L ABNER Glory Road! By Al Capp

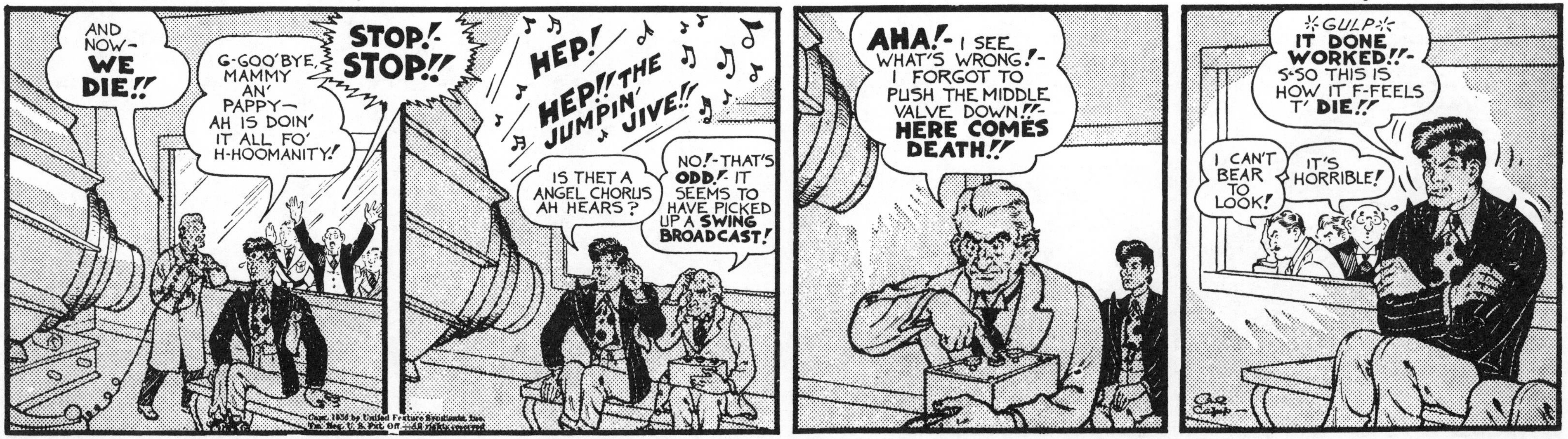
AND NOW-WE DIE!!
G-GOO'BYE, MAMMY AN' PAPPY-AH IS DOIN' IT ALL FO' H-HOOMANITY!
STOP!-STOP!!
HEP! HEP!! THE JUMPIN' JIVE!!
IS THET A ANGEL CHORUS AH HEARS?
NO!-THAT'S ODD!-IT SEEMS TO HAVE PICKED UP A SWING BROADCAST!
AHA!-I SEE WHAT'S WRONG!-I FORGOT TO PUSH THE MIDDLE VALVE DOWN!!-HERE COMES DEATH!!
GULP IT DONE WORKED!!-S-SO THIS IS HOW IT F-FEELS T' DIE!!
I CAN'T BEAR TO LOOK!
IT'S HORRIBLE!

LI'L ABNER It's a Small World! By Al Capp

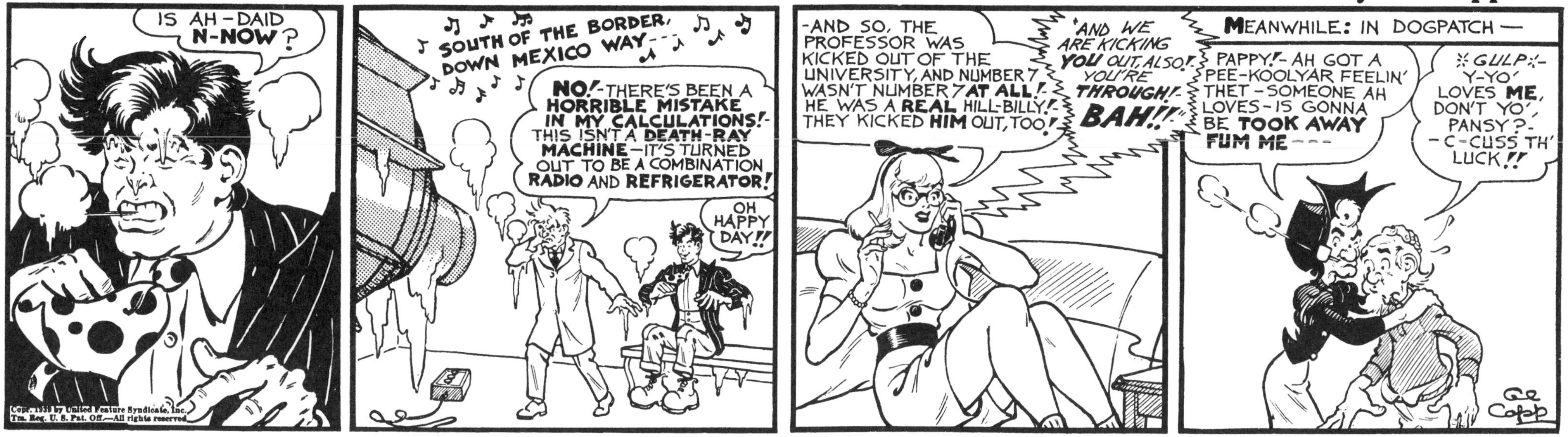

IS AH-DAID N-NOW?
Copr. 1939 by United Feature Syndicate, Inc. Tm. Reg. U. S. Pat. Off.—All rights reserved
SOUTH OF THE BORDER, DOWN MEXICO WAY---
NO!-THERE'S BEEN A HORRIBLE MISTAKE IN MY CALCULATIONS!-THIS ISN'T A DEATH-RAY MACHINE-IT'S TURNED OUT TO BE A COMBINATION RADIO AND REFRIGERATOR!
OH HAPPY DAY!!
-AND SO, THE PROFESSOR WAS KICKED OUT OF THE UNIVERSITY, AND NUMBER 7 WASN'T NUMBER 7 AT ALL!-HE WAS A REAL HILL-BILLY!-THEY KICKED HIM OUT, TOO!
"AND WE ARE KICKING YOU OUT, ALSO!-YOU'RE THROUGH!-BAH!!"
MEANWHILE: IN DOGPATCH—
PAPPY!-AH GOT A PEE-KOOLYAR FEELIN' THET-SOMEONE AH LOVES-IS GONNA BE TOOK AWAY FUM ME---
GULP-Y-YO' LOVES ME, DON'T YO', PANSY?-C-CUSS TH' LUCK!!
Al Capp

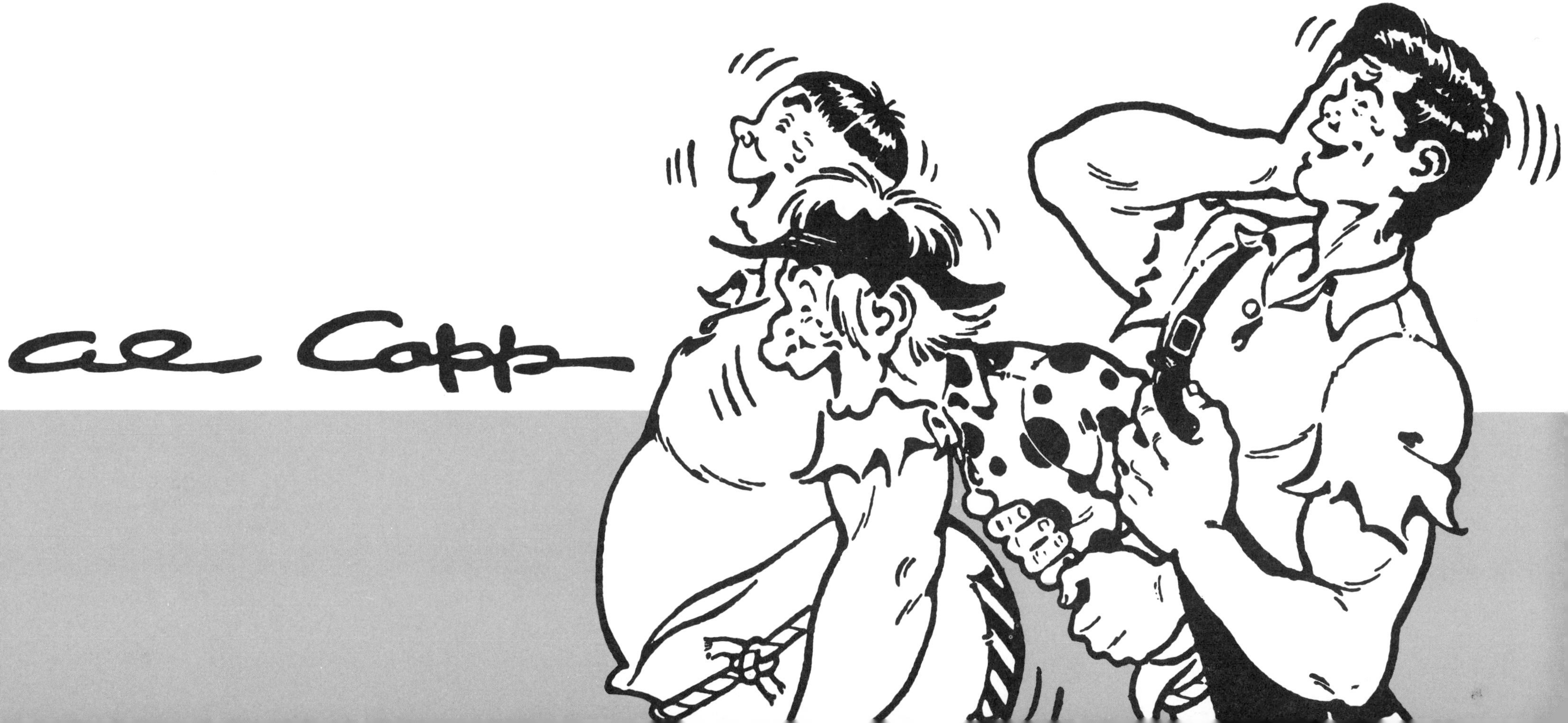

Al Capp

The black and white daily *Li'l Abner* strips are being collected chronologically in their entirety. At some point we will begin a separate series of volumes of chronological Sunday strips, hopefully in full color. Readers should note that the Sunday strips involved a separate continuity from the Monday through Saturday adventures. Any readers possessing original *Li'l Abner* artwork, related merchandise, Al Capp correspondence or other related historical material are encouraged to contact the publisher.